Accounting Information Systems
The Crossroads of Accounting & IT
Second Edition

Donna Kay, MBA, PhD, CPA, CITP
Maryville University of Saint Louis

Ali Ovlia, MS, DM
Webster University

PEARSON

Boston   Columbus   Indianapolis   New York   San Francisco   Upper Saddle River
Amsterdam   Cape Town   Dubai   London   Madrid   Milan   Munich   Paris   Montréal   Toronto
Delhi   Mexico City   São Paulo   Sydney   Hong Kong   Seoul   Singapore   Taipei   Tokyo

Editor in Chief: Donna Battista

Editorial Project Manager: Nicole Sam

Editorial Assistants: Jane Avery and Lauren Zanedis

Director of Marketing: Maggie Moylan Leen

Marketing Assistant: Kimberly Lovato

Managing Editor: Jeff Holcomb

Associate Production Project Manager: Alison Eusden

Senior Manufacturing Buyer: Carol Melville

Permissions Project Supervisor: Jill Dougan

Manager, Visual Research: Rachel Youdelman

Art Director: Anthony Gemmellaro

Cover Designer: Anthony Gemmellaro

Senior Media Producer: Melissa Honig

Media Producer: James Bateman

Production Coordination and Composition: Integra

Printer/Binder: R.R. Donnelly/Jefferson City

Cover Printer: Lehigh-Phoenix Color/Hagerstown

Text Font: Times LT Std, 10/12

Text Credits: Page 6: *Based on The New Value Chain From the Imagination Challenge: The Strategic Foresight and Innovation in the Global Economy* by Alexander Manu published peachpit.com/articles/ (accessed July 2009). Pages: 13–14, 38, 47, 54, 67, 69, 70, 86–88, 396, 101, 102, 104, 107, 136, 140, 149: Screenshots © Intuit Inc. All rights reserved. Page 165: "The Big Squeeze" by Molly Rose Teuke from *Profit Magazine*, May 2006. Page 216: Courtesy of International Business Machines Corporation, © 2011 International Business Machines Corporation. Pages 241–243: "Sustainable Economics" by Tom Niemeier, Founder of SPACE. Copyright © 2009 by the author, reprinted by permission. Pages 244–245: "Accounting for Sustainability in the Built Environment" by Tim Gaidis, Senior Associate at HOK. Copyright © 2009 by the author, reprinted by permission. Page: 256: "XBRL Benefits for U.S. Federal Financial Institutions Examination Council (FFIEC)" from *Business Case for XBRL* by Charles Hoffman, Bryce Pippert and Phil Walenga. Copyright © July 2005 UBMatrix. Pages: 263, 264, 365: Figure was created using Altova XMLSPY (Copyright 2003-2010 Altova GmbH) and is reprinted with permission of Altova. XML Spy and Altova are trademarks of Altova GmbH and are registered in numerous countries. Photo Credits: Cover: Darqowski/Shutterstock, Benchart/Shutterstock, Elenamiv/Shutterstock; Page 19: Olegganko/Shutterstock; Pages 276–277: Photo courtesy of Tom Niemeier; Page 278–280: Photo courtesy of Tom Niemeier; Page 344: Photo courtesy of Tim Gaidis; Page 413: Stephen Mcsweeny/Shutterstock; Page 415: Russal/Shuttersock.

Library of Congress Cataloging-in-Publication Data is on file at the Library of Congress

10 9 8 7 6 5 4 3 2 1

PEARSON

ISBN 10:   0-13-299132-2

ISBN 13: 978-0-13-299132-2

Brief Contents

Contents

What's New in This Edition?

To bring you the latest, each chapter text has been carefully updated to reflect changes in the accounting and IT fields.

- Business process mapping has been entirely overhauled to focus on flowcharts as the process mapping tool preferred by accounting professionals. The new Business Process Modeling and Notation (BPMN) 2.0 is also presented in Chapters 4 and 5 because it is the business process mapping notation preferred in business to meet the simplicity requested by accounting professionals while providing more technical detail than flowcharts to meet the needs of IT professionals.

- Coverage of business process mapping using data flow diagrams (DFDs) is moved to Chapter Extensions 4 and 5, available online at www.pearsonhighered.com/kay.

- Chapter 6, *Enterprise Information Systems*, has been updated to include the portion of the enterprise system that is increasingly in the cloud, with a new section on cloud computing.

- Chapter 8, *Accounting and Sustainability Intelligence*, keeps you at the forefront of sustainability and how it affects your accounting system. Chapter 8 is updated to include coverage of integrated reporting that integrates traditional financial reporting and sustainability reporting. Novo Nordisk's Integrated Report appears in Chapter Extension 8 (located at www.pearsonhighered.com/kay) so you can learn from a leader in integrating reporting on financial, social, and environmental performance.

- *Cybersecurity*, Chapter 11, includes a new chapter extension with two leading IT control frameworks—ISO 27k IT controls and COBIT.

- Each chapter has updated assignments prepared by Ali Ovlia.

- The latest emerging trends and technologies, such as mobile technology and robotics, are covered in online Chapter 15, to keep you up to date on technologies impacting accounting.

It's All About You!

This book is all about you—the student!

- To save you time...
  The materials focus on the key topics and skills you need to be successful in this course and on the job.

- To make your life easier...
  The concepts and materials are presented in a friendly manner so the subject matter makes sense.

- To give you a competitive advantage...
  Everything in this text is focused on aiding you in the successful navigation of the crossroads of accounting and IT.

Best wishes for your continued success!

What Gives Me a Competitive Advantage as an Accounting Professional?

This book is designed to assist you in developing the following top five core competencies for accounting professionals (AICPA):

1. Communication and leadership
2. Strategic and critical thinking
3. Customer focus
4. Interpretation of converging information
5. Technological skills

Technology is integral to accounting today. To fully understand accounting, the accounting professional must understand the crossroads of accounting and information technology. To navigate the crossroads, this book equips you to communicate using two different languages: the language of the accounting professional and the language of the IT professional.

This text contains straightforward presentation of leading edge technologies at the crossroads of accounting and IT. From business intelligence to XBRL, from integrated enterprise systems to cybersecurity, and from enterprise risk management to sustainability accounting, this text offers you the latest in accounting and technology in easy to understand terms.

This gives you a competitive advantage and better prepares you to successfully launch your career as an accounting professional.

How Can I Study Less and Learn More?

The art and science of effective learning is simple: It's not how long you study—it's how *effectively* you study.

How do you study effectively? *Connect new information to what you already know.* Build on what you already know to construct new knowledge.

If you can't connect new knowledge to something you can relate to, keep asking questions until you can build a bridge from what you know now to the new information.

Effective learning can be compared to global travel. Let's say your professor is very excited about exploring the city of Prague, so he or she gives you a Prague city map. The map has limited usefulness to you, however, if you are in Chicago, New York, or Los Angeles. Before the map has real meaning or significance to you, first you must travel to Prague.

In the same way, if your professor is excited about the latest development in accounting and business intelligence, for example, but you are unable to connect the new information to what you already know, you will not be able to construct new meaning. Connect the new information to something you already know.

By the way, this learning approach is called constructivist pedagogy, and it is woven throughout this text. The questions, examples, illustrations, and assignments are all designed to create an experience that provides an opportunity for you to construct deeper meaning and a memorable personal discovery.

Top Ten Tips for Studying AIS

1. Connect new information to what you already know.

2. If you can't do Tip No. 1, then build a learning bridge. Ask your professor questions. Perform an online search and read more about the topic. Find something about the new topic that you can use to build a bridge to what you already know.

3. Clarify your learning. Clear up any misunderstandings by asking questions. Don't give up when you feel confused. Persist and keep asking questions to clear up any confusion.

4. Streamline your learning. For example, this text uses models that streamline learning large amounts of new information. One baseline accounting system model is representative of most accounting systems. This saves you from learning dozens of different accounting systems. If you can connect your current knowledge to the new model, you can dramatically improve the effectiveness of your study.

5. Connect to your classmates. Classmates can help you build the bridge to connect new knowledge to what you already know. Or maybe you can assist in building the bridge for a classmate. Sometimes when we teach others, we learn the most.

6. Learn to see things in a new way. In this book, we use GPS as a reminder to see both the details of accounting and the global picture of an entire accounting system.

7. Discover the relevance. Are you ever frustrated in courses when you are asked to learn things that do not seem relevant? Discover the relevance of AIS topics and give yourself a reason to learn.

8. Write down your questions. It's amazing how the process of formulating questions can clarify your own thinking. Don't be surprised if during the process of writing down your question, you discover the answer.

9. Review the chapters and your notes three times. Read the chapter and make notes. Review the chapter a day later and again one week later. You will retain more information if you review the material three times instead of just once. This will save you time and improve your grades!

10. Remember: AIS is SASSY. The main areas of AIS are shown on the inside front cover and listed below:

    - **S**tore accounting data.
    - **A**nalyze accounting data.
    - **S**afeguard accounting data.
    - **SY**stem design.

How Do I Navigate the Crossroads of Accounting and IT?

The roadmap to navigating the crossroads of accounting and IT is shown on the inside front cover.

Remember – AIS is SASSY:

Part 1: **S**tore accounting data.

Part 2: **A**nalyze accounting data.

Part 3: **S**afeguard accounting data.

Part 4: **SY**stem design.

The fifth and final part of the book is a capstone, integrating AIS topics.

If you want to know more, here is a brief summary for you. By the way, don't be surprised if your professor covers the chapters in a different order. There are many different approaches to teaching and learning AIS.

Part 1: Enterprise Accounting Systems: People, Processes, and Technology

introduces you to the design, development, and functioning of accounting systems today. In *Chapter 1: Accounting System Insights* we provide you with insights into understanding how accounting systems function in today's business environment. *Chapter 2: Accounting Databases* provides an introduction to databases and their integral role in accounting systems. *Chapter 3: Accounting Interface: Database Forms, Queries, and Reports* describes the accounting system interface and its role in the accounting system. In *Chapter 4: Accounting Systems and Business Processes*, we share with you how to read and develop business process maps that document business processes. *Chapter 5: Business Processes: Purchasing, Sales, and Payroll Cycles* covers documentation for business processes using business process maps for purchasing, sales, and payroll cycles. In *Chapter 6: Integrated Enterprise Systems and Cloud Computing* we explore how the accounting system is integrated into the larger enterprise system and how cloud computing is being used by enterprises.

Part 2: Accounting and Intelligence Systems

explores the impact of intelligent systems on accounting. *Chapter 7: Accounting and Business Intelligence* discusses how enterprises use analytics to create business intelligence for improved decision making and business performance. *Chapter 8: Accounting and Sustainability Intelligence* provides an overview of the emerging field of accounting for sustainability and the resulting impact on the accounting system. *Chapter 9: XBRL: Intelligent Business Reporting* explores the who, what, where, when, and how of eXtensible Business Reporting Language (XBRL) that electronically tags each piece of financial data.

Part 3: Security, Controls, and Risk

focuses on safeguarding information assets stored in accounting systems. *Chapter 10: Fraud and Internal Control* introduces COSO's Internal Control Framework and COBIT's IT controls framework. *Chapter 11: Cybersecurity* explores the threats posed by cybercrime to an accounting system. This chapter introduces you to the International Information Systems Security Certification Consortium (ISC)[2] 10 domains for cybersecurity. *Chapter 12: The Risk Intelligent Enterprise: Enterprise Risk Management* introduces COSO's enterprise risk management (ERM) framework. The chapter presents the top 10 tips for spreadsheet risk management.

Part 4: Designing and Developing Accounting Systems

provides an overview of different approaches to developing accounting systems and the related accounting database. *Chapter 13: Accounting System Development* explores the phases of the system development life cycle (SDLC) as applied to developing an accounting system. *Chapter 14: Database Design: ERD, REA, and SQL* compares and contrasts two approaches to accounting database design: entity relationship diagram (ERD) and resources, entities, and agents (REA). This chapter also explores how data is extracted from the database using Structured Query Language (SQL).

Part 5: Enterprise Accounting Systems: Capstone

provides a capstone experience for integrating accounting system topics. *Chapter 15: Emerging Trends and Technologies* is an online chapter that explores the latest trends in information technology and the impact on accounting systems. *Chapter 16: Accounting Systems in Action: LIVE Projects* provides opportunities for LIVE projects to develop your project management and team building skills, two critical skills for your future success as an accounting professional at the crossroads of accounting and IT.

How Can Features of This Book Streamline My Learning?

Every feature in this book has been designed for you and your success in learning the content of this course.

- Real and relevant makes the content come alive!

- Accounting Insights simplify the complex!

Online materials keep you current!

- Online Chapter 15 – Emerging Trends and Technologies
- Online Chapter 16 – Live Projects

It's Your Call

This is your training ground. These scenarios provide you with the opportunity to use your knowledge and professional skills.

2.33 Since your background is in AIS, you have been asked to provide training to the other accountants in your company about the new accounting system design. How would you explain to your colleagues about the three tiers in an accounting system architecture? (Q2.1)

2.34 You have been called in as a consultant to act as a liaison between the accountants and the IT professionals at a company. The accountants are complaining that they must re-enter all the customer information each time an order is placed. The accountants see this as inefficient and time consuming with no value added.

The only response from the IT professionals has been to say that the database tables need to be normalized. The accountants have asked you what this means. Communication between the two groups of professionals has deteriorated.

How would you facilitate communication between the accountants and the IT professionals? How would you explain to both sides what is needed to resolve the issue? (Q2.4)

2.35 Your company is expanding its operations to include overseas markets. Your supervisor asked you to prepare a summary explaining changes to the CUSTOMER database table that need to be implemented as a result of the overseas expansion. (Q2.3, 2.4)

2.36 You work at a university and have been assigned to a project team to update the university database to include information about employee dependents. The university provides tuition free to all employee dependents and wants to track dependent information to estimate free tuition in the future.

One of the project team members has suggested simply adding the employee dependent information to the EMPLOYEE database table. What do you think? Is this advisable? Prepare your notes to respond to his suggestion at the next team meeting. (Q2.3, 2.4)

2.37 Your supervisor would like to know why calculated fields are typically not included as database fields in accounting software. Prepare a short report on advantages and disadvantages of including and not including the calculated field for your supervisor. (Q2.3, 2.4)

Tech in Practice

These technology in practice exercises are perfect for individuals and teams.

Tech Exercises

Sharpen your skills with these technology exercises. Watch the software videos at www.pearsonhighered.com/kay.

2.38
Tech Tool: Database Software
Software Videos: Database Tables, Database Table Relationships

EspressoCoffee asked for your assistance in building database tables to record sales transactions.
1. Using Microsoft Access database software and information in Figure 2.21, build the following database tables. Identify the primary key for each table.
   - CUSTOMER table
   - SALES ORDER table
   - SALES ORDER LINE table
   - ITEM table

2.20 An item table's record has 5 fields: Item code, Item name, description, location ID, and warehouse ID. Which of these fields is a good candidate for the primary key?
a. Location ID
b. Item Code
c. Warehouse ID
d. Item name

2.21 An item may appear on many orders. An order contains many items. The relationship between Item table and Order table is:
a. Many-to-one
b. Many-to-many
c. One-to-many
d. One-to-one

2.22 Sandy, an accountant, wants to search for a specific customer address. She should search using:
a. Customer name
b. Customer address
c. Customer ID
d. a and b

2.23 Which of the following is NOT a database essential?
a. Form
b. Table
c. Query
d. DBMS

Exercises

Each Exercise relates to one of the major questions addressed in the chapter and is labeled with the question number in green.

Short Exercises

Warm up with these short exercises.

2.24 Match the following database fields with the appropriate database table. (Q2.3)
a. VENDOR table
b. CUSTOMER table
c. EMPLOYEE table
d. ACCOUNTS table
e. SALES ORDER table
f. SALES ORDER LINE table
g. PURCHASE ORDER table
h. PURCHASE ORDER LINE table

_____ 1. Customer name
_____ 2. Account number
_____ 3. Customer number
_____ 4. Employee address
_____ 5. Item quantity sold
_____ 6. Item quantity purchased
_____ 7. Sales order number
_____ 8. Sales order date
_____ 9. Purchase order date
_____ 10. Purchase order number
_____ 11. Vendor address
_____ 12. Sales order total

What Online Resources Go with My Textbook?

To make your life a little easier, the following online resources are provided for you on your textbook Web site (www.pearsonhighered.com/kay).

- **Part 5: Enterprise Accounting Systems: Capstone** found online on your text Web site includes the following two online chapters.

  - **Chapter 15: Emerging Trends and Technologies (Online Chapter).** A complete version of this chapter, including the latest technology trends impacting accounting, is available online.

  - **Chapter 16: Accounting Systems in Action: LIVE Projects (Online Chapter).** A complete version of Chapter 16, including templates for project deliverables, is available online.

- **Chapter Extension 4,** covering business process maps using data flow diagrams (DFDs), is available online.

- **Chapter Extension 5,** covering business process mapping using DFDs for the sales, purchasing, payroll, and financial cycles, is available online.

- **Software videos** referenced in the end-of-chapter assignments will assist you in completing the tech exercises.

- **Tech Exercise data files** to use when completing your assignments can be downloaded from your text Web site.

- **Presentation slides** summarizing important points in each chapter to streamline your learning are available online.

- **And more....**

What Certifications Can Give Me a Competitive Advantage as an Accounting Professional?

Some of the certifications you may want to consider as an accounting professional include the following.

- **Certified Public Accountant (CPA):** Up to 20% of some CPA exam sections relate to accounting and IT topics covered in this book. Some text assignments are designed to assist you in preparing for the new writing assignments on the CPA exam. For more information about requirements to take the CPA Exam, visit www.aicpa.org/BecomeACPA.

- **Certified Information Technology Professional (CITP):** If you are a CPA and enjoy being at the crossroads of accounting and IT, you might consider obtaining the Certified Information Technology Professional (CITP) credential. To learn more about the CITP credential, visit www.aicpa.org/CITP.

- **Certified Information Systems Auditor (CISA):** CISA is a certification for IT auditors. For more information, see www.isaca.org/CISA.

- **Certified Internal Auditor (CIA):** This certification is for accounting professionals who specialize in internal audit. See www.theiaa.org for more information.

- **Certified Information Systems Security Professional (CISSP):** The CISSP is a globally recognized credential for professionals in the information security field. For more information, see www.isc2.org/CISSP.

- **Certified in Financial Forensics (CFF):** The Certified in Financial Forensics credential is exclusively for CPAs who pass the CFF Exam and possess the necessary experience requirements. If you would like to learn more about the CFF credential, visit www.aicpa.org/CFF.

Acknowledgments

We would like to acknowledge the following individuals:

Pearson Education Team:

    Donna Battista, Editor in Chief

    Nicole Sam, Editorial Project Manager

    Jeffrey Holcomb, Managing Editor

    Alison Eusden, Production Project Manager

    Anthony Gemmellaro, Art Director

Brian Behrens for his steadfast support

Pam Horwitz, Dean of Business, Maryville University of Saint Louis, for her kind words of encouragement

The Maryville Team: Kim Temme, Karen Tabak, John Lewington, and the late Mark Roman for support and encouragement

Benjamin Akande, Dean of Business, Webster University, for his encouragement

Al Cawns, Chair of Mathematics and Computer Science, Webster University, for his support

To the following individuals for their engaging sidebar contributions to the text:

    Tim Gaidis, HOK

    Tom Niemeier and Matt Lung, SPACE LLC

To the following reviewers for thoughtful comments and constructive feedback:

    Wael Aguir, *University of Texas – San Antonio*

    T. S. Amer, *Northern Arizona University*

    Fred Barbee, *University of Alaska – Anchorage*

    Katherine Boswell, *University of Louisiana at Monroe*

    Joyce Bryer, *Indiana University*

    Mark Cecchini, *University of South Carolina*

    Lewis Chasalow, *University of Findlay*

    Deb Cosgrove, *University of Nebraska – Lincoln*

    Sandra Devona, *Northern Illinois University*

    David Dulany, *Aurora University*

    Doris Duncan, *California State University – East Bay*

    Kurt Fanning, *Grand Valley State University*

    Marilyn Griffin, *Virginia Tech*

    Rita Hays, *Southwestern Oklahoma State University*

    Kenneth Henry, *Florida International University*

    Steven Hornik, *University of Nebraska – Lincoln*

    Constance Hylton, *George Mason University*

    Andrew Jansma, *SUNY Buffalo*

    Grover Kearns, *University of South Florida – St. Petersburg*

Frank Klaus, *Cleveland State University*

Michael Lavine, *University of Maryland*

Maria Leach, *Auburn Montogmery*

Deborah Lee, *Northeastern State University – Broken Arrow*

Chan Li, *University of Pittsburgh*

Robert Lin, *California State University – East Bay*

Maureen Mascha, *Marquette University*

Sue Minke, *Indiana University – Purdue University at Fort Wayne*

Vishal Munsif, *Florida International University*

Brandis Phillips, *North Carolina A&T*

Theresa Phinney, *Texas A&M University*

Erik Rolland, *University of California – Riverside*

Ward Thrasher, *University of Bridgeport*

Barbara Uliss, *Metropolitan State College*

Patrick Wheeler, *University of Missouri – Columbia*

Lu Zhang, *Benedictine University*

Meet the Authors

Dr. Donna Kay is an Associate Professor of Accounting and Accounting Systems & Forensics at Maryville University of Saint Louis. Dr. Kay teaches in the accounting, accounting systems & forensics, and MBA programs.

Dr. Kay earned BS and MBA degrees from Southern Illinois University at Edwardsville before receiving a PhD from Saint Louis University, where she conducted action research on the perceived effectiveness of technology and instructional techniques. Named to *Who's Who of American Women*, Dr. Kay holds certifications as both a Certified Public Accountant (CPA) and Certified Informational Technology Professional (CITP). She is an active member of the American Institute of Certified Public Accountants, the Missouri Society of CPAs (MSCPA), the American Accounting Association (AAA), Teachers of Accounting at Two-Year Colleges (TACTYC), the Missouri Association of Accounting Educators (MAAE), and the AIS Educator Association (AISEA). Dr. Kay serves on the Information Technology Committee of the MSCPA.

Donna Kay's other publications include *Computer Accounting with QuickBooks* and *Pacioli's Secret*.

Dr. Ali Ovlia, an Associate Professor of Computer Science at Webster University in Saint Louis, teaches in the computer science, information systems, decision support systems, and Master of Science in Distributed Systems programs.

Dr. Ovlia earned a BS from the Italian Naval Academy of Livorno, Italy, a BS and MS in Computer Science from the University of Oklahoma, and a Doctorate of Management from Webster University. His doctoral dissertation research investigated the impact of electronic commerce on small and medium-size organizations. Prior to teaching at Webster University, Dr. Ovlia taught at Harris-Stowe State University, where he developed and implemented the i960 processor performance monitoring technique for aerospace manufacturer McDonnell Douglas. Dr. Ovlia is a member of the Association of Computing Machinery (ACM), the Institute of Electrical and Electronics Engineers (IEEE), the Association of Information Technology Professionals (AITP), and the American Accounting Association (AAA).

Part One *Enterprise Accounting Systems: People, Processes, and Technology* focuses on how people, processes, and technology are used to process and store accounting data.

Part One
Enterprise Accounting Systems: People, Processes, and Technology

Store Accounting Data

Chapter 1
Accounting System Insights

Chapter 2
Accounting Databases

Chapter 3
Accounting Interface: Database Forms, Queries, and Reports

Chapter 4
Accounting Systems and Business Processes

Chapter 5
Business Processes: Purchasing, Sales, and Payroll Cycles

Chapter 6
Intergrated Enterprise Systems and Cloud Computing

1

Accounting System Insights

How Can the Data in Your Accounting System Create Value?
Meet Business Intelligence.

Can you imagine how the data stored in your accounting system can make millions of dollars for your business?

Meet business intelligence. Business intelligence (BI) uses data in smarter ways. BI involves analyzing data to glean insights for improved decisions and performance. The accounting system stores data, such as sales data, that can be used in BI analytics.

- Southwest Airlines used BI to increase profitability.
- Travelocity, a leader in the online travel industry, used BI to personalize customer service, increasing its gross bookings and earnings by 100% in the first year.
- Coca-Cola Bottling Company used BI about sales from vending machines to better forecast demand, increasing sales by 10%.
- The state of Texas used BI to recover over $600 million in taxes from noncompliant taxpayers by crosschecking returns with other sources of data.
- Wells Fargo & Co., a leader in online financial services, used BI to provide its customers with a 360-degree view of their spending, credit and debit card transactions, checking accounts, and online bill payments.

My Questions

Q 1.1 How do I navigate the crossroads of accounting and IT?

Q 1.2 How is the accounting system related to the enterprise system?

Q 1.3 What are the secrets of my success at the crossroads of accounting and IT?

Q 1.4 What are three keys to opportunity at the crossroads of accounting and IT?

How Do I Navigate the Crossroads of Accounting and IT?

Imagine that you just landed a new job! You have been hired as the IT auditor for EspressoCoffee Company, an online retailer of Italian espresso beans and espresso machines. You are responsible for auditing the accounting system and the related information technology (IT).

Can you conduct a successful audit if you don't understand the IT used by the system? How do you evaluate IT security for the accounting system if you don't understand the underlying IT? Did you know IT auditors often receive higher salaries because of their specialized knowledge of accounting and IT?

To audit accounting systems, IT auditors must be able to communicate with both accounting and IT professionals. Often accountants and IT professionals appear to be speaking different languages. The specialties of their unique fields often have terms and definitions that differ. For example, what an IT professional might call a *computer application*, the accountant might refer to as *software*. Some enterprises have addressed this need by hiring professionals with experience in both accounting and IT who serve as liaisons between the organization's accounting and IT professionals.

In today's business environment, the accounting professional stands at the crossroads of accounting and information technology. The goal of this text is to assist you in navigating the crossroads. We will equip you with IT terminology to facilitate communication with IT professionals, give you tools that IT professionals use, and provide you with insights to understand better the role of the accounting professional at the crossroads of accounting and IT. Having IT knowledge gives you a competitive advantage as an accounting professional.

> **Crossroads**
> This feature will appear throughout your book to clue you in to important terms and topics at the crossroads of accounting and IT.

> To guide you through the crossroads of accounting and IT, this book is organized around three major functions of the accounting system:
> 1. **Store.** People, processes, and technology to store accounting data are covered in Part 1.
> 2. **Analyze.** Financial analytics and business intelligence for decision making are covered in Part 2.
> 3. **Safeguard.** Safeguarding information assets stored in the accounting system using security, controls, and risk management is covered in Part 3.

Numbers...2 Digits or 10?

Both accounting and IT professionals deal with numbers. Computers are digital and can process only *0*s and *1*s, so computer scientists distill everything down to two digits: *0*s and *1*s.

Accountants distill business transactions into numbers. The difference is that accountants use all 10 digits instead of just 2. So at the crossroads of accounting and IT, it all comes down to numbers.

When the Numbers Change....

One enterprise found that its accounting staff and IT professionals were in a heated disagreement about a relatively minor update to an accounting program needed by the accounting staff. The IT staff wanted to charge thousands of dollars to the accounting department for the minor change. When a liaison was called in, she facilitated communication and discovered that all the numbers in the accounting program had been "hard keyed" into the program. Thus, actual numbers, such as 127 or 580, had been used in the program instead of using spreadsheet cell addresses for the source data. The only way to update the program was to manually replace the numbers that had been hard-keyed into the program with updated numbers. This time-consuming, labor-intensive approach was costly.

Imagine if an accounting professional with IT knowledge had been present at the meeting when the initial program was designed. If cell addresses had been used, results would have updated automatically when the numbers changed. Imagine the resources and time that the enterprise might have saved had this oversight never occurred. This example of accounting and IT professionals who need to work together and communicate well underscores the need for accountants who understand accounting and IT. It also underscores your value as an accounting professional if you understand the crossroads of accounting and IT.

My Connection...

How do I study less and learn more? Make connections. Try the following:
• Active Review 1.9
• It's Your Call 1.26

What Is Your Competitive Advantage?

To understand how to be a valued accountant, you need to understand how the accounting system (and you) fit into the larger enterprise system. What value do you add to the enterprise?

Throughout your book the terms *enterprise* and *organization* are used interchangeably.

Crossroads

As an accounting professional, you will encounter symbols and terminology used by IT professionals. A cloud is used by IT professionals to represent the enterprise network. This is known as a network cloud (Figure 1.1).

How Is the Accounting System Related to the Enterprise System?

Imagine that you just received your first paycheck on your new job! How was the data collected to create your paycheck? Who collected the data? Who created the paycheck?

When you were hired, the human resources department collected personal data about you, such as your name, address, and Social Security number. Human resources also collected data about your salary, pay grade, and benefits. That information was shared with the accounting department to generate your paycheck.

Within an enterprise there are numerous activities performed by various departments. These activities are often interconnected, such as human resources and accounting working together to create your paycheck.

An **enterprise system** supports people conducting business activities throughout the enterprise. Three basic functions of an enterprise system involve the following:

- Input: Capturing information to store in the system (such as your salary data)
- Processing: Sorting and storing information (such as calculating the amount of your paycheck)
- Output: Summarizing information to generate documents and reports used by executives, managers, and employees (such as your paycheck)

Because people performing different activities (such as human resources and accounting) have different needs, unique software may be required to meet their specific needs. For example, accountants use an accounting system to meet their needs. This accounting system is a subsystem of the larger enterprise system (Figure 1.1).

An accounting system captures accounting information about transactions, processes the accounting information captured, and generates financial reports, such as income statements and sales reports.

In addition to the accounting system (see Figure 1.1) additional modules or subsystems of an enterprise system might include the following:

- Supply chain management (SCM)
- Operations/production system (OPS)
- Human resource management (HRM)
- Customer relationship management (CRM)

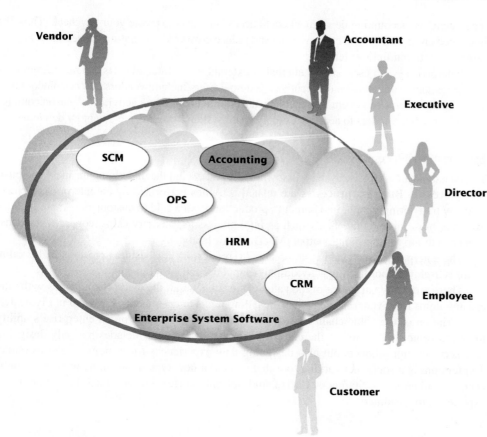

FIGURE 1.1

Enterprise System

How do you see the accounting system interacting with HRM to create your paycheck? When you make an online purchase, how do you interact with an enterprise system?

An **integrated enterprise system** shares data across functional areas within the enterprise. The same information is often used by different departments, as in the case of your paycheck. In an integrated enterprise system, when human resources enters your personal salary data into

> **Integrated Enterprise Systems...**
>
> ...share data across the enterprise. For example, when data is entered into the supply chain management system to record the receipt of an inventory order, the same data can be shared with the accounting system to record the related accounting transactions. This is a good news/bad news situation. The good news is that other people are entering accounting data for you. The bad news is that they may not enter it correctly.

The Road to Integrated Enterprise Systems...How Did We Get Here?

Enterprise resource planning or ERP software of the 1990s was developed as an enterprise-wide system to help managers plan and control organizational resources. ERPs focused on resource planning for the enterprise, integrating information flows across an entire enterprise including accounting, human resources, supply chain, production, and marketing.

In the 2000s ERPs evolved further into the next generation of integrated business processing software called **enterprise software**. Enterprise software goes beyond resource planning. It encompasses all the information processing needs of the entire enterprise, including, but not limited to, resource planning. Enterprise software integrates the various business functions and transaction processing in the enterprise system. One widely used enterprise software is SAP (Systems, Applications, and Products in Data Processing) AG headquartered in Germany. A SAP enterprise system offers modules to assist in managing business processes including the following:

- Financials
- Human resources
- Operations
- Customer relationship management (CRM)
- Supply chain management (SCM)
- Enterprise resource planning (ERP)

If the modules are integrated with the capability to pass electronic documents and information from one module to another, the system is called an integrated enterprise system (IES).

How many times today have you re-entered the same information?

the system, the accounting department could access that data to create your paycheck. Thus, the integrated enterprise system can save time and reduce errors by eliminating the need to rekey the same data into multiple systems.

Enterprise system users can be internal or external users. Internal users can include employees, accountants, directors, and executives. External users include vendors and customers given access to the enterprise system to streamline and coordinate business activities. Amazon.com, for example, permits vendors to access its supply chain system to coordinate inventory deliveries.

Business Processes

To understand an enterprise system, first you must understand the underlying business and business processes. **Business processes** are related activities performed by an enterprise to create value by transforming input into output (a product or service sold to customers). Apple Inc., for example, buys input (components such as Intel processors, memory chips, copper wire, transformers, etc.) to transform into output (MacBook Air laptops).

The enterprise value chain is an organizing framework for business processes. The **value chain** is useful in coordinating activities with suppliers and customers.

There are many variations of the value chain. In general, the value chain begins with purchasing items from vendors and ends with selling items to customers. As shown in Figure 1.2, one variation of the value chain includes the impact of innovation on an enterprise's ability to create value. Innovation in the current business environment includes not only designing new services and products but also designing new experiences for customers. For example, Twitter.com is a social networking tool that created a new type of social networking experience for online users. Starbucks Coffee sold not only coffee, but provided the coffee house experience to customers.

> Asking the following key questions about an enterprise can provide a deeper understanding of the underlying business the enterprise system serves:
> - How does the enterprise create value?
> - What are its business operations?
> - What are the enterprise's business processes for conducting operations?
> - Can the business processes be streamlined or improved?

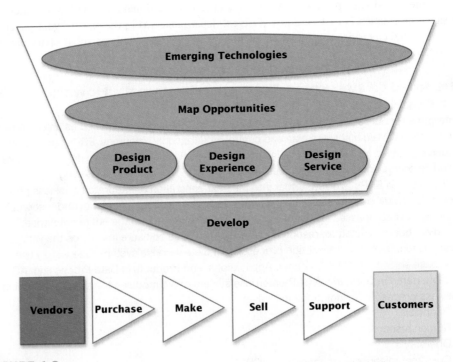

FIGURE 1.2

Value Chain and Innovation

Pair and Share: Share with a classmate your response to the following question: How do you think emerging technologies will create opportunities for accounting?

Based upon The New Value Chain from The *Imagination Challenge: The Strategic Foresight and Innovation in the Global Economy* by Alexander Manu. peachpit.com/articles/ (accessed July 2009).

By Any Other Name...

The system that supports financial and accounting activities in an organization can be called many different names. In academia, such a system is often called an *accounting information system* or *AIS*. However, if you use that term on the job, be prepared for responses such as "What are you talking about?" Typically, AIS is not a term that is used in practice. Instead, terms used may be *accounting system*, *enterprise accounting system*, *financial system*, or *general ledger system*. Boeing, for example, uses the term *enterprise accounting system*.

For simplicity, this book uses the term *accounting system* to refer to systems that support financial and accounting activities within an enterprise. Keep in mind as you are reading that the term *accounting system* may be used interchangeably with *accounting information system* or *enterprise accounting system*.

As shown in Figure 1.2, in addition to research and development for new services, products, and experiences, the value chain is comprised of a series of business processes. These processes include the following:

- Purchase items from vendors.
- Make the service, product, or experience.
- Market and sell the service, product, or experience to customers.
- Support and maintain the service, product, or experience.

The enterprise system supports these business processes. As shown in Figure 1.3, the supply chain management (SCM) system supports the business process of purchasing items from vendors. The operations/production system (OPS) provides the resources to support tracking

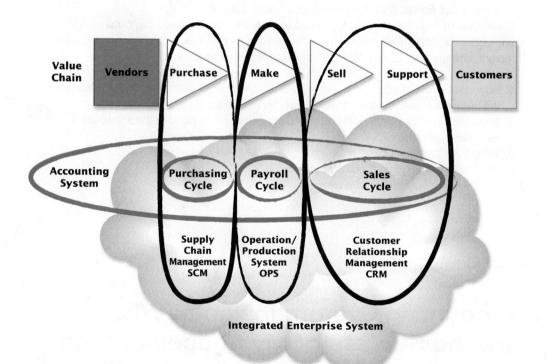

FIGURE 1.3

Business Processes, Transaction Cycles, and the Integrated Enterprise System

Pair and Share: Share with a classmate your response to the following question: Of all the systems, why is the accounting system the most indispensable in the integrated enterprise system?

and coordinating operations of the business to make the service, product, or experience. The customer relationship management (CRM) system supports marketing and sales activities. The accounting system is unique in that it spans the value chain, tracking transaction information from the purchase of items from vendors through the sale to customers (Figure 1.3).

Transaction Cycles

An enterprise's business processes and accounting system are interrelated. The accounting transactions related to specific business processes are frequently called **transaction cycles**. Figure 1.3 shows the relationship between the business processes in the value chain and the accounting transaction cycles. As the figure illustrates, the **purchasing cycle** consists of transactions related to purchasing items from vendors. Sometimes the purchasing cycle is referred to as the *vendors transaction cycle* or *purchasing transaction cycle*. The purchasing cycle relates to transactions between an enterprise and its vendors, including suppliers and consultants.

The **payroll cycle** consists of employee and payroll transactions. These expenditures make it possible to conduct operations to create a service, product, or experience for the enterprise's customers. Together, the purchasing cycle and payroll cycle are referred to as the *expenditure transaction cycle*.

The **sales cycle** in the accounting system corresponds to the selling component of the value chain. The sales cycle may also be called the *revenue cycle* or *revenue transaction cycle*. The sales cycle involves exchanges or transactions between an enterprise and its customers.

To understand the accounting system for an enterprise, it is essential to understand the underlying business processes and transaction cycles. Next, we share with you some accounting system insights. These insights will aid you in navigating the crossroads of accounting and IT.

Crossroads
What IT professionals may refer to as *business processes*, accounting professionals may call *transaction cycles*.

Crossroads
Some IT professionals may mistakenly use the term *accounting cycle* to refer to the purchasing, payroll, and sales cycle.

Accounting professionals typically use the term *accounting cycle* to refer to the accounting activities that span the accounting period, such as preparing a trial balance, making adjusting entries, and creating financial statements.

My Connection...
How do I study less and learn more? Make connections. Try the following:
• Active Review 1.8
• Short Exercise 1.29

Have You Ever Purchased a Used Car?
CARFAX.com is an online service for used car buyers. For a fee, you can obtain information about the car you would like to purchase, such as previous owner(s), prior accidents, repairs, and the resale value. What is the value of this information to a used car buyer?
What do you think?
1. How does CARFAX.com create value? What is the enterprise's value chain? What are the business processes that make up the value chain for the enterprise?
2. What are the accounting events or transactions that correspond to the enterprise's business processes?
3. What transactions make up the purchasing cycle for the business?
4. What are the transactions in the payroll cycle?
5. What is the sales cycle for the enterprise?

Would You Like to Know a Secret?
We will share with you some secrets about accounting that you may not have heard about in your previous accounting classes. These secrets will provide you insights to effectively prepare you for your transition into the world of accounting/IT professionals.

Accounting System Insights: What Are the Secrets of My Success at the Crossroads of Accounting and IT?

Imagine that you take your first paycheck to the bank and deposit it using the ATM. Accountants are well known for focusing on details, such as recording your single bank deposit accurately.

Now imagine the accounting system required to track all deposits made at Wells Fargo's 12,000 ATMs. In addition to getting the details right, the accounting/IT professional must also be able to understand the overall accounting system, such as Wells Fargo's system's ability to track deposits made at over 12,000 ATMs.

Can't See the Forest for the Trees?

Studying accounting systems is very different from studying other areas of accounting, such as financial, tax, or managerial accounting. Financial accounting focuses on external reporting for creditors and investors. Tax accounting focuses on tax reports for the Internal Revenue Service (IRS), state departments of revenue, and local tax agencies. Managerial accounting focuses on providing accounting information to internal users, primarily management. Successful accountants are well known for focusing on details, which is imperative for a successful accounting professional. However, understanding accounting systems involves seeing the overall system as well as focusing on details.

FIGURE 1.4

**Satellite Mapping
(learn.arc.nasa.gov)**

Your prior accounting courses, such as financial, managerial, and tax accounting, focused more on details. You may find that this course requires you to think differently about accounting. To aid you in this transition, we share with you some accounting system insights.

Accounting Insight No. 1: Think Satellite Mapping

Viewing an accounting system can be compared to satellite mapping. With satellite mapping, you can use an aerial satellite view to see the entire globe or zoom in to see cities or even streets (Figure 1.4). Obtain the level of detail needed by zooming in or out until the satellite map is in focus.

The aerial view of accounting is the enterprise-wide view of the accounting system. To see the detailed view of accounting, zoom in (drill down) to focus on specific, detailed information, events, and transactions recorded in the accounting system.

ACCOUNTING INSIGHT NO. 1
Use Satellite Mapping
to View Accounting Systems...
Zoom out for Aerial View...
Zoom in for Detail View....

BASELINE ACCOUNTING SYSTEM MODEL To assist you in envisioning a global view of an accounting system, Figure 1.5 shows an accounting system model that is representative of most enterprises. This will be referred to as a baseline accounting system model.

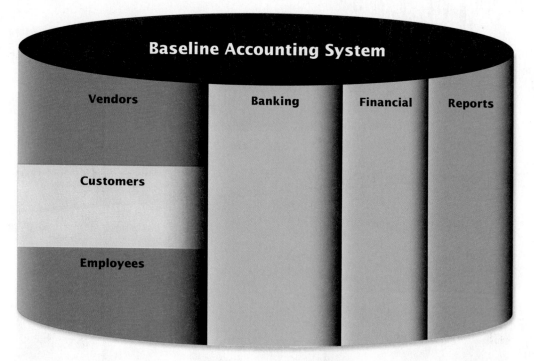

FIGURE 1.5

Baseline Accounting System Model

The **baseline accounting system** model provides an enterprise-wide view of the firm's accounting similar to the aerial, global view for satellite mapping.

The baseline accounting system typically consists of the following modules that most enterprises use:

- Vendors module
- Customers module
- Employees module
- Banking module
- Financial module
- Reports module

Each module contains business processes with related accounting transactions. The baseline accounting system with transactions common to most business operations is shown in Figure 1.6. The baseline accounting system with corresponding transaction cycles is shown in Figure 1.7. Next, we explore further each module in the baseline accounting system.

VENDORS MODULE: PURCHASING CYCLE The **vendors module** is composed of transactions with vendors, such as purchasing goods or services. An example of a vendor transaction would be when Apple Inc. purchases components to use for building iPads.

The vendors module relates to the purchasing cycle. Vendor transactions that are common to the purchasing cycle for many enterprises include the following:

- Create purchase orders.
- Receive items.
- Enter bills.

CUSTOMERS MODULE: SALES CYCLE The **customers module** consists of transactions with customers, such as selling the customer a product or service. An example of a customer transaction would be when an Apple retail store sells you, the customer, an iPad.

The customers module relates to the sales cycle. Customer transactions that are commonly performed as part of the sales cycle include the following:

- Create invoices.
- Receive customer payments.

A Model...

...is a symbolic representation of a real system or product. For example, a car manufacturer designs a car, then builds a working model (prototype) of the car to test the design before actually building the entire car. Similarly, we will use a baseline model of the accounting system to represent how accounting information flows through most enterprises.

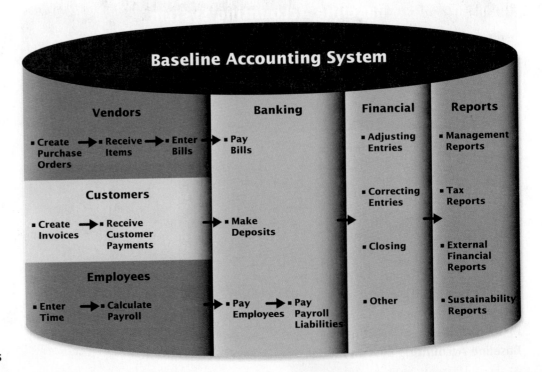

FIGURE 1.6

Baseline Accounting System with Transactions

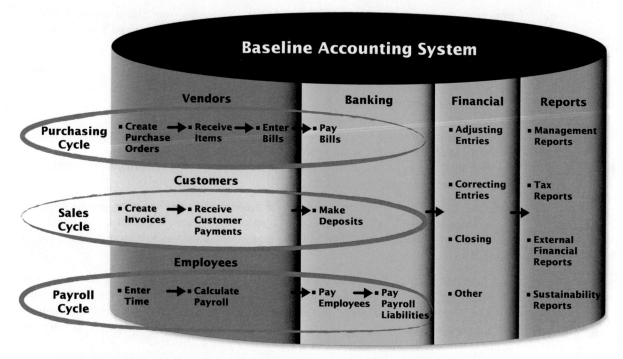

FIGURE 1.7

Baseline Accounting System with Transaction Cycles

Pair and Share: Share with a classmate your response to the following:
Explain how Figures 1.5, 1.6, and 1.7 use satellite mapping for accounting.

EMPLOYEES MODULE: PAYROLL CYCLE The **employees module** consists of transactions with employees for payroll. If you work at an Apple store as an employee, an example of an employee (payroll) transaction is when Apple pays you a salary.

The employees module relates to the payroll cycle. Employee transactions often completed as part of the payroll cycle include the following:

- Enter time.
- Calculate payroll.

BANKING MODULE The **banking module** involves cash received (deposits) or cash paid (checks/withdrawals) by the enterprise. An example of a banking transaction would be if you, the customer, paid cash to Apple Inc. for your new iPad. Apple would deposit this cash in a bank.

You will notice in Figure 1.6 that the banking module is typically a continuation of other modules:

- Pay bills is a continuation of the vendors module components.
- Make deposits is a continuation of the customers module components.
- Pay employees and pay payroll liabilities are continuations of the employees module components.

FINANCIAL MODULE: FINANCIAL CYCLE The **financial module** consists of other events and transactions that do not fall into the prior modules. Sometimes it is referred to as the *financial cycle*.

The financial module includes the following items:

- **Adjusting entries** at year end to bring accounts up to date, such as recording depreciation for the period
- **Correcting entries** to correct errors
- **Closing entries** to close out Income and Expense accounts at year end so the enterprise can begin the new year with $-0- balances in all Income and Expense accounts.

REPORTS MODULE The **reports module** relates to output from the accounting system. Reports can be in electronic form or in hardcopy printouts. In general, there are four types of reports produced by the accounting system:

- **Financial reports**, such as the financial statements included in a company's annual report given to investors. For example, Apple Inc. includes an income statement, balance sheet, and statement of cash flows in its annual report to investors.
- **Tax reports** used when filing federal, state, and local taxes.
- **Management reports** provided to management of the enterprise. These reports are prepared as needed to assist management in decision making.
- **Sustainability reports** used for decision making and performance evaluation related to an enterprise's sustainability practices.

Reports generated by the reports module of the accounting system are often summaries of the output from the other baseline modules, (i.e., vendors, customers, employees, banking, and financial modules). Next, we will look at how the modules in the baseline accounting system are incorporated into accounting software.

ACCOUNTING SOFTWARE Accounting software often includes a navigation screen that represents the major modules within the accounting system. QuickBooks accounting software uses a Home page as shown in Figure 1.8. The QuickBooks Home page aids you in seeing the entire accounting system at a glance. It is your satellite map for the accounting software. If you zoom in closer, you see the modules and related transaction cycles:

- Vendor transactions in the purchasing cycle
- Customer transactions in the sales cycle
- Employee transactions in the payroll cycle

To zoom in or drill down to see details, you simply click on the icons. For example, if you click on the Write Checks icon (Figure 1.9), you can drill down to view the detail of an onscreen check (Figure 1.10).

Your Competitive Advantage...

In your book you see the approach frequently used in practice:

1. Start with a baseline system.
2. Customize the baseline for enterprise-specific needs.

With this approach, you can handle virtually any accounting system you encounter in practice, giving you a competitive advantage.

ABCs of Accounting Systems

Today, developing an accounting system is as easy as ABC. Divide the accounting system into two stages: baseline and customized. The dilemma facing enterprises has been:

- *Do we change our business processes to fit a generic baseline accounting system?*
- *Do we custom build an accounting system that fits our unique business needs?*

This dilemma is addressed by using the accounting system ABCs. The baseline accounting system is a generic accounting system that includes the workflow and business processes frequently used by most enterprises. Modules in a baseline accounting system include the vendors, customers, employees, banking, financial, and reports modules as shown in the baseline accounting system model in Figures 1.5, 1.6, and 1.7.

To create a customized accounting system, we configure or customize the baseline accounting system to accommodate the unique requirements and needs of the specific enterprise. This involves customizing each of the modules shown in the baseline model to fit the specific needs of the enterprise.

$$\text{Accounting System} =$$
$$\text{Baseline System} +$$
$$\text{Customized System}$$

Debits and Credits...

A transaction is an exchange between an enterprise and another entity. Double-entry accounting using debits and credits is based upon receiving and giving. When Apple sells an iPhone, Apple receives cash and gives an iPhone. Thus, an exchange of cash and merchandise inventory occurs. An event may not involve an exchange, but may still need to be recorded in the accounting system. Accrued interest expense needs to be recorded at the end of the accounting period to bring accounts up to date but does not involve an exchange.

Debits and Credits...

Debits and credits play an important role when learning double-entry accounting.

Accounting Insight No. 2: Debits and Credits?

Today, most accounting information is *not* entered using debits and credits. Debits and credits may be used to make adjusting entries at year end to bring accounts up to date. However, debits and credits typically are not used to enter transactions and events into the accounting system.

ACCOUNTING INSIGHT NO. 2
Most Accounting Information
Is NOT Entered...
Using Debits and Credits

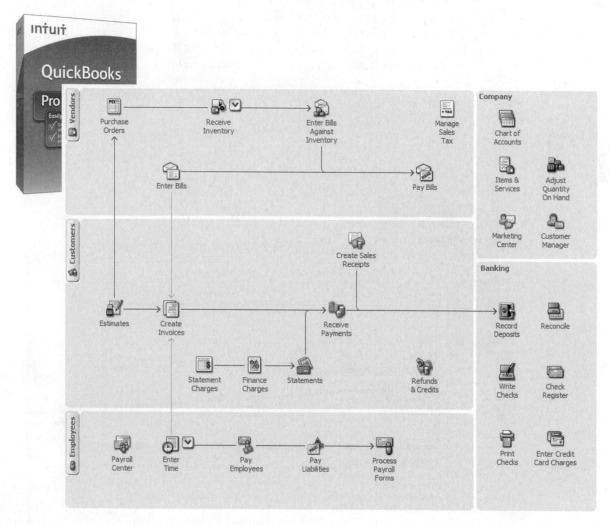

FIGURE 1.8

QuickBooks Home Page

On the QuickBooks Home page, can you find the vendors module? The employees module? The customers module? Does the QuickBooks Home page have a financial module?

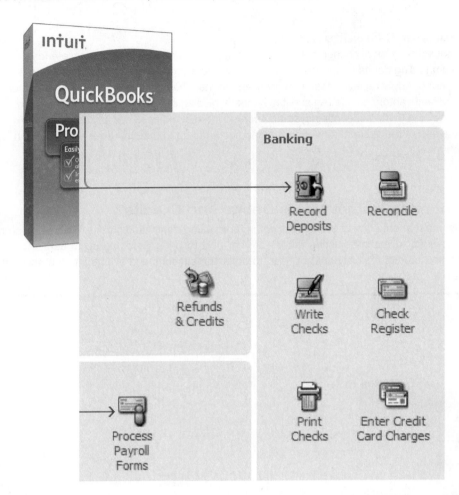

FIGURE 1.9

QuickBooks Drill Down

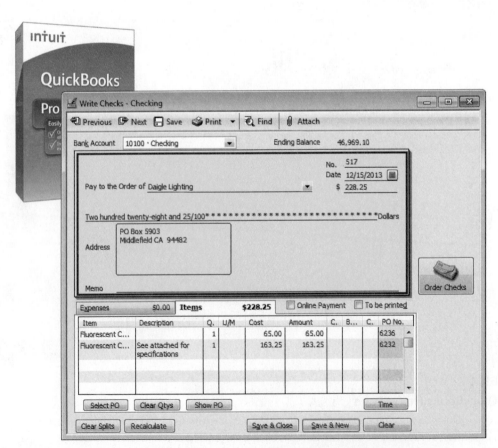

FIGURE 1.10

Onscreen Check Detail

Accounting Insight No. 3: Onscreen Forms

Accounting information is frequently entered using onscreen forms, such as the onscreen check shown in Figure 1.10.

These onscreen forms are actually database forms designed to look like frequently used paper forms, such as checks, invoices, and purchase orders. The onscreen forms often mirror the paper forms to speed data entry.

ACCOUNTING INSIGHT NO. 3
Accounting Information Is Often Entered...
Using Onscreen Forms:
• Checks
• Invoices
• Purchase Orders
• and More....

Accounting Insight No. 4: Databases

This brings us to Accounting Insight No. 4: Today, virtually without exception, accounting systems use databases to store accounting information. From QuickBooks for small business to SAP for large-scale enterprises, accounting systems use databases to store accounting data. Thus, the database is a key component of the accounting system.

ACCOUNTING INSIGHT NO. 4
Accounting Systems
Use DATABASES to Store
Accounting Information

Accounting software is often classified into three categories:

■ Small business
■ Midsize
■ Large scale

Small business software includes QuickBooks, Peachtree, and SAP Business One. Accounting software for midsize enterprises includes QuickBooks Enterprise and SAP Business All-in-One. Large-scale accounting systems would use enterprise software such as SAP Business Suite and Oracle E-Business Suite (Figure 1.11).

With small business accounting software, such as QuickBooks or Peachtree, the database is integrated. When you install the software, the database is installed also. This is similar to an integrated sound system, such as a BOSE speaker with sound components integrated into one unit.

For large-scale enterprises using enterprise software, such as SAP, there is a front-end software application (client) that is the user interface. The user interface consists of the input and output forms seen on the computer screen. A database software application, such as an Oracle database, is installed as a separate component. Large-scale enterprise software with a front-end software application on screen and a behind-the-screen database can be compared to a high-end Bang & Olufsen sound system with separate components of woofers, subwoofers, and so on.

Although the size and number of databases may differ, accounting systems use databases to collect and store accounting information.

Accounting Databases...
In your book, to clearly identify databases used to store accounting data, the term *accounting database* is used.

In Your Book...
We use illustrations from different accounting software to give you stronger transitional skills.

We begin your book using QuickBooks software examples because it is easy to learn. Then you can transition your skills to use accounting software designed for larger enterprises.

Your Competitive Advantage...
Transitional skills permit you to learn one type of accounting software and transition your knowledge to other accounting software packages. For example, if you learn the fundamentals of accounting software for small business, you can transition that knowledge to learning mid- and large-scale accounting software.

Accounting Insight No. 5: Behind the Screen

This leads us to Accounting Insight No. 5: To understand accounting systems, the accountant must understand databases. Understanding databases can be tricky because databases are *behind the screen*. The accounting software appears on the accountant's computer screen. The accounting database that stores the accounting data runs behind the screen of the accounting software.

ACCOUNTING INSIGHT NO. 5
To Understand Accounting Systems the Accountant Today Must Understand
DATABASES...
Behind the Screen

FIGURE 1.11

Accounting Software

Did you know that QuickBooks Enterprise software has a larger market share than all other midsize accounting software combined? Did you know that QuickBooks accounting software has almost 95% of the small business accounting software market?

ACCOUNTING INSIGHT NO. 6
When Designing a Database Begin with the Outcome in Mind

Accounting Software		
Small Business	**Mid-Size Enterprise**	**Large-Scale Enterprise**
▪ QuickBooks	▪ QuickBooks Enterprise	▪ SAP Business Suite
▪ Peachtree	▪ SAP Business All-in-One	▪ Oracle E-Business Suite
▪ SAP Business One	▪ Oracle's JD Edwards EnterpriseOne	▪ Oracle's PeopleSoft Enterprise

Accounting Insight No. 6: Outcome in Mind

Accounting Insight No. 6 states that when designing an accounting database, begin with the outcome in mind. What reports or outcomes do you need from the accounting system? The outcomes are called user requirements. Collecting and anticipating user requirements is a crucial part of designing an effective accounting system. For example, let's say you are designing a database for EspressoCoffee. EspressoCoffee would like to send a mailing to all customers in the 63141 ZIP code. Thus, it is necessary to design and store the address information in the database in such a way that EspressoCoffee can search by ZIP code.

Begin with the Outcome in Mind...
For example, if you needed to mail your customers in the 63141 ZIP code, you must be able to sort by ZIP.

User Requirements...
Outcomes required by the user are called user requirements.

EspressoCoffee Company
EspressoCoffee is a company that will be used throughout your book to illustrate accounting system concepts.

2-D Databases...
A spreadsheet can be viewed as a two-dimensional or flat database (see Figure 1.13).

What are the database essentials that you need to know as an accounting professional? Database essentials include the following:

- Fields
- Records
- Tables

To illustrate these database essentials, we will assist EspressoCoffee in setting up a system for tracking customer information. EspressoCoffee would like to set up a system for tracking information about its customers who buy espresso beans and machines. For ease of use, EspressoCoffee would like to organize the information in a spreadsheet.

Database Essentials

Field: A piece of information about events, people, or objects
Record: A collection of related fields
Table: A collection of related records with a unique table name
Database: A collection of related tables

DATABASE FIELDS: PIECES OF INFORMATION Each piece of information that EspressoCoffee collects about a customer is called a **field**. For example, customer name, street, city, state, and ZIP would be considered fields.

DATABASE RECORDS: COLLECTION OF RELATED FIELDS Each row in EspressoCoffee's spreadsheet contains information about a specific customer. This is called a **record**. A database record is a collection of related database fields populated with data about a specific customer (Figure 1.12).

The **primary key** is a unique identifier for each record. For example, for EspressoCoffee to retrieve a specific customer, it needs a unique identifier for each customer. If EspressoCoffee had two customers named John Smith, when John Smith placed an order for espresso beans, the company would have no way to know which John Smith placed the order—unless EspressoCoffee had a unique identifier for each customer. Customer No. is the primary key that uniquely identifies each customer for EspressoCoffee. Each customer has a unique customer number so that no two customers have the same number (Figure 1.12).

Field

	A	B	C	D	E	F	G	H
1	CUSTOMER No	LAST NAME	FIRST NAME	COMPANY NAME	STREET ADDRESS	CITY	STATE	ZIP
2	127127	Ashuer	Angela		13 Joseph Ave	Appleton	WI	54911
3	913691	Pico	Vincent	EspressoBar	58 Dante	Pisa	Tuscany	56100
4								
5								

Record →

⫷ ◀ ▶ ⫸ Customer

FIGURE 1.12

Fields and Records

How many fields do you see in Figure 1.12?
How many records are in Figure 1.12?

DATABASE TABLES: COLLECTION OF RELATED RECORDS A database table is a collection of related records. You can think of a spreadsheet as a two-dimensional or flat database because it is only one table (Figure 1.13).

Each database table has a unique name. For example, we will name the database table in Figure 1.13 the CUSTOMER table because it stores data about EspressoCoffee's customers.

ACCOUNTING DATABASES: COLLECTION OF RELATED TABLES A database is a collection of related tables. A relational database is three dimensional with many interrelated tables (Figure 1.14). In a **relational database**, the tables are related or connected through fields that are common to two or more tables.

> Note that the address is broken into separate fields so that you can search by ZIP, for example.

1st Dimension →

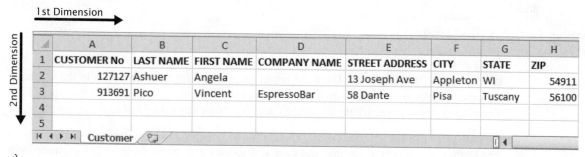

2nd Dimension ↓

	A	B	C	D	E	F	G	H
1	CUSTOMER No	LAST NAME	FIRST NAME	COMPANY NAME	STREET ADDRESS	CITY	STATE	ZIP
2	127127	Ashuer	Angela		13 Joseph Ave	Appleton	WI	54911
3	913691	Pico	Vincent	EspressoBar	58 Dante	Pisa	Tuscany	56100
4								
5								

⫷ ◀ ▶ ⫸ Customer

FIGURE 1.13

Excel Spreadsheet as a 2-Dimensional Database Table

3rd Dimension

1st Dimension →

2nd Dimension ↓

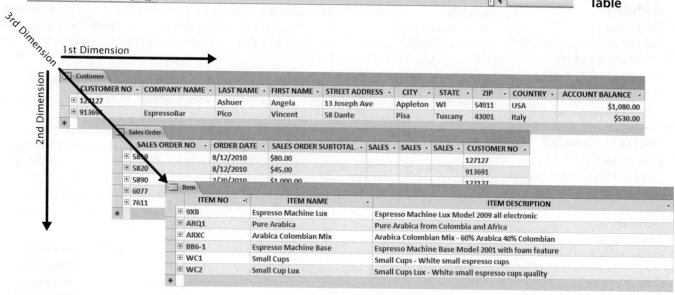

Customer

CUSTOMER NO	COMPANY NAME	LAST NAME	FIRST NAME	STREET ADDRESS	CITY	STATE	ZIP	COUNTRY	ACCOUNT BALANCE
127127		Ashuer	Angela	13 Joseph Ave	Appleton	WI	54911	USA	$1,080.00
913691	EspressoBar	Pico	Vincent	58 Dante	Pisa	Tuscany	43001	Italy	$530.00

Sales Order

SALES ORDER NO	ORDER DATE	SALES ORDER SUBTOTAL	SALES	SALES	SALES	CUSTOMER NO
5819	8/12/2010	$80.00				127127
5820	8/12/2010	$45.00				913691
5890	7/20/2010	$1,000.00				127127
6077						
7611						

Item

ITEM NO	ITEM NAME	ITEM DESCRIPTION
9XB	Espresso Machine Lux	Espresso Machine Lux Model 2009 all electronic
ARQ1	Pure Arabica	Pure Arabica from Colombia and Africa
ARXC	Arabica Colombian Mix	Arabica Colombian Mix - 60% Arabica 40% Colombian
BB6-1	Espresso Machine Base	Espresso Machine Base Model 2001 with foam feature
WC1	Small Cups	Small Cups - White small espresso cups
WC2	Small Cup Lux	Small Cups Lux - White small espresso cups quality

FIGURE 1.14

Database Tables in Three Dimensions

Can you identify the three dimensions to a database?

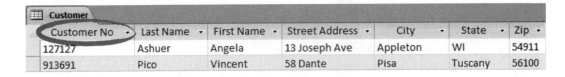

FIGURE 1.15

CUSTOMER Table

Customer No	Last Name	First Name	Street Address	City	State	Zip
127127	Ashuer	Angela	13 Joseph Ave	Appleton	WI	54911
913691	Pico	Vincent	58 Dante	Pisa	Tuscany	56100

FIGURE 1.16

ORDER Table

Why don't we need to repeat the customer information in the ORDER table?

Invoice No	Date	Customer No
5819	12.21.2010	127127
5820	12.23.2010	913691

EspressoCoffee
Company

For example, after EspressoCoffee builds a CUSTOMER database table, it will need to track information about customer orders in a separate table called the ORDER table. The ORDER table also needs a unique identifier or primary key, such as Order No.

The customer information is stored in the CUSTOMER table and the order information is stored in a separate table, the ORDER table. Note that we do not need to reenter all of the customer information again in the ORDER table. We can simply enter the customer number and then connect the related tables (CUSTOMER table and ORDER table). This is why it is called a relational database: The table relationships are used to connect the tables in the database (Figure 1.15 and 1.16). In a relational database, the tables are related or connected using fields that are common to two or more tables.

In an accounting database, there will be many tables including a table for customers, vendors, employees, sales orders, purchase orders, and many more. Each table in the database will consist of records comprised of fields.

Three more database essential terms that an accountant needs to understand are:

- Database forms
- Database queries
- Database reports

DATABASE FORMS: INPUT Database forms are forms used to input data into the database. Onscreen checks and onscreen invoices in accounting software are actually database forms designed to resemble paper source documents, making data entry easier and faster (Figure 1.10).

DATABASE QUERIES: SEARCHES Database queries are questions. Database queries search the database to answer a specific question and extract a specific piece of information from one or more tables. For example, you might ask the question "How many customers does EspressoCoffee have in the 54911 ZIP code?" You could query the database to search on the ZIP field using the criteria of ZIP = 54911.

DATABASE REPORTS: OUTPUT After you search or query the database, you will need a way to view or output the information. Database reports provide a format for viewing the results of your query. You can usually view a report onscreen or print out a copy of a report.

For example, if you wanted to create a 2012 income statement for EspressoCoffee using accounting information stored in a database, first the system would run a query to retrieve revenue and expense account balances for 2012. Then the results of the query would display in a database report using an income statement format.

Accounting Insights No. 3 through 6 relate to how accounting data is stored in a database. Storing accounting data is one of three vital functions that the accounting system serves. Basically, three functions of the accounting system include:

1. Storage of accounting transactions and financial data. The accounting transactions that result from the operations of the business are typically stored in a relational database. Sometimes the relational database that stores operational transactions is referred to as an **operational database**. Accounting Insights No. 3 through 6 relate to this first function of storing accounting data in a database.

2. Business intelligence and financial analytics for decision making. Business intelligence employs data analytics and predictive modeling to gain insights from data to improve the

Database Queries...
Note that the customer address must be broken into separate fields so that you can search on the ZIP Code field.

Database Queries...
SQL (Structured Query Language) is a query language used to query a relational database.

More Database Essentials
Database form: Database screen to input data
Database query: Database searches
Database report: Database screen for output data

quality of business decisions. Accounting Insight No. 7 relates to this second function of how accounting data is used for decision making.

3. **Safeguarding information assets.** One of the functions of the accounting system is to have appropriate security and controls to safeguard the information assets that it contains. Accounting Insight No. 8 relates to this third function of accounting systems, safeguarding information assets.

My Connection...

How do I study less and learn more? Make connections. Try the following:

- Active Review 1.3
- Tech in Practice 1.27
- Short Exercise 1.30
- Tech in Practice 1.40

Accounting Insight No. 7: Business Intelligence

ACCOUNTING INSIGHT NO. 7
Business Intelligence
Provides Organizations with
Competitive Advantage

Businesses may invest millions of dollars to create financial systems to collect and store data. The total cost of ownership (TCO) for a large enterprise system has been estimated to be as high as $300 million. To increase the return on this sizable investment, enterprises seek to derive value from the data to make more intelligent decisions to improve business performance. A growing trend in organizations today is the use of **business intelligence (BI)**. Data analysis and predictive modeling are used to gain insights from data to improve the quality of business decisions. The value of information often derives from its ability to improve decision making. Business intelligence provides organizations with a competitive advantage.

Accounting and financial systems play an important role, not only in collecting and storing financial data, but also in providing information for decision making and BI. If the accounting system does not collect the information needed, makes errors in storing the information, or is unable to retrieve the information once stored, then the information needed for decisions is flawed or unavailable. If the information is flawed, the decision may be misguided, sometimes costing enterprises millions of dollars—simply because the accounting system did not provide useful information to decision makers.

Increasingly, systems today are expected to have the capability to convert data into information and, through further analysis, into BI for improved decisions. The transformation of data to intelligence can be illustrated with the following example for Apple Inc.

- **Data:** The amount of a single sale of an Apple computer would be accounting data.
- **Information:** Apple's income statement for the year showing sales by type of customer would be information. Which customers purchased what products last year?
- **Intelligence:** Financial analytics and predictive modeling that allows Apple to predict the number of customers who will purchase a new product. Which customers will purchase what products next year?

Decisions. Decisions. Decisions...

An important role of the accounting system is to provide information to decision makers.

Enterprise decisions: Should Apple Inc. open new stores? Should Apple raise prices of the iPad? Would making a greener Apple computer be more competitive?

Investor decisions: Should an investor buy stock in Apple Inc? Should an investor buy or sell Google stock?

Creditor decisions: Should Duetsch Bank make a loan to a new start-up enterprise? Will the borrower be able to repay loan interest and principal?

How many decisions do you make in one day? What information do you use when you make those decisions?

Kroger supermarket chain used BI to increase its coupon redemption rate to 50% as compared to a typical redemption rate of 1% to 3%.

Two approaches to BI and financial analytics are:

- Shadow data
- BI technologies

SHADOW DATA Many organizations use shadow data consisting of internally developed spreadsheets. Shadow data is data that shadows the formal accounting system. For example, shadow data is often data extracted from the relational database to perform financial analyses.

Queries of the operational database are combined with financial analytics to derive BI. BI using daily accounting sales transactions stored in the operational database can answer such questions as "Which customers purchased what products *last* year?"

MS Excel has the capability to extract data from databases using Open DataBase Connectivity (ODBC). After the data is imported into Excel, the spreadsheet software can be used to perform analysis that is cumbersome, if not impossible, to perform within the relational database. Significant amounts of an accountant's time may be spent extracting information from the relational database into spreadsheets and then analyzing the data using spreadsheet software. Some accountants estimate that 90% of their time is spent using spreadsheets.

There are several reasons for the popularity of shadow data. One of the main reasons is that it is easier to perform analysis using spreadsheet features than performing the analysis using a relational database. Another reason is that using a relational database to perform analysis often requires the assistance of IT staff to program the necessary queries, which creates dependency on IT availability and knowledge.

A disadvantage of shadow data is that often there is little or no documentation. When the employee who created the spreadsheet leaves, no one else may know how to use the application. The same application must be redeveloped by someone else or abandoned. Another disadvantage is that while security and control may be adequate to prevent unauthorized access to the relational database, security and control for shadow data is often inadequate or nonexistent.

BUSINESS INTELLIGENCE TECHNOLOGIES An increasing trend in business is the use of BI technologies. BI technologies are basically software applications that perform data mining and advanced mathematical analysis. Organizations use BI technologies to find patterns and insights, such as Kroger using BI to target consumers with specific coupons. The insights gained can be used as BI to improve decision making.

The advent of integrated enterprise systems led to the development of data warehouses storing massive amounts of enterprise data. Data warehouses permit extensive data analytics to provide BI for improved decision quality.

By analyzing historical and current data, past and present performance, and vast data stores contained in data warehouses, decision makers can gain valuable insights. BI using data warehouses employ financial analytics and predictive modeling to forecast future business trends. For example, BI using predictive modeling might answer the following question: Which customers will purchase what products *next* year?

BI using a data warehouse employs an extract, transform, and load (ETL) approach. Data is extracted from the operational database, transformed by analytical processing, and then loaded into an online application. These online applications are called online analytical processing or **OLAP cubes**. Data cubes permit users to view the data in a multidimensional manner. For example, sales can be viewed in terms of geographic region, market segment, and type of customer.

The disadvantage to this type of BI is that often there is a lag between when the data, such as sales transactions for example, is entered into the relational database and when it is available for viewing in an OLAP cube. Sometimes the lag can be 24 hours or longer.

Accounting Insight No. 8: Safeguarding Information

Organizations seek to collect and store valuable information to improve business performance; yet by doing so, the information asset becomes a prime target. Fighting cybercrime has become an ongoing battle for some enterprises as they try to prevent and detect cyberattacks on information assets. Because information assets have value, the accounting system must safeguard the information stored.

In today's business environment with financial frauds, lapses in ethics, and cybercrime, a crucial aspect of accounting systems is security and controls to safeguard information assets stored in the system.

To protect information assets, organizations implement security and controls to prevent fraud, unauthorized access, modification, destruction, or disclosure. Internal control is the set of policies and procedures enterprises use to safeguard assets, including information assets, and to prevent and detect errors. Limiting access to your enterprise's accounting system by requiring a valid user ID and password is an example of an internal control.

In the aftermath of the Enron financial scandal, which involved massive fraud, there is increased emphasis upon preventing and detecting fraud. There is also an increased focus upon ethics within the accounting profession. The Sarbanes-Oxley Act of 2002 (SOX), the U.S. legislation passed after the Enron scandal, requires that publicly traded companies assess the effectiveness of their system of internal controls and that an independent CPA firm audit this assessment. IT audit plays a critical role in assessing security and controls for an enterprise's IT and accounting applications.

When designing an accounting system, it is crucial that security for information assets is considered to prevent fraud and unauthorized access. Security and controls are needed for accounting systems, accounting databases, shadow data systems, and BI applications.

Fraud, ethics, SOX, and other security and control standards and frameworks are discussed in detail in later chapters.

> **Information Assets...**
> Information assets consist of information contained within the information system including electronic records, files, and databases.

> **$11,000,000 Spreadsheet Error...**
> Kodak, the world's largest film maker, announced it was adjusting earnings due to an $11,000,000 spreadsheet error. Kodak's chief financial officer (CFO) explained how the $11 million error occurred: "There were too many zeros added to the employee's accrued severance." (marketwatch.com, 2005)

> **You're The Boss...**
> If you were the CFO of Kodak, how would you explain to the public that one of your employees had mistakenly entered too many zeros in a spreadsheet and overstated your earnings by $11,000,000? How would you explain that the error went undetected before you announced earnings and issued your financial results to your investors and the public?

> **My Connection...**
> How do I study less and learn more? Make connections. Try the following:
> • Active Review 1.10
> • Short Exercise 1.31
> • It's Your Call 1.34

What Are Three Keys to Opportunity at the Crossroads of Accounting and IT?

Successful accounting systems consider the impact of three key factors: people, processes, and technology. These three keys are a triage that you can use as an accounting/IT professional to assess and address virtually any systems issues or opportunities (Figure 1.17).

People, Processes, and Technology

If you are evaluating a new accounting system, you can use these three keys to address its impact:

1. What is the impact of the new system on **people**? *Who* will be affected? *How* will they be impacted? Will we downsize? Upsize? Will training be required? How will our employees manage the changes required by the new system?
2. What is the impact of the new system on **processes**? How will our business processes change? Will the new system require us to change the way we enter information into our accounting system?
3. What is the impact on **technology**? Will our existing technology be adequate? What new technology will we need to purchase? How much will the new technology cost?

> Triage means "to sort." Medical professionals triage or sort patients based on need. Triage your accounting IT issues by sorting into people, processes, or technology.

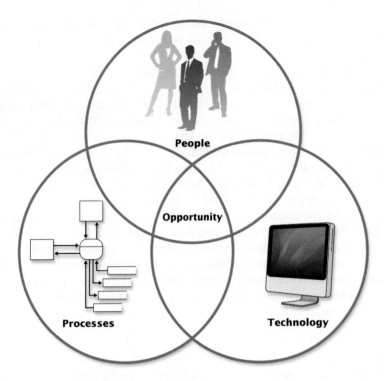

FIGURE 1.17

Three Keys
Pair and Share: Share with a classmate your response to the following:
How can you use the three keys to triage an issue or opportunity that you are currently facing?

International Financial Reporting Standards (IFRS)...

When addressing the impending changes required by the anticipated adoption of IFRS in the United States, sort the impacts into people, processes, and technology:

1. What is the impact of IFRS on people?
2. What is the impact of IFRS on processes?
3. What is the impact of IFRS on technology?

> Transactions are exchanges. If Apple Inc. sells a laptop to a customer, Apple gives the customer the laptop and receives cash from the customer. Thus, there is an exchange of a laptop for cash.

PEOPLE People involved in the accounting system are sometimes referred to as agents. People can be internal agents, such as employees. Agents can also be external to the enterprise, such as vendors. People to consider when evaluating the impact of a proposed action can include the following:

- Vendors: People from whom your enterprise purchases goods and services. This includes consultants hired by the enterprise.
- Customers: People who buy your goods and/or services.
- Employees: People employed by the enterprise.

PROCESSES Processes are related activities or events that create value. These activities and events can be grouped into related areas, such as vendor transactions, customer transactions, and employee transactions:

- Vendor transactions: Purchase transactions resulting from when an enterprise purchases goods and services from vendors
- Customer transactions: Sales transactions related to an enterprise selling goods and services to customers
- Employee transactions: Payroll transactions related to processing payments to enterprise employees and governmental agencies

As we study processes, we want to view how the information flows through your enterprise and accounting system. When and how is information captured? For example, Figure 1.7 shows how information flows through a baseline accounting system. We will explore business processes further in Chapters 4 and 5.

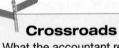

Crossroads
What the accountant refers to as *software*, the IT professional may refer to as *applications*.

TECHNOLOGY The third key, technology, is ever changing. We are going to focus specifically on **information technology (IT)** when we are evaluating accounting systems. IT consists of software, hardware, and network technology used by the organization.

Software consists of computer programs. These programs tell the computer what steps to perform. Hardware consists of electrical and electronic components used in IT, such as laptops. A network is the technology used to connect computers. A database is a technology used to store data. For example, an accounting system uses a database to store data about accounting transactions.

IT architecture is the design or blueprint for an enterprise's information technology. **IT infrastructure** is how specific software, hardware, and networks are used to build IT architecture for your enterprise.

After triaging the system issues into people, processes, and technology, what is the next step? How are accounting systems designed and developed? Who decides what features the system will have? What data will be collected? What reports will be generated by the system?

As you can imagine, this is a complex undertaking, so a well-organized approach to system development is required. A structured approach to developing systems frequently used by IT professionals is called the system development life cycle or SDLC.

System Development Life Cycle (SDLC)

The **system development life cycle (SDLC)** provides a roadmap or framework for organizing the complex, multifaceted undertaking of developing a system. SDLC is increasingly important to accountants because now we are required to audit the SDLC as the system is being developed. Imagine trying to audit a new system under development if you don't understand SDLC. To introduce you to SDLC, the following are six main phases for developing new systems:

Plan the system project including scheduling, budgeting, and staffing.

Analyze the new system requirements, such as what reports are required and what data needs to be collected by the system.

Design business processes and databases for the new system.

Build/buy and test databases and computer programs for the new system.

Install new IT hardware, software, and databases.

Deploy the new system, using the system on an ongoing basis and maintaining and updating it as necessary.

Advantages to using SDLC include the following:

- The SDLC provides an organized, systematic approach to modeling and documenting a new system.
- The SDLC provides a better understanding about the role of data, accounting activities, and users, such as accountants.
- The SDLC provides an overview of the interrelationships of databases, computer programs, business processes, and security and controls.
- The SDLC facilitates project management for a new system.
- The SDLC may appear on professional certification exams, such as the certified public accountant (CPA) examination, the certified information technology professional (CITP) examination, and the certified information systems auditor (CISA) examination.

> IT architecture is the equivalent of a house blueprint, and IT infrastructure is the equivalent of an actual house built from the blueprint.

> **PAD-BID**
> Notice that the acronym for the six phases of the SDLC is PAD-BID: plan, analyze, design, build/buy, install, and deploy.

> **My Connection...**
> How do I study less and learn more? Make connections. Try Short Exercise 1.32.

Your GPS for Navigating the Crossroads of Accounting and IT

Our book is your GPS for navigating the crossroads of accounting and IT. Your roadmap to this book is shown in Figure 1.18. Seeing a roadmap now will save you time later. It provides you with an overview of the entire accounting systems field. As you progress through this book, the roadmap will assist you in navigating your journey through the crossroads of accounting and IT.

Part 1
Enterprise Accounting Systems: People, Processes, and Technology

Store Accounting Data

Chapter 1
Accounting System Insights

Chapter 2
Accounting Databases

Chapter 3
Accounting Interface:
Database Forms, Queries, and Reports

Chapter 4
Accounting Systems and Business Processes

Chapter 5
Business Processes: Purchasing, Sales, and Payroll Cycles

Chapter 6
Integrated Enterprise Systems and Cloud Computing

Part 2
Accounting and Intelligence Systems

Analyze Accounting Data

Chapter 7
Accounting and Business Intelligence

Chapter 8
Accounting and Sustainability Intelligence

Chapter 9
XBRL: Intelligent Business Reporting

Part 3
Security, Controls, and Risk

Safeguard Accounting Data

Chapter 10
Fraud and Internal Control

Chapter 11
Cybersecurity

Chapter 12
The Risk Intelligent Enterprise: Enterprise Risk Management

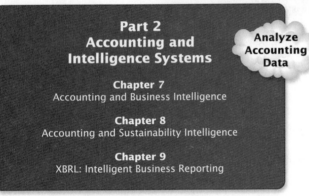

Part 4
Designing and Developing Accounting Systems

System Design

Chapter 13
Accounting System Development

Chapter 14
Database Design: ERD, REA, and SQL

Part 5
Enterprise Accounting Systems: Capstone

Chapter 15
Emerging Trends and Technologies

Chapter 16
Accounting Systems in Action: LIVE Projects

FIGURE 1.18

Your Roadmap to This Book

Pair and Share: Share with a classmate your responses to the following questions:
Which area of accounting systems interests you the most? Which chapter captures your interest? Which topics would you like to learn more about?

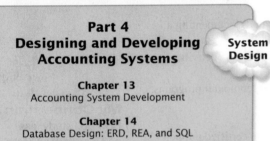

As you navigate the cross-roads of accounting and IT using the roadmap in Figure 1.18, remember that AIS is SASSY:

1. **S**tore accounting data.
2. **A**nalyze accounting data.
3. **S**afeguard accounting data.
4. **SY**stem design.

The first three parts of the book relate to three functions of the accounting system: storing, analyzing, and safeguarding data. The fourth part covers designing and developing accounting systems. The final part integrates the topics covered throughout the book. Next is a preview of the chapters in each part.

Part 1, *Enterprise Accounting Systems: People, Processes, and Technology*, introduces you to the design, development, and functioning of accounting systems today. In Chapter 1, *Accounting System Insights*, we provide you with insights into understanding how accounting systems function in today's business environment. Chapter 2, *Accounting Databases*, provides an introduction to databases and their integral role in accounting systems. Chapter 3, *Accounting Interface: Database Forms, Queries, and Reports*, describes the accounting system interface and its role in the accounting system. In Chapter 4, *Accounting Systems and Business Processes*, we will share with you how to read and develop business process maps. Chapter 5, *Business Processes: Purchasing, Sales, and Payroll Cycles*, covers documentation for business processes using business process mapping for purchasing, sales and payroll cycles. In Chapter 6, *Integrated Enterprise Systems and Cloud Computing*, we explore how the accounting system is integrated into the larger enterprise system.

Part 2, *Accounting and Intelligent Systems*, explores the impact of intelligent systems on accounting. Chapter 7, *Accounting and Business Intelligence*, discusses how enterprises use analytics to create business intelligence for improved decision making and business performance. Chapter 8, *Accounting and Sustainability Intelligence*, provides an overview of the emerging field of accounting for sustainability and the resulting impact on the accounting system. Chapter 9, *XBRL: Intelligent Business Reporting*, explores the who, what, where, when, and how of eXtensible Business Reporting Language (XBRL) that electronically tags each piece of financial data.

Part 3, *Security, Controls, and Risk*, focuses on safeguarding information assets stored in accounting systems. Chapter 10, *Fraud and Internal Control*, introduces COSO's Internal Control Framework and COBIT's IT controls framework. Chapter 11, *Cybersecurity*, explores the threats posed by cybercrime to an accounting system. This chapter introduces you to the International Information Systems Security Certification Consortium's (ISC)^2 10 domains for cybersecurity. Chapter 12, *The Risk Intelligent Enterprise: Enterprise Risk Management*, introduces COSO's enterprise risk management (ERM) framework. The chapter presents the top 10 tips for spreadsheet risk management.

Part 4, *Designing and Developing Accounting Systems*, provides an overview of different approaches to developing accounting systems and the related accounting database. Chapter 13, *Accounting System Development*, explores the phases of the system development life cycle as applied to developing an accounting system. Chapter 14, *Database Design: ERD, REA, and SQL*, compares and contrasts two approaches to accounting database design: entity relationship diagram (ERD) and resources, entities, and agents (REA). This chapter also explores how data is extracted from the database using Structured Query Language (SQL).

Part 5, *Enterprise Accounting Systems: Capstone*, provides a capstone experience for integrating accounting system topics. Chapter 15, *Emerging Trends and Technologies*, is an online chapter that explores the latest trends in information technology and its impact on accounting systems. Chapter 16, *Accounting Systems in Action: LIVE Projects*, provides opportunities for LIVE projects to develop your project-management and team-building skills, two critical skills for your success as an accounting professional at the crossroads of accounting and IT.

Additional online resources to assist you are available on your text website including presentation slides and software videos.

Chapter Highlights

What is the importance and value of information as an asset? Today, the value of information assets for some businesses exceeds the value of other assets, such as land and buildings.

What is the role of the accounting system within the larger enterprise system? The accounting system spans the entire value chain of an enterprise, tracking transaction information from the purchase of items from vendors through the sale of products or services to customers. Business processes are associated with the related accounting transactions known as transaction cycles. The purchasing cycle consists of transactions related to purchasing items from vendors. The payroll cycle consists of employee and payroll transactions. The sales cycle

involves exchanges or transactions between an enterprise and its customers. In addition to the accounting system, other modules or subsystems of an enterprise system can include supply chain management (SCM), operations/production system (OPS), human resource management (HRM), and customer relationship management (CRM).

What are the modules and associated transaction cycles in a baseline accounting system? The modules in a baseline accounting system include the following:

1. Vendors module relating to transactions with vendors, such as creating purchase orders, receiving items, and entering bills. This module is associated with the purchasing cycle.

2. Customers module relating to transactions with customers, such as creating invoices and receiving payments. This module is associated with the sales cycle.

3. Employees module relating to transactions with employees, such as entering time and calculating payroll. This module is associated with the payroll cycle.

4. Banking module relating to transactions involving financial institutions, such as writing checks and recording deposits.

5. Financial module relating to transactions not recorded in the prior four modules, as well as adjusting, correcting, and closing entries.

6. Reports module relating to the four major types of reports generated by accounting systems: financial and regulatory reports, tax reports, management reports, and sustainability reports.

What are the database essentials that today's accounting professional needs to know? Database essentials include the following:

1. A field is a piece of data, such as customer first name.

2. A record is a collection of related fields, such as a customer record.

3. A table is a collection of related records, such as a CUSTOMER table.

4. A database is a collection of related tables, such as an accounting database.

5. A database form is a computer-based form for entering data into the database.

6. A database query is used to extract data from a database, such as searching for a customer's account balance.

7. A database report is a computer-based output to display.

What are the SDLC phases? The system development life cycle organizes the activities involved in developing a new system into the following six distinct phases:

1. Plan the system project including scheduling, budgeting, and staffing.

2. Analyze the new system requirements, such as what reports are required and what data needs to be collected by the system.

3. Design business processes and databases for the new system.

4. Build/buy and test databases and computer programs for the new system.

5. Install new IT hardware, software, and databases.

6. Deploy the new system, using the system on an ongoing basis and maintaining and updating it as necessary.

Why is it important to safeguard information assets? To protect information assets, organizations implement security and controls to prevent fraud, unauthorized access, modification, destruction, or disclosure. Internal control is the set of policies and procedures enterprises use to safeguard assets, including information assets, and to prevent and detect errors.

What are three functions of an accounting system in today's business environment? Three functions of an accounting system are:

1. Collecting, recording, and storing financial and accounting data.

2. Providing financial analytics and business intelligence for improved decision making and business performance.

3. Safeguarding information assets stored in accounting systems using security, controls, and risk management.

Accounting System Insights

Insight No. 1 Use satellite mapping to view accounting systems. Zoom out to see the entire system...zoom in to focus on detail.

Insight No. 2 Most accounting information is *not* entered using debits and credits.

Insight No. 3 Accounting information is often entered using onscreen forms, such as checks and invoices.

Insight No. 4 Nearly all accounting systems use databases to store accounting information.

Insight No. 5 To understand accounting systems, the accountant must understand databases.

Insight No. 6 When designing databases, begin with the outcome in mind.

Insight No. 7 Business intelligence provides organizations with competitive advantage.

Insight No. 8 Because information assets have value, the accounting system must safeguard the information stored.

Active Review

Study less. Learn more. Make connections.

1.1 Refer to the chapter opener, *Meet Business Intelligence*. In your opinion, how can business intelligence create value using the accounting system?

1.2 Refer to the chapter opener, *Meet Business Intelligence*. Discuss the importance of sales data in creating business intelligence for an organization.

1.3 Pick your favorite Accounting Insight from Chapter 1. Discuss why it's your favorite.

1.4 What are the modules in the baseline accounting system model? Discuss the purposes and transactions associated with each module.

1.5 Discuss how the features of a spreadsheet and a database are similar and how they are different.

1.6 Discuss the potential risks if a company's accounting system is not well secured.

1.7 Discuss the benefits of an integrated enterprise system.

1.8 Discuss how value chain activities are related to accounting transaction cycles.

1.9 Discuss the significance of information technology to the accounting professional.

1.10 Discuss problems that enterprises may experience with shadow data.

Key Terms Check

Understanding the language used at the crossroads of accounting and IT is key to your success.

1.11 Match the following terms and definitions.

a. enterprise system
b. integrated enterprise system
c. business processes
d. value chain
e. transaction cycles
f. purchasing cycle
g. payroll cycle
h. sales cycle
i. baseline accounting system

_____ 1. An organizing framework for business processes, beginning with vendors and ending with customers

_____ 2. Exchanges or transactions between an enterprise and its customers

_____ 3. Accounting transactions related to specific business processes

_____ 4. Shares data across functional areas within the enterprise

_____ 5. Transactions with employees

_____ 6. Related activities performed by an enterprise to create value by transforming input into output

_____ 7. A system that supports business activities throughout the enterprise, including inputs, processing, and outputs

_____ 8. Transactions related to purchasing items from vendors

_____ 9. A model that provides an enterprise-wide view of the firm's accounting system

1.12 Match the following terms and definitions.

a. vendors module
b. customers module
c. employees module
d. banking module
e. financial module
f. reports module
g. adjusting entries
h. correcting entries
i. closing entries
j. financial reports
k. tax reports
l. management reports
m. sustainability reports

_____ 1. A module that relates to output from the accounting system
_____ 2. A module that includes adjusting and correcting entries
_____ 3. A module related to purchasing goods and services
_____ 4. A module that involves cash received and cash paid
_____ 5. A module related to the payroll cycle
_____ 6. A module related to selling the customer a product or service
_____ 7. Reports used to evaluate an enterprise's sustainability performance
_____ 8. Reports used when filing federal, state, and local returns
_____ 9. Reports prepared to assist managers in making decisions
_____ 10. Reports that include a company's income statement, balance sheet, and statement of cash flows
_____ 11. Entries to bring accounts up to date at year end
_____ 12. Zeros out revenue and expense accounts at year end
_____ 13. Entries to correct errors

1.13 Match the following terms and definitions.

a. field
b. record
c. primary key
d. relational database
e. operational database
f. business intelligence
g. OLAP cubes

_____ 1. A unique identifier for each record
_____ 2. An online application that permits users to view data in a multidimensional way
_____ 3. A collection of related database fields
_____ 4. Data analytics and predictive modeling used to gain insights from data to improve the quality of business decisions
_____ 5. A piece of information
_____ 6. A database that stores transactions related to business operations
_____ 7. A collection of related database tables

1.14 Match the following terms and definitions.

a. people
b. processes
c. technology
d. information technology (IT)
e. IT architecture
f. IT infrastructure
g. system development life cycle (SDLC)
h. plan
i. analyze
j. design
k. build/buy
l. install
m. deploy

_____ 1. A framework for organizing the complex, multifaceted undertaking of developing a system
_____ 2. Includes testing databases and computer programs for the new system
_____ 3. Includes scheduling, budgeting, and staffing a project
_____ 4. Includes evaluating new system requirements
_____ 5. Using the new system on an ongoing basis and maintaining and updating it as necessary
_____ 6. Setting up new IT hardware, software, and databases
_____ 7. Prepare models for business processes and databases for the new system
_____ 8. One of the three keys of opportunity that focuses on how business activities are impacted
_____ 9. One of the three keys of opportunity that focuses on software, hardware, and networks
_____ 10. One of the three keys of opportunity that focuses on how employees, customers, and vendors are impacted
_____ 11. Consists of software, hardware, and network technology used by an organization
_____ 12. How specific software, hardware, and networks are used to build IT architecture for an enterprise
_____ 13. The design or blueprint for an enterprise's information technology

Practice Test

1.15 In addition to accounting systems, which of the following are members of enterprise systems?

a. SCM and OPS
b. CRM and SCM
c. HRM and Financial
d. SCM, OPS, CRM, and HR

1.16 The value chain is useful for:

a. Coordinating accounting system activities.
b. Coordinating activities with suppliers and customers
c. Linking business values like a chain.
d. Everything we do in a business.

1.17 In businesses, the system that supports financial and accounting activities in an organization is often called:

a. Accounting system
b. General ledger
c. Enterprise accounting system
d. All of the above

1.18 In which of the baseline accounting system modules are pay employee and pay payroll liabilities included?

a. Employee module
b. Reports module
c. Banking module
d. All of the above

1.19 Which of the following modules are included in the purchasing cycle?

a. Vendors and customers
b. Vendors and banking
c. Employees and vendors
d. Vendors, banking, and reports

1.20 In the accounting systems context, which of the following is NOT correct?

a. To understand accounting, the accountant today must understand databases.
b. Most accounting information is not entered using debits and credits.
c. The accounting information system is used to perform accounting activity faster.
d. Business intelligence provides organizations with a competitive advantage.

1.21 The three key factors that impact the accounting system are:

a. Customer, supplier, and employee
b. People, technology, and accounting processes
c. Computers, networks, and accounting software
d. Business processes, database, technology

1.22 An accounting system does all the following except:

a. Capture accounting information about a transaction
b. Reduce the cost of accounting transactions
c. Generate financial reports
d. Process the captured accounting information

1.23 Which of the following is not an accounting transaction?

a. Payroll cycle
b. Purchasing cycle
c. Accounting cycle
d. Sales cycle

1.24 When IT professionals say business processes, they mean:

a. Computer programs
b. Accounting cycles
c. Accounting modules
d. Accounting system

Exercises

Each Exercise relates to one of the major questions addressed in the chapter and is labeled with the question number in green.

Short Exercises
Warm up with these short exercises.

1.25 Match each of the following accounting events to the baseline accounting system module in which it occurs. **(Q1.3)**

> Vendors module
> Customers module
> Employees module
> Banking module
> Financial module
> Reports module

1. Create purchase orders _____
2. Adjusting entries _____
3. Make deposits _____
4. Calculate payroll _____
5. Receive customer payments _____
6. Pay bills _____
7. Tax reports _____
8. Enter time _____
9. Enter bills _____
10. Create invoices _____
11. Pay employees _____
12. Receive items _____
13. Sustainability reports _____
14. Pay payroll liabilities _____
15. Correcting entries _____
16. Management reports _____
17. Closing _____
18. Financial reports _____

1.26 Match each of the following accounting events to the accounting transaction cycle. **(Q1.3)**

> Purchasing cycle
> Sales cycle
> Payroll cycle

1. Create purchase orders _____
2. Create invoices _____
3. Make deposits _____
4. Calculate payroll _____
5. Receive customer payments _____

   6. Pay bills _____
   7. Enter time _____
   8. Enter bills _____
   9. Receive items _____
  10. Pay employees _____

1.27 Identify which of the following are internal agents to an enterprise and which are external agents. **(Q1.4)**

   1. Vendors
   2. Customers
   3. Employees
   4. Delivery service
   5. Internal Revenue Service
   6. Bank

1.28 Can you match the following terms used by accounting professionals to those used by IT professionals? **(Q1.1)**

   a. Rows
   b. Columns
   c. Software
   _____ 1. Applications
   _____ 2. Records
   _____ 3. Fields

1.29 Match each of the following transaction cycles to the integrated enterprise system module that generates the transactions. **(Q1.2)**

   a. Purchasing cycle
   b. Payroll cycle
   c. Sales cycle
   _____ 1. Human resources management (HRM)
   _____ 2. Supply chain management (SCM)
   _____ 3. Customer relationship management (CRM)
   _____ 4. Operation/production system (OPS)

1.30 Look at the CUSTOMER table for EspressoCoffee appearing in Figure 1.12. Can you answer the following questions? **(Q1.3)**

   1. How many fields do you see in the database table in Figure 1.12?
   2. How many records do you see in the database table?
   3. Are there any other fields that you would recommend that EspressoCoffee add to the CUSTOMER table? Is there any additional information that EspressoCoffee might need about customers?

1.31 For the following functions of the accounting system, identify technologies used by each function. **(Q1.3)**

   1. Storing accounting data
   2. Analyzing accounting data
   3. Safeguarding accounting data

1.32 Using the three keys of opportunity, describe the impact on people, processes, and technology of an enterprise changing accounting software. **(Q1.4)**

It's Your Call

This is your training ground. These scenarios provide you with the opportunity to use your knowledge and professional skills.

1.33 Your firm has announced that in order to meet earnings targets, 10% of its workforce must be let go. As chief financial officer you have been asked to explain the value that your staff of accounting and IT professionals provide to the firm. You realize that your response may affect the number of staff that you keep employed. What would you say? **(Q1.1)**

1.34 You are working as an intern in the payroll department of a large company. Your best friend, who helped you get the job, works at the same company in sales. Your friend calls you when he is traveling and says his login for the system is not working. IT told him it might take up to 24 hours to fix it. He asks you to share your login with him so he can access the system. What would you do? **(Q1.3)**

1.35 To meet a tight deadline, you download spreadsheet files to your company laptop to take work home with you. What are the risks to safeguarding the information on your laptop? **(Q1.3)**

1.36 Your younger brother calls you from college. He is registering for classes. He wants to know why he needs to take an accounting information systems course. How will the course help him to be successful in his future career? What do you tell him? **(Q1.3)**

Tech in Practice

These technology in practice exercises are perfect for both individuals and teams.

Tech Exercises

Sharpen your skills with these technology exercises. Watch the software videos and download data files for these Tech Exercises at www.pearsonhighered. com/kay.

1.37
Tech Tool: Spreadsheet Software
Software Video: Spreadsheet Data Tables

EspressoCoffee has given you the following work assignment.

1. Using spreadsheet software and the following information, create a CUSTOMER table for EspressoCoffee.

	A	B	C	D	E	F	G	H
1	CUSTOMER NO.	LAST NAME	FIRST NAME	COMPANY NAME	STREET ADDRESS	CITY	STATE	ZIP
2								
3								
4								
5								
6								
7								
8								

2. Identify the primary key by highlighting the column in yellow.
3. Populate the CUSTOMER table by entering the following customer information.

   Customer No.: 127127
   Name: Angela Ashuer
   Address: 13 Joseph Ave, Appleton, WI, 54911

   Customer No.: 913691
   Name: Vincent Pico, EspressoBar
   Address: 58 Dante, Pisa, Tuscany, 56100

   Customer No.: 127000
   Name: Becky Cornell
   Address: 1203 N Lake Shore Drive, Chicago, IL 60610

Customer No.: 1958361
Name: David Kolse, Creamy Coffee
Address: 702 Ensenada Street, Orlando, FL 32825

Customer No.: 532700
Name: Fred Olhman, Coffee Shoppe
Address: 7011 Second Street, San Francisco, CA 94102

1.38

Tech Tool: Database Software
Software Video: Database Tables

EspressoCoffee has given you an assignment to create a database table for tracking customer information.

1. Using Microsoft Access database software and the following fields, create a CUSTOMER table for EspressoCoffee.

Customer No.	State
Last Name	ZIP
First Name	Country
Company Name	Email Address
Street Address	Web Site
City	

2. Using Microsoft Access, select the primary key for the CUSTOMER table.
3. Populate the CUSTOMER table by entering the following customer information.

Customer No.: 127127
Name: Angela Ashuer
Address: 13 Joseph Ave, Appleton, WI, 54911, USA
Email: ang@gmail.com

Customer No.: 913691
Name: Vincent Pico, EspressoBar
Address: 58 Dante, Pisa, Tuscany, 56100, Italy
Email: vpico@yahoo.com
Web site: espressobar.it

Customer No.: 127000
Name: Becky Cornell
Address: 1203 N Lake Shore Drive, Chicago, IL 60610, USA

Customer No.: 1958361
Name: David Kolse, Creamy Coffee
Address: 702 Ensenada Street, Orlando, FL 32825, USA
Email: creamycoffee@flash.net
Web site: creamycoffee.com

Customer No.: 532700
Name: Fred Olhman, Coffee Shoppe
Address: 7011 Second Street, San Francisco, CA 94102, USA
Email: coffeeshoppe@gmail.com
Web site: coffeeshoppe.com

1.39

Tech Tool: Database Software

Software Video: Database Tables

EspressoCoffee has asked you to create an ORDER database table.

1. Using Microsoft Access database software and the following fields, create an ORDER table for EspressoCoffee.

   Order No.
   Date
   Customer No.

2. Using Microsoft Access, select the primary key for the ORDER table.
3. Populate the ORDER table by entering the following order information.

   Order No.: 5819
   Date: 12.21.2010
   Customer No.: 127127

   Order No.: 5820
   Date: 12.23.2013
   Customer No.: 913691

   Order No.: 7200
   Date: 07.01.2014
   Customer No.: 127000

   Order No.: 9723
   Date: 12.21.2014
   Customer No.: 1958361

   Order No.: 12631
   Date: 12.27.2013
   Customer No.: 1958361

1.40

Tech Tool: Spreadsheet Software

Software Video: Spreadsheet Data Tables

1. Using spreadsheet software, construct a table that will collect data for an application of your choice (for example, data regarding dogs for a dog walking business).
2. Identify the appropriate fields.
3. Identify the primary key.
4. Populate at least two records with test data.

1.41

Tech Tool: Database Software

Software Video: Database Tables

1. Select an authentic enterprise of your choice. Using Microsoft Access database software, develop a CUSTOMER table for the enterprise, identifying the appropriate fields.
2. Using Microsoft Access, select the primary key for the CUSTOMER table.
3. Populate the CUSTOMER table by entering test data for at least three customers.
4. What customer reports would the enterprise need to create? Would the database table you created be able to provide the information required?

1.42 (Continuation of TIP 1.41)

Tech Tool: Database Software

Software Video: Database Tables

1. Using Microsoft Access database software and information from the prior exercise, create an ORDER table, identifying the appropriate fields.
2. Using Microsoft Access, select the primary key for the ORDER table.
3. Populate the ORDER table by entering test data for three orders.
4. What queries can you envision that the enterprise might need that would use information from both the CUSTOMER table and the ORDER table?

1.43

Tech Tool: Database Software

Software Video: Database Tables

1. Download the data file for this exercise.
2. Open the Microsoft Access database file.
3. How many tables exist in the database?
4. How many records are in the CUSTOMER table?
5. What is the primary key in the CUSTOMER table?
6. What field in the CUSTOMER table connects it to the ORDER table?

1.44

Tech Tool: Spreadsheet Software

Software Video: Spreadsheet Graph and Data Organization

1. Download the data file for this exercise.
2. Graph the items on-hand quantity.
3. Identify items with on-hand quantity less than the re-order quantity.
4. Sort items based on their on-hand quantity.

Hint: To answer the third question, use the pivot table tool to select item name, quantity on hand, and reorder point. Use an IF statement to identify items that must be reordered.

1.45

Tech Tool: Spreadsheet Software

Software Video: Spreadsheet Graph and Data Organization

1. Download the data file for this exercise.
2. Find out who is the most long-standing and most recent customer.
3. Find out who is the customer with the highest balance.
4. What is the average of customers' balances?
5. Graph customer balances to identify the customer with highest and lowest balance.

Go Online

In the fast-paced world of technology, your skill at finding answers fast can be vital. Go online and experience typical assignments you may encounter as a professional.

1.46 You have decided to start your career planning. Your first step is to go online and search for job openings for entry-level accounting professionals. What skills and competencies do the job openings require? Compare the requirements with your current status. How do you plan to gain the skills and knowledge needed?

1.47 You have been in your current accounting position for five years. You want to continue advancing in your career. Go online and search for your ideal accounting professional position five years after you graduate from college. What are the positions that you would apply for? What skills and competencies do the job openings require? Compare the requirements with your current status. How do you plan to gain the skills and knowledge needed?

1.48 You have been asked by the CFO to prepare a brief presentation to management about how business intelligence could benefit your company. Go online to research how business intelligence is being used by other companies. Prepare a brief presentation as requested by the CFO.

1.49 You are working for a business solutions consulting company that hired you because of your knowledge of accounting systems and IT. You have been asked to select the two accounting software applications that you believe have the best features. Go online and search for two accounting software applications commercially available. Identify whether the software is predominantly used by small, midsize, or large enterprises. List the features these products offer to customers. Briefly summarize the advantages and disadvantages of each and why these two are your top picks.

1.50 Your accounting colleagues are debating the differences between data, information, and business intelligence. Go online and search for definitions of data, information, and business intelligence. Construct your own definition for each that you like best that you can share with your colleagues.

Technology Projects

These technology projects are perfect for both individuals and teams.

Technology Project 1

Tech Tool: Spreadsheet Software, Database Software
Software Videos: Spreadsheet Data Tables, Database Tables

iSportDesign, an online retailer of sporting goods that the customer can custom design, needs help in modernizing its accounting system. Nick, the owner and operator, has asked for your assistance. He wants to hire you as an intern. This is your opportunity to get some experience with accounting and technology, so you agree.

The first project he has for you is putting customer data into electronic form for easier retrieval. You decide to put the customer data into both a spreadsheet and a database so Nick can choose which he likes best for his company.

Your deliverables for the project include the following:

Deliverable 1. A spreadsheet containing customer data for iSportDesign

Deliverable 2. A Customer database table

Visit www.pearsonhighered.com/kay to do the following:
1. Download Technology Project 1 instructions.
2. Download files provided online for your convenience in completing the project deliverables.
3. Watch the videos with software instructions to complete this project at www.pearsonhighered.com/kay.

LIVE Project 1

LIVE projects give you an opportunity to apply your accounting and technology skills to LIVE applications.

LIVE Project 1 lets you explore emerging trends and technologies at the crossroads of accounting and IT.

To view the LIVE projects, visit www.pearsonhighered.com/kay and click on online Chapter 16, "LIVE Projects." You will find the following:

1. LIVE Project 1 with milestones and deliverables.
2. Project management training.
3. Team coaching.

2

Accounting Databases

Can a Faulty Database Cost American Consumers Billions?

Meet Ingenix.

You're the Boss...
If you were the CFO of United Healthcare, what would you say to the American consumer? How would you explain they were overcharged billions for their healthcare because of a flawed database?

A U.S. Senate Committee found that due to a faulty database "American consumers have paid billions of dollars for health care services that their insurance companies should have paid." Basically, the database was undercharging the insurance companies for their share of medical bills and overcharging the patients by billions of dollars. Two-thirds of U.S. healthcare insurers, including United HealthCare and Aetna, used the flawed database operated by Ingenix.

Crossroads
At the crossroads of accounting and IT, we focus on the integral role that databases play in accounting today.

My Questions

Q 2.1 What role does the database play in an accounting system?

Q 2.2 What is the role of the database in an enterprise?

Q 2.3 How do I build an accounting database?

Q 2.4 What is database integrity?

Q 2.5 What are the differences between a manual accounting system and a database accounting system?

What Role Does the Database Play in an Accounting System?

Do you shop online? When you make a purchase online, what information do you enter? Where do you think your information is stored? Have you ever purchased items more than once from the same online retailer? Does your information, such as shipping address, automatically appear on the screen?

Imagine you place an online order with Amazon.com, the world's largest online retailer. The information you enter into the online order form is stored in a database. Databases store information about online purchases, shipping addresses, billing addresses, and various accounting transactions.

One of the benefits of a database is that the information, such as your shipping address for online purchases, can be stored and retrieved to be reused at a later time. Also, your shipping address can be shared electronically with the delivery service, such as FedEx. As a customer, you can track the status of your shipment in real-time over the Internet. The use of databases permits the data to be shared between you, Amazon, and FedEx.

This brings us to Accounting Insight No. 9.

Accounting Insight No. 9: Enter Data Once

Insight No. 9 states that when you enter data into a database, you want to enter the data once. One of the advantages of the relational database is that we can enter data into the database once, and then reuse that data in various locations when and where it is needed.

Imagine that as an accounting professional for EspressoCoffee you will be entering customer orders. If EspressoCoffee has a customer named Vincent Pico whose address is 58 Dante, Pisa, Italy, would you want to enter the customer's address every time the customer placed an order? Wouldn't you prefer to enter the customer's address once and then store it in the CUSTOMER table? The address in the CUSTOMER table could be reused each time the customer places an order, with the address appearing on the order invoice. Better yet, wouldn't you prefer that customers entered their addresses so you didn't have to enter it for them?

ACCOUNTING INSIGHT NO. 9
Enter Data Once

When Data Needs Scrubbing....
Dirty data occurs when errors are entered into a system.

Consider the case of a stock trader erroneously entering a "b" (for billion) instead of an "m" (for million), causing the New York Stock Exchange to plummet. This actual event occurred in May 2010. After the "b" was entered, programmed trading using algorithms kicked in, resulting in the stock market plummet. Accenture, a technology consulting firm, saw its stock drop from over $40 at 2:47 PM to less than a penny one minute later at 2:48 PM that day.

Imagine that you go to your local bank to wire $1,800 to your brother in Zurich, Switzerland. A couple of days later when you log in to your online bank account, you notice that your account balance is much less than you anticipated. Then you see a withdrawal for $18,000. When you return to your local bank to unravel what has happened, you discover that the bank manager mistakenly entered an extra "0," resulting in $18,000 being withdrawn from your account, instead of $1,800. Your brother was gracious enough to authorize the Zurich bank to return the excess funds, after the bank deducted $1,700 in service charges. So an extra "0" cost the bank $1,700 and one unhappy bank customer, who cautioned the bank manager to always check the number before pressing the Enter key.

How many times do you check a number before pressing the Enter key?

When Data Needs Scrubbing....
The sales manager for EspressoCoffee has just landed a large customer order. He is eager to close the deal and has asked for your assistance. He wants to know if the customer he is working with is the same as the customer already in your database. Is Espresso Cafe, 5858 Grande Avenue, Sainte Louis, Missouri, the same customer as Expresso Cafe, 5858 Grand Ave, Saint Louis, MO?

What do you say? Is this the same customer? Will your database view it as the same customer?

There are three main benefits associated with entering data once:

- It is more efficient. You do not spend non-value-added time reentering the same information again and again.
- Reentering the same data again and again increases the chances of entering erroneous data, such as misspellings and transpositions.
- When you need to update the customer's address, you only need to update it once. This eliminates the possibility of updating some, but not all, of the other entries.

Accounting Insight No. 10: 80/20 Rule

Use the 80/20 Rule to design accounting databases. Invest 80% of your time and energy on the planning and design of the database. If there is a sound design, then only 20% of your time will be spent on maintaining and updating the database.

If the 80/20 Rule is reversed and you spend 20% of your time and energy designing the database, then you can expect to spend 80% of your time maintaining a poorly designed accounting database.

Accounting Databases: Behind the Screen

Nearly all accounting information today is stored in databases. As you learned in Insight No. 5, to understand accounting systems, the accountant must understand databases. Large-scale accounting systems, such as SAP, and even small business software like QuickBooks use databases to store accounting data.

Behind the front-end accounting software screen is an accounting database and database management system (DBMS) software. As you can see in Figure 2.1, accounting data is entered into accounting software using onscreen forms. The data is passed to the DBMS software, which stores it in the appropriate database table.

80/20 Rule...
The 80/20 Rule is also called the Pareto Principle, named after the Italian economist Vilfredo Pareto, who noticed that 20% of the population in Italy received 80% of the income.

Some businesses find that 20% of their customers generate 80% of their revenues. Of course, the key is to know which customers make up that 20%.

Can you think of any other ways you can use the 80/20 Rule?

Accounting Software...
provides an interface for the user to:
1. Input data using onscreen forms.
2. Output data using reports.

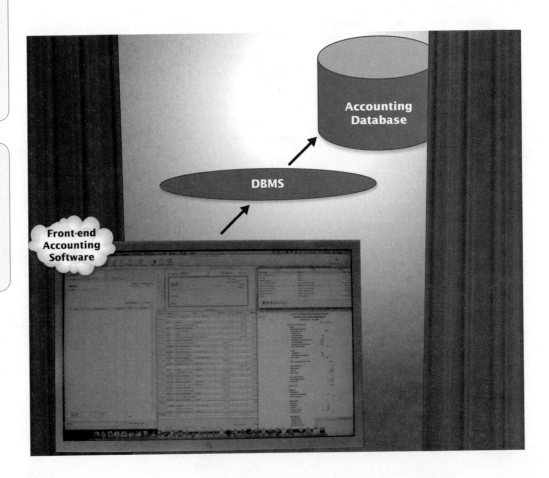

FIGURE 2.1

Accounting Database Behind the Screen

Pair and Share: Share with a classmate your response to the following:
When you enter data into accounting software, what happens behind the screen?

DBMS...

is software used to:

1. Create database tables.
2. Transfer data from the accounting software to the database.
3. Update data in the database.
4. Delete data from the database.
5. Sort database tables.
6. Run queries.

**Crossroads...
What drives
a database
engine?**

When IT professionals talk about a database engine, what are they talking about?

A database engine is a database program, such as MS Access, that includes DBMS software. The DBMS software drives the database engine.

The DBMS software processes the accounting data and the accounting database stores accounting data. When you request an accounting report, the accounting software interacts with the DBMS software to retrieve the requested data from the specified tables in the accounting database to generate the report.

Figure 2.2 shows the three tiers in the accounting system architecture:

- Database tier
- Application tier
- User tier

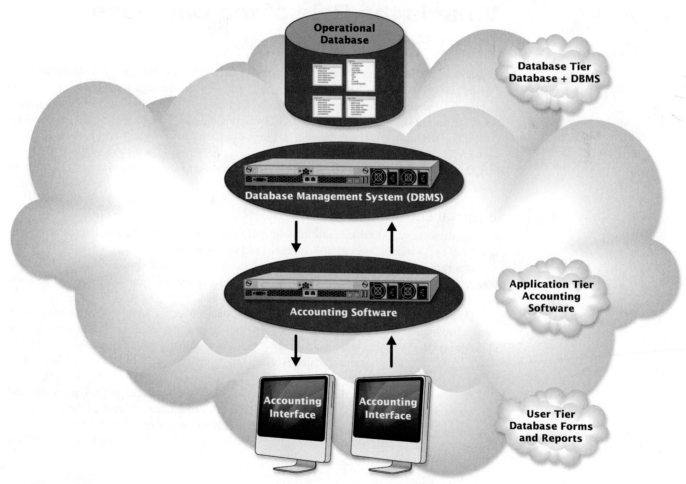

FIGURE 2.2

Accounting System Architecture

Pair and Share: Share with a classmate your response to the following:
When you enter new customer information into accounting software, can you trace that data in this figure to the database table in which it would be stored?

**Oracle...A
Database Giant...**
Oracle has over 30 million
lines of programming code.
When a defect in the code
is detected, a patch of programming code is used to
fix the defect. One Oracle
defect required 78 patches
at a cost of over $1 million.

My Connection...
Make connections. Try:
• Active Review 2.5
• Short Exercise 2.30

The database tier consists of the database and the DBMS. DBMS software is used to insert, update, and delete data in the database. All database engines, from Microsoft Access to large Oracle databases, use DBMS software.

The application tier consists of software applications, such as accounting software. The accounting software interacts with a DBMS to add, update, and delete accounting data in the database. The user tier consists of the user interface that appears on the accountant's computer screen.

As an example, a QuickBooks Customer List is related to the CUSTOMER database table. Each time you add a customer to your QuickBooks Customer List, you are adding a new record to the CUSTOMER table. When you enter a customer name on a sales invoice in QuickBooks, customer information from the Customer List, such as address and contact information, is automatically completed on the sales invoice. Behind the screen, QuickBooks is retrieving this data from the CUSTOMER database table and inserting it into the sales invoice form on your computer screen.

When the accounting professional understands how the accounting data is stored and retrieved in a database, it is easier to trace errors. An accounting database is one of several types of databases used by enterprises. Next, we will look at the different types of databases an enterprise might employ.

What Is the Role of the Database in an Enterprise?

Databases provide enterprises with the capability to collect and use data that simply was not possible or cost effective before the advent of databases. For example, databases can be used to collect large amounts of data about customers that later is analyzed for business intelligence.

The **database administrator (DBA)** is responsible for managing the enterprise's databases. The DBA, together with internal auditors, establish policies and procedures for database security, including backup and disaster recovery.

Databases used by an enterprise can be considered as one of two types: internal databases or external databases (Figure 2.3).

Internal Databases

Internal databases are databases in which the data belongs to the organization. Internal databases consist of two varieties: operational databases and data warehouses.

Operational databases are used to store data related to operating the business. For example, Apple Inc. would use an operational database to store and track data about business operations, such as sales of iPads.

Data stored in operational databases include data collected from enterprise accounting transactions, such as vendor transactions, customer transactions, and employee payroll. The operational database also includes data about people, including vendors, customers, and employees. Data in the operational databases are stored using a unique identifier or primary key so specific data can be retrieved.

Data warehouses store data from a variety of sources. Data stored in the data warehouse may be current data, historical data, or future estimates. The difference between the operational database and the data warehouse is that the data warehouse is not used for routine business activities. Instead, the data warehouse is often used for business intelligence purposes to improve management decision making.

External Databases

External databases are databases containing data collected by other organizations, including:

- Governmental agencies, such as the Internal Revenue Service (IRS) and the Securities and Exchange Commission (SEC)
- Research organizations, such as Gartner, Inc., and Marketing Research Association (MRA)

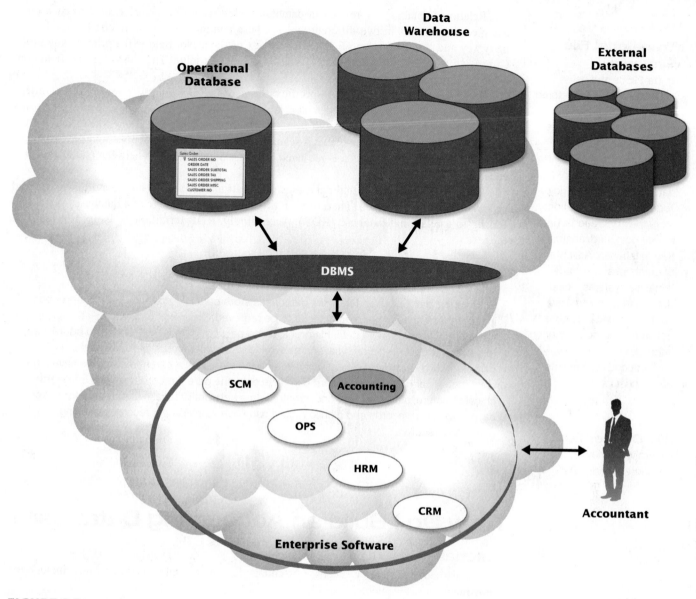

FIGURE 2.3

Enterprise Databases

As an accounting professional, which of the enterprise databases do you think you would use?

- Financial organizations, such as Dow Jones
- National and international trade organizations, such as Organic Trade Association

Data that can be obtained from these external databases include industry market indices data, market forecasting data, census data, and unemployment data. For example, your enterprise might use data from Gartner, Inc., for information about IT technology research and trends.

> When we use the term *database* we are referring to the operational database.

Database Structures

The databases that an enterprise uses can be structured in different ways. The structure of a database pertains to how the stored data within the database is related to other stored data. How the data is stored, or structured, in a database affects how the data is retrieved. There are three basic database structures:

- Relational database
- Hierarchical database
- Network database

Database vs. Traditional File Systems...

In the 1950s and early 1960s, organizations stored their operational data in files instead of databases. Each file was designed independently of other files, resulting in data redundancy and inconsistency. Today, most organizations store their operational data in well-designed, anomaly-free databases. Advantages of databases over traditional file systems include data sharing, centralized control, redundancy control, improved data integrity, improved data security, and reduced data maintenance cost.

My Connection...
• Active Review 2.2
• Short Exercise 2.29

Relational databases store data in database tables. These tables are related to each other using common fields in two different tables. These common fields are referred to as the primary key and the foreign key. For example, the Customer No. field is the primary key in the CUSTOMER table and the foreign key in the SALES ORDER table. The Customer No. field connects these two database tables.

To retrieve information about a specific customer, such as name, address, and recent orders, the enterprise would search two database tables: the SALES ORDER table and the CUSTOMER table. The SALES ORDER table would be searched for a specific Customer No. to retrieve the sales order data. The CUSTOMER table is searched for the same Customer No. to retrieve the customer's name and address. Data is retrieved by using the relationship between tables, thus it is called a relational database.

Currently, most operational databases are relational databases due to storage space and processing time advantages. Therefore, in this text, when we refer to a database, we are referring to a relational database (RDB). Accordingly, RDB terminology is used throughout the text.

Hierarchical and Network Databases...
Hierarchical databases and network databases store data in records that are not grouped into database tables. When data needs to be retrieved, instead of using the relationships between tables to retrieve data, hierarchical and network databases use record addresses to search for data. In hierarchical and network databases, records are categorized as parent or child records. In a hierarchical database structure, a parent record can have many child records and each child record can have only one parent record, resulting in a hierarchical structure, similar to your ancestry tree. In a network database, a parent record can have many child records and a child record can have many parent records, resulting in a network of records.

How Do I Build an Accounting Database?

Database Essentials Revisited

As you learned in Chapter 1, database essentials that an accountant needs to know include the following database elements:

- Fields: Pieces of information about events, people, or objects
- Records: Collection of related fields
- Table: Collection of related records with a unique table name
- Database: Collection of related tables

Database fields are pieces of information about events, people, and objects. In the CUSTOMER table shown in Figure 2.4, there are 10 fields:

Customer No.
Company Name
Last Name
First Name
Street Address
City
State
ZIP
Country
Account Balance

As shown in Figure 2.4, the field First Name contains the names of specific customers: Angela and Vincent.

	CUSTOMER NO	COMPANY NAME	LAST NAME	FIRST NAME	STREET ADDRESS	CITY	STATE	ZIP	COUNTRY	ACCOUNT BALANCE
⊞	127127		Ashuer	Angela	13 Joseph Ave	Appleton	WI	54911	USA	$1,080.00
⊞	913691	EspressoBar	Pico	Vincent	58 Dante	Pisa	Tuscany	43001	Italy	$530.00

FIGURE 2.4

Customer Table

Pair and Share: How many fields do you see in this database table? How many records?

Database records are a collection of related fields, populated with data. The table in Figure 2.4 contains two records (rows). Each record is populated with data about properties of the specific customer. For example, the first record relates to the customer named Angela Ashuer who is located in Appleton, Wisconsin, and her Customer No. is 127127. In order to retrieve data stored in the database, each record must have one or more fields that are unique identifiers for each record in the database. The unique identifier is called a primary key. For example, in the CUSTOMER table, the unique identifier is the customer number field (Customer No.) because each customer should have a different customer number.

A **database table** is a collection of related records with a unique table name. A table stores records of the same type, such as customer records. For example, the table in Figure 2.4 contains data about two specific customers and accordingly is called the CUSTOMER table.

A **database** is a collection of related tables. In a relational database, the database tables are related or connected through fields common to two or more tables. For example, the Customer No. field appears in the CUSTOMER table, and the Customer No. field would also appear in the SALES ORDER table. Thus, the Customer No. field connects or relates the CUSTOMER table to the SALES ORDER table.

Figure 2.5 illustrates the database elements and hierarchy of field, record, table, and database.

Notice that the First Name field, Angela, appears in the CUSTOMER record, which appears in the CUSTOMER table. Also note that the four database tables (CUSTOMER, SALES ORDER, SALES ORDER LINE, and ITEM) are related. A customer places an order, the order has one or more order lines, and each order line contains an item. The Customer No. field appears in both the CUSTOMER table and the SALES ORDER table, connecting or relating those two tables.

In addition to fields, records, and tables, the database essentials that every accountant should know include:

- Database forms: A means to input data into a database
- Database queries: Tools for searching and extracting data from a database
- Database reports: Output of the database queries

Database forms are onscreen forms or screen interfaces used for entering and updating data. Many of the onscreen database forms used for accounting systems are designed to resemble paper source documents, such as onscreen checks or onscreen invoices (Figure 2.9).

Database queries are used to search the database and retrieve specific data from one or more database tables. For example, if you need to know customer Angela's city, you would enter her Customer No. 127127; the query uses this information to retrieve Angela's record with the customer city.

Database reports are the output of the accounting system. After the query retrieves information from the accounting database, the database report provides a format for viewing the results of your query. Often, you can display the report onscreen or print the report. For example, Figure 2.6 shows a database report.

Accounting Databases: People, Things, and Transactions

An accounting database collects data about *people*, *things*, and *transactions*. Imagine the number of database tables required to collect accounting data for an entire enterprise. To simplify the enormity of this undertaking, we will focus on the transaction cycles in the baseline accounting system model shown in Figure 2.7.

Database tables can consist of data about objects (*people* or *things*) or events (*transactions*). The *people* shown in the baseline accounting system model are vendors, customers, and

> ### Database Logical View...
> The database table's logical view is a structured format. This is the view the user sees on his or her computer screen, with field, record, and table format. In the logical view, fields are located at the intersection of rows and columns, similar to a spreadsheet view. In the logical view, a row in a database table represents a record.

> ### DBMS and RDBMS...
> When using a relational database, the database management system (DBMS) is called a relational database management system (RDBMS). The RDBMS uses tools such as Structured Query Language (SQL) to query a relational database.

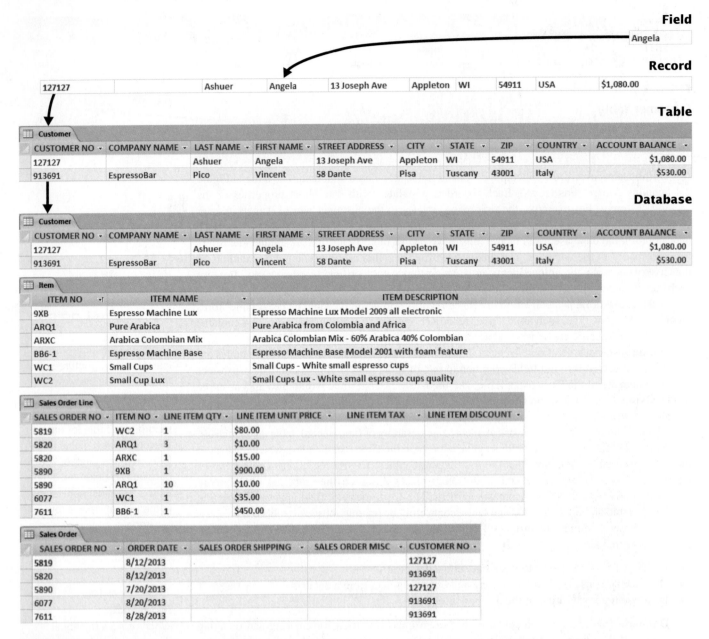

FIGURE 2.5

Database Essentials: Field, Record, Table, Database

Can you trace the First Name field, Angela, through the hierarchy of record, table, and database?

employees. We know that we need a database table for each. So we need a VENDOR table, a CUSTOMER table, and an EMPLOYEE table.

Things shown in the baseline accounting system model are items purchased. So we will need an ITEM table.

Transactions in the model require various database tables to record the transactions in the transaction cycles:

- Purchasing cycle transactions
- Sales cycle transactions
- Payroll cycle transactions

By using business transactions to identify accounting database tables, we ensure that the database will support data needed by the enterprise. You can collect information about a specific enterprise's business transactions by reviewing source documents, interviewing users, and observing procedures and operations.

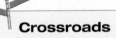

Crossroads

What IT professionals call objects, accounting professionals usually refer to as people or things.

EspressoCoffee Annual Sales Report

Sales Region	Quarter	Espresso Sales
Austria	1	$610,911.00
	2	$901,574.00
	3	$465,460.00
	4	$671,190.00
	Total	$2,649,135.00
Canada	1	$635,144.00
	2	$777,186.00
	3	$338,432.00
	4	$226,018.00
	Total	$1,976,780.00
China	1	$61,241.00
	2	$643,284.00
	3	$834,940.00
	4	$497,871.00
	Total	$2,037,336.00
France	1	$969,279.00
	2	$61,797.00
	3	$353,502.00
	4	$779,811.00
	Total	$2,164,389.00
Germany	1	$486,259.00
	2	$355,135.00
	3	$150,321.00
	4	$248,347.00
	Total	$1,240,062.00

FIGURE 2.6

Report

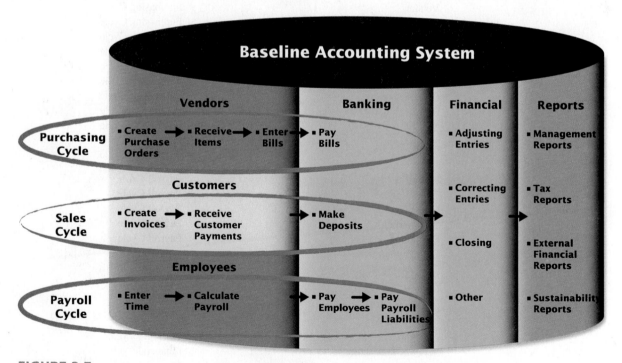

FIGURE 2.7

Baseline Accounting System with Transaction Cycles

Can you imagine the number of database tables needed to collect data about the people, things, and transactions for a baseline accounting system?

A sample of database tables used in an accounting system is shown in Figure 2.8. Notice that the tables correspond to the transaction cycles and that some of the tables are used in more than one transaction cycle. To illustrate how an accounting database is built, we will focus on the sales cycle for EspressoCoffee Company. In particular, we will use the sales order/create invoice transaction to show how database tables are created.

Illustration: EspressoCoffee Accounting Database

To demonstrate the fundamentals of building an accounting database, we will use MS Access to build a portion of an accounting database for EspressoCoffee. The abbreviated steps we will use to build EspressoCoffee's accounting database are:

1. Identify and build database tables. We divide the database into tables based on objects (people and things) and events (transactions). For example, customers are people so we build a CUSTOMER table. Sales are transactions so we build a SALES ORDER table.

> We will explore the fundamentals of building accounting databases using MS Access. We use MS Access because of its availability and simplicity. However, most enterprise databases are built with more sophisticated and powerful database software, such as MS SQL Server or Oracle DBMS.

EspressoCoffee
Company

FIGURE 2.8 Sample of Database Tables for an Accounting System

Can you think of any other database tables that an enterprise might need for its accounting system?

Database table	Transaction Cycle
Customer	Sales Cycle
Sales Order	Sales Cycle
Sales Order Line	Sales Cycle
Item	Sales Cycle
Cash Receipts	Sales Cycle
Cash Account	Sales Cycle
Sales Shipment	Sales Cycle
Sales Shipment Line	Sales Cycle
•	Sales Cycle
•	Sales Cycle
•	Sales Cycle
Vendor	Purchasing Cycle
Purchase Order	Purchasing Cycle
Purchase Order Line	Purchasing Cycle
Item	Purchasing Cycle
Item Received	Purchasing Cycle
Item Received Line	Purchasing Cycle
Cash Payments	Purchasing Cycle
Cash Account	Purchasing Cycle
•	Purchasing Cycle
•	Purchasing Cycle
•	Purchasing Cycle
Employee	Payroll Cycle
Time Worked	Payroll Cycle
Labor Type	Payroll Cycle
Withholding	Payroll Cycle
Exemption	Payroll Cycle
Cash Payments	Payroll Cycle
Cash Account	Payroll Cycle
•	Payroll Cycle
•	Payroll Cycle
•	Payroll Cycle
Accounts	Financial Cycle
Account Transactions	Financial Cycle
General Ledger	Financial Cycle
•	Financial Cycle
•	Financial Cycle
•	Financial Cycle

2. Identify and enter fields in each database table. We divide the database tables into fields or pieces of data. For example, the CUSTOMER table will contain fields for customer number, first name, last name and so on.

3. Select the primary key for each table. We select or create a unique identifier for each table that can be used for record retrieval, such as Customer No.

4. Identify and build relationships among database tables. We identify common fields in two or more tables that can be used to connect the tables.

To illustrate the accounting database behind the screen of EspressoCoffee's accounting system, we will build database tables for EspressoCoffee's sales order transactions.

STEP 1: IDENTIFY AND BUILD DATABASE TABLES When building a database using database software, such as MS Access, we will first identify the database tables needed. As shown in Figure 2.9, tables can consist of data about objects, such as people, or events, such as transactions.

In this illustration, we focus on EspressoCoffee customer transactions. By analyzing the EspressoCoffee sales invoice shown in Figure 2.10, database designers can determine that database tables are needed to store data about customers, sales orders, and items. At least three tables will be needed:

- CUSTOMER table
- SALES ORDER table
- ITEM table

STEP 2: IDENTIFY AND ENTER FIELDS FOR EACH DATABASE TABLE Next, for each database table, we identify the fields for that table. When determining the fields that are needed for each table, it is important to consider how the data will be used. What reports will be needed? What analysis is required? What information is needed to perform that analysis?

For EspressoCoffee, what data do we need to collect about its customers? What data could we collect that might give us a competitive advantage? How can the data and information be transformed into business intelligence? At a minimum, we want to collect information about name, address, phone number, and email address. Then we must consider the specifics of how we want to store this information. For example, if we store a customer's name in a single field called Name, what if there is a company name and an individual's contact name?

FIGURE 2.9 Database Entities and Database Tables

People, Things, or Transactions	Database Tables
Customers	CUSTOMER table
Inventory Items	ITEM table
Sales Orders	SALES ORDER table

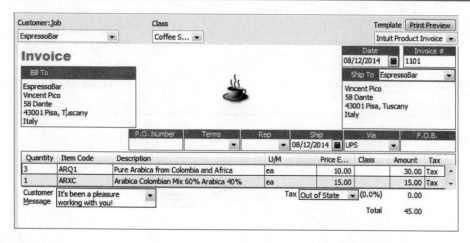

FIGURE 2.10

EspressoCoffee Sales Invoice

How many different items did EspressoBar order?

FIGURE 2.11

EspressoCoffee Customer, Sales Order, and Item Tables

Can you identify the primary keys in these database tables?

Selected fields for three database tables for EspressoCoffee are shown in Figure 2.11. The Name field has been broken into three separate name fields: Company Name, Last Name, and First Name. The Address field has been divided into separate fields: Street Address, City, State, ZIP, and Country. This permits EspressoCoffee to search for all customers in a specific country or ZIP code. If the data were not divided into separate fields, EspressoCoffee would be limited in its ability to retrieve information to reach its target markets.

Note that calculated amounts, such as the sales order subtotal and sales order tax amounts, are not included as fields in the SALES ORDER table. Calculated amounts would be redundant data. In general, calculated amounts are not stored in database fields to avoid overlooking updating the calculated field, which would result in inconsistent data. Instead, database queries perform the calculations.

STEP 3: SELECT PRIMARY KEYS Each record in a table must have a unique identifier or primary key. For example, Customer No. is the primary key for EspressoCoffee's CUSTOMER table. Figure 2.12 lists the database tables and associated primary keys. Notice in Figure 2.11 that MS Access identifies the primary keys in the CUSTOMER, SALES ORDER, and ITEM tables with a key symbol.

STEP 4: IDENTIFY AND BUILD RELATIONSHIPS AMONG DATABASE TABLES In a relational database, each database table must be related to at least one other table in the database. A database table cannot be a freestanding island with no connections; there must be at least one connection or relationship with another table in the relational database.

How are database tables connected? First, you identify a relationship between two tables, (for example, customer places an order). Second, you build the relationship between the tables using one or more fields common to the two tables. For example as shown in Figure 2.13, the CUSTOMER table and the SALES ORDER table are related through a field that is common to both tables, the Customer No. field.

> **Would You Like to Know More?**
>
> Some database modeling techniques, such as ERD (entity relationship diagram), show maximum and minimum occurrences for relationships. In MS Access, only the maximum number is used.
>
> If you would like to know more, see Chapter 14.

FIGURE 2.12 Primary Keys

Database Table	Primary Key
CUSTOMER table	Customer no.
SALES ORDER table	Sales order no.
ITEM table	Item no.

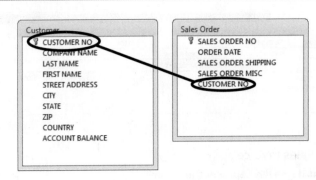

FIGURE 2.13

EspressoCoffee Customer and Sales Order Table Connections

Why don't you need to repeat all the customer fields in the SALES ORDER table?

The Customer No. field appears in both the CUSTOMER table and the SALES ORDER table. The SALES ORDER table must show which customer placed a specific order; therefore, the Customer No. is included in the SALES ORDER table in order to identify the customer placing that order.

In the CUSTOMER table, the Customer No. is the primary key. In the SALES ORDER table, the Customer No. is known as a foreign key. A foreign key is a primary key in one table (CUSTOMER table) that appears in a second table (SALES ORDER table) to connect or relate the two tables.

The next step is to identify the type of relationship between tables. There are three possible types of relationships:

- One-to-one relationships
- One-to-many relationships
- Many-to-many relationships

The relationship type refers to the maximum number that one record in a table might relate to other records in another table.

One-to-One Relationships If a relationship is one-to-one, for each one record in one database table there is one record in the related table. In the example shown in Figure 2.14, there is one record for each employee in EspressoCoffee's EMPLOYEE table, and there is one corresponding record in the 401K RETIREMENT ACCOUNT INFORMATION table for that specific employee.

One-to-Many Relationships One-to-many relationships are the most common. If a relationship is one-to-many, for each one record in one database table, there may be many records in the related table. For example as shown in Figure 2.15, one of EspressoCoffee's customers can place many orders. Thus, one record in the CUSTOMER table could relate to many records in the SALES ORDER table. MS Access uses the ∞ symbol to represent *many*. If one customer placed five orders, then that one customer record would be related to five records in the SALES ORDER table. However, each order relates to only one customer. See Figure 2.16 for a two-part process used to identify the relationship type.

Many-to-Many Relationships If a relationship is many-to-many, there may be many records in one table that relate to many records in the related table. As shown in Figure 2.17 for EspressoCoffee, one sales order can contain many items. A specific item might appear on many sales orders. So there is a many-to-many relationship between the SALES ORDER table and the ITEM table. A many-to-many relationship is problematic when building a database and must be eliminated using a special database table called an intersection table.

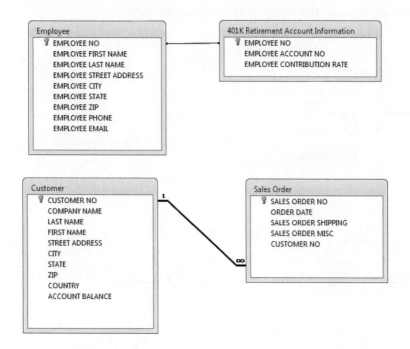

FIGURE 2.14

One-to-One Relationship

How many 401K accounts does each employee have? For each employee record in the EMPLOYEE table, how many related records are in the 401K RETIREMENT ACCOUNT Information table?

FIGURE 2.15

One-to-Many Relationship

How many orders can one customer place? How many customers can place one specific order?

Step 1: What is the *maximum* number of *orders* a customer can place? **Many**

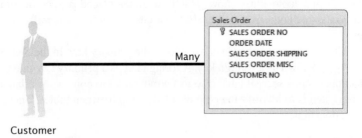

Step 2: What is the *maximum* number of *customers* who can place a specific order? *1*

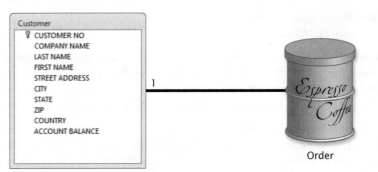

FIGURE 2.16

One-to-Many Relationship Detail

To summarize, at this point EspressoCoffee shows:

- Three tables: CUSTOMER, SALES ORDER, and ITEM
- The relationship between the CUSTOMER and SALES ORDER tables: One-to-many
- The relationship between the SALES ORDER and ITEM tables: Many-to-many

The next step is to remove the many-to-many relationship between the SALES ORDER and ITEM tables. Database software, such as Access, is unable to build database tables with many-to-many relationships. Therefore, you must remove all many-to-many relationships. This is accomplished using a special type of database table called an Intersection table.

Intersection tables, also called junction tables, are placed at the intersection or junction of the two tables with a many-to-many relationship. For example, EspressoCoffee's SALES ORDER table and ITEM table have a many-to-many relationship as shown in Figure 2.17. We must eliminate the many-to-many relationship using an intersection table.

FIGURE 2.17

Many-to-Many Relationship

How many items can appear on one sales order? On how many sales orders can one item appear?

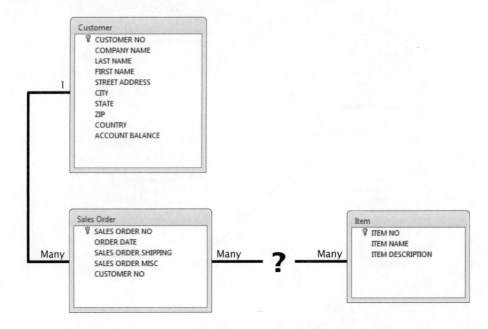

Intersection Table

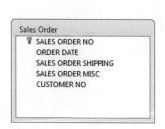

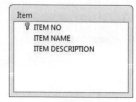

FIGURE 2.18
Intersection Table

Let's go back to the EspressoCoffee sales invoice in Figure 2.10. We see in this sales order form that for each item ordered the item (code) number, description, quantity, unit price, and total price are written on one line of the sales order (line item).

If we add an intersection table named SALES ORDER LINE at the intersection of the SALES ORDER table and the ITEM table, the many-to-many relationship is removed. The relationships between the new SALES ORDER LINE intersection table and the two original tables (SALES ORDER and ITEM tables) automatically become one to many.

The following shows how we convert a many-to-many relationship into two one-to-many relationships by adding an intersection table.

1. For each many-to-many relationship, create an intersection table at the intersection of the many-to-many relationship. The relationship between the SALES ORDER and ITEM tables is a many-to-many relationship. As shown in Figure 2.18, we create an intersection table and place it at the intersection of the SALES ORDER and ITEM tables. In this case, we name the intersection table SALES ORDER LINE.

2. Create two new one-to-many relationships, each of which connects the tables involved in the many-to-many relationship to the new intersection table. The many-to-many relationship is eliminated. The relationship between the SALES ORDER and SALES ORDER LINE tables is now one-to-many. The relationship between the ITEM table and SALES ORDER LINE table is also one-to-many.

3. The intersection table's primary key is a **composite primary key**, which means that more than one field is required to uniquely identify a record in the intersection table. The intersection table will inherit as its own primary key the primary keys of the two tables involved in the many-to-many relationship. The primary key for the intersection table includes the foreign keys of the tables involved in the many-to-many relationship (SALES ORDER table and ITEM table). In this case as shown in Figure 2.19, the primary key for the SALES ORDER LINE table is a combination of Sales Order No. (the primary key for the SALES ORDER table) and Item No. (the primary key for the ITEM table).

Figure 2.20 summarizes the steps to remove a many-to-many relationship by inserting an intersection table.

Figure 2.21 shows the four database tables used for recording sales order transactions for EspressoCoffee. Notice that the tables are connected or related with one-to-many relationships. Inserting the intersection table, SALES ORDER LINE, eliminated the many-to-many relationship.

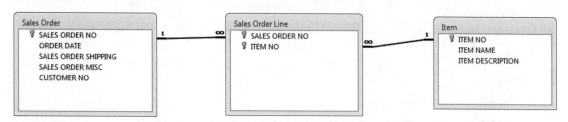

FIGURE 2.19
Intersection Table with Primary Keys

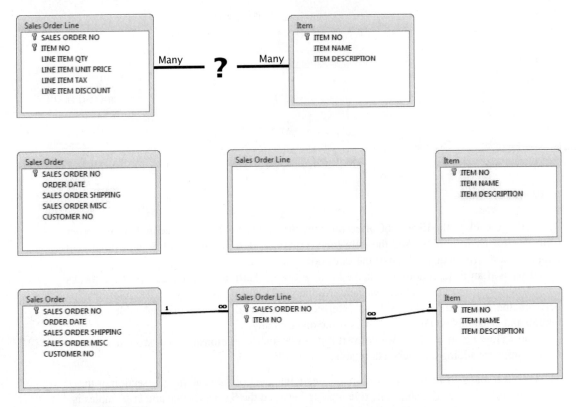

FIGURE 2.20

Using an Intersection Table to Remove Many-to-Many Relationship

Pair and Share: Explain how the intersection table removes the problematic many-to-many relationship.

Next, we need to build the relationship lines between the database tables to connect the tables. For example, the primary key (Customer No.) of the CUSTOMER table, which is also the foreign key in the SALES ORDER table, is used to connect the CUSTOMER table and the SALES ORDER table.

In MS Access, you insert the relationship lines by clicking on the primary key (Customer No.) in the CUSTOMER table and dragging and dropping it into the SALES ORDER table. The customer number is the primary key in the CUSTOMER table and the foreign key in the SALES ORDER table.

The field Sales Order No. connects the SALES ORDER table and the SALES ORDER LINE table. Also, the field Item No. connects the ITEM table to the SALES ORDER LINE table. Figure 2.21 shows the EspressoCoffee sales order transaction database in MS Access. Notice in Figure 2.21 that all the relationships are one-to-many relationships. Now that the database tables are related, a

My Connection...
- Short Exercise 2.24
- Short Exercise 2.25
- Tech in Practice 2.38
- Tech in Practice 2.39

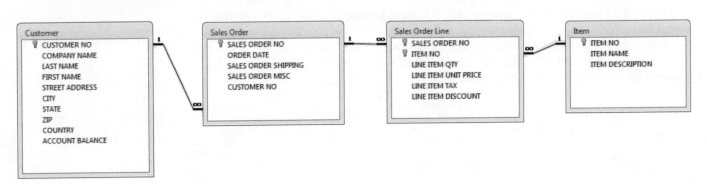

FIGURE 2.21

MS Access Sales Transaction Database Tables for EspressoCoffee

Can you imagine what the diagram of all the database tables for the entire accounting system looks like, instead of only four tables?

database query can be used to search and retrieve data stored in the tables. Note that the Line Item Total amount is calculated using Line Item Qty, Line Item Unit Price, Line Item Tax, and Line Item Discount fields. To eliminate redundant data, the Line Item Total amount can be calculated using a database query instead of storing it as a database field.

Accounting Databases and SDLC

As mentioned in Chapter 1, accounting systems are designed and developed using the system development life cycle (SDLC). The accounting database is considered in each of the SDLC phases (PAD-BID: plan, analyze, design, build/buy, install, and deploy).

Plan In the first phase of the SDLC, the feasibility of updating a current database or building a new database is evaluated.

Analysis During the analysis phase, we analyze the current accounting database and what users require from the database, such as new accounting reports. Based on the user requirements, modifications to the accounting database are analyzed.

Design In the design phase, we design a new accounting database model that satisfies user requirements. The database model can be designed and documented using entity relationship diagrams (ERD) or other database-modeling tools, such as unified modeling language (UML) class and object diagrams. Special software for modeling, such as Microsoft Visio or CASE tools, can be used to document the database models. In the system design phase, IT architecture for hardware and software for the new database is identified.

Build/Buy During this phase, we build the new accounting database using database software such as MS Access, MS SQL Server, or Oracle. Another option is to buy a database. For example, if you purchase MS Dynamics GP accounting software, the database is included with the software.

During the system build phase, system builders and software engineers transform the database model into an actual accounting database using DBMS software. The newly developed databases are tested using test data. Final fine-tuning is completed.

Install The system install phase involves installing the database and computer programs on the organization servers and user workstations. The database is populated with real data from the enterprise.

Deploy During this phase, we operate, maintain, and support the database on an ongoing basis.

What Is Database Integrity?

What Would You Do?

Imagine that as an accounting professional at EspressoCoffee you are charged with tracking customer orders. Joey, your coworker in IT, developed the database shown in Figure 2.22 for you to use in tracking orders. Joey tells you that the primary key is a composite of three fields: the Customer No., the Order No., and the Item No.

> ### Database Anomalies...
> Three types of database anomalies (problems) are DUI:
> - Deletion problem
> - Update problem
> - Insertion problem

Your supervisor has asked you to complete the following steps:

1. Delete Vincent as a customer. He will no longer be purchasing from EspressoCoffee. Keep a record of his sales orders, however, because this information is needed to prepare EspressoCoffee's income statement.
2. Update Angela's address to 123 Lakeshore Drive, Chicago, IL 60611.
3. Add Nick as a customer to the database. He will be placing an order later.

> ### Crossroads
> At the crossroads of accounting and IT, you need to know about three database realms:
> 1. Database designer realm: Database designers perform the plan, analysis, and design phases of the SDLC.
> 2. Database builder/ programmer realm: Database programmers build the database during the SDLC build and install phases.
> 3. Database user realm: Database users are most familiar with the SDLC deploy phase.
>
> Each database realm (designer, builder, and user), has its own terminology. As accounting professionals, we may be accustomed to the terminology of the user realm; however, accountants today need to communicate with IT professionals who are database designers and builders.
>
> In this chapter, we use the database builder terminology. See Chapter 14 if you want to learn the database designer terminology.

EspressoCoffee
Company

> ### The Cost of Inaccurate Data...
> Globally, the cost of inaccurate data is estimated to be between $100 billion and $600 billion (Daley, 2003).
>
> *Has inaccurate data ever cost you money?*

Customer Order											
CUSTOMER NO	NAME	ADDRESS	TOTAL BALANCE	ORDER NO	ORDER DATE	ORDER BAL	ORDER LINE BAL	ITEM NO	QTY	UNIT PRICE
913691	Vincent	58 Dante	$530.00	5820	8/12/2013	$45.00	$30.00	ARQ1	3	$10.00
913691	Vincent	58 Dante	$530.00	5820	8/12/2013	$45.00	$15.00	ARXC	1	$15.00
913691	Vincent	58 Dante	$530.00	6077	8/20/2013	$35.00	$35.00	WC1	1	$35.00
913691	Vincent	58 Dante	$530.00	7611	8/28/2013	$450.00	$450.00	BB6-1	1	$450.00
127127	Angela	13 Joseph Ave	$1,080.00	5890	7/20/2013	$1,000.00	$900.00	9XB	1	$900.00
127127	Angela	13 Joseph Ave	$1,080.00	5890	7/20/2013	$1,000.00	$100.00	ARQ1	10	$10.00
127127	Angela	13 Joseph Ave	$1,080.00	5819	8/12/2013	$80.00	$80.00	WC2	1	$80.00

FIGURE 2.22

Joey's Database Table for Tracking Customer Orders

Pair and Share: Share with a classmate your response to the following question:
Can you find the deletion, update, and insertion anomalies in Joey's database?

> **You're the Boss...**
> If you were Joey's boss, what feedback would you give him on his database design? How would you work with Joey to improve it?

What Would You Do?

If you delete Vincent as a customer, you also delete a record of his sales orders, which is needed for preparing the income statement. To update Angela's address, you must update her address in three records. You cannot add Nick to the database, because he has no order number, which is needed for the primary key.

You have just encountered something called database anomalies.

Database Anomalies

Database anomalies are problems in the design of a database. They can result in inaccurate, incomplete, or unreliable data. Poorly designed databases may contain problems with inserting, updating, and deleting data.

Let's look again at Joey's database table for EspressoCoffee shown in Figure 2.22. Three types of issues or anomalies found in the database table are:

1. Deletion problem
2. Update problem
3. Insertion problem

Deletion Problem Deleting Vincent as a customer will cause the deletion of four records. These four records hold vital information about four orders and four items that will also be deleted.

Update Problem To update Angela's customer address, three records would need to be updated. In addition, there are no fields for recording the city, state, and ZIP code.

Insertion Problem To identify a unique record, we have to use the customer number, order number, and item number. That means these three fields together form the primary key. If we want to insert a customer who hasn't placed an order yet, then the order number and item number are empty (null), and we do not have a primary key for retrieving the record.

Poorly designed databases can provide incorrect data and create problems in searching and retrieving data. A well-designed database is free of deletion, update, and insertion anomalies.

Database Normalization

Database anomalies can be removed through a process called **normalization**. Through normalization, redundancy and inconsistencies are removed.

The problem with the database table that Joey developed for EspressoCoffee shown in Figure 2.22 is that it contains data about multiple objects and events: two objects (item and customer) and an event (sales order).

Separating the database into related tables instead of using just one large table helps to eliminate the deletion, update, and insertion problems. The EspressoCoffee database tables in Figure 2.23 contain the same data but stored in database tables free of anomalies.

Using the divide-and-conquer principle, we divide the two objects (item and customer) into two different, but related, tables: Customer table and Item table. We record the event in yet another table: Sales Order table. The Sales Order table has information about only the order event.

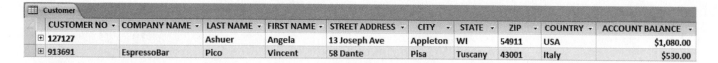

Customer

CUSTOMER NO	COMPANY NAME	LAST NAME	FIRST NAME	STREET ADDRESS	CITY	STATE	ZIP	COUNTRY	ACCOUNT BALANCE
⊞ 127127		Ashuer	Angela	13 Joseph Ave	Appleton	WI	54911	USA	$1,080.00
⊞ 913691	EspressoBar	Pico	Vincent	58 Dante	Pisa	Tuscany	43001	Italy	$530.00

Sales Order

SALES ORDER NO	ORDER DATE	SALES ORDER SHIPPING	SALES ORDER MISC	CUSTOMER NO
⊞ 5819	8/12/2013			127127
⊞ 5820	8/12/2013			913691
⊞ 5890	7/20/2013			127127
⊞ 6077	8/20/2013			913691
⊞ 7611	8/28/2013			913691

Sales Order Line

SALES ORDER NO	ITEM NO	LINE ITEM QTY	LINE ITEM UNIT PRICE	LINE ITEM TAX	LINE ITEM DISCOUNT
5819	WC2	1	$80.00		
5820	ARQ1	3	$10.00		
5820	ARXC	1	$15.00		
5890	9XB	1	$900.00		
5890	ARQ1	10	$10.00		
6077	WC1	1	$35.00		
7611	BB6-1	1	$450.00		

Item

ITEM NO	ITEM NAME	ITEM DESCRIPTION
⊞ 9XB	Espresso Machine Lux	Espresso Machine Lux Model 2009 all electronic
⊞ ARQ1	Pure Arabica	Pure Arabica from Colombia and Africa
⊞ ARXC	Arabica Colombian Mix	Arabica Colombian Mix - 60% Arabica 40% Colombian
⊞ BB6-1	Espresso Machine Base	Espresso Machine Base Model 2001 with foam feature
⊞ WC1	Small Cups	Small Cups - White small espresso cups
⊞ WC2	Small Cup Lux	Small Cups Lux - White small espresso cups quality

FIGURE 2.23

EspressoCoffee Anomaly-Free Database Tables

Pair and Share: Compare the tables in this figure to the tables in Figure 2.21. What is the same? What is different?

As you will recall, we cannot build a many-to-many relationship in a database program. When we remove many-to-many relationships by adding a new intersection table (SALES ORDER LINE table), we also remove the duplicate records from two tables (ITEM table and SALES ORDER table) that have a many-to-many relationship.

Notice that the customer's address is stored in the CUSTOMER table, permitting the customer's address to be stored only once. Any time the customer's address is desired, it is retrieved from the CUSTOMER table.

Well-designed databases permit you to search and retrieve desired information. Relational database designers and builders follow specific database design rules to create well-structured database tables.

Database Integrity Rules

Database integrity means that the database contains accurate, valid data. Database integrity is especially important for accounting databases that must be accurate in order to produce reliable accounting reports. Database developers follow certain rules in order to ensure database integrity.

When building databases, the following four rules are used to ensure database integrity:

Rule 1: Entity integrity
Rule 2: Primary key integrity

Rule 3: Domain integrity
Rule 4: Referential integrity

DATABASE INTEGRITY RULE 1: ENTITY INTEGRITY Each record in the database must have a unique identifier (i.e., a unique primary key). No two records in the database table can have the same primary key value. This ensures that each record can be retrieved from the database using the unique identifier, such as customer number.

DATABASE INTEGRITY RULE 2: PRIMARY KEY INTEGRITY The primary key value cannot be null (empty). Each record must have a value for the primary key field.

DATABASE INTEGRITY RULE 3: DOMAIN INTEGRITY The field values must be from a pre-defined domain. For example, the Date field must have a date and not any other values. In MS Access, this is referred to as a validation rule.

DATABASE INTEGRITY RULE 4: REFERENTIAL INTEGRITY Data referenced and stored in related tables must be consistent across the database. For example, a customer address should be the same in any table in which it is referenced. Referential integrity is improved when the customer address, for example, is stored in one location only, eliminating the possibility of the address differing from table to table.

> **My Connection...**
> • Short Exercise 2.27

What Are the Differences between a Manual Accounting System and a Database Accounting System?

The differences between a manual accounting system that you learned about in your introductory accounting courses and a database accounting system used in practice are summarized in Figure 2.24. Notice that many of the manual steps are performed automatically with a database accounting system.

> **My Connection...**
> • Active Review 2.10

FIGURE 2.24 Manual vs. Database Accounting System

How many tasks can a database accounting system perform automatically that you must perform by hand in a manual accounting system?

Task	Manual Accounting System	Database Accounting System
Transactions Entered: ■ Vendor Transactions ■ Customer Transactions ■ Employee Transactions	Debit and credit journal entries made manually	Transactions entered using onscreen database forms such as onscreen invoices and checks; totals automatically calculated
Financial Cycle: ■ Adjusting Entries ■ Correcting Entries	Debit and credit journal entries made manually	Adjustments made using onscreen journal
Financial Cycle: ■ Closing Entries	Debit and credit journal entries made manually	Completed automatically
Account Balances	Entries in journal manually posted to General Ledger accounts and account balances recalculated	Account information stored in database tables; balances automatically calculated
Financial Statements and Reports	Reports prepared manually using General Ledger account balances	Database queries retrieve information from various database tables and generate reports

Chapter Highlights

What data is stored in accounting databases? Organizations store data about assets, liabilities, operations, transactions, employees, customers, vendors, and more in databases. Accounting databases need to be well structured, redundancy-free, consistent, and current.

What are the three tiers in accounting system architecture? Behind the front-end accounting software screen is a back-end database management system and accounting database. The three tiers in accounting system architecture are:

- Database tier: The back-end accounting database stores accounting data in database tables. A back-end database management system (DBMS) sorts, stores, inserts, updates, and deletes accounting data and runs queries.
- Application tier: Accounting software applications interact with the DBMS to access the back-end accounting database.
- User tier: The user tier consists of the interface appearing on the accountant's computer screen. The user interface consists of database forms and reports.

What are enterprise databases? Enterprise databases used by an enterprise for business purposes can be considered as one of two types: internal databases or external databases.

- Internal databases are databases in which the data belongs to the organization. Internal databases consist of two varieties: operational databases and data warehouses. Operational databases, such as an accounting database, store enterprise transactions. Data warehouses store data from a variety of sources.
- External databases are databases containing data collected by other organizations.

What problems can result from poorly designed databases? Poorly designed databases may contain database problems or anomalies, such as problems with inserting, updating, and deleting data. This can result in inaccurate, unreliable accounting data.

What are the database essentials? Database essentials that an accounting professional needs to know include the following database elements:

- Fields: Pieces of information about events, people, or objects
- Records: Collection of related fields
- Table: Collection of related records with a unique table name
- Database: Collection of related tables
- Forms: Onscreen forms or screen interfaces used for entering and updating data
- Queries: Commands used to search the database and retrieve specific data from one or more database tables
- Reports: Output of the accounting system in a report format to view the results of queries

What are the steps used to build an accounting database? The steps use to build an accounting database are:

1. Identify and build database tables.
2. Identify and enter fields in each database table.
3. Select the primary key for each table.
4. Identify and build relationships among database tables, removing any many-to-many relationships by creating intersection tables.

What are the differences between a manual accounting system and a database accounting system? Differences between a manual and database accounting system are summarized in Figure 2.24.

Accounting System Insights

Insight No. 9   Enter data once.

Insight No. 10 Design accounting databases using the 80/20 Rule. Invest 80% of the time designing the database and 20% of the time maintaining the database.

Active Review

Study less. Learn more. Make connections.

2.1 Refer to the chapter opener, *Meet Ingenix*. In your opinion, what could have been done to prevent the faulty database from costing consumers billions of dollars? How would you clean up the Ingenix database?

2.2 Discuss the differences between an operational database and a data warehouse. Is the accounting database considered an operational database or a data warehouse?

2.3 What is a DBMS? Discuss its role in the accounting system.

2.4 Discuss the importance of primary keys to the accounting database.

2.5 Discuss the role of the accounting database in the accounting system. Which components are behind the screen?

2.6 Discuss the roles of accounting professionals in designing and building accounting databases. Why it is important for accounting professionals to know about enterprise databases?

2.7 Discuss how modern database systems support the growth of large enterprises, such as Wal-Mart.

2.8 What is an intersection table? Why is it created?

2.9 What is a foreign key? Discuss its importance to a relational database.

2.10 Discuss the advantages of a database accounting system versus a manual accounting system.

Key Terms Check

Understanding the language used at the crossroads of accounting and IT is key to your success.

2.11 Match the following terms and definitions.

a. database fields
b. database records
c. database tables
d. database
e. database forms
f. database queries
g. database reports

_____ 1. Onscreen interface used for entering and updating data
_____ 2. Used to view output of the accounting system
_____ 3. A collection of related records with a unique name
_____ 4. Pieces of information about events, people, or objects
_____ 5. Used to search the database and retrieve data from one or more database tables
_____ 6. A collection of related fields
_____ 7. A collection of related tables

2.12 Match the following terms and definitions.

a. operational database
b. data warehouse
c. database administrator
d. intersection table
e. composite primary key
f. normalization
g. database integrity

_____ 1. Responsible for managing the enterprise's databases
_____ 2. Ensures that the database contains accurate, valid data
_____ 3. Stores data from a variety of sources and is used for business intelligence
_____ 4. Databases used to store data related to business operations and transactions
_____ 5. A process for removing database anomalies or problems
_____ 6. Used when more than one field is required to uniquely identify a record
_____ 7. Placed at the junction of two tables to eliminate a many-to-many relationship

2.13 Which of the following statements are true?

_____ 1. Accounting transactions are stored in the operational database.

_____ 2. A database administrator is responsible for designing the database.

_____ 3. The result of a query could be a report.

_____ 4. Deletion, insertion, and update problems are solved by normalization.

_____ 5. A data warehouse stores only future data.

_____ 6. An intersection table refers to the intersection of queries and reports.

_____ 7. A composite primary key consists of more than one field.

Practice Test

2.14 Enter data once means:

a. Data is entered into the database only one time and it is reused from various locations when it is needed.

b. Data is entered only one time and it cannot be entered again.

c. Data is used only one time and it can not be reused.

d. Data is entered into the database from various locations at the same time.

2.15 _____ transfers data from the accounting software to the database.

a. CRM

b. DBMS

c. User Interface

d. Relational database

2.16 Internal databases consist of:

a. DBMS

b. Operational database

c. The database stored in the employee computer

d. Operational and data warehouse

2.17 While auditing the Account Receivable records, the auditor discovers an entry for Cambiz Coffee shop with an address of 721 Sweet Water Pond, St. Peters MO and another entry for Cambiz Coffee shop with an address of 721 Sweet Water Pond, Saint Peters MO. Each entry has a different customer number. Which of the following statements is false?

a. The DBMS views these as two separate accounts.

b. Data is entered into the computer incorrectly.

c. Customer has two shops.

d. The data needs scrubbing.

2.18 _____ is a collection of related records.

a. Database engine

b. Database table

c. Database field

d. Object Oriented database

2.19 Which tier in the accounting system architecture consists of accounting software?

a. Accountant tier

b. Database tier

c. User tier

d. Application tier

2.20 An item table's record has 5 fields: Item code, Item name, description, location ID, and warehouse ID. Which of these fields is a good candidate for the primary key?

a. Location ID
b. Item Code
c. Warehouse ID
d. Item name

2.21 An item may appear on many orders. An order contains many items. The relationship between Item table and Order table is:

a. Many-to-one
b. Many-to-many
c. One-to-many
d. One-to-one

2.22 Sandy, an accountant, wants to search for a specific customer address. She should search using:

a. Customer name
b. Customer address
c. Customer ID
d. a and b

2.23 Which of the following is NOT a database essential?

a. Form
b. Table
c. Query
d. DBMS

Exercises

Each Exercise relates to one of the major questions addressed in the chapter and is labeled with the question number in green.

Short Exercises
Warm up with these short exercises.

2.24 Match the following database fields with the appropriate database table. **(Q2.3)**

a. VENDOR table
b. CUSTOMER table
c. EMPLOYEE table
d. ACCOUNTS table
e. SALES ORDER table
f. SALES ORDER LINE table
g. PURCHASE ORDER table
h. PURCHASE ORDER LINE table

_____ 1. Customer name
_____ 2. Account number
_____ 3. Customer number
_____ 4. Employee address
_____ 5. Item quantity sold
_____ 6. Item quantity purchased
_____ 7. Sales order number
_____ 8. Sales order date
_____ 9. Purchase order date
_____ 10. Purchase order number
_____ 11. Vendor address
_____ 12. Sales order total

____ 13. Purchase order total
____ 14. Vendor number
____ 15. Account type

2.25 Identify the relationship between the following tables. **(Q2.3)**

a. one-to-one
b. one-to-many
c. many-to-many
  1. STUDENT table and COURSE table
  2. TEACHER table and STUDENT table
  3. EMPLOYEE table and DEPARTMENT table

2.26 Suppose data about vendors and the items they sell are stored in a single database table. Do you think this table is anomaly-free? Why or why not? If you think there are anomalies in this table can you suggest a solution for removing them? **(Q2.4)**

2.27 Which of the following database tables would be used in a purchase order form? **(Q2.3)**
  1. SALES ORDER table
  2. PURCHASE ORDER table
  3. ITEM table
  4. VENDOR table
  5. CUSTOMER table
  6. PURCHASE ORDER LINE table
  7. SALES ORDER LINE table
  8. CASH RECEIPTS table

2.28 An enterprise's EMPLOYEE table contains the following fields. Which of these employee fields is a good choice for the EMPLOYEE table primary key? Why? **(Q2.3, 2.4)**

- First Name
- Last Name
- ID No.
- Address
- Phone Number
- Hours Worked
- Hourly Pay
- Deductions

2.29 Identify the following as either internal or external databases. **(Q2.2)**

a. Internal database
b. External database
____ 1. Data warehouse for business intelligence
____ 2. EDGAR Online containing annual reports for publicly traded companies
____ 3. Accounting database
____ 4. Eurostat containing economic and financial statistics about the European Union
____ 5. Operational databases for storing business transactions
____ 6. Factiva, a database with financial data provided by Dow Jones & Reuters Company

2.30 Identify in which tier each of the following items belong. **(Q2.1)**

a. Database tier
b. Application tier
c. User tier
____ 1. DBMS
____ 2. CUSTOMER table
____ 3. Accounting software
____ 4. Customer data entry form
____ 5. Vendor report
____ 6. ITEM table

2.31 Using the following database tables, answer the following questions. (Q2.3)

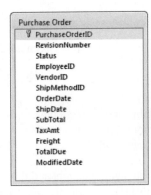

1. What is the relationship between the VENDOR table and the PURCHASE ORDER table?
2. What is the primary key for the VENDOR table?
3. What is the primary key for the PURCHASE ORDER table?
4. What is the foreign key for the PURCHASE ORDER table?

2.32 Using the following purchase order for EspressoCoffee, answer the following questions. (Q2.3)

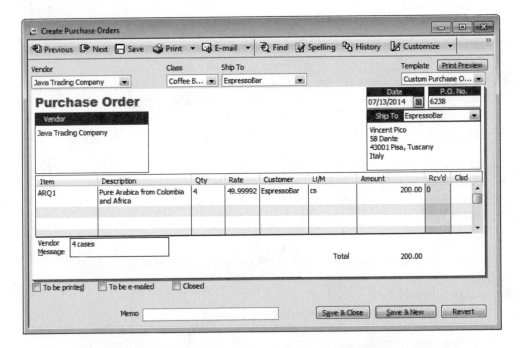

1. Name the database tables that EspressoCoffee should use to record its purchase transactions.
2. Identify the primary key(s) for each table that would uniquely identify each record in the table.
3. Identify the relationships among the tables as one-to-one, one-to-many, or many-to-many.
4. Identify the intersection table that should be used to remove any many-to-many relationships.
5. Identify foreign keys used to connect the tables.

It's Your Call

This is your training ground. These scenarios provide you with the opportunity to use your knowledge and professional skills.

2.33 Since your background is in AIS, you have been asked to provide training to the other accountants in your company about the new accounting system design. How would you explain to your colleagues about the three tiers in an accounting system architecture? **(Q2.1)**

2.34 You have been called in as a consultant to act as a liaison between the accountants and the IT professionals at a company. The accountants are complaining that they must re-enter all the customer information each time an order is placed. The accountants see this as inefficient and time consuming with no value added.

The only response from the IT professionals has been to say that the database tables need to be normalized. The accountants have asked you what this means. Communication between the two groups of professionals has deteriorated.

How would you facilitate communication between the accountants and the IT professionals? How would you explain to both sides what is needed to resolve the issue? **(Q2.4)**

2.35 Your company is expanding its operations to include overseas markets. Your supervisor asked you to prepare a summary explaining changes to the CUSTOMER database table that need to be implemented as a result of the overseas expansion. **(Q2.3, 2.4)**

2.36 You work at a university and have been assigned to a project team to update the university database to include information about employee dependents. The university provides tuition free to all employee dependents and wants to track dependent information to estimate free tuition in the future.

One of the project team members has suggested simply adding the employee dependent information to the EMPLOYEE database table. What do you think? Is this advisable? Prepare your notes to respond to his suggestion at the next team meeting. **(Q2.3, 2.4)**

2.37 Your supervisor would like to know why calculated fields are typically not included as database fields in accounting software. Prepare a short report on advantages and disadvantages of including and not including the calculated field for your supervisor. **(Q2.3, 2.4)**

Tech in Practice

These technology in practice exercises are perfect for both individuals and teams.

Tech Exercises

Sharpen your skills with these technology exercises. Watch the software videos at www.pearsonhighered.com/kay.

2.38

Tech Tool: Database Software

Software Videos: Database Tables, Database Table Relationships

EspressoCoffee asked for your assistance in building database tables to record sales transactions.

1. Using Microsoft Access database software and information in Figure 2.21, build the following database tables. Identify the primary key for each table.
   - CUSTOMER table
   - SALES ORDER table
   - SALES ORDER LINE table
   - ITEM table

2. Identify the table relationships between the CUSTOMER, SALES ORDER, SALES ORDER LINE, and ITEM tables. Use database software to create the database table relationships.
3. Print the table relationships.

2.39 (Continuation of TE 2.27)

Tech Tool: Database Software

Software Video: Database Tables

This is a continuation of the previous exercise.

EspressoCoffee asked for your assistance in entering data into database tables to record sales transactions.

1. Using Microsoft Access database software and your database file from the previous exercise, enter the following customer information into the CUSTOMER table.

Customer No	Company Name	Last Name	First Name	Street Address	City	State	ZIP	Country	Account Balance
127127		Ashuer	Angela	13 Joseph Ave	Appleton	WI	54911	USA	$1080.00
913691	EspressoBar	Pico	Vincent	58 Dante	Pisa	Tuscany	43001	Italy	$ 530.00

2. Enter the following items into the ITEM table.

Item No	Item Name	Item Description
9XB	Espresso Machine Lux	Espresso Machine Lux Model 2009 all electronic
ARQ1	Pure Arabica	Pure Arabica from Colombia and Africa
ARXC	Arabica Colombian Mix	Arabica Colombian Mix - 60% Arabica, 40% Colombian
BB6-1	Espresso Machine Base	Espresso Machine Base Model 2001 with foam feature
WC1	Small Cups	Small Cups - White small espresso cups
WC2	Small Cup Lux	Small Cups Lux - White small espresso cups quality

3. Enter the following sales into the SALES ORDER table and the SALES ORDER LINE table.
   - On December 5, 2012, customer Angela Ashuer places an order to buy the following items:
   a. (2) Item No. ARXC for $40 each
   - On December 22, 2012, customer Vincent Pico places an order to buy the following items:
   a. (1) Item No. 9XB for $400 each
   b. (12) Item No. WC1 for $15 each
4. Print the CUSTOMER, SALES ORDER, SALES ORDER LINE, AND ITEM tables.

2.40

Tech Tool: Database Software

Software Videos: Database Tables, Database Table Relationships

Complete the following:

1. Select an authentic enterprise of your choice. Using Microsoft Access database software, develop the following tables for the enterprise, identify appropriate fields, and select the primary keys.
2. ■ CUSTOMER table
   ■ SALES ORDER table
   ■ SALES ORDER LINE table
   ■ ITEM table
3. Identify the relationships between the tables as one-to-one, one-to-many, or many-to-many.

4. Use Microsoft Access database software to create the database table relationships.
5. Print the table relationships.
6. Populate the tables with at least three records of test data.

2.41

Tech Tool: Database Software

Software Videos: Database Tables, Database Table Relationships

EspressoCoffee buys coffee beans from vendors in South America and Africa and needs a database table to collect information about the company's vendors.

1. Use the following fields to build a VENDOR table.

Vendor No.	Vendor ZIP
Vendor Name	Vendor Country
Vendor Street Address	Vendor Email
Vendor City	Vendor Web Site
Vendor State	

2. Identify and add the primary key for the VENDOR table.

2.42

Tech Tool: Database Software

Software Videos: Database Tables, Database Table Relationships

EspressoCoffee has asked for your assistance in building database tables to record purchase transactions. Use the following EspressoCoffee purchase order and MS Access database software to complete the following.

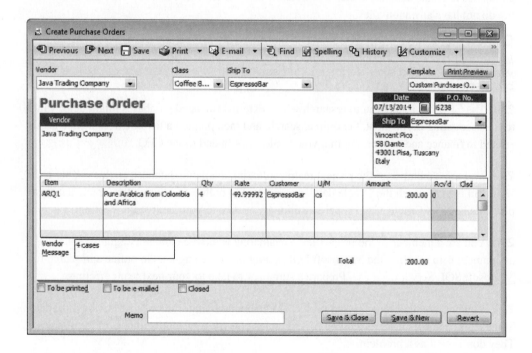

1. Build the database tables for EspressoCoffee purchase transactions. (Hint: You should have four tables.)
2. Enter the fields you think appropriate for each database table.
3. Select the primary key(s) for each database table.
4. Remove any many-to-many relationships using intersection tables.
5. Build the relationships among the tables and print.

2.43

Tech Tool: Database Software

Software Video: Database Tables

Ethan, your coworker, who unfortunately didn't take an accounting information system course while studying accounting, wants you to help him to understand database anomalies. To help your coworker, build a table in MS Access with the following fields and data. Show Ethan deletion, update, and insertion anomalies.

Vendor No	Item Code	Vendor First Name	Vendor Last Name	Vendor City	Item Name	Item Description	Quantity	Unit Price
120	23MX	Mark	Kwinsky	St. Louis	Accx 202	Accelerator gas pedal	3	$60
234	10SP	Jim	Maranda	Chicago	SW6B	Switch pin	12	$7.20
127	10U2	Mary	Vedette	Tulsa	52SET	Under seat bar	1	$56
120	PP10	Mark	Kwinsky	St. Louis	BrkL	Left Brake	1	$150
120	WX30	Mark	Kwinsky	St. Louis	BrkR	Right Brake	1	$150

2.44

Tech Tool: Database Software

Software Video: Database Tables

Use information provided in the 2.43 exercise table and your understanding of the database anomalies to create database tables that hold the same data, which is in the exercise 2.43 table but do not have any anomalies.

Go Online

In the fast paced world of technology, your skill at finding answers fast can be vital. Go online and experience typical assignments you may encounter as a professional.

2.45 The CFO has asked you to research which external financial databases might be of value to the accounting department. Go online, search, and then prepare a list of external databases related to finance and accounting that you would recommend to the CFO.

2.46 You are a member of the project team evaluating available database engines. Your assignment is to research the Oracle database engine. Go online and search for Oracle database products, such as Oracle 11g. Prepare a summary to take to your next team meeting.

2.47 You are a member of the project team evaluating available database engines. Your assignment is to research the Microsoft SQL Server database engine. Go online and search for Microsoft SQL Server database. Prepare a summary to take to your next team meeting.

2.48 You have been talking to your project team about the importance of scrubbing dirty data. Some team members have asked you for examples of dirty data and its impact on companies. They don't see it as a problem.

Go online and search for examples of dirty data to present to your team at the next team meeting.

Technology Projects

These technology projects are perfect for both individuals and teams.

Technology Project 2

Tech Tool: Database Software

Software Videos: Database Tables, Database Table Relationships

Technology Project 2 is your opportunity to practice building database tables and relationships for iSportDesign. With this project, you will use Microsoft Access database software.

Your deliverables for this project include:

Deliverable 1. CUSTOMER table
Deliverable 2. SALES ORDER table
Deliverable 3. SALES ORDER LINE table
Deliverable 4. ITEM table
Deliverable 5. VENDOR table
Deliverable 6. PURCHASE ORDER table
Deliverable 7. PURCHASE ORDER LINE table
Deliverable 8. Table relationships

Visit www.pearsonhighered.com/kay to:

1. Download Technology Project 2 instructions.
2. Download files provided online for your convenience in completing the project deliverables.
3. Watch the videos with software instructions to complete this project at www.pearsonhighered.com/kay.

3 Accounting Interface: Database Forms, Queries, and Reports

Does the Accounting Interface Matter? Meet Scott Cook.

Can you imagine creating an accounting software interface that turns into a billion dollar business?

Meet Scott Cook. Scott heard his wife complaining about paying bills and saw an opportunity for personal accounting software, which became Quicken. Entrepreneurs began using Quicken for business use, and Cook saw an opportunity to create the small business accounting software QuickBooks. Today, QuickBooks has 95% of the small business accounting software market with over 4 million users. One reason QuickBooks is so successful is because of the user-friendly accounting interface.

Today, Scott Cook is worth over $1 billion. The company he founded, Intuit, is worth over $15 billion.

Crossroads

At the crossroads of accounting and IT is the accounting interface that connects the accountant as user to the database behind the screen.

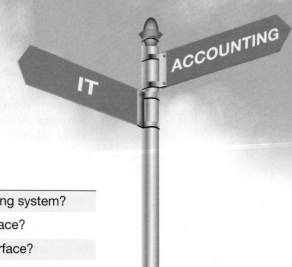

My Questions

Q 3.1   What is the role of the accounting interface in the accounting system?

Q 3.2   What is the role of database forms in the accounting interface?

Q 3.3   What is the role of database reports in the accounting interface?

Q 3.4   What is the role of queries in the accounting interface?

What Is the Role of the Accounting Interface in the Accounting System?

Imagine that in your job at EspressoCoffee your boss wants to know how much EspressoCoffee was sold in the United States for the last quarter. You would enter your request into the accounting software interface, which interacts with the DBMS. The DBMS runs the query to retrieve the information from the accounting database. The retrieved data then appears on your computer screen (Figure 3.1).

EspressoCoffee
Company

Virtually all accounting software use databases to store accounting data. The accounting interface connects the accountant to the database behind the computer screen (Figure 3.1).

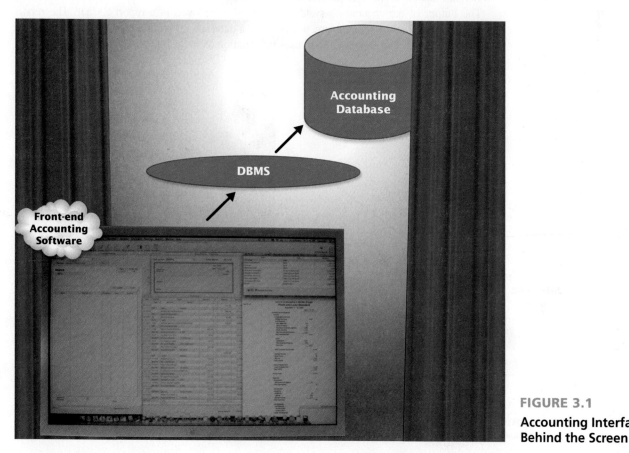

FIGURE 3.1

Accounting Interface and Behind the Screen

The front-end user interface is served by three database essentials: database forms, database queries, and database reports. Database forms are used to input information. Database reports are used to present the output of the system (Figure 3.2). Database queries are used to search and retrieve the accounting data that appears in either the database form or report. These three database essentials serve the user interface that appears on the accountant's computer screen.

An effective accounting system has a user-friendly interface that meets the enterprise's needs for entering and retrieving accounting data. Accounting software interfaces today are more user-friendly then ever. The user doesn't need to know about databases to use the accounting software. However, knowledge of databases is essential if the accountant wishes to understand what is occurring behind the screen of the accounting software.

User Interface Components

The accounting interface consists of four main interface components:

- Navigation
- Database forms
- Database queries
- Database reports

The Home page of QuickBooks accounting software (Figure 3.3) is an important part of its interface for navigating the software. Its **graphical user interface (GUI)** consists of icons that streamline navigation and display the logical flow of tasks within each transaction cycle. QuickBooks' user-friendly interface has led to immense popularity with entrepreneurs. The interface navigation permits the user to navigate or move through the software to access the other three interface components: forms, queries, and reports.

Typically, database forms are used to input the data into the system. These database forms may be designed to look like paper copy documents, such as checks and invoices, to facilitate data entry and make the interface more user-friendly. This is the approach that is used by Intuit's QuickBooks product where the onscreen database form resembles a document that a user already understands, such as a check or invoice (Figure 3.4).

The output of the accounting system is typically displayed in a report format. The report displayed on the user's computer screen is actually a database report that is formatted to meet the user's requirements. The database report uses information from the database to populate the report.

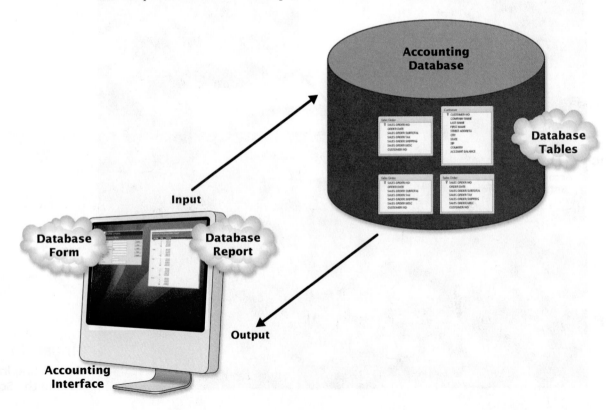

FIGURE 3.2

Accounting Interface

If you were adding queries to this image, where would you put them?

Accounting Database

Database Tables

Input

Database Form

Database Report

Output

Accounting Interface

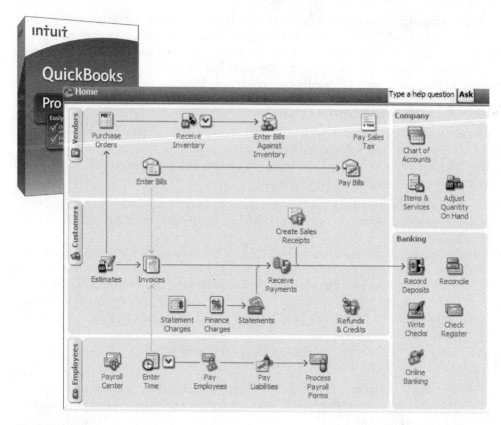

FIGURE 3.3

QuickBooks Graphical User Interface

Pair and Share: Compare the QuickBooks Home page shown here to the baseline accounting system in Figure 3.6. What are the similarities? What are the differences?

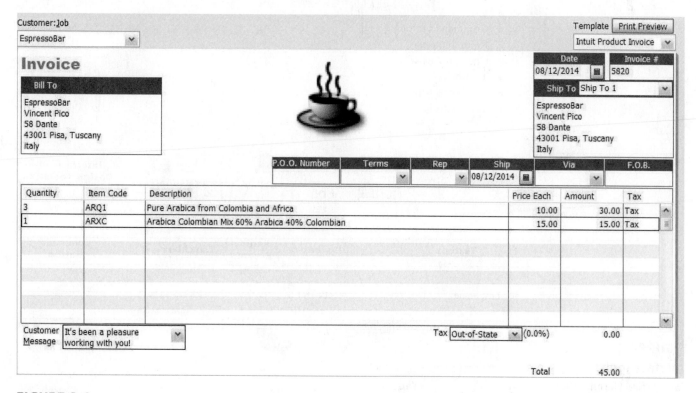

FIGURE 3.4

QuickBooks User Interface: Invoice

A third component of the user interface is queries. The user poses a question or inquiry and the database is searched and the data retrieved. The user interface must provide a means for the user to enter the query. Sometimes the interface will call this a search and may provide a form where the question can be entered. In other instances, the query may be run to prepare a report, retrieving data from the database to enter into the database report that appears on the user's computer screen.

User-Friendly Interface

What makes an interface user-friendly? Think about different software that you have used. What do you like best about these software interfaces? What do you like least? Some user interfaces are more user-friendly than others. In general, some of the characteristics considered to make software more user-friendly include the following:

- Streamlined, uncluttered design. A crowded interface can create a TMI (too much information) situation. This can be a source of confusion for the user, resulting in errors and frustration.
- Effortless navigation and guidance. The interface should guide the user in a self-explanatory, logical manner. A complex interface can result in only a small percentage of the features being used, because the user does not know the feature exists or understand how to use it.
- Customizable preferences. The interface might provide the ability for the user to customize screen colors and move the toolbar or palette to the top, side, or bottom of the screen based on the user's preference.
- Enhanced productivity. Designing the interface to minimize keystrokes and time required to enter and retrieve data increases productivity of the user.

Although as an accountant you may not be expected to design the accounting interface, you may be asked to evaluate the interface when making a purchase selection. The user friendliness of the interface is an important selection criterion.

User Interface Tools

User interface screens contain various interface tools to help the user interact with the system. As shown in Figure 3.5, interface tools include the following:

- Icons
- Command buttons
- Radio buttons
- Check boxes
- Text boxes
- List boxes (drop-down lists)
- Tab controls

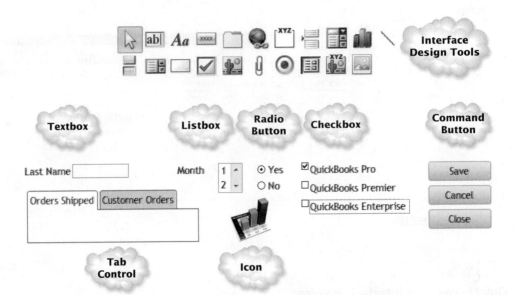

FIGURE 3.5

Interface Tools

Can you find the interface tools used in Figures 3.3 and 3.4?

Interface tools can appear on database forms, queries, and reports. Interface tools, such as text boxes, can be used for data entry on database forms (for example, entering the quantity ordered on an invoice form). Some interface tools provide for enhanced data entry to reduce errors and increase efficiency. For example, to enter a state, the interface may use a drop-down list of state abbreviations. This eliminates the possibility of a user entering an incorrect abbreviation for a state.

A well-designed accounting interface employs interface tools effectively so that only valid data is entered to ensure data integrity and quality.

Next, we will explore three of these components that make up the user interface:

- Database forms for input
- Database queries for retrieval
- Database reports for output

> **My Connection...**
> Try the following:
> • Active Review 3.2
> • Active Review 3.4

What Is the Role of Database Forms in the Accounting Interface?

Database forms are commonly used to input data into accounting systems. See Figure 3.4 for an example of a database form used as part of an accounting system interface. The database forms are frequently designed to look like commonly used and familiar items, such as an invoice or a check. Even an onscreen journal is really a database form that is designed to look similar to a paper journal used in a manual accounting system.

As you learned, a baseline accounting system model, representative of most accounting systems, includes vendors, customers, employees, banking, financial, and reports modules (Figure 3.6). The baseline accounting system shows how business processes or transaction cycles are divided into well-defined sequences of activities. Database forms are used to record the accounting transactions resulting from these activities for the following modules:

- Vendors
- Customers
- Employees
- Banking
- Financial

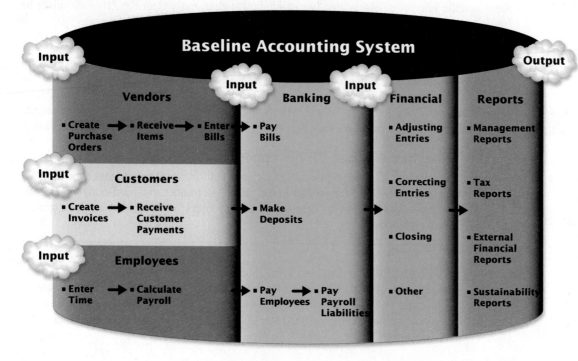

FIGURE 3.6

Baseline Accounting System with Transactions

Can you identify which modules use database forms and which modules use database reports?

Database Form Design

Well-designed database forms are designed to save time and minimize data entry errors. A few general guidelines for database form design include the following:

- Enter data once.
- Use data validation.
- Enable auto entry.
- Mirror paper forms.
- Design user-friendly forms.
- Implement appropriate security.

Accounting Insight No. 9: Enter Data Once

ACCOUNTING INSIGHT NO. 9
Enter Data Once

Accounting Insight No. 9 (enter data once), which was introduced in Chapter 2, can be applied to database form design. The database form should require the user to enter the data only one time, reusing data automatically as needed. Some organizations have streamlined data entry using bar code scanning instead of keying data into an onscreen form. Another means of streamlining data entry is to use default values when possible. These values automatically appear in the field as the default. For example, the current date might appear as the default value on invoices, and the user only needs to change the date if the current date is not correct. This saves significant time when entering data because default values automatically appear and just require review instead of re-entry.

DATA VALIDATION **Data validation** tools help to ensure that only valid data is entered. An onscreen form can use data validation features to minimize entry errors. For example, the Month field can be a drop-down list of 1 through 12. This prevents the user from mistyping *13*, for instance, into the Month field.

Another example is a global company that discovered that data entry for the country name was problematic because employees used the country names in their native languages. In the United States, employees entered *Germany*; in Italy, the employees entered *Germania*; and in Germany, employees entered *Deutschland*. This is dirty data. When the company searched the Country field for *Germany*, only partial results were retrieved. One solution to this problem is the use of a drop-down list of countries using standard naming. This prevents mistyping or inconsistent data entry.

Other data validation techniques include using an input mask to format the Data Entry field for a specific number of characters. For example, the Data Entry field for ZIP code might be limited to five spaces. Data validation can include limit checks (for example, under $100) and range checks (for example, between $200 and $500).

AUTO ENTRY Database forms are often designed to automatically complete portions of the form after you make a selection. For example, when you select a customer's name for an invoice in QuickBooks accounting software, QuickBooks will automatically complete the customer address and sales terms. When you select the customer's name, behind the screen QuickBooks is executing a database query to retrieve the customer address from the CUSTOMER table in the database.

Accounting Insight No. 11: Mirror Paper Forms

ACCOUNTING INSIGHT NO. 11
To Save Time Entering Data...
Mirror Database Forms and
Paper Forms

Accounting Insight No. 11 is to mirror database forms and paper forms to save time entering data. For example, if sales representatives in the field collect data using hard-copy forms, then the onscreen data entry form and the hard-copy data collection form should correspond to save time and reduce data entry errors.

USER-FRIENDLY FORMS The database form should be easy to use and understand. An accounting professional typically does not want to take time to look up how to enter accounting data into an onscreen form. Instead, the onscreen form should be self-explanatory or provide onscreen prompts that eliminate the need to refer to other resources to properly enter data.

APPROPRIATE SECURITY MEASURES When you enter your password into a login form, what appears when you type your password? This feature of concealing the password is a security mask that prevents others from viewing your password. Web-based entry forms that online customers use to order products might use encryption for confidential customer information such as credit card numbers. Database forms should have appropriate security measures to prevent unauthorized access to data.

Accounting Data Entry Forms

An accounting system requires specialized database forms to meet specific accounting requirements and needs. The end user, such as the accountant, enters data into the onscreen accounting forms. The data entered is stored in the operational accounting database. As shown in Figure 3.6, the modules in the baseline accounting system labeled *Input* would have corresponding data entry forms.

CUSTOMER MODULE Some of the typical database forms used in a baseline customer module of an integrated accounting system might include an order form, invoice, credit memo, customer payment receipt, and accompanying deposit ticket. Additional database forms may be required to satisfy the enterprise-specific needs for a customized accounting system.

VENDOR MODULE Database forms used for a baseline vendor module might include a purchase order, receiving form, bill entry form, and a check form. Other database forms would be added as required to meet enterprise-specific needs.

EMPLOYEE MODULE The baseline employee module might include database forms for adding employees, time tracking, and calculating payroll. Once again, additional database forms can be created to meet specific organizational needs for payroll.

BANKING MODULE The banking module might include database forms for writing checks, making deposits, and reconciling bank statements.

FINANCIAL MODULE For the financial module, an onscreen journal database form might be used to enter adjusting entries to bring accounts up to date at year end. The onscreen journal could also be used to make correcting entries. Another onscreen form might be used for closing the accounts at year end.

Building Database Forms

Database programs provide tools for building database forms for accounting interface development. These tools include text boxes, media holders for photos and audio, spreadsheet holders, text table holders, and calendar holders. Command buttons, radio buttons, check box buttons, icons, and drop-down lists are included in the database form development toolkit. The developer drags and drops the appropriate tool into the database form.

Some of these accounting interface forms may be completely text based while other forms may make extensive use of graphics, such as onscreen checks. Multimedia forms may include audio and video components, such as an employee form that displays the employee's photo or a short movie that demonstrates how to use the form.

Using MS Access, Figure 3.7 demonstrates how to build a database form for updating customer information. To view the resulting database form for EspressoCoffee, see Figure 3.8. Notice the use of text boxes and command buttons.

Because of its availability, MS Access is useful for learning database fundamentals and how accounting data is stored using relational databases. Large database programs, such as Oracle and IBM DB2, offer additional functionality, including increased security and control, the ability to maintain thousands of database tables, and more complex queries.

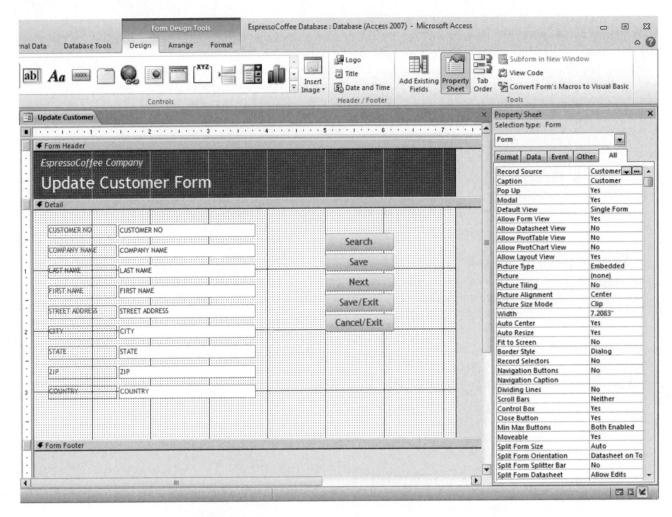

FIGURE 3.7

Building Database Forms Using MS Access

Database Forms

To build a database form, the developer uses a form design template as shown. The developer selects the fields required on the form. The fields correspond to one or more tables in the database. The developer adds control tools (for example, checkbox, button).

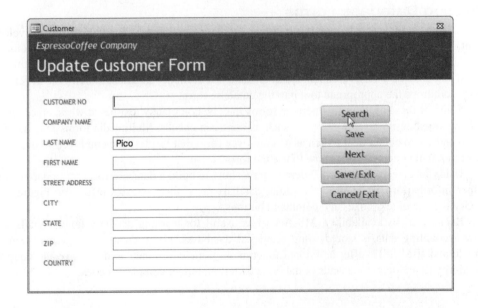

FIGURE 3.8

EspressoCoffee Database Form

Do you see any changes you would like to make?

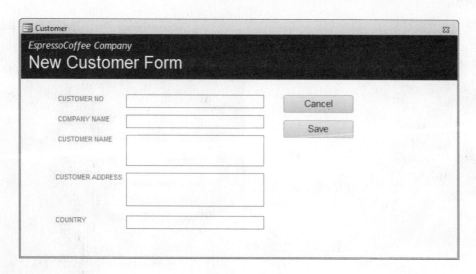

FIGURE 3.9

Joey's Database Form

What Would You Do?

Imagine that Joey, your coworker in IT, showed you the database form in Figure 3.9. You met Joey in Chapter 2 when he developed a database for you to track orders. After you worked with Joey to remove the anomalies from that database, you and Joey agreed that in the future the two of you would communicate on an ongoing basis while Joey was developing IT solutions for you.

Joey has asked for your signature to approve the database form in Figure 3.9 for entering new customer data. What would you do?

a. Sign the approval form.
b. Sign the approval form and ask Joey to make changes.
c. Send Joey an email letting him know you will not be signing the approval form.
d. Send Joey an email thanking him for his work and listing the changes you need.

What changes, if any, would you ask Joey to make?

While this section discussed how to input data into the accounting system using data forms, the next section covers accounting system output using database reports.

EspressoCoffee
Company

> **My Connection...**
> • Short Exercise 3.22
> • It's Your Call 3.34
> • Tech in Practice 3.38

Accounting Interface Forms Mapped to the Accounting Database

Microsoft GP Dynamics, formerly MS Great Plains, is accounting software for midsize companies. MS Dynamics has a setting that permits you to see the associated database tables. Figure 3.10 shows you how to access the database tables through the MS Dynamics menus.

FIGURE 3.10

Accessing MS Dynamics Database Tables

MS Dynamics accounting software lets you access the database tables behind the screen.

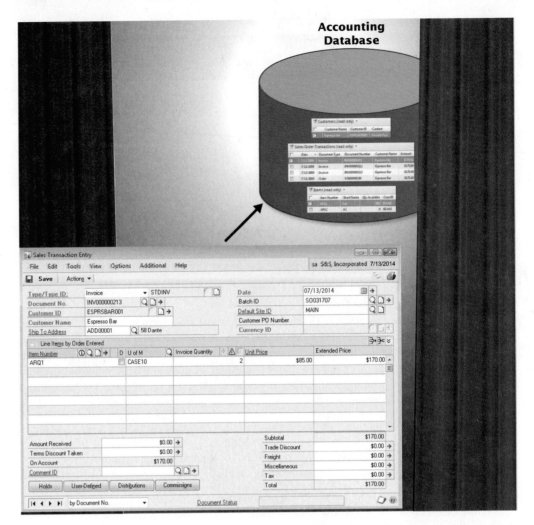

FIGURE 3.11

MS Dynamics Accounting Interface Mapped to Database Tables

The MS Dynamics invoice form (sales transaction entry form) is shown in Figure 3.11 along with the MS SQL Server database tables. As you can see,

- Customer ID on the MS Dynamics invoice maps to the Customer ID field in the CUSTOMER database table.
- Document No. on the MS Dynamics invoice maps to the Document Number field in the SALES ORDER table.
- Item Number maps to the Item Number field in the ITEM table.
- Other fields on the MS Dynamics form can be mapped to corresponding fields in the corresponding database tables.

What Is the Role of Database Reports in the Accounting Interface?

The reports module relates to output from the accounting system (see Figure 3.6). In the baseline accounting system model, the reports module focuses on baseline reports common to most enterprises.

Accounting Reports

In general, we will classify accounting reports into the following four basic types.

- Financial accounting and regulatory reports given to investors, creditors, and regulatory agencies. An example of a regulatory agency would be the Securities and Exchange Commission (SEC).

- Tax reports used when filing federal, state, and local taxes. Examples of tax reports would include tax returns filed with the Internal Revenue Service (IRS).
- Management reports provided to internal users of accounting information. These reports can be used in carrying out the management functions of planning, control, and decision making.
- Sustainability accounting reports are increasingly demanded by stakeholders to evaluate an enterprise's responsiveness to economic, environmental, and social sustainability challenges.

Note that the first two categories, financial and tax, are external reports given to outside parties, and the third category, management reports, is directed to internal users and decision makers. Typically financial and tax reports are standardized to meet the requirements of external reporting agencies. Management reports, however, are tailored to meet the management's needs and can consist of ad hoc reports that are created as needed.

FINANCIAL REPORTS Financial reports are used by external parties to make decisions. For example, a banker might use the financial statements to decide whether to make a loan to a company. A prospective investor might use the financial statements to decide whether to invest in a company.

The three financial statements most frequently used by external users are as follows:

- Profit and loss (also called the income statement): lists income and expenses
- Balance sheet: lists assets, liabilities, and owners' equity
- Statement of cash flows: lists cash flows from operating, investing, and financing activities

TAX REPORTS The objective of the tax return is to provide information to the Internal Revenue Service (IRS) and state tax authorities. When preparing tax returns, a company uses different rules from those used to prepare financial statements. The Internal Revenue Code is the highest level of authority for federal income tax law, but there are other primary and secondary sources of tax law that would be followed when preparing a return.

Tax forms include the following:

- Federal income tax return (for example, Form 1040, 1120, 1120S)
- State income tax return
- Payroll tax forms (for example, Forms 940, 941, W-2)

MANAGEMENT REPORTS Financial reports used by internal users (managers) to make decisions regarding company operations. These reports do not have to follow a particular set of rules and can be created to satisfy a manager's information needs.

Examples of reports that managers use include the following:

- Contribution margin income statement
- Cash budget
- Accounts receivable aging summary
- Accounts payable aging summary
- Cost-volume-profit (CVP) analysis
- Operating and capital budgets
- Variance analysis
- Special order analysis
- Insource or outsource analysis
- Segment performance analysis

Accounting Database Report Design

Typically the report output is displayed onscreen, in electronic files, or as hard-copy printouts. Information broadcasting can be used to email electronic reports to end users on a scheduled basis. For example, if an accountant needs a monthly tax report, information broadcasting can be used to send the electronic tax report on the first of each month.

Database reports can be historical data, real-time, or live. **Real-time reports** provide up-to-the-minute data without a time lag. **Live reports** continuously provide live, up-to-the-minute data.

Database reports can be interactive where the user can drill down to source documents simply by clicking on an amount displayed in the report. For example, in the check register for some accounting software, you can click on a check amount in the check register and drill down to the check source document.

Would You Like to Know More?
Sustainability Reports... and their implications for the accounting system are covered in greater detail in Chapter 8, *Accounting and Sustainability Intelligence*.

Would You Like to Know More?
Management Reports... will be explored further in Chapter 7, *Accounting and Business Intelligence*.

The design of the accounting database reports should be consistent with the user requirements. For example, if up-to-date information is essential to better decision making, then a live or real-time report should be used.

Building Database Reports

Database programs provide tools for building database reports for the accounting system interface. Most accounting software provides predesigned accounting reports. Customized accounting reports can be developed to meet the enterprise's specific needs.

Database report tools include text boxes, field labels, command buttons, headers, footers, chart holders, and other data visualization tools. The database report content is frequently linked to queries.

Building a database report using MS Access is illustrated in Figure 3.12. As you can see, MS Access provides many tools for developing database reports. The resulting database report is shown in Figure 3.13.

What Would You Do?

EspressoCoffee
Company

Joey from IT has asked for your signature approving the database report shown in Figure 3.14. You requested an aging of accounts receivable report to use in following up on slow paying customers. What would you do?

a. Sign the approval form.
b. Sign the approval form and ask Joey to make changes.
c. Send Joey an email letting him know you will not be signing the approval form.
d. Send Joey an email thanking him for his work and listing the changes you need.

What changes, if any, would you ask Joey to make?

Database reports display the formatted results of database queries. Database queries are searches to retrieve information from the database. Next, we will explore database queries and how they are used in an accounting system.

My Connection...
• Short Exercise 3.13
• It's Your Call 3.25
• Tech in Practice 3.29

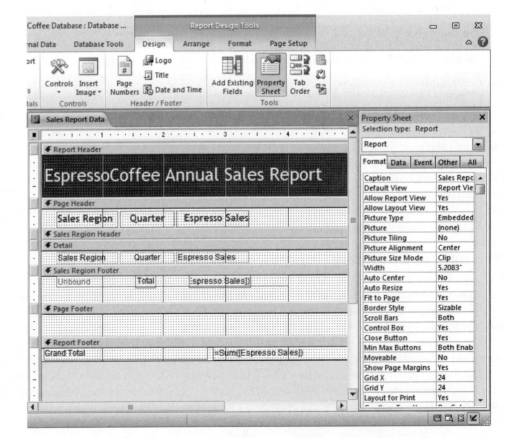

FIGURE 3.12

Building Database Reports Using MS Access

Database Reports
To build a database report, the developer uses a report design template as shown. The developer formats and enters the report header, detail, and footer. The required fields are placed in the desired location on the report layout.

EspressoCoffee Annual Sales Report

Sales Region	Quarter	Espresso Sales
Austria	1	$610,911.00
	2	$901,574.00
	3	$465,460.00
	4	$671,190.00
	Total	$2,649,135.00
Canada	1	$635,144.00
	2	$777,186.00
	3	$338,432.00
	4	$226,018.00
	Total	$1,976,780.00
China	1	$61,241.00
	2	$643,284.00
	3	$834,940.00
	4	$497,871.00
	Total	$2,037,336.00
France	1	$969,279.00
	2	$61,797.00
	3	$353,502.00
	4	$779,811.00
	Total	$2,164,389.00
Germany	1	$486,259.00
	2	$355,135.00
	3	$150,321.00
	4	$248,347.00
	Total	$1,240,062.00
Greece	1	$379,479.00
	2	$884,916.00
	3	$41,013.00
	4	$941,831.00
	Total	$2,247,239.00
Italy	1	$449,484.00
	2	$592,636.00
	3	$913,037.00
	4	$84,420.00
	Total	$2,039,577.00

FIGURE 3.13

EspressoCoffee Database Report

Do you see any changes you would like?

What Is the Role of Database Queries in the Accounting Interface?

Have you ever searched the Internet using Google? Have you ever used "Help" to learn about a software feature? If so, then you have used a query.

Queries are questions you ask about data stored in a database. Database queries conduct the search and retrieval functions required to obtain the data to display in database forms and reports. When you use the search feature in accounting software, the system is executing a query to search for the keywords you entered.

Queries can be used with database forms to update information in the database. Imagine that you need to update the address information for an EspressoCoffee customer, Vincent Pico. First, you would search for his customer record by entering his name or customer number into a database form (Figure 3.8). The relational database management system (RDBMS) executes a query to locate Vincent's customer record in the Customer table of the accounting database.

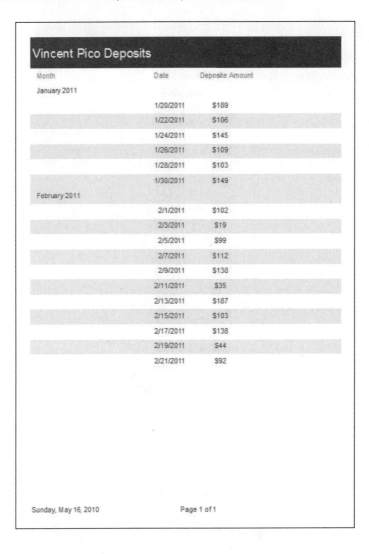

FIGURE 3.14

Joey's Database Report

His customer information is retrieved and displayed on the customer form on your computer screen, permitting you to update Vincent's customer address.

In addition to displaying query results in database forms, query results are also displayed in database reports (Figure 3.13).

Accounting Insight No. 12: Database Queries

ACCOUNTING INSIGHT NO. 12
Use Database Queries to Extract Data from Multiple Related Database Tables

Accounting Insight No. 12 relates to queries: Use database queries to extract data from multiple related database tables. Queries may retrieve data from multiple fields in multiple database tables and present the data in a report format. For example, a database report for a balance sheet would display the account no., account name, and account balance for all asset, liability, and stockholders' equity accounts. The database reports can be onscreen, in electronic files, or on paper printouts. Regardless of how the query results are displayed, the execution of the query is the same.

For relational databases, such as those used for accounting systems, the relational database is searched and data is retrieved using **structured query language (SQL)**. Queries can be constructed using one of two approaches: using query builder tools or writing the SQL programming code. Next we will explore each of these ways to construct queries.

Query Builder Tools

Today, most database engines, such as MS Access, MS SQL Server, Oracle, and IBM DB2, provide user-friendly **query builder tools** to streamline query development. Query builder tools make it possible to build queries without using programming code.

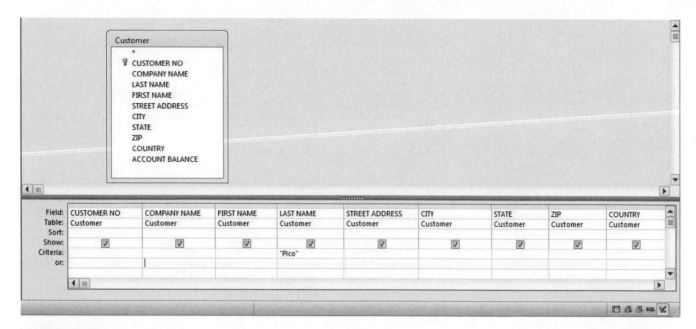

FIGURE 3.15

Building Database Queries Using MS Access

Database Queries
To build a database query, the developer can use a Query by Example (QBE) template as shown.
The developer displays the tables involved in the query. From those tables, the developer
selects the fields required by the query. Search criteria are specified (for example, Customer
Last Name = "Pico" as shown).

MS Access, for example, offers a query builder tool to assist you in building a database query.
In the background, Access is converting the steps into SQL programming code that runs a query
to accomplish the search and retrieval functions. See Figure 3.15 for an example of a query tool
and Figure 3.16 for the accompanying SQL programming code that is generated behind the screen.

Query builder tools may be referred to as query-by-example (QBE). This type of query tool
shows the database tables with fields on the user's computer screen. The user simply selects the
fields to include in the query. Search criteria, such as Customer Last Name = Pico, is entered in
the QBE to identify the data to retrieve (Figure 3.15). Another example of a query built using a

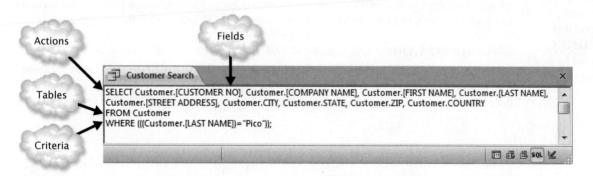

FIGURE 3.16

SQL Programming Code in MS Access

SQL Database Queries
After building a database query with Query by Example, developers can view the SQL
programming code for the database query as shown. Developers can edit and modify the SQL
code as needed. Each SQL statement contains action(s), table(s), field(s), and criteria.

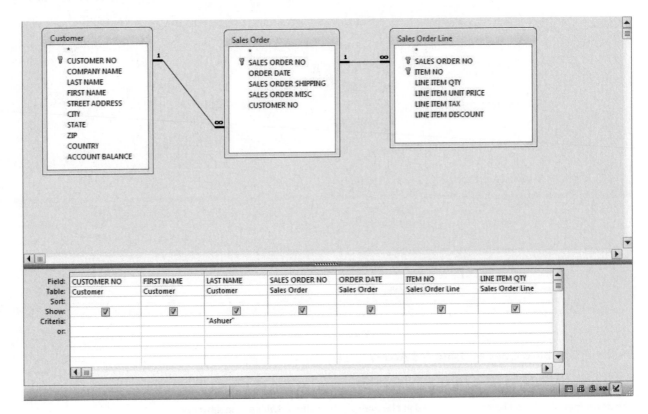

FIGURE 3.17

Customer Order Query in MS Access

Compare this query with the query in Figure 3.16. What differences do you see?

query builder tool is shown in Figure 3.17. This query uses multiple database tables to search and retrieve information about customer orders. The results of the query are shown in Figure 3.18.

MS SQL Server, Oracle, and IBM DB2 databases also provide query building tools, such as SQL Assist, to streamline the query development process. These tools generate the SQL programming code that is required to execute the query.

Sometimes, however, the query builder tools cannot accomplish the user requirements because of complexity, content, or display format. In these cases, programming code must be used to create the required query. Some accountants find that learning SQL programming code reduces their dependence on IT developers to code queries. Furthermore, it provides the accountant with flexibility to experiment and test various queries to accomplish the desired results.

Structured Query Language (SQL)

SQL queries permit the user to search, insert, update, and delete data from a relational database. The RDBMS translates the query statements into action. For example, the SQL programming code to search and retrieve the customer address from the CUSTOMER table for a customer with

CUSTOMER NO	FIRST NAME	LAST NAME	SALES ORDER NO	ORDER DATE	ITEM NO	LINE ITEM QTY
127127	Angela	Ashuer	5890	7/20/2010	9XB	1
127127	Angela	Ashuer	5890	7/20/2010	ARQ1	10
127127	Angela	Ashuer	5819	8/12/2010	WC2	1

FIGURE 3.18

Customer Order Query Results

Compare the fields in the query builder in Figure 3.17 to the query results in this figure. What is the search criteria?

the last name "Pico" appears in Figure 3.16. Notice there are four main clauses to the SQL statement. First, an action is specified, such as SELECT. The second clause consists of the field names to display in the query results. The third clause specifies the table name from which the field contents are extracted. This clause begins with the word FROM. The fourth clause begins with the word WHERE and specifies the condition or criteria for the search. The SELECT statement will search the Customer Name field until it locates the database record containing the specified criteria of "Pico." Then the query retrieves the selected field contents.

Writing SQL statements requires precision. The programmer must use the proper syntax for SQL statements. Each SQL statement must end with a semicolon and contain specific words, such as SELECT, FROM, and WHERE. To streamline query building, database programs provide query builder tools.

> ### Would You Like to Know More?
> If you would like to know more about SQL, see Chapter 14, *Database Design: ERD, REA, and SQL*.

Crossroads
Increasingly, cyberattacks are using SQL injections, malicious SQL programming code injected into an enterprise's SQL queries, to extract confidential data, such as customer credit card numbers. Therefore, knowledge of SQL is becoming increasingly vital to accounting IT professionals in detecting SQL injection cyberattacks.

What Would You Do?

Joey from IT provided you with the SQL code for a database query you requested (Figure 3.19). You asked Joey to create a database query for the aging of accounts receivable showing the age of customer accounts. Joey requested your feedback and signature for approval. What would you do?

EspressoCoffee
Company

a. Sign the approval form.
b. Email Joey that you would like to speak with him about changes you would like made.
c. Email Joey the changes you would like him to make.
d. Call your supervisor.
e. Call his supervisor.

What changes, if any, would you ask Joey to make?

You're the Boss...
If you were Joey's boss, what would you say to Joey about his SQL code for the database query?

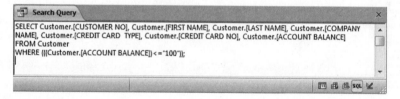

FIGURE 3.19
Joey's Database Query

My Connection...
• Short Exercise 3.14
• It's Your Call 3.27
• Tech in Practice 3.30

Illustration: MS SQL Server Database Query Builder

MS SQL Server is a database engine for mid- to large-scale enterprises. Using MS SQL Server, database developers can create database tables and SQL queries. Figure 3.20 shows the MS SQL Server query builder. To build a query in MS SQL Server, the developer types the SQL programming code, such as SELECT. As the developer types, database tables and fields will appear onscreen from which the developer can choose.

Figure 3.21 shows the SQL query after it is built. Notice that the query builder displays the SQL programming code in the upper section of the screen. Also notice that this SQL query contains the same four main clauses (ACTION, TABLES, FIELDS, and CRITERIA) as you saw with SQL queries built using MS Access.

You can create database forms and reports for a database created in MS SQL Server. To create database forms and reports, database developers use MS Visual Studio (Figure 3.22). It is an application development workbench used to create interface software, such as for accounting systems.

Your Competitive Advantage...
At the crossroads of accounting and IT, transitional skills become important. For example, you may learn about databases using MS Access. The skills learned allow you to transition to larger databases, such as MS SQL Server or Oracle.

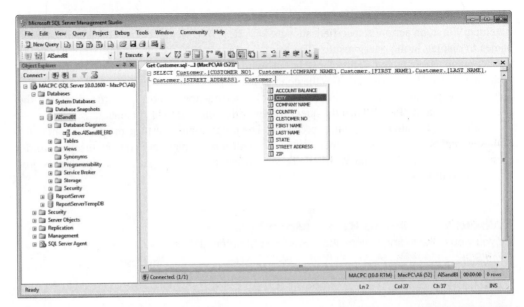

FIGURE 3.20

MS SQL Server Query Builder

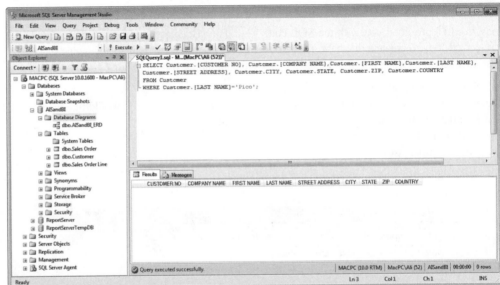

FIGURE 3.21

MS SQL Server Query

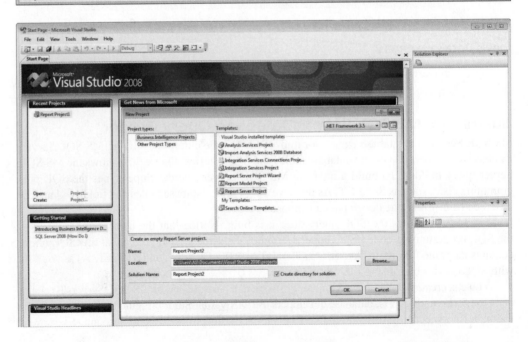

FIGURE 3.22

MS Visual Studio Developer Screen

Chapter Highlights

What is the role of the accounting system interface?
The accounting system user interface plays an important role in entering accounting data and retrieving accounting information. The accountant views the interface on the screen, and the RDBMS and database are behind the screen. The accounting software interface interacts with the RDBMS using database forms, queries, and reports. Features of a well-designed interface include user-friendly, effortless navigation, and customizable preferences.

What is the role of database forms? Database forms are commonly used to input data into accounting systems. The database forms are frequently designed to look like commonly used and familiar items, such as an invoice or a check.

What is the role of database reports? The output of the accounting system is typically displayed in a report format. The report displayed on the user's computer screen is actually a database report that is formatted to meet accounting requirements. The database report uses information from the database to populate the report.

What is the role of database queries? One component of the user interface is retrieval or query. Sometimes the interface will call this a search and provide a form where the search question can be entered. In other instances, a query may be run to prepare a report, retrieving data from the database to enter into the database report that appears on the user's computer screen.

Accounting System Insights

Insight No. 9   Enter data once.

Insight No. 11 To save time entering data, mirror database forms and paper forms.

Insight No. 12 Use database queries to extract data from multiple related database tables.

Active Review

Study less. Learn more. Make connections.

3.1 Refer to the chapter opener, *Meet Scott Cook*. In your opinion, why is the QuickBooks accounting interface user friendly and so successful?

3.2 Discuss why the user interface is important in an accounting system.

3.3 What features would you like to see in an accounting interface to make it more user friendly? Why?

3.4 Discuss the features of an accounting interface that could reduce data entry errors.

3.5 Discuss the differences between a database form to enter data and a database form to search for data. How would these differences affect the way you design these forms?

3.6 Discuss the relationship of queries to database forms and reports used by the accounting interface.

3.7 Discuss the impact that voice data entry could have on the accounting interface database forms.

3.8 Discuss the impact that an avatar (graphical computer images of a person) could have on the accounting interface.

3.9 Discuss how database forms can streamline accounting data entry for online accounting applications, such as NetSuite or QuickBooks Online.

3.10 Discuss the differences between live and real-time reports. Which would you prefer?

Key Terms Check

Understanding the language used at the crossroads of accounting and IT is key to your success.

3.11 Match the following terms and definitions.
a. graphical user interface (GUI)
b. data validation
c. real-time reports
d. live reports
e. structured query language (SQL)
f. query builder tools

_____ 1. Tools used to minimize data entry errors, such as drop-down lists

_____ 2. Streamlines query development

_____ 3. Code used to search and retrieve data

_____ 4. Reports that provide up-to-the-minute data without a time lag

_____ 5. Reports that provide up-to-the-minute data continuously

_____ 6. User interfaces containing images and icons

Practice Test

3.12 Which of the following is NOT an accounting interface component?

a. Navigation
b. Database management system
c. Database queries
d. Reports

3.13 In an accounting system, what is NOT behind the screen?

a. Database
b. DBMS
c. Report
d. Database query

3.14 Graphical user interface tools are used to:

a. Make the software appear more complex than necessary
b. Help the user to interact with the system
c. Increase the amount of time needed to enter data
d. Decrease the cost of the software

3.15 _____ are used to enter data into the database.

a. Reports
b. Queries
c. Forms
d. Radio Buttons

3.16 _____ are used to conduct the search and retrieval functions.

a. Database navigation
b. Forms
c. Reports
d. Queries

3.17 Which SQL statement is used to search one ore more database tables?

a. SELECT
b. SEARCH
c. FIND
d. LOOK

3.18 The ability of an interface to guide the user in a self-explanatory, logical manner is part of which user interface characteristics?

a. Streamlined, uncluttered design
b. Effortless navigation
c. Customizable preferences
d. Enhanced productivity

3.19 Which of one of the user interface tools is used to start an action?

a. Text box
b. List box
c. Radio button
d. Command button

3.20 Which one of the following baseline accounting systems doesn't have a data entry form?

a. Vendor

b. Banking

c. Report

d. Customer

3.21 Real-time reports:

a. Continuously provide live, up-to-the-minute data

b. Are used by external parties to make decisions

c. Are used by stakeholders to evaluate an enterprise's responsiveness to economic, environmental, and social sustainability challenges

d. Provide up-to-the-minute data without a time lag

Exercises

Each Exercise relates to one of the major questions addressed in the chapter and is labeled with the question number in green.

Short Exercises

Warm up with these short exercises.

3.22 For the following accounting interface forms identify the appropriate accounting system module. **(Q3.2)**

a. Vendors module

b. Customers module

c. Employees module

d. Banking module

e. Financial module

f. Reports module

1.

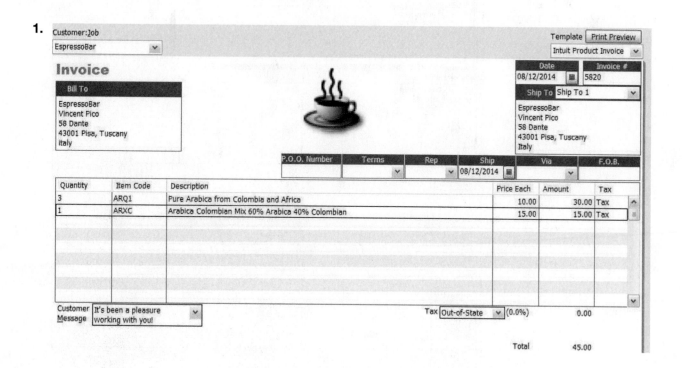

2.

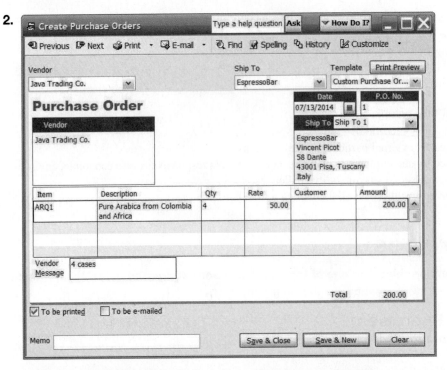

3.

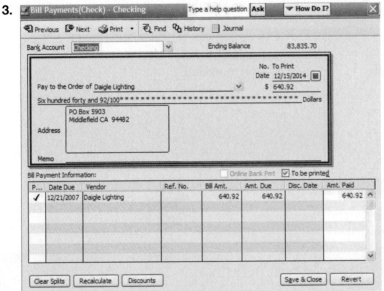

4.

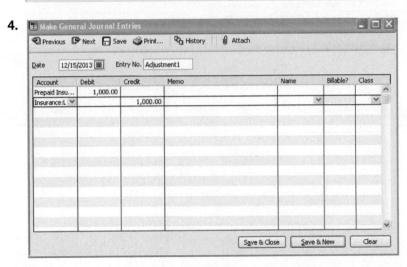

5.

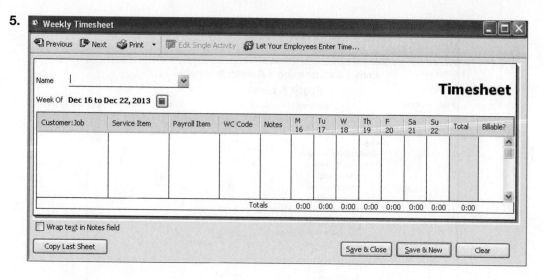

3.23 For the following reports identify the type of report. **(Q3.3)**

a. Financial report

b. Tax report

c. Management report

d. Sustainability report

1.

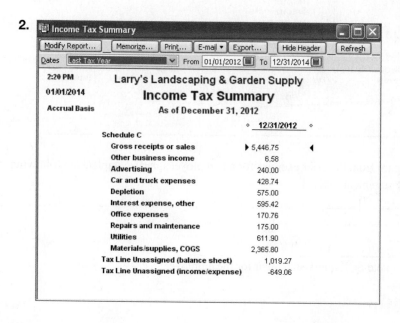

2.

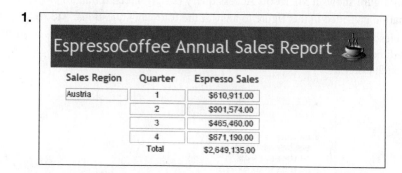

3.

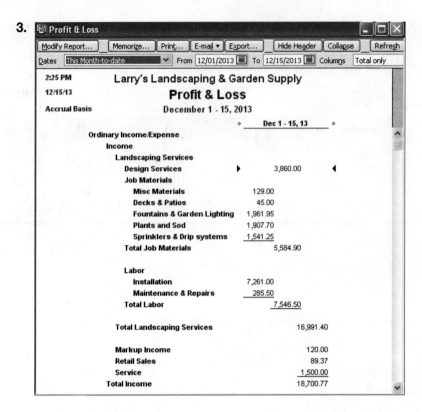

3.24 The following figure shows a Microsoft Access query design screen for an employee query. Use information provided in this figure to answer the following questions: **(Q3.4)**

1. How many tables are used in this query?
2. What fields will be displayed when the query is run?
3. What is the search criteria?

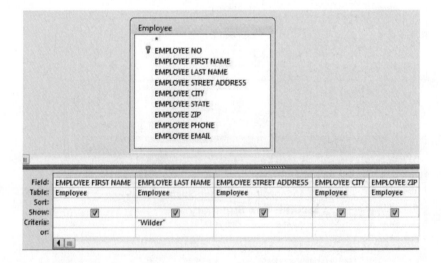

3.25 Using the figure from the prior exercise for an employee query, complete the following for the SQL query statement: **(Q3.4)**

1. SELECT _____.[_____], _____.[_____], _____.[_____], _____.
   [_____], _____.[_____]
2. FROM _____
3. WHERE (((_____.[_____])=" "_____"));
4. Write the complete SQL query statement for the employee query.

3.26 The following figure shows a Microsoft Access query design screen for a vendor query. Use information provided in this figure to answer the following questions: **(Q3.4)**

1. How many tables are used in this query?
2. What fields will be displayed when the query is run?
3. What is the search criteria?

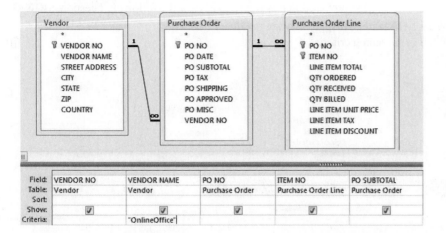

3.27 When RDBMS processes the following SQL SELECT statement: **(Q3.4)**

SELECT Customer No, Customer Name, Invoice No, Date
FROM Customer, Invoice
WHERE Customer No = "3099";

1. What tables are accessed?
2. What fields are retrieved when the query is run?
3. What is the search criteria?

3.28 You have been asked to build a database form for entering vendor data into a VENDOR table. The VENDOR table has the following fields: **(Q3.2)**

- Vendor ID
- Vendor Name
- Vendor Street Address
- Vendor City
- Vendor State
- Vendor ZIP Code
- Vendor Email
- Vendor Phone

1. What text boxes do you need to use on the database form?
2. How would you label the text boxes?
3. What command buttons would you use?

3.29 Using information from the previous exercise, design a user-friendly vendor data input form. Sketch the design on paper or use Microsoft Excel (clip art, shapes, and text boxes) to design your interface. **(Q3.1, 3.2)**

3.30 What are the database fields you might see on a database report for an aging of accounts receivable? **(Q3.3)**

3.31 Now that you know how database forms and queries are used, for the next week track the following: **(Q3.2, 3.3)**

1. How many database forms do you use? List the various database forms you use during the week.
2. What database queries do you use? List the different types of database queries you used during the week.

3.32 You have been asked to write an SQL query to retrieve information about customer's sales orders. **(Q3.4)**

1. What database tables would be used in the query?
2. What database fields would be used in the query?

3.33 The following figure shows a Microsoft Access query design screen for a rental items query. Use information provided in this figure to answer the following questions: **(Q3.4)**

1. What fields will be displayed when the query is run?
2. What is the search criteria?

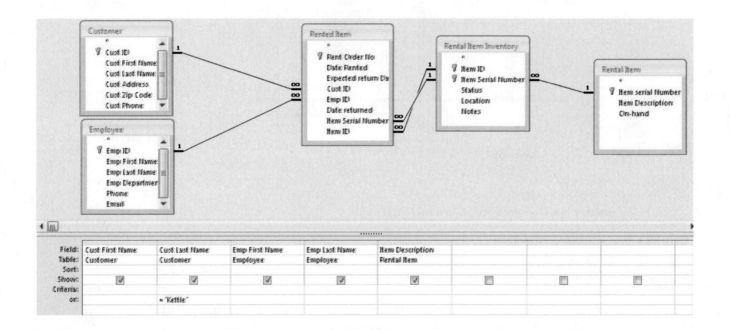

It's Your Call

This is your training ground. These scenarios provide you with the opportunity to use your knowledge and professional skills.

3.34 Your colleague in IT has designed the following New Employee database form. You have been asked to sign the approval authorization for the form, indicating that you have reviewed and approved the form. List all the changes that you would ask your IT colleague to make to the form. What would you say to the designer? **(Q3.1, 3.2)**

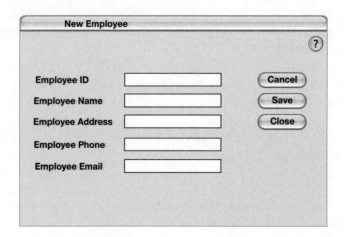

3.35 A pharmaceutical company is planning to evaluate its regional sales for the past year. Your coworker, a newly hired accountant with limited database experience, prepared the following report design. Do you have any advice for her design? Document your answer, including a reason for each design issue you see. Provide her with possible solutions for each issue. **(Q3.1, 3.3)**

Regional Painkiller Medication Sales

DESCRIPTION	ADVIL
MEDICATION CODE	6122041
PACKAGE SIZE	100 CT
STORE CODE	100
WHOLE SALES VOLUME	0

DESCRIPTION	ADVIL
MEDICATION CODE	6122061
PACKAGE SIZE	165 CT
STORE CODE	105
WHOLE SALES VOLUME	0

DESCRIPTION	ADVIL
MEDICATION CODE	6122041
PACKAGE SIZE	100 CT
STORE CODE	101
WHOLE SALES VOLUME	0

3.36 You have been asked to prepare a report showing monthly sales by geographic region. Most of the managers using the report are not accountants, so your supervisor thought they would be more likely to use the report if it contained some images instead of just numbers. Your supervisor has asked you to add some charts and graphs to the report since "one picture is worth a thousand words." **(Q3.1, 3.3)**

1. What types of graphs and charts do you think are best to show the monthly sales by geographic region?
2. What data would you display in the charts and graphs?
3. How would your answer change if the company had international sales?

3.37 You have been called in as a consultant liaison for a dispute between sales, accounting, and IT professionals. The sales professionals are claiming that sales reports are distorted and are blaming the accounting department for a decrease in their sales bonuses. The accounting professionals have reviewed the sales reports and are concerned that the queries used to retrieve the sales data are not reporting all the sales for each region. So the accounting professionals are blaming the IT staff. The IT professionals reply that they are just doing what they are told. IT claims they are understaffed and doing the best they can shorthanded.

You have been called in to facilitate a resolution of this dispute. When reviewing the database tables used by the sales query, you notice that the names of countries in which sales occurred were not entered consistently. For example, you found that *Italy* was entered by the French as *Italie*, by the Italians as *Italia*, by the Germans as *Italien*, and by the English as *Italy*. When the query was run, you notice that the search criteria was *Italia*.

How do you resolve this dirty data dispute? **(Q3.1, 3.2, 3.3, 3.4)**

Tech in Practice

These technology in practice exercises are perfect for both individuals and teams.

Tech Exercises

Sharpen your skills with these technology exercises. Watch these software videos at www.pearsonhighered.com/kay.

3.38

Tech Tool: Database Software

Software Video: Database Forms

EspressoCoffee has asked for your assistance in completing the Update Customer database form.

1. Download the Microsoft Access database file for this exercise.
2. Using Microsoft Access database software and information in Figure 3.7, complete the Update Customer database form.
3. Print the Update Customer database form.

3.39

Tech Tool: Database Software

Software Video: Database Reports

EspressoCoffee has asked for your assistance in completing an annual sales database report.

1. Download the Microsoft Access database file for this exercise.
2. Using Microsoft Access database software and the information in Figure 3.12, complete the EspressoCoffee annual sales report.
3. Print the annual sales report.

3.40

Tech Tool: Database Software

Software Video: Database Queries

EspressoCoffee has asked for your assistance in creating a query to retrieve customer information.

1. Download the Microsoft Access database file for this exercise.
2. Using Microsoft Access database software, create the query shown in Figure 3.15.
3. Run the query and print the result.
4. Select the SQL view. Copy and paste into Excel and print.

3.41

Tech Tool: Database Software

Software Video: Database Queries

EspressoCoffee has asked for your assistance in creating a customer order query.

1. Download the Microsoft Access database file for this exercise.
2. Using Microsoft Access database software, create the query shown in Figure 3.17.
3. Run the query and print the result.
4. Select the SQL view. Copy and paste into Excel and print.

3.42

Tech Tool: Database Software

Software Video: Database Forms

EspressoCoffee has asked for your assistance in creating a Vendor database form.

1. Download the Microsoft Access database file for this exercise.

2. Using Microsoft Access database software, create a Vendor database form that displays the following fields:

Vendor No.	State
Vendor Name	ZIP
Street Address	Country
City	Telephone

3. Print the Vendor database form.

3.43

Tech Tool: Database Software
Software Video: Database Reports

EspressoCoffee has asked for your assistance in creating a database report.

1. Download the Microsoft Access database file for this exercise.
2. Using Microsoft Access database software and the following information, create the EspressoCoffee vendor list.
3. Print the vendor report.

Vendor List

STATE	VENDOR NAME	NO	STREET ADDRESS	CITY	ZIP	COUNTRY	PHONE
CA							
	Touring Equipment C	101	22 North South Street	Santiago	91740	USA	(909) 213-9812
CO							
	Anderson's Custom	11	3100 E 60 Ave	Denver	80221	USA	(303) 674-6221
FL							
	Fitness Association	102	201 Sunset Blvd	Miami	33101	USA	(305) 901-2610
KS							
	Professional Athletic	104	620 Bradly Rd	Whichita	67201	USA	(318) 909-0909
MI							
	Image Makers Bike C	16	Magnolia Street	Auborne	68540	USA	(517) 892-1121
MO							
	Paperless Office	13	1204 Forsyth	Clayton	63112	USA	(314) 783-4221
NE							
	International	5	600 Time Center Ct	Grande Island	68501	USA	(308) 211-0982
	Trey Research	10	10 Market Lane	Valentine	68552	USA	(402) 551-7612

3.44

Tech Tool: Database Software
Software Video: Database Queries

EspressoCoffee has asked for your assistance in creating a query to retrieve vendor information.

1. Download the Microsoft Access database file for this exercise.
2. Using Microsoft Access database software, create a query to retrieve information about vendors from the state of Texas. When your query is run, your results should appear as follows (see table below).
3. Run the query and print the result.
4. Select the SQL view. Copy and paste into Excel and print.

Vendors Living in Texas					
VENDOR NAME	STREET ADDRESS	CITY	STATE	ZIP	COUNTRY
Compete, Inc.	11231 Main Street	Austin	TX	78737	USA
Light Speed	431 Golf View Dr.	Houston	TX	77053	USA
Holiday Skate & Cycle	6 10th Street	Dallas	TX	75252	USA

3.45

Tech Tool: Database Software and Spreadsheet Software

Software Video: Database Search

EspressoCoffee's management has asked your assistance in searching the vendor table. They wish to search this table in Microsoft Access as well as Excel.

1. Download the Microsoft Access and Microsoft Excel data files for this exercise.
2. Use the Microsoft Access query-by-example (QBE) to retrieve vendor information with name equal to "International."
3. Use the Microsoft Excel search tool to retrieve vendor information with name equal to "International."

Notice that the search tool in Microsoft Excel is different than the *Find* tool. The Find tool shows only the search item, but the search tool shows the record (row) containing the search item.

3.46

Tech Tool: Database Software

Software Video: Database Search

EspressoCoffee's management has asked your assistance in viewing all records in a database table. They want you to build a form that allows a user to browse vendors' information, starting from the first.

1. Download the Microsoft Access data file for this exercise.
2. Create a vendor form that satisfies the EspressoCoffee requirement.
3. Print the form.

Go Online

In the fast-paced world of technology, your skill at finding answers fast can be vital. Go online and experience typical assignments you may encounter as a professional.

3.47 Your company is considering expanding its retail operations to an online storefront. You have been asked to make recommendations for the design of the storefront interface. Go online and find two examples of online storefronts with user-friendly interfaces. Prepare a briefing to the design team summarizing the features of these two storefronts that you liked best.

3.48 Your firm is considering the purchase of new small business accounting software. The options have been narrowed to QuickBooks software and SAP Business One. You have been assigned to the project team to evaluate these two software options. The team has asked you to evaluate the user interface for each option. (See Chapter 4 for samples of the QuickBooks interface. See Chapter 6 for samples of the SAP Business One interface.)

Go online to research and view the user interfaces for each option. What would you report back at the next team meeting? Which interface would you prefer? Why?

Technology Projects

These technology projects are perfect for both individuals and teams.

Technology Project 3

Tech Tool: Database Software

Software Videos: Database Forms, Database Reports, Database Queries

Technology Project 3 is your opportunity to practice building database forms, queries, and reports for iSportDesign. With this project, you will use Microsoft Access database software.

Your deliverables for this project include the following:

Deliverable 1. Update customer database form

Deliverable 2. New customer database form

Deliverable 3. New item database form

Deliverable 4. Sales order database form

Deliverable 5. Sales report

Deliverable 6. Customer report

Deliverable 7. Inventory report

Deliverable 8. Customer query

Deliverable 9. Sales order query

Deliverable 10. Item query

Visit www.pearsonhighered.com/kay to do the following:

1. Download Technology Project 3 instructions.
2. Download files provided online for your convenience in completing the project deliverables.
3. Watch the videos with software instructions to complete this project at www.pearsonhighered.com/kay.

4 Accounting Systems and Business Processes

How Can You Update Business Process Management with Today's Technologies?

Meet Social Business.

Can you imagine keeping track of every activity you performed today on sticky notes that you could post online and share with your friends? Then what if together with your friends you analyze and rearrange the stickies so that tomorrow you can be more efficient?

Business process management meets social networking. Software AG's ArisAlign is social networking and business process management combined. It uses Amazon's cloud computing to allow you to collaborate with others in the discovery of business processes. ArisAlign uses the equivalent of electronic whiteboards and sticky notes. Each activity is placed on a sticky note. The sticky notes can be moved and rearranged to show the workflow for a business process. Similar to Facebook, it gives you information about recent updates.

Crossroads

At the crossroads of accounting and IT, the business processes that IT professionals document correspond to the accountant's transaction cycles.

My Questions

What Is the Role of Business Processes in the Accounting System?

Can you recall the last time that you purchased fast food or made a purchase at a convenience store? Do you recall, step-by-step, who did what during that purchase?

This is exactly what enterprises attempt to do when they undertake the implementation of a new accounting system. The enterprise must document, step-by-step, who does what. Understanding business processes is key to developing an effective accounting system.

As you know from previous chapters, business processes are a related set of activities that create value. The value chain is a related set of business processes (Figure 4.1). Transaction cycles (purchasing, sales, and payroll cycles) are associated with the business processes in the value chain. The business processes result in accounting transactions. The accounting system must be able to capture and store this transaction data.

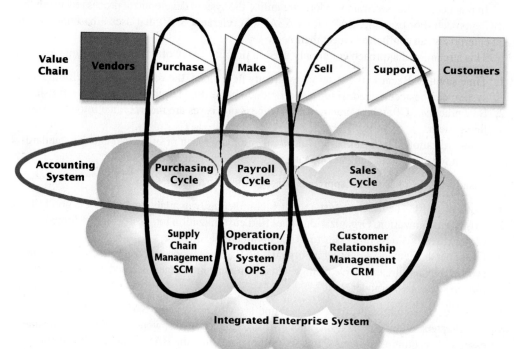

FIGURE 4.1

Business Processes and the Transaction Cycles

ACCOUNTING INSIGHT NO. 13
ABCs of Accounting Systems Are...
Accounting System =
Baseline System + Customization

Accounting Insight No. 13: ABCs of Accounting Systems

Accounting Insight No. 13 states the ABCs of accounting systems: The accounting system equals the baseline system plus customization.

The dilemma facing enterprises has been:

- Do we change our business processes to fit a generic baseline accounting system?
  or
- Do we custom-build an accounting system that fits our unique business needs?

This dilemma is addressed by using the ABCs of accounting systems. The baseline accounting system is a generic accounting system that includes the workflow and business processes frequently used by most enterprises. To create a customized accounting system, we configure or customize the baseline accounting system to accommodate the unique needs of the specific enterprise.

The Car of Your Dreams...

Imagine you are purchasing a new car! Your hard work at EspressoCoffee is paying off, and you can afford to purchase the car of your dreams. What car would you purchase? What features would you select for your car?

The car model you select can be compared to the baseline accounting system. The features that you select, such as sunroof and navigation system, can be compared to customizing the accounting system.

When the automobile was first invented, each car was made by hand. Now most cars are made using an assembly line where the models are standardized to streamline production. Today, most car buyers select the make and model they want to purchase. Then they select the options and features, such as power windows, sunroof, heated seats, and navigation system.

This same evolution has occurred in the development of accounting systems. Instead of building each accounting system with custom programming as in the past, today most enterprises purchase a baseline system and then customize it with features to meet enterprise-specific needs. The process is similar to selecting a base model car, such as an Audi S5, and adding features, such as a sunroof.

In practice, several software vendors streamline the system development process by using this ABC approach. For example, SAP offers ASAP (Accelerated SAP) that uses a baseline system that enterprises can configure to meet their needs.

This streamlined approach commonly used in practice today offers several advantages:

1. Time savings. Because the baseline is already developed, the timeline for developing a system can be accelerated, significantly reducing the time required from start to finish.
2. Best practices. Often best practices for business processes are incorporated into the baseline system.
3. Standardization. The baseline-plus-customization approach offers advantages of standardization for the system and customization for unique requirements.

Disadvantages of the ABC approach to accounting systems include:

1. Not a good fit. The baseline system that is commercially available may not be a good fit.
2. Costly customization. Organizations may find customization too costly and be forced to change their business processes to fit the commercial software.
3. Change management. Adapting an organization's business processes to meet the baseline system may require extensive change. Change management may be needed to reduce employee stress and turnover.

BASE...
Remember the baseline accounting system as BĀS (pronounced /bās/).

Next, we share with you again the baseline accounting system (BAS) model that you saw in prior chapters. We developed this model to make it easier for you to learn about business processes and accounting systems. Then we will explore how the BAS model can be customized using business process maps.

Buy? Or Build?

Today, more and more enterprises prefer to buy their accounting systems instead of building them from scratch using custom programming. Enterprises can select commercially available accounting systems such as SAP, Oracle, Oracle's JD Edwards, Microsoft Dynamics, and QuickBooks.

What motivates enterprises to buy instead of build their accounting systems? The benefits. Benefits offered by these off-the-shelf products include best practices design, lower cost, tighter security, more control, scalability, regular maintenance, and international compliance.

My Connection...
• Try Active Review 4.8

What Are the Business Processes in a Baseline Accounting System?

Can you imagine looking at each and every enterprise in the entire world as having a unique and different accounting system? Can you imagine how many business processes you would need to learn if you looked at each and every business process within each enterprise as being unique? Thousands? Millions?

Here is the good news. Using a baseline accounting system model (Figure 4.2) will streamline your study of business processes. We introduced you to this model in previous chapters and now you will see the power of the model in saving you time.

Instead of learning each and every accounting system as having unique business processes, the baseline accounting system model standardizes the business processes that are common to almost all organizations. By studying this model, you can quickly understand business processes for most organizations.

Your Competitive Advantage....
The baseline accounting system model gives you a competitive advantage. Instead of learning business processes for only one or two enterprises, you will be able to apply the model to any organization. The baseline accounting system and its events can be customized to fit enterprise-specific needs.

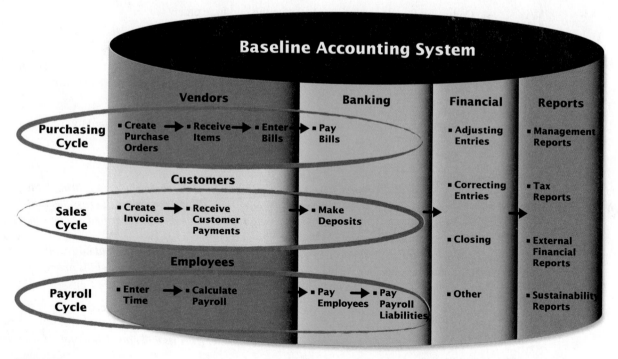

FIGURE 4.2

Baseline Accounting System with Transaction Cycles

Crossroads

What IT professionals call business processes (a series of related activities), accounting professionals may refer to as transaction cycles (a series of related transactions).

As you know, Accounting Insight No. 1 is that we use satellite mapping for viewing the accounting system, zooming out for an overview of the entire system or zooming in to view the detail of specific events. The BAS model in Figure 4.2 illustrates the business processes and transaction cycles common to most enterprises. This model is a high-level view similar to the satellite mapping view of the entire globe at a glance. The model in Figure 4.2 shows the six major modules common to most enterprises:

- Vendors
- Customers
- Employees
- Banking
- Financial
- Reports

Each module contains business processes or related activities that are basic elements for business operations. Our focus is on the accounting transactions that accompany the business processes.

The vendors, customers, and employees modules correspond to the purchasing, sales, and payroll transaction cycles. As shown in the model, the vendors, customers, and employees modules are expanded to show the common events within each of these transaction cycles. Now we drill down in each module to explore the business processes in the baseline accounting system in greater detail.

Vendors Module

The vendors module relates to the purchasing cycle for the organization and the accompanying purchase transactions. The vendors module consists of the following transactions with vendors typically found in most accounting systems:

1. **Create Purchase Orders.** A purchase order is a document that lists items to be ordered, purchase order number, vendor, date, etc. A copy of this document is kept by the enterprise and another copy is sent to the vendor.

   For example, EspressoCoffee Company prepares purchase orders to purchase espresso beans and espresso machines from its Italian suppliers.

2. **Receive Items (Inventory).** The items received by the enterprise are:

   a. Compared to items ordered as listed on the purchase order
   b. Recorded as received on a receiving report

   When EspressoCoffee receives shipments of espresso beans and espresso machines, the receiving department compares the items on the purchase order to verify the order is correct. Items received are recorded on the receiving report and in the accounting system.

3. **Enter Bills.** The enterprise receives a bill for the goods. The bill is compared to:

   a. The purchase order
   b. The receiving report that lists the items received

   EspressoCoffee's vendors send bills separately from the shipment, either through the mail or electronically. When EspressoCoffee receives the bill for orders, it crosschecks the bill with the purchase order and the receiving report. Once the bill is verified as correct, it is entered into the accounting system.

   When EspressoCoffee receives bills for services, such as insurance and utility bills that are not accompanied by purchase orders and receiving reports, those bills are reviewed and entered into the accounting system.

4. **Pay Bills.** When the bill is paid, the company's Checking account is reduced for the amount of the payment.

   EspressoCoffee Company pays its bills when due from its company Checking account.

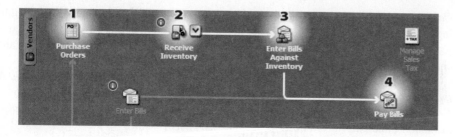

FIGURE 4.3

QuickBooks Vendors Transactions

The vendors section of the QuickBooks Home page (Figure 4.3) shows the activities in the purchasing cycle. Notice the icons for the following:

- Purchase Orders
- Receive Inventory
- Enter Bills Against Inventory
- Pay Bills

Customers Module

The customers module relates to the sales cycle and the accompanying transactions. As shown in Figure 4.2, the customers module consists of typical transactions with customers, including the following:

1. ***Create Invoices.*** When a customer places an order, the sale is recorded on an invoice (or sales receipt). When the accrual basis of accounting is used, the sale is recognized when the good or service is provided, regardless of when the cash is received. A document, such as an invoice or sales receipt, is prepared when the good is provided in order to record the sales revenue at that time.

   EspressoCoffee Company emails invoices to customers when sales are made.

2. ***Receive Customer Payments.*** The customer payment is recorded when it is received. Cash can be received before the sale (as a customer deposit), at the same time as the sale occurs (cash sale), or after the sale is made (credit sale).

   EspressoCoffee records customers' payments when received.

3. ***Make Deposits.*** The customer's payment is deposited in the bank.

   EspressoCoffee deposits customers' payments into the company Checking account.

The customers section of the QuickBooks Home page (Figure 4.4) shows the activities in the sales cycle. Notice the icons for the following:

- Create Invoices
- Receive Payments
- Record Deposits

FIGURE 4.4

QuickBooks Customers Transactions

Employees Module

The employees module (Figure 4.2) corresponds to the payroll cycle and the corresponding payroll transactions. Payroll consists of wages and salaries paid to employees as well as withholdings and payroll liabilities. Typical events in the payroll cycle include the following:

1. ***Enter Time.*** To calculate payroll, employee time must be tracked and entered into the system.

   EspressoCoffee Company tracks employee time using employee time tracking.

2. *Calculate Payroll.* To create paychecks, it is necessary to calculate the gross pay, withholdings, and net pay for each employee. Amounts withheld from employee pay can include federal and state withholdings, health insurance deductions, retirement contributions, and charitable donations.

   EspressoCoffee Company pays its employees monthly, on the first of each month. At that time, it calculates employee gross pay, withholdings, and net pay. EspressoCoffee Company calculates payroll liabilities for federal and state withholdings, health insurance deductions, and other deductions from employee paychecks.

3. *Pay Employees.* Employee paychecks are printed and distributed or directly deposited into employee bank accounts.

   EspressoCoffee prepares and distributes employee paychecks, paid from the company Checking account.

4. *Pay Payroll Liabilities.* Payroll liabilities are paid to the appropriate governmental agencies or entities.

   EspressoCoffee Company pays all payroll liabilities when due.

The employees section of the QuickBooks Home page (Figure 4.5) shows the activities in the payroll cycle for QuickBooks software.

FIGURE 4.5

QuickBooks Employees Transactions

Banking Module

The banking module (Figure 4.2) consists of transactions involving cash received and cash paid. The typical banking transactions covered thus far consist of the following:

- Cash paid to vendors
- Cash received from customers
- Cash paid to employees
- Cash paid for payroll liabilities

As Figure 4.2 illustrates, the banking module is typically a continuation of other modules:

- Pay Bills is a continuation of the purchasing cycle transactions (vendors module).
- Make Deposits is a continuation of the sales cycle transactions (customers module).
- Pay Employees and Pay Payroll Liabilities are continuations of the payroll cycle transactions (employees module).

The banking section of the QuickBooks Home page (Figure 4.6) shows the following icons to record banking transactions:

- Record Deposits
- Write Checks

FIGURE 4.6

QuickBooks Banking Transactions

Financial Module

The financial module consists of other activities and transactions that do not fall into the prior modules. Such items would include:

- Adjusting entries: Entries to bring accounts up to date, such as recording depreciation for the period
- Correcting entries: Entries necessary to correct errors
- Closing entries: All entries needed to close temporary Income and Expense accounts at year end
- Other: All other transactions and entries needed to properly maintain and operate the accounting system

The financial module includes all tasks necessary to maintain the enterprise's General Ledger. The General Ledger is the listing of accounts and their balances, including the transactions affecting each account. The accounts in the enterprise's General Ledger are the building blocks of the entire accounting system. Accounts are used to sort accounting data into similar categories. For example, a company's Checking account is affected by the following banking transactions:

- Pay bills for vendor transactions to purchase goods and services.
- Deposit payments from customers for goods and services.
- Make payments to employees for payroll.
- Pay payroll liabilities.

Since most accounting systems use databases to store accounting data, the account balances are calculated using various database tables. Recall from Chapter 1 that each table needs a unique identifier or primary key. For accounts, the unique identifier is usually the account number. Each account is assigned a different number. The collection of all the accounts and account numbers used by an enterprise is called a chart of accounts (Figure 4.7).

A well-designed chart of accounts uses a coding system for account numbers. For example, assets might be numbered 1000–1999; liabilities numbered 2000–2999; equities numbered 3000–3999; revenues numbered 4000–4999; and expenses numbered 5000–5999.

> In practice, the baseline accounting system is typically selected from among available commercial accounting or enterprise software. For example, a small enterprise might select QuickBooks financial software. A midsize organization might purchase Oracle's JD Edwards. A large enterprise, such as Nestlé, purchases SAP.
>
> After the baseline accounting system is selected, the baseline system is configured or customized to meet the unique requirements and needs of the specific enterprise.

EspressoCoffee
Account Listing

Account	Type
EspressoCoffee	Bank
Inventory Asset	Other Current Asset
Accumulated Depreciation	Fixed Asset
Furniture and Equipment	Fixed Asset
Security Deposits Asset	Other Asset
Sales Tax Payable	Other Current Liability
Opening Balance Equity	Equity
Owners Draw	Equity
Owners Equity	Equity
Merchandise Sales	Income
Sales Discounts	Income
Merchant Account Fees	Cost of Goods Sold
Advertising and Promotion	Expense
Automobile Expense	Expense
Bank Service Charges	Expense
Computer and Internet Expens...	Expense
Depreciation Expense	Expense
Insurance Expense	Expense
Interest Expense	Expense
Janitorial Expense	Expense
Meals and Entertainment	Expense
Office Supplies	Expense
Professional Fees	Expense
Rent Expense	Expense
Repairs and Maintenance	Expense
Telephone Expense	Expense
Uniforms	Expense
Utilities	Expense
Ask My Accountant	Other Expense
Estimates	Non-Posting

FIGURE 4.7
Chart of Accounts

Reports Module

The reports module relates to output from the accounting system. Reports can be onscreen, in electronic files, or on hardcopy printouts. In general, we can classify reports into the following four basic types.

- Financial accounting and regulatory reports given to investors, creditors, and regulatory agencies. An example of a regulatory agency would be the Securities and Exchange Commission (SEC). Reports filed with the SEC by publicly traded companies include a Form 10-K.
- Tax reports used when filing federal, state, and local taxes. Examples of tax reports would include tax returns filed with the Internal Revenue Service (IRS), such as Form 1120 filed by corporations.
- Management reports provided to internal users of accounting information. These reports can be used in carrying out the management functions of planning, control, and decision making. Management reports can be numerous and varied depending upon management needs. An example of a management report would be a sales report classifying sales by geographic region and store.
- Sustainability reports provided to current and potential investors, consumers, and humanitarian and environmental organizations. Sustainability reports provide information about the sustainability of an organization's economic, social, and environmental performance and impact. The format of sustainability reports can vary widely because at this time there is no required framework or regulation of sustainability reporting.

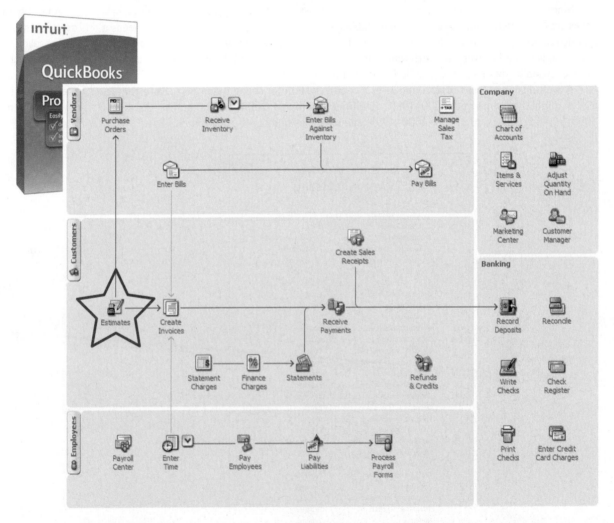

FIGURE 4.8
QuickBooks Customized with Estimates

Note that the first two categories, financial and tax, are external reports given to outside parties. Management reports are directed to internal users and decision makers. The last category, sustainability reports, can be used by both internal and external users for evaluating performance and making decisions.

When designing an accounting system, it is often useful to begin with the end report in mind. What accounting reports will the users require? Then the system can be designed to ensure that it generates the required reports.

This baseline accounting system, comprised of modules and events common to most enterprises, can be customized to meet enterprise-specific needs. In the customization stage, the enterprise drills down to develop a more detailed view of the accounting system.

Customizing Accounting Software...

QuickBooks accounting software has over 4 million small business users.

When you set up a new company in QuickBooks, you begin with a baseline accounting system. Then there are two ways to customize QuickBooks for your specific business:

1. Use a specialized version of QuickBooks, such as QuickBooks for contractors, retailers, and not-for-profits. These versions include customized features to meet the needs of the specific type of enterprise.

2. Use QuickBooks Preferences to modify the software settings to meet your specific business needs, such as adding the Estimates feature as shown in Figure 4.8.

My Connection...
• Short Exercise 4.26

How Do I Customize an Accounting System Using Business Process Mapping?

What Is Business Process Mapping?

Just as a roadmap is a graphical representation of roads, highways, and streets on which you drive a car, business process mapping graphically describes the processes of the accounting system. A business process map diagrams step-by-step the activities performed in a process.

A streamlined, effective approach to business process mapping is to start with the baseline accounting system. Each module in the baseline system is mapped for business processes and activities performed within that module. The baseline modules for vendors, customers, employees, banking, financial, and reports are expanded and customized to show the detail of the business processes for the specific enterprise. The employees module, for example, might be customized by adding payroll features to meet enterprise requirements for payroll with holdings, such as health insurance, 401(k) contributions, and charitable donations.

Just as satellite mapping can zoom in to see the detailed street view, we can zoom into see a detailed view of business processes. For example, we can zoom in to see the detailed step-by-step tasks to create an invoice. At a minimum, business process mapping for the accounting system should include the purchasing, sales, and payroll transaction cycles.

Why Use Business Process Mapping?

Can you imagine driving a cross-country roadtrip without a paper or electronic roadmap? You could waste time getting lost, taking wrong turns, and perhaps even ending up at a different destination than you desired.

A business process map for an accounting system accomplishes some of the same purposes as a roadmap for a cross-country roadtrip. With the business process map, you can plan in advance and think through contingencies when needed. You can plan for each step of the process and the most effective path to accomplish required activities.

In general, reasons to use business process maps for accounting systems include:

- Communication tool. The business process map is a communication tool between the accounting professionals who use the system and the IT professionals who develop the accounting system. Accounting and IT professionals need a communication tool so together they can design together an effective, reliable accounting system. The business process map facilitates communication between the accounting and IT professionals so each can see and reach a common understanding of the overall design requirements and activities.
- Documentation tool. The business process map documents the various activities to be performed and the order in which the activities must occur. A business process map can be a valuable tool for a new employee trying to learn a new accounting system fast. When you start a new job, consider asking if there is a business process map for the activities you are assigned. If not, consider drawing your own business process map to learn the job faster.

Duct Tape Accounting Systems...

Duct tape accounting systems use patches to fix problems as they arise. A duct tape accounting system often proves true the adage *Every problem began life as a solution.* A solution to one problem creates another problem later. In this type of system, rarely is time taken to think of the accounting system in a global view or to document changes implemented. Sometimes these duct tape systems appear to work fine until a key employee leaves. Then remaining employees often do not know how the system works, and there is no documentation to assist remaining employees. That is why business process documentation is important.

- Streamlining tool. Sometimes tasks are performed a certain way because they have always been done that way—instead of because it is the most effective way to perform the task. By streamlining operations, companies can cut costs. Business process mapping is a valuable tool to envision how an accounting system can be improved and streamlined, while at the same time maintaining security and control over confidential information.

Business Process Management...

When a new accounting system is developed, organizations often streamline business processes to improve effectiveness. This is sometimes referred to as business process management or BPM. How can the enterprise's business processes be improved? Can any steps be eliminated?

What Notation Does a Business Process Map Use?

Just as different roadmaps have different symbols and notations for identifying different elements on the map (interstates, highways, cities, towns, and so on), a business process map can be drawn using different types of symbols and notations. Some of the standard notations that you may see used for business process maps include:

- Flowcharts
- Data flow diagrams (DFD)
- Unified modeling language (UML)
- Business Process Model and Notation (BPMN)

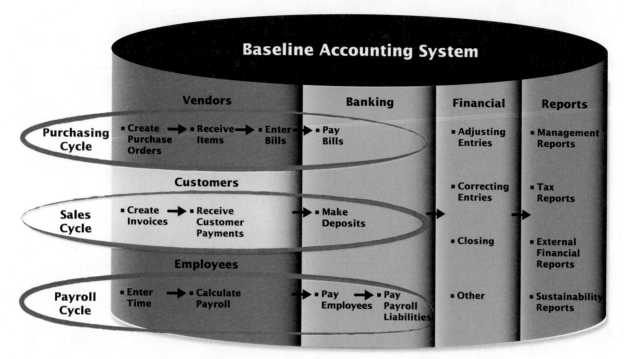

FIGURE 4.9

Baseline Accounting System Sales Cycle

Next, for you to see how business process mapping notations differ, we show the sales cycle in the baseline accounting system (Figure 4.9) diagrammed using various business process mapping notations.

FLOWCHARTS First used in the 1920s, flowcharts are still used today to graphically describe a series of activities and decisions. Accounting professionals may prefer flowcharts for business process maps because of simplicity. Flowcharts are an easy option for accounting professionals to learn quickly. The advantage of simplicity for flowcharts is also a disadvantage. Flowcharts do not always provide the level of detail that IT professionals need to develop accounting systems and applications. This can lead to miscommunication and flawed systems. (See Figure 4.10 for a flowchart example.)

FIGURE 4.10

Sales Cycle Flowchart

DATA FLOW DIAGRAMS (DFD) First used in the 1970s, data flow diagrams use only four symbols to graphically describe processes and data flow: agent (square), process (rounded rectangle), data store (three-sided rectangle), and data flow (line and arrow). The advantage of a DFD over a flowchart is that DFDs specify agents (individuals performing the processes). One disadvantage of DFDs is that there is no symbol for decisions. Another disadvantage of DFDs is that there are more modern methods of business process mapping that have become more widely used. (See Figure 4.11 for an example of a DFD.)

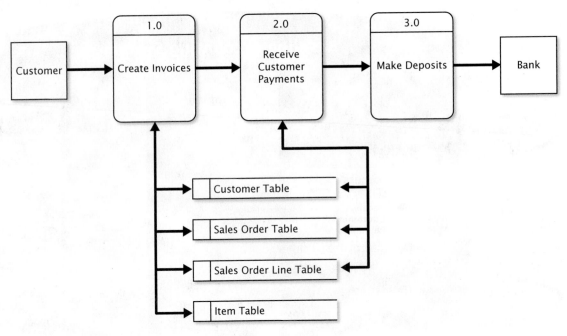

FIGURE 4.11

Sales Cycle Data Flow Diagram

UNIFIED MODELING LANGUAGE (UML) UML has gained widespread use among IT professionals, but it is an extremely complex business processing mapping tool that has hundreds of different symbols. The level of complexity possible with UML has made it popular with IT professionals and at the same time makes it challenging and time consuming for accounting professionals to learn and use as a communication tool. (See Figure 4.12 for examples of the numerous UML symbols that can be used with UML diagrams.)

BUSINESS PROCESS MODEL AND NOTATION VERSION 2.0 (BPMN 2.0) Introduced in 2011, BPMN 2.0 provides a business process mapping standard for bridging the gap between IT professionals and business users, such as accountants. BPMN 2.0 doesn't require extensive training to use, making it a better choice for accounting professionals to understand and use to communicate with IT professionals. On the other hand, BPMN 2.0 provides greater detail than flowcharting to meet the needs of IT professionals for successful system implementation. So BPMN provides a balance between simplicity and complexity to facilitate communication between the accounting and IT professionals. (See Figure 4.13 for an example of a BPMN 2.0 diagram.)

Which business process mapping notation do you need to know? Since accounting professionals may prefer flowcharts, you need to be familiar with flowcharting. However, flowcharts may not meet the needs of IT professionals building the system. Since BPMN 2.0 was developed to bridge the communication gap between IT and business users who must work together as a team to design, develop, and implement systems, knowledge of BPMN 2.0 diagrams could make you a valued team member to bridge the communication gap. Knowledge of both flowcharts and BPMN 2.0 can satisfy the demands placed on you by both accountants and IT professionals. A fundamental knowledge of flowcharts and BPMN 2.0 could give you a competitive advantage, so we will use both to illustrate business process maps for an accounting system.

FIGURE 4.12

UML Diagram Symbols

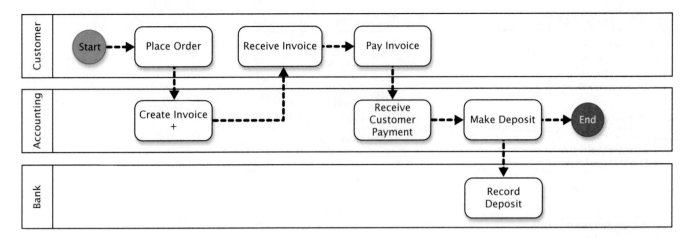

FIGURE 4.13

Sales Cycle BPMN 2.0 Diagram

> **My Connection...**
> How do I study less and learn more? Make connections. Try Short Exercise 4.27.

How Do I Read a Flowchart?

Friday Night Flowchart

How do you decide what to do on Friday night? What process do you use to make a decision? Could you map that process? Do you consider a series of questions, such as:

- Do I have homework?
- Do I have money?
- Do I have time?
- Do I have other commitments to family, friends, classmates, etc.?
- Do I text my friends to see what they are doing?
- What are my food preferences (pizza, burgers, sushi...)?
- What are my location preferences (walking distance, two miles, ten miles, or more)?

A flowchart of a possible scenario for deciding what to do on Friday night appears in Figure 4.14, Friday Night Flowchart. Just as your Friday night decision process follows a typical series of steps, businesses conduct operations following a typical series of steps that can be mapped using a flowchart. For example, a flowchart for creating a customer invoice appears in Figure 4.15.

Create Customer Invoice Flowchart

Notice that the Create Customer Invoice flowchart in Figure 4.15 begins with the start symbol. Next, Process Customer Order is shown in a process symbol. The diamond-shaped symbol represents a decision. In this case, the decision is whether to proceed with the customer order. If the customer credit is confirmed and the order is complete, then the order is shipped. After that, the invoice is generated.

Some commonly used flowchart symbols are summarized for you in Figure 4.16. These symbols are used to graphically model the data flow including input, processing and output.

Figure 4.17 shows how the flowchart for creating a sales invoice connects to the sales cycle flowchart shown earlier. The Sales Cycle flowchart is a Level 1 flowchart that can be expanded and shown in greater detail in a Level 2 flowchart. The Create Invoices flowchart is a Level 2 flowchart. There can be up to four levels of detail shown for flowcharts (Levels 1, 2, 3, and 4). Basically you are drilling down into greater and greater detail about tasks performed, similar to drilling down in satellite mapping to see greater and greater mapping detail.

How Do Accountants Use Flowcharts?

Accountants may use flowcharts during audits to map systems they are auditing or to map the steps performed in an audit. Also, flowcharts have been known to appear on CPA Examination questions.

How Do IT Professionals Use Flowcharts?

Software engineers use flowcharts when writing software programs. Flowcharts are well suited for programming development because of the ability to chart a series of steps and decisions involved in a process that then can be converted to programming code.

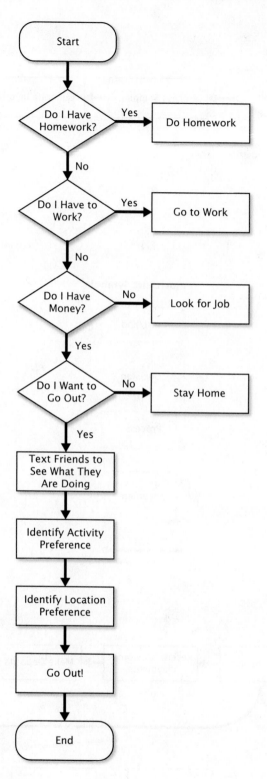

FIGURE 4.14
Friday Night Flowchart

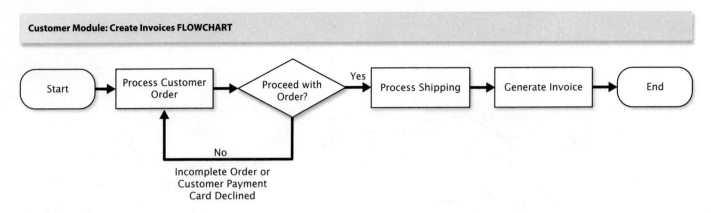

Customer Module: Create Invoices FLOWCHART

FIGURE 4.15

Create Customer Invoices Flowchart

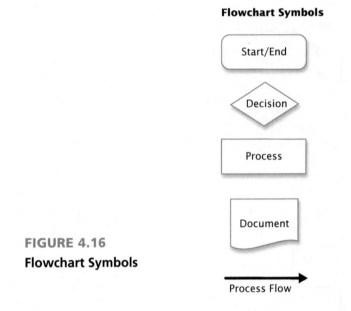

FIGURE 4.16

Flowchart Symbols

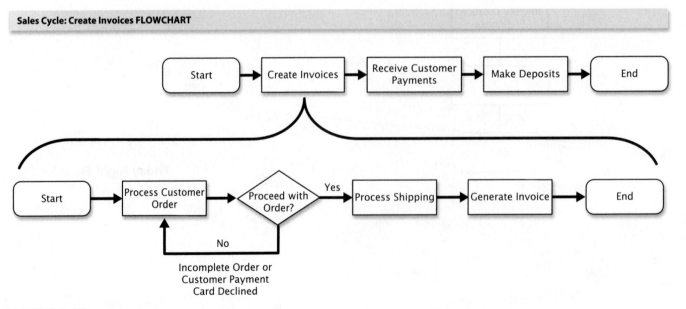

Sales Cycle: Create Invoices FLOWCHART

FIGURE 4.17

Sales Cycle Flowchart Level 1 and 2

My Connection...
How do I study less and learn more? Make connections. Try Short Exercise 4.32.

How Do I Read a BPMN 2.0 Diagram?

OMG BPMN
Business Process Model and Notation is sponsored by OMG (Object Management Group, Inc.). OMG is a not-for-profit industry standards consortium. OMG maintains specifications including UML and BPMN (www.omg.org).

BPMN 2.0 was developed as an easily understandable, standardized language to communicate business processes effectively between all business users and IT professionals. Figure 4.13 shows an example of a BPMN diagram for the sales cycle. Some frequently used BPMN 2.0 symbols are shown in Figures 4.18 and 4.19.

Just as satellite mapping shows the detailed street view, BPMN diagrams can drill down and show greater detail. Figure 4.20 shows a BPMN 2.0 diagram for EspressoCoffee to map its business process for a component of the sales cycle: create a customer invoice. (See Figure 4.21 for a sample EspressoCoffee customer invoice.) Notice how a BPMN diagram is used to expand the activity Create Invoice to show details about where the invoice is sent and data is stored.

BPMN diagrams answer the question: Who does what, where, when, and how? Figure 4.20 documents the following activities EspressoCoffee performs to create a customer invoice:

EspressoCoffee
Company

- A customer places an online order with EspressoCoffee.
- The customer identity is verified with EspressoCoffee's CUSTOMER database table.

Bpmn Diagrams Can Be Used in Multiple Ways
1. As documentation to describe the current accounting system
2. As a blueprint to describe a new, proposed accounting system
3. As a tool for streamlining a current or proposed accounting system

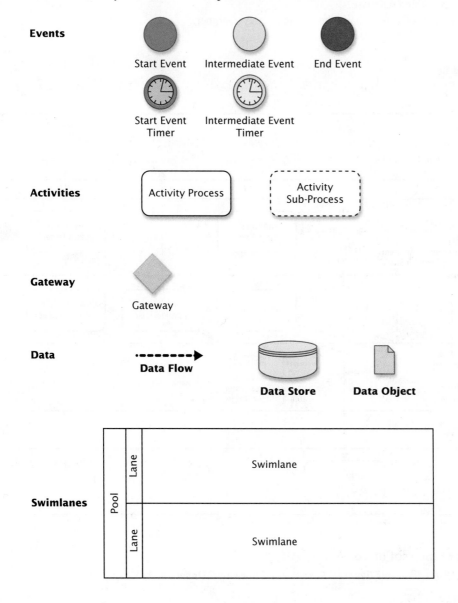

FIGURE 4.18
BPMN 2.0 Symbols

FIGURE 4.19

BPMN Example

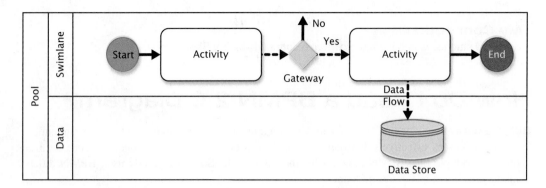

- Item availability is verified with the Iᴛᴇᴍ table.
- The customer credit card standing is verified with the credit card company.
- After verifications, shipping is authorized, and the shipping information is sent to the warehouse.
- The warehouse picks the items from stock.
- The warehouse ships the items to the customer with the pick list.
- The warehouse notifies accounting that the items are shipped.
- EspressoCoffee creates an invoice, querying and updating data as needed using the accounting database.
- EspressoCoffee emails the invoice to the customer.

Customer Module: Create Invoices BPMN 2.0 DIAGRAM

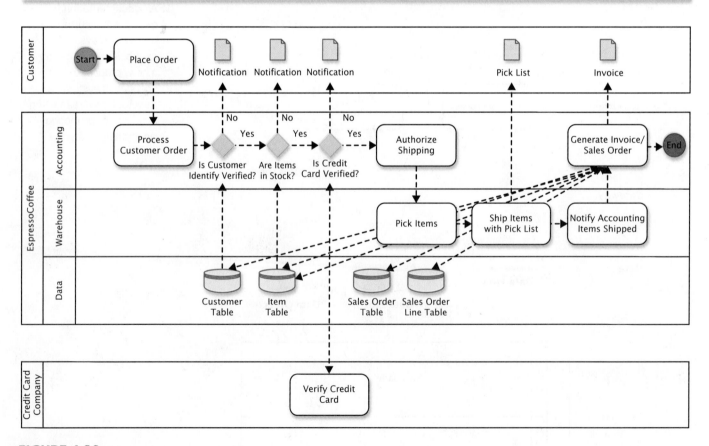

FIGURE 4.20

Create Invoices BPMN Diagram for EspressoCoffee

Can you identify the swimlanes in this BPMN diagram? Events? Activities? Gateways? Database tables?

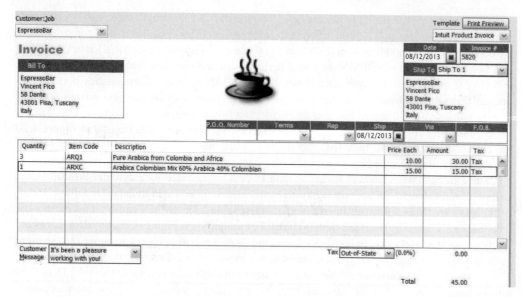

FIGURE 4.21

QuickBooks Invoice

As you can see in Figure 4.20, the detailed view for creating an EspressoCoffee invoice uses the following BPMN symbols to map the process:

- Events
- Activities
- Gateways
- Data
- Swimlanes
- Pools

Events

An event triggers, interrupts, or ends a process. Events are represented by circles. The circles are stoplight coded:

- Start—Green
- Intermediate—Yellow
- End—Red

Notice in Figure 4.18 that in addition to Start, Intermediate, and End symbols for events, there are also Start and Intermediate symbols with a clock in the center of the symbol. These symbols represent events scheduled at specific times.

Activities

Activities are actions performed. An activity is represented by a rounded rectangle. Notice in Figure 4.20 that activities start with an action verb, such as *generate*, *process*, *ship*, and so on. Sometimes a plus sign (+) is placed inside the activity symbol to indicate there is more detail about the activity in another BPMN diagram.

Gateways

Gateways are used for forking and merging process flows. Gateways, shown as diamond shapes, represent decisions or possible outcomes to an activity. For example, in Figure 4.20 gateways result in a Yes/No outcome. If the item is out of stock, the customer is notified and the order is not placed. If the customer's credit card standing cannot be verified, then the customer is notified and the order is not placed.

Data

Data symbols in a BPMN diagram can include the following:

- Data flow
- Data object
- Data store

Data flow is represented by lines and arrows on the BPMN diagram. Data flow shows how data enters a system, how it moves through a system from process to process, where it is stored, and how it exits the system. In addition, data flows can show when data is inserted, updated, or deleted.

For simplicity, in the BPMN diagrams here, we use a dotted line and arrow used by some BPMN 2.0 software to indicate data flows. Some BPMN software distinguishes between sequence flows (a solid line and arrow) versus message flows (dotted line and arrow). For our purposes, we will use a dotted line and arrow for data flows in general.

A **data object** can be a document or data record. Examples of data objects in Figure 4.20 are customer notifications, pick list, and invoice. Data objects are sometimes called artifacts. Data objects are represented by a rectangle with one corner folded over.

Data store is where data is stored. A data store is represented by a cylinder typically used to represent databases. For accounting system purposes, data is stored in database tables. An accounting system uses numerous interrelated database tables. The BPMN can designate either the database or the specific database table(s) used. For example, in Figure 4.20, the data stores are the Customer, Sales Order, Sales Order Line, and Item database tables. Customer information, such as customer number, name, and address are stored in the CUSTOMER table. Information about each line on the invoice or sales order is stored in the SALES ORDER LINE table. Data flow arrows from the activity to the database table indicate data is stored. Data flow arrows coming out of the database table indicate data is extracted. To make the BPMN easier to read, data stores can be grouped together into a Data swimlane.

Swimlanes

Swimlanes and **pools** are rectangles used to group and organize activities in a BPMN diagram. Pools represent major participants in the process and are often used to identify separate organizations. For example, Figure 4.20 shows pools for each entity in the diagram: Customer, EspressoCoffee, and Credit Card Company.

Just like a swimming pool, the BPMN pool can contain swimlanes. These swimlanes are used to organize activities based on function or role. In Figure 4.20, EspressoCoffee's pool is divided into swimlanes for Accounting, Warehouse, and Data.

Who Does What, When, Where, and How?

When reading a BPMN diagram, we want to know who does what, when, where, and how. One approach to reading a BPMN diagram is:

Step 1: Identify the Start event that triggers the process. In the BPMN diagram in Figure 4.20, the customer triggers the start of the create invoice process.

Step 2: Identify the activities. Activities begin with an action verb. For example, activities in Figure 4.20 are:

- Place Order (Customer)
- Process Customer Order (EspressoCoffee Accounting)
- Authorize Shipping (EspressoCoffee Accounting)
- Pick Items (EspressoCoffee Warehouse)
- Ship Items with Pick List (EspressoCoffee Warehouse)
- Notify Accounting Items Shipped (EspressoCoffee Warehouse)
- Generate Invoice/Sales Invoice

Step 3: Identify gateways where forking or merging data flows occur. Three gateways shown in Figure 4.20 are:

- Is Customer Identify Verified?
- Are Items in Stock?
- Is Credit Card Verified?

Step 4: Identify data objects. In Figure 4.20, the data objects are:

- Customer Notifications
- Pick List
- Customer Invoice

Step 5: Identify data stores. In Figure 4.20, the data stores consist of the following database tables:

- CUSTOMER table
- SALES ORDER table
- SALES ORDER LINE table
- ITEM table

Step 6: Trace data flows. The data flows in Figure 4.20 connect the flow objects: events, activities, and gateways.

Step 7: Identify the End event. The End event in Figure 4.20 designates the end of the create invoice process.

What Would You Do?

Joey, your colleague in IT, asked for your signature approving his business process map for creating a customer invoice for EspressoCoffee (Figure 4.22).
What would you do?

a. Sign the approval form.
b. Sign the approval form and email Joey your suggested changes.
c. Do not sign the approval form and email Joey your requests for modifications.
d. Do not sign the approval form and email Joey with a meeting request to review the business process map.

What are the changes you would request?

> As an accounting professional, you may be asked to approve business process diagrams prepared by IT professionals. If you fail to identify flaws in the diagram, flaws in the accounting system may result.

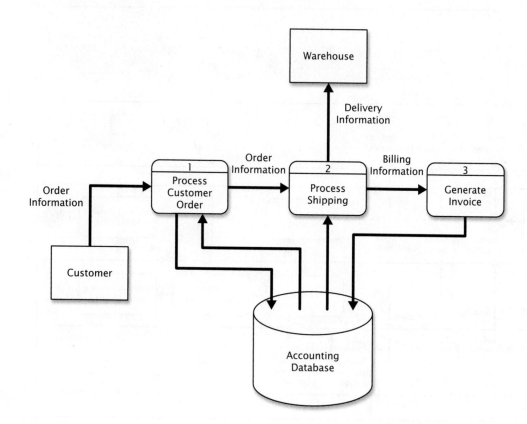

FIGURE 4.22

Joey's Business Process Map

> **My Connection...**
> How do I study less and learn more? Make connections. Try Short Exercise 4.33.

How Do I Build a Business Process Map?

Now that you know how to *read* a business process map, the next task is to learn how to *build* a business process map. Remember that when building a business process map, you continue to use satellite mapping—zooming in for greater and greater detail. For example, Figure 4.23

Sales Cycle BPMN 2.0 DIAGRAM

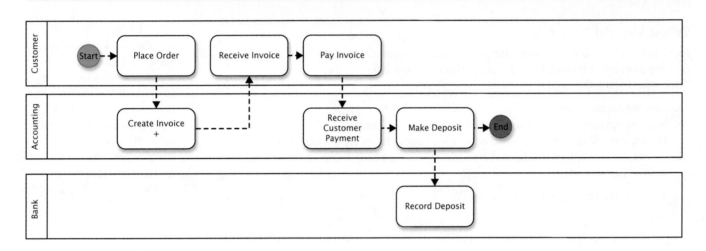

Customer Module: Create Invoices BPMN 2.0 DIAGRAM

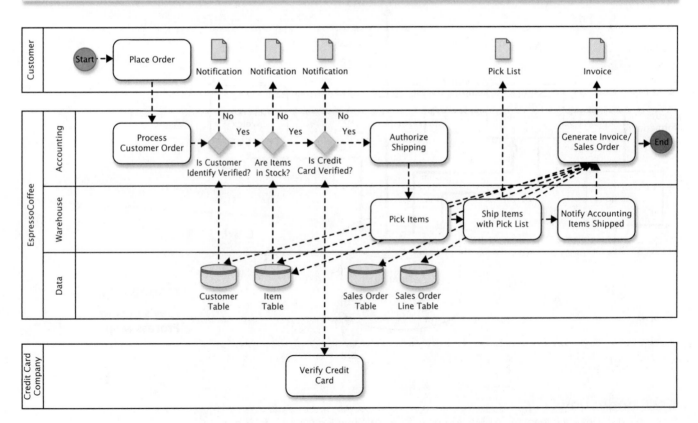

FIGURE 4.23

Sales Cycle and Create Invoices BPMN Diagrams

shows how the sales cycle BPMN diagram can zoom in to show greater detail of the create invoice activity. Notice the (+) sign in the create invoice activity for the sales cycle. This indicates there is a more detailed BPMN to show another level of the create invoice activity.

Five Steps to Build a Business Process Map

The steps to build a business process map are basically the same whether you are building a flowchart or a BPMN diagram. You can build a business process map using the following five steps:

Step 1: Write narrative for a business activity.
Step 2: Annotate the narrative.
Step 3: Create a business process map to organize activities.
Step 4: Develop a business process map using the information from the business process map organizer.
Step 5: Repeat steps 1 through 4 for each subprocess as needed.

If a greater level of detail is needed, steps 1 through 4 are repeated again for the next level of detail, and so on. The steps to create a business process map using BPMN for an EspressoCoffee customer invoice follow.

Step 1: Write a narrative for the business process. This narrative should be a general description of the business process and only include major activities. It describes how the business activity is conducted. See Figure 4.24 for a narrative example for EspressoCoffee.

Step 2: Annotate the narrative. After a narrative is prepared, annotate the narrative by underlining the activities in the narrative. Typically, the narrative is told in chronological order, so if you prefer, you can identify the activities as Activity 1, 2, and so on. See Figure 4.25 for an example of an annotated narrative. Notice that the activities typically describe an action, such as *process customer order*.

Step 3: Create a business process map organizer to organize activities. After annotating the narrative, create a table to organize activities (see Figure 4.26). The number of columns in the business process map organizer will vary based upon whether you are using a flowchart or a BPMN to diagram the business process. If used for a BPMN diagram, the organizer might have four columns: activity, gateway, swimlane, and data store. The organizer contains as many rows

EspressoCoffee
Company

> EspressoCoffee customers place an online order. EspressoCoffee processes the customer order by verifying the customer identity, verifying the items are available, and sending a request to the credit card company to verify the customer's good credit standing. The shipment authorization is sent to the warehouse. The warehouse picks the items from stock. The items are shipped to the customer with a pick list enclosed. The warehouse notifies accounting that the items have shipped. Accounting generates an invoice from the sales information and emails the invoice to the customer. The corresponding database tables are updated.

FIGURE 4.24

Narrative for EspressoCoffee Create Invoices

> EspressoCoffee customers _place an online order_. EspressoCoffee _processes the customer order_ by verifying the customer identity, verifying the items are available, and sending a request to the credit card company to verify the customer's good credit standing. The _shipment authorization is sent_ to the warehouse. The warehouse _picks the items_ from stock. The _items are shipped_ to the customer with a pick list enclosed. The warehouse _notifies accounting_ that the items have shipped. Accounting _generates an invoice_ from the sales information and emails the invoice to the customer. The corresponding database tables are updated.

FIGURE 4.25

Annotated Narrative for EspressoCoffee Create Invoices

Business Process Map Organizer

Activity	Gateway (Decision)	Swimlane (BPMN Only)	Data Store (BPMN Only)
Place Order		Customer	
Process Customer Order		Accounting	
	Verify Customer Identity	Accounting	Customer Table
	Verify Items Available	Accounting	Item table
	Verify Credit Standing	Accounting	
Authorize Shipping		Accounting	
Pick Items		Warehouse	Item table
Ship Items with Pick List		Warehouse	
Notify Accounting Items Shipped		Warehouse	
Generate Invoice		Accounting	Customer table Sales Order table Sales Order Line table Item table

FIGURE 4.26

Business Process Map Organizer

as the number of activities plus gateways for the business process. To prepare the organizer, complete the following steps:

a. Place the first activity (or gateway) in the first row. Place the second activity (or gateway) in the second row. Continue until all annotated activities (and gateways) are placed in the organizer. Make sure that these activities (and gateways) are placed in the organizer in the order performed.

b. For each activity or gateway, identify the swimlane in which the activity or gateway should appear. Insert the name of the swimlane in the swimlane column for the activity or gateway.

c. For each activity or gateway listed in the organizer, identify database tables used. Insert database tables in the data store column for the activity or gateway.

Step 4: Develop a business process map using information in the business process map organizer. Using the notation for flowcharting or BPMN 2.0, create a business process map. Build the business process map so that you have one activity or gateway to correspond to each row in the organizer (see Figure 4.23).

Step 5: Repeat steps 1 through 4 for subprocesses as needed. If additional detail is needed for a process, add a (+) sign to the process symbol. To map the additional detail, repeat steps 1 through 4 to develop a BPMN diagram for the subprocesses (see Figure 4.23).

> **My Connection...**
> Try Short Exercises 4.39 and 4.40.

> **Building BPMN Diagrams....**
> With the increasing popularity of BPMN 2.0 diagrams, you have several software options to make building BPMN diagrams easier. Software for building BPMN diagrams includes:
> - OmniGraffle
> - Visio
> - Altova

How Do I Collect Information to Build a Business Process Map?

When creating a business process map, information about the tasks and activities involved in an enterprise's business processes can be collected using various techniques, including the following:

1. Review current accounting system documentation.
2. Observe business processes.
3. Interview employees.
4. Conduct surveys.
5. Prepare narratives.

REVIEW CURRENT ACCOUNTING SYSTEM DOCUMENTATION Typically, the first step in collecting information for business processes documentation is to review the documentation for the current system. Some organizations may have little, if any, formal documentation for their accounting system. Many times the accounting system evolves as the need arises, so there may not be any current system documentation to review. If well documented, each step of the design of the accounting system including business process mapping should have been documented and saved.

One of your first tasks when preparing a business process map is to collect, review, and organize all the documentation you can find. This includes any business process maps that document the current system.

OBSERVE BUSINESS PROCESSES After collecting and reviewing the documentation available for the current system, you need to observe operations to verify that the business operates the same as the documentation shows. There are a couple of reasons why this may not be the case.

First, the documentation may be outdated. The system may have been updated, but the documentation was not. Secondly, the system may be outdated. Business processes may have changed, but the system did not. So the system and the documentation may agree, but the actual processes used by employees are different. The business processes may have changed due to technological advances, streamlined operations, and cutting "red tape" by bypassing control procedures to name a few reasons.

When you observe, it is important to note ways in which the business operations and business processes can be improved. Business process management (BPM) is frequently used by firms during difficult financial times to reduce costs and improve efficiency, such as during the financial crisis commencing in 2008. Also, firms use BPM when new accounting systems are developed to improve and streamline business processes.

It is often wise to observe business operations and accounting procedures in action without anyone realizing that you are observing them. Imagine that EspressoCoffee opens a local coffee shop to sell its coffee and serve its espresso. You work at the local coffee shop to launch it and learn the business. Procedures require you to double count the cash drawer at shift changes, but because the coffee shop is so busy, nobody has time to double count the drawer. If you knew that an employee from company headquarters was going to be in the shop to observe today, would you double count the cash drawer?

When you observe business operations and procedures, often you can collect better information about actual business procedures if employees do not know they are being observed.

INTERVIEW EMPLOYEES Typically, you will want to interview employees who work in the various areas for which you are creating business process maps. First, prepare a list of employees that you want to interview.

Second, prepare a list of questions that you will be asking each employee.

Third, be organized and have a system for recording the employee responses. You may want to use a laptop to enter responses as you conduct the interview. Sometimes, however, the interviewee is less forthright if you are typing everything he or she says. Frequently, the best way to elicit information, if not the most time effective, is to take minimal notes during the interview to avoid concern on the interviewee's part. As soon as the interview is over, type the rest of your notes using your jotted notes as an outline and reminder. If you use this approach, you will want to allow 10 minutes or so between interviews to enter your notes before continuing with the next interview.

You may consider an electronic interview in the form of an electronic survey or questionnaire. Although surveys permit the employee to enter the responses electronically, saving you time, it prevents you from asking immediate follow-up questions if the response is partial or ambiguous.

Fourth, schedule interviews. Specify the amount of time you will require from the employee, and plan accordingly so you can stay within the time limit. To obtain maximum cooperation from employees, you will want to be considerate of the effect on the employees' work schedules.

Fifth, conduct the interviews. At the beginning of the interview, state the reason for the interview. Keep in mind that employees may be concerned about performance evaluations or job elimination as they are speaking with you, and this could influence their responses. Interviewing employees on-site at their work area instead of conducting the interviews in a conference room might be less convenient for you. However, on-site interviews provide the greatest opportunity for you to observe further how the procedures and processes are carried out by each employee. On-site interviews also provide the opportunity for you to ask the employee if he or she would mind showing you how he or she performs a task, demonstrating the procedures the employee uses. On the other hand, an employee who works in an open area might feel uncomfortable being interviewed if other employees can overhear the conversation. A conference room offers more privacy, if needed.

Sixth, compile your documentation from the interviews. Index and/or code the results of your interview for easier retrieval later.

CONDUCT SURVEYS Information can also be collected from employees using surveys. These instruments ask questions to collect information about how employees perform their responsibilities. The questions can be either open-ended or close-ended. Close-ended questions have defined answers from which the employee chooses. For example, if the employee is asked if he or she counts the cash drawer before starting a shift, the defined answers would *Yes* or *No*. On the other hand, an open-ended question would ask the employee to list the steps he or she performs when there is a shift change. Open-ended questions are preferred to elicit the most useful information.

PREPARE NARRATIVES After you collect the documentation from the current system as well as documentation you prepare from observations, interviews, and surveys, you will need to organize all the documentation into a workable form. Sometimes a narrative is prepared that tells the story of the processes and procedures used to conduct business. Occasionally, it works out well to ask the employees to tell the story, or narrative, of what they do each day, preferably in an electronic form.

Figure 4.24 is an example narrative for EspressoCoffee used to describe the process for creating a sales invoice.

Secrets of a Well-Designed Business Process Map: Avoid Black Holes, Miracles, and Gray Holes

As you can see from the business process maps in this chapter, ten different people might draw the same business process in ten different ways. Some business process maps are more well designed than others. One way to improve the design of your business process map is to verify

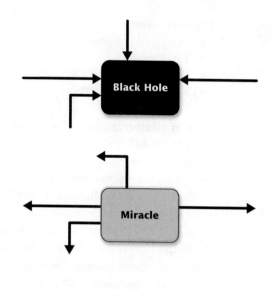

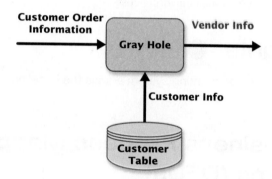

FIGURE 4.27

Common Errors: Black Hole, Miracle, and Gray Hole

that you do not have any of the three most common errors of business process mapping shown for you in Figure 4.27:

- Black hole
- Miracle
- Gray hole

The **black hole** error occurs when the data is shown going into an activity, but no data exits. A black hole in the universe has high gravity force, which attracts and absorbs everything, including light. In a business process map, a black hole takes in data, but there is no output data.

The **miracle** error occurs when miraculously something comes out of a process, but there was no input into the process. As illustrated in Figure 4.27, there are four data flow lines coming out of the process, but there is no data flow line going into the process.

The **gray hole** error occurs when the input data does not generate the output information. For example, if you enter customer information into an activity *process customer order* but the output data is vendor information, there is an inconsistency between the input data and the output data.

My Connection...
- Short Exercise 4.31

Chapter Highlights

How are accounting systems developed today? Today, most accounting systems are developed in two stages. First, baseline accounting software is selected. Then the accounting software is customized to meet the enterprise's specific needs.

What are the modules and transactions in a baseline accounting system? The modules and

transactions in the baseline accounting system model consist of the following:

Vendors module
- Create Purchase Orders
- Receive Items
- Enter Bills

Customers module
- Create Invoices
- Receive Customer Payments

Employees module
- Enter Time
- Calculate Payroll

Banking module
- Pay Bills
- Make Deposits
- Pay Employees
- Pay Payroll Liabilities

Financial module
- Adjusting Entries
- Correcting Entries
- Closing Entries
- General Ledger/Other

Reports module
- Management Reports
- Tax Reports
- Financial/Regulatory Reports
- Sustainability Reports

How is customization of accounting systems documented? Customizing an accounting system involves documenting the specific needs of the enterprise using business process maps to provide a detailed view of the enterprise's business processes. Business process mapping notations include flowcharts, data flow diagrams, UML, and BPMN diagrams. Each module of the baseline model can be customized to meet the enterprise's needs. Additional modules might also be needed to provide the required customization, such as a production module to track manufacturing costs.

Accounting System Insights

Insight No. 13 The ABCs of accounting systems are the accounting system equals the baseline system plus customization.

Chapter Extension 4: Business Process Mapping Using Data Flow Diagrams (DFDs)

See the text website for the Chapter 4 Extension: Business Process Mapping Using Data Flow Diagrams (DFDs).

Active Review

Study less. Learn more. Make connections.

4.1 Refer to the chapter opener, *Meet Social Business.* In your opinion, is it easier to document business processes when working together as a team? Or as an individual?

4.2 Refer to the chapter opener, *Meet Social Business.* In your opinion, how important is it to document business processes?

4.3 Discuss how the baseline accounting system model corresponds to the value chain shown in Figure 4.1.

4.4 List activities in the customers module of the baseline accounting system. Why are these events commonly found in most enterprises?

4.5 List activities in the vendors module of the baseline accounting system. Why are these events commonly seen in most enterprises?

4.6 Discuss how information is collected to prepare business process maps.

4.7 Discuss the process of developing annotated narratives.

4.8 Discuss how Accounting Insight No. 13 solves a dilemma that many enterprises face.

4.9 Discuss the advantages and disadvantages of BPMN 2.0 compared with other process mapping techniques.

4.10 Discuss why an enterprise might need to customize the baseline accounting system.

4.11 Discuss how BPMN 2.0 process mapping can allow accountants to customize accounting processes.

4.12 Discuss the similarities and differences between flowcharting and process mapping.

Key Terms Check

Understanding the language used at the crossroads of accounting and IT is key to your success.

4.13 Match the following terms and definitions.

a. Process map diagrams.	____ 1. A series of activities and decisions
b. Flowchart	____ 2. A modeling language popular among IT professionals
c. DFD	____ 3. Graphically, describes process and data flow
d. d.UML	____ 4. Provides greater detail than flowcharting
e. BPMN 2.0	____ 5. Graphically describes the process of accounting system

4.14 Match the following BPMN 2.0 terms and definitions.

a. Event	____ 1. A red circle, it is used to show a process termination in a BPMN 2.0 diagram.
b. Activity	____ 2. A rectangle, it is used to group and organize activities in a BPMN 2.0 diagram.
c. Gateway	____ 3. Are used for forking and merging process flows
d. Data Store	____ 4. Triggers, intermediate, and end process
e. Data Object	____ 5. It shows actions performed in a process map.
f. Swimlane	____ 6. Documents or data records
g. Start	____ 7. Database
h. End	____ 8. A green circle, it is used to show a process initiation in a BPMN 2.0 diagram.

Practice Test

4.15 A business process typically associated with the vendors module of the baseline accounting system is:

a. Create invoices

b. Receive payments

c. Make deposits

d. Receive items

4.16 A business process typically associated with the customers module of the baseline accounting system is:

a. Pay bills

b. Receive items

c. Make deposits

d. Create purchase orders

4.17 A business process typically associated with the employees module of the baseline accounting system is:

a. Enter time

b. Make deposits

c. Pay bills

d. Receive payments

4.18 Which of the following is most likely to happen as a result of Business Process Management?

a. Business processes will be streamlined to reduce costs and improve efficiency.

b. The accounting database table will be updated.

c. More complexity is added to accounting processes.

d. Business size is increased.

4.19 In a BPMN diagram, a gateway:

a. Triggers, interrupts, or ends a process

b. Is an activity performed

c. Is used for forking and merging process flows

d. Shows how data enters a system, how it moves through a system from process to process, where it is stored, and how it exits the system.

4.20 A decision symbol in the flowchart is similar to the _____ symbol in a BPMN diagram.

   a. Data Object
   b. Activity
   c. Gateway
   d. Event

4.21 In a process, there are five major participants. Three of these participants are internal to the company and two are external. How many swimlanes are there in the process map depicting this process?

   a. 2
   b. 3
   c. Cannot be determined at this time
   d. 5

4.22 Annotating a narrative involves:

   a. Creating a business process map organizer
   b. Writing a general description of the business activity
   c. Identifying and underlining the activities in the narrative
   d. Identifying and underlining the participants in the narrative

4.23 Which columns of the business process map organizer do you use if you are developing a flowchart?

   a. Activity, Gateway, and Swimlane
   b. Data store, Activity, and Gateway
   c. Activity, Swimlane, and Gateway
   d. All columns

4.24 A streamlined, effective approach to business process mapping is to:

   a. Learn about different process map modeling languages
   b. Start with the baseline accounting system
   c. Start to draw flowchart for the business process
   d. Identify activities included in the business process

Exercises

Each Exercise relates to one of the major questions addressed in the chapter and is labeled with the question number in green.

Short Exercises

Warm up with these short exercises.

4.25 Match the following BPMN 2.0 terms with the appropriate example. **(Q4.5)**

a. Activity	___ 1. Customer
b. Gateway	___ 2. CUSTOMER table
c. Data store	___ 3. Verify customer credit
d. Data object	___ 4. Credit Card Company
e. Swimlane	___ 5. Generate shipping labels
	___ 6. Customer lack of credit notification email
	___ 7. Is customer credit verified?
	___ 8. Authorize shipping
	___ 9. Shipping confirmation notification
	___ 10. Warehouse

4.26 Match the following processes and their sequence with the appropriate baseline accounting system module. **(Q4.2)**

a. Create invoices
b. Receive items.
c. Enter bills.
d. Create purchase orders.
e. Enter time.
f. Pay employees.
g. Calculate payroll.
h. Pay bills.
i. Make deposits.
j. Receive customer payments.
k. Pay payroll liabilities.

Transaction Cycle	Process
Purchasing Cycle	
Purchasing Cycle	
Purchasing Cycle	
Sales Cycle	
Sales Cycle	
Sales Cycle	
Payroll Cycle	
Payroll Cycle	
Payroll Cycle	
Payroll Cycle	

4.27 Write the following activities in the correct sequence flow? **(Q4.4, 4.5)**

a. Authorize payroll
b. Calculate withholding
c. Calculate net pay
d. Calculate gross pay

4.28 For a bank ATM transaction, identify the following: **(Q4.6)**

1. Swimlanes (major participants)
2. Activities
3. Gateways
4. Data Stores
5. Data Objects

4.29 Select an authentic enterprise of your choice, and describe how the enterprise processes sales transactions with customers. **(Q4.6)**

List the following:

1. Swimlanes (major participant)
2. Activities
3. Gateways
4. Data Stores
5. Data Objects

4.30 Annotate the following narrative, labeling and numbering the activities. **(Q4.6)**

Customers select items to purchase and place them in their online shopping cart on Amazon.com. When customers are ready to check out, the credit card information is entered. To process the order, customers click the checkout button.

4.31 Identify errors in the following BPMN 2.0 diagram. **(Q4.5, Q4.6)**

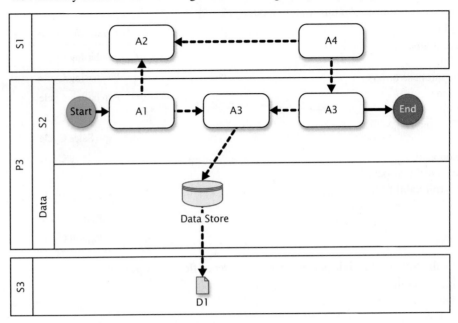

4.32 Write a narrative for the following flowchart. **(Q4.4)**

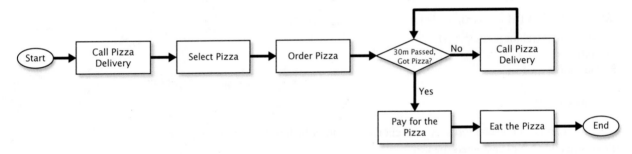

4.33 Write a narrative for the following BPM 2.0 diagram. **(Q4.5)**

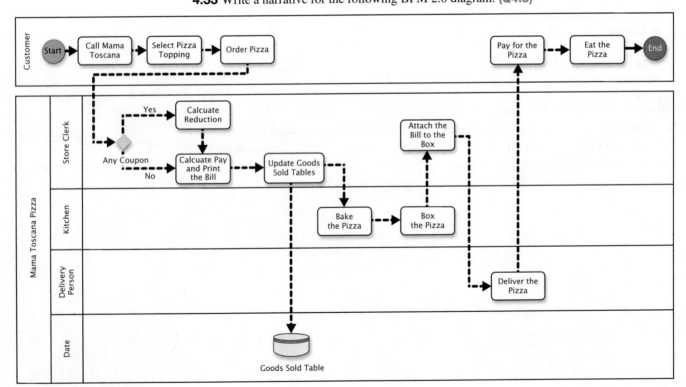

It's Your Call

This is your training ground. These scenarios provide you with the opportunity to use your knowledge and professional skills.

4.34 You have been called in as a consultant to verify the accuracy of the BPMN 2.0 diagrams documenting Soleil Corporation's current business processes. What steps would you take to verify the accuracy of the BPMN? How would you document any discrepancies to include in your consultant's report?

Prepare a short email to the president of the company outlining your plan for verifying the accuracy of the BPMN diagrams. **(Q4.2, 4.3, 4.5, 4.6)**

4.35 Your supervisor has asked you to represent the accounting department on a project team charged with streamlining business processes to cut costs. Your assignment is to observe and document all current business processes as performed by accounting professionals. Some of your coworkers have approached you and asked if your job is to eliminate their jobs. What do you say? How do you communicate with your accounting colleagues what you are doing? **(Q4.3, 4.4, 4.5, 4.6)**

4.36 You are the accounting representative on a project team to streamline business processes for your company. The team leader has asked you to prepare a short email for the team that outlines the steps that would be used to document the business processes using flow charts and BPMN 2.0 diagrams. He asked that you keep it short and simple so that team members can use it as a checklist.

Prepare a short email to the team leader responding to his request. **(Q4.3, 4.4, 4.5)**

4.37 MiaPizza is a small family-run pizza parlor that accepts only cash. One of the owner's sons has just graduated from college and is urging his dad to begin accepting credit cards in order to increase sales. The son is one of your good friends. Knowing that you are taking an AIS course, he offers a free pizza dinner in exchange for talking to him about how to implement credit card processing into the business. He wants to know more about the steps (activities) you would advise he take to document the new business process.

To prepare for your free pizza dinner, write a short summary of your notes, with the steps he should use to document the proposed business process. **(Q4.6)**

4.38 Your supervisor has asked you to represent the accounting department on a process-improvement team charged with optimizing processes workflow. Your assignment is to observe and document the online current sales process as performed by accounting professionals. What do you include in your document? **(Q4.5, 4.6)**

Tech in Practice

These technology in practice exercises are perfect for both individuals and teams.

Tech Exercises

Sharpen your skills with these technology exercises. Watch these software videos at www.pearsonhighered.com/kay.

4.39

Tech Tool: Spreadsheet Software or Visio Software

Software Videos: MS Excel BPMN Diagram Drawing or Ms Visio BPMN Diagram Drawing

Use the following business process map organizer to complete the corresponding BPMN 2.0 and flowchart diagrams.

Business Process Map Organizer			
Activity	Gateway	Swimlane (BPMN Only)	Date Stores (BPMN Only)
Place Order		Customer	
Process Customer Order		Accounting	
	Verify Customer Identity		
	Verify Customer Credit	Accounting	Customer Table
	Verify Items Available	Accounting	Item Table
Authorize Shipping		Accounting	
Pick Items		Warehouse	Item Table
Ship Items with Pick List		Warehouse	
Notify Accounting Items Shipped		Warehouse	
Generate Invoice		Accounting	Customer Table
Sales Order Table
Sales Order Line Table
Item Table
Account Receivable Table

Notice in this business process that customers do not pay when they receive their orders' items. They will pay on the due date stated on the billing statement.

4.40

Tech Tool: Spreadsheet Software or Visio Software

Software Videos: MS Excel BPMN Diagram and Flowchart Drawing or MS Visio Flowchart or Diagram Drawing

MiaPizza customers place an order by calling the store. They place their order after selecting the type of pizza. Often, customers will call the store if their order is not delivered after 60 minutes. They pay for the pizza when it is delivered. (This exercise is only focused on customer's side ordering and receiving, not the pizza delivery process.)

1. Annotate the narrative.
2. Create business process map organizer.
3. Build the corresponding flowchart.
4. Build the corresponding BPMN.

4.41

Tech Tool: Spreadsheet Software or Visio Software

Software Videos: MS Excel BPMN Diagram and Flowchart Drawing or MS Visio Flowchart or BPMN Diagram Drawing

Use the following narrative to complete the accompanying requirements.

MiaPizza is a small family-run pizza parlor that accepts only cash. A customer places a pizza order by calling the store. MiaPizza takes the order over the phone. The order is entered into the system. Customer pizza is prepared and boxed. A customer receipt is printed and taped to the pizza box. Then the pizza is delivered.

1. Annotate the narrative.
2. Prepare a business process map organizer.
3. Build the corresponding flowchart.
4. Build the corresponding BPMN 2.0 diagram.

4.42

Tech Tool: Spreadsheet Software or Visio Software

Software Videos: MS Excel BPMN Diagram and Flowchart Drawing or MS Visio Flowchart or BPMN Diagram Drawing

Select an authentic enterprise of your choice.

1. Observe the sales transactions of this enterprise.
2. List the swimlanes, activities, gateways, data stores, and data objects that you observe.
3. Draw a flowchart to document the sales transaction, showing activities as well as flow of activities.
4. Draw a BPMN diagram to document the sales transactions, showing swimlanes, activities, gateways, data stores, and data objects.
5. Do you see any improvements the enterprise might make? List your recommendations to streamline and improve the business process.

4.43

Tech Tool: Spreadsheet Software or Visio Software

Software Videos: MS Excel BPMN Diagram and Flowchart Drawing or MS Visio Flowchart or BPMN Diagram Drawing

Use the following BPMN 2.0 diagram for Bamboo Furniture and the narrative to complete the accompanying requirements.

Subprocess Process Customer Order narrative:

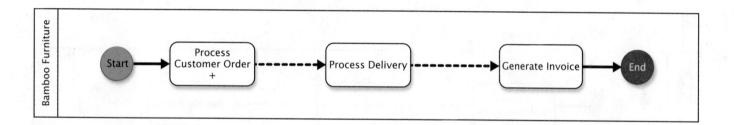

Bamboo Furniture customers view and make furniture selections on the showroom floor. Employees check item availability using the enterprise database. If the items are available in the warehouse, the employee obtains the customer information to place the sales order. If the items are not available, the customer is notified. If the customer chooses to still place the order, the customer information is obtained and the order is placed with the manufacturer. Customer credit is verified by sending an authorization request to the credit card company for the amount of the purchase. After the customer credit is verified, sales order information is stored in the SALES ORDER and SALES ORDER LINE tables. If the customer does not have a good credit standing, the customer order is rejected and the customer is notified.

1. Annotate the narrative.
2. Create a business process map organizer.
3. Build a flowchart diagram for the Process Customer Order subprocess.
4. Build a BPMN diagram for the Process Customer Order subprocess.

4.44

Tech Tool: Spreadsheet Software or Visio Software

Software Videos: MS Excel BPMN Diagram and Flowchart Drawing or MS Visio Flowchart or BPMN Diagram Drawing

Process Delivery subprocess narrative:

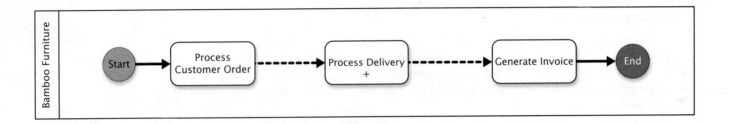

After a customer order is placed with Bamboo Furniture and the furniture is located in the warehouse, the delivery date for the furniture is scheduled. The customer is notified of the delivery date, the customer address is verified, and the appropriate database tables are updated.

1. Annotate the narrative.
2. Create a business process map organizer.
3. Build a flowchart for the Process Delivery subprocess.
4. Build BPMN diagram for the Process Delivery subprocess.

4.45

Tech Tool: Spreadsheet Software or Visio Software
Software Videos: MS Excel BPMN Diagram and Flowchart Drawing or MS Visio Flowchart or BPMN Diagram Drawing

Generate Invoice subprocess narrative:

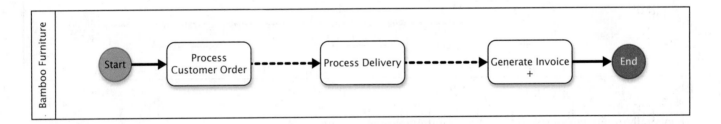

After the delivery date is scheduled, customer and sales order information is updated. The invoice is printed and delivered with the furniture to the customer.

1. Annotate the narrative.
2. Create a business process map organizer.
3. Build a flowchart for the Generate Invoice subprocess.
4. Build a BPMN diagram for the Generate Invoice subprocess.

4.46

Tech Tool: Spreadsheet Software or Visio Software
Software Videos: MS Excel BPMN Diagram and Flowchart Drawing or MS Visio Flowchart or BPMN Diagram Drawing

An employee at the English Oak Furniture, after observing the sales quoting approval process, prepares the following short document.

Salesperson sets up an account detail, checks the product availability, and prepares customer price quote. The salesperson verifies if discount approval is needed. If an approval is needed, then a sales manager approves sales discounts. Then a salesperson sends a quote to the customer and update the sales data. Customer receives and reviews quote.

Prepare a business process map organizer for the sales quoting approval process.

4.47

Tech Tool: Spreadsheet Software or Visio Software

Software Videos: MS Excel BPMN Diagram and Flowchart Drawing or MS Visio Flowchart or BPMN Diagram Drawing

Use the English Oak Furniture sales quoting approval business process map organizer that you prepared for the preceding exercise and build a flowchart and BPMN diagram.

Go Online

In the fast-paced world of technology, your skill at finding answers fast can be vital. Go online and experience typical assignments you may encounter as a professional.

4.48 You have been assigned to the project team responsible for documenting business processes for accounting. You are scheduled to make a short presentation about the pros and cons of different modeling tools used for documenting business processes. Go online and search for business process modeling techniques. What would you say in your presentation summary?

4.49 You have been called in as a consultant to conduct a feasibility study for a new accounting system for a client, LaLune Enterprises. You have been asked to speak to the accounting department about purchasing a baseline system versus customizing their existing baseline system to meet the organization's specific needs. Go online and research the advantages and disadvantages of customizing baseline systems. What would you say to the accounting department on this topic? Prepare your speaking notes for the meeting. Write a short email draft that you prepare in advance to send right after the meeting.

4.50 You have been assigned to the process-improvement team responsible for documenting business processes for accounting. You are scheduled to make a short presentation about the pros and cons of different process mapping tools used for documenting business processes. Go online and search for business process mapping techniques. What would you say in your presentation summary?

Technology Projects

These technology projects are perfect for both individuals and teams.

Technology Project 4

Tech Tool: Spreadsheet Software or Visio Software

Software Videos: MS Excel BPMN Diagram and Fowchart Drawing or MS Visio Flowchart or BPMN Diagram Drawing

Technology Project 4 is your opportunity to practice building BPMN diagrams for iSportDesign. With this project, you will use either spreadsheet software or Visio software. (Ask your instructor which software you will be using to complete this technology project.) Your deliverables for the project include the following:

Deliverable 1. A business process map organizer
Deliverable 2. A flowchart diagram
Deliverable 3. A BPMN 2.0 diagram

Visit www.pearsonhighered.com/kay to do the following:

1. Download Technology Project 4 instructions.
2. Download files provided online for your convenience in completing the project deliverables.
3. Watch the videos with software instructions to complete this project at www.pearsonhighered.com/kay.

5

Business Processes: Purchasing, Sales, and Payroll Cycles

What Do You Do When Your Employer Is Transferring Your Promising Project? Meet SAP.

Can you imagine working on a promising project, only to learn that your employer is transferring the project to someone else? Would you think about founding your own company in order to keep working on the project? That's exactly what five IBM engineers did. The five engineers were working on a systems project for IBM when the project was transferred to another unit. The five engineers thought the project was so promising they founded their own company so they could continue working on it. Meet SAP.

What did the former IBM engineers see that made the project look so promising? They had noticed that client after client was developing similar computer programs, and they saw an opportunity to create standardized enterprise software. SAP was based on the premise that business processes could be modeled in a standard way.

The first version of SAP was an accounting software named R/1 issued in 1973. Headquartered in Walldorf, Germany, SAP AG products today are used by AT&T, Coca-Cola, and approximately 76,000 other customers in 120 countries. Employing more than 51,800 people in more than 50 countries, SAP developed a commercially available universal baseline system based on best practice business processes.

By the way, do you know what SAP stands for? *Systeme, Anwendungen, und Produkte in Datenverarbeitung Aktiengesellschaft* (English translation: Systems, Applications, and Products in Data Processing AG or SAP AG).

Crossroads

At the crossroads of accounting and IT, business processes designed using IT tools such as business process maps are the underpinning for the design of the accounting system.

My Questions

Q 5.1	How do I customize an accounting system?
Q 5.2	How do I customize the sales cycle?
Q 5.3	How do I customize the purchasing cycle?
Q 5.4	How do I customize the payroll cycle?
Q 5.5	How do I customize the financial cycle?

How Do I Customize an Accounting System?

Accounting Insight No. 14: Gap Analysis

Accounting Insight No. 14 states that when customizing a baseline accounting system, perform a gap analysis: Determine the gap between the baseline system and the customization desired.

In a **gap analysis**, the gap between the baseline modules and the customization required to meet enterprise-specific needs is analyzed. Once the gap analysis is completed, there are two general approaches to completing the customization: big bang and stages.

ACCOUNTING INSIGHT NO. 14
Gap Analysis =
Baseline System −
Customization Desired

Big Bang vs. Stages Customization

The **big bang** approach to customization involves customizing and installing customer, vendor, employee, and remaining modules for the entire enterprise at the same time. The advantage to this approach is that the new system goes "live" all at once. This is also the biggest disadvantage. The enormity of installing an enterprise system for a huge enterprise can be overwhelming in terms of resources and logistics. If there are unresolved issues when the entire system goes live, it can be crippling for the enterprise. Hershey Foods Corp. (now Hershey Company) experienced big bang system implementation difficulties that prevented the company from shipping orders to customers during its busiest season. When using the big bang approach, timing of the implementation can play a crucial role in its success. Troubleshooting a complex new system implementation may take weeks. This is easier to accomplish when it is not during an enterprise's busy season (CFO.com).

The **stages** approach customizes one module or geographic location at a time, stage by stage, until the entire enterprise has been converted to the new system. This approach permits developers to pilot the modules, testing and resolving issues before moving to the next stage. There are advantages and disadvantages to this approach as well. One advantage is the ability to test and resolve issues on a smaller scale, one stage at a time. The disadvantage is that the timeline for such a project may seem prolonged.

Whether you use the big bang or stages approach when customizing an accounting system, workflow (the flow or order in which work is performed) must be considered.

Workflow Management System

Each step in the business process and workflow must be documented using a business process map. Some enterprise software uses a workflow management system that automates the workflow, automatically forwarding the electronic document to the next step in the business process. Some accounting software may facilitate, but not automate the steps. For example, as seen in the previous chapter QuickBooks accounting software uses a coach on its Home page to designate the order of the steps in the workflow. The steps in the workflow are numbered in the order they are to be completed. However, the software does not automatically forward documents for approval.

Enterprise software, such as Oracle (oracle.com) or SAP (sap.com), provides a workflow management system that automatically forwards documents to the next user in the workflow. For example, many colleges and universities have installed enterprise software with automated workflow management systems. A purchase order may be authorized electronically by the marketing department chairperson. The electronic purchase order is then automatically forwarded to the next step in the business process, review by the business school dean. When the dean logs in, he or she is notified of any items that require attention, such as the pending purchase order awaiting approval. The dean then electronically approves the pending purchase, and the purchase order is automatically forwarded to the next step in the workflow, the purchasing department.

As business processes for a new system are planned, workflow management is also considered.

Customize or Not?

Customizing a baseline system can prove costly with unexpected cost overruns and delays. Some enterprises discovered it was more cost effective to re-engineer their business processes, adapting their processes to fit the baseline commercial system. Changing their business processes to match the baseline system, the enterprises eliminated the need for costly custom programming. Programming to customize the baseline system may not carry forward into later versions, costing some enterprises millions of dollars for customizations that must be abandoned or redone.

Next, we will look at how to customize EspressoCoffee's sales, purchasing, payroll, and financial cycles using business process mapping.

How Do I Customize the Sales Cycle?

EspressoCoffee
Company

In this chapter, we continue to focus on customizing modules in the baseline accounting system model (Figure 5.1). In the previous chapter, you saw how business process maps were used to document EspressoCoffee's business process for creating an invoice. Figure 5.2 shows the flowchart for creating an invoice. Figure 5.3 shows the BPMN diagram for creating an invoice and the corresponding database tables. The four database tables used by the create invoice BPMN diagram are CUSTOMER, SALES ORDER, SALES ORDER LINE, and ITEM tables. Each database table is shown with its related fields. A sample invoice is shown in Figure 5.4 for EspressoCoffee. This is the end result of the create invoice business process.

Now, we will illustrate business process maps for the remainder of the sales cycle. As shown in Figure 5.5, you can see that the activities making up the sales cycle include the following activities in the customer module:

- *Create invoices.*
- *Receive customer payments.*

The activity in the banking module that relates to the sales cycle is:

- *Make deposits.*

Next, the *receive customer payments* and *make deposits* activities will be customized to meet EspressoCoffee's specific needs using business process maps. We will show example business

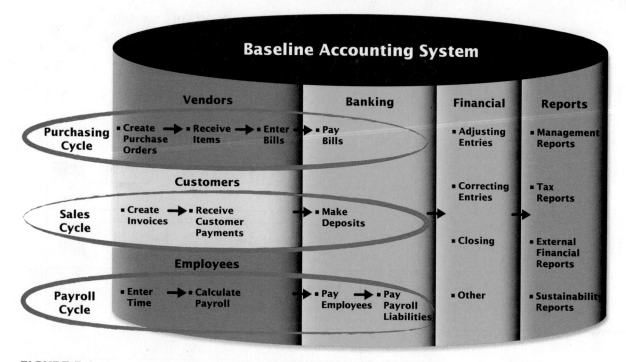

FIGURE 5.1

Baseline Accounting System with Transactions

process maps using flowchart and BPMN 2.0 notations. As you may recall from Chapter 4, one advantage to using flowchart notation is simplicity. For this reason, accounting professionals may prefer flowcharts. However, flowcharts may not include the detail that IT professionals need. So IT professionals may prefer more detailed process maps. BPMN 2.0 notation was developed to bridge the communication gap between business users, such as accountants, and IT professionals. To prepare you to work with both accounting and IT professionals, both flowchart and BPMN 2.0 notation will be demonstrated for business process maps in this chapter.

> The details of the database tables are shown at the bottom of Figure 5.3, including the fields and table relationships.
>
> As we proceed through this chapter, database table names are shown on the BPMN diagrams in the Data swimlane. Keep in mind that when data flow is shown going into or from a database table, data will be entered, updated, and retrieved using database field contents within the table.

My Connection...
- Short Exercise 5.25
- Tech Exercise 5.33

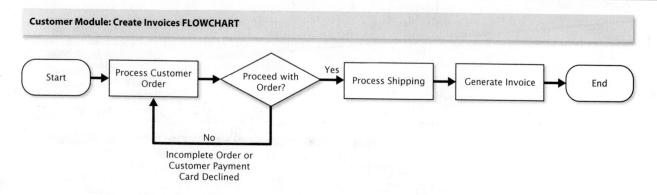

Customer Module: Create Invoices FLOWCHART

FIGURE 5.2

Create Invoices Flowchart for EspressoCoffee

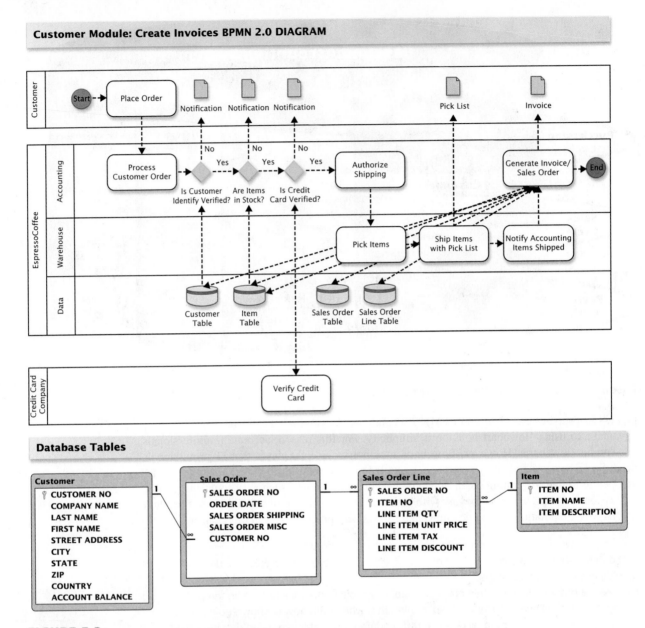

Customer Module: Create Invoices BPMN 2.0 DIAGRAM

Database Tables

FIGURE 5.3

EspressoCoffee Create Invoices BPMN Diagram with Database Tables

Pair and Share: Can you match the database tables in the BPMN diagram with the MS Access database tables displaying fields?

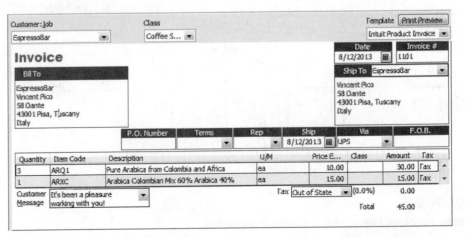

FIGURE 5.4

EspressoCoffee Customer Invoice

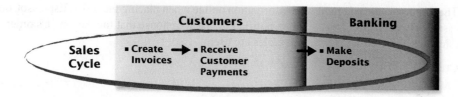

FIGURE 5.5

Sales Cycle

Can you find this sales cycle in Figure 5.1?

Receive Customer Payments Business Process Map

The business process maps to document EspressoCoffee's process for recording customer payments are shown in Figures 5.6A and 5.6B. Note that the baseline *receive customer payments* activity has been customized for EspressoCoffee's specific needs.

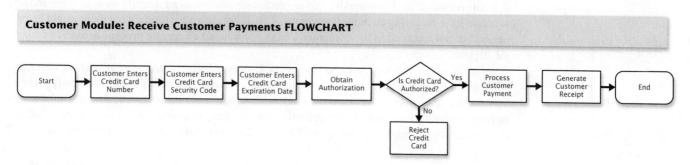

FIGURE 5.6A

Receive Customer Payments Flowchart for EspressoCoffee

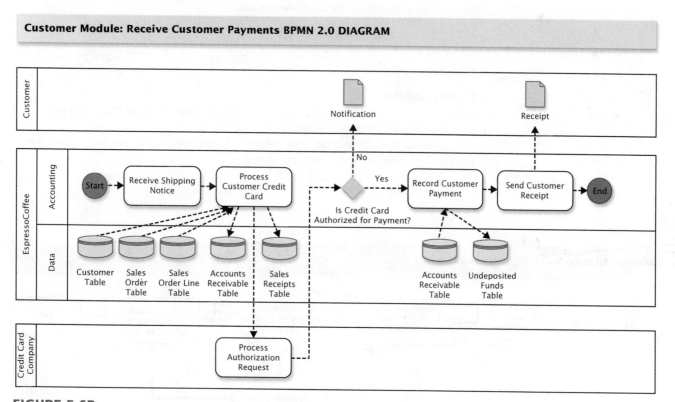

FIGURE 5.6B

Receive Customer Payments BPMN Diagram for EspressoCoffee

Pair and Share: How would an UNDEPOSITED FUNDS table be used when recording customer payments?

The customer entered credit card information online when placing the order. EspressoCoffee processes the credit card payment when notified by the warehouse that the customer's order has been shipped. The following database tables are used:

- CUSTOMER table
- SALES ORDER table
- SALES ORDER LINE table

Data is retrieved from these database tables to process the customer credit card payment with the credit card company. Then a customer receipt is emailed to the customer. The database tables are updated.

Make Deposits Business Process Map

After EspressoCoffee processes the customers' online payments, it records the associated bank deposit. As mentioned previously, this is commonly shown as an activity in a baseline model separate from receiving customer payments. This is because a customer's payment might be received but not recorded in the company's bank account, so a separate process is used to record the deposit.

The business process maps to document EspressoCoffee's process for making deposits (Figures 5.7A and 5.7B) have been customized for EspressoCoffee's specific needs. When the credit card company receives the customer credit card information, it sends customer payment information, such as the authorization number, to EspressoCoffee. EspressoCoffee then processes the bank deposit. The following database tables are updated accordingly:

- CUSTOMER table
- CASH RECEIPTS table
- CASH ACCOUNT table
- GENERAL LEDGER table

This completes the sales cycle for EspressoCoffee.

Crossroads

Accountants refer to a customer's balance as an account receivable. So this would be placed in an ACCOUNTS RECEIVABLE database table.

An IT professional, such as a database designer, might also put the customer balance as a field in the CUSTOMER table to speed up retrieval.

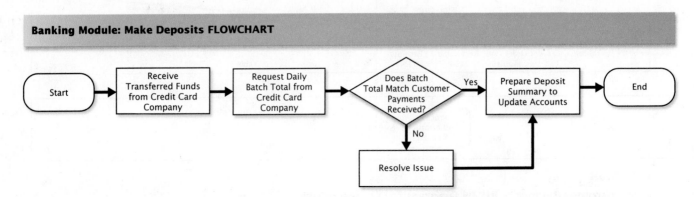

Banking Module: Make Deposits FLOWCHART

FIGURE 5.7A

Make Deposits Flowchart for EspressoCoffee

Banking Module: Make Deposits BPMN 2.0 DIAGRAM

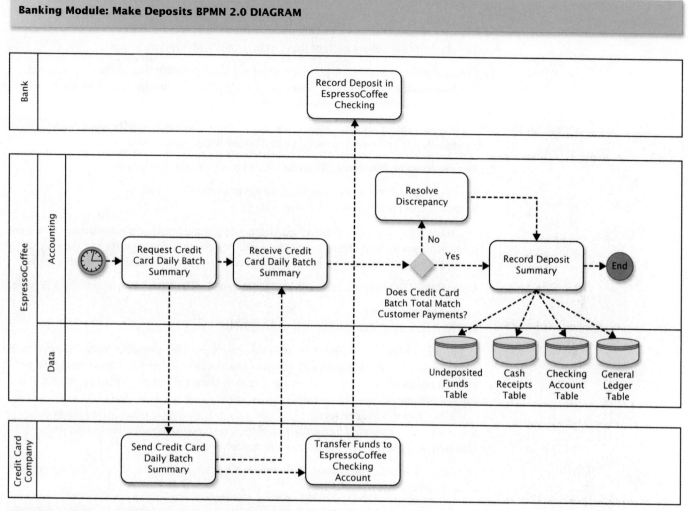

FIGURE 5.7B

Make Deposits BPMN Diagram for EspressoCoffee

Pair and Share: How do the flowchart and BPMN diagram for making deposits differ? How are they the same?

How Do I Customize the Purchasing Cycle?

Next, you will learn about customizing the purchasing cycle for EspressoCoffee using business process maps. As shown in Figure 5.8, the components that make up the vendor module include the following:

- *Create purchase orders.*
- *Receive items.*
- *Enter bills.*

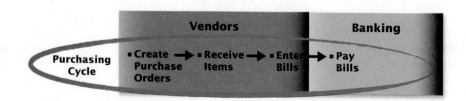

FIGURE 5.8

Purchasing Cycle

Can you find this purchasing cycle in Figure 5.1?

In the banking module, the activity that relates to the purchasing cycle is as follows:

- *Pay bills.*

Additional information about each of these transactions with vendors follows.

1. ***Create Purchase Orders.*** A purchase order is a document that lists items to be ordered, purchase order number, vendor, date, etc. A copy of this document is kept by the enterprise, and another copy is sent to the vendor.

   For example, EspressoCoffee Company prepares purchase orders to purchase espresso beans and espresso and cappuccino machines from its Italian suppliers.

2. ***Receive Items or Inventory.*** The items received by the enterprise are:

   a. compared to items ordered as listed on the purchase order, and
   b. recorded as received on a receiving report.

   When EspressoCoffee receives shipments of espresso beans and espresso machines, the receiving department compares the items on the purchase order to verify that the order is correct. Items received are recorded on the receiving report and in the accounting system.

3. ***Enter Bills.*** The enterprise receives a bill for the goods. The bill is compared to the following:

   a. The purchase order
   b. The receiving report listing the items received

   EspressoCoffee's vendors send bills separately from the shipment, either through mail or electronically. When EspressoCoffee receives the bill for orders, it crosschecks the bill with the purchase order and the receiving report. Once the bill is verified as correct, it is entered into the accounting system.
   When EspressoCoffee receives bills for services, such as insurance and utility bills that are not accompanied by purchase orders and receiving reports, those bills are reviewed and entered into the accounting system.

4. ***Pay Bills.*** When the bill is paid, the company Checking account is reduced for the amount of the payment.

   EspressoCoffee Company pays its bills when due from its company Checking account.

Create Purchase Orders Business Process Map

A flowchart (Figure 5.9A) and a BPMN diagram (Figure 5.9B) document EspressoCoffee's process for creating purchase orders. Notice in the BPMN diagram that the Start event symbol displays a clock in the center of the symbol. This indicates the event is scheduled at a specific time. In this case, each day at 9:00 PM, EspressoCoffee's system automatically checks inventory stock levels in the ITEM table.

For items that need to be reordered, a purchase order (PO) is processed. To process a purchase order, the following four database tables are used:

- VENDOR table
- PURCHASE ORDER table
- PURCHASE ORDER LINE table
- ITEM table

After reviewing the PO, an employee authorizes it by entering his or her user ID. The database tables are updated. EspressoCoffee then generates a PO that is emailed to the vendor. A sample EspressoCoffee purchase order is shown in Figure 5.10.

Intersection Table...
The PURCHASE ORDER LINE table is an intersection table required to eliminate the many-to-many relationship between the PURCHASE ORDER table and the ITEM table.

My Connection...
- Short Exercise 5.26
- Tech Exercise 5.34

Vendor Module: Create Purchase Orders FLOWCHART

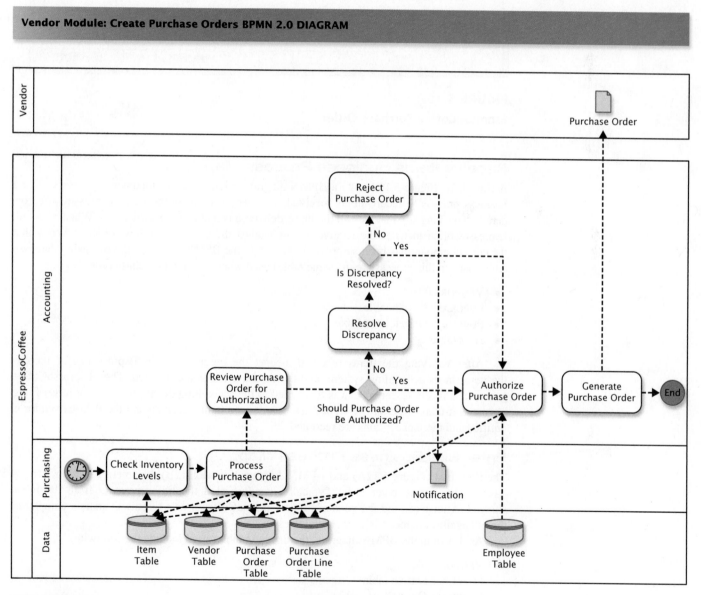

FIGURE 5.9A

Create Purchase Orders Flowchart for EspressoCoffee

Vendor Module: Create Purchase Orders BPMN 2.0 DIAGRAM

FIGURE 5.9B

Create Purchase Orders BPMN Diagram for EspressoCoffee

Pair and Share: Why is the activity, Authorize Purchase Order, necessary?

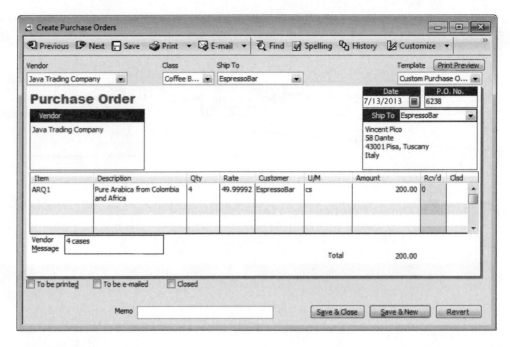

FIGURE 5.10

EspressoCoffee Purchase Order

Receive Items Business Process Map

A flowchart (Figure 5.11A) and a BPMN diagram (Figure 5.11B) document EspressoCoffee's business process to record items received. The vendor delivers the items EspressoCoffee ordered. A packing slip that lists all the items delivered is included with the items. When received, EspressoCoffee matches the received items against the original purchase order to verify that the correct amount has been shipped. As shown in the BPMN diagram, the following database tables used in this process are the same tables used when placing a purchase order.

- VENDOR table
- PURCHASE ORDER table
- PURCHASE ORDER LINE table
- ITEM table

After verifying the items received against the purchase order, EspressoCoffee records the items in its accounting system, and the database tables are updated. Then EspressoCoffee generates a receiving report that is forwarded to the accounting department for use in verifying payment. If there were any discrepancies between the items received and the PO, the vendor is notified and these exceptions are recorded.

Enter Bills Business Process Map

The flowchart (Figure 5.12A) and BPMN diagram (Figure 5.12B) document EspressoCoffee's business process to enter bills. Typically, vendors mail the bill separately from the items shipped. After receiving the vendor's bill, EspressoCoffee uses a three-way match, comparing the bill against the receiving report and the PO.

As shown in the BPMN diagram, the database tables used include the following:

- VENDOR table
- PURCHASE ORDER table
- PURCHASE ORDER LINE table
- ACCOUNTS PAYABLE table

After verifying the bills with the items received and the items ordered, EspressoCoffee records the bill in its accounting system, and the database tables are updated. If there are any discrepancies in the bill, the vendor is notified and the exceptions are recorded.

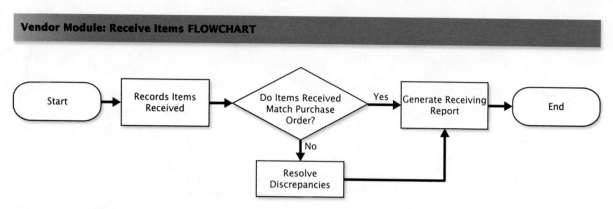

FIGURE 5.11A

Receive Items Flowchart for EspressoCoffee

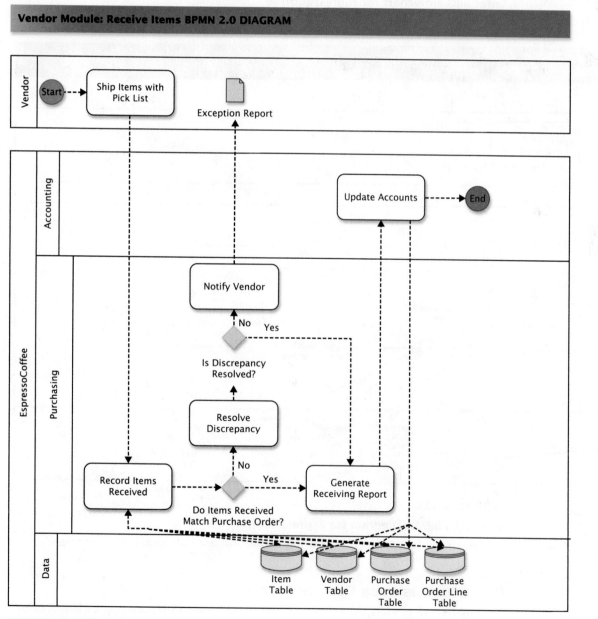

FIGURE 5.11B

Receive Items BPMN Diagram for EspressoCoffee

Pair and Share: Why is the activity Notify Vendor necessary?

Vendor Module: Enter Bills FLOWCHART

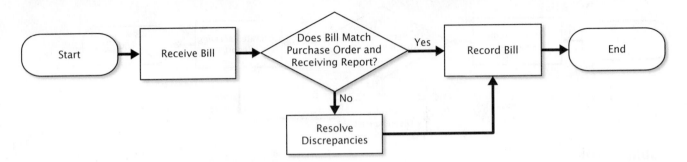

FIGURE 5.12A

Enter Bills Flowchart for EspressoCoffee

Vendor Module: Enter Bills BPMN 2.0 DIAGRAM

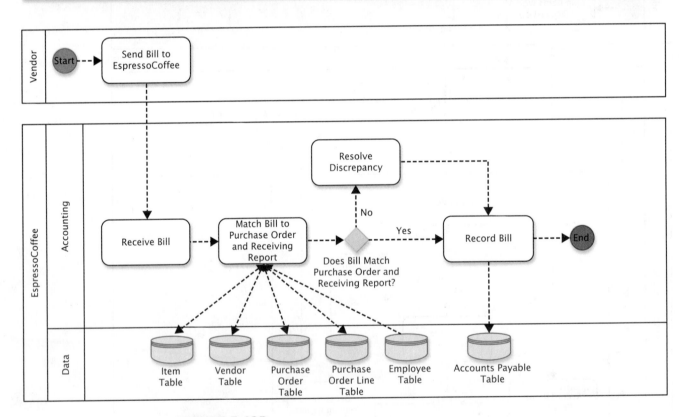

FIGURE 5.12B

Enter Bills BPMN Diagram for EspressoCoffee

Pair and Share: Can you find the three-way match that occurs in this business process?

Pay Bills Business Process Map

The flowchart (Figure 5.13A) and BPMN diagram (Figure 5.13B) document EspressoCoffee's business process for paying bills. This process is initiated by an EspressoCoffee accountant who selects bills to pay considering due dates, interest charges, and cash available.

Banking Module: Pay Bills FLOWCHART

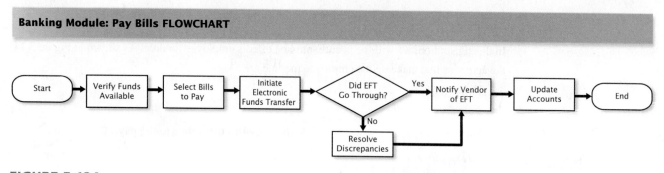

FIGURE 5.13A

Pay Bills Flowchart for EspressoCoffee

Banking Module: Pay Bills BPMN 2.0 DIAGRAM

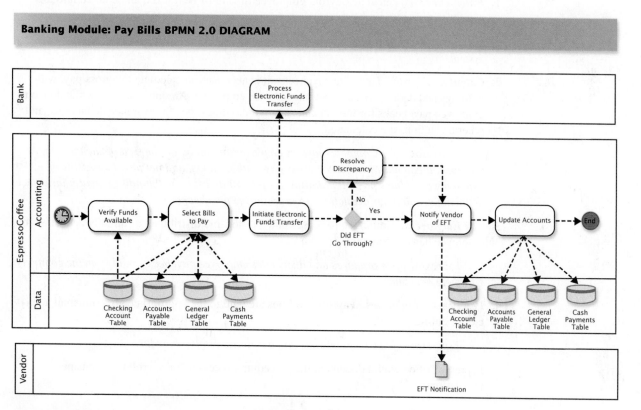

FIGURE 5.13B

Pay Bills BPMN Diagram for EspressoCoffee

Pair and Share: How would this BPMN diagram change if a check is sent to the vendor instead of electronic funds transfer?

EspressoCoffee initiates an electronic funds transfer (EFT) through its bank to make payment to the vendor. A payment notification is sent to the vendor. As shown in the BPMN diagram, the following database tables are updated accordingly:

- ACCOUNTS PAYABLE table
- CASH PAYMENTS table
- CASH ACCOUNT table
- GENERAL LEDGER table

This completes the purchasing cycle for EspressoCoffee. Next, we focus on the payroll cycle.

> Note the *pay bills* activity has been customized for EspressoCoffee's specific needs and might differ for other enterprises.

How Do I Customize the Payroll Cycle?

In this illustration, we will focus on EspressoCoffee's employee module. As shown in Figure 5.14, the activities that make up the employee module are:

- *Enter time.*
- *Calculate payroll.*

Furthermore, in the banking module the activities that relate to the payroll cycle are:

- *Pay employees.*
- *Pay payroll liabilities.*

The employee module consists of transactions related to payroll. Payroll consists of wages and salaries paid to employees. Typical activities in the payroll cycle include the following:

1. ***Enter Time.*** To calculate payroll, employee time must be tracked and entered into the system.

   EspressoCoffee Company tracks employee time using the employee computer login system.

2. ***Calculate Payroll.*** To create paychecks, it is necessary to calculate the gross pay, withholdings and deductions, and net pay for each employee. Amounts that are withheld from employee paychecks for federal and state withholdings, health insurance deductions, and other deductions are calculated.

   EspressoCoffee Company pays its employees monthly, on the first of each month. At that time, it calculates employee gross pay, withholdings, and net pay. EspressoCoffee Company calculates payroll liabilities for federal and state withholdings, health insurance deductions, and other deductions from employee paychecks.

3. ***Pay Employees.*** Employee paychecks are printed and distributed or directly deposited into employee bank accounts.

   EspressoCoffee prepares and distributes employee paychecks, paid from the company Checking account.

4. ***Pay Payroll Liabilities.*** Payroll liabilities are paid to the appropriate governmental agencies or entities.

   EspressoCoffee Company pays all payroll liabilities when due.

EspressoCoffee would document the preceding processes for payroll using business process maps.

Enter Time Business Process Map

The flowchart (Figure 5.15A) and the BPMN diagram (Figure 5.15B) document EspressoCoffee's business process for entering employee time. When an employee logs in using his or her employee ID, the system logs the time. When the employee logs out, the system logs that time. Then the system calculates and stores the time worked.

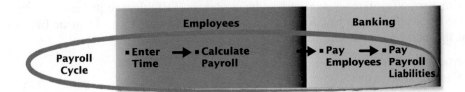

FIGURE 5.14

Payroll Cycle

Can you find this payroll cycle in Figure 5.1?

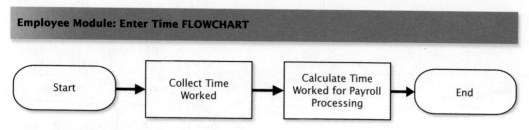

FIGURE 5.15A

Enter Time Flowchart for EspressoCoffee

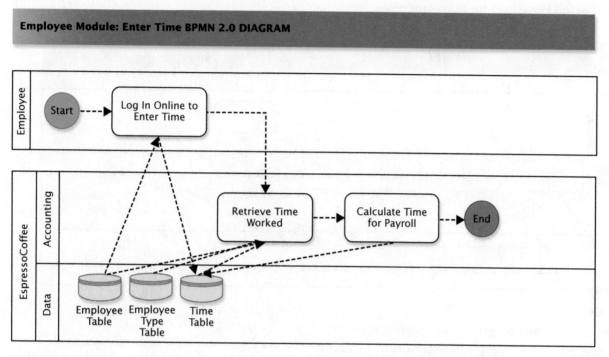

FIGURE 5.15B

Enter Time BPMN Diagram for EspressoCoffee

Pair and Share: How might this BPMN diagram change if employees tracked time manually using time cards?

The database tables used for entering time include the following:

- EMPLOYEE table
- EMPLOYEE TYPE table
- TIME table

The EMPLOYEE table stores information, such as employee name, address, Social Security number, and employee type. The EMPLOYEE TYPE table has two fields: Employee Type Code and Employee Type Description. The employee type code is the primary key for the EMPLOYEE TYPE table and the foreign key for the EMPLOYEE table.

The TIME table stores log in and log out times. It also stores time worked.

Calculate Payroll Business Process Map

The flowchart (Figure 5.16A) and the BPMN diagram (Figure 5.16B) document EspressoCoffee's business process for calculating payroll. As you can see, this process is scheduled to start at a specific date and time. In EspressoCoffee's case, the *calculate payroll* activity is triggered on the 29th of each month at midnight. In a BPMN diagram, this is represented by a Start event symbol with a clock. Notice that an annotation can be added to the BPMN diagram to indicate

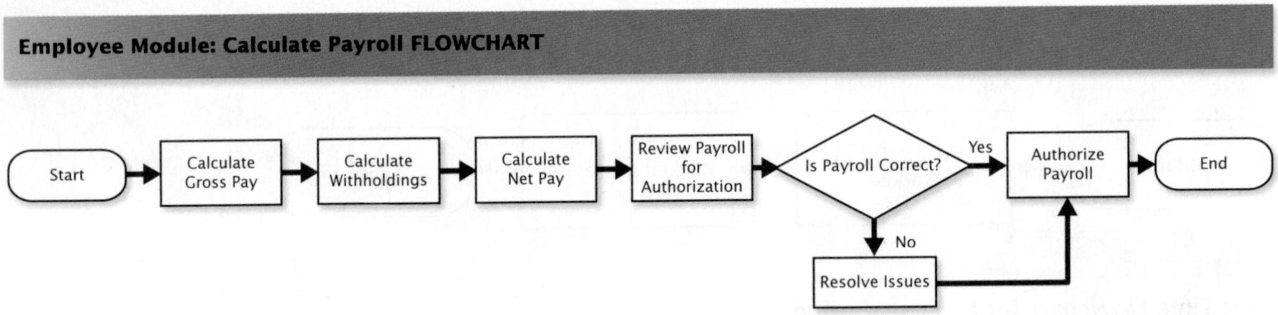

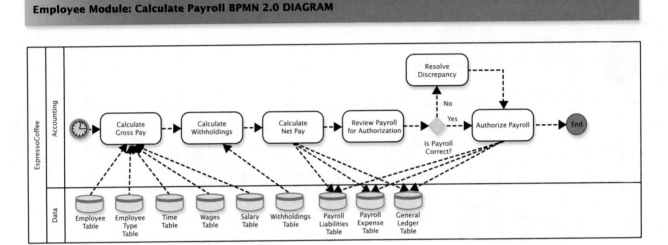

FIGURE 5.16A

Calculate Payroll Flowchart for EspressoCoffee

FIGURE 5.16B

Calculate Payroll BPMN Diagram for EspressoCoffee

Pair and Share: Why is the activity, Authorize Payroll, necessary?

date and time when an activity starts. Gross pay is calculated using information from the following database tables:

- EMPLOYEE table
- WAGES table
- EMPLOYEE TYPE table
- SALARY table
- TIME table

Withholdings are calculated using the gross pay calculations and information from the WITHHOLDINGS table. Next, net pay is calculated using the gross pay and withholdings information. The employee payroll and withholdings information is stored in the following database tables:

- PAYROLL LIABILITIES ACCOUNT table
- PAYROLL EXPENSE ACCOUNT table
- GENERAL LEDGER table

The accountant is notified when payroll has been processed. The accountant reviews payroll calculations and authorizes payroll.

Pay Employees Business Process Map

The flowchart (Figure 5.17A) and the BPMN diagram (Figure 5.17B) document EspressoCoffee's business process for the *pay employees* activity. At a scheduled time, the accountant initiates payroll payment processing. Payroll information is retrieved from the appropriate database tables.

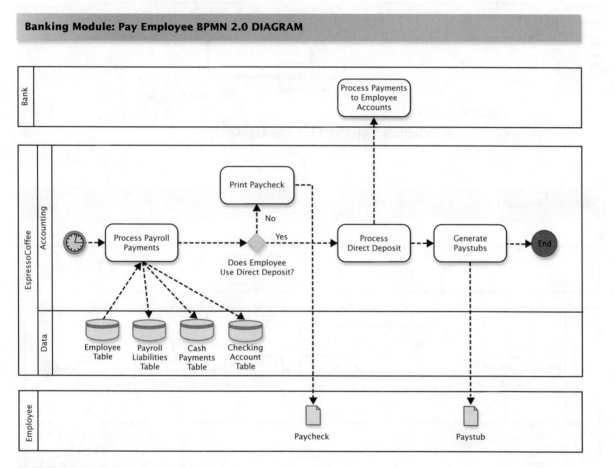

Banking Module: Pay Employees FLOWCHART

FIGURE 5.17A

Pay Employees Flowchart for EspressoCoffee

Banking Module: Pay Employee BPMN 2.0 DIAGRAM

FIGURE 5.17B

Pay Employees BPMN Diagram for EspressoCoffee

Pair and Share: If all employees elect direct deposit, what would change in this business process map?

If the employee has elected to use direct deposit, then the electronic deposit is processed and deposited in the employee's bank account. The paystub is printed and distributed to the employee.

If the employee elects to receive a printed check, the payroll check and paystub are printed and then distributed to the employee.

Pay Payroll Liabilities Business Process Map

The flowchart (Figure 5.18A) and BPMN diagram (Figure 5.18B) document EspressoCoffee's business process for the *pay payroll liabilities* activity. The payment of payroll liabilities is scheduled for specific times based upon the due dates of the specific payroll liability (for example, federal withholding).

At that time, the electronic deposits for payroll liabilities are processed. The accountant is notified and authorizes the payment. The appropriate database tables are updated.

This completes the payroll cycle for EspressoCoffee.

My Connection...
- Short Exercise 5.28
- Tech Exercise 5.39

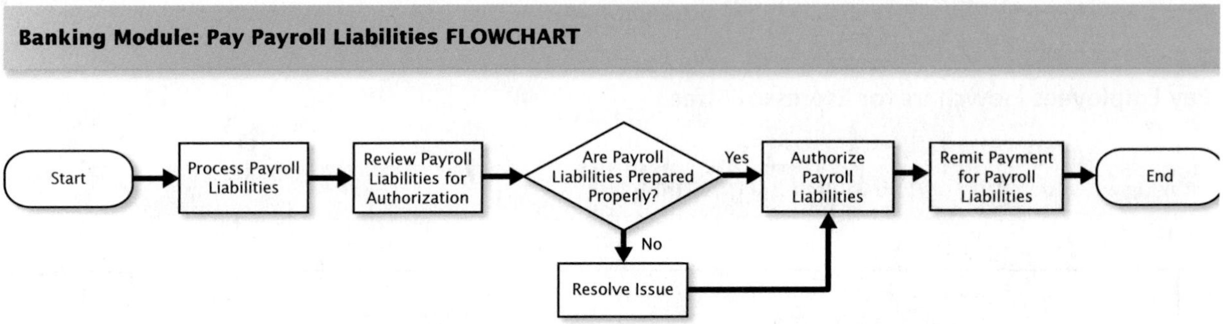

Banking Module: Pay Payroll Liabilities FLOWCHART

FIGURE 5.18A

Pay Payroll Liabilities Flowchart for EspressoCoffee

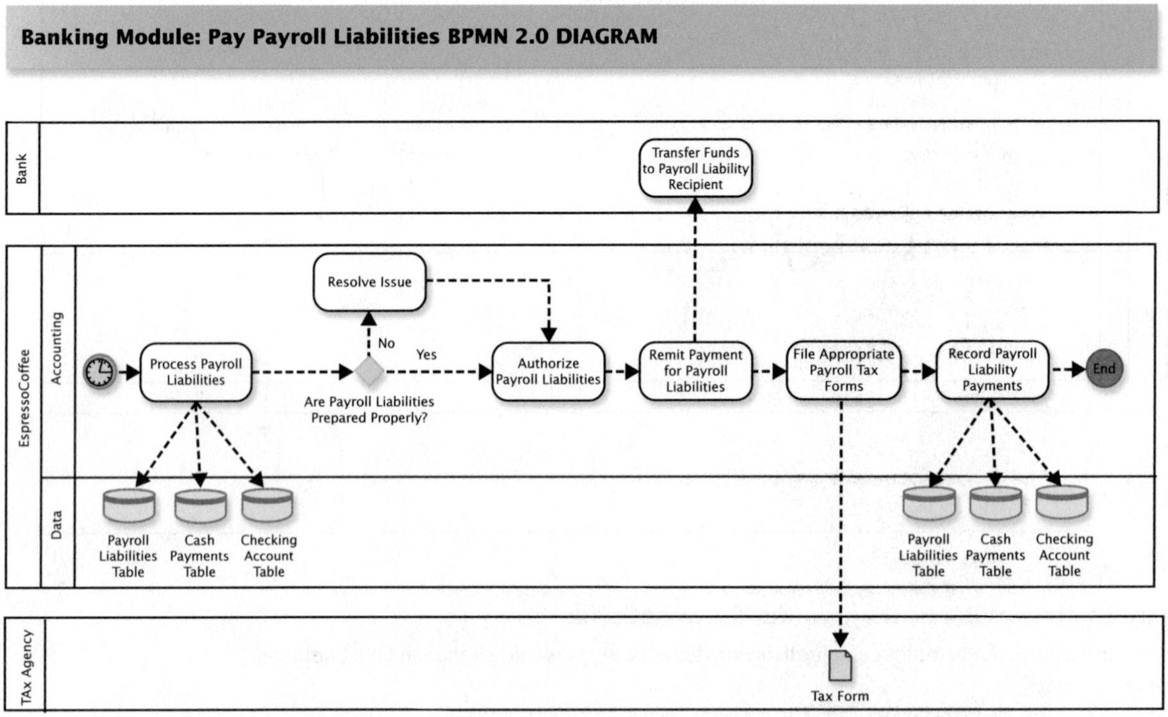

Banking Module: Pay Payroll Liabilities BPMN 2.0 DIAGRAM

FIGURE 5.18B

Pay Payroll Liabilities BPMN Diagram for EspressoCoffee

Pair and Share: How are the flowchart and BPMN diagram for the business process, Pay Payroll Liabilities, similar? How do the flowchart and BPMN diagram differ?

How Do I Customize the Financial Cycle?

Now, we will turn to the financial module. Recall that the financial module (Figure 5.19) consists of other activities and transactions that do not fall into the vendor, customer, employee, or banking modules. Typically, such items could include the following:

- Adjusting entries. Entries to bring accounts up to date
- Correcting entries. Entries necessary to correct errors
- Closing entries. All entries needed to close temporary Income and Expense accounts at year end
- General ledger. All maintenance tasks necessary to maintain the enterprise's general ledger of accounts
- Other. All other transactions and entries needed to properly maintain and operate the accounting system

As an example of how business process maps can be used to document processes for the financial cycle, the flowchart (Figure 5.20A) and BPMN diagram (Figure 5.20B) document EspressoCoffee's process for year-end adjustments. Notice that first a trial balance is prepared to ensure the accounting system is in balance. Information about adjustments is gathered. Then adjusting entries are entered into the system (Figure 5.21). An adjusted trial balance is prepared to ensure that the accounting system is still in balance after adjusting entries are made.

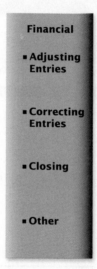

FIGURE 5.19

Financial Cycle

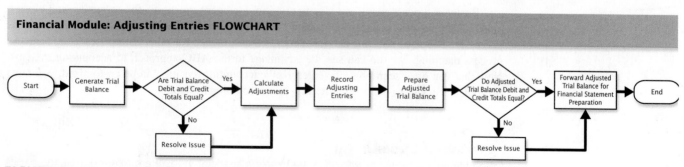

Financial Module: Adjusting Entries FLOWCHART

FIGURE 5.20A

Adjusting Entries Flowchart for EspressoCoffee

Financial Module: Adjusting Entries BPMN 2.0 DIAGRAM

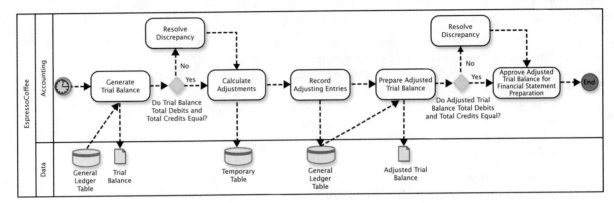

FIGURE 5.20B

Adjusting Entries BPMN Diagram for EspressoCoffee

Pair and Share: Why is the temporary database table necessary?

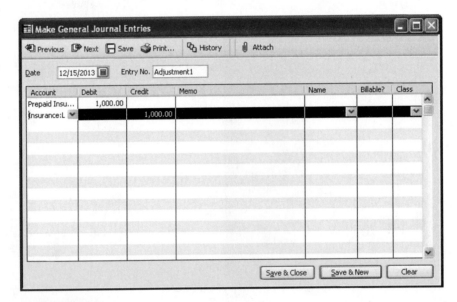

FIGURE 5.21

EspressoCoffee Journal

Business process maps can also be used to document processes for correcting and closing entries. The business process maps shown in this chapter described EspressoCoffee's business processes. The same baseline activities could be customized for other enterprises using business process mapping. So you can see the advantage to the ABC approach to accounting systems. Now that you have seen how one enterprise's accounting system can be customized, you have the tools necessary to document virtually any accounting system.

Financial Cycle...

Sometimes the activities shown in the baseline financial module are referred to as the *financial cycle* or *accounting cycle*.

My Connection...
• Tech Exercise 5.43

Chapter Highlights

How are business processes documented? The baseline accounting system can be customized using data flow diagrams (DFDs) to document the enterprise's business processes.

What is gap analysis? A gap analysis identifies the gap between the selected baseline system, such as SAP, and the customization required by the specific enterprise.

What is the difference between the big bang approach and stages approach to customization? The two approaches to customization are the big bang and stages. The big bang approach is used when all the modules are built and implemented for the entire enterprise at the same time. The stages approach involves completing modules or locations stage by stage instead of all at once.

What is a workflow management system? Workflow management systems automate workflow by automatically forwarding the electronic document to the next step in the business process.

Accounting System Insights

Insight No. 14 Gap analysis is the difference between the baseline system and the customization desired.

Chapter Extension 5: Business Processes: Purchasing, Sales, and Payroll Cycles Using Data Flow Diagrams (DFDs)

See the text website for this chapter extension using Data Flow Diagrams (DFDs) for business process mapping of the purchasing, sales, and payroll transaction cycles.

Active Review

Study less. Learn more. Make connections.

5.1 Refer to the chapter opener, *Meet SAP*. In your opinion, why was the first version of SAP accounting software?

5.2 Refer to the chapter opener, *Meet SAP*. In your opinion, can business processes be modeled in a standard way? How do you think businesses can benefit from software that incorporates best practices for business processes?

5.3 Discuss why accounting professionals should learn about a business process mapping notation that is the best for communicating with IT professionals.

5.4 Discuss how an organization can customize the baseline accounting system to meet its specific needs.

5.5 What is a gap analysis, and when is it typically conducted? Can you think of any other applications for which you could use a gap analysis?

5.6 Discuss how a workflow management system can improve employee productivity.

5.7 Discuss why a company might decide to change its business processes rather than customize a new accounting system.

5.8 What are the benefits of documenting an enterprise's business processes?

5.9 Discuss how business sales processes differ for an online furniture retailer and a physical furniture store.

5.10 Discuss what information about a business process is not documented by a flowchart but is documented by the corresponding business process.

Key Terms Check

Understanding the language used at the crossroads of accounting and IT is key to your success.

5.11 Match the following terms and definitions.

a. SAP
b. big bang
c. stages
d. gap analysis

_____ 1. Standardized enterprise software
_____ 2. Analyzing the gap between the actual cost of the accounting system project and the budgeted cost
_____ 3. Analyzing the gap between the baseline modules and the customization required to meet enterprise-specific needs
_____ 4. An IBM supercomputer
_____ 5. When all system modules are built and implemented for the entire enterprise at the same time
_____ 6. When modules or locations for a new system are built and implemented stage by stage instead of all at once
_____ 7. System analysis and program development
_____ 8. Analyzing the gap between the IT capacity and the IT demand

Practice Test

5.12 The big bang approach to customization involves

a. Customizing and installing one module at a time
b. Piloting modules, testing, and resolving issues before moving on to the next subsystem
c. Resolving issues on a small scale
d. Customizing and installing all the modules for the company at the same time

Gran Prix Auto Part Sales Narrative:

Gran Prix Auto Part Company sells luxury car spare parts online to car dealers and repair shops. Gran Prix Auto Part customers place an online order. Gran Prix Auto Part processes the customer order by verifying with the accounting department that the customer's credit is in good standing with the company (the customer's account is paid on time). The items are verified for availability from company stores near the customer. The nearest store is selected. The shipment is processed and sent to the customer's store. An invoice is generated from the sales information and emailed to the customer. The corresponding database tables are updated.

5.13 Who are the major participants in the Gran Prix Auto Part sales narrative?

a. Customer, Credit Card Company, Gran Prix Auto Part stores
b. Customer, Accounting Department, Gran Prix Auto Part stores, Gran Prix Auto Part
c. Bank, Gran Prix Auto Part stores, Credit Card Company
d. Gran Prix Auto Part, Bank, Gran Prix Auto Part stores

5.14 What are the processes in the Gran Prix Auto Part sales narrative?

a. Process customer order, Process shipping, Generate invoice
b. Verify customer's credit, Verify item availability, Update the database tables
c. Receive customer's order, Verify customer's credit, Send shipment to customer
d. Verify customer's credit, Send shipment to customer, Generate invoice

5.15 The Create Invoices and Receive Customer Payments are in which baseline accounting system module?

a. Employees
b. Vendors
c. Customers
d. Banking

5.16 The Create Purchase Orders, Receive Items, and Enter Bills are in which baseline accounting system?

a. Banking
b. Customer
c. Vendor
d. Reporting

Gran Prix Purchase Narrative:

Gran Prix needs to purchase more Audi spare parts. Gran Prix submits an order to the Audi Company online. When Gran Prix receives the spare parts shipment, the receiving department processes the shipment. Gran Prix receives an invoice and processes the bill. The corresponding database tables are updated.

5.17 Who are the major participants in the Gran Prix purchase narrative?

a. Gran Prix, Receiving department, Accounting department
b. Gran Prix, Receiving department
c. Audi, Receiving department
d. Audi, Receiving department, Accounting department

5.18 What are the activities in the Gran Prix purchase narrative?

a. Submit Purchase Order, Process Shipment, Process Bills
b. Submit Purchase Order, Process Shipment, Receive Invoice
c. Submit Purchase Order, Receive Shipment, Receive Invoice
d. Submit Purchase Order, Receive Shipment, Enter Bills

Gran Prix Process Payroll Liabilities:

Gran Prix has an automated process for paying the payroll liabilities. On the appropriate date, the accounting system automatically initiates the Process Payroll Liabilities. Data from the EMPLOYEE and PAYROLL LIABILITIES ACCOUNT database tables are used in this process. At the completion of this process, the CASH PAYMENTS ACCOUNT and CASH ACCOUNT database tables are updated and an email is sent to the accountant. The accountant authorizes the payroll liabilities. The EMPLOYEE, PAYROLL LIABILITIES ACCOUNT, CASH PAYMENTS ACCOUNT, and CASH ACCOUNT database tables are updated. Payment is sent to the appropriate government entities.

5.19 Who are the major participants in the Gran Prix Process Payroll Liabilities narrative?

a. Employee and Accountant
b. Government Entities and Bank
c. Schedule and Employee
d. Accountant and Government Entities

5.20 What are the activities in the Gran Prix Process Payroll Liabilities narrative?

a. Send Payment and Process Payroll Liabilities
b. Process Payroll Liabilities and Authorize Payroll Liabilities
c. Update database tables and Authorize Payroll Liabilities
d. Email Accountant and Send Payment

5.21 The financial modules usually include the following processes except:

a. Pay interest expense
b. Make correcting entries
c. Make closing entries
d. Make adjusting entries

Exercises

Each Exercise relates to one of the major questions addressed in the chapter and is labeled with the question number in green.

Short Exercises

Warm up with these short exercises.

5.22 Compare and contrast using a baseline system versus customizing a system to meet enterprise-specific needs. Use the following organizer for your answer. (Q5.1)

Compare (Same)	and	Compare (Different)

5.23 Compare and contrast the big bang approach and the stages approach to customizing and implementing a system. What are the advantages and disadvantages of each approach? Use the following organizer for your answer. (Q5.1)

Compare (Same)	and	Compare (Different)

5.24 EspressoCoffee is considering permitting vendors to access certain parts of its vendor module, such as verifying orders placed and tracking items received by EspressoCoffee. This would represent significant time and cost savings to EspressoCoffee since its employees would not use time checking information for vendors. The vendors would be able to access the information themselves.

In order to permit vendors to access EspressoCoffee's system, the vendor would need to be authenticated by logging on with a specified user ID and password. EspressoCoffee would then verify the vendor and provide the vendor with access to the appropriate areas of EspressoCoffee's system. (Q5.1, 5.2, 5.3)

1. Identify which process maps and flowchart shown in Chapter 5 would need to be modified to provide vendor access to EspressoCoffee's system.
2. Describe how the process map and flowchart would need to be modified if this change were made to EspressoCoffee's system.

5.25 EspressoCoffee is considering opening a chain of espresso cafes that would sell the EspressoCoffee brand of coffee beans and espresso machines. (Q5.1, 5.2)

1. Identify which process maps and flowcharts for EspressoCoffee in Chapter 5 would need to be modified.
2. Which processes should be modified to accommodate this change in operations?

5.26 Sam's Sports Car Galaxy, a supplier of sports car auto parts, uses a bar-code system for inventory of the auto parts. Inventory is automatically checked on a regular basis to determine when reorders are needed. The system automatically generates a purchase order (PO) that is sent electronically to an employee for authorization. After approval, the PO is sent electronically to the vendor. (Q5.3)

1. Annotate the preceding narrative.
2. Identify major participants.
3. Identify activities.

4. Identify possible gateways.
5. Identify database tables.

5.27 Kayla Company pays its employees on the 30th of each month. An accounting employee initiates the process. Employee pay is calculated based on a fixed salary or an hourly pay. Withholdings are deducted from the gross pay to calculate net pay. An accounting supervisor reviews and authorizes payroll. (Q5.4)

1. Annotate the preceding narrative.
2. Identify major participants.
3. Identify activities.
4. Identify possible gateways.
5. Identify database tables.

5.28 When processing payroll, Kayla Company gives employees the option of receiving their paychecks in the mail or having a direct deposit made to their bank accounts. (Q5.4)

1. Annotate the preceding narrative.
2. Identify activities.
3. Identify possible gateways.
4. Identify major participants.
5. Identify database tables.

5.29 Kayla Company has decided to go paperless throughout the organization. When processing payroll, the company will use direct deposit for all employees. (Q5.4)

1. Annotate the preceding narrative.
2. Identify activities.
3. Identify possible gateways.
4. Identify major participants.
5. Identify database tables.

It's Your Call

This is your training ground. These scenarios provide you with the opportunity to use your knowledge and professional skills.

5.30 You have been hired as a consultant to MIPS Electronics, a chain of successful electronics stores. MIPS would like to implement a workflow management system to streamline accounting procedures. Prepare an email summary to the president of MIPS Electronics summarizing the benefits and limitations of a workflow management system. (Q5.1)

5.31 You are a member of the project team for a new integrated enterprise system for Justin Enterprises. The CEO has acquired a number of different companies over the past few years. This has resulted in different accounting systems that are not compatible, so the CEO has made the decision to convert to an integrated enterprise system. She has asked you to summarize in a short email whether you would recommend using the big bang or stages approach to the conversion and why. (Q5.1)

5.32 You are the accounting representative on a project team for a new integrated enterprise system that will include a new accounting system. The team is evaluating the following two options:

- Option A: Use the SAP baseline system and modify the company's business processes to match the baseline system.
- Option B: Customize the SAP system to correspond to your current business processes.

You are charged with preparing an update for the president of the company regarding a recommendation for which option to pursue and the rationale. (Q5.1)

Tech in Practice

These technology in practice exercises are perfect for both individuals and teams.

Tech Exercises

Sharpen your skills with these technology exercises. Watch these software videos at www.pearsonhighered.com/kay.

5.33

Tech Tool: Spreadsheet Software or Visio Software

Software Videos: MS Excel BPMN Diagram Drawing or MS Visio BPMN Diagram Drawing

Use the following business process map organizer for Ariel Enterprises. The company sells to customers on account. The following business process map organizer summarizes the activities, major participants (swimlanes), gateways, and database tables for the *receive customer payment* process for Ariel Enterprises.

1. Build a flowchart.
2. Build a BPMN 20 diagram.

Activity	Gateway (decision)	Swimlane	Data Store
Customer Sends Cash Payment		Customer	
Process Customer Payment		Accounting	• CUSTOMER • SALES ORDER • SALES ORDER LINE • ACCOUNT RECEIVABLE
Record Customer Payment	Verify Cash Amount	Accounting	• UNDEPOSITED • ACCOUNT RECEIVABLE
Send Customer Receipt		Accounting	

5.34

Tech Tool: Spreadsheet Software or Visio Software

Software Videos: MS Excel BPMN Diagram Drawing or MS Visio BPMN Diagram Drawing

Use the following narrative to answer the accompanying questions.

iBacci Chocolate sells fine European chocolates and candies. The company buys from local Italian artisans and sells the items online. The company's ITEM database table used to account for inventory is automatically checked at a specific time of the day to determine if the quantity has dropped below the reorder point. If so, the system automatically processes a purchase order and forwards it to the appropriate employee. The employee reviews it for authorization. If there are no discrepancies, then PO is authorized; otherwise, the purchasing department is notified. The PO is generated and sent to the specified vendor.

1. Annotate the narrative.
2. Create a business process map organizer.
3. Build a flowchart.
4. Build a BPMN 2.0 diagram.

5.35

Tech Tool: Spreadsheet Software or Visio Software

Software Videos: MS Excel BPMN Diagram Drawing or MS Visio BPMN Diagram Drawing

Use the following narrative to answer the accompanying questions.

iBacci Chocolate sells fine European chocolates and candies. The company buys from local Italian artisans and sells the items online. Vendor ships purchased items. When the items are received from the vendors, a purchasing department employee records the items. Another iBacci employee completes a two-way match by counting the items received and comparing the count to the original PO. If there is no discrepancy, then employee records the items received in the system. A receiving report is generated and sent to the accounting department. Accounting department updates the accounts. If there were discrepancies, then the purchasing department would attempt to resolve them and generate a receiving report; otherwise, discrepancies are recorded, a discrepancy notification is generated, and this is sent to the vendor.

1. Annotate the narrative.
2. Create a business process map organizer.
3. Build a flowchart.
4. Build a BPMN 2.0 diagram.

5.36

Tech Tool: Spreadsheet Software or Visio Software
Software Videos: MS Excel BPMN Diagram Drawing or MS Visio BPMN Diagram Drawing
Use the following narrative to answer the accompanying questions.

iBacci Chocolate sells fine European chocolates and candies. The company buys from local Italian artisans and sells the items online. A vendor sends a bill. When the bill is received from the vendor, the accounting department completes a three-way match, comparing the vendor's bill with the receiving report and the original PO. If the bill matched the purchasing order and receiving report, then the bill is recorded. If there are any discrepancies, then the accounting department would try to resolve and record the bill; otherwise, the discrepancies are recorded and a discrepancy notification is sent to the vendor.

1. Annotate the narrative.
2. Create a business process map organizer.
3. Build a flowchart.
4. Build a BPMN 2.0 diagram.

5.37

Tech Tool: Spreadsheet Software or Visio Software
Software Videos: MS Excel BPMN Diagram Drawing or MS Visio BPMN Diagram Drawing
Use the following narrative to answer the accompanying questions.

iBacci Chocolate sells fine European chocolates and candies. The company buys from local Italian artisans and sells the items online. On the first of each month, the accountant reviews and selects bills to pay. Checks are prepared and printed. The controller reviews the checks and supporting documents and signs the checks. The checks are mailed to the vendors.

1. Annotate the narrative.
2. Create a business process map organizer.
3. Build a flowchart.
4. Build a BPMN 2.0 diagram.

5.38

Tech Tool: Spreadsheet Software or Visio Software
Software Videos: MS Excel BPMN Diagram Drawing or MS Visio BPMN Diagram Drawing
iBacci Chocolate needs your assistance in documenting its business processes for the payroll cycle for entering time worked. The following is a narrative for recording employee time.

When an hourly employee arrives at work, he or she logs on to his or her computer station with a unique user ID and password. The log-on activity is recorded by the system as the starting time and saved in a TIME database table. When the employee leaves for the day, he or she logs off, activating the system to record the end of the time worked.

Every Friday, the payroll clerk uses a database query with the TIME table to calculate the length of time worked for the week by each hourly employee. Total hours worked is stored in the TIME table. Complete the following.

1. Annotate the narrative.
2. Create a business process map organizer.
3. Build a flowchart.
4. Build a BPMN 2.0 diagram.

5.39

Tech Tool: Spreadsheet Software or Visio Software

Software Videos: MS Excel BPMN Diagram Drawing or MS Visio BPMN Diagram Drawing

iBacci Chocolate needs your assistance in documenting its business processes for the payroll cycle for calculating payroll. The following is a narrative.

Every Friday, the payroll clerk runs a database query to retrieve hours worked by each hourly employee. The clerk runs another query to retrieve the pay information from the WAGES and SALARY tables. The clerk then runs an application to calculate withholding amounts. Net pay for employee paychecks is calculated and stored in database tables. Payroll is reviewed for authorization. The payroll supervisor authorizes correct payrolls. Unauthorized payrolls are resolved and authorized by payroll supervisor.

Complete the following.

1. Annotate the narrative.
2. Create a business process map organizer.
3. Build a flowchart.
4. Build a BPMN 2.0 diagram.

5.40

Tech Tool: Spreadsheet Software or Visio Software

Software Videos: MS Excel BPMN Diagram Drawing or MS Visio BPMN Diagram Drawing

iBacci Chocolate needs your assistance in documenting its business processes for the payroll cycle for paying employees. The following is a narrative.

Every Friday after calculating time and payroll, a second payroll clerk runs a database query to retrieve payroll information. This payroll clerk performs a random check of employee time and pay to verify accuracy and validity. Then the payroll clerk, for accuracy, inserts check forms and paystubs into a dedicated laser printer and prints the paychecks and pay stubs. Pays with discrepancies are reviewed and discrepancies are resolved; then pays are forwarded to the payroll clerk for printing. The controller reviews the paychecks and signs the checks. The payroll clerk inserts the checks and stubs into window envelopes and mails the checks to employees.

Complete the following.

1. Annotate the narrative.
2. Create a business process map organizer.
3. Build a flowchart.
4. Build a BPMN 2.0 diagram.

5.41

Tech Tool: Spreadsheet Software or Visio Software

Software Videos: MS Excel BPMN Diagram Drawing or MS Visio BPMN Diagram Drawing

Select an authentic enterprise of your choice.

1. Write a narrative to describe how the enterprise processes customer payments.
2. Annotate the narrative.
3. Create a business process map organizer.
4. Build a flowchart.
5. Build a BPMN 2.0 diagram.
6. After reviewing the process map and flowchart diagrams you created, do you see any improvements the enterprise could make? List your recommendations to streamline and improve the business process.

5.42

Tech Tool: Spreadsheet Software or Visio Software

Software Videos: MS Excel BPMN Diagram Drawing or MS Visio BPMN Diagram Drawing

Go to your college's office that collects student tuition payments and observe the steps used in this business process. Then complete the following:

1. Write a narrative summarizing what you observed.
2. Annotate the narrative.
3. Create a business process map organizer.
4. Build a BPMN 2.0 diagram and a flowchart for *receive students (customers) payments*, documenting the steps to collect and record student tuition payments.

5.43

Tech Tool: Spreadsheet Software or Visio Software

Software Videos: MS Excel BPMN Diagram Drawing or MS Visio BPMN Diagram Drawing

The new CFO has asked you to update documentation for accounting procedures using BPMN 2.0 and flowchart. You have decided to start with a BPMN 2.0 diagram and flowchart for the *closing* process at year end.

1. Create a business process map organizer.
2. Build a BPMN 2.0 diagram and flowchart to document *closing*.

5.44 The following table shows a series of business activities as well as how these activities are performed. Next to each activity there are series of options. For each activity, select one of the options. Notice that the option you pick for an activity should match the choice you make for the preceding activities.

- Write a narrative for the resulting sequence of activities and the options that you have selected.
- Annotate your narrative.
- Create a business process map organizer.
- And build a flowchart and BPMN 2.0 diagram.

What do you think of the activities 10 and 11 sequences in the table? Do you have any other options for conducting these activities?

Sequence	Activity	Execution Options
1	Customer selects items	1. Selects from a hard-copy catalog. 2. Selects from an online catalog. 3. Selects from store display.
2	Customer places an order	1. Enters selected items online. 2. Calls the store and store employee enters the items into the system. 3. Takes the items to the cashier.
3	Check item availability	1. Customer sees item availability confirmation on the computer screen. 2. On the phone, store employee confirms items availability.
4	If items are in stock, then pull items from stock	N/A
5	Items are not in stock	1. Customer sees item availability confirmation on the computer screen. 2. On the phone, store employee tells you items are not in stock.
6	Proceed with order (items are not in stock)	1. Store employee records your order in the backlog order book. 2. Automated system saves backlog information.
7	Notify customer of delay in delivery (items are not in stock)	1. Delay information is emailed to customer. 2. Delay information is mailed to the customer.
8	Proceed with customer order (items are in stock)	1. Ship items.
9	Generate the invoice	N/A
10	Give invoice to the customer	1. Invoice is emailed to the customer. 2. Customer can download the invoice in PDF format. 3. Invoice is mailed to the customer.
11	Customer pays	1. Customer pays the cashier and receives the receipt. 2. Customer pays online with credit card. 3. On the phone, customer gives credit card number to the store employee.

5.45 The following process map diagram shows the shipping process for Soccer Sport Store. As you see, Soccer Sport uses the US Postal service to deliver sporting goods to its customers. Management in Soccer Sport would like to provide other delivery options to its customers. You have been selected to help management implement this requirement.

1. Identify activities that must be added or changed.
2. Write a narrative to describe the new process.
3. Annotate your narrative.
4. Create a business process map organizer.
5. Build a flowchart for the new shipping process.
6. Build a BPMN 2.0 diagram for the new shipping process.

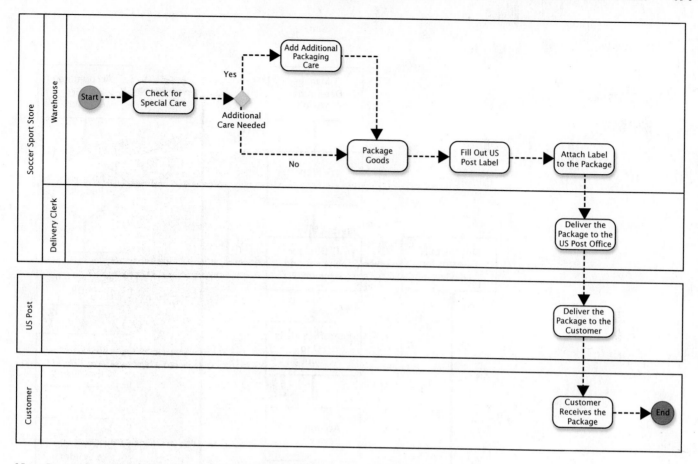

Note: In your business process map organizer, include, if it is required, any gateway and data store.

5.46 The following flowchart shows a fully manual purchasing process for an IT department.
1. Write a narrative to fully computerize this process.
2. Annotate your narrative.
3. Create a business process map organizer.
4. Build a flowchart.
5. Build a BPMN 2.0 diagram.
6. Write a summary and explain why your new computerized process is more efficient than the manual one. Remember that computerized processes are not always more efficient than manual ones!

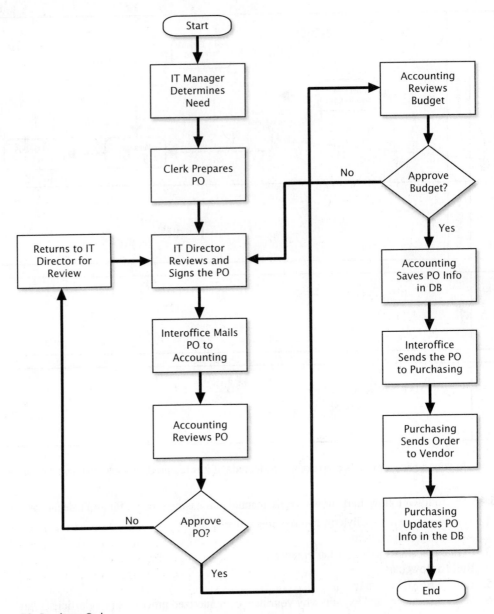

PO: Purchase Order
DB: Database

5.47 Fashion One, a department store in St. Louis, has two sales channels. Customers can purchase at the company store in downtown St. Louis or place their orders over the phone. To place an order over the phone, customers browse the company's mailed catalog and select their items, then call Fashion One to place their order. Customers provide the salesperson with their personal and order information. The salesperson verifies the customer information. New customers are added to the CUSTOMER table. The salesperson verifies item availability and customer credit card, and then sends the order information to accounting. The salesperson would notify the customer in case of a problem with item availability or the credit card.

Management at Fashion One has noticed the following problems with their over-the-phone sales process.

1. Cost of printing and mailing catalogs is becoming too high for the company—currently, $500,000 per year.
2. About 25% percent of the items sold are returned due to customer dissatisfaction with color, size, or fabric texture. This costs the company about $1 million per year.

3. In recent years, some customers have become more reluctant to provide their credit card number on the phone; therefore, the number of customers buying over the phone has reduced drastically. The exact cost of losing customers due to this problem is unknown, but the data analytic department is trying to estimate it.

4. Often items in the mailed catalogs do not match with the available items in the inventory. Therefore, salespersons spend time just telling customers what items are available. This year, Fashion One had to add 10 more salespersons for its over-the-phone sales section. The cost of this problem is unknown, but data analytic is trying to estimate it.

The sales channel project team has provided the following BPMN 2.0 diagram for the over-the-phone sales process. You are a member of this team from the accounting department. Suggest a different sales channel that is more efficient and less costly than the current process. Identify new activities and document your suggestion with a BPMN 2.0 diagram. State how the new sales process could eliminate the current problems and create new opportunities. Do you see any changes in the control the accounting department has over the new sales process?

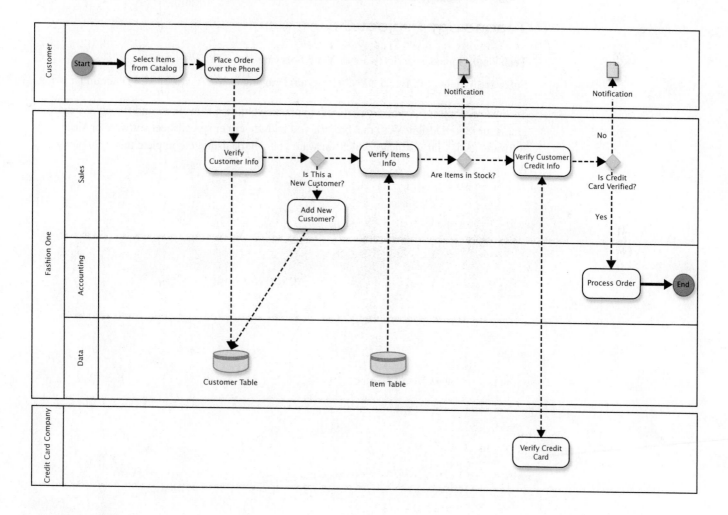

Go Online

In the fast-paced world of technology, your skill at finding answers fast can be vital. Go online and experience typical assignments you may encounter as a professional.

5.48 The CEO of Beth&Company has announced that she believes the best return on investment in the future is going to be attained by improving operational performance through improved business processes. Recent advances in technology have created even greater opportunities.

She has asked you to research the business process management suites currently available and to make a recommendation. Go online and research business process management suites. Prepare a short email to the CEO with an executive summary of your findings.

5.49 The CEO of Beth&Company has asked you to get her up to speed on best practices in business process management. Go online and search for *BMP and best practices*. Prepare a short email to the CEO with an executive summary of your findings.

5.50 Go online and research how business process mapping helps management streamline their business processes.

Technology Projects

These technology projects are perfect for both individuals and teams.

Technology Project 5

Tech Tool: Spreadsheet Software or Visio Software

Software Videos: MS Excel BPMN Diagram Drawing or MS Visio BPMN Diagram Drawing

Technology Project 5 is your opportunity to practice building flowcharts and BPMN 2.0 diagrams for iSportDesign. With this project, you will use either spreadsheet software or Visio software. (Ask your instructor which software you will be using to complete this technology project.)

Your deliverables for the project include the following:

Deliverable 1. Create a business process map organizer for *create purchase orders* process.

Deliverable 2. Build a BPMN 2.0 and a flowchart for *create purchase orders* process.

Deliverable 3. Create a business process map organizer for *receive items* process.

Deliverable 4. Build a BPMN 2.0 and a flowchart for *receive items* process.

Deliverable 5. Create a business process map organizer for *enter bills* process.

Deliverable 6. Build a BPMN 2.0 and a flowchart for *enter bills* process.

Deliverable 7. Create a business process map organizer for *pay bills* process.

Deliverable 8. Build a BPMN 2.0 and a flowchart for *pay bills* process.

Visit www.pearsonhighered.com/kay to complete the following:

1. Download Technology Project 5 instructions.
2. Download files provided online for your convenience in completing the project deliverables.
3. Watch the videos with software instructions to complete this project at www.pearsonhighered.com/kay.

6 Integrated Enterprise Systems and Cloud Computing

Who Has the Largest Integrated Enterprise System in the World?

Meet Nestlé.

Have you ever purchased a Nestlé Crunch bar? Baby Ruth bar? SweeTarts? Toll House cookies?

Meet Nestlé S.A., the company that makes those products and many more. Nestlé, headquartered in Vevey, Switzerland, is a global enterprise with approximately 200 operating companies and subsidiaries in over 80 countries.

Nestlé had 9 different general ledgers and multiple purchasing systems. It was paying 29 different prices for vanilla—to the same vendor—because Nestlé's various divisions used different numbers and names to identify vanilla.

Nestlé turned to SAP to integrate its global operations. Large-scale enterprise systems, such as SAP, make it possible for enterprises to integrate and share data, including accounting data, throughout the organization.

What would you recommend Nestlé do about the vanilla issue?

Crossroads

At the crossroads of accounting and IT, technological advances in the past 15 to 20 years make it possible to integrate the accounting system with other systems (such as human resources, customer relationship management, supply chain, and operations).

My Questions

Q 6.1 What is an integrated enterprise system and how did we get here?

Q 6.2 What are the benefits and challenges of an integrated enterprise system?

Q 6.3 What IT architecture does an integrated enterprise system use?

Q 6.4 What do I need to know about SAP?

Q 6.5 How do I integrate my enterprise system with the Cloud?

What Is an Integrated Enterprise System and How Did We Get Here?

Imagine that when you go to register for your college classes you have to enter all your personal and course information into the computer. Now imagine going to the business office at your college to pay your tuition bill and having to re-enter all your personal and course information again. To sign up for financial aid, you must re-enter all the data yet again. Imagine if every department at your college required you to re-enter the same data because its computers couldn't communicate with other departments.

That is exactly how some systems still operate today. The accounting system doesn't communicate with the human resources system. The operations system doesn't communicate with either of them. Each system functions as a stand-alone silo (see Figure 6.1). Because the systems don't communicate, the data has to be re-entered into each system.

> **How Many Database Tables Does an SAP System Have?**
> It is estimated that an SAP enterprise system may contain 10,000 database tables. Can you imagine building table relationships for 10,000 database tables?

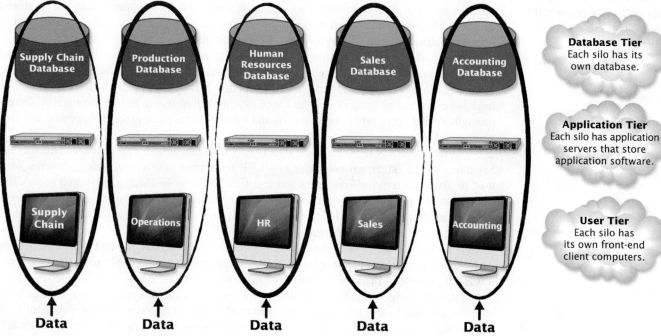

FIGURE 6.1

Silo Architecture

> **Share Data...**
> Integrated enterprise systems make it possible for you to track your online purchases with Amazon.com.

As you know, the accounting system interacts with all aspects of an organization, capturing and providing information to virtually all areas within an enterprise. Sales, purchasing, human resources, shipping, receiving, operations, production, customer service, and others rely upon the accounting system to capture and retrieve data needed to meet their needs. For optimal effectiveness, the accounting system needs to be integrated throughout the enterprise, and technological advances have made this possible.

Integrated Enterprise Systems: How Did We Get Here?

How did enterprises move from stand-alone silos with separate information systems for each department to an integrated enterprise system (IES) that shares data throughout the organization? To understand how we reached this state of integrated enterprise systems, we must take a brief look back.

In modern times, with the advent of the computer, it was quickly realized that the computer could be used to assist in accounting tasks. In the late 1950s, businesses started using IBM mainframe computers for transaction processing. The mainframes could execute a relatively large volume of transactions in a short time. However, these mainframe computers were not accessible to the accountant. The accountant had to work with IT professionals to utilize computing power. Sometimes this resulted in time lags and misinterpretation of the accountant's requests.

Heterogeneous systems arose to meet the needs of individual departments. Custom programming using languages, such as COBOL, were used. Often these silo systems were on different platforms (hardware and operating systems) that best fit the individual department needs, such as the needs of the accounting department.

Crossroads
What IT professionals refer to as an integrated enterprise system, accounting professionals might refer to as an ERP. ERP is actually only one module in the larger integrated enterprise system.

With the appearance of the personal computer in the early 1980s, the individual accountant could now sit at his or her desk and use the computer to perform accounting functions. At that time the personal computer was a stand-alone machine. Accounting data could not be shared electronically between personal computers. Data had to be moved to portable storage, such as floppy disks, to move the data to another personal computer.

In the early 1990s, local area networks (LANs) became available to businesses to connect stand-alone personal computers. This permitted accountants to share accounting data electronically between computers, resulting in the birth of computer networks. Later, to improve electronic sharing of data and applications, client server architecture added servers (computers that serve other computers on the network with more processing power and disk storage space).

The founders of SAP AG saw the opportunity to create an integrated system. This was the beginning of the integrated enterprise era. ERP (enterprise resource planning) systems were used to plan an enterprise's resources and logistics. The term ERP came to be used generically to refer to integrated enterprise systems. Modules added to the integrated enterprise system included accounting (financials), human resources, production, customer relationship management, and supply chain management.

Figure 6.1 illustrates how the functional silos, such as accounting and human resources, each had a separate information system. The same data had to be rekeyed into each system since it was not possible to share the data between systems.

Spaghetti code was sometimes used to connect the separate systems using custom written programming code (Figure 6.2). This permitted some of the systems to share some of their data. In many cases, however, some data still had to be rekeyed. Finally, as shown in Figure 6.3, integrated enterprise systems using enterprise databases made it possible to enter data once and share the data between departments and functional areas.

Y2K...

Why did so many large enterprises make the shift to integrated enterprise systems at the turn of the millennium? One impetus for the shift to integrated enterprise systems was Y2K, or the year 2000.

When database storage space was relatively costly, programmers would save storage space by saving only the required characters. In the case of the year, only the last two characters were usually stored. This solution worked well for years 1953, 1976, and 1981. However, with the advent of the new millennium, if only the last two digits were stored, how would the system know if 53 referred to 1953 or 2053?

In this case, software application programs would not run properly, integrated processors in production equipment might not function, and database queries would not retrieve needed data.

Many large enterprises, such as Ralston Purina, Anheuser Busch, and Deutsche Bank, installed integrated enterprise systems to address the Y2K issue. This involved massive investments in IT components needed to implement the IES. New, centralized operational databases, such as Oracle and IBM databases, were used. Front-end applications included SAP. Business processes were redesigned to improve business operations and meet requirements of the new integrated systems.

Although the integrated enterprise systems were often installed to fix the Y2K issue, they enabled enterprises to use the Internet more effectively, update business processes, and better coordinate activities throughout the organization.

With many of the Y2K enterprise systems now a decade old, some organizations are choosing to use cloud computing to update their enterprise systems.

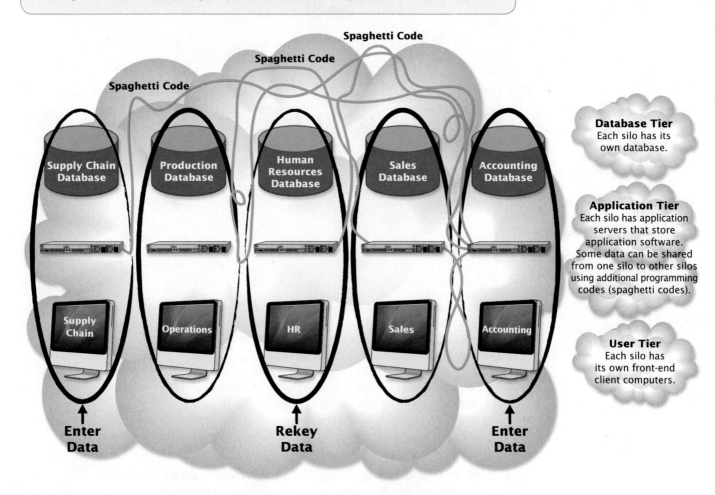

FIGURE 6.2

Silo Architecture with Spaghetti Code

Can you trace data flow from the other systems to accounting?

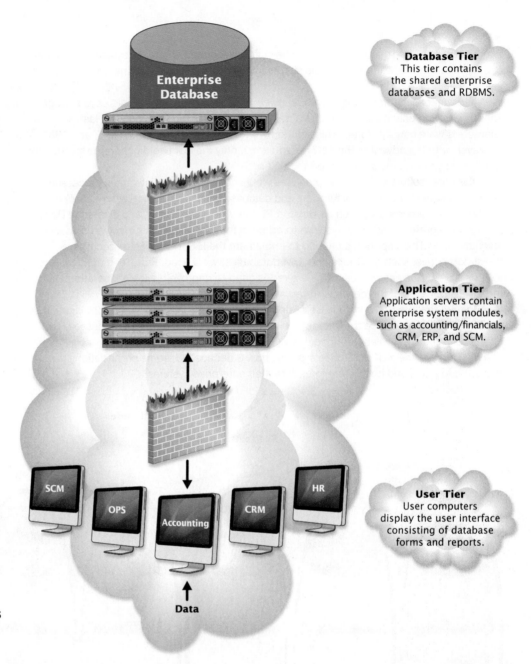

FIGURE 6.3

Integrated Enterprise System Three-Tier Architecture with Firewalls

Why is a firewall necessary between these tiers?

From a value chain and business process perspective, the integrated enterprise system technology now permits data to flow through functional areas as it passes through the value chain (Figure 6.4). As you can see from the figure, data entered for supply chain management (SCM) can be reused by the accounting system in the purchasing cycle. Time worked by shop floor employees, tracked by the operations/production system (OPS), is used in the accounting payroll cycle. Customer transaction information can be shared by customer relationship management (CRM) and the accounting system sales cycle.

Integrated enterprise systems integrate workflow and business processes within and among enterprises. The integrated enterprise system offers a business process management system (BPMS) that combines:

- Automated workflow: automating the flow of documents among employees
- Automated business processes: automating the flow of information among software modules and functional areas
- Internet technologies: automating information flow among enterprise segments and other enterprises at remote sites

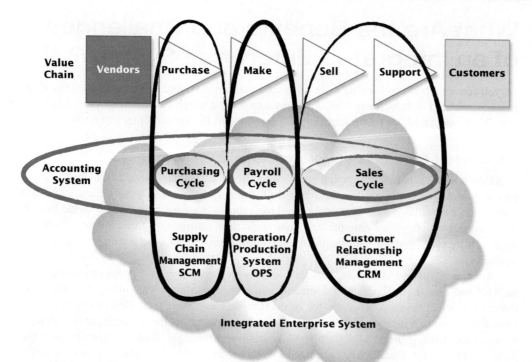

FIGURE 6.4

Integrated Enterprise Systems and Value Chain

What data does the accounting system need from the other system modules? List as many as you can.

The Internet permits remote sites to use a central database more efficiently. Additionally, the Internet has provided e-business opportunities for enterprises to further integrate their systems with customers and vendors. Today, integrated enterprise systems provide an opportunity to use the shared data to create business intelligence and build digital financial dashboards that monitor enterprise performance.

Accounting Insight No. 15: Share Data

Accounting Insight No. 15 states that integrated systems share data...let others enter data for you.

By integrating the accounting system into the larger enterprise system, employees in other parts of the organization can enter data that will automatically feed into the accounting system. Better yet, have customers do the data entry for you. For example, Southwest Airlines has customers place their ticket orders online and print their own boarding passes. Why pay an employee to enter the data when customers are happier to enter the data themselves, which is faster and cheaper? The data is then shared throughout the enterprise.

ACCOUNTING INSIGHT NO. 15
Integrated Systems Share Data...
Let Others Enter Data For You.

Integrated modules share information using an integrated database system, thus eliminating the need to rekey the same data. Each time data is rekeyed, it presents another opportunity for errors to enter the system.

Before installing an SAP integrated enterprise system, Microsoft estimated that as much as 90% of the data being processed may have been redundant (Kalakota, 1999). Microsoft installed an SAP R/3 relational database system, replacing a "tangle of 33 financial-tracking systems in 26 subsidiaries" (White, 1997). Spending $25 million to install the SAP system, Microsoft estimated the system would save $18 million a year.

> **Share Data...**
> With an integrated enterprise system, an Owens-Corning factory-floor employee can enter shipments of roofing shingles to customers into the system, updating accounting records at the same time.

My Connection...
Make connections. Try Short Exercise 6.24.

What Are the Benefits and Challenges of an Integrated Enterprise System?

As you can see, there are benefits to an integrated enterprise system. There are also many challenges associated with such a system. An organization must weigh the advantages and disadvantages of an integrated system to determine if it is a good fit for the particular enterprise.

Integrated Enterprise System Benefits

In addition to data sharing, integrated enterprise systems offer many other advantages to complex organizations with facilities scattered around the globe. Today, these organizations are faced with the need to be resilient and respond to rapidly changing markets and world events. A well-designed integrated enterprise system offers live information that facilitates business agility. Integrated systems can improve communication, coordinate activities, and reduce duplication.

Another advantage of IES besides data sharing is that integrated system providers, such as SAP and Oracle, incorporate best practices into their products. This offers the enterprise the most efficient business processes for an integrated enterprise system. Best practices can facilitate compliance with regulatory and accounting requirements of the Securities and Exchange Commission (SEC), the Public Company Accounting Oversight Board (PCAOB), and the Sarbanes-Oxley Act. Because the integrated system product offers best practices, an enterprise may choose to modify its business processes to conform with the provider's baseline system and eliminate costly customization.

Yet another advantage of integrated enterprise systems is that suppliers and customers may be granted access to track shipments and orders within the system. This feature can reduce the amount of employee time and cost spent tracking shipments in response to vendor and customer inquiries. Sharing information with supply chain partners can improve efficiency and coordination, thereby reducing costs.

Integrated Enterprise System Challenges

Although the integrated enterprise system offers many advantages, challenges also accompany an IES. Two challenges some enterprises have faced when implementing integrated enterprise systems are shifting from functional silos to integrated system business processes and managing the change required by such a shift.

The transition from functional silos to an integrated system focuses on **business process management (BPM)**. BPM may involve changing how business operations are conducted. The integrated system product already contains best practices. Some organizations choose to redesign their current business practices to fit the baseline enterprise product adopted. This can result in significant changes for employees in even routine tasks.

The other option is to customize the baseline enterprise system to fit the current business processes. This can prove prohibitively costly. Another disadvantage to customizing the baseline system is that when a later version of the integrated system is adopted, often the expensive custom programming must be completed again or abandoned.

To reduce costs, organizations might prefer not to customize, but the baseline system may not meet industry- or enterprise-specific requirements. In that case customization may be the only option. For example, public and private universities have different policies, regulations, and accounting requirements. In some cases, customization may be the only option to meet specific university requirements.

Change management involves managing the change that individuals within the organization experience as a result of the newly integrated system. One company implementing an integrated system experienced a 60% turnover rate in accounting and order entry staff. Another organization found that after implementing an SAP integrated enterprise system, its managers insisted on the old reports they had received from the prior system—even though the new reports were more comprehensive. Developers spent hours reformatting the new reports to appear like the old reports in order to satisfy manager demands. One of the SAP

Top Reasons for Failed ERPs...

Top reasons why ERPs fail include the following:
1. Unrealistic budget. Underestimated costs. Overestimated benefits.
2. Unrealistic schedule. Not enough time allowed for project completion.
3. Not a good fit. User requirements are not met. Baseline system not a good fit with business processes.
4. Too much change. Failure to educate employees on changes to expect. Lack of adequate change management.
5. Lack of project champion at the top. Commitment by top management is lacking to champion the project.

$130 Million Later and No ERP....

Kmart wrote off $130 million for a failed ERP that was never completed.

team members at that organization stated that he would give everything he knew about SAP to know more about change management.

Yet another challenge to implementing an integrated enterprise system is whether to link current heterogeneous systems or to start anew. One organization with two autonomous divisions found that one division chose to go with SAP. This required the division to start anew and abandon its legacy systems. The other division decided to use a "bolt-on" approach. This division linked its current heterogeneous systems for production and distribution together. Then it "bolted on" new Oracle systems for human resources and accounting.

Organizations may reach a point where linking heterogeneous systems together no longer meets their needs. For example, Welch's chief information officer (CIO), Larry Rencken, stated, "It really started with the fact that we had an old and fragile infrastructure with three platforms and some products up to 25 years old—applications that were so customized they were not upgradable....We had an infrastructure with a lot of spaghetti code keeping it together, and we now have a desire for one fully integrated enterprise" (Teuke, 2006).

Although a fully integrated enterprise system, such as the one depicted in Figure 6.3, offers many advantages over heterogeneous systems held together with spaghetti code (Figure 6.2), the conversion to an integrated system may not be pain free. In the case of Hershey, conversion and implementation difficulties with a $112 million ERP prevented the company from delivering $100 million of Hershey's Kisses and other candy during its peak Halloween season. The *Wall Street Journal* likened installing an integrated SAP R/3 system to "the corporate equivalent of a root canal" (White, 1997).

One of the challenges of implementing an integrated enterprise system is staying on time and on budget. Integrated enterprise system implementations tend to be large investments, sometimes costing millions of dollars. One of the challenges is staying within the budget for the project implementation to avoid cost overruns. Underestimating implementation costs is a leading cause of project failures.

> **My Connection...**
> • Active Review 6.7.

What IT Architecture Does an Integrated Enterprise System Use?

A large-scale integrated enterprise system, such as SAP, uses a modular approach and three-tier architecture.

Integrated Enterprise Systems: Three-Tier Architecture

In order for an accountant to trace errors or audit the accounting system effectively, the accountant must understand the three-tier architecture of the integrated enterprise system. Failure to understand how the accounting data is entered, processed, stored, and retrieved can result in overlooking opportunities for error prevention and detection.

As shown in Figure 6.3, **three-tier architecture** means that the system relies upon three tiers of information technology components:

- Database tier
- Application tier
- User tier (for example, accountant)

In three-tier architecture, the database tier and application tier are considered the back-end. The user tier is called the front-end.

> **Crossroads**
> What is a thin client? Accounting professionals might think of a slender person.
>
> IT professionals, on the other hand, might think of an interface.
>
> Oracle Financials by Oracle Corporation is a high-end accounting application for large-scale enterprises. Using a thin client user interface called network computing architecture or NCA, Oracle Financials requires only a Web browser on the end-user client computer to access and run the accounting application.

> **What Is a Database Server?**
> When you go out to eat dinner, you are the customer and the server serves you food.
>
> When you want to retrieve data from the database, you are the client and the database server serves you data.

Would You Like To Know More?

To discover more about accounting system security measures, see Chapter 11, *Cybersecurity*.

The **database tier** is comprised of a large centralized relational database. As you know, the relational database uses software called relational database management system (RDBMS). The RDBMS executes commands to add, update, retrieve, and delete data from the database.

The database and RDBMS are stored on database servers or specialized computers designed to maintain the database. Large-scale database applications, such as Oracle 11g database or IBM DB2, are examples of the types of databases used with large-scale integrated enterprise systems.

The **application tier** consists of application servers, specialized computers that store and run the applications, such as Oracle Financials or SAP. Applications are the software programs that interact with the RDBMS. The application tier contains the modules for accounting, operations, sales, supply chain, and human resources. For example, in an accounting software application, the accountant might enter adjusting entries to bring accounts up to date at year end. The accounting application software would interact with the RDBMS to update the appropriate account balances.

The **user tier** consists of front-end client computers. This would include the user interface that appears on the accountant's computer screen. The user interface may be text-based or a graphical user interface (GUI). Accounting applications may use database forms that resemble the hardcopy paper forms in order to streamline data entry. In an earlier chapter, you discovered how the user interface is created using database forms and reports.

To mitigate risk of unauthorized access and possible data theft or destruction, security and control measures are used to safeguard the information assets stored in the integrated enterprise system. Each tier of the three-tier architecture has unique security and control requirements. As Figure 6.3 illustrates, typically there are firewalls constructed between each tier of the three-tier architecture. A **firewall** is a program on the router, an electronic device that routes data being transferred on the network. The firewall program is like a communication policeman monitoring traffic to and from the servers, preventing unauthorized access.

Integrated Enterprise Systems: A Modular Approach

In an integrated enterprise system, the modules in the system are interrelated. The baseline accounting system model (Figure 6.5) shows you the modules commonly used by most enterprises. These are the basic building blocks for accounting systems.

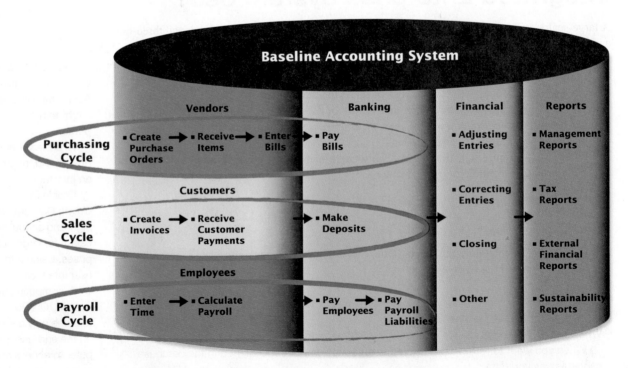

FIGURE 6.5

Baseline Accounting System with Transaction Cycles

FIGURE 6.6 Integrated Enterprise System Modules (Oracle.com, SAP.com)

Pair and Share: Can you map the modules listed here to the baseline accounting system model?

Oracle E-Business Applications	Financial Management Enterprise Resource Planning (ERP) Customer Relationship Management (CRM) Human Capital Management Supply Chain Management (SCM) Manufacturing Procurement
SAP Business Suite Modules	Financials Enterprise Resource Planning (ERP) Manufacturing Human Capital Management Customer Relationship Management (CRM) Supply Chain Management (SCM) Supplier Relationship Management (SRM)

Although the particular IES module names can vary, basically there are modules to account for customer, vendor, employee, banking, and financial transactions. Figure 6.6 lists the names of modules for two large-scale enterprise systems. These modules run on an application server and interact with the user interface on the client computer, such as the accountant's computer screen.

The data that the accountant enters using the interface is processed by the appropriate application module, which then interacts with the RDBMS. The RDBMS processes the commands and interacts with the database to insert, update, retrieve, and delete data. The advantage to the integrated system is that the modules are integrated so data can be shared between modules. Accounting can share payroll data with human resources. The sales department can share data with accounting. The supply chain can share inventory data with the accounting system.

Next, you will see the user interface for SAP, an integrated enterprise system. The purpose is to illustrate for you a few of the modules in an integrated system.

My Connection...
- Short Exercise 6.25
- Short Exercise 6.26
- Short Exercise 6.27

What Do I Need to Know about SAP?

SAP was the vision of five IBM computer engineers who realized that enterprises could standardize and integrate processes. SAP software is used around the globe by large enterprises to integrate supply chain, operations, sales, human resources, and accounting functions. Integrated enterprise systems, such as SAP, have the capability to do the following:

- Integrate enterprise modules to share data among modules.
- Integrate with customer systems to share data with customers.
- Integrate with vendor systems to share data with vendors.

This means that a customer can check his or her account balance. A vendor can check its shipments. Employees can schedule vacations. Accounting can access data entered by other modules.

Access to the SAP system is determined by the role assigned to a specific employee. For example, a sales representative might see certain screens while an accountant might have access to other screens. Next, you have the opportunity to see an SAP interface. We will demonstrate some of the SAP modules to introduce you to SAP.

Your Competitive Advantage...
SAP Business One is designed for small to midsize enterprises yet provides many of the advantages of the large-scale SAP applications.

An introduction to SAP Business One gives you a competitive advantage. It is simpler to learn than large-scale SAP and provides you with transitional skills so you can quickly transition to larger-scale applications.

Sales Forms...
Note that some systems may use one form for sales orders and invoices. SAP uses three forms: sales order, delivery, and A/R Invoice.

SAP for Small and Midsize Companies

SAP offers a range of products and services. SAP products for small and midsize companies include the following:

- SAP Business All-in-One designed for midsize businesses wanting an integrated enterprise system
- SAP Business One designed for small and midsize businesses seeking an integrated solution that goes beyond accounting-only software

Both of these SAP products integrate accounting with other business processes. These SAP solutions for small and midsize companies use the same integrated enterprise approach that SAP for larger-scale enterprises uses. In the following illustration, for brevity, we will use SAP to refer to SAP Business One.

The user interface for SAP is shown in Figure 6.7. Notice the navigation pane on the left side of the screen. The navigation tabs correspond to the modules that you know from the baseline accounting system model (Figure 6.5). The SAP navigation contains tabs for Financials, Sales, Purchasing, Banking, and Reports in addition to other tabs. Each of these tabs expands to show underlying activities and tasks. In Figure 6.7, you can see that the Sales - A/R tab expands to show associated activities including the following:

- Sales order: SAP uses separate forms for sales orders and invoices.
- Delivery: SAP uses a separate form to track shipping and delivery of the product to customers.
- A/R Invoice: This SAP form corresponds to the baseline model's customer invoice. A/R is an abbreviation for accounts receivable, an amount that the company expects to receive in the future.
- A/R Invoice + Payment: This SAP form corresponds to the *receive customer payments* activity on the baseline model.

Integrated Sales Module: Order-to-Cash

SAP calls the sales cycle **order-to-cash**. This is because the sales cycle starts with the customer's order and ends with the collection of cash.

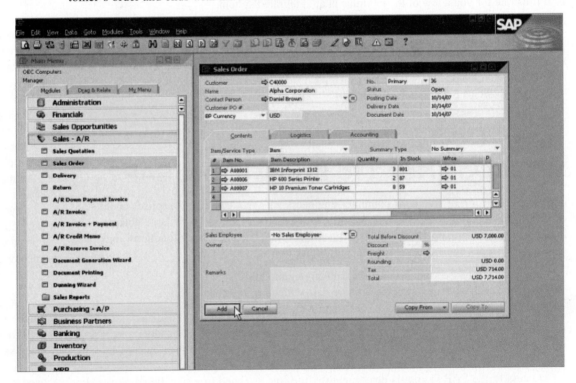

FIGURE 6.7

SAP Business One Interface

Can you name some of the database tables that are used to build the sales order form?

As you know, the sales cycle relates to the customer module events of *entering orders/ invoices* and *receiving customer payments*. As shown on the right side of Figure 6.7, the sales order in SAP consists of three parts:

- Header: contains customer information and dates.
- Middle section: contains Contents, Logistics, and Accounting tabs. The Contents tab contains information about the items ordered, including item number, item description, and quantity. The Logistics tab contains shipping and billing addresses. The Accounting tab contains general ledger account information. Automatic journal entries result from the transaction when it is recorded.
- Footer: contains calculated totals for items appearing on the sales order, including freight and tax.

To enter information into the sales order form, you can select from existing data already in the system or you can type the information into the form.

Employees can check real-time inventory data to see if the items ordered are in stock. Notice that the SAP item master data form in Figure 6.8 permits employees to check the availability of the item.

After the order data is entered in an integrated system, the data can be accessed by others to coordinate business activities, such as filling and shipping the order. For example, the order data can trigger the purchase of materials and components needed to fulfill the sales order. With some systems, customers are able to track orders through online access to the integrated system so they can stay up to date on the order status.

Information about delivery of the customer orders can be entered into a delivery form (shown in Figure 6.9). Note that in the lower right corner of the delivery form you can copy from another document, such as a sales order form. This time-saving feature lets you reuse the data from the sales order form instead of re-entering it. When the order is picked up by the shipping carrier, the sales order information is automatically updated to show the status. When the order is shipped, inventory levels are updated.

An SAP A/R Invoice (Figure 6.10) can be copied from other forms, such as the sales order and delivery form. The A/R Invoice is used to bill customers for the order.

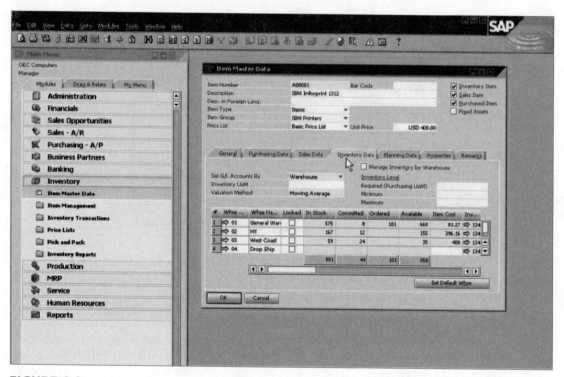

FIGURE 6.8

SAP Business One Inventory Availability

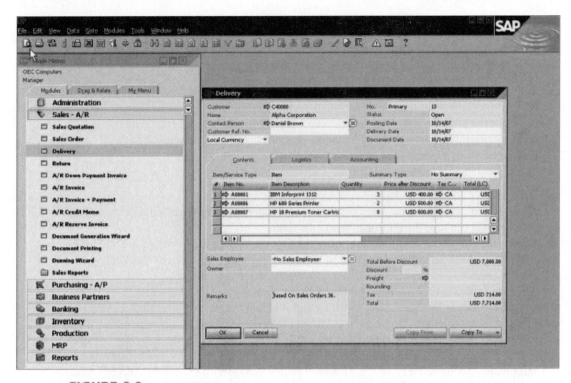

FIGURE 6.9

SAP Business One Delivery Form

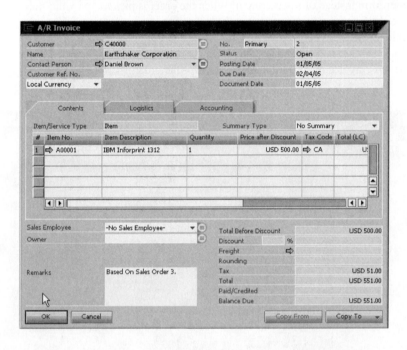

FIGURE 6.10

SAP Business One A/R Invoice Form

Can you find where this form could occur in the business process maps shown in Chapter 5?

When the customer's payment is received, an SAP deposit form (shown in Figure 6.11) is used to record the bank deposit. Notice that the deposit form is accessed from the banking module.

SAP Business All-in-One for midsize companies also includes a customer cockpit. As shown in Figure 6.12, the customer cockpit uses traffic light alerts to track the order status from order placement to picking and delivery. An SAP Business All-in-One sales workcenter (Figure 6.13) permits employees to view sales analytics. If an employee wants to see how well an item is selling, a search can be conducted using SAP. For example, to see how many sales orders contain material M-13, a sales order query could be run. The search criteria, material M-13, is entered into the SAP sales order search form (Figure 6.14).

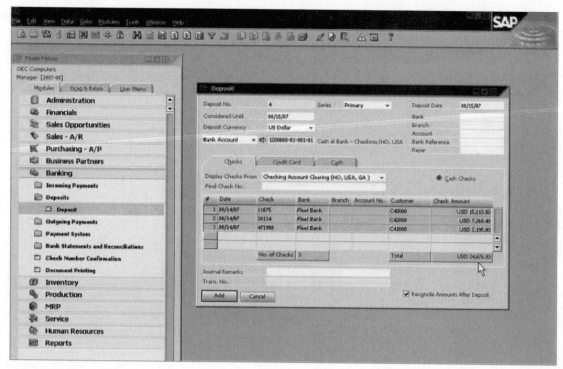

FIGURE 6.11

SAP Business One Deposit Form

Can you match the navigation tabs shown on the left of the SAP screen with the modules in
the baseline accounting system model?

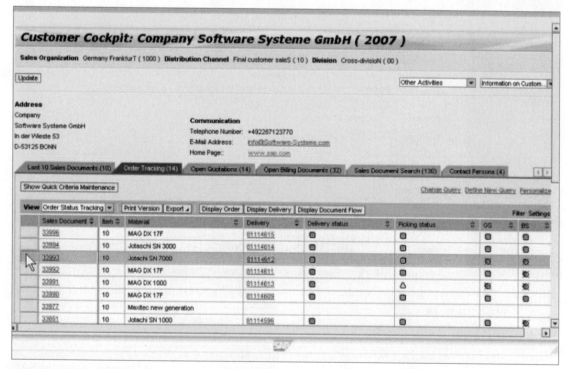

FIGURE 6.12

SAP Customer Cockpit

Which sales order has a warning regarding its picking status?

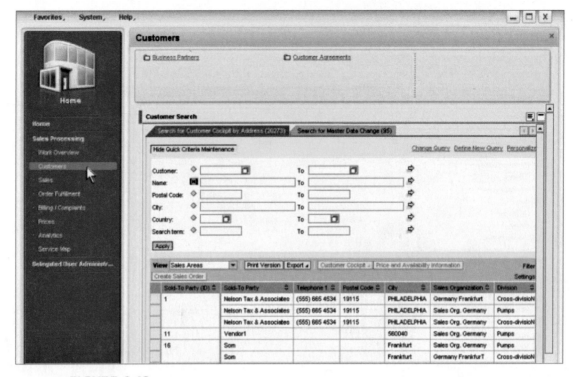

FIGURE 6.13

SAP Sales Workcenter

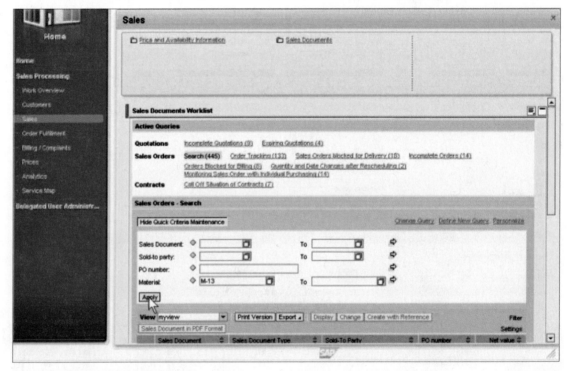

FIGURE 6.14

SAP Sales Order Search

SAP sales analytics can be displayed in charts or reports. Notice in Figure 6.15 that the SAP sales analytics form allows the employee to use a filter to select the criteria for a specific report or chart. Buttons in the lower left corner of the screen permit the employee to send the sales analytics via email (information broadcasting) or to download to Excel.

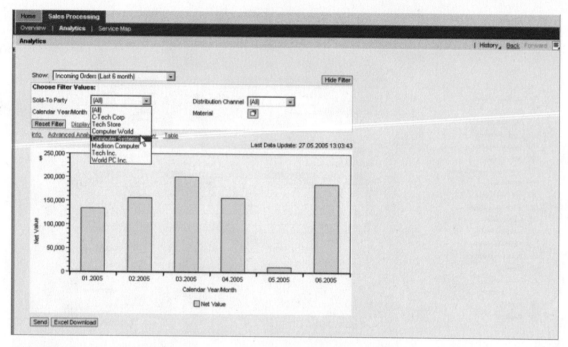

FIGURE 6.15

SAP Sales Analytics

Integrated Purchasing Module: Procure-to-Pay

The SAP purchasing module corresponds to the vendor module in the baseline model. SAP refers to this as **procure-to-pay**. As shown in Figure 6.16, events in the SAP purchasing module include the following:

- Purchase order: The SAP purchase order form is used to place an order for a purchase.
- Goods Receipt PO: This SAP form corresponds to the baseline receive items event.
- A/P Invoice: This SAP form corresponds to the baseline model's enter bills event. A/P is an abbreviation for accounts payable, an amount that the company expects to pay in the future.

An SAP purchase order form is shown in Figure 6.16. SAP permits you to select from existing vendors and items or enter new ones.

In an integrated system, the workflow can be built into the system so electronic purchase orders are automatically forwarded to appropriate parties for their approval. When the next person in the workflow approval process logs onto his or her computer, the pending purchase order awaiting his or her approval will appear in a queue. The person approves or disapproves the purchase order and then it is electronically forwarded to the next person in the approval process.

The integrated system increases efficiency by automatically forwarding the purchase order to the next person. After the final approval is received, the purchase order may be electronically forwarded to the appropriate vendor, again speeding up the process.

To record items received, SAP uses a form called a Goods Receipt PO (Figure 6.17). Notice the Copy From button in the lower left corner of the Goods Receipt PO. This permits the employee to copy data from the PO to the Goods Receipt PO instead of re-entering the data. Copying information from an existing PO saves time and reduces the opportunity for error.

The receiving report may be electronically forwarded to the accounting department to inform it that the items have been received. Typically the bill is sent by the vendor to the accounting department. When the bill is received, the accounting department performs a three-way match to verify the bill. The accounting department compares three documents: the PO, the Goods Receipt PO, and the vendor's bill. Then the bill is entered into an A/P (Accounts Payable) Invoice form.

Who Has the Best Supply Chain?
One survey found that the companies with the best supply chains included Apple, Cisco, P&G, and Wal-Mart (cio.com, 2010).

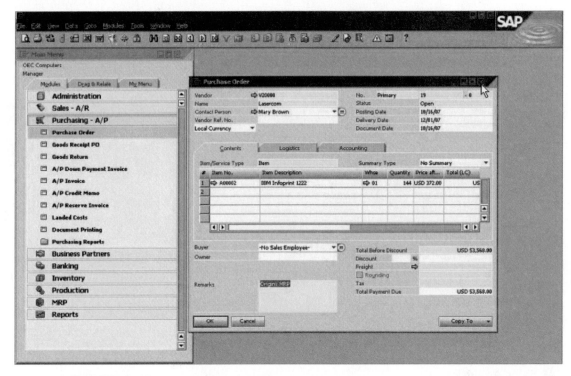

FIGURE 6.16

SAP Business One Purchase Order

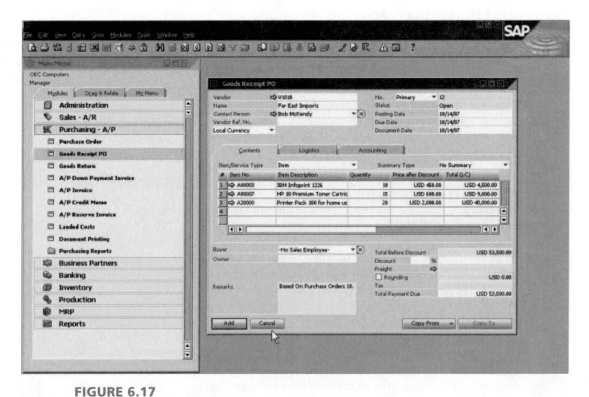

FIGURE 6.17

SAP Business One Goods Receipt PO

SAP Business All-in-One facilitates tracking of purchase orders, goods received, and invoices (bills). SAP Business All-in-One automatically initiates a three-way match, comparing the PO, the goods received, and the bill entered (A/P Invoice). After the system compares these three items, it lists any exceptions.

What happens when your three-way match doesn't match? Figure 6.18 shows an SAP accounts payable invoice management workcenter where employees can see exceptions that the system has flagged. Figure 6.19 shows an invoice (bill) exception for missing goods receipts. The company received a bill for items it had ordered, but the system could not find a matching receipt for the goods received. With a three-way match, the company will not pay the bill until the goods are confirmed as received. SAP provides the capability for the accountant to email the employee responsible for receiving to inquire about the status.

Figure 6.20 shows another exception that the SAP system flagged. From the invoice management workcenter, select duplicate invoice exceptions to drill down to the list of duplicate bills found in the SAP system. Invoice No. 13872 is a duplicate invoice, and this needs to be resolved before the associated bill is paid.

Integrated Employee Module

The employee module focuses on the transactions related to payroll and employees. The functions completed by this module include the ability to track employee time worked, calculate payroll and withholding amounts, create employee paychecks, and pay payroll liabilities to appropriate governmental agencies and organizations.

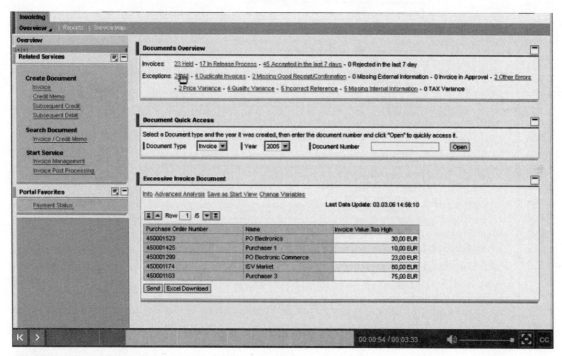

FIGURE 6.18

SAP Accounts Payable Invoice Management Workcenter

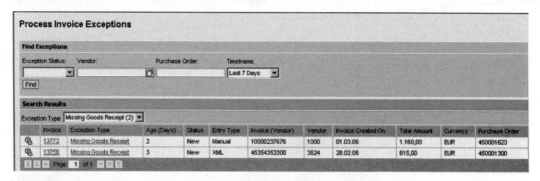

FIGURE 6.19

SAP Invoice (Bill) Exceptions Missing Goods Receipt

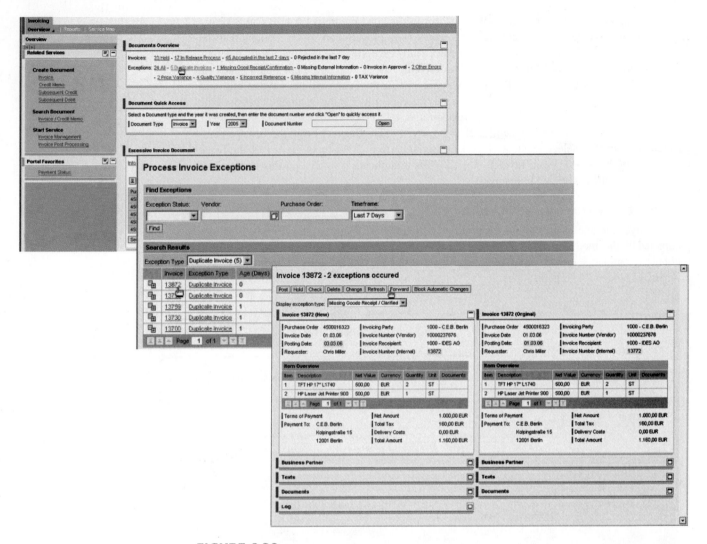

FIGURE 6.20

SAP Duplicate Invoices (Bills)

Integrated enterprise systems permit the employee time worked to be used in multiple ways. For example, the time worked can be used to calculate payroll and also transferred to invoices to bill customers.

Figure 6.21 shows the SAP screens for employees to record working time. Employees can use a daily or weekly format for entering their working time. After time is entered, the employee reviews and confirms the hours worked. Notice the Synchronize button on the left side of the third screen. The employee clicks this button and enters his or her password to synchronize the time entered with the back-end enterprise database.

Integrated Financial Module

The financial module focuses on events related to completing the accounting cycle and recording transactions that are not entered into the other modules. In an integrated enterprise system, this module is sometimes referred to as a general ledger module.

SAP automatically converts data entered from the sales and purchasing forms into journal entries, updating the general ledger. There are times, however, when it is necessary to enter journal entries into the system. For example, adjusting entries often must be calculated and entered by an accountant at year end.

Figure 6.22 shows the SAP onscreen journal used to make journal entries. Notice that there is a column for account number, account name, debit amount, and credit amount. The system requires that debits and credits for the entry must equal.

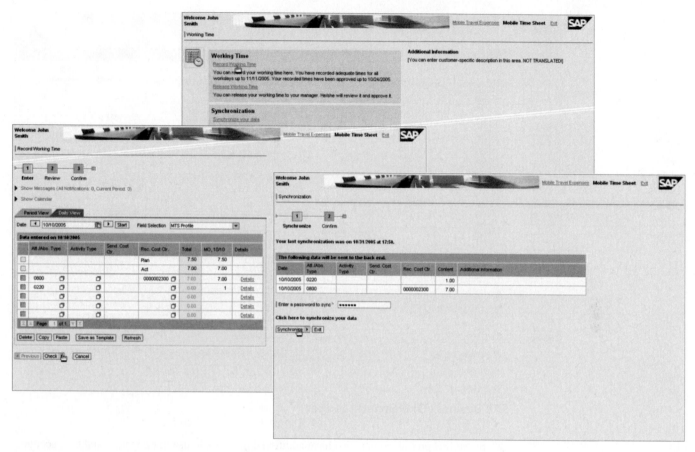

FIGURE 6.21

SAP Business One Record Working Time

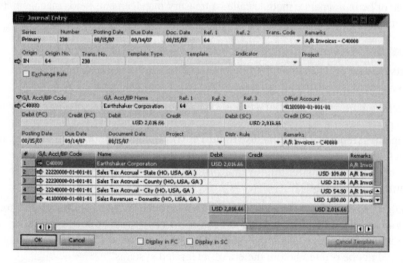

FIGURE 6.22

SAP Business One Journal Entry

Figure 6.23 shows the General Ledger account activity for several revenue and expense accounts. Notice the debit/credit column to track changes in each of the accounts. The balance column shows the cumulative balance of an account after each transaction.

At year end, an IES may streamline consolidation of numerous entities using different currencies and from various geographic locations. The integrated system may also be designed to implement accounting standards, such as generally accepted accounting principles (GAAP) or International Financial Reporting Standards (IFRS), as well as regulations and legislation, such as Sarbanes-Oxley.

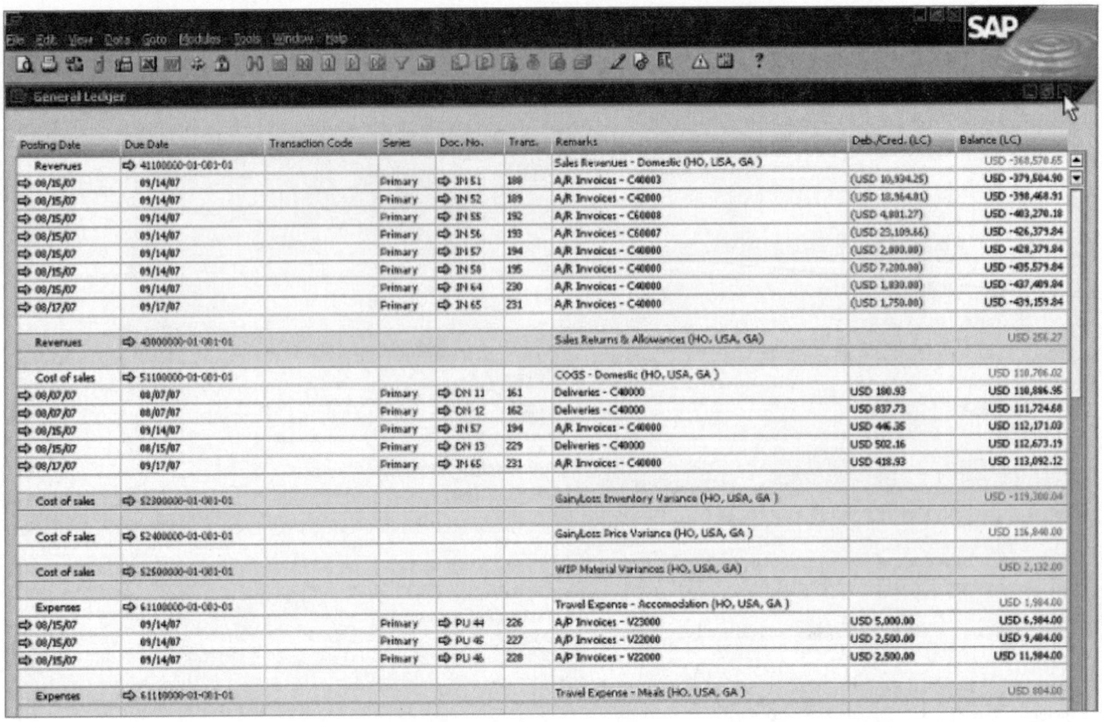

FIGURE 6.23

SAP Business One General Ledger

Some IES providers may also have additional modules to use in budgeting and cost accounting functions. For organizations involved in manufacturing, yet another module may be added for production and operations management. Treasury management functions may be part of the financial module or be in a separate module called a treasury management, funds management, or cash management module.

Integrated Reports Module

The reports module provides the reporting or output function for the entire integrated system. In general, we can classify accounting reports into one of four categories:

- Financial reporting for external users, such as investors, creditors, and regulatory agencies
- Tax reports used for filing with federal, state, and local taxing agencies
- Management reports for internal use to provide information for decision making, including business intelligence
- Sustainability reporting for improved decision making related to economic, social, and environmental sustainability

An integrated enterprise system makes it possible to retrieve data from various modules and functional areas when compiling reports to meet the needs of users throughout the organization. The integrated database management system offers the enterprise additional reporting capabilities that could not be offered before the era of integrated systems.

SAP provides several different options for creating reports. Figure 6.24 shows the Reports tab in SAP. Notice how the tab expands to show different types of reports, such as Financials. Under Financials is listed Accounting reports. Figure 6.24 shows an Aging report.

SAP also permits users to create reports using MS Excel as the interface. An example of a digital dashboard created using SAP report designer is shown in Figure 6.25. Notice that the digital dashboard is displayed using MS Excel. SAP Business All-in-One includes business intelligence software to provide additional analysis for improved decision making.

SAP has a query wizard (Figure 6.26) that employees can use to create custom reports. The query wizard gives real-time access to the enterprise database. It is accessed from the Reports tab. The employee can build a report by selecting database tables using the query wizard. Then database fields for the report are selected. Search criteria are entered, such as a customer balance greater than $-0-.

What Does [dbo] Tell You?

Notice the [dbo] in the SQL statement shown in Figure 6.27. The [dbo] tells you that this query is used with an MS SQL Server database. Table names in MS SQL Server start with the prefix [dbo]. [dbo] stands for database object.

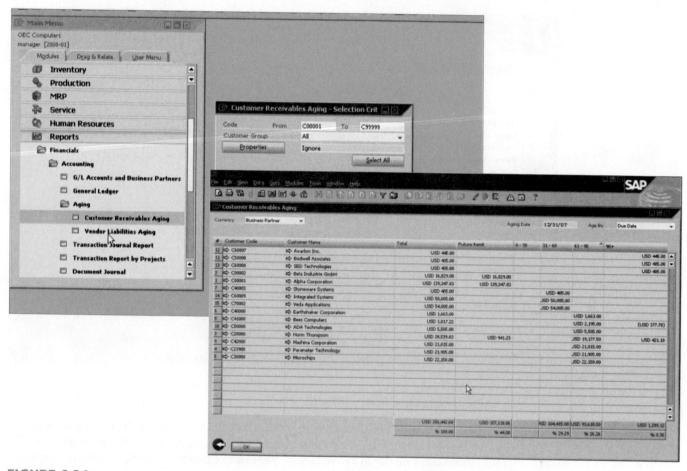

FIGURE 6.24

SAP Business One Aging Report

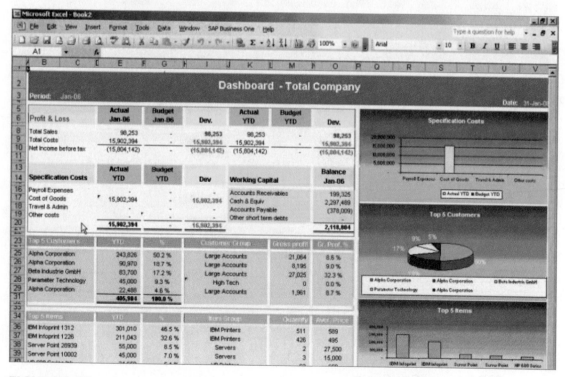

FIGURE 6.25

SAP Business One Digital Dashboard

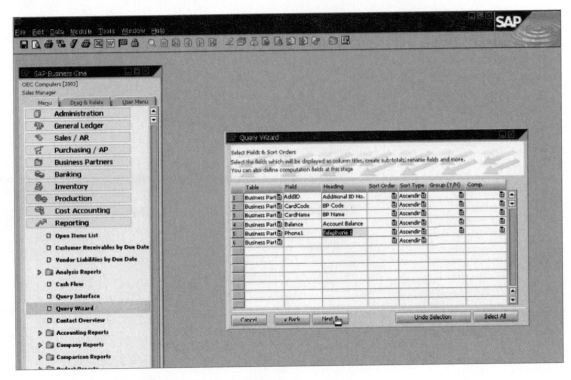

FIGURE 6.26

SAP Business One Query Wizard

The query result is shown in Figure 6.27. The fields selected and the field contents appear in the query results. Notice the SQL statement appearing at the top of the query window. The SQL statement is similar to the SQL query you saw in Chapter 3. The SQL statement shows the selected fields from the specified tables using the search criteria.

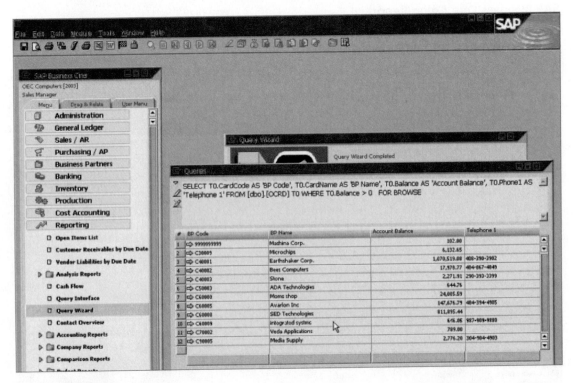

FIGURE 6.27

SAP Business One Query

What are the database tables and fields used by the SQL statement in this query?

Cloud Computing...
Cloud computing is an emerging trend in the area of accounting software applications. As enterprises strive to reduce their IT costs for hardware and software, more are turning to cloud computing, in which they basically lease the software as a service (SaaS). The provider owns the server, database, and accounting software. The enterprise leases or rents use of the software from the provider.

My Connection...
- Short Exercise 6.28
- Short Exercise 6.30
- Tech in Practice 6.43

How Do I Integrate My Enterprise System with the Cloud?

Cloud Computing

Do you use a Web-based email account? Store files online? Store photos online? Then you are using cloud computing. Cloud computing uses remote computing facilities owned by third parties to run software applications and store files. Typically, the cloud is accessed over the Internet, and increasingly the cloud is accessed using apps, such as Apple's iCloud.

With cloud computing, instead of owning the IT hardware and software on-site, you rent the computing services from a third party off site, which is referred to as "in the cloud."

There are many benefits to the cloud. No longer do businesses have to buy complicated software applications with dedicated servers. Costly and hard to find IT personnel to install, maintain, and upgrade complicated software may be reduced or eliminated. There are also some downsides to cloud computing, including security concerns. For example, a cyberattack on Sony Playstation in the cloud resulted in almost a month of downtime.

Three service models of cloud computing (Figure 6.28) that you can rent from providers are:

- IaaS (Infrastructure-as-a-Service)
- PaaS (Platform-as-a-Service)
- SaaS (Software-as-a-Service)

Apple's iCloud...
Apple's iCloud streamlines syncing of files and apps among desktop, laptop, iPad and iPhone. All devices are synced through the cloud. Cloud computing has made it possible to do more and more with mobile devices that no longer need large storage capacity. Documents can be stored in the cloud and accessed only as needed.

Where Is the Cloud?
A third-party provider, such as Amazon Web Services or Rackspace, has huge cloud server farms in carefully monitored and highly secure locations. Instead of being located in a cloud, these server farms are frequently located underground, making it easier to maintain cooler temperatures needed for highly sensitive equipment.

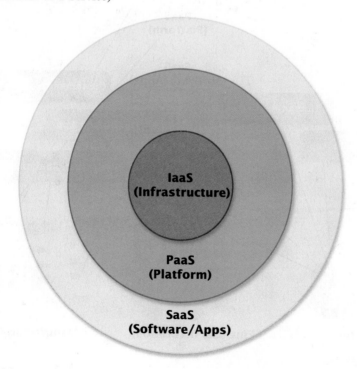

FIGURE 6.28

Cloud Computing Services

Which are the risks of cloud computing for SaaS, PaaS, and IaaS?

IaaS (Infrastructure-as-a-Service). This cloud service model lets you outsource the IT equipment needed to support your operations, including data storage, hardware, servers, and networks. An IaaS provider owns the equipment. You basically rent the computing resources, while the provider houses, runs, and maintains it. Infrastructure-as-a-Service may also be referred to as Hardware-as-a-Service.

PaaS (Platform-as-a-Service). With PaaS, the cloud provider provides the platform (programming languages, operating systems, networks, servers, and storage) needed for you to deploy or develop applications (software). For example, if you needed a specialized app for your accounting needs, you could rent the platform needed to develop the app without the expense of buying the networks, operating systems, and programming languages.

SaaS (Software-as-a-Service). With SaaS, the cloud provider rents you use of the provider's software application, such as accounting software. Instead of running the software on your own on-site computers, you typically use a Web browser or mobile app to access the cloud application. QuickBooks Online, Net Suite, and SAP ByDesign are examples of SaaS for accounting apps.

As shown in Figure 6.29, you can use one or more of the cloud computing service layers: software, platform, or infrastructure. The main idea to remember about cloud computing is that instead of purchasing the software, platform, or infrastructure, you rent them as needed on demand. Cloud providers to choose from include:

- Amazon Web Services
- Oracle Public Cloud
- Google Cloud Services

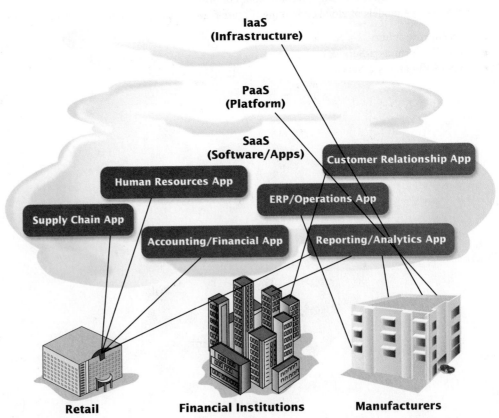

Cloud Computing

FIGURE 6.29

Cloud Computing SaaS, PaaS, and Iaas

Which cloud services do you think would be best suited for an accounting firm: SaaS? PaaS? Iaas?

- Terremark Cloud Computing
- Microsoft Azure
- Rackspace

Rent or Buy?

Assume you are considering whether to buy a home or rent an apartment. If you buy a home, you will be responsible for maintenance and security. If you rent, the landlord owner is responsible for maintenance and security. If you decide to rent an apartment instead of buying a home, this can be compared to companies choosing to rent cloud computing services instead of buying the infrastructure, platforms, and software.

Accounting in the Cloud

Cloud accounting applications include QuickBooks Online, NetSuite, and SAP ByDesign. While QuickBooks Online focuses on accounting and financial services, NetSuite and SAP ByDesign offer an integrated enterprise system in the cloud, integrating the accounting/financial module with other modules, such as human resources, CRM, and supply chain.

When the accounting application is in the cloud, instead of installing the accounting software on a company-owed, on-site hard drive or server, you rent the accounting software as a computing service. You access the accounting application over the Internet using a Web browser, such as Google Chrome. For integrated enterprise systems in the cloud, the accounting module is one module within the larger integrated system.

An example of cloud-based SAP ByDesign interface appears in Figure 6.30. SAP ByDesign is accessed using a Web browser and offers modules for sales/customers, purchases/vendors, human resources, financials, and reporting.

Compare the SAP cloud computing interface in Figure 6.30 with the integrated SAP Business One interface in Figure 6.7. The navigation is slightly different, with the ByDesign navigation bar to access modules appearing across the top of the window instead of on the left with Business One. However, many of the database forms for entering data, such as invoices and purchase orders, function in the same manner.

One of the big advantages of cloud-based integrated enterprise systems is that in addition to integrating your accounting system with other related modules, such as human resources and CRM, a cloud-based system facilitates integrating your enterprise system with vendors and

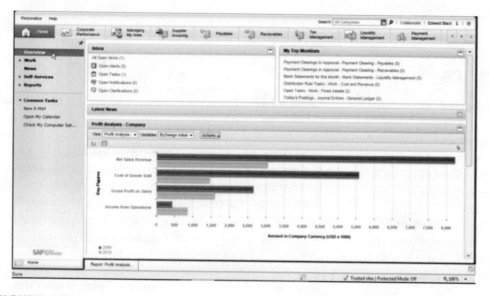

FIGURE 6.30

SAP ByDesign Interface

Can you find the navigation bar?

customers. For customers to access their account balance in the cloud, they use a Web browser with login and password.

> **All about Databases**
> Whether an accounting system, an on-site integrated enterprise system, or a cloud-based enterprise sytem, it's all about databases. When you enter data in a cloud-based system, the data is still stored in a database.

Cloud Computing Benefits and Challenges

Cloud computing offers many benefits to organizations. But for every benefit, there may be a corresponding challenge. The following is a brief list of a few benefits and accompanying challenges presented by cloud computing.

1. Investment. If you use cloud computing, you may be able to avoid the ongoing investments in upgrades and new technologies. The downside is that you may lose control over when upgrades and new technologies are implemented in the cloud.
2. Security. You no longer have to worry about on-site security for your computing needs that are outsourced to the cloud, and a cloud provider may be able to specialize in the special security needs for cloud computing. The downside is that you lose control over security and must rely upon the cloud provider to provide intrusion detection systems, video surveillance and more.
3. Accessibility. You can access the cloud whenever you need to so long as you have an Internet connection. However, the challenge is ensuring that others cannot also access your information because it is stored in the cloud.
4. Data. One benefit of cloud computing is that your data is stored in the cloud and someone else is responsible for storing and backing it up. The challenge to this is that if a cloud provider goes down, how do you access your data and backups?
5. Mobility. When you use cloud computing, you can be mobile, accessing the data from mobile devices such as a laptop, tablet or smartphone. The challenge is to ensure that your security is not compromised as a result. When you use a Web browser, there are additional security considerations, such as using HTTPS (Hypertext Transfer Protocol Secure) and using encryption so others cannot see your data in transmission. Also, the mobile device may be outside a secure firewall, so this security challenge must be addressed as well.

> **My Connection...**
> • Active Review 6.11

In many cases, the benefits of cloud computing, such as mobility and access, can create the greatest challenges and risks.

Chapter Highlights

What are advantages of an integrated enterprise system? The integrated enterprise system offers many advantages over the functional silo approach to enterprise systems. The accounting functions are integrated into the larger enterprise system, permitting accounting to share data with other functional areas and better coordinate activities.

What are challenges associated with an integrated enterprise system? Challenges of an integrated enterprise system include business processes that may need to be redesigned and managing the changes required by the new system.

How is data entered in an integrated enterprise system? Database forms that relate to business process activities permit users to enter data once into the IES and have

the data shared throughout the enterprise, eliminating the need for different functional areas to rekey the same data.

How does an integrated enterprise system relate to the accounting system? Integrated enterprise systems use a modular approach that is consistent with the baseline accounting system model. The basic module names may vary but the functions are basically the same. Integrated enterprise systems integrate accounting with other modules for an enterprise. Customer and vendor systems can also be integrated.

How Do I Integrate My Enterprise System with the Cloud? Cloud computing involves enterprises that rent remote computing facilities owned by third parties to provide software applications, platforms and IT infrastructure.

Accounting System Insights

Insight No. 15 Integrated systems share data... let others enter data for you.

Active Review

Study less. Learn more. Make connections.

6.1 Refer to the chapter opener, *Meet Nestlé*. In your opinion, what should Nestlé do about the vanilla issue? How can an integrated enterprise system address such issues?

6.2 Discuss the role of networks, such as LANs and the Internet, in the evolution of integrated enterprise systems.

6.3 Compare the silo and integrated architectures. Do you see any advantages associated with the silo architecture? Explain.

6.4 Discuss the differences between an accounting system integrated with other enterprise system modules and a stand-alone accounting system.

6.5 Discuss the impact of an integrated enterprise system on an organization's value chain and supply chain.

6.6 Discuss the advantages of an integrated enterprise system when creating reports.

6.7 Discuss the obstacles an organization faces when it decides to implement a new enterprise system.

6.8 Discuss why implementing an integrated enterprise system can be more cost effective than a nonintegrated system.

6.9 Discuss the role of each tier in three-tier architecture.

6.10 Discuss security and control measures used in three-tier architecture.

6.11 Discuss why, with all the tremendous benefits of the cloud computing, some companies are still reluctant to migrate their systems into the cloud.

Key Terms Check

Understanding the language used at the crossroads of accounting and IT is key to your success.

6.12 Match the following terms and definitions.
a. order-to-cash
b. procure-to-pay
c. spaghetti code
d. three-tier architecture
e. database tier
f. application tier
g. user tier
h. firewall
i. business process management (BPM)

_____ 1. Programming code used to connect stand-alone systems
_____ 2. Transforming business processes to improve efficiency
_____ 3. Corresponds to the purchasing cycle
_____ 4. Corresponds to the sales cycle
_____ 5. Consists of front-end client computers and the user interface
_____ 6. Software programs on a router that monitor network traffic
_____ 7. Comprised of a centralized relationship database and an RDBMS
_____ 8. Consists of servers and application software
_____ 9. When an enterprise system uses layers of IT components: enterprise database, application, and client computers

6.13 Match the following terms and definitions.
a. Software as a service
b. Infrastructure as a service
c. Cloud computing
d. Platform as a service

_____ 1. Provides the programming language and operating systems, networks, and servers needed for application development
_____ 2. Providing on-demand off-site computing services
_____ 3. Rents you the use of software applications such as an accounting system
_____ 4. Lets you outsource the IT equipment needed to support your operations

Practice Test

6.14 Which of the following best explains an enterprise IT silo architecture?

a. All enterprise systems are connected to a centralized database.

b. Except the accounting system, various systems are integrated throughout the enterprise.

c. Stand-alone systems within an enterprise

d. It was installed to fix the Y2K issue.

6.15 In the early 1990s, stand-alone computers were connected using

a. The Internet

b. Local Area Networks

c. The intranet

d. Wide-area network

6.16 The three-tier architecture consists of

a. Database tier, application tier, and user tier

b. Server computer tier, network tier, and personal computer tier

c. User interface tier, database management system tier, and accounting tier

d. None of the above

6.17 Which of the following is offered by BPMS?

a. Automating the flow of documents among employees

b. Automating the flow of information software modules and functional area

c. Automating information flow among enterprise segments and other enterprises at remote sites

d. All the above

6.18 The term ERP is used generally to refer to

a. Enterprise three-tier architecture

b. Stand-alone systems connected with spaghetti programming code

c. Enterprise resource planning

d. Integrated enterprise systems

6.19 What is the minimum number of firewalls protecting three-tier architecture?

a. Three

b. One

c. Four

d. Two

6.20 The SAP order-to-cash is the equivalent of which modules in the baseline accounting system?

a. Customers and banking

b. Vendors and banking

c. Employees and banking

d. Customers, banking, and financial

6.21 Which of the following best explains cloud computing?

a. Third-party off-site and on-demand IT services to an organization

b. Off-site IT services owned by an organization

c. An organization's IT infrastructure residing in a remote location

d. An organization's IT infrastructure spread over many remote locations

6.22 Which of the following cloud computing services include accounting software?

a. SaaS

b. PaaS and IaaS

c. aaS

d. PaaS

6.23 Which of the following is NOT a benefit of cloud computing?

a. Cloud computing helps organizations avoid the ongoing investments in upgrades and new technologies.

b. Cloud computing provider will offer the security needed for cloud services.

c. Cloud can be accessed whenever it is needed as long as there is an Internet connection.

d. Cloud computing increases an organization's control over IT services.

Exercises

Each Exercise relates to one of the major questions addressed in the chapter and is labeled with the question number in green.

Short Exercises
Warm up with these short exercises.

6.24 Sales reps for Hamid Enterprises enter prospective customer information into customer prospects software. Sales reps use the data to periodically follow up on prospective customers.

When a prospective customer places a sales order, the accounting department currently must re-enter all the customer contact information into the accounting system.

When sales reps need to obtain information about whether a customer has placed an order, they are unable to access the accounting database. In addition, the prospective customer number used in the sales rep database is different than the customer number that the accountants use. In some cases, the customer's name has been spelled differently in the two systems and there is no way to retrieve the proper information.

How can you apply Accounting Insight No. 15 to improve this situation? **(Q6.1)**

6.25 An organization's integrated enterprise system that includes accounting has the following components. Match the components with the appropriate tier. **(Q6.1)**

a. Database tier
b. Application tier
c. User tier

_____ 1. Oracle database
_____ 2. Back-end SAP applications for accounting and finance module
_____ 3. Oracle 11g RDBMS
_____ 4. Employee computers running the accounting interface for entering data and producing reports
_____ 5. Application server
_____ 6. Database server

6.26 An organization's accounting system consists of the following hardware and software:

- Hardware:
  Dell Workstation and Dell Servers
- Software:
  Unix platform
  Oracle 11g database engine
  Oracle's JD Edwards financial software
  Microsoft Excel

In the same organization, the human resource department uses a system with the following characteristics:

- Hardware:
  Sun Microsystems servers and workstation
- Software:
  Microsoft.Net platform
  Microsoft SQL Server database
  Oracle PeopleSoft human resources module

Answer the following questions that an auditor asked you: (Q6.1, 6.2, 6.3)

1. Is this an integrated enterprise system? Why or why not?
2. What is the process for accounting employees to access the human resource database and extract useful information?

6.27 Most integrated enterprise systems consolidate enterprise operational databases into a single database. Using what you know about database forms, queries, and reports, explain the advantages of a centralized database. (Q6.3)

6.28 Refer to the SAP Business One sales order form shown in Figure 6.7. For each of the following database fields shown in the form, identify the database table in which the field is stored. (Q6.4)

a. CUSTOMER table
b. SALES ORDER table
c. SALES ORDER LINE table
d. ITEM table

_____ 1. Contact Person
_____ 2. Name
_____ 3. Delivery Date
_____ 4. Sales Employee
_____ 5. Item Description
_____ 6. Quantity
_____ 7. In Stock
_____ 8. Freight
_____ 9. Tax
_____ 10. Total

6.29 Refer to the SAP Business One purchase order form shown in Figure 6.16. For each of the following database fields shown in the form, identify the database table in which the field is stored. (Q6.4)

a. VENDER table
b. PURCHASE ORDER table
c. PURCHASE ORDER LINE table
d. ITEM table

_____ 1. Contact Person
_____ 2. Name
_____ 3. Delivery Date
_____ 4. Buyer
_____ 5. Item Description
_____ 6. Quantity
_____ 7. Discount
_____ 8. Freight
_____ 9. Tax
_____ 10. Total Payment Due

6.30 Refer to the SAP duplicate invoices shown in Figure 6.20. What process does the SAP integrated enterprise system use to identify the duplicate invoices? If you were not using an integrated system, would the system be able to identify duplicate invoices? (Q6.4)

6.31 Refer to the SAP Business One SQL query shown in Figure 6.27. The SQL statement is shown in the top of the Queries window. What is the search criteria in the SQL statement? What database table(s) are referenced in the SQL statement? (Q6.4)

6.32 A bank wishes to use accounting software and data storage from a cloud computing provider. What type of cloud computing services would the bank be seeking? Should the bank request all required disk space at the beginning? Explain. (Q6.4, 6.5)

It's Your Call

This is your training ground. These scenarios provide you with the opportunity to use your knowledge and professional skills.

6.33 You have been called in as a consultant in the role of liaison between the accounting and IT professionals. The IT department has put forth a plan for an integrated enterprise system. The plan calls for the accounting database to be integrated into an enterprise relational database. IT asserts that accounting can be improved when an enterprise system is integrated. An integrated system can improve management decision making.

The accounting department is resisting this change. The accountants have a strong preference for keeping a stand-alone accounting system. They are concerned about the security of the confidential data stored in the accounting database. They are worried that after the integration the accounting database will be vulnerable to access by other employees.

Your job is to facilitate communication between the accounting and IT professionals to reach a resolution regarding the integrated enterprise system issue. Describe how you would handle this situation. **(Q6.2, 6.3)**

6.34 The CFO of Rosewater Corporation has asked you to prepare an executive summary for him to present at the next leadership team meeting. Currently, Rosewater uses stand-alone silo systems. The CFO would like you to summarize the problems experienced with the current silo systems and how these problems could be eliminated with an integrated enterprise system. He has asked that you address any risks associated with an integrated enterprise system. **(Q6.2, 6.3)**

6.35 Your boss, the CFO, has asked you to resolve an issue between accounting and human resources. You investigate to obtain the facts. Your friend in accounting tells you that in recent months after payroll checks are run, human resources complains that a few employees have not received their paychecks. When you talk to human resources, you learn that the department enters all new employees immediately into the database. The department is baffled as to why accounting can't seem to get it right. The new employees are very upset when they call human resources after they do not receive their first paycheck.

Your next step is to talk to IT to try to unravel what is occurring. When you explain the situation to IT, the database administrator tells you that accounting and human resources have stand-alone databases. Although human resources enters new employees into its database immediately, the updated data is transferred to the accounting database on the first of each month. Payroll is run on the last day of each month.

After gathering the facts, how would you resolve this issue? What do you tell the CFO? What do you say to accounting? What do you tell human resources? **(Q6.2, 6.3)**

6.36 Your company is evaluating the option of renting some of its computing services from a cloud provider. After many discussions, your company is considering renting only the accounting module. Your supervisor has asked you to develop, as soon as possible, a short document about how this type of service is provided by a cloud computing provider and the necessary steps that should be taken to implement this service. **(Q6.4, 6.5)**

Tech in Practice

These technology in practice exercises are perfect for both individuals and teams.

Tech Exercises

Sharpen your skills with these technology exercises. Watch these software videos at www.pearsonhighered.com/kay.

6.37
Tech Tool: Database Software
Software Videos: Database Tables

Refer to the SAP Business One sales order form for an integrated enterprise system shown in Figure 6.7. Your assignment is to build the database tables and fields to link to a database form similar to the one shown in Figure 6.7.

Use Microsoft Access database software and the following figure of MS Access tables to build the tables and fields.

1. Build the CUSTOMER table and select the primary key.
2. Build the SALES ORDER table and select the primary key.
3. Build the SALES ORDER LINE table and select the composite primary key.
4. Build the ITEM table and select the primary key.
5. Build the table relationships.
6. Print the table relationships.
7. Enter the following customer data into the CUSTOMER table and print.

   Customer No.: C40000
   Company Name: Alpha Corporation
   Contact Person: Daniel Brown

   Customer No.: C42000
   Company Name: Beta Company
   Contact Person: Adam Green

8. Enter the following item data into the ITEM table and print.

   Item No.: A00001
   Item Description: IBM Inforprint 1312
   In Stock: 801

   Item No.: A00006
   Item Description: HP 600 Series Printer
   In Stock: 87

   Item No.: A00007
   Item Description: HP 10 Premium Toner Cartridges
   In Stock: 59

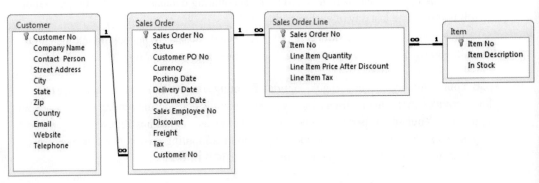

6.38

Tech Tool: Database Software

Software Videos: Database Forms

Your assignment is to build a database form to enter customer information into an integrated enterprise system.

1. Download the data file for this exercise.
2. Use Microsoft Access database software and the following sample to build a Customer form.

6.39

Tech Tool: Database Software

Software Videos: Database Queries

Your assignment is to build queries to retrieve customer and item information using Microsoft Access database software. These are typical queries that would be used when completing a sales order form as shown in Figure 6.7.

1. Download the data file for this exercise.
2. Build a query to retrieve the company name and contact person when the customer number is entered. For this query, use a search criteria of Customer No. = C40000.
3. Build a query to retrieve item description and in stock information when the item number is entered. For this query, use a search criteria of Item No. = A00001.

6.40

Tech Tool: Database Software

Software Videos: Advanced Database Forms and Queries

Your assignment is to build a database form to enter sales orders into an integrated enterprise system.

1. Download the data file for this exercise.
2. Use Microsoft Access database software and the following sample to build a Sales Order form for entering sales orders.

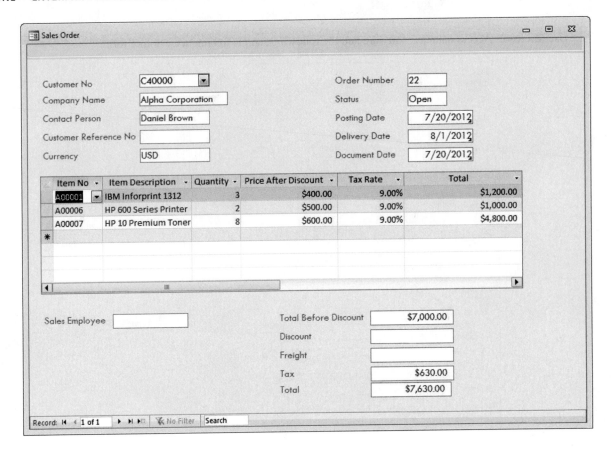

6.41

Tech Tool: Database Software

Software Videos: Database Tables

Refer to the SAP Business One purchase order form for an integrated enterprise system shown in Figure 6.16. Your assignment is to build the database tables and fields to link to a database form similar to the one shown in Figure 6.16.

Use Microsoft Access database software and the following figure of MS Access tables to build the required tables and fields.

1. Download the data file for this exercise.
2. Build the VENDOR table and select the primary key.
3. Build the PURCHASE ORDER table and select the primary key.
4. Build the PURCHASE ORDER LINE table and select the composite primary key.
5. Build the table relationships.
6. Print the table relationships.
7. Enter the following vendor data into the VENDOR table and print.

    Vendor No.: V20000
    Vendor Name: LaserCom
    Contact Person: Mary Brown

    Vendor No.: V21000
    Vendor Name: SportMax
    Contact Person: Tina Sharp

    Vendor No.: V22000
    Vendor Name: Soccer World
    Contact Person: Tomas Angel

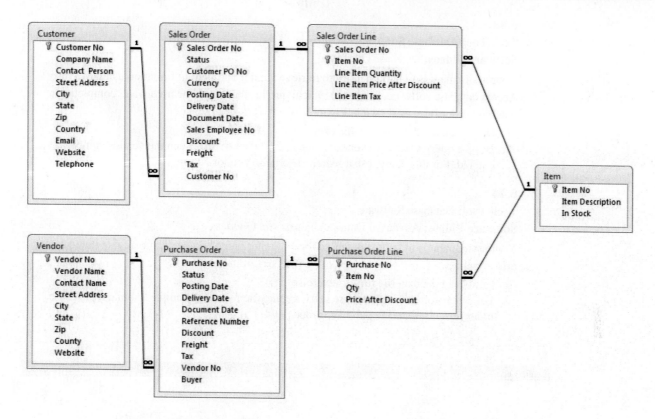

6.42

Tech Tool: Database Software

Software Videos: Database Forms

Your assignment is to build a database form for entering vendor information into an integrated enterprise system.

1. Download the data file for this exercise.
2. Use Microsoft Access database software and the following sample to build a Vendor form.

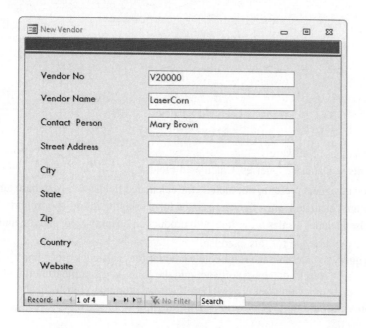

6.43

Tech Tool: Database Software

Software Videos: Database Queries

Your assignment is to build queries to retrieve vendor and item information using Microsoft Access database software. These are typical queries that would be used when completing a purchase order form as shown in Figure 6.16.

1. Download the data file for this exercise.
2. Build a query to retrieve vendor name and contact person when the vendor number is entered. For this query, use a search criteria of Vendor No. = V20000.

6.44

Tech Tool: Database Software

Software Videos: Advanced Database Forms and Queries

Your assignment is to build a database form to enter purchase orders into an integrated enterprise system.

1. Download the data file for this exercise.
2. Use Microsoft Access database software and the following sample to build a purchase order form for entering purchase orders.

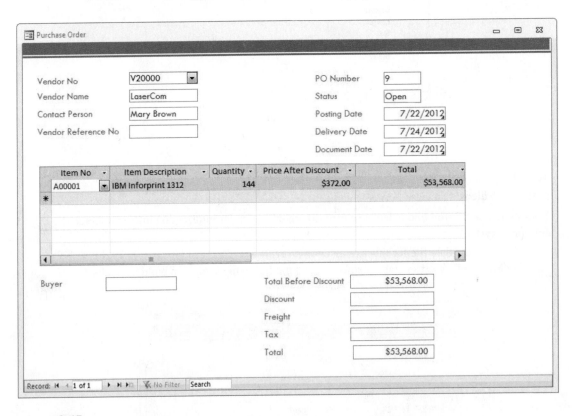

6.45

Tech Tool: Database Software

Software Videos: Database Queries, Calculated Fields

Some database designers prefer to not include the calculated fields in the database tables. These fields' values are calculated when they are needed for displaying in forms or reports. The data file for this exercise includes a sales order line with product id, quantity sold, and the unit price.

1. Download the data file for this exercise.
2. Create a query to calculate the total dollar amount for each sales order line.
3. Use Microsoft Access database software and the following sample to build a form to display each sales order line fields as well as line total amount. Your form should display the total amount of sales at the bottom of the form.

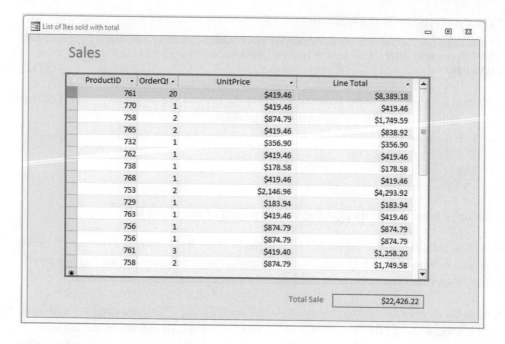

6.46

Tech Tool: Database Software

Software Videos: Database Queries, Calculated Fields

1. Download the data file for this exercise.
2. Create a query to calculate the total dollar amount for each sales order line.
3. Use Microsoft Access database software and the following sample to build a form to display each invoice form with invoice line fields as well as line total amount. Your form should display the total amount of that sales order at the bottom of the form.

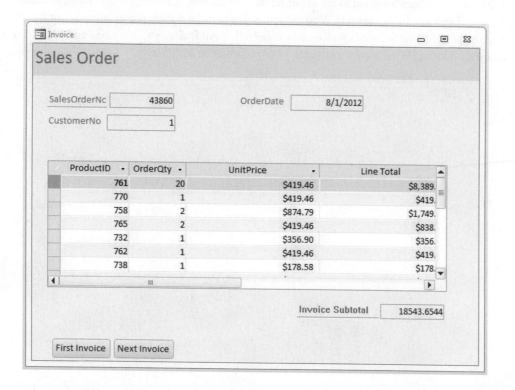

Go Online

In the fast-paced world of technology, your skill at finding answers fast can be vital. Go online and experience typical assignments you may encounter as a professional.

6.47 You are a member of the project team exploring integrated enterprise systems. Your role is to go online and research the following SAP products:

- SAP Business One
- SAP Business All-in-One
- SAP ByDesign
- SAP Business Suite

Summarize your findings for reporting back to the rest of the project team.

6.48 You are a member of the project team exploring integrated enterprise systems. Your role is to go online and research Oracle E-Business applications. Summarize your findings for reporting back to the rest of the project team.

6.49 In the elevator on the way to your office this morning, the CEO of the company asked you what you knew about ERP versus integrated enterprise systems. He mentioned that his leadership team keeps throwing these terms around, but nobody can give him a straight answer about what the difference is between the two. Are they the same? As he steps off the elevator, he asks you to send him a quick email with the answer so he can keep his leadership team on its toes. You race to your desk and go online to research the answer. What do you put in your email to the CEO?

6.50 You have landed a consulting job for AsciBusiness Solutions, a firm that is contemplating an integrated enterprise system. Although the CFO realizes there are many benefits of integrating the accounting system with other systems and sharing data, she has asked you to prepare an executive summary of the challenges associated with converting from a stand-alone to an integrated system. The CFO is especially interested in the challenges related to business processes. Go online and research this issue. Then summarize your findings for the CFO.

6.51 You have been assigned to the cloud services evaluation team responsible for documenting cloud services for accounting. You are scheduled to make a short presentation about the different types of cloud accounting providers, especially SAP ByDesign. Go online and search for cloud accounting. What would you say in your presentation summary?

Technology Projects

These technology projects are perfect for both individuals and teams.

Technology Project 6

Tech Tool: Spreadsheet Software, Database Software

Software Videos: DFD Drawing or Visio DFD Drawing, Database Tables, Database Queries, Database Forms, Database Reports, Advanced Database Forms and Queries

iSportDesign, an online retailer of sporting goods that the customer can custom design, has asked for your assistance with its new integrated enterprise system.

Your deliverables for the project include the following:

Deliverable 1. A DFD to document integrated purchasing and sales functions (Ask your instructor whether you should use spreadsheet or Visio software to complete this deliverable.)

Deliverable 2. Database tables

Deliverable 3. Database queries

Deliverable 4. Database forms

Deliverable 5. Database reports

Visit www.pearsonhighered.com/kay to do the following:

1. Download Technology Project 6 instructions.
2. Download files provided online for your convenience in completing the project deliverables.
3. Watch the videos with software instructions to complete this project at www.pearsonhighered.com/kay.

Part Two *Accounting and Intelligence Systems* explores how accounting is an integral part of analytic and intelligence systems for business intelligence, sustainability reporting, and intelligent business reporting with XBRL.

Part Two
Accounting and Intelligence Systems

Analyze Accounting Data

Chapter 7
Accounting and Business Intelligence

Chapter 8
Accounting and Sustainability Intelligence

Chapter 9
XBRL: Intelligent Business Reporting

7 Accounting and Business Intelligence

Can Business Intelligence Be Used to Improve Business Performance? Meet Kroger.

> The data mining firm, Dunnhumby, provides data mining services not only to Kroger, but also to Procter & Gamble, Macy's, Pepsico, Coca-Cola, Kellogg's, Kraft Foods, and Panera Bread.

How did the supermarket chain Kroger use data mining and business intelligence tools to improve its business performance? Working with a data mining firm, Dunnhumby, Kroger used sales data gathered by its loyalty cards to send customers promotional offerings. Intelligent data mining of billions of sales transactions a month allowed Kroger to target coupons and promotions to match customer preferences. Instead of sending the same coupons and promotions to all its customers, Kroger targeted customers with the coupons they are most likely to use. The result: Kroger's coupon redemption rate is 50%, as compared to a typical redemption rate of 1% to 3%.

Kroger used data mining and accounting data about sales transactions to create business intelligence. The insights gained through business intelligence were used to improve business performance.

What do you think? Would you prefer low prices on all merchandise? Or would you prefer coupons with discounts on the items that you typically purchase?

Crossroads

At the crossroads of accounting and IT, accounting data can be mined to create business intelligence.

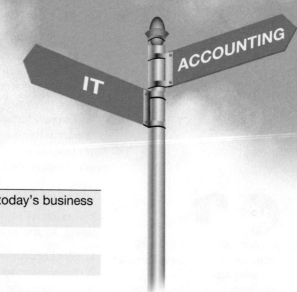

My Questions

Q 7.1	How is business intelligence used for decision making in today's business environment?
Q 7.2	What is the integrated decision model (IDM)?
Q 7.3	What makes an enterprise system intelligent?
Q 7.4	Can shadow data create business intelligence (BI)?
Q 7.5	How are BI technologies used to create business intelligence?
Q 7.6	How do shadow data and BI technologies compare?

How Is Business Intelligence Used for Decision Making in Today's Business Environment?

What was the last purchase decision you made? How did you arrive at that decision? What information did you use when making the decision? Did online product reviews influence your decision?

Just like you, businesses make decisions. And just like you, businesses strive to collect and use data to make better decisions. While you might ask a friend or read online product reviews before making a purchase decision, businesses today use business intelligence to make better decisions.

A rapidly changing business environment, technological advances, and informed consumers drive enterprises to use their information assets in more intelligent ways.

How can enterprises create greater value from the data stored in their databases? How can enterprises transform data into business intelligence?

Data is transformed into information (meaningful data) when the data is processed and organized in a systematic manner. Information can be transformed into business intelligence by further processing and analysis. Intelligence involves the ability to see meaningful interrelationships and glean insights, and business intelligence can be used to improve decision making and business performance.

For example, Kroger collects data about daily sales transactions. This data is stored in the accounting database. It can be used to answer such questions as "What products did customers buy *today*?" (Figure 7.1).

> The concept of business intelligence was first introduced in 1958 by Hans Peter Luhn, an IBM researcher, who defined intelligence as "the ability to apprehend the interrelationships of presented facts in such a way as to guide action towards a desired goal" (Luhn, 1958).

> In 2009 Gartner Group predicted "Through 2012, more than 35 percent of the top 5,000 global companies will regularly fail to make insightful decisions about significant changes in their business and markets" (Gartner Business Intelligence Summit, 2009).

FIGURE 7.1 Transforming Data to Information to Business Intelligence

Data	Information	Business Intelligence
Sales figures for one day for Kroger	Income statement for Kroger for one year	Data mining and analysis of Kroger sales transactions to target customers with coupons and promotions to increase sales
What products did customers buy *today*?	What products did customers purchase *last* year?	What products will customers purchase *next* year?

Kroger's sales data is transformed into information when it is sorted and summarized as total sales on the corporate annual income statement. It then becomes meaningful data, or information. This information can be used to answer such questions as "What products did customers purchase *last* year?"

Through further analysis, such as data mining and predictive modeling, Kroger transforms the sales information into business intelligence. The business intelligence can provide Kroger with insights to improve future business performance. Business intelligence can be used to answer questions such as "What products will customers purchase *next* year?"

Accounting Insight No. 16: Data Analysis

One reason we capture and store accounting data is so it can be analyzed and used for decision making. As shown in Figure 7.2, three main functions of the accounting system are as follows:

1. Store accounting data.
2. Analyze accounting data to use in decision making.
3. Safeguard the accounting data.

Most accounting systems store accounting data using relational databases. Accounting Insight No. 16 states that while relational databases are well suited for storing data, intelligence tools are better suited for data analysis to create business intelligence. For this reason, most organizations employ analysis tools in addition to their relational databases.

Some organizations create shadow data consisting of "homegrown" spreadsheets. These spreadsheets are often created on an ad hoc basis as the need arises. Performing analysis in a spreadsheet is often easier for accountants than performing the same analysis using a database.

Some organizations may use business intelligence technologies, such as data mining and predictive modeling, for data analysis. **Data mining** uses mathematical algorithms to find patterns, trends, and relationships among data, such as customer purchasing patterns. **Predictive modeling** uses mathematical algorithms to predict future trends, such as future customer purchases.

ACCOUNTING INSIGHT NO. 16
Relational databases are well suited for storing data.
Intelligence tools are better suited for data analysis to create business intelligence.

Can you imagine a carpenter trying to cut lumber with a hammer? The hammer is a tool well suited for hammering nails into lumber, but not well suited for cutting lumber. Likewise, different IT tools serve different purposes. Relational databases are IT tools suited for storing data, but have limitations for analyzing data.

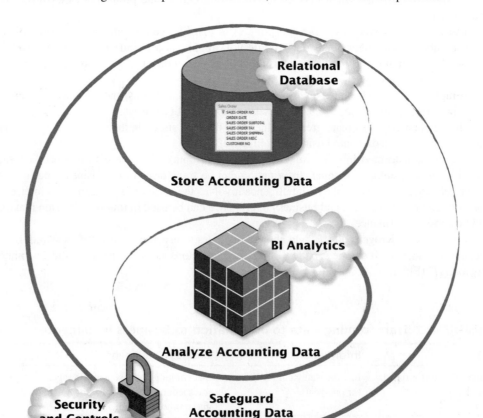

FIGURE 7.2

Accounting System Functions: Store, Analyze, and Safeguard Data

In prior chapters we focused on how accounting data was stored, the first function of the accounting system. In this chapter, we will shift our focus to the second function of the accounting system—how accounting data can be analyzed for use in making decisions.

Decision Models

As an accounting professional, you may be responsible for collecting, organizing, and presenting information to directors and executives so they can make decisions. How can you anticipate all the various types of data, information, and intelligence management will need?

One approach is to begin with the outcome in mind. What types of decisions will management be making? Basically, there are three types of business decisions:

1. Routine operational decisions (structured decisions)
2. Tactical decisions (semi-structured decisions)
3. Strategic decisions (unstructured decisions)

Routine operational decisions are recurring and typically relate to ongoing business operations. After a routine decision is made once, the same decision can be applied until the environment or business operation requires reevaluation. An example of a routine decision would be the most cost effective shipping procedure. Routine operational decisions are also called structured decisions, and they have the least ambiguity.

Tactical decisions are typically short term, impacting one year or less. Examples of tactical decisions are outsourcing and special orders. These decisions are considered semi-structured, with more ambiguity than routine decisions but less ambiguity than strategic decisions.

Strategic decisions are usually long term in nature and unstructured with a high degree of ambiguity. Examples of strategic decisions include mergers and acquisitions, diversification, and divestiture.

How does a system collect, organize, analyze, and provide the information and intelligence needed for routine, tactical, and strategic decisions? To serve these varied decision needs can be a daunting challenge for an accounting system. Although there are many different types of decisions, a decision model helps to identify data that must be collected for decision making. Next, we share with you the integrated decision model (IDM) to assist you in understanding how the accounting system serves decision making.

> **How Did We Get Here?**
>
> In the past, enterprise resource planning (ERP) systems provided information for routine, operational decisions. Decision support systems, or DSS, provided information for tactical, semi-structured decisions. Executive information systems provided support for strategic decisions. These systems were the predecessors of today's sophisticated intelligence tools used for data analysis.

> **My Connection...**
> Try Short Exercise 7.29.

What Is the Integrated Decision Model (IDM)?

The **integrated decision model (IDM)** provides a framework to structure and organize the decision-making process. IDM integrates consideration of both quantitative factors, such as dollars of revenue and costs, and qualitative factors that cannot be quantified in dollars. Qualitative factors might include product quality or customer satisfaction. An IDM spreadsheet template (Figure 7.3) includes both quantitative (financial) and qualitative (nonfinancial) analysis.

As the business environment becomes more complex and diverse, more and more factors must be considered when making decisions. For example, as environmental considerations, diversity, and corporate social responsibility are increasingly considered when evaluating a firm's performance, enterprises may include these factors in the decision process. Some of these considerations cannot be quantified in dollars, however. Though difficult to place a dollar amount on the factor, there are times when the factor can be overriding, such as product safety.

The IDM (Figure 7.4) serves to integrate both qualitative and quantitative factors into the decision. This process of integrating financial and nonfinancial factors into the decision process can improve the quality of the decision.

FIGURE 7.3

Integrated Decision Model (IDM) Template

	A	B	C
1	**INTEGRATED DECISION MODEL (IDM)**		
2	**1. ISSUE/OPPORTUNITY**	**< Identify Issue or Opportunity >**	
3	**2. OPTIONS**	< Identify Option A >	< Identify Option B >
4	**3. QUANTITATIVE ANALYSIS**	Financial Factors Option A	Financial Factors Option B
5	Benefits	$ <Insert Benefits>	$ <Insert Benefits>
6	Costs	$ <Insert Costs>	$ <Insert Costs>
7	Net Cost/Benefit	$ <Insert Net>	$ <Insert Net>
8	**4. QUALITATIVE ANALYSIS**	Nonfinancial Factors Option A	Nonfinancial Factors Option B
9	Advantages	• <Insert Advantages>	• <Insert Advantages>
10	Disadvantages	• <Insert Disadvantages>	• <Insert Disadvantages>
11	**5. DECISION**	**< Select Option A or B >**	

Decisions in Seven Steps

IDM consists of seven basic steps as a framework for the decision-making and evaluation process. As Figure 7.4 shows, the seven steps to reach and implement a decision are the following:

1. Define the opportunity or issue.
2. Identify options to address the opportunity or issue.
3. Analyze quantitative (financial) factors.
4. Analyze qualitative (nonfinancial) factors.
5. Make recommendation and/or decision with supporting rationale.
6. Implement decision.
7. Evaluate performance.

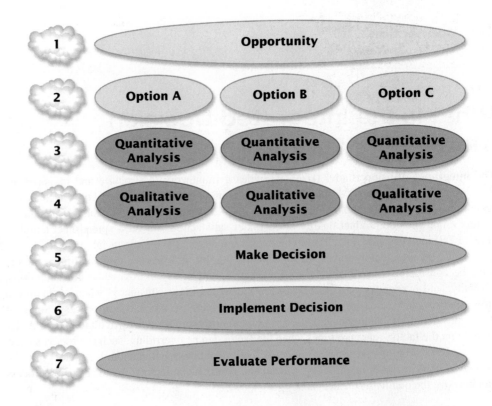

FIGURE 7.4

Integrated Decision Model (IDM)

Additional explanation of each of these steps follows.

1. ***Define the opportunity or issue.*** What is the core issue or opportunity? Make certain you have identified and are addressing the core issue rather than a symptom. For example, is the issue a sudden drop in sales? Or is the issue the decline in product quality that *caused* the sudden drop in sales?

2. ***Identify options to address the opportunity or issue.*** What are the options to address the issue? Use creative solutions and brainstorming techniques to identify options that turn challenges into opportunities. A combination of options should also be considered. For example, assume you identify two options: Option 1 is to increase the sales force; Option 2 is to increase advertising expenditures. A third option might be to combine Option 1 and Option 2 to increase the sales force and increase advertising expenditures but at a lower level than in the other options.

3. ***Analyze quantitative (financial) factors.*** Collect financial information for each of the alternatives. As you collect information, other options may become apparent. Revisit step 2 if necessary and then proceed. Quantitative analysis may consist of cost-benefit analysis, cost-volume-profit analysis, capital budgeting, and more. Basically, you are attempting to compare the financial costs and benefits of each option and determine the differences.

4. ***Analyze qualitative (nonfinancial) factors.*** Have you ever purchased a product that is not the lowest cost alternative? Why? Nonfinancial factors can often influence a decision. Step 4 is to gather nonfinancial information for each option to address qualitative factors, such as product quality, timeliness, the stress factor, streamlining, ease of use, overall satisfaction, and so on. See Figure 7.3 for a template to use in organizing qualitative factors. Basically, you list qualitative factors for each option, categorizing the factors as advantages or disadvantages.

5. ***Make recommendation and/or decision with supporting rationale.*** After considering the quantitative and qualitative analysis for each option, arrive at a recommendation and concisely state your supporting rationale. The recommendation should be clearly stated, but caveats based on changing circumstances are acceptable so long as the decision maker is given a clear course of action. As accountants, we are often asked to make recommendations to management, but management makes the final decision.

6. ***Implement decision.*** Take action. Operationalize the decision using the appropriate people and resources.

7. ***Evaluate performance.*** Obtain feedback about the performance resulting from the decision. Did you meet your estimated targets? If not, why not? Use this information to make appropriate adjustments such as modifying your future estimates or better controlling operations and implementation.

Illustration: EspressoCoffee Integrated Decision Model (IDM)

In this illustration, we will focus on EspressoCoffee customers in the United States who are deciding whether to purchase an espresso machine and espresso beans from EspressoCoffee. EspressoCoffee wants to understand the customer decision process in order to better serve customer information needs when making the purchase decision.

To do so, we will apply the IDM to this scenario to illustrate how the model is used when there are qualitative factors involved in the decision. The IDM steps are summarized in Figure 7.5.

First, define the issue, opportunity, or problem. In this case, the customer is deciding whether to purchase an EspressoCoffee machine to make his or her own espresso.

Second, identify options. For the average customer, there are two options: either purchase espresso at a local coffee shop or purchase an espresso machine and espresso beans to make it at home.

Third, collect, summarize, and analyze quantitative information. In this decision, a cost-benefit analysis is used in which the costs and benefits of each option are compared.

Fourth, collect, summarize, and analyze qualitative information related to the decision. The qualitative factors are grouped by advantages and disadvantages.

Fifth, make a recommendation or decision, including the supporting rationale for the decision. What are your reasons for reaching your recommendation or decision?

As you can see from the IDM in Figure 7.5 for EspressoCoffee customers, the qualitative factors may play an important role in the final decision. A system must be able to capture and

EspressoCoffee
Company

FIGURE 7.5 EspressoCoffee IDM

1	Define the Issue	Purchase an espresso machine and espresso beans?	
2	Identify Options	Option A: Purchase espresso from local coffee shop	Option B: Purchase an espresso machine and espresso beans from EspressoCoffee Company
3	Quantitative (Financial) Analysis	Benefits*: $ -0- Costs: Daily espresso ($5.00 × 360) ($1,800) Total ($1,800)	Benefits*: $ -0- Costs: Espresso machine ($300) Espresso beans ($14 × 12 months) ($168) Total ($468)
4	Qualitative (Nonfinancial) Analysis	Advantages: ■ Enjoy coffee shop atmosphere ■ Conduct meetings at coffee shop over espresso Disadvantages: ■ Time consuming ■ Waiting in line ■ Inconsistent quality of espresso	Advantages: ■ Convenience at home ■ Saves time ■ Saves fuel ■ Better quality espresso beans Disadvantage: ■ Time to learn to make espresso
5	Recommendation / Decision		Based on cost savings and additional convenience and quality, consumer purchases an espresso machine and beans from EspressoCoffee.

*In this case, there are no financial benefits.

store the needed qualitative information. This is a unique challenge for a relational database, but is significant in arriving at intelligence from raw data.

Quantitative data often tells us *how much* (such as the cost of espressos from a coffee shop for one year). Qualitative data often tells us *why*. Why would EspressoCoffee customers choose to pay significantly more for espresso at a coffee shop? If a customer highly values the friends he or she meets at the coffee shop, the customer might choose to pay more for the espresso because, in fact, he or she is also paying for the atmosphere and the companionship (Figure 7.5). The results of the IDM analysis are further summarized in Figure 7.6. Espresso made at home has a higher initial cost, lower total cost, and saves you time. Purchasing espresso at the coffee shop has a higher annual cost and requires more drive time, weighed against the opportunity to see your friends.

How does the accounting system provide support for decision making? The illustration for EspressoCoffee shows that even with a relatively simplistic decision, information is required for decision analysis.

My Connection...
• Active Review 7.9

FIGURE 7.6 EspressoCoffee Customer Decision

Option	$Benefits	–	$Cost	–	Disadv	+	Adv	=	Decision
Homemade espresso	Save $	–	Initial cost	–		+	Save time		
Coffee shop espresso	N/A	–	Higher annual cost	–	More drive time	+	See friends		

What Makes an Enterprise System Intelligent?

An enterprise system is considered intelligent when it uses IT tools and technologies to create business intelligence. These intelligence tools provide the opportunity to view the data in many different ways, thus creating intelligence from the data through analysis. The data for BI may be viewed in a multidimensional cube. This data cube can be thought of as similar to a Rubik's cube. You can turn and twist the Rubik's cube to create different variations of the same cube.

In the same way, a data cube allows you to view the same data in different ways (see Figure 7.7). For example, sales can be viewed from different perspectives: geographic region, time period, and/or type of customer.

For our purposes in studying accounting systems, two approaches to business intelligence are shadow data and BI technologies.

Shadow data. Shadow data is used when data is stored in spreadsheets and other tools that shadow the formal accounting system. Shadow data is frequently under the control of the accounting professional.

Business intelligence (BI) technologies. BI technologies include analytics, data mining, and predictive modeling. They are typically under the control of the enterprise's IT professionals.

An intelligent enterprise system may use one or both types of BI. Some organizations, for example, may use only shadow data while others may use both shadow data and BI technologies.

Intelligent System Components

The four common components in an intelligent enterprise system are:

1. data storage
2. data extraction and transfer
3. data analysis
4. data visualization

The components work together to analyze multidimensional data cubes and identify meaningful interrelationships (Figure 7.8). These meaningful relationships can provide insights for more intelligent business decisions.

Crossroads

At the crossroads of accounting and IT, you can see that BI may come down to a "control issue." Accounting professionals tend to control shadow data. IT professionals tend to control BI technologies.

FIGURE 7.7

Multidimensional Data Cube

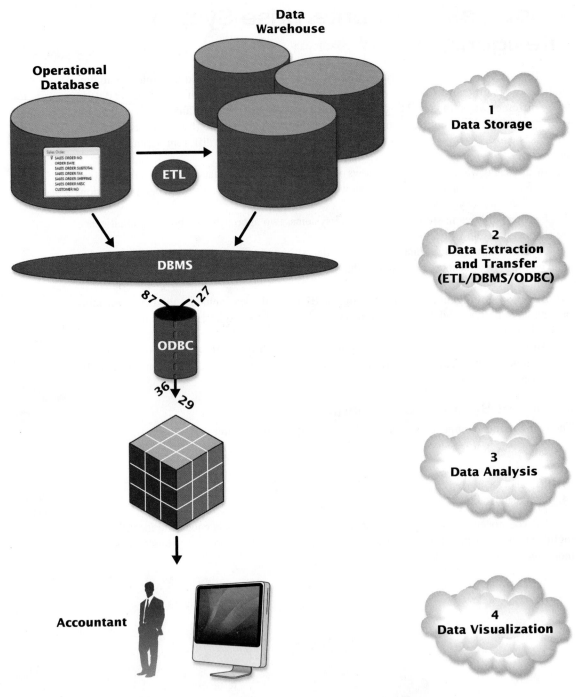

FIGURE 7.8

Intelligent System Components

DATA STORAGE Data is stored using operational databases, data warehouses, and other data storage. Data from recurring transactions and operations is stored in an operational database. Data from the operational database and other sources may be loaded into a data warehouse. The data warehouse is a large database that serves as a central location for aggregating and storing an enterprise's data. When an organization uses a data warehouse, data is often transferred from various sources throughout the organization, including the operational database, spreadsheets, and company e-commerce Web sites, into the data warehouse where the data is integrated.

DATA EXTRACTION AND TRANSFER Data extraction and transfer tools are used to extract data stored in databases (operational databases and data warehouses) and transfer the data into data analysis tools. As mentioned previously, the operational database that is well suited for storing data is not well suited for data analysis. Thus, it is necessary to transfer the data from the operational database into an analysis tool.

The exact steps for data extraction and transfer may differ based upon the intelligence tool used; however, the process is basically the same.

DATA ANALYSIS Data analysis tools are used to analyze data to identify interrelationships and insights that can be used to create intelligence for better business decisions. The data analysis shown in Figure 7.9 includes two approaches to BI: shadow data and BI technologies. Data analysis can be performed using statistical, mathematical, financial, and data mining functions.

DATA VISUALIZATION Visualization tools include user interface applications that display results of the data analysis on the user's computer. For example, shadow data might use a spreadsheet display. A BI technology might display results using OLAP (Online Analytical Processing) cubes that permit the user to view data from various multidimensional perspectives.

Tools for visualizing the results in an understandable, user-friendly form can consist of charts, graphs, figures, tables, and cubes. These tools are sometimes combined to create digital dashboards. The **digital dashboard** is often interactive, permitting the viewer to see the effect of changes in various scenarios, parameters, and variables.

Next, we explore further the two approaches to BI: shadow data and BI technologies.

> **Informatics**
>
> Informatics is a term more widely used in Europe to refer to the use of information technology to solve problems. Business informatics focuses on how to use information technology to solve business problems. Intelligence tools can be viewed as a subset of informatics.

> **My Connection...**
> Active Review 7.6

Can Shadow Data Create Business Intelligence (BI)?

What Would You Do?

Imagine that you were just promoted at EspressoCoffee. Your duties now include responsibility for tracking international accounting and tax issues. EspressoCoffee sells products in many different countries, and each country has different accounting requirements. Italy, for example, requires that invoice numbering restart with No. 1 each year. This means that your first invoice for January 2013 and January 2014 will both be No. 1—but only for Italian invoices. All other invoices are consecutively numbered. Your accounting system is unable to accommodate this requirement.

What would you do? Would you set up a spreadsheet to track the Italian invoice numbers, cross matching them to the corresponding consecutive invoice numbers?

This is exactly how shadow data of homegrown spreadsheets are born. A business has a need for data that the formal accounting system cannot satisfy, frequently with tight deadlines and time pressure. So spreadsheets come to the rescue. They are easy to create and fast to implement. The data in the spreadsheet shadows the formal accounting system, so it is called shadow data.

Although spreadsheets are the most common form of shadow data, other tools include user-developed databases, such as MS Access and Lotus Notes. One large organization discovered that it had over 10,000 free-standing Lotus Notes databases outside the formal enterprise system under IT supervision. These shadow databases were often repetitious and failed to interchange data efficiently, requiring re-entry of the same data into multiple databases.

Since spreadsheets are so widely used, we will focus on how shadow data spreadsheets create BI for decisions.

Shadow Data and Intelligent Components

Why is the spreadsheet the most frequently used tool to create shadow data? Spreadsheets are convenient. The accounting professional can design and build his or her own spreadsheet to meet data analysis and reporting needs.

Spreadsheet software, such as MS Excel, makes it relatively easy to extract data from a database. Once the data has been transferred to the spreadsheet, Excel tools can be used to analyze the data and print reports.

Shadow data also includes data not currently stored in a database but collected from other sources. Some enterprises use spreadsheets to create two-dimensional databases to collect and store data that the accounting system does not store.

EspressoCoffee
Company

> **Shadow Data**
> Some organizations use spreadsheets extensively to prepare consolidated financial statements.

> **Shadow Data Emails...**
> Have you ever needed information, such as a name, address, phone number, or attachment contained in an email, but you were unable to locate the email? For enterprises, crucial information may be stored in vendor and customer emails, such as customer specifications. One of the challenges of a well-designed system is to capture, organize, store, and retrieve such data (see Inmon, 2008).

Figure 7.9 illustrates the four components of an intelligent system using shadow data for BI. The areas in a secured and controlled environment are shaded green for safe zone. The unsecured and uncontrolled environment is shaded red for danger zone. As you can see, shadow data may be vulnerable to unauthorized access.

Next, let's look more closely at the four intelligent components for shadow data: data storage, data extraction, data analysis, and data visualization.

SHADOW DATA STORAGE Data storage for shadow data may be scattered throughout an organization. Data stored in the accounting database may be extracted and stored in spreadsheets on computer desktops and laptops throughout the enterprise. Other shadow data may never be

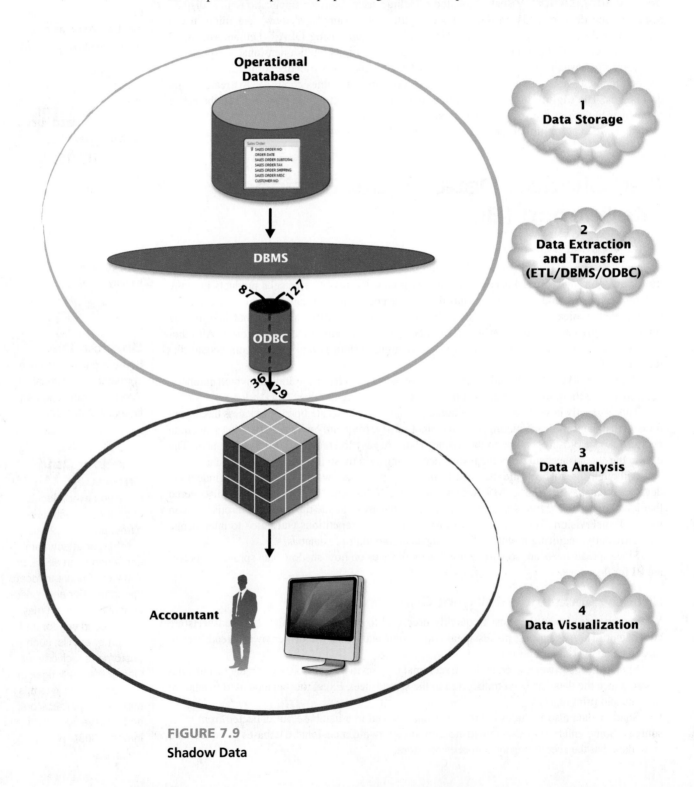

FIGURE 7.9
Shadow Data

stored in the accounting database but might be collected to store in spreadsheet files as a way of tracing data that the formal accounting system doesn't. For example, an enterprise may need to evaluate different loan financing options with different interest rates and terms. This data is not stored in the accounting system and might be compiled and analyzed using a spreadsheet to evaluate loan financing options.

Figure 7.10 shows an example of an Excel data list used to store data for an NGO (Non-Governmental Organization). This data list will be used to assist the NGO in evaluating which fundraising events to conduct in order to maximize the benefits of fundraising efforts. **Data lists**, also called data tables, use columns for fields and rows for records.

SHADOW DATA EXTRACTION AND TRANSFER Given the widespread use of spreadsheets by accounting and business professionals, ways to transfer data from the accounting database into spreadsheets have been streamlined to meet this demand.

A relational database management system (RDBMS), discussed in Chapter 2, is used to extract data from the operational database using queries. Because the data analysis application may not be compatible with the database's RDBMS query commands, software called **Open DataBase Connectivity (ODBC)** may be necessary to translate the data analysis query commands into commands that are compatible with RDBMS commands.

You can think of the ODBC as a pipeline between the database and the spreadsheet. As shown in Figure 7.9, you can see the ODBC is the pipeline or connection between the database that stores data and the spreadsheet that analyzes the data. The user can open an ODBC or data

Crossroads

What IT professionals call ODBC (Open Database Connectivity) accounting professionals may think of as data pipelines used to extract and transfer data from the database into a spreadsheet.

	A	B	C	D	E	F	G	H
1	MONTH	DAY	YEAR	TRANSACTION	CHECK NO.	PAYEE/PAYER	CATEGORY	AMOUNT
2	5	8	2013	Deposit	1275	Jeff Hanley	Donation	$ 500
3	5	8	2013	Deposit	5800	Annie Gunne	Donation	$ 400
4	5	8	2013	Deposit	1237	Adam Hartland	Donation	$ 200
5	5	8	2013	Deposit	1976	Franco Rosi	Donation	$ 1,000
6	5	8	2013	Deposit	1953	Lauren Madison	Donation	$ 800
7	5	8	2013	Deposit	2700	Jim Jackson	Donation	$ 500
8	5	8	2013	Deposit	860	Mary Toulousse	Donation	$ 200
9	5	8	2013	Deposit	1585	Joseph Haretz	Donation	$ 900
10	5	8	2013	Check	11025	Golf Club	Other Expenses	$ (4,000)
11	5	8	2013	Check	11026	P&J Advertising Agency	Advertising	$ (800)
12	5	8	2013	Check	11027	Office Plus	Supplies	$ (500)
13	5	8	2013	Check	11028	Payroll	Wages	$ (250)
14	11	12	2013	Deposit		Various	Donation	$ 10,800
15	11	12	2013	Check	13029	P&J Advertising Agency	Advertising	$ (450)
16	11	12	2013	Check	13030	Office Plus	Supplies	$ (125)
17	6	28	2013	Deposit		Various	Donation	$ 25,000
18	6	28	2013	Check	11130	P&J Advertising Agency	Advertising	$ (800)
19	6	27	2013	Check	11129	Office Plus	Supplies	$ (500)
20	7	1	2013	Check	11131	Payroll	Wages	$ (250)
21	9	15	2013	Deposit		Various	Donation	$ 1,000
22	9	10	2013	Check	11132	Pffice Plus	Supplies	$ (800)
23	9	15	2013	Check	11134	World Circus	Supplies	$ (8,000)
24	9	12	2013	Check	11133	P&J Advertising Agency	Advertising	$ (2,000)

FIGURE 7.10

STAR for Autism Data List

Data lists use columns for fields and rows for records.

pipeline from the database to the spreadsheet. After the ODBC is established, data is extracted, transferred, and loaded into a spreadsheet.

MS Excel includes an ODBC (Open Database Connectivity) feature that can be used to extract data from a relational database and import the data into Excel (Figure 7.11).

SHADOW DATA SPREADSHEET ANALYSIS TOOLS One reason often cited for the popularity of spreadsheets among accountants is the ease of performing data analysis. The end-user accountant can perform relatively complex data analysis from a desktop computer using spreadsheet analysis tools.

Spreadsheet software offers an array of analysis tools. MS Excel analysis tools include AutoFilter, Subtotal, Conditional Formatting, and PivotTables. PivotTables can also be used as

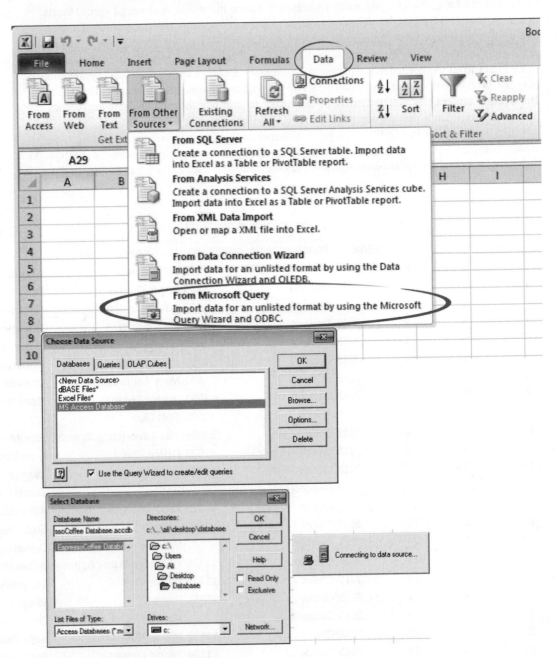

FIGURE 7.11

Extracting Data with ODBC

Create ODBC Data Connection

To extract data from a database, spreadsheet applications, such as MS Excel, allow users to establish an ODBC to a specific database, open the database tables, and extract data into the spreadsheet application.

a visualization tool to view the analysis results. MS Excel also offers additional analysis tools such as mathematical and statistical functions, Solver, and Analysis Toolkit Add-Ins. **Macros** can be used with Excel to automatically perform a sequence of analysis tasks, step by step. Macros can be saved with the spreadsheet and conveniently reused as needed. Data validation and PivotTables are illustrated in Figures 7.12 and 7.13.

QuickBooks Accounting Software...
Even small business accounting software, such as QuickBooks, has streamlined extracting and transferring data from the accounting database into Excel. The QuickBooks reports window displays a button labeled Export. When this button is selected, the user is given choices on how to export the data from QuickBooks into Excel. For example, let's say that your company has experienced unusually high levels of payments for accounts payable. If you wanted to investigate further, you could pull up the Audit Trail report in QuickBooks, export the report into Excel, sort on payments for Accounts Payable, and then review the User ID of the employee making the payments.

SAP and Microsoft...
SAP and Microsoft worked collaboratively to develop Duet, a product that extracts data from the SAP R3 relational database and transfers the data into Excel.

SHADOW DATA VISUALIZATION TOOLS For an example of an Excel PivotTable that permits the end user to pivot the data to visualize the analysis results from different perspectives, see Figure 7.13. As shown in the figure, the first PivotTable displays the events in columns. In the second PivotTable, the events are pivoted to appear as rows. In addition to PivotTables, OLAP cubes can be used with MS Excel to view the analysis results in a multidimensional format. Spreadsheet charts and graphs can be used to visualize data analysis.

Illustration: STAR for Autism Shadow Data

As part of EspressoCoffee's social initiatives, the organization donates time and resources to support STAR for Autism (Society to Aid Research for Autism). It is a foundation that funds research on the causes, treatments, and therapies for autism.

	A	B	C	D	E	F	G	H	I	J
1	MONTH	DAY	YEAR	TRANSACTION	CHECK NO.	PAYEE/PAYER	CATEGORY	AMOUNT	EVENT	
2	5	8	2013	Deposit	1275	Jeff Hanley	Donation	$ 500	Golf Benefit	
3	5	8	2013	Deposit	5800	Annie Gunne	Donation	$ 400	Golf Benefit	
4	5	8	2013	Deposit	1237	Adam Hartland	Donation	$ 200	Golf Benefit	
5	5	8	2013	Deposit	1976	Franco Rosi	Donation	$ 1,000	Golf Benefit	
6	5	8	2013	Deposit	1953	Lauren Madison	Donation	$ 800	Golf Benefit	
7	5	8	2013	Deposit	2700	Jim Jackson	Donation	$ 500	Golf Benefit	
8	5	8	2013	Deposit	860	Mary Toulousse	Donation	$ 200	Golf Benefit	
9	5	8	2013	Deposit	1585	Joseph Haretz	Donation	$ 900	Golf Benefit	
10	5	8	2013	Check	11025	Golf Club	Other Expenses	$ (4,000)	Golf Benefit	
11	5	8	2013	Check	11026	P&J Advertising Agency	Advertising	$ (800)	Golf Benefit	
12	5	8	2013	Check	11027	Office Plus	Supplies	$ (500)	Golf Benefit	
13	5	8	2013	Check	11028	Payroll	Wages	$ (250)	Golf Benefit	
14	11	12	2013	Deposit		Various	Donation	$ 10,800	Silent Auction	
15	11	12	2013	Check	13029	P&J Advertising Agency	Advertising	$ (450)	Silent Auction	
16	11	12	2013	Check	13030	Office Plus	Supplies	$ (125)	Silent Auction	
17	6	28	2013	Deposit		Various	Donation	$ 25,000	Walkathon	
18	6	28	2013	Check	11130	P&J Advertising Agency	Advertising	$ (800)	Walkathon	
19	6	27	2013	Check	11129	Office Plus	Supplies	$ (500)	Walkathon	
20	7	1	2013	Check	11131	Payroll	Wages	$ (250)	Walkathon	
21	9	15	2013	Deposit		Various	Donation	$ 1,000	Golf Benefit / Silent Auction	
22	9	10	2013	Check	11132	Pffice Plus	Supplies	$ (800)	Walkathon	
23	9	15	2013	Check	11134	World Circus	Supplies	$ (8,000)	Carnival / Raffe	
24	9	12	2013	Check	11133	P&J Advertising Agency	Advertising	$ (2,000)	Carnival	

FIGURE 7.12

STAR for Autism Data List with Event Field and Data Validation
Spreadsheet applications include data validation tools to improve the accuracy of data entered into the spreadsheet. Data validation tools in MS Excel include drop-down lists restricting what can be entered into a specific cell.

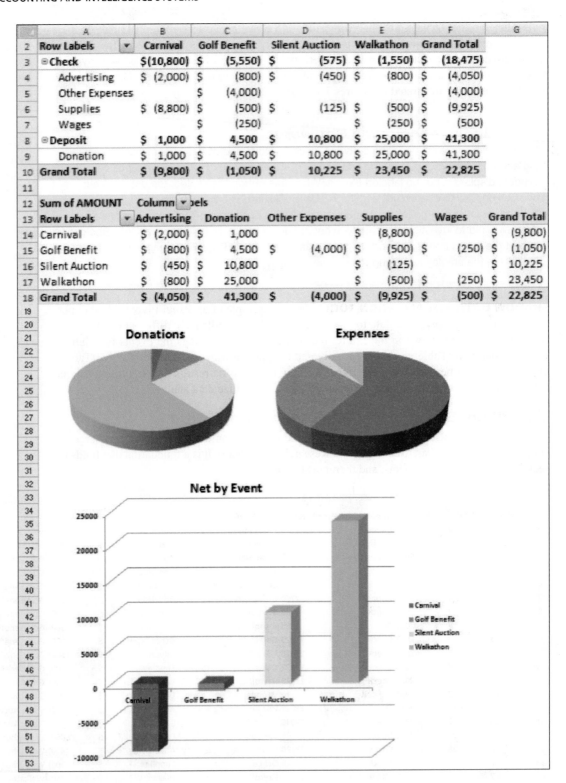

	A	B	C	D	E	F	G
2	Row Labels ▾	Carnival	Golf Benefit	Silent Auction	Walkathon	Grand Total	
3	⊟Check	$(10,800)	$ (5,550)	$ (575)	$ (1,550)	$ (18,475)	
4	Advertising	$ (2,000)	$ (800)	$ (450)	$ (800)	$ (4,050)	
5	Other Expenses		$ (4,000)			$ (4,000)	
6	Supplies	$ (8,800)	$ (500)	$ (125)	$ (500)	$ (9,925)	
7	Wages		$ (250)		$ (250)	$ (500)	
8	⊟Deposit	$ 1,000	$ 4,500	$ 10,800	$ 25,000	$ 41,300	
9	Donation	$ 1,000	$ 4,500	$ 10,800	$ 25,000	$ 41,300	
10	Grand Total	$ (9,800)	$ (1,050)	$ 10,225	$ 23,450	$ 22,825	
11							
12	Sum of AMOUNT	Column ▾ bels					
13	Row Labels ▾	Advertising	Donation	Other Expenses	Supplies	Wages	Grand Total
14	Carnival	$ (2,000)	$ 1,000		$ (8,800)		$ (9,800)
15	Golf Benefit	$ (800)	$ 4,500	$ (4,000)	$ (500)	$ (250)	$ (1,050)
16	Silent Auction	$ (450)	$ 10,800		$ (125)		$ 10,225
17	Walkathon	$ (800)	$ 25,000		$ (500)	$ (250)	$ 23,450
18	Grand Total	$ (4,050)	$ 41,300	$ (4,000)	$ (9,925)	$ (500)	$ 22,825

FIGURE 7.13

Shadow Data Dashboard

Create PivotTable

Spreadsheet applications may include PivotTable and PivotChart data analysis tools. These tools can be used to create digital dashboards.

STAR for Autism conducts several fundraising events each year. Even though the staff felt that the fundraising events were an overall success, the events were not generating the funds expected. This prompted one of the board members to ask for additional analysis to create intelligence that could be used for improved decisions regarding which events to continue and discontinue. The foundation's accounting system was unable to provide the data analysis requested by the board member.

You volunteered to assist STAR for Autism in evaluating which fundraising activities should be continued in the upcoming year. Working with staff members, you created a shadow data spreadsheet to conduct data analysis and create intelligence that could be used by the foundation board for more informed decision making.

EXTRACTION AND TRANSFER A database connection was established to connect to the accounting system database (Figure 7.11). Then the selected data stored in the accounting system was extracted and imported into a spreadsheet, such as the data list shown in Figure 7.10.

ANALYSIS AND VISUALIZATION After the data was transferred to a spreadsheet, the foundation wanted to perform a cost-benefit analysis for each event to determine which events provided the most benefit for the costs incurred. To conduct this analysis, an additional field, Event, was added to the spreadsheet. Additional information was entered into this field for each record (row). This additional data permits the foundation to track the costs and benefits to specific events.

When entering the additional information, data validation can be used to ensure that only valid data is entered into the selected cells. For example, in this case, the only events that should be entered are golf benefit, silent auction, carnival, and walkathon. Figure 7.12 shows an example of data validation.

After the event information is entered, the organization can use spreadsheet features to perform analysis, such as AutoFilter, Subtotal, and Conditional Formatting. The AutoFilter feature permits the user to filter data to view only selected items. The Subtotal feature can calculate the subtotal for each event as well as a grand total for all events. For example, conditional formatting can be applied so that the events with negative cash flows are displayed in red.

Another useful MS Excel feature is a PivotTable. Once an Excel data list is prepared, a PivotTable can be created to further analyze and report the results. An Excel PivotTable permits analysis of the data by pivoting the perspective from which the data is viewed. The same PivotTable can provide multiple perspectives of the same data with a simple click of the mouse (Figure 7.13). A shadow data dashboard can be created using PivotTables and PivotCharts for the foundation to monitor fundraising in the future.

DECISION AND ACTION As shown in Figure 7.14, the results of the analysis can be summarized in a decision model, such as the IDM, to clearly show the comparisons between the various options. IDM integrates qualitative factors into the decision process by listing the nonquantifiable factors that impact the decision, even though dollar amounts cannot be assigned to the factors.

As you can see in this case, the walkathon and the silent auction generate the most cash donations. The golf benefit shows a net cash drain resulting from the event. However, the qualitative considerations, such as building donor relationships and the positive public relations from the event, may prompt the foundation to continue offering this fundraising event even though the event actually costs the foundation instead of bringing in additional funds. The fourth fundraising event, the carnival, shows a net cost to the foundation of $9,800. Based on this analysis, the foundation board made the decision to discontinue the carnival event.

My Connection...
- Tech in Practice 7.35
- Tech in Practice 7.36

Shadow Data Advantages and Disadvantages

Shadow data offers several advantages for the accounting professional, including convenience and availability. The spreadsheet is easy to learn and use. Extensive training is not required to create, use, or maintain spreadsheets. Also, spreadsheets have extensive analytic features, such as PivotTables, Solver, and Crystal Ball. Spreadsheets offer reporting features that do not require custom programming to produce a professional looking report.

Spreadsheet software is readily available. The accounting professional can develop the spreadsheet solution when needed and does not have to wait on IT to produce the required analysis. To have value to the end user, intelligence must be timely (i.e., received in time to be used). Another advantage is that the accounting professional often better understands the requirements and needs for applications that have specific requirements unique to accounting. IT professionals may not have the requisite accounting knowledge to meet the analysis and reporting needs of the accounting professional.

The convenience and availability of spreadsheets for shadow data, however, are accompanied by a number of serious disadvantages. Since the shadow data is developed on an ad hoc basis, often it is not well documented. This can lead to issues in the future when the accountant who developed the spreadsheet application leaves the organization. The application may have to be redeveloped because no one else knows how to use the prior spreadsheet. Another consideration of shadow data is that there may not be adequate or regular backups for disaster recovery.

Since shadow data is typically not developed by an IT professional, the shadow data may not undergo adequate testing to detect errors. This could result in material misstatements in accounting reports.

Also, since shadow data is outside the formal data systems under IT control, there are concerns about data security and irregularities. This is illustrated in the first section of Figure 7.9 where the area outlined in green represents the portion of the shadow data that is secured. The area outlined in red represents the portion of the system that is open to unauthorized access and is unsecured. Notice that a large portion of shadow data is unsecured.

Imagine that you extract data from your company's database and transfer the data through an ODBC to an Excel spreadsheet stored on your laptop. Then you take your laptop on a business trip. When you pass through airport security, you place your laptop on the conveyor belt for screening. You are delayed during security screening and your laptop has disappeared by the time you make it through the checkpoint. The shadow data on your missing laptop is unsecured. What would you do?

FIGURE 7.14 STAR for Autism Integrative Decision Model (IDM)

		Option A Golf Benefit	Option B Carnival	Option C Walkathon	Option D Silent Auction
1	Define the Issue	Which fundraising events should be continued or discontinued?			
2	Identify Options	Option A Golf Benefit	Option B Carnival	Option C Walkathon	Option D Silent Auction
3	Quantitative (Financial) Analysis	Benefits $ 4,500 Costs (5,550) Net ($1,050)	Benefits $1,000 Costs (10,800) Net ($9,800)	Benefits $25,000 Costs (1,550) Net $23,450	Benefits $10,800 Costs (575) Net $10,225
4	Qualitative (Nonfinancial) Analysis	Advantages: ■ Builds donor relationships ■ Good public relations	Advantage: ■ Fun event	Advantage: ■ Loyal event supporters	Advantage: ■ Minimal investment/ low risk
		Disadvantages: ■ Time consuming ■ Subject to weather	Disadvantages: ■ Time consuming to conduct ■ Uses large amounts of volunteer time	Disadvantage: ■ Subject to weather	Disadvantage: ■ Dependent upon select volunteers
5	Decision	Continue	Discontinue	Continue	Continue

Managing the risk that spreadsheets and shadow data bring may involve implementing tighter security and controls over spreadsheets. Another option is to move shadow data into an IT secured and controlled environment.

Shadow Data Global Spreadsheet Analysis

Remember Accounting Insight No. 10: 80% of time and resources should be invested in the accounting system design and 20% should be invested in maintenance of the system. When using shadow data, this is often reversed, with minimal time spent on design and significant amount of time spent on maintaining or recreating the shadow data. To address some of the disadvantages discussed, next we briefly look at a framework for integrating spreadsheets globally throughout an enterprise.

Shadow data spreadsheets are often scattered throughout an organization, located on various computer servers, desktops, and laptops. Furthermore, the design, formatting, and data can vary dramatically from spreadsheet to spreadsheet.

William Inmon (2008), widely recognized as the "father of data warehousing," offers several suggestions with regard to standardizing spreadsheets to permit global spreadsheet analysis within an organization.

First of all, just as each record in a database table has a unique identifier called the primary key, Inmon recommends that each spreadsheet in an organization be assigned a unique identifier called a **spreadsheet identifier** or **SSID**. For example, a spreadsheet might be assigned an identifier, such as SSID1001. The data within the numerous spreadsheets in an organization can then be referenced by the SSID and cell address as shown in Figure 7.15.

Secondly, implementing a global identification system for shadow data stored in spreadsheets can facilitate standardization in design and development. For example, guidelines might specify that the column labels are located in the first row as opposed to being scattered throughout the spreadsheet. This formatting is consistent with a data list format as shown in Figure 7.10. A data list is easily analyzed with PivotTables and other data analysis tools. If the design is more standardized across spreadsheets, global spreadsheet analysis is possible using queries that extract and integrate data from several spreadsheets (Figure 7.16).

Finally, an enterprise using global spreadsheet identification may require that all spreadsheets be stored on an enterprise server instead of desktops and laptops throughout an organization. This permits IT professionals to further standardize and organize the spreadsheets while at the same time heightening security and control.

> ### Would You Like to Know More?
>
> If you would like to know more about security and risk management for spreadsheets, see Chapter 12, *The Risk Intelligent Enterprise: Enterprise Risk Management.*

What Do Ants, Algorithms & Business Have in Common?

Businesses are turning to complex mathematical formulas called algorithms to analyze data to make better decisions and gain competitive advantage. Netflix uses algorithms to match customer preferences. Major League Baseball teams use Moneyball theory to draft future star players.

Algorithms are used by businesses to:

- streamline supply chains
- assess the fastest way to deliver products to customers
- analyze consumer purchases to decide what products to stock and where to place the products in the store
- decide where to locate new stores to maximize sales
- analyze how to cut airline fuel costs by changing flight times and refueling locations
- assist criminal justice systems to process cases faster

So what do ants have to do with algorithms and business? Have you ever noticed how a trail of ants will quickly adapt if something blocks their established route? Dr. George Danner, director of a UK analytics firm, says how foraging ants rapidly adapt can provide insights for algorithms. Algorithms can use insights from foraging ants to determine optimal solutions to business problems, such as rerouting product shipments efficiently. (www.bbc.co.uk)

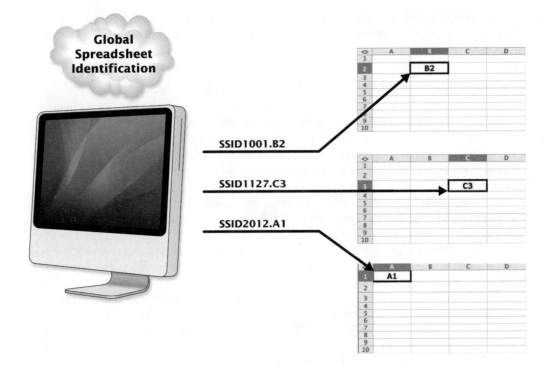

FIGURE 7.15

Global Spreadsheet Identification

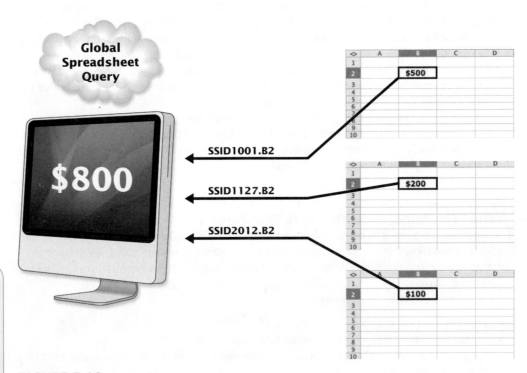

FIGURE 7.16

Global Spreadsheet Query

> **Business Intelligence Technologies...**
> are a type of advanced data analytics used to support business decision making. Leading business intelligence tools that Gartner Research identified for 2012 included Oracle Business Intelligence, MicroStrategy, IBM Cognos, and SAP BusinessObjects (Gartner's 2012 Magic Quadrant for Business Intelligence Platforms).

How Are BI Technologies Used to Create Business Intelligence?

Eight hours. That's how long it took one large enterprise to run an accounting report using an operational database query. The SAP database query required 8 hours to process, and if the report needed any changes, then *another* 8 hours was required to reprocess the report.

Two minutes. That's how long it took the enterprise to process the same accounting report when BI technologies were used. If you were the accountant waiting for the report, which would you choose: the 8-hour operational database query or the 2-minute BI query?

Let's follow the path of the data when BI technologies were used to create the report. As you can see in Figure 7.17, the accounting data in the operational database was extracted and transferred to a data warehouse. ETL (Extract/Transform/Load) applications are used to accomplish this data transfer.

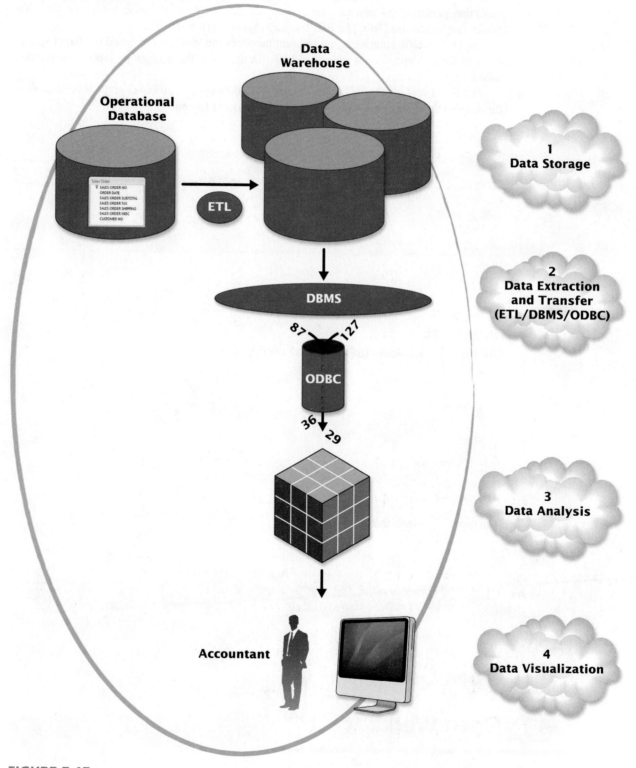

FIGURE 7.17
BI Technologies

In the data warehouse, the data is prepared for analysis. You can think of the data warehouse as a staging area for data analysis. IT professionals working with BI technologies develop the BI applications to run the query and analysis.

In the case of this particular enterprise, the next step was to use an SAP BEx Analyzer (Business Explorer Analyzer). The BEx Analyzer is an analysis and reporting tool that works with SAP and MS Excel. When the BEx Analyzer is installed, MS Excel displays a Business Explorer toolbar as shown in Figure 7.18. BEx Analyzer employs a macro (step-by-step program) that performs the analysis and exports the queried data into an Excel spreadsheet. The queries can be accessed from the BEx toolbar (Figures 7.19 and 7.20).

For this specific enterprise, information broadcasting was used to email the Excel spreadsheets to the accountant on a scheduled basis. In this case, the accounting report was required twice a year.

The Excel spreadsheet would appear in the accountant's email inbox at the scheduled time. The accountant would review the report and then request any needed changes.

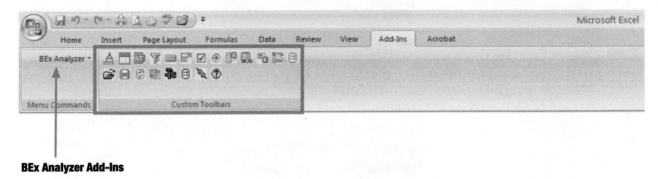

BEx Analyzer Add-Ins

FIGURE 7.18
SAP Business Explorer (BEx) Toolbar and Excel

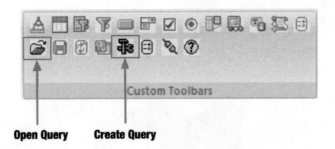

FIGURE 7.19
SAP BEx Queries   **Open Query**   **Create Query**

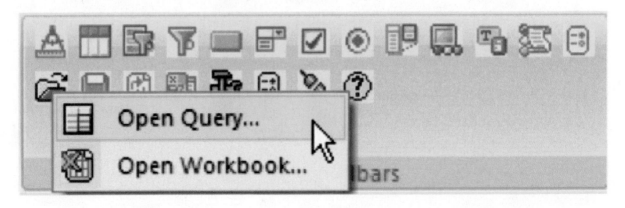

FIGURE 7.20
SAP BEx Open Query

With BI technologies, the reprocessing of the report required only a couple of minutes instead of the 8 hours required to process the report when an operational database query was used. This illustrates one of the advantages of BI technologies: processing speed.

BI Technologies and Intelligent Components

BI technologies use the same four intelligent components that shadow data does: data storage, data extraction, data analysis, and data visualization. The difference between BI technologies and shadow data is how the four components are used. First, let's compare shadow data and BI technologies so you can see some of the differences.

As you already know, shadow data relies upon operational databases. These operational databases store data about accounting transactions, such as sales. Typically, operational databases are relational databases where tables are related using common fields (primary keys and foreign keys). The relational database is well suited for storing data, but less well suited for retrieving data.

To see why, let's look at Figure 7.21 which shows four database tables: CUSTOMER, SALES ORDER, SALES ORDER LINE, and ITEM. If you were to write a query to extract items ordered by a specific customer on a specific invoice, the query would need to traverse three database tables: the CUSTOMER table, the SALES ORDER table, and the SALES ORDER LINE table.

Now imagine that you needed to write queries for the relational database shown in Figure 7.22. This database has 66 tables. Your queries might require traversing many tables in order to extract data. Some databases have thousands of tables. In a massive relational database, a complex query might require traversing hundreds of database tables. In addition, the operational database is used on an ongoing basis to process transactions. Running queries against the operational database can slow down transaction processing. So a relational database is well suited for storing data, but BI technologies are better suited for retrieving and analyzing data.

BI TECHNOLOGIES DATA STORAGE How is data stored when using BI technologies? Data warehouses. Large data warehouses store data used with BI technologies.

Instead of the relational structure used by an operational database (Figure 7.22), the data warehouse uses a dimensional database structure. One of the more popular dimensional structures is the star structure shown in Figure 7.23. Notice the two types of database tables in the dimensional database:

- Fact table
- Dimension table

A **dimensional database** has one fact table and two or more dimension (Dim) tables. The dimension tables in a star database are dimensions of the database, such as time dimension, product information, sales territory, currency, and so on. In Figure 7.23, the dimension tables provide multidimensional views of data about Internet sales.

Notice that the primary keys of the dimension tables are foreign keys in the fact table at the center of the star. In this case, the fact table contains facts about AdventureWorks Internet sales. The foreign keys in the center fact table create links to the other dimensions of the star structure.

> ### Your Competitive Advantage...
> Typically IT professionals with specialized knowledge are needed to develop the applications to run BI technologies. As an accounting professional, knowledge of BI essentials will assist you in working with IT professionals to meet your analysis and reporting needs.

> ### Relational Database or Dimensional Database?
> A dimensional database has one fact table at its center. A relational database does not have one central database table. Instead, it resembles an interlocking chain, linked together without a center.

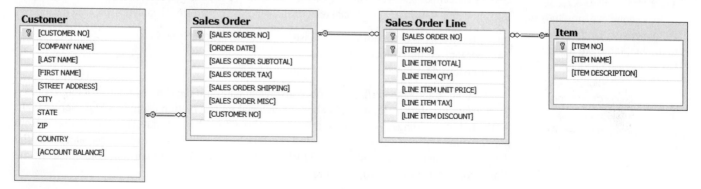

FIGURE 7.21

Relational Database Structure

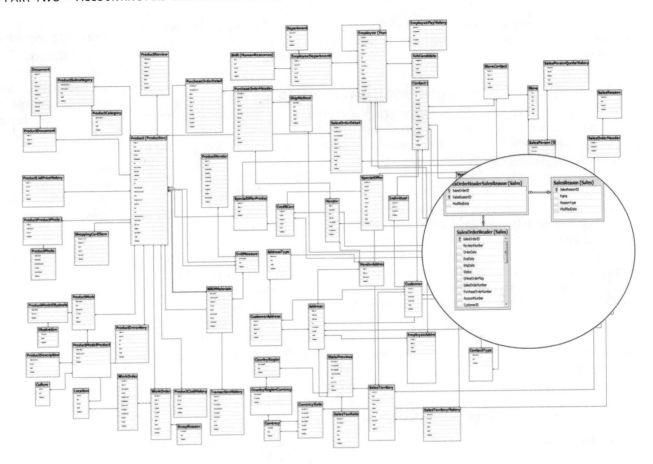

FIGURE 7.22

MS SQL Server AdventureWorks Relational Database

A star structure has one fact table at the center. All dimension database tables are related only to the fact table, creating a star shape. This dimensional structure allows faster access and retrieval of massive amounts of data. Notice that when data is retrieved, the query traverses only two tables: the fact table and one of the dimension tables. So at most, even complex queries traverse only two database tables (Figure 7.23).

A data warehouse includes data transferred from the operational database. It can also include data from other sources, including shadow data. The data warehouse may contain data duplication and inconsistencies. This does not present the problem for the data warehouse that it does for an operational database.

BI TECHNOLOGIES EXTRACTION AND TRANSFER The steps in the extraction and transfer process for BI technologies vary based upon the data source. For example, companies often store accounting transaction data in an operational relational database. To perform BI analytics, the data must be

- extracted from the relational database,
- reorganized into dimensions, and
- transferred and loaded into data warehouse tables.

ETL (Extract/Transfer/Load) tools convert the data into the dimensional structure required for the data warehouse. Figure 7.24 shows a pictorial representation using MS SQL Server ETL. At the top of the image, you can see the relational database table, SALESTERRITORY, that is from the AdventureWorks relational database. The ETL process extracts, transforms, and loads the data into a dimension database table, DIMSALESTERRITORY. This dimension table is part of the dimensional database shown in Figure 7.23.

BI TECHNOLOGIES DATA ANALYSIS BI technologies use a variety of data analysis tools, including data mining and predictive modeling. Data mining consists of mathematical, statistical, logical, and heuristic algorithms for discovering new relationships and patterns among data. An

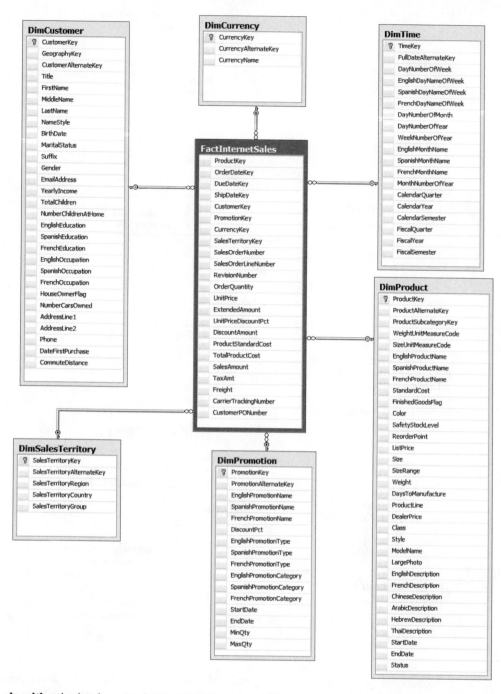

FIGURE 7.23
Dimensional Database Star Structure

algorithm is simply a step-by-step solution to a problem. Data mining techniques rely on pattern recognition, clustering, and neural networks. For example, cluster analysis is used for credit card fraud detection by analyzing the locations in which a credit card is used frequently. When the credit card is used outside the identified clusters, it is flagged for investigation (Turban, 2008).

Macros can be used to automate the steps in the algorithm. A macro can be initiated by the user or can be programmed to automatically run at scheduled times.

Other BI analysis tools include text mining and Web mining. **Text mining** is typically used on relatively unstructured data. Text mining can be used to mine text stored in various enterprise documents, including emails, word processing documents, and reports (Inmon, 2008).

Web mining is similar to the searches you conduct when you use the Google search engine. **Web mining** searches the Internet for specific patterns on Web sites. For example, social networking sites can be mined for patterns and trends to predict customer preferences.

Predictive modeling also uses algorithms to identify patterns and trends and then predict future behavior. For example, predictive modeling is used to predict what products consumers will purchase in the future.

Fact or Dimension Table?
How do I tell a fact database table from a dimension table? The word *Fact* is added to the fact database table name. *Dim* is added to the dimension database table name.

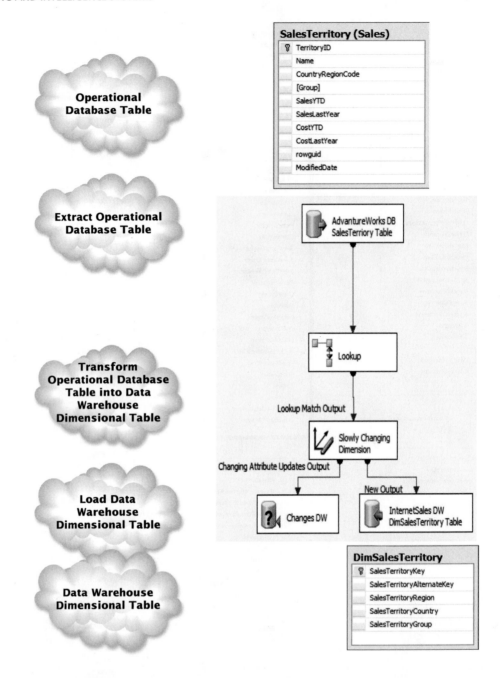

FIGURE 7.24

ETL For Loading DimSalesTerritory Table Using MS SQL Server

BI developers are specialized IT professionals who use BI technologies. BI developers work with accountants and other end users to identify user requirements and develop business intelligence data analysis to fulfill those requirements. BI developers can use information broadcasting to distribute the BI results on a scheduled basis to end users.

BI TECHNOLOGIES VISUALIZATION TOOLS BI technologies are complex. The role of the BI developer is to have specialized knowledge to use the complex BI technologies. No matter how complex the BI technologies, the role of the accounting professional typically involves only a data visualization tool, which should be easy for the accountant to use. So spreadsheets are an ideal choice for a BI visualization tool.

For example, the SAP BEx Analyzer mentioned earlier displays the BI results in an Excel spreadsheet. In other cases, SAP Web Analyzer can be used to export the BI results in graphical form into a Web browser. SAP BusinessObjects is yet another BI tool to enhance the user interface.

Whether a spreadsheet or Web browser output is selected may depend upon the end user preference. For example, accountants may prefer reports in Excel while the human resources department may prefer a Web browser that shows results in graphical output.

Digital dashboards are a powerful and flexible user interface. A digital dashboard graphically presents BI, allowing the user to manipulate data and view the resulting changes.

To understand BI dashboards, imagine your car dashboard with the speedometer showing your car's speed, the odometer showing your mileage, your fuel gauge showing gas level, the temperature gauge showing the engine temperature, and the RPM gauge showing the revolutions per minute of engine rotation. In sum, these gauges show your car's performance. By monitoring the dashboard, a car's driver can see how increased speed increases RPM and distance traveled reduces the fuel gauge. The temperature gauge alerts the driver when the car engine becomes overheated.

Sophisticated digital dashboards reveal patterns, trends, progress, and anomalies. See Figure 7.25 for an SAP sales monitoring dashboard. A digital dashboard shows not only BI

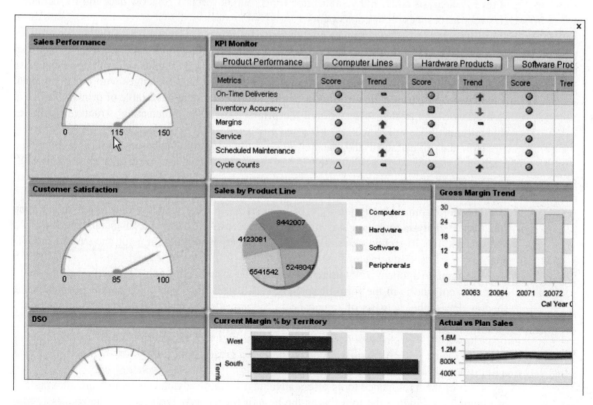

FIGURE 7.25

SAP Business One Sales Monitoring Dashboard

analysis results, but also when business performance variables reach critical threshold levels. By continuously monitoring the dashboard, business and accounting professionals can see changing, real-time business performance measures.

BI Technologies Advantages and Disadvantages

BI technologies offer enterprises many advantages. Two of the main advantages include faster processing of massive amounts of data and discovery of new knowledge through data mining and predictive modeling. BI technologies have the capability to integrate data from the operational database as well as multiple other sources of data including the Internet. Furthermore, BI technologies offer security and control advantages over shadow data. As shown in Figure 7.17, the entire BI system is secured. BI technologies reside under the control of the IT department providing the opportunity for standardization of controls to secure the system.

Although processing time for BI applications may be faster, one of the disadvantages of the BI system is a longer development time due to the use of BI developers. Another disadvantage is that some BI systems are not real-time, experiencing a time lag caused by batch updates run only periodically. This can result in outdated intelligence. Since the investment required for BI technologies can be significant and the benefits difficult to quantify, an enterprise may find a BI system cost prohibitive.

> **My Connection...**
> - Active Review 7.5
> - Short Exercise 7.31
> - It's Your Call 7.32
> - Go Online 7.47

How Do Shadow Data and BI Technologies Compare?

Business intelligence can be divided into two general categories: shadow data and BI technologies. The four components of an intelligent system are data storage, extraction and transfer (type of query), analysis tools, and visualization tools (output format). Shadow data and BI technologies vary across these four components.

How data is stored determines how the data is retrieved. The database structure determines how the database is stored, accessed, and retrieved. An operational database uses a relational database structure that connects database tables through common fields. The relational database is well suited for storing data, such as transaction data, but has challenges with retrieving data. A data warehouse uses a dimensional structure, such as star, that has a table of primary keys and then accesses the related table through the primary key. The dimensional structure facilitates data retrieval.

How data is extracted and transferred depends upon the database structure. A relational database structure, such as that used by an operational database, uses queries such as SQL (Structured Query Language). A dimensional structure used by a data warehouse, such as star, requires a different query language, which is more effective at searching and extracting data.

The third component is the type of analysis tools used. Shadow data often relies upon spreadsheet analysis tools, such as spreadsheet macros, statistical and financial functions, and analysis add-ins. BI technologies rely on BI developers who program using the system specific analysis tools, including macros.

The final component of intelligence tools is the visualization tool. The output of the intelligent system can be in the form of spreadsheets, dashboards, charts, or graphs. Typically the shadow data output consists of spreadsheets and spreadsheet charts and graphs. Output for BI can include spreadsheets as well as Web graphics and dashboards.

The security for shadow data is illustrated in Figure 7.9. Security for BI technologies is shown in Figure 7.17. As the figures show, there is a greater opportunity for unauthorized access with the use of shadow data.

Each of the intelligence tools offers advantages and disadvantages, which are summarized in Figure 7.26. Finding the tool that is the best fit for meeting the needs of the end user, considering data quality, data integrity, accuracy, reliability, processing cost, and response time, is essential to business competitive advantage.

FIGURE 7.26 Comparison of Business Intelligence Tools

Business Intelligence Technologies	Shadow Data
Interactive reporting	Possibly interactive reporting
Integrated data from operational database and data warehouse	Data from various internal and external sources
Three to six months to implement	Quick to implement
Large number of users	Typically a single user
Data and application located on secure servers	Data and application may not be located on secure servers
Possibly Sarbanes-Oxley (SOX) compliant	Typically not SOX compliant
Fully documented and supported by IT department	Typically not documented and supported by IT department

As you can see from this chapter, BI can take many forms. In the following two chapters, we will share with you two additional forms of BI. XBRL is required by some publicly traded companies for reporting financial results. The electronic tags used by XBRL permit the user to slice and dice data for multidimensional data analysis. Another form of BI that has increasing importance for more organizations is intelligence related to sustainability.

> **My Connection...**
> Active Review 7.8

Chapter Highlights

What is an integrated decision model? Decision models facilitate data collection for the decision-making process. The Integrated Decision Model (IDM) considers both quantitative and qualitative factors in decision making. The seven steps in the IDM are:

1. Define the issue or opportunity.
2. Identify the options to address the issue or opportunity.
3. Analyze the quantitative (financial) factors, considering the costs and benefits of each option.
4. Analyze the qualitative (nonfinancial) factors for each option.
5. Make a decision.
6. Implement the decision.
7. Evaluate performance.

What are the four components of an intelligent enterprise system? The four components of an intelligent enterprise system are:

- Data storage
- Data extraction and transfer
- Data analysis
- Data visualization

What are two approaches to business intelligence? Two approaches to business intelligence are:

1. Shadow data. Shadow data shadows the formal accounting system and often resides in spreadsheets on computer desktops and laptops.
2. Business intelligence technologies. BI technologies include business analytics, data mining, and predictive modeling.

What is global spreadsheet identification? To improve security over shadow data in spreadsheets, global spreadsheet identification is recommended. Each spreadsheet is assigned a spreadsheet identifier, or SSID, similar to a primary key for database record identification.

What database structure does a data warehouse use? Data warehouses use a dimensional database structure, such as the star structure. This dimensional structure allows faster access and retrieval of massive amounts of data for BI technologies.

How do shadow data and BI technologies compare? The advantages and disadvantages of shadow data and BI technologies are summarized in Figure 7.26.

Accounting System Insights 🔑

Insight No. 16 While relational databases are well suited for storing data, intelligence tools are better suited for analysis.

Active Review

Study less. Learn more. Make connections.

7.1 Refer to the chapter opener, *Meet Kroger*. In your opinion, if you are the consumer, would you prefer to receive targeted coupons even if it means the company is tracking your purchasing data?

7.2 Discuss security concerns related to shadow data and business intelligence technologies.

7.3 Discuss how centralizing the operational database and data warehouse improves the performance of intelligence queries.

7.4 Discuss differences between an operational database and a data warehouse.

7.5 Discuss why running business intelligence queries using an operational database can be a slow process. Why is it faster to use BI technologies with a data warehouse?

7.6 Discuss the role of accounting professionals in the development of shadow data.

7.7 Discuss the role of accounting professionals in the development of business intelligence technologies.

7.8 Discuss the benefits and limitations of using shadow data versus BI technologies.

7.9 Discuss the advantages of using a decision model. How does it help standardize your accounting system? Why is it important to consider qualitative factors when making a decision?

7.10 Discuss the advantages of a dimensional database structure used for data warehouses.

Key Terms Check

Understanding the language used at the crossroads of accounting and IT is key to your success.

Select the single best answer.

7.11 Long-range, unstructured decisions with a high degree of ambiguity are called
a. routine operating decisions.
b. tactical decisions.
c. strategic decisions.
d. all of the above.

7.12 Decisions typically related to ongoing business activities are considered
a. routine operating decisions.
b. tactical decisions.
c. strategic decisions.
d. all of the above.

7.13 Semistructured decisions that are typically short term in nature and impact one year or less are considered
a. routine operating decisions.
b. tactical decisions.
c. strategic decisions.
d. all of the above.

7.14 A business intelligence technique that uses mathematical algorithms to predict future trends is
a. data mining.
b. text mining.
c. Web mining.
d. predictive modeling.

7.15 A business intelligence technique used on relatively unstructured data such as emails is called

a. data mining.
b. text mining.
c. Web mining.
d. predictive modeling.

7.16 A business intelligence technique used to search social networking sites for customer preferences would be referred to as

a. data mining.
b. text mining.
c. Web mining.
d. predictive modeling.

7.17 A business intelligence technique used to search data stored in a data warehouse using mathematical algorithms to find patterns, trends, and relationships among data is referred to as

a. data mining.
b. text mining.
c. Web mining.
d. predictive modeling.

7.18 Match the following terms and definitions.

a. integrative decision model (IDM)
b. digital dashboard
c. open database connectivity (ODBC)
d. macros
e. spreadsheet identifier (SSID)
f. dimensional database
g. algorithm

_____ 1. Translates data analysis query commands into commands that are compatible with RDBMS commands to extract data from an operational database
_____ 2. A step-by-step solution to a problem
_____ 3. Contains one fact database table and one or more dimension database tables
_____ 4. Each spreadsheet is assigned a unique identifier.
_____ 5. Automatically perform a sequence of analysis tasks, step by step
_____ 6. A framework to structure the decision-making process and incorporate both qualitative and quantitative considerations in the decision
_____ 7. An interactive form that combines charts, graphs, figures, tables, and data cubes

Practice Test

7.19 Business intelligence is used to

a. Streamline business processes
b. Make better business decisions
c. Make the enterprise database more intelligent
d. Remove redundant data from the enterprise database

7.20 Tactical decisions are

a. Routine operational decisions
b. Semi-structured
c. Unstructured
d. Made for merger and acquisition

7.21 Total sales on the corporate annual income statement is

a. Data
b. Information
c. Intelligence
d. All the above

7.22 _____ provides an organization with insights to improve future business performance.

a. Customer relationship management
b. An information system
c. Enterprise resource planning
d. Predictive analysis

7.23 _____ provides a framework for structuring and organizing the decision-making process.

a. An integrated decision model
b. A predictive model
c. Data mining
d. A mathematical model

7.24 Data cubes allow

a. Databases to have more than one table
b. More data from various tables be stored in one table
c. A multidimensional view of the data
d. a and b

7.25 Shadow data is

a. Test data
b. Data currently stored in the organization databases
c. Data collected from sources other than the organization databases
d. b and c

7.26 ODBC

a. Is an operational database component
b. Processes user queries
c. Is the pipeline between the database and the data analysis application
d. Provides the database reports

7.27 Inmon recommend that each

a. Spreadsheet in an organization be assigned login and password
b. Spreadsheet in an organization carry the developer name and identification
c. Spreadsheet in an organization be encrypted before being stored
d. Spreadsheet in an organization be assigned a unique identifier

7.28 Which of the following is true?

a. Shadow data is quick to implement.
b. Shadow data is used by a large number of users.
c. Shadow data is fully documented and supported by the IT department.
d. Shadow data is highly secure and protected.

Exercises

Each Exercise relates to one of the major questions addressed in the chapter and is labeled with the question number in green.

Short Exercises

Warm up with these short exercises.

7.29 Identify which of the following numbered items are data, information, or intelligence. **(Q7.1)**

a. data
b. information
c. intelligence

_____ 1. Sequence of numbers stored in a table
_____ 2. A chart depicting sales of a specific item for specific regions and average income in those regions
_____ 3. A table containing one hundred names
_____ 4. A graph showing sales amounts for a specific year
_____ 5. A pie chart showing sales in different regions
_____ 6. A graph depicting sales in relation to customer age
_____ 7. A graph showing the average price of a product in the marketplace

7.30 Match the following intelligent system components with the appropriate example. **(Q7.3, 7.4)**

a. data storage
b. data extraction and transfer
c. data analysis
d. data visualization

_____ 1. ODBC
_____ 2. digital dashboard
_____ 3. spreadsheet financial functions
_____ 4. relational database
_____ 5. query
_____ 6. star data warehouse structure
_____ 7. ETL
_____ 8. predictive modeling
_____ 9. OLAP cube
_____ 10. data mining

7.31 Number the following steps for an ETL in the order in which the steps would be executed. **(Q7.5)**

a. Load data warehouse dimensional table
b. Extract operational relational database table
c. Choose operational database table
d. Use data warehouse dimensional table
e. Transform operational database table into data warehouse dimensional table

It's Your Call

This is your training ground. These scenarios provide you with the opportunity to use your knowledge and professional skills.

7.32 Both accounting and IT report to the CFO of Lawrence Enterprises. The IT professionals have been lobbying him for a data warehouse to use for business intelligence. While the CFO can see the value of using business intelligence to improve decisions, he is not sure that it is warranted by the cost of the data warehouse. The accounting professionals are saying that it will put them over budget if they have to purchase a data warehouse. Why can't IT just use the operational database that was purchased last year?

The CFO has called you in to act as a liaison between accounting and IT. He wants some straight answers from you: Does he need to invest in a data warehouse or not? Can the company just use the operational database for business intelligence? Draft a short email to the CFO with your response. **(Q7.3, 7.4, 7.5)**

7.33 Because of your background in accounting and IT, the vice president of sales and marketing asked you to create a digital dashboard for his sales managers. For his review, he would like you to send him a short email summarizing your ideas for the digital dashboard. Draft a short email to the vice president outlining your thoughts. Include the following:

1. What information and intelligence would you put on the digital dashboard for the sales managers?
2. What would be the source of your data for the digital dashboard?
3. What decisions could the digital dashboard help the sales managers make? **(Q7.3, 7.4, 7.5)**

7.34 Because of your stellar performance in your accounting information systems course, you have been called to the office of the university's controller. The controller tells you that the university's annual audit begins next month. The controller has heard from other universities that they experienced audit issues with numerous spreadsheets that did not have proper controls. The controller has asked you to complete an internship with his office. Your assignment would be to devise a plan to improve spreadsheet controls. What would you say in your executive summary to the controller? **(Q7.4)**

Tech in Practice

These technology in practice exercises are perfect for both individuals and teams.

Tech Exercises

Sharpen your skills with these technology exercises. Watch these software videos at www.pearsonhighered.com/kay.

7.35

Tech Tool: Spreadsheet Software
Software Videos: Spreadsheet Data Tables, Spreadsheet PivotTables and PivotCharts

This technology exercise is a continuation of the Chapter 7 illustration, STAR for Autism Shadow Data.

Although the foundation board voted to continue the golf benefit, the walkathon, and the silent auction, but to discontinue the carnival, one of the board members requested additional analysis be conducted regarding the carnival. The board member was concerned that the board was making a hasty decision and felt that the carnival had been a successful fundraiser in past years.

One of the staff members collected the following additional data and has asked your assistance in analyzing it. In particular, the staff member asked if you could organize the information in a data list for 2008 and 2009 for the carnival as has been done for 2010. In addition, the board members had asked for a dashboard to summarize the analysis using PivotTables and PivotCharts.

1. Download the spreadsheet data file for this exercise for STAR for Autism.
2. Using the downloaded spreadsheet data file, create a digital dashboard that compares prior years to the current year results, including a PivotTable and PivotChart.
3. What relationships and insights do you see? What intelligence can you glean from your analysis?

7.36

Tech Tool: Spreadsheet Software, Database Software

Software Videos: Spreadsheet ODBC, Spreadsheet Data Tables, Spreadsheet PivotTables and PivotCharts

EspressoCoffee has asked for your assistance with the following tasks.

1. Download the EspressoCoffee file for this exercise.
2. Set up open database connectivity (ODBC) to import data from the Microsoft Access file you downloaded into a spreadsheet.
3. Format the imported data into a data table in Excel.
4. Create a PivotTable to analyze the sales data.
5. Create a pie chart with totals for each country.
6. Create a bar chart by quarter.
7. Using the PivotTable and charts you created, develop a digital dashboard that could be used to monitor and track EspressoCoffee sales.
8. Analyze the information provided by your digital dashboard to create intelligence. What intelligence can you glean from your analysis?

7.37

Tech Tool: Spreadsheet Software

Software Videos: Spreadsheet Data Tables, Spreadsheet PivotTables and PivotCharts

You have just been hired as the new accounting intern. Your first assignment is to reformat a spreadsheet that your predecessor created. Complete the following steps.

1. Download the file for this exercise.
2. Reformat the spreadsheet into a data table format.
3. Create a PivotTable to analyze the data.
4. Create a chart that best summarizes intelligence.
5. Develop a digital dashboard that can be used to monitor results in the future.

7.38

Tech Tool: Spreadsheet Software

Software Videos: Spreadsheet Data Tables, Spreadsheet PivotTables and PivotCharts

Now that you have a full-time position, you have decided to start investing. You have invested in three different companies. You are using a spreadsheet to track stock prices for the three different companies for a 12-month period.

1. Download the spreadsheet data file for this exercise.
2. Create a PivotTable to analyze the data.
3. Create a line chart to contrast the stock performance of the three companies.
4. Develop a digital dashboard that can be used to monitor stock performance.

7.39

Tech Tool: Spreadsheet Software

Software Videos: Spreadsheet Data Tables, Spreadsheet PivotTables and PivotCharts

Have you ever been asked for your ZIP code when you made a purchase at a store? From American Eagle to Williams Sonoma, stores ask customers for ZIP codes when a sale is made. Why?

ZIP codes can be used to identify pockets of customers in specific geographic regions that then can be targeted with coupon mailings and advertisements. When the sales transactions are recorded in the accounting system, also recording the customers' ZIP codes can provide additional intelligence for making future sales.

As the new accounting intern, you just received your first information broadcast email containing the results of a business intelligence query. This BI query retrieved data from the company's data warehouse about customer ZIP codes and amount of purchase, using information that had been stored in both the CUSTOMER table and the ORDER table. The query results were exported to a spreadsheet, and then using information broadcasting it was sent to your email inbox.

Complete the following steps to obtain a sense of how additional insights and business intelligence can be obtained through analysis.

1. Download and open the file for this exercise.
2. Format the data as a spreadsheet data table.
3. Create a PivotTable to analyze ZIP codes and purchases.
4. Create a chart that best depicts the location of customers making purchases. Does your chart provide a means for gauging the dollar amount of the purchases? If not, can you think of a way to create a chart that would reveal this additional type of business intelligence?
5. Develop a digital dashboard that the company can use for BI purposes in the future.

7.40
Tech Tool: Spreadsheet Software
Software Videos: Spreadsheet Data Tables

Explore the data analysis tools provided by Microsoft Excel.

1. Open Microsoft Excel.
2. List all the data analysis tools that you can discover in Excel.
3. Explain how these tools can be used to create business intelligence using shadow data.

7.41
Tech Tool: Spreadsheet Software
Software Videos: Spreadsheet Data Tables

Explore the data visualization tools provided by Excel.

1. Open Microsoft Excel.
2. List all the data visualization tools that you can discover in Excel.
3. Explain how these tools can be used for digital dashboards.

7.42
Tech Tool: Spreadsheet Software
Software Videos: Spreadsheet Data Analysis Tools

The following table shows the increase of the teenage population in the past 10 years in a European country as well as the increase in demand for a specific nonalcoholic drink.

1. Download the exercise data file.
2. Graph the teenage population for the past 10 years.
3. Graph the demand for the past 10 years.
4. Plot the teenager population (x, independent variable) versus the demand (y, dependent variable).

Year	Demand	Teenage population
1	487000	9123000
2	560000	10189000
3	601000	11570000
4	689000	12584000
5	788000	13965000
6	854000	15191000
7	902000	17321000
8	957000	19247000
9	991000	21096000
10	1010000	23095000

7.43
Tech Tool: Spreadsheet Software
Software Videos: Spreadsheet Data Analysis Tools

A marketing manager says that there is a relationship between the marketing budget and sales volume. He provided the following table of the marketing budget (in thousand $) and the amount of sales (in million $). He insists that if the marketing budget increases to 23, 25, and 27 thousand dollars, the sales will increase accordingly. Is he correct? To support your answer, you may need to use Microsoft Excel to:

1. Put the data in the spreadsheet.
2. Decide between the marketing budget and the sales amount—which one depends on the other (x and y of the curve).
3. Plot the marketing budget versus sales volume.

Use the Microsoft Trendline data analysis tool to:

4. Determine the curve that best fits the plotted data and the curve equation.
5. Find out the R^2 value. The closer to 1, the stronger the relationship.

Analyze the result.

Marketing Budget (in thousand $)	Sales Amount (in million $)
10	260
12	410
13	515
14	580
15	680
17	707
20	750
23	640
25	510

7.44

Tech Tool: Spreadsheet Software
Software Videos: Spreadsheet ODBC

You are asked to build a spreadsheet graph to monitor different products' sales amounts. Management is interested in seeing changes in the sales display data when the sales of different products are changed.

1. Download the MS Access data file for this exercise and open it.
2. Set up ODBC to import data from the Microsoft Access file you downloaded into a spreadsheet.
3. Graph sales of different products.
4. Go back to the exercise data file (MS Access data file) and change the sales volume of a product.
5. Verify changes in your graph.
6. Prepare a summary for this process.

7.45

Tech Tool: Spreadsheet Software
Software Videos: Spreadsheet ODBC

Add a PivotTable and PivotChart to the preceding exercise solution. Verify changes in the data file in the pivot chart. Prepare a summary of this process.

MS Excel 2010 and above: Add a slicer tool to be able to focus only on the selected products.

Go Online

In the fast-paced world of technology, your skill at finding answers quickly can be vital. Go online and experience typical assignments you may encounter as a professional.

7.46 You are the accounting representative for a project team assigned to evaluate business intelligence solutions. The team leader has asked you to research BI vendors and the BI solutions that each provides. Go online and search for business intelligence solution providers. Prepare a short summary of the list of BI vendors and their products that you can present at the next team meeting.

7.47 The CFO has just asked you to get her up to speed on data warehousing. The IT staff will be in her office this afternoon asking for funding. She wants to be able to have an intelligent conversation but they are using terms such as *snowflakes* and *stars*. What do stars and snowflakes have to do with a data warehouse? Go online and research dimensional database structures, and create a short summary for the CFO to prepare her for the afternoon meeting.

7.48 You are CFO of Vienna SA. Recently your company has faced decreasing sales as a result of competitors using business intelligence. The CEO wants to implement a data warehouse for BI purposes. Since IT reports to you, you need to learn about data warehousing fast. Go online and search for companies providing data warehouse solutions, such as Teradata and Sybase. Prepare your notes for your upcoming meeting with IT to discuss data warehousing options.

7.49 You are completing a summer internship with Laura Inc. The company makes extensive use of shadow data for data analysis. The controller has asked you to research a spreadsheet add-in called Analysis Toolpak. Go online and search for information about this product. Write a short email to the controller about what you learn.

7.50 You are completing a summer internship with Laura Inc. The company makes extensive use of shadow data for data analysis. The controller has asked you to research a spreadsheet-based application called Crystal Ball used for predictive modeling. Go online and search for information about this product. Write a short email to the controller about what you learn about Crystal Ball.

Technology Projects

These technology projects are perfect for both individuals and teams.

Technology Project 7

Tech Tool: Spreadsheet Software, Database Software

Software Videos: Spreadsheet ODBC, Spreadsheet Data Tables, Spreadsheet PivotTables and PivotCharts

Nick, the owner of iSportDesign, would like to start using business intelligence to improve decision making. He has asked you to complete the following assignments for this initiative. Your deliverables for the project include:

Deliverable 1. Shadow data: Data list for sales data for iSportDesign created using an ODBC and a relational database

Deliverable 2. Shadow data: Data list with data validation and analysis added

Deliverable 3. Shadow data: PivotTable and PivotChart

Deliverable 4. Shadow data: Digital dashboard

Deliverable 5. BI technologies: Digital dashboard created from a data warehouse table for iSportDesign sales

Visit www.pearsonhighered.com/kay to:

1. Download Technology Project 7 instructions.
2. Download files provided online for your convenience in completing the project deliverables.
3. Watch the videos with software instructions to complete this project at www.pearsonhighered.com/kay.

LIVE Project 2: Business Intelligence Using Excel

LIVE projects give you an opportunity to apply your accounting and technology skills to LIVE applications.

LIVE Project 2 provides you with a structured approach to using spreadsheets to create business intelligence for a real company.

To view the LIVE projects, visit www.pearsonhighered.com/kay and click on Chapter 16: LIVE Projects. You will find the following:

1. LIVE Project 2 with milestones and deliverables.
2. Project management training.
3. Team coaching.

8 Accounting and Sustainability Intelligence

What's the Bottom Line?
Meet the Triple Bottom Line.

When accountants would like someone to get to the point, they are well known for saying, "What's the bottom line?" The bottom line also refers to the bottom line of the income statement, or profit.

Can you imagine an income statement that doesn't have a bottom line? What about an income statement with a triple bottom line? Yes, that's right: three bottom lines.

In 2010, a sea change in accounting occurred quietly in the United States. The state of Maryland passed legislation creating a new type of corporation. This corporation doesn't have one bottom line, but three bottom lines. The new class of corporation will report on economic, social, and environmental performance (or profit, people, and the planet). At the time, 10 other states, including California, Oregon, and Washington, were considering similar legislation.

What do you think? Should corporations report their economic, social, and environmental results? How will this new reporting affect your accounting system?

Crossroads
At the crossroads of accounting and IT, initiatives for sustainability accounting can affect the accounting system and IT requirements.

My Questions

Q 8.1	What's the triple bottom line?
Q 8.2	What is sustainability accounting? And how will it impact my accounting system?
Q 8.3	How is sustainability accounting used in decision making?
Q 8.4	How is sustainability accounting used for reporting performance?
Q 8.5	What is integrated reporting?
Q 8.6	Who's a leader in integrated reports?

What's the Triple Bottom Line?

Do you recycle? Do you reuse your shopping bag? Do you buy products that use recycled materials? Do you prefer organic foods?

Have you ever considered not only the cost of your choices but also their effect on society and the environment? How would you measure the effect of your choices on society? The effect on the environment?

Today, that is exactly what companies around the globe are attempting to do: measure the effect of their choices on society and the environment. Why are companies undertaking this challenge?

More and more, consumers, investors, and society are placing greater demands on enterprises and voicing their expectations with dollars—how they invest and what products they purchase. As increasing pressure is placed upon organizations to demonstrate social and environmental responsibility, these organizations seek new ways to manage, measure, and report their performance.

Enterprises and society have discovered that focusing only on bottom line profit can lead to dysfunctional results both for corporations and for society. Efforts to expand the decision making focus of corporations to include a more comprehensive picture of the results of their actions has led to the triple bottom line. The **triple bottom line**, as its name implies, considers three results: the effect on people, profit, and the planet (Savitz, 2006). The triple bottom line measures the economic, social, and environmental results of corporate decisions. While this is an attractive theory, it has proven challenging to measure in practice. In addition, short-term results that might appear favorable for all three bottom lines might in fact be detrimental in the long run. This brings us to another framework that offers the advantage of timeframe, considering short-term and long-run effects of decisions: sustainability.

> The triple bottom line is sometimes called 3BL.

> Although the triple bottom line and sustainability are related, sustainability considers a longer run perspective.

> **My Connection...**
> Try Active Review 8.1.

What Is Sustainability Accounting? And How Will It Impact My Accounting System?

Sustainability focuses on the ability to sustain an action in the future on an ongoing basis. Is the decision and resulting action sustainable in the long run? Is the organization's performance sustainable in the long run?

Sustainability is transformational business, transforming business from a focus on bottom line profit to a holistic view of the business as an integral part of a larger system.

ACCOUNTING INSIGHT NO. 17
Use Satellite Mapping for
Sustainability Accounting…
Zoom Out to See Business in a
Global World View Considering
Economic, Social, and Environmental
Sustainability

Accounting Insight No. 17: Sustainability Accounting

In Accounting Insight No. 17, we use satellite mapping for sustainability accounting: Zoom out further to see business in a global world view, considering economic, social, and environmental sustainability.

For many corporations, their decisions in the short run may produce extraordinary profits, but in the long run the results are not sustainable. This can lead to situations in which managers rotate out of positions every two to five years, just before the adverse long-term consequences become reality. Then, the next manager, who bears the results of the prior manager's myopic decisions, may appear to be incompetent. The prior manager appears to have been the star performer when in fact, he or she just had the foresight to leave before negative consequences began showing up in the financial results.

Sustainability requires a new perspective on firm operations. Not only does it require the ability to view the enterprise in a global perspective, but it also requires the ability to consider the long view of decisions, actions, and consequences. While one can argue that it is not possible to predict with complete certainty the results of actions, management can be cognizant of possible negative effects of actions and decide if it wants a few extra dollars of profit today in order to risk those negative future consequences.

The focus then shifts from *How can we increase profits this year?* to *Is our organization making decisions that are economically sustainable? Socially sustainable? Environmentally sustainable?*

> *Unless the accountancy profession embraces sustainability, we will become less and less relevant to society.*
> —Nick Shepherd
> President, EduVision

What Do You Think?
Will accountants become less relevant to society if they don't embrace sustainability? If accountants are not the professionals responsible for sustainability, who will be?

Sustainability accounting is also called enterprise sustainability accounting (ESA).

You're the Boss...
Imagine you own a business with only one asset: an oil well. You are pumping crude oil as fast as you can and making a lot of money!

The oil well is not endless, however. Eventually the oil well runs out of oil. Then you have *no* money.

How could you make your business more sustainable? How could you account for results of your operations differently to assist you in making better long-run decisions?

Sustainability accounting involves collecting, storing, organizing, and reporting economic, social, and environmental information for two general purposes:

1. Making decisions
2. Evaluating performance

Sustainability accounting places new demands on the accounting system. The challenge for the accounting system is how to capture and report the additional data needed to account for sustainability. The accounting system must now be capable of capturing data and providing sustainability information for decision making and performance evaluation (Figure 8.1).

The decision model and sustainability reports used by an organization must be considered when designing the accounting system to ensure that the appropriate data is captured by the

FIGURE 8.1

Sustainability Information for Decision Making and Performance Evaluation

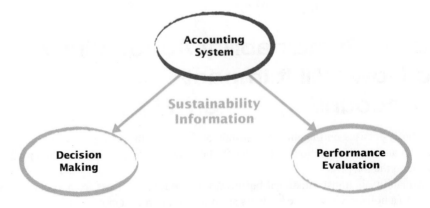

system. To analyze the impact on the accounting system of new demands for sustainability information, we will use the three keys of opportunity, which we shared with you in Chapter 1.

Three Keys to Sustainability Accounting

The three keys of people, processes, and technology can be used to analyze the impact of sustainability accounting on the accounting system (Figure 8.2). We will explore the following questions:

1. How does sustainability accounting impact people?
2. How does sustainability accounting affect your organization's processes?
3. How does sustainability accounting impact your organization's technology?

PEOPLE Sustainability accounting can impact people inside and outside the organization. Employees, including accounting and IT professionals as well as customers and vendors, may be affected. Accountants will be asked to collect and report new types of data, such as an organization's effects on society and the environment. This will require new ways of measuring data that are different from what accountants have used in the past. Accountants are often asked to provide recommendations for decision making. So when an accountant analyzes decision options, he or she will need to consider information related to sustainability.

Customers may demand more people- and eco-friendly products. Sometimes, companies must educate customers regarding the benefits of new products, such as energy efficiency and cost savings of a new refrigerator purchase.

New expectations may be placed upon vendors to reduce packaging and provide more people- and eco-friendly products. With respect to employees, some firms create a culture of sustainability throughout an organization that impacts all employees. For example, some organizations have adopted a company-wide sustainability policy to use virtual meetings instead of employee travel.

At the crossroads of accounting and IT, professionals responsible for the accounting system will need to evaluate how sustainability impacts processes and technology, which we explore next.

PROCESSES How does sustainability impact an organization's processes? How does an organization integrate sustainability into its processes? How can business processes be managed to meet strategic enterprise sustainability goals?

Some organizations use a value-chain approach. Each link in the chain (Figure 8.3) is analyzed and managed to implement sustainability practices. The organization systematically reviews the links in the value chain for possible sustainability improvements. For example, when making

> **Did You Know?**
> The total amount of resources required to make a computer is about the same as what is required to make an SUV.

> Business processes are a related set of activities that add value. The value chain is a related set of business processes.

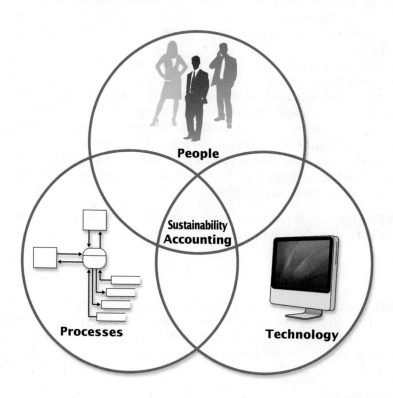

FIGURE 8.2

Three Keys to Sustainability Accounting

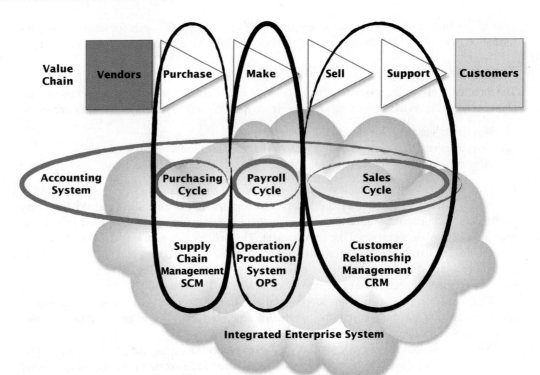

FIGURE 8.3

Business Processes and Transaction Cycles

a product, an organization might reduce energy usage and toxic waste. In the support link of the value chain, an organization might implement recycling of its used products.

As Figure 8.3 shows, the business processes in the value chain are related to the transaction cycles used in the accounting system:

1. The purchasing cycle relates to vendor transactions.
2. The sales cycle relates to customer transactions.
3. The payroll cycle relates to employee transactions.

Each of the business processes and related transaction cycles can be evaluated for ways to integrate sustainability. The business processes related to the purchasing cycle, for example, might be analyzed and updated to improve economic, social, and environmental sustainability.

Some organizations have focused on nurturing vendor relationships with suppliers in developing geographic regions. In addition to improved quality of life for individuals in those areas, potential benefits to the organization include a sustainable supply of scarce resources.

Another example of managing business processes to meet economic and environmental sustainability targets would be working with vendors to implement a paperless electronic purchasing process to reduce paper, postage, and related environmental costs.

The transaction cycles (purchasing, sales, and payroll) generate transaction data stored in the accounting system using technology. So next we will focus on the impact of sustainability on technology needs for the accounting system.

TECHNOLOGY How does sustainability impact technology? For our purposes, we can divide sustainability's impact on technology into two categories:

1. **Green IT**
2. Sustainability and accounting technology needs

Green IT. Did you know that your computer can contain lead, mercury, cadmium, and other heavy metals? Did you know that if your computer is not disposed of properly, those heavy metals can leach into the groundwater, contaminating water supplies? This applies to other electronics that you use as well, such as cell phones, laptops and netbooks.

A Greener Apple....

Apple redesigned the MacBook and iMac computer displays to use mercury-free LED backlight technology.

Apple estimates that 53% of the greenhouse gas emissions result from the power Apple products consume when used by the customer. To reduce the environmental impact, the products are designed to be more energy efficient.

Sustainability concerns may impact decisions regarding the IT hardware used. Hardware selection decisions might be impacted by the unique challenges of proper disposal or recycling of electronic waste.

E-cycling or electronic recycling programs may be implemented by organizations to improve sustainability performance. Consider a firm that has hundreds, even thousands, of computers. An aggressive e-cycling program and careful IT purchasing decisions can have a significant impact. Some computer manufacturers, such as Apple, are working to redesign their electronics products to reduce or eliminate toxic components. Some companies have implemented recycling programs for their products. HP, for example, has implemented a recycling program for inkjet and laser printer cartridges.

The European Union (EU) addressed the mounting e-cycling problem by enacting legislation in 2003 that places more responsibility on the manufacturer for proper disposal. Currently, manufacturers of the electrical and electronics equipment must accept consumers' e-waste free of charge.

Sustainability and Accounting Technology Needs. How will sustainability impact the technology needs for an accounting system? To answer that question, let's consider the primary functions of the accounting system:

1. Store accounting data, including sustainability data. Typically we use a database to store the data. So we will need to consider the impact on the accounting database.
2. Use data, including sustainability data. Two uses of sustainability accounting data are decision making and performance evaluation. Analytics and business intelligence techniques may be employed to generate sustainability intelligence for decision making and performance reporting.
3. Safeguard information assets, including sustainability information. The information collected about sustainability performance and decision making may be closely guarded by an organization in order to prevent misuse.

How do you design databases to organize and store sustainability data? To accommodate the need for tracking sustainability information, additional database fields may be needed. For example, additional fields might be necessary to identify whether the impact is economic, social, or environmental.

Financial or quantitative data, such as dollar amounts, can easily be stored and retrieved using a database. However, much of sustainability reporting uses nonfinancial or qualitative data. Storing qualitative data in a database often requires use of specific techniques to prepare the data for database storage.

To store and retrieve data related to sustainability, additional tags or identifiers might be attached to the data, such as XBRL tags. The advent of XBRL for reporting purposes has the potential to simplify accounting for sustainability. XBRL uses electronic tags for data, both quantitative and qualitative. This is especially useful for sustainability accounting that involves significant amounts of qualitative data. Furthermore, the XBRL tags can be used for external performance reporting or for internal decision making and evaluation.

What additional data analytics and business intelligence is needed for sustainability decisions and performance evaluation? Several providers of enterprise systems have already responded with business intelligence tools for sustainability. Business intelligence tools, such as Oracle Business Intelligence, provide graphical sustainability dashboards to monitor sustainability patterns, trends, progress, and anomalies. One area of enterprise sustainability accounting gaining increased attention is enterprise carbon accounting (ECA). Carbon accounting focuses on measuring the amount of carbon (CO_2) emissions as a result of an organization's operations and activities. Emission sources include fossil fuel consumption, onsite emissions, transportation of people and products, product packaging, and waste disposal.

To address the growing demand for carbon accounting, some software providers, such as Microsoft and SAP, now offer carbon accounting software applications. For example, MS Dynamics offers an Environmental Sustainability Dashboard for tracking an organization's energy usage and carbon footprint.

Next, we will show you how sustainability analytics can be used in the decision making process.

What Do You Think?

California places responsibility on the consumer for e-cycling. The consumer pays a fee when purchasing electronics to cover the cost of e-cycling.

Missouri places responsibility on the manufacturer to accept e-waste from consumers free of charge.

Does one approach incentivize the consumer to recycle? Which approach incentivizes the manufacturer?

What do you think?

SAS...

Notice that three functions of the accounting system are SAS:
1. Store data.
2. Analyze and use data.
3. Safeguard data.

XBRL: Electronic Tags...

Would you like to know more about XBRL? See Chapter 9.

Groom Energy Solutions, a consulting firm specializing in technology to make companies more energy-efficient estimates that almost 90% of companies use spreadsheets for carbon accounting.

My Connection...

- Short Exercise 8.22
- Go Online 8.37

How Is Sustainability Accounting Used in Decision Making?

How does the accounting system capture and report the additional sustainability data needed for decision making? How do we know what data to collect and store in the accounting system?

Sustainability requires a new decision making perspective. Instead of short-term profit maximization, true sustainability focuses on creating long-term value. Sustainability recognizes the interdependencies of economic, social, and environmental factors in creating value. It offers a new approach to decision making in the business environment, resulting in a dramatic shift in data requirements, data analysis, and decision models.

Using a decision model streamlines the data collection process. We have a better idea of what data we need to collect and store in the accounting system if we know how the data will be used in the decision process. In the last chapter, we shared with you a decision model, IDM or integrated decision model, to assist in organizing data needed for decision making. Next, we will share with you a decision model developed to assist in weighing sustainability information in the decision-making process.

Sustainability IDa Model

The traditional cost-benefit decision model (Figure 8.4) considers only economic factors that can be quantified in dollars. This traditional model was the one used in the Ford Pinto case (see Unsustainable Decisions: A Case Study).

The IDM, or integrated decision model, shared with you in Chapter 7 considers both the financial (quantitative) and nonfinancial (qualitative) factors. For example, the IDM would consider customer satisfaction and product quality even if a dollar amount could not be placed on the factor (Figure 8.5).

The IDM can be expanded to encompass the additional dimension of economic, social, and environmental factors in decision making. We expand the quantitative analysis to consider economic, social, and environmental (ESE) costs and benefits. We expand the qualitative analysis to consider economic, social, and environmental advantages and disadvantages. This expanded decision model, the **sustainability IDa (Integrated Decision analysis) model** provides you with an organizing framework for grappling with complex and sometimes conflicting sustainability issues.

The sustainability IDa model shown in Figure 8.6 uses a seven-step process.

1. Identify the opportunity or issue.
2. Identify options to address the opportunity or issue.
3. Analyze the costs and benefits using quantitative data, considering ESE impacts.
4. Analyze the advantages and disadvantages of qualitative factors, considering ESE impacts.
5. Make a decision: What will we do?
6. Implement or deploy the decision: How will we do it?
7. Evaluate performance: How did we do? Compare projected results of the decision to actual performance. Then, there are three basic choices: continue status quo, make changes in the decision, or change the implementation.

> **Would Like to Know More?**
> If you would like to know more about a third dimension to the sustainability IDa model, see the book *Pacioli's Secret*.

FIGURE 8.4 Traditional Decision-Making Model

STAR for Autism Traditional Decision Model

1	Define the Issue	Which fundraising events should be continued or discontinued?			
2	Identify Options	Option A Golf Benefit	Option B Carnival	Option C Walkathon	Option D Silent Auction
3	Quantitative (Financial) Analysis	Benefits $4,500 Costs (5,550) Net ($1,050)	Benefits $1,000 Costs (10,800) Net ($9,800)	Benefits $25,000 Costs (1,550) Net $23,450	Benefits $10,800 Costs (575) Net $10,225
4	Qualitative (Nonfinancial) Analysis	OMITTED			
5	Decision	Discontinue	Discontinue	Continue	Continue

FIGURE 8.5 Integrated Decision Model (IDM)

STAR for Autism Integrated Decision Model (IDM)

1	Define the Issue	Which fundraising events should be continued or discontinued?			
2	Identify Options	Option A Golf Benefit	Option B Carnival	Option C Walkathon	Option D Silent Auction
3	Quantitative (Financial) Analysis	Benefits $4,500 Costs (5,550) Net ($1,050)	Benefits $1,000 Costs (10,800) Net ($9,800)	Benefits $25,000 Costs (1,550) Net $23,450	Benefits $10,800 Costs (575) Net $10,225

4	Qualitative
	(Nonfinancial)
	Analysis
		Advantages:
		■ Builds donor
		   relationships
		■ Good public relations
			Advantage:
			■ Fun event
				Advantage:
				■ Loyal event
				   supporters
					Advantage:
					■ Minimal investment/
					   low risk

		Disadvantages:
		■ Time consuming
		■ Subject to weather
			Disadvantages:
			■ Time consuming
			   to conduct
			■ Uses large amounts
			   of volunteer time
				Disadvantage:
				■ Subject to weather
					Disadvantage:
					■ Dependent upon select
					   volunteers

5	Decision	Continue	Discontinue	Continue	Continue

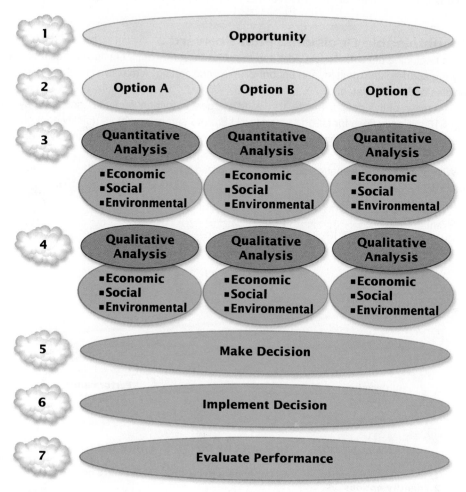

FIGURE 8.6

Sustainability IDa Model

Unsustainable Decisions: A Case Study...

An unfortunate example where sustainability was not considered was the infamous Ford Pinto case. In the 1970s Ford Motor Company introduced the Pinto, a car with a safety-related defect that resulted in fuel tank rupture in rear-end collisions, causing an explosion and fire. Passenger death and injuries occurred because of this defect. Many of the deaths were children.

Ford was indicted for reckless homicide and the jury trial ended with a judgment against Ford for $125 million in punitive damages. Ford's decision to proceed with the production of the defective car was found to be based on a cost-benefit study. The cost was $11 per car for the improvement needed to eliminate the defect. One hundred and eighty deaths resulted from this decision. Ford's cost-benefit analysis showed costs to repair ($137 million) were greater than the estimated benefits of avoided damages for lost life and injury ($49.5 million). The prosecution alleged that Ford "deliberately chose profit over human life" (Fisse, 1983).

Do you think Ford's decision would have been different if economic, social, and environmental factors were considered?

Notice that the sustainability IDa model encompasses the two uses of sustainability information: making decisions and evaluating performance. Steps 1 through 5 of the sustainability IDa model relate to decision making. Step 7 relates to performance evaluation (Figure 8.7).

The IDa model integrates sustainability into decision making by considering the following dimensions:

- Dimension 1: Economic, social, and environmental factors
- Dimension 2: Financial (quantitative) and nonfinancial (qualitative) factors

Unsustainable Decisions: Fast Forward...

At the beginning of 2010, Toyota admitted that it had a safety defect in its vehicles that was causing sudden, unexpected, and uncontrollable acceleration. A massive recall of 8 million vehicles occurred belatedly.

As a result of this defect, Toyota, the world's largest auto manufacturer, agreed to pay over $16 million in fines for failing to alert the U.S. auto-safety regulators quickly enough. Over 300 lawsuits have been filed against Toyota. Approximately 90 deaths are believed linked to the defect.

Why didn't Toyota respond sooner when it realized it had a problem with sudden acceleration of its cars?

Do you think Toyota was remiss?

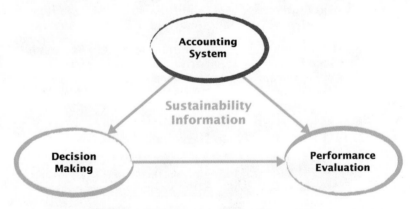

WHAT WILL WE DO?   **HOW WILL WE DO IT?**   **HOW DID WE DO?**

1. Identify opportunity	6. Implement decision	7. Evaluate performance
2. Identify options		
3. Analyze quantitative factors		
4. Analyze qualitative factors		
5. Make decision		

FIGURE 8.7

Sustainability IDa Model: Closing the Loop

Massey Coal Mine Explosion....

In April 2010, an explosion at the Upper Big Branch mine in West Virginia left 29 people dead. Massey Energy Co., which owns the mine, was fined $382,000 in the prior year for safety violations. Massey was accused of putting profit before people's safety.

You're the Boss...

If you were the CFO of Massey Energy Co., what dollar value would you place on the 29 lives lost?

How would you explain the accounting for this disaster to the press and the public?

BP and the Gulf of Mexico

An explosion at an oil rig in the Gulf of Mexico in 2010 resulted in massive amounts of oil spewing into the waters of the gulf, causing record amounts of damage to the water, coastline, wildlife, and economic vitality of the region.

Could British Petroleum (BP) have taken more proactive measures to ensure that if such a catastrophe occurred, there would be a better way to cap the damaged oil well?

You're the Boss...

If you were the CFO of BP, how would you account for sustainability in this instance?

How would you explain your accounting for sustainability to the press and an outraged public?

ECONOMIC/SOCIAL/ENVIRONMENTAL SUSTAINABILITY The first dimension of the sustainability IDa model is economic, social, and environmental sustainability. The sustainability question is applied to each aspect of the decision. Is the decision and resulting action sustainable economically? For example, if in August you overdraw your bank account in order to pay your bills is this action sustainable in the long run? Can you overdraw your bank account every month in order to pay your bills? Obviously, the answer is no.

Let's say that then you turn to charging purchases on your credit card in order to "balance" your budget. Is this action sustainable? Can you continue to charge items you cannot afford to a credit card indefinitely? Again, the obvious answer is no. There comes a day when the credit card bill must be paid. To be economically sustainable, it is necessary to have a balance of cash inflows and cash outflows that can be maintained in the long run. Although you might charge extra purchases in one month, it is not sustainable to do this every month.

In the IDa model, next we consider social sustainability. The action may be sustainable economically, but is it sustainable socially? Will society tolerate a dangerous product? A toxic product? Adverse health effects?

Next, environmental sustainability is considered. If the production of a particular product entails large amounts of toxic waste, is this sustainable in the long run? Are there other avenues to produce the product without the adverse consequences? Environmental factors can be further categorized into their impact on air, water, and land.

Many of the factors impacting sustainability cannot be quantified in financial terms, such as overall employee health. If your employees are healthier, are they more productive? How do you quantify this? Simply because an item cannot be quantified does not mean it should be eliminated from consideration. Which brings us to the next dimension of the sustainability IDa model: quantitative versus qualitative factors.

QUANTITATIVE AND QUALITATIVE FACTORS The second dimension to consider in accounting for sustainability is another challenge to the typical accounting system. Many times if a factor affecting a decision could not be quantified in dollars and cents, it was not considered, often with disastrous results. There are some nonquantifiable factors that override all other

> The future of financials—is nonfinancials.
> —Sir David Tweedie

What Do You Think?

What do you think Sir David Tweedie meant by his statement: *The future of financials—is nonfinancials?*

quantifiable factors, such as loss of life. In the Ford Pinto case, the jury was so outraged at the lack of consideration for the loss of life, especially children's lives, that it awarded many times the damages that Ford had anticipated.

Much of the information related to sustainability is qualitative data that is challenging or impossible to quantify, yet crucial to sound decisions. The second dimension of integrated decision analysis involves integrating both quantitative and qualitative factors into your decision.

The challenge for the accounting system is to organize, sort, and store the qualitative (nonfinancial) factors as well as the quantitative (financial). When designing the database, this requires special design considerations to allow for storage, retrieval, and analysis.

One approach to storing qualitative data is to quantify it using numerical ranking. For example, if you have identified safety as an important qualitative factor for your production employees, then you might develop a numerical ranking or Likert scale of 1 to 5 to identify the safety level. The safety level 1 might be the most hazardous to employees while 5 might be the safest. Even though safety is a qualitative factor, there are measures that can be used to quantify safety for comparison and storage in a database.

Another method of addressing how to store qualitative data is to quantify it by developing estimates of dollar amounts that are indicative of the level of risk and value. For example, if a suggested course of action is considered relatively hazardous to employees, the safety aspect of the action could be quantified by estimating workers' compensation claims, increased health insurance costs, and cost of employee absenteeism. In the 1990s, Ontario's Hydro, a hydroelectric power company, attempted to identify and quantify the external impacts of operations, including environmental and health effects. The company used modeling techniques to estimate how emissions affected the environment and people, and then estimated the costs of the impact (see Epstein 2008).

Yet another way to store qualitative data in a database is to use predefined labels that can be entered in the database and later retrieved using business intelligence tools. For example, predefined labels for safety levels might be as follows:

- Hazardous for human consumption
- Hazardous above 90 degrees Fahrenheit
- Hazardous when mixed with water

The predefined labels would be stored in an alphanumeric database field of a specified length. The field would be searchable using database queries and analyzed using business intelligence tools.

The power of the database is its ability to store and retrieve large amounts of data. Thus, it is important that the qualitative data is stored in the database in such a way that it can later be retrieved. To summarize, three ways to store qualitative data so it can be retrieved for decision making and performance evaluation purposes are (1) numerical ranking, (2) estimated dollar amounts, and (3) predefined labels.

ILLUSTRATION: SUSTAINABILITY IDA MODEL Could business intelligence techniques be used to create sustainability intelligence for better decision making?

Imagine you are in the C-Suite for a computer manufacturing company. You learn that e-cycling legislation similar to EU regulations is expected. The legislation would require manufacturers of electronic devices to be responsible for the disposal costs of the devices containing toxic elements, such as lead, cadmium, and mercury. You have identified two options:

Option A: Redesign the computers to reduce or eliminate the use of toxic elements in the product and manufacturing process.

Option B: Continue the status quo with the current manufacturing process and use of toxic elements. Maintaining the same production process will result in increased disposal costs to meet the proposed legislation requirements.

Data collected about the two options are summarized in the spreadsheet shown in Figure 8.8. The spreadsheet illustrates how the data can be tagged for use with the sustainability IDa model. The first dimension tag is economic, social, or environmental. The second dimension tag is quantitative (QT) or qualitative (QL).

The sustainability IDa model is used to analyze the data as shown in Figure 8.9. A sustainability dashboard shows the results of the analysis and the multidimensionality of the data. This

	A	B	C	D	E
1	OPTION	ITEM	AMOUNT	1ST DIMENSION	2ND DIMENSIION
2	A: REDESIGN	Research cost	-1000000	ECONOMIC	QT
3	A: REDESIGN	Design prototype	-2000000	ECONOMIC	QT
4	A: REDESIGN	Test prototype	-500000	ECONOMIC	QT
5	A: REDESIGN	Redesign prototype	-1000000	ECONOMIC	QT
6	A: REDESIGN	Market test	-1500000	ECONOMIC	QT
7	A: REDESIGN	Final redesign	-500000	ECONOMIC	QT
8	A: REDESIGN	Increased green sales	10000000	ECONOMIC	QT
9	A: REDESIGN	Reduced hazardous disposal cost	6000000	ENVIRONMENT	QT
10	A: REDESIGN	Residual hazardous waste disposal	-500000	ENVIRONMENT	QT
11	A: REDESIGN	New packaging requirements costs	-2000000	ENVIRONMENT	QT
12	A: REDESIGN	Reduced health costs	2000000	SOCIAL	QT
13	A: REDESIGN	Reduced toxic waste	-	ENVIRONMENT	QL
14	A: REDESIGN	Employee well being	-	SOCIAL	QL
15	A: REDESIGN	Improved public relations	-	SOCIAL	QL
16	B: STATUS QUO	Increased collection costs	-2000000	ECONOMIC	QT
17	B: STATUS QUO	Properly contain hazardous waste	-1000000	ENVIRONMENT	QT
18	B: STATUS QUO	Additional safety equipment	-500000	ENVIRONMENT	QT
19	B: STATUS QUO	Increased hazardous disposal cost	-6000000	ENVIRONMENT	QT
20	B: STATUS QUO	Increased safety packaging cost	-1000000	ENVIRONMENT	QT
21	B: STATUS QUO	Estimated damages and settlements	-5000000	ENVIRONMENT	QT
22	B: STATUS QUO	Toxic environmental waste	-	ENVIRONMENT	QL
23	B: STATUS QUO	Toxic exposure (employees & community)	-	SOCIAL	QL
24	B: STATUS QUO	Expected increased health care costs	-	SOCIAL	QL

FIGURE 8.8

Sustainability Decision Data

Spreadsheet Data List This data list contains data about a sustainability decision. Notice that the dimension of economic, social, and environmental is included in column D. Column E indicates whether the data is quantitative (QT) or qualitative (QL).

dashboard includes a pivot table and sustainability chart. As the IDa model and dashboard show, if social and environmental costs are included in the analysis, the redesign option is more advantageous. Notice that in Figure 8.6 the first five steps in the IDa model facilitate decision making: What will we do?

After a decision is made, it is implemented. This is step 6 of the sustainability IDa model, which addresses how we will implement the decision.

Finally, we want to measure the results of that decision by evaluating actual performance as compared to projections. Step 7 asks the following: How did we do?

Sustainability and Decision Making: Creating Value

Sustainability, a new approach to decision making, shifts the decision focus from minimizing risk to creating value. The questions that decision makers ask change from *How does our firm minimize the risk of lawsuits from defective products? Toxic pollution? Groundwater contamination?* to *How do we create value for our customers, society, and the global community?*

Value creation approaches include redesigning the product and process, adopting a cradle-to-cradle/zero-waste model, and using life-cycle assessment as illustrated by the following company examples.

- Redesign the product to reduce social and environmental impacts. For example, Nike redesigned the Nike Air shoe to use nitrogen in the air pocket to reduce adverse environmental impact.
- Redesign the process to reduce adverse social and environmental impacts, such as reducing consumption, waste, or toxicity. FedEx uses hybrid-powered delivery trucks to increase fuel efficiency by 50% and reduce maintenance and environmental emissions.
- Adopt a cradle-to-cradle or zero-waste model to strive for zero waste as opposed to reduced waste. For example, Ford Motor Company redesigned one of its Michigan facilities to use a green roof, replacing paved surfaces with green space to reduce stormwater runoff, capture harmful particulates, create a bird habitat, and provide additional insulation to reduce energy use and costs.
- Use life-cycle assessment to better understand the total impact of an organization's activities, processes, and products and to improve decisions. Sony's Corporate Sustainability Report diagrams the life-cycle assessment of the environmental impact of its products by showing resources used, energy consumed, CO_2 emissions, waste, and products recycled (Epstein, 2008).

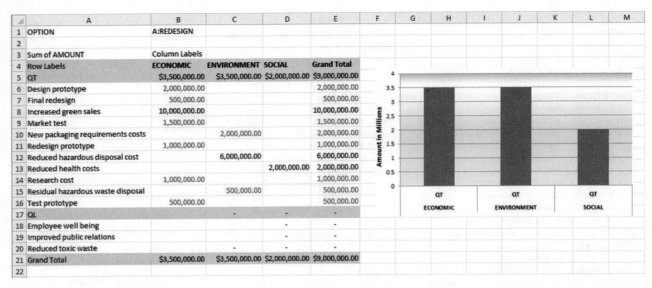

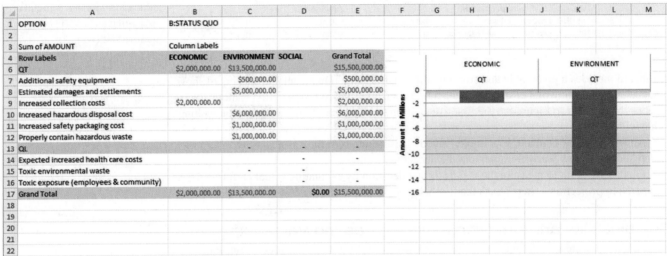

FIGURE 8.9

Sustainability IDa Model and Dashboard

PivotTables and PivotCharts
The sustainability dashboard uses data from the data list to create PivotTables and
PivotCharts. Option A, redesign, shows a more positive overall result.

My Connection...
- Active Review 8.6
- It's Your Call 8.26
- Tech in Practice 8.29

Integrating sustainability into decision making often involves innovation, looking at issues as opportunities and envisioning new sustainable solutions. Next, we take a look at some of the frameworks that have been proposed for measuring and evaluating sustainability performance.

How Is Sustainability Accounting Used for Reporting Performance?

Increasingly, companies are providing sustainability reports in addition to their traditional financial reports. Firms such as Southwest Airlines, Canon and Puma provide sustainability reports to the public.

Sustainability reporting expands a firm's performance report to include not only economic performance, but also a firm's performance as it relates to social and environmental responsibility. These sustainability reports are used by stakeholders, such as investors, consumers, society, and others, to evaluate the firm's performance in terms of economic, social, and environmental results.

Ninety-five percent of the Fortune Global 250 issue sustainability reports, almost half of which reported gaining financial value from sustainability initiatives. At the current time, Denmark, Norway, and Sweden require sustainability reporting. Europe has been a leader in recommending or requiring sustainability reports. In the United States, sustainability reporting is voluntary, but an increasing number of U.S. organizations are choosing to provide sustainability reports. Currently, organizations choose the format and content of their sustainability reports. Some companies, such as Novus International, choose to use the global reporting initiative framework. Other companies, such as Apple Inc., choose to develop their own metrics for measuring sustainability performance. Whatever sustainability reporting framework is used, the accounting system must collect, organize, store, and analyze the data.

> Buildings in the United States account for 72% of the electrical usage and 39% of carbon emissions. As a result, enterprises striving to improve sustainability performance often target building design and construction.

Green Winners...

A 2009 A.T. Kearney study revealed that during the financial crisis, companies demonstrating a "true" commitment to sustainability outperformed industry peers. Furthermore, the sustainability-focused companies were well protected from value erosion. Over a three-month period the differential was 10% higher while over a six-month period the differential rose to 15%. For more information, see www.atkearney.com (accessed 2009).

> In an MIT Sloan Management Review survey, two-thirds of the respondents indicated sustainability was critically important to being competitive (MIT, 2012).

Sustainability Reporting Criteria

Sustainability frameworks provide a common language for discussing sustainability issues. In order for a model to be accepted throughout an organization and provide a common language for communicating and understanding issues, the sustainability reporting model must be transparent and effective. So we will use these two criteria to evaluate frameworks for reporting and evaluating sustainability performance.

> **Business Sustainability...**
> ...focusing solely on financial and economic performance, without capitalizing on value creation from social and environmental innovation, is a business dead-end.
> —Kevin McKinley, ISO Deputy Secretary-General

TRANSPARENCY The sustainability report must provide a clear, accurate, and complete representation of the organization's sustainability practices and performance. The measurements used to account for sustainability performance must be clearly articulated so that all can see what is being used to measure the performance.

EFFECTIVENESS The success of a framework or model is often based not upon perfection, but effectiveness. This is sometimes referred to as the KIS principle: Keep It Simple. If a system is overly complex, it is difficult to communicate clearly to stakeholders. Thus, the framework must be simple enough to be understood by all stakeholders, regardless of background or perspective. Furthermore, it is imperative that everyone have a common understanding. Otherwise, individuals may think they are in agreement but actually be working at cross purposes.

In order to be effective, the sustainability report must provide information about the organization's sustainability performance in a relatively straightforward and understandable manner. In business, this is described as the three-minute elevator test. If you can't explain something in a three-minute elevator ride, it is too complicated to be effective.

To be effective, sustainability reports must be comprehensible. Furthermore, the sustainability report must be useful in terms of providing information for making decisions and assessing an organization's sustainability performance.

Thus, a complicated sustainability framework may provide greater detail and complexity; however, it may not be as effective as a more simplistic sustainability model. Furthermore, the accounting system must be able to capture and analyze the data in order to provide the sustainability measures needed for decision making and performance evaluation. Thus, the accounting system plays a crucial role in the success of sustainability reporting.

Sustainability Reporting Frameworks

A number of sustainability frameworks are being used, each with different advantages and disadvantages. ISO 14000, established by the International Organization for Standardization based in Geneva, Switzerland, focuses on environmental management. The European Union uses Eco-Management and Audit Scheme (EMAS) as a framework for sustainability. The Global Reporting Initiative (GRI) Sustainability Reporting Framework was used by almost 4,000 organizations in 2012.

Next, we will look briefly at some of the frameworks currently being used to report on sustainability performance.

ISO 14000 ENVIRONMENTAL MANAGEMENT The ISO 14000 family is a framework of guiding principles for establishing an environmental management system (EMS). This framework was established by the same organization, International Organization for Standardization, that established ISO 9000 for quality management standards that have become accepted around the globe.

The EMS standards enable organizations to identify and control their environmental impact, continuously improve their environmental performance, and implement a systematic approach to setting and achieving environmental targets.

What this framework does not do is specify specific levels of environmental performance for an organization. Instead, the focus is upon providing guidance to organizations in creating an environmental management system.

EMAS EUROPEAN UNION The European Union Eco-Management and Audit Scheme (EMAS) was proposed in 1995 as a management tool for organizations to report environmental performance. EMAS now requires ISO 14001 as the environmental management system. Only organizations operating in the European Union (EU) and the European Economic Area (EEA) are eligible to participate.

Four basic steps are required for an organization to receive EMAS registration. The organization must conduct a review of environmental aspects of the organization's operations, legal and regulatory framework, and environmental management practices and procedures. Based upon the environmental review, the organization must establish an effective environmental management system (EMS) aimed at achieving the organization's environmental policy. The organization is required to conduct an environmental audit to assess the environmental management system, conformity with the organization's policies, and compliance with environmental regulations. Finally, the organization must provide a statement of environmental performance as well as future actions to continuously improve its environmental performance.

SIGMA GUIDELINES The SIGMA (Sustainability Integrated Guidelines for Management) project was a joint undertaking of the British Standards Institution, Forum for the Future, AccountAbility, and the UK Department of Trade and Industry. The SIGMA Guidelines offer guiding principles for sustainability and a framework that integrates sustainability into management decision making.

INTERNATIONAL FEDERATION OF ACCOUNTANTS (IFAC) SUSTAINABILITY FRAMEWORK The International Federation of Accountants' (IFAC) Web site provides a resource summarizing various frameworks used in accounting for sustainability. Furthermore, additional information, articles, and links are provided as resources (www.ifac.org).

GLOBAL REPORTING INITIATIVE (GRI) Of the various approaches to sustainability reporting, the **Global Reporting Initiative (GRI)** is the most widely used. GRI offers a sustainability reporting framework of which the G3 guidelines are the cornerstone. G3 guidelines include reporting principles and guidance to define report content and quality as well as standard disclosures related to strategy and profile, management approach, and performance indicators. Examples of performance indicators in the G3 guidelines include measures related to environmental and social issues. For example, categories of performance indicators for social issues include the following:

- Labor practices and decent work conditions such as health and safety, training, and diversity
- Human rights, including child labor, disciplinary practices, and indigenous rights

- Society, including community, corruption, and competition
- Product responsibility, such as customer health and safety, advertising, and respect for privacy

To achieve a grade of A under the GRI, a company must report on all indicators. To attain an A+, the company must report on all indicators and have external assurance. For grades of B or C, the company can choose on which indicators it will report, with more indicators needed to receive a grade of B. If assurance services are used to verify the reporting, the company can raise the grade, from B to B+ or C to C+.

In addition to the G3 guidelines, some sectors, such as electrical utilities, financial services, and media, have supplemental disclosure requirements.

GRI (globalreporting.org) developed an XBRL taxonomy for sustainability reporting. XBRL adds electronic tags to amounts, similar to a bar code on an energy bar. The electronic tag contains data about the data (metadata). Furthermore, XBRL offers the ability to tag qualitative data in the sustainability report. This feature permits users to search for specific economic, social, and environmental performance indicators, such as carbon footprint, and then compare these among different organizations.

> **What's Your Water Footprint?**
> What's your sustainability performance?
>   Calculate your water footprint at www.h20conserve.org.

> **My Connection...**
> - Active Review 8.2
> - Go Online 8.35

What Is Integrated Reporting?

An integrated report consists of one report containing both financial and nonfinancial information about a company's economic, social, and environmental performance.

The International Integrated Reporting Committee (IIRC), formed in August of 2010, is overseeing the development of an integrated reporting model that integrates financial and sustainability performance into a single report. Instead of organizations preparing a financial report, using U.S. GAAP or IFRS, and a separate sustainability report, IIRC suggests using one report that integrates both financial and sustainability performance.

Who Uses Integrated Reporting?

Early issuers of integrated reports include: Phillips (the Netherlands), United Technologies (United States), Southwest Airlines (United States), and Novo Nordisk (Denmark). In 2010, South Africa mandated integrated reporting for all companies listed on the Johannesburg Stock Exchange.

The IIRC started a pilot project in 2011 in which companies could participate in creating integrated reports. Some companies participating in the pilot project, such as Novo Nordisk, make their integrated reports available to the public. Other companies in the pilot project may create integrated reports, but not make the reports available for public viewing.

How Is Integrated Reporting Different?

According to the IIRC, integrated reporting offers eight major differences from traditional financial reporting.

1. *Thinking.* Thinking progresses from silo thinking used for traditional financial reporting to integrated thinking about the value creation process and long-term success.
2. *Stewardship.* Stewardship of financial capital shifts to stewardship of all forms of capital, including human and intellectual capital.
3. *Focus.* Focus on the past financial performance shifts to focus on the past and the future, including the connection between performance and strategic objectives.
4. *Timeframe.* Timeframe moves from short term to short, medium and long-term considerations.
5. *Trust.* Trust is improved by shifting from narrow disclosures to greater transparency.
6. *Adaptive.* Integrated reporting moves from rule-bound reporting to adaptive reporting to respond to individual company circumstances.
7. *Concise.* Long, complex reports are replaced with reports that are concise, covering material information.
8. *Technology Enabled.* Integrated reporting uses emerging technologies, such as XBRL.

Five Guiding Principles of Integrated Reporting

Five guiding principles are the foundation for the proposed integrated reporting framework:

1. Strategic focus
2. Connectivity of information
3. Future orientation
4. Responsiveness and stakeholder inclusiveness
5. Conciseness, reliability, and materiality

Principle 1: Strategic Focus. The integrated report moves from a short-term, historical, "what happened?" perspective to a forward looking, strategic focus. The integrated report is intended to communicate an organization's strategic objectives, how its performance relates to its strategy, and how the strategy relates to creating and sustaining value over time.

Principle 2: Connectivity of Information. The integrated report attempts to show how business decisions and performance are connected—how strategies connect to key performance indicators and key risk indicators. Currently when an organization reports its performance in an annual report, stakeholders may be left wondering: *How does the organization's performance relate to its strategy?* The integrated report attempts to connect an organization's strategy to its performance so the stakeholders can assess an organization's strategy and the attainment of the strategy through performance indicators.

Principle 3: Future Orientation. While traditional financial reporting primarily focuses on past data, an integrated report attempts to provide stakeholders with management's expectations about the future, such as targets, projections, and sensitivity analysis. This better enables stakeholders to assess future risks, uncertainties, and opportunities that the organization faces. The future orientation of an integrated report provides information that is useful in assessing the sustainability of the organization's business model.

Principle 4: Responsiveness and Stakeholder Inclusiveness. An integrated report provides insights into the organization's relationships with its key stakeholders. An integrated report attempts to improve the transparency of reporting to stakeholders on key economic, social, and environmental issues. An integrated report can answer questions such as:

- Does the organization understand stakeholder needs?
- Does the organization respond to stakeholder needs and concerns?
- Does the organization present information to stakeholders in a transparent manner that builds trust?

Principle 5: Conciseness, Reliability, and Materiality. Integrated reporting should focus on providing concise information that is sufficiently reliable and material to stakeholders' assessment about the organization's ability to create and sustain value over time. Management must exercise judgement in determining if information is concise, reliable, and material, and the expectation is that management discloses both positive, as well as negative, issues to stakeholders.

Benefits of Integrated Reporting and Associated Accounting System Challenges

Benefits of integrated reporting are many, but two primary benefits are:

1. Increased efficiency. Instead of preparing multiple reports (one for financial, another for sustainability reporting), the organization prepares only one integrated report. In addition, it is more efficient for stakeholders to find information in one concise report instead of numerous lengthy reports.
2. Improved communication. One report created in a clear concise, transparent style could improve communication with stakeholders.

While integrated reporting offers benefits, questions to address include:

1. What are the performance metrics that best measure integrated economic, social, and environmental performance?
2. How will nonfinancial, qualitative information be appropriately measured and stored in the accounting system to integrate financial and nonfinancial performance into one report?

3. What assurance services will be needed and provided? How will integrated reports be audited?
4. What technology will be needed to accommodate integrated reporting?

So at the same time integrated reporting offers advantages, such as increased efficiency and improved communication, it also presents unique challenges for the accounting system and supporting IT. Next, some additional benefits of integrated reporting and associated accounting system challenges are summarized for you.

Benefit. Integrated reporting offers a broader explanation than traditional reporting. For example, integrated reporting reports on not only an organization's stewardship of financial capital, but also other forms of capital, such as manufactured, intellectual, natural, and social capital. Consider that in 1975, 83% of market value was physical and financial capital. In 2009, it had decreased to 19% for physical and financial capital with other forms of capital accounting for 81%.

Challenge. Reporting on other forms of capital places new demands on the accounting system to account for these various types of capital.

Benefit. Integrated reporting better conveys critical connectivity of information presented. While traditional financial reporting continues to add more and more information, integrated reporting attempts to remove the clutter, focusing on making key connections clear.

Challenge. The integrated reporting challenge is to identify how to remove the clutter without removing valuable information—how to streamline reporting while improving the value provided stakeholders by the reporting. Once again, this presents an additional challenge for the accounting system to collect, store, and analyze de-cluttered information for integrated reporting.

Benefit. The IIRC has brought together key organizations to achieve an integrated reporting framework, including leaders in the field, such as Dr. Robert Eccles of Harvard University, the four international accounting firms, the IRG, and XBRL among other influential organizations. This approach increases the probability of coordinated international action to develop an international integrated framework.

Challenge. As always, one challenge with an undertaking of this magnitude is addressing diverse perspectives of various stakeholders and organizations. Even if a consensus is reached, integrated reporting will require significant change for organizations, including major changes in accounting systems to collect, store, analyze, and communicate the additional information needed for integrated reporting. Managing these changes to attain integrated reporting goals may also prove challenging.

Benefit. Integrated reporting reflects an integrated thinking approach. The Integrated Decision analysis (IDa) model shared with you earlier in this chapter also is based on integrated thinking. An integrated decision process aligns with integrated thinking for performance evaluation. As Figure 8.7 illustrates, sustainability information can be used for:

1. Integrated Decisions: *What Will We Do?*
2. Integrated Reporting for Performance Evaluation: *How Did We Do?*

This alignment of integrated decision making and integrated reporting for performance evaluation closes the loop to better evaluate decisions, both for short term and long term impact.

Challenge. Both integrated decision making and integrated performance evaluation (integrated reporting) require financial and nonfinancial information. The challenge for the accounting system is to capture, store, and retrieve the nonfinancial information in an expedient, value-added way. As mentioned earlier, nonfinancial information presents unique challenges to database accounting systems that must be addressed in order to provide useful information.

> ## Integrated Thinking....
> *It will increasingly be through this process of "integrated thinking" that organizations are able to create and sustain value. The effective communication of this process can help investors, and other stakeholders, to understand not only an organization's past and current performance, but also its future resilience.*
>
> *—Towards Integrated Reporting, Communicating Value in the 21st Century*

Benefit. While traditional financial reporting is typically focused on the past, short-term performance, integrated reporting provides an opportunity to also provide a future, strategic approach to performance evaluation.

Challenge. For the accounting system tracking historical transactions can be much easier than tracking future focused, strategic information.

Benefit. By combining different strands of reporting (financial, management commentary, governance, and sustainability reporting) into a single report, the integrated report can better explain an organization's ability to create and sustain value. Integrating various reports into a single report can reduce the reporting burden and at the same time create added value for the stakeholders using the information.

Challenge. The systems and IT currently used for the multiple strands of reporting may not be compatible. The accounting system must be able to integrate the multiple sources of financial and nonfinancial information. To prepare an integrated report, the accounting system must be designed to collect and store both financial and nonfinancial data that can be used to measure performance. Most accounting systems are well suited to storing financial data measured in dollars. But how will such a system store nonfinancial, strategic data that is not measured in dollars? One of the proposed solutions to meeting the unique challenges of integrated reporting is to use eXtensible Business Reporting Language (XBRL). XBRL electronically tags data (similar to putting a bar code on products) for easier analysis and retrieval. XBRL can tag financial and nonfinancial data, so XBRL appears promising for collecting and reporting financial and nonfinancial data to streamline integrated reporting. If you would like to learn more about XBRL, see the next chapter, *XBRL: Intelligent Business Reporting.*

> **My Connection...**
> Short Exercise 8.25
> It's Your Call 8.28

Who's a Leader in Integrated Reports?

To provide you with an actual integrated report from one of the leaders in publicly issuing integrated reports, selected portions of Novo Nordisk's Integrated Report are included in Chapter Extension 8. *(Note that page numbers referenced here about Novo Nordisk's Integrated Report refer to page numbers appearing in the Integrated Report Chapter Extension 8.)*

Novo Nordisk, a Danish company, uses a triple bottom line management approach to grow business in ways that are both profitable and responsible—financially responsible, socially responsible, and environmentally responsible.

Novo Nordisk's Integrated Report consistently presents information divided into three categories:

1. Financial performance
2. Social performance
3. Environmental performance

Financial Performance

Discussion of Novo Nordisk's performance begins on page 5 of its integrated report, with information about financial performance. Novo Nordisk clearly defines its long-term financial targets as:

1. Operating profit growth.
2. Operating margin.
3. Operating profit after tax to net operating assets.
4. Generation of cash as measured by cash conversion (cash to earnings).

Then 2011 financial performance is compared against the long-term financial targets. Novo Nordisk met targets for three of its four performance indicators (PI).

Social Performance

Novo Nordisk (page 9 of its integrated report) clearly defines three dimensions of its social performance:

1. Customers: improving health care for people Novo Nordisk serves.
2. Employees: developing employees and providing a healthy, safe work environment.
3. Community: contributing to the communities in which Novo Nordisk operates.

After defining three dimensions of its social performance, Novo Nordisk then compares its 2011 social performance against its long-term social targets so stakeholders can assess the organization's social performance.

Environmental Performance

Novo Nordisk (page 11 of its integrated report) compares its 2011 environmental performance with its long-term environmental targets. Its environmental performance metrics are divided into two categories: inputs and outputs.

Input metrics included water and energy consumption, which decreased in 2011 by 34% and 21% respectively. Novo Nordisk's consumption performance in 2011 was better than the long-term target of 11% reduction from a 2007 baseline. Notice the graphs on page 11 that compare Novo Nordisk's target performance with actual (realised) performance. In all three charts, Novo Nordisk's actual performance was better than the targeted environmental performance.

Output environmental metrics included recycled waste and CO_2 emissions. Although Novo Nordisk's total waste increased from 2010 to 2011, the amount of recycled waste increased from 51% in 2010 to 70% in 2011.

Consolidated Financial, Social, and Environmental Statements

Novo Nordisk's consolidated financial, social, and environmental statements for 2011 begin on page 55 of its integrated report. Notice that the income statement (page 56), the balance sheet (page 57), and the statement of cash flows (page 58) appear similar to what you would expect to see in a traditional financial annual report.

After footnotes to the financial statements, the statement of social performance appears on page 91 of the integrated report. The statement of social performance contains key performance indicators grouped by patients, employees, and assurance. Notes to the statement of social performance appear on pages 92 to 96 and provide additional supporting detail about Novo Nordisk's social performance.

The statement of environmental performance appears on page 97 of the integrated report. Key performance indicators for environmental performance are grouped into inputs (energy, water, and raw material consumption) and outputs (CO2 emissions, wastewater, waste, and so on). Notes to the statement of consolidated performance appears on pages 98 and 99, providing additional supporting detail and explanations about Novo Nordisk's environmental performance.

Novo Nordisk's Consolidated Financial, Social, and Environmental Statements also include an independent auditor's report on the consolidated financial statements provided by Novo Nordisk's auditor, PricewaterhouseCoopers. In addition, Novo Nordisk's Integrated Report includes an independent assurance report by PwC on Novo Nordisk's social and environmental reporting.

After you have reviewed Novo Nordisk's Integrated Report, what do you think the future holds for integrated reporting? Will there be a one report that integrates financial and sustainability reporting? Will integrated reporting become required? Will the trend continue? Or fade away? What do you think?

Sustainable Economics
Meet Tom Niemeier, Founder of SPACE LLC (shown on left). Meet Matt Lung of SPACE Constructors, LLC (shown on right). Web: www.spacestl.com Twitter: @spacearchitects
© SPACE LLC 2011

Hi, I'm Tom, founder of SPACE LLC. I established SPACE, an ARCHITECTURE + DESIGN firm, in March of 2005. As seems to be our luck, many things fell into place for us. When we were ready to design and build a first class studio to showcase our design talents, we determined that we would utilize all the "best practices" of sustainable design, but that we would not attempt LEED certification. By our estimates, for our project we would spend $40,000 to $50,000 more to go through the LEED process, with the required paperwork and documentation. We made a conscious decision to use that money instead to create a more sustainable building.

Our first thoughts turned to solar PV panels or possibly wind turbines. We wanted to do something visible so it would be clear to our clients where we stood on the issue of sustainability. To our dismay, we learned that these technologies still do not have an impressive ROI. Spending $20,000 to get $7 off the monthly electric bill simply was not very enticing!

Reluctantly, we assumed that we would need to install the traditional heating and cooling systems, complete with rooftop condensing units and forced air ducted units. It was around this time that we met Artic Solar, a fledgling alternative energy system distributor. It was through that company that we learned of solar thermal panels that do not attempt to convert the sun's energy to electricity. These panels simply heat water, and that is the energy we had to harness.

While we could use the hot water for our shower and domestic use, we were not heavy users of hot water. The best use of hot water is to install a radiant heat floor, but we had an existing concrete slab already. But since we had hazardous waste removed through our Brownfield remediation, we figured we could pour a new slab as a form of "encapsulation" so it would be paid for through the Brownfield tax credits. We had our alternative energy system for heat, but what about cooling?

Our building purchase came with an adjacent 7,500 square foot parking lot. Artic Solar suggested using that land to install geothermal wells. The wells would cool water down to around 55 degrees and then pump the water to a heat pump to cool the water down to 45 degrees. The cold water would be distributed in pipes to "cooling cassettes," which are basically small fan motors that blow air across a cold water coil. While this would work, the bulky cassettes did not fit into our open to structure wood ceiling design.

The Europeans commonly use a cooling system known as a "chilled beam" system, basically a large metal plate with a chilled water pipe system connected to the backside of it. We were interested in using this system, but the surface area needed to "chill" a space the size of ours was quite large. Most of our beautiful wood ceiling would be covered by the metal plates. It was at this point an idea emerged where aesthetic desires met functional needs. Instead of large metal plates, perhaps they could be many narrow linear plates that could simply be clamped around a pipe and stacked adjacent to each other. This way both sides of the plate would be "cooling surfaces." A further design innovation rotated the plates vertically so a reverse "chimney" effect could take place, with the air dropping through the plates as heat is absorbed. We finally had an energy system that we could be truly proud of…but what would it cost?

Our lowest bid for a traditional heating and cooling system was $58,000. The Artic Solar design stood at $105,000. It was difficult to find a way to pay for it through our conventional bank loan. There was more to consider. PNC Bank had its *Green Technology* division head-quartered here in St. Louis. We met with Terry Stark, who explained that the Artic Solar system could be purchased through a lease buyout program. This would enable us to use our construction loan on things other than the heating and cooling system.

We also determined that the Artic Solar system qualified for a federal reimbursement of 30%, which effectively reduced the energy system cost by over $30,000. Our local electrical power company, AmerenUE offers an alternative energy system incentive package. The energy model (which the company paid for) showed that we had improved the building baseline energy use by 51%, something it had never seen. The improvements entitled us to over $17,000 in incentives. Suddenly the Artic Solar system bid was very competitive with the traditional heating and cooling bids. When considered with the long-term life-cycle cost benefits of the Artic Solar system, it was an easy decision.

So now as I sit here in our new studio, I am struck by the fact that we were so successful in taking risks and leading by doing. In the face of the worst economy since the Great Depression, working in an industry especially hard hit, we pulled off something very special. While I am surrounded by the great aesthetic design that many talented people in this office helped make a reality, I am especially comforted by the fact that our building is not only good for us, but good for the earth as well.

Accounting for Sustainability in the Built Environment...HOK Hellmuth, Obata + Kassabaum, Inc.

Meet Tim Gaidis, Sustainable Design Practice Leader, HOK © HOK 2009. www.hok.com

Have you ever considered the amount of energy and resources required not just to construct, but to operate and maintain the buildings in which we live, work and learn? Energy for lighting, heating, ventilating and air conditioning, running appliances like computers and refrigerators... How about the quantity of materials and waste flows that go into and out of a building? The treated water that we use for drinking, food preparation, cooling equipment, wastewater conveyance and more...?: According to the United States Green Building Council (USGBC), buildings in the United States alone account for:

72% of electricity consumption

39% of energy use

38% of all carbon dioxide (CO_2) emissions

40% of raw materials use

30% of waste output (136 million tons annually)

14% of potable water consumption

Carbon...

We are very adept at measuring elements of our built environment with economic currency, but as triple bottom line thinking gains traction, the emerging form of common currency in the built environment that relates most completely to other natural and contrived systems is carbon. All aspects of buildings can be measured in terms of their carbon impact:

- Embedded carbon can be measured in materials and products from the original resource extraction to system re-introduction at the end of a product's useful life.
- Energy-related carbon dioxide emissions related to material and product fabrication and energy used for building operations can be measured as well.

The wonderful aspect of carbon is that it can be measured in natural systems also. Consider the following:

- Emitted carbon, released as a greenhouse gas (CO2) from fossil fuels when we burn, process, or ship these items
- Embedded carbon found in once-living organisms such as limestone (the calcium carbonate that makes up fossilized seashells)
- The process carbon cycle of plant evapotranspiration during photosynthesis (plants "breathe in" CO2 and "breathe out" oxygen)

If a currency value is placed on carbon, the systems would be linked, and we could measure the value of building components and operations more clearly and directly against the value of natural systems. To the preceding list of building metrics we could add the following:

- Emitted CO_2
- Embedded CO_2
- Processed CO_2

Could there be a "net-present value of carbon"?

Architects and engineers as well as developers of all facets of our built environment are shifting toward systems and reporting that more openly recognize metrics in addition to first-time cost, especially ones that relate to long-term life cycles. These include operating and maintenance costs, interior renovations, deconstruction at the end of a building's useful life, and even the salaries and productivity of people who use these facilities as part of a facility's "whole" cost.

Designers are also integrating systems that achieve synergistic relationships. Consider how the harvesting of "free" daylight in a cooling-load-dominated building favorably impacts multiple building systems and metrics through performance-based (as opposed to aesthetic only) design of windows and sunlight optimization/control devices like exterior louvers:

DAYLIGHTING…

reduces the need for electric lighting (lower capital and operating costs)
which reduces the amount of interior heat generated
which reduces the amount of cooling required
which reduces the size of cooling equipment (lower capital cost)
and reduces the constructed area required to house cooling equipment (lower capital cost)
and reduces the amount of energy used for cooling (lower operating cost)
and reduces the need for fossil fuels (lower operating and environmental costs)
and reduces emissions from fossil fuels (lower environmental costs)

All of these impacts must be measured to show the WHOLE VALUE of daylighting. Another example: Designers are creating buildings that capture stormwater both to use within building systems such as plumbing fixtures, irrigation, and in-cooling systems:

STORMWATER CAPTURE…

reduces the need for stormwater drainage infrastructure (lower capital and community costs)
reduces the need for treated potable water (lower operating and environmental costs)
reduces stormwater/sewer treatment in combined systems (lower community and environmental costs)
both of which reduce the energy used to pump water (lower community costs)
which reduces the need for and emissions from fossil fuels (lower operating, community, and environmental costs)

And the list goes on…. You can see how many of these impacts have opportunities for multiple metrics and multiple bottom lines when accounting for their "whole" value.

When Will We Reach Sustainability?

At every moment, we can see the future becoming the present. We harvest the sun for light and energy, we draw energy from the wind and tides, we recycle the water that we use, we build from renewable resources, and we create new environments that make living and working together more productive, effective, and healthy. Our challenge is to advance the scale of our emerging abilities and technologies to the point at which we are in balance with and are enhancing our environment while truly achieving our cultural aspirations.

The ability to accurately and completely measure our current state and our proposed interventions within the context of multiple systems and variables is critical to our ability to define, adjust, and adapt our activities through comparative analysis and feedback loops. We must see the forest AND the trees at the same time, and if we ignore the accounting of integral linked systems, we will inevitably fall prey to unintentional outcomes.

HOK...

is an architectural design firm founded in St. Louis, Missouri, in 1955. Today, the firm's members collaborate in unprecedented ways and incorporate sustainability into the design process for every project regardless of its location, building type, or budget. HOK's formal commitment to sustainable design began while the movement was in its infancy: Awareness was limited, resources and expertise were scarce, and measurement tools were nonexistent. In 1993, the

firm's seven-person Executive Committee established sustainable design as a core value that should drive all HOK projects. This public declaration helped guide HOK and the entire design profession. By developing solutions to enhance aesthetic goals while limiting resource consumption, improving building performance, and promoting occupant health and productivity, HOK is leading the way to an increasingly sustainable future. In recognition of HOK's 50th anniversary in 2005, the firm donated $500,000 to fund a solar-powered diagnostic and treatment center in southeastern rural Kenya. HOK worked with Africa Infectious Disease Village Clinics, Inc., to launch the most comprehensive tuberculosis (TB) diagnosis and treatment initiative in the region. The contribution exemplifies HOK's long-standing commitment to enriching lives and creating more sustainable communities.

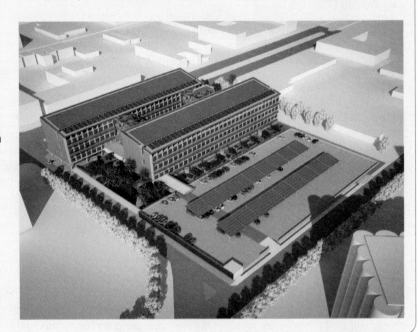

Chapter Highlights

What is the triple bottom line? The triple bottom line measures a company's economic, social, and environmental performance.

How is sustainability used in decision making? Sustainability focuses on an organization's ability to sustain its performance on an ongoing basis in the future. Decisions are made based upon whether the action is economically, socially, and environmentally sustainable.

What is a sustainability decision model? The sustainability IDa model provides a framework for decision

making considering the economic, social, and environmental dimension of decisions. It also integrates consideration of quantitative and qualitative factors that impact a decision.

How is sustainability performance measured? The Global Reporting Initiative (GRI) is currently the most widely used sustainability framework for performance evaluation.

What is integrated reporting? Integrated reporting integrates financial and sustainability reporting into one report. An integrated report typically includes information about financial, social, and environmental performance.

Accounting System Insights

Insight No. 17 Use satellite mapping for sustainability accounting. Zoom out to see business in a global world view considering economic, social, and environmental sustainability.

Chapter Extension 8: Novo Nordisk Integrated Report

See the text website for the Chapter 8 Extension: Novo Nordisk Integrated Report.

Active Review

Study less. Learn more. Make connections.

8.1 Refer to the chapter opener, *Meet the Triple Bottom Line.* In your opinion, should companies be required to report their performance using a triple bottom line?

8.2 In today's global market economy, one could argue that implementing sustainability could cost corporations enormous amounts of money, draining resources. So why is the corporate trend toward including sustainability in business activities?

8.3 Discuss the importance of the criteria of transparency and effectiveness for a sustainability framework.

8.4 Some company sustainability reports indicate that it is not adequate to focus on only corporate social responsibility (people). Discuss your opinion about how social and environmental considerations are interrelated. Do you think the three categories (economic, social, and environmental) are necessary and adequate to address sustainability? Why or why not?

8.5 Discuss why the future of financials might be nonfinancials.

8.6 Discuss how sustainability affects decision making.

8.7 Discuss the role of accounting systems and business intelligence in assisting organizations to improve sustainability.

8.8 Discuss the role of XBRL in accounting for sustainability. In your opinion, how can XBRL facilitate the organization's sustainability measurements?

8.9 Discuss why the amount a company spends on social and environmental issues may not be the best indicator or measure of its sustainability intelligence.

8.10 Discuss the future of the integrated reporting. In your discussion, include your answers to the questions put forward at the end of the *Who's a Leader in Integrated Reports?* section.

Key Terms Check

Understanding the language used at the crossroads of accounting and IT is key to your success.

8.11 Match the following terms and definitions.
a. triple bottom line
b. sustainability
c. sustainability accounting
d. green IT
e. e-cycling
f. sustainability Integrated Decision analysis (IDa) model
g. global reporting initiative (GRI)
h. integrated reporting

_____ 1. Involves collecting, storing, organizing, and reporting economic, social, and environmental information for making decisions and evaluating performance

_____ 2. Most widely used framework for sustainability performance reporting

_____ 3. The ability to sustain an action in the future on an ongoing basis

_____ 4. A report consisting of financial and nonfinancial information about a company's economic, social, and environmental performance

_____ 5. A framework for considering both qualitative and quantitative economic, social, and environmental factors

_____ 6. Measures an organization's performance in terms of economic, social, and environmental results

_____ 7. Recycling of electronic equipment such as computers and monitors

_____ 8. Environmentally friendly information technology equipment

Practice Test

8.12 Sustainability accounting means:
a. The ability to sustain future environmental risks
b. Including the air, water, and land pollution into the accounting
c. The ability to sustain an action in the future on an ongoing basis
d. The ability to quantify, in dollar amount, the air, water, and land pollution

8.13 _____ measures the economics, social, and environmental results of corporate decisions.

a. Sustainability accounting
b. Corporate energy consumption
c. Corporate carbon accounting
d. Triple bottom line

8.14 The three keys to sustainability accounting are:

a. People, processes, and technology
b. People, data, and processes
c. Sales, purchasing, and employee
d. Social, environmental, and economics

8.15 Sustainability IDa is the same as integrated decision model IDM, except…

a. It has four more steps.
b. It includes the economic, environmental, and social dimensions in the decision process.
c. It is designed for quick decision making.
d. It is used for unsustainable decisions making.

8.16 Sustainability shifts the business focus to:

a. A holistic view of the business as an integral part of a larger system
b. Viewing the business as an insignificant part of a larger system
c. The environmental impacts
d. Bottom line profit

8.17 One way to store qualitative data is to:

a. Track it in the spreadsheets
b. Ignore it—qualitative data is not relevant to sustainability decision making
c. Guess its financial value
d. Quantify it using numerical ranking

8.18 Which method of creating value is best defined as striving for zero waste as opposed to reduced waste?

a. Redesign the product
b. Life cycle assessment model
c. Cradle-to-cradle model
d. Redesign the processes and product

8.19 The _____ family is a framework of guiding principles for establishing an environmental management system.

a. EMAS European Union
b. Sigma guideline
c. International Federation of Accountants (IFAC)
d. ISO 14000 environmental management

8.20 Which two criteria are used to evaluate frameworks for reporting and sustainability performance?

a. Effectiveness and efficiency
b. Transparency and effectiveness
c. Consistency and timeliness
d. Relevancy and accuracy

8.21 Which of the following is NOT one of the guiding principles for the proposed integrated reporting framework?

a. Connectivity of information
b. Effectiveness, reliability, and relevancy
c. Strategic focus
d. Future orientation

Exercises

Each Exercise relates to one of the major questions addressed in the chapter and is labeled with the question number in green.

Short Exercises

Warm up with these short exercises.

8.22 Select a family member, friend, acquaintance, or complete stranger and explain the concept of sustainability to him or her. Explain the interrelationships of sustainability and accounting. Evaluate your effectiveness at explaining sustainability successfully. **(Q8.1, 8.2, 8.3, 8.4)**

8.23 How is qualitative sustainability data stored in a database? List at least three ways to store qualitative data in a database with examples for each. **(Q8.3)**

8.24 Choose three qualitative measures for sustainability and try to quantify them. Is it always possible to quantify qualitative measures? Why or why not? Give an example to support your answer. **(Q8.3)**

8.25 Give two reasons that support the importance of the integrated reporting to the future of sustainability reporting. You may use the Novo Nordisk integrated report that is included in this chapter's extension. **(Q8.5, 8.6)**

It's Your Call

This is your training ground. These scenarios provide you with the opportunity to use your knowledge and professional skills.

8.26 It is the first day of your new job as an accounting intern. In the elevator on the way to your cubicle, a gentleman in the elevator (that you later learn is the controller of the company) says to you, "I just don't get it." Shaking his head, he repeats, "I just don't get it." Then he adds, "Just how is sustainability relevant to accounting? Don't we have enough problems to keep track of instead of creating more problems to account for?"

Unsure how to answer, you remain silent. So he continues, "You are our new intern, aren't you? Well, why don't you send me an email by this afternoon explaining how sustainability is relevant to accounting. Tell me why I should care about this latest trend, sustainability, and how it could affect our accounting system."

Prepare an email to the controller of the company to respond to his request. **(Q8.1, 8.2, 8.3, 8.4)**

8.27 As CFO you have been asked to evaluate the sustainability of two different enterprise software systems for your company.

1. A system that uses an SAP baseline system. Your company would not customize the system but would need to modify some of its business processes in order to adapt to the baseline system.
2. A system that customizes the SAP baseline system to fit your current business processes. You would not need to modify your business processes.

Evaluate the sustainability of each system. Which system would you recommend your company adopt: the baseline system or the customized system? Why? **(Q8.2, 8.3)**

8.28 Your supervisor has asked you to join him in a meeting about a possible change in the organization reporting method. He says your organization is considering replacing several reports with an integrated report. He wants you to prepare a presentation for him about the integrated reporting.

Prepare a summary and guideline for this presentation. In your work, state what an integrated reporting model is, what types of reports are combined together in this report, what are the benefits and challenges. **(Q8.5, 8.6)**

Tech in Practice

These technology in practice exercises are perfect for both individuals and teams.

Tech Exercises

Sharpen your skills with these technology exercises. Watch these software videos at www.pearsonhighered.com/kay.

8.29

Tech Tool: Spreadsheet Software

Software Videos: Spreadsheet Data Tables, Spreadsheet PivotTables and PivotCharts

EspressoCoffee has asked for your assistance in building a sustainability dashboard.

1. Download the spreadsheet file for this exercise.
2. Use the data table to build a sustainability dashboard.
3. Print the dashboard.

8.30

Tech Tool: Spreadsheet Software

Software Videos: Spreadsheet Data Tables, Spreadsheet PivotTables and PivotCharts

This exercise is a continuation of the sustainability decision model used in the chapter. The computer manufacturer would like to add rankings to the qualitative factors that would affect the decision whether to redesign computers or continue with the status quo.

1. Download the spreadsheet file for this exercise.
2. Update the spreadsheet data table by adding the following rankings for the qualitative factors in the Amount column. The company will use a Likert scale of 1 to 5, with 5 as the most desirable ranking and 1 the least.

Rating	Item
4	Reduced toxic waste
5	Employee well-being
4	Improved public relations
1	Toxic environmental waste
1	Toxic exposure (employees and community)
2	Expected increased healthcare costs

3. Create the following PivotTables and PivotCharts to use in the sustainability dashboard. Add these PivotTables and PivotCharts to the Sustainability Dashboard sheet.
   a. Option A Redesign, Quantitative, Sum Amount. This PivotTable and PivotChart will provide the sum for economic, social, and environmental dimensions for option A.
   b. Option A Redesign, Qualitative, Average Amount. This PivotTable and PivotChart will provide the average for the Likert scale rating for economic, social, and environmental dimensions for option A.
   c. Option B Status Quo, Quantitative, Sum Amount. This PivotTable and PivotChart will provide the sum for economic, social, and environmental dimensions for option B.
   d. Option B Status Quo, Qualitative, Average Amount. This PivotTable and PivotChart will provide the average for the Likert scale rating for economic, social, and environmental dimensions for option B.

8.31

Tech Tool: Spreadsheet Software

Software Videos: Spreadsheet Data Tables, Spreadsheet PivotTables and PivotCharts

1. Select two cars that you would consider purchasing, one of which is a hybrid or electric powered.
2. Using the sustainability IDa model and spreadsheet software, analyze the sustainability of each option, including safety and environmental considerations.
3. Is there an external database you can use to assist you in making a more informed decision?
4. Make your decision regarding which car to purchase. Did your analysis change your thinking regarding which car you would purchase?

8.32

Tech Tool: Spreadsheet Software

The Nature Way Company is one of the leading companies in the snack food market. Nature Way is considering a sustainability strategy to produce and sell snacks to benefit consumers and the environment. The Nature Way sustainability strategy would impact its potato chip product with the following policies:

- Use organic potatoes: Using organic fertilizer reduces the carbon footprint.
- Use fuel-efficient farming equipments: This policy helps to reduce carbon emissions and fossil fuel consumption.
- Use less salts in potato chips.
- Invest in advising and helping the Nature Way potato suppliers around the world with efficient water consumption.
- Invest in the well-being of Nature Way potato suppliers around the world.
- Use healthy vegetable oil for making potato chips.
- Invest in consumer health benefits through advertisement for physical activities, health awareness programs, and health club coupons.
- Use smaller bags to allow consumer to better control potato chip consumption.

Develop a spreadsheet to document environmental, social, and economic impacts of the Nature Way sustainability strategy policies.

8.33

Tech Tool: Spreadsheet Software

Software Videos: Spreadsheet Data Tables, Spreadsheet PivotTables and PivotCharts
This exercise is a continuation of the preceding exercise.

Identify quantitative and qualitative factors of the Nature Way sustainability strategy policies and come up with an estimated dollar value (credit or debit). Use your best guess for the dollar values.

Create a chart showing the profit or loss from these policies. Assume that the Nature Way previous-year potato chip sales were $25,000,000, and estimate that because of these sustainability policies there will be an increase of 10% in sales amount.

Go Online

In the fast-paced world of technology, your skill at finding answers fast can be vital. Go online and experience typical assignments you may encounter as a professional.

8.34 The CFO is receiving more and more pressure from the board of directors and consumers to issue a sustainability report. She has asked you to research examples of sustainability reports that are well done. Go online and search for sustainability reports of two different companies that you think are good examples to show the CFO. Compare and contrast the two reports. What aspects of the reports would you recommend that your company use for sustainability reporting?

8.35 The CFO has asked you why different companies often use different criteria to measure sustainability performance. Go online and search for the sustainability reports of two corporations that use different criteria to measure sustainability performance. Why do you think the two corporations have selected different criteria?

8.36 Your organization would like to nurture vendor relationships with suppliers in developing geographic regions to improve sustainability. Go online and search for examples of organizations that are using this sustainability approach. Summarize your results to present to the president of the company.

8.37 You are starting a consulting service and believe that carbon accounting is one of the fastest-growing areas of accounting. Go online and research carbon accounting and carbon accounting software packages. Prepare a short summary of your findings that you can give to prospective clients.

8.38 You are just hired by a consulting firm based in New York City. Your job is to consult with companies located in the Midwest on various reports, including financial and sustainability reporting. Your firm wants you to consult your clients on integrated reporting benefits. Go online and search for the benefits of integrated reporting as stated by Dr. Robert Eccles, one of the leaders in the integrated reporting field. Prepare a short report, in Q & A format, of findings that you can put in a PowerPoint presentation.

Technology Projects

These technology projects are perfect for both individuals and teams.

Technology Project 8

Tech Tool: Spreadsheet Software

Software Videos: Spreadsheet Data Tables, Spreadsheet PivotTables and PivotCharts

iSportDesign would like to consider sustainability when making decisions and evaluating its performance. Nick, the owner, has asked you to build a sustainability dashboard for him. Your deliverables for the project include the following:

Deliverable 1. A sustainability data table for iSportDesign

Deliverable 2. A sustainability dashboard

Visit www.pearsonhighered.com/kay to do the following:

1. Download Technology Project 8 instructions.
2. Download files provided online for your convenience in completing the project deliverables.
3. Watch the videos with software instructions to complete this project at www.pearsonhighered.com/kay.

9

XBRL: Intelligent Business Reporting

Who Is the Father of XBRL?
Meet Charlie Hoffman.

Can you imagine coming up with an idea to revolutionize financial reporting and then working on it for years until it becomes widely accepted?

Meet Charlie Hoffman. In 1998, Charlie Hoffman, an accountant for a small accounting firm in Washington state, conceived the idea of XBRL for preparing, analyzing, and communicating financial information. He saw the opportunity to adapt the programming language XML used for Web sites to create a new programming language for intelligent business reports, eXtensible Business Reporting Language (XBRL).

Charlie, who has become known as the *Father of XBRL*, received the 2006 Special Recognition Award from the American Institute of Certified Public Accountants (AICPA) for his contributions to the development of XBRL. At the time Charlie received the award, XBRL was used on six continents (AICPA, 2006).

My Questions

Q 9.1	What is XBRL?
Q 9.2	Who uses XBRL?
Q 9.3	Where is XBRL used?
Q 9.4	Why use XBRL?
Q 9.5	When is XBRL used?
Q 9.6	How does XBRL work?

Crossroads

At the crossroads of accounting and IT, a new programming language, such as XBRL, can revolutionize financial reporting.

What Is XBRL?

EspressoCoffee
Company

Imagine you are given a spreadsheet containing account titles and balances from which you will prepare an income statement for EspressoCoffee. Mistakenly, you hit a key that sorts the amounts but not the associated account titles. The account titles and balances are scrambled. The $2,000,000 that appeared next to the account title, Net Income, now appears as advertising expense. How would you unscramble the numbers?

With XBRL, each amount is electronically tagged with a description of the data. Each account balance has its own unique identifier, or tag, so you can identify the type of data, time period, and more.

XBRL (eXtensible Business Reporting Language) is now used for digital financial reporting around the globe. In the United States, the Securities and Exchange Commission (SEC) mandated the largest public companies begin using XBRL as of June 2009. All publicly traded companies were required to use XBRL for SEC filings by June 2011. Credit rating agencies must use XBRL for reporting all ratings beginning in August 2009 (SEC.gov, 2009; XBRL.US, 2009).

> **XBRL Is Used Around the Globe...**
> Australia, Belgium, Canada, China, Denmark, France, Germany, Ireland, Israel, Japan, Korea, Luxembourg, the Netherlands, New Zealand, Norway, Singapore, Spain, Sweden, Thailand, the United Kingdom, and the United States.

HTML to XML to XBRL: How Did We Get Here?

Let's take a brief look back to see how we reached this point.

HTML or HyperText Markup Language is a programming language used to develop Web pages. However, HTML is static. The data in the Web page is static and has to be reprogrammed to be changed and updated. This presents challenges in keeping Web sites up-to-date. For example, let's say that you want to post pricing updates for your customers on your Web site. Every time there is a price change, you not only need to update your records, but also see that your Web site programming code is updated as well. This brings us to XML or eXtensible Markup Language.

XML is a programming language also used for Web site development. The advantage to using XML for Web sites is that it is dynamic. The Web site content can be updated on a dynamic basis. For example, your prices for customers posted on your Web site could be linked to your database. This permits you to update the sales price listed in your database and have your Web site price update automatically! If you recall Accounting Insight No. 9, our goal is to enter data once in order to save time and reduce errors. The use of XML for Web sites permits enterprises to enter data once in their databases and have the update ripple through to the Web site. Furthermore, data can be entered in the Web site, such as a customer order, and the database updates automatically. While XML offers enterprises the advantage of dynamic data updates, XML does not provide the capability for metadata: data about data. For example, numbers such as 100; 1,200; or 18,000 might be transmitted; however, unique identifiers about the data are not included. Is 100 the amount of sales or advertising expense? Is it for the year 2000 or the year 2010? This brings us to XBRL or eXtensible Business Reporting Language.

XBRL was developed to standardize and streamline financial and business reports. It is a programming language that includes metadata, data about data. For example, XBRL has the capability to include data about the number 100. It can include metadata to identify the number 100 as advertising expense for the month of January 2010 for a specific company.

XBRL offers many advantages for reporting financial data, including improved data analytics for intelligence and streamlined communication of financial and business reports. Financial analysts and investors can swiftly perform data analysis without rekeying data. Enterprises such as Fujitsu have pursued opportunities to use XBRL to create business intelligence for improved decision making.

Financial reports in the past have often been presented using a variety of noninterchangeable formats, such as spreadsheets, text files, HTML, and Adobe PDF. Sharing data between applications and users was challenging and sometimes impossible. At times, the only option was to rekey the data, resulting in errors and delays. XBRL provides standardization that permits data to be shared across different applications and IT platforms (hardware and operating systems).

XBRL, a programming language that is an extension of eXtensible Markup Language (XML), adds electronic tags to each piece of data in reports. The electronic tags are **metadata**: data about data. The tags describe the data, such as company name, time period, account title, and currency. XBRL tags enable computers to process data intelligently by storing, updating, searching, analyzing, transmitting, and communicating with greater speed, standardization, and capabilities.

XBRL in computer readable form is shown in Figure 9.1. The same XBRL data is shown in Figure 9.2 in human readable form. Notice that the electronic tags in Figure 9.1 describe the data listed in Figure 9.2.

One way to envision XBRL is in the context of unique identifiers. Just as each record in a database table has a unique identifier or primary key, XBRL provides the capability to have a unique identifier for each amount or fact appearing in a financial report. You can think of the XBRL tags as primary keys for data contained in financial reports.

XBRL has the ability to tag both numerical and nonnumerical data. Consequently, both quantitative (financial) and qualitative (nonfinancial) data can be tagged electronically. So XBRL offers many advantages in terms of more comprehensive reporting and analysis. As you know from Chapters 7 and 8, the integrative decision models, such as IDM and sustainability IDa model, use qualitative and quantitative data for improved decision making. XBRL facilitates the integration of financial and nonfinancial data by the ability to electronically tag both types of data.

My Connection...
Try Active Review 9.1

FIGURE 9.1

Sample XBRL Program Code in Computer Readable Form

Pair and Share: Can you find the XBRL code for Cash and Cash Equivalents?

```
<ifrs-gp:AssetsHeldSale contextRef="Current_AsOf" unitRef="U-Euros"
   decimals="0">10000</ifrs-gp:AssetsHeldSale>
<ifrs-gp:Inventories contextRef="Current_AsOf" unitRef="U-Euros"
   decimals="0">100000</ifrs-gp:Inventories>
<ifrs-gp:TradeOtherReceivablesNetCurrent contextRef="Current_AsOf" unitRef="U-
   Euros" decimals="0">30000</ifrs-gp: TradeOtherReceivablesNetCurrent>
<ifrs-gp:PrepaymentsCurrent contextRef="Current_AsOf" unitRef="U-Euros"
   decimals="0">40000</ifrs-gp:PrepaymentsCurrent >
<ifrs-gp:CashCashEquivalents contextRef="Current_AsOf" unitRef="U-Euros"
   decimals="0">40000</ifrs-gp: CashCashEquivalents>
<ifrs-gp:OtherAssetsCurrent contextRef="Current_AsOf" unitRef="U-Euros"
   decimals="0">50000</ifrs-gp: OtherAssetsCurrent>
<ifrs-gp:AssetsCurrentTotal contextRef="Current_AsOf" unitRef="U-Euros"
   decimals="0">270000</ifrs-gp: AssetsCurrentTotal >
```

FIGURE 9.2

Sample XBRL Report in Human Readable Form

CURRENT ASSETS	
Assets Held for Sale	$ 10,000
Inventories	100,000
Trade and Other Receivables, Net Current	30,000
Prepayments, Current	40,000
Cash and Cash Equivalents	40,000
Other Assets, Current	50,000
Current Asset, Total	$270,000

Who Uses XBRL?

XBRL is used by stock exchanges, companies, governmental and regulatory agencies, banks and banking regulators, financial and investment analysts, and accountants. XBRL can be used by preparers, reviewers, and users of financial information.

Beginning in 2009, the SEC mandated the use of XBRL for SEC filings for selected large public companies. The use of XBRL for financial reporting permits the SEC to review a greater number of filings, faster and in greater detail. The financial analysts and investors who use the financial reports can conduct financial analysis faster and with greater accuracy. Banking regulators in the United States and Europe have also found XBRL to be useful in standardizing and streamlining their work. The U.S. Federal Deposit Insurance Corporation (FDIC) is using XBRL to process filings by some banks.

Some companies realized that XBRL can also be used to generate intelligence for internal decision making. Fujitsu, for example, uses data tagging to facilitate data analytics for business intelligence purposes.

> **SEC.GOV...**
> You can view XBRL filings at the SEC Web site (www.sec.gov).

> **My Connection...**
> • Active Review 9.2

Where Is XBRL Used?

XBRL is being used around the globe for digital reporting purposes. Europe, Asia, and the Americas are seeing XBRL used by organizations and governmental entities to facilitate financial reporting and analysis.

Asia and XBRL

XBRL has been used for financial reporting in China since 2004 when it was the first capital market in the world to adopt XBRL. XBRL is now mandated by stock exchanges in China, Japan, Singapore, and South Korea. In Japan, companies such as Fujitsu and Wacoal have started to use XBRL for internal management applications. Since 2006 the Bank of Japan has used a voluntary XBRL program. China is using XBRL for data mining in addition to risk profiling and communication of financial information.

Europe and XBRL

XBRL is used in 17 countries in Europe including Belgium, Spain, the United Kingdom, the Netherlands, Luxembourg, Denmark, Sweden, Germany, France, Italy, and Ireland. Europe was faced with regulating 25 different central banks with different regulations for financial institutions as well as different languages. XBRL was implemented by BASEL II to standardize and streamline the work of European banking regulators.

Spain's banking industry was the first in Europe to adopt XBRL to make banking more efficient with plans to expand XBRL to government-wide use. In Belgium, XBRL has been required for filings with the National Bank of Belgium since January 2008. France's national bank has adopted XBRL for regulating banking. Some German companies are filing reports in XBRL while Italy has implemented XBRL for chamber of commerce filings. In the United Kingdom, XBRL was used on a voluntary basis for tax reporting, until 2011, when this became mandatory.

The Americas and XBRL

In South America, central banks are exploring XBRL, while in Chile, XBRL is being considered for capital markets. In North America, Canada has implemented a voluntary XBRL filing program. In the United States, the FDIC is using XBRL for some bank reporting requirements. The U.S. Securities and Exchange Commission implemented a voluntary XBRL program in 2005 with mandatory XBRL filings required for selected companies beginning in June 2009 (Kernan, 2008).

> **My Connection...**
> • Active Review 9.6

The Bank of Spain...

is one of many XBRL success stories. Implementing XBRL permitted credit institutions to validate reports prior to submission, resulting in better data quality and reduced manual verification (Fujitsu, 2009).

My Connection...
• Active Review 9.8

Why Use XBRL?

Why do companies use XBRL? XBRL complies with reporting regulations, simplifies and streamlines financial reporting, increases transparency, and improves data quality.

As XBRL is mandated by more and more capital markets globally, companies are using XBRL to meet those requirements. Furthermore, banks and other financial institutions are expected to comply with banking regulations that require XBRL. Dan Roberts, chair of the XBRL-US Steering Committee Consortium commented that the FDIC "went from 66 percent data accuracy to 95 percent accuracy within the first quarter it was implemented" (edgar-online.com, 2009).

While XBRL may be required for external reporting purposes, another reason for using XBRL is that it is effective for data analysis for internal applications. Fujitsu refers to this as Straight Through Reporting (STR). Other benefits of using XBRL include cost savings, reduced rekeying, error reduction, increased timeliness, and improved data quality (Figure 9.3).

XBRL converts unstructured data into structured data, automating data exchange by making the data interchangeable across formats, software applications, and platforms. Many enterprises use shadow data stored in spreadsheets to track data not captured by the formal accounting system. However, the unstructured spreadsheet data often causes new problems. The data is often not exchangeable with other software applications and reporting formats. XBRL offers the benefit of making the financial data interchangeable across different applications and platforms, facilitating transmission and communication of the financial and business reports. Furthermore, XBRL addresses some of the unique challenges that spreadsheets cause in meeting Sarbanes-Oxley requirements for internal controls (Hoffman, 2005).

FIGURE 9.3 XBRL Benefits for U.S. Federal Financial Institutions Examination Council (FFIEC)

Characteristic	Old System without XBRL	New System with XBRL	Benefit
Total processing cost (over 10-year period)	$65 Million	$39 Million	Savings of $26 Million
Processing time	60 to 75 Days	2 Days	Savings between 58 to 73 days
Source of data	Multiple sources	Single source	Reduction of errors
Errors in data received	18,000 Errors	0 Errors	System allowed for the validation of the data automatically at time of submission, communicating errors to filers and allowing them to correct data prior to submission; system would not accept reports with errors.
Submission method	Proprietary Value-Added Network (VAN)	Secure Internet Connection (HTTPS)	Cost savings
Software updates	Manual from Excel, Word, PDF	Automated using XBRL-based metadata	Automated updates of vendor software, more flexibility

Source: C. Hoffman, et al., Business Case for XBRL, xml.coverpages.org/UBmatrix-BusinessCaseForXBRL.pdf, July 2005. (Accessed June 2009.) Reprinted with permission.

When Is XBRL Used?

The last time you purchased a bottled or canned beverage, when you went to the checkout counter to pay, how did the cashier ring up your order? Did the cashier scan the bottle over the barcode scanner? Did the price of the beverage appear automatically on your receipt?

XBRL has been compared to product barcodes. Barcodes contain information about products in digital form.

The barcode system scans the barcode on the beverage bottle, retrieves the corresponding price and product information from the database, and displays the price on the cashier's screen while printing it on your receipt. The system automatically updates the inventory count, reducing inventory by the number of bottles you purchased. Some systems are so advanced that when inventory reaches a predetermined level, the system automatically reorders the inventory item from a specified supplier.

The use of barcodes dramatically improved the efficiency of managing inventory and recording sales transactions. In the same way, XBRL shows promise to streamline financial reports and data processing by using digital tagging that is the equivalent of barcode scanning for financial reports.

When barcodes were first introduced, the barcodes were stuck on the cans and bottles at the end of the manufacturing process before the product was shipped (Figure 9.4). Then companies realized that it would be more efficient and less expensive to simply print barcodes on bottles and cans as they were manufactured. So instead of an afterthought, adding barcodes became part of the manufacturing process, thereby reducing the cost and time required (Figure 9.5). The same is true for XBRL.

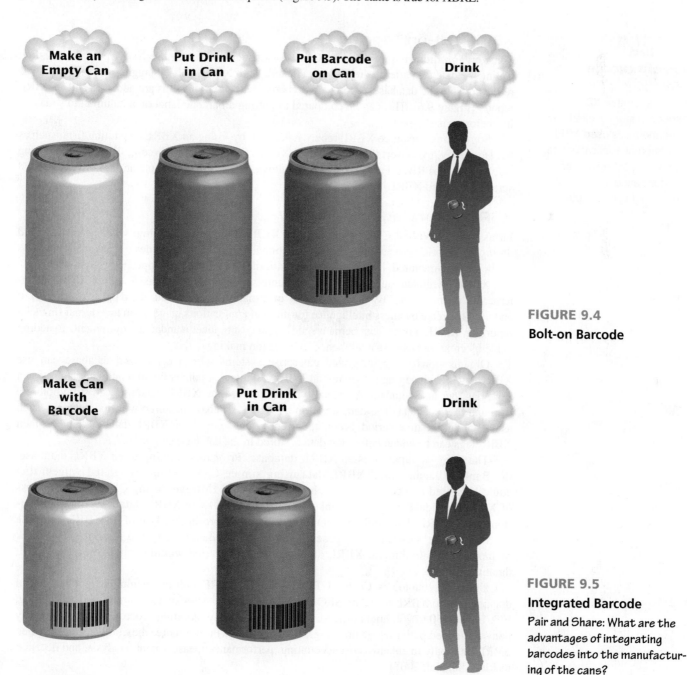

FIGURE 9.4

Bolt-on Barcode

FIGURE 9.5

Integrated Barcode

Pair and Share: What are the advantages of integrating barcodes into the manufacturing of the cans?

Accounting Insight No 18: XBRL Tagging

Accounting Insight No. 18 states that XBRL electronic tags for financial data are added using bolt-on tagging or integrated tagging. Bolt-on tagging adds tags after reports are prepared, just as barcodes were added to bottles at the **end** of the manufacturing process. Integrated tagging adds tags as information is processed, similar to adding barcodes **during** the manufacturing process.

My Connection...
- Short Exercise 9.24
- Short Exercise 9.27
- It's Your Call 9.30

United Technologies Corp.

UTC is another XBRL success story. United Technologies used XBRL for internal applications to improve cost accounting, performance, and decision making (Fujitsu, 2009).

XBRL Bolt-on Tagging

Some organizations required to use XBRL for financial reporting use **XBRL bolt-on tagging**, adding the data tags after the reports are created. With XBRL bolt-on tagging, data for reports is retrieved from the database, reports are prepared, and electronic tags are added to create XBRL reports (Figure 9.6). This can be compared to putting a barcode label on an aluminum soda can just before it is shipped.

Some firms outsource XBRL report generation by hiring an XBRL consulting firm, such as RR Donnelley, to convert their reports into XBRL. Other firms insource XBRL reports by using software such as Rivet, Fujitsu XWand, or Altova. These software applications convert text and spreadsheets into XBRL.

XBRL Integrated Tagging

Firms such as Wacoal Corporation employ **XBRL integrated tagging**, where data is tagged during information processing. This can be compared to adding barcodes to cans while the cans are being manufactured, instead of waiting until the can of soda is shipped.

XBRL integrated tagging permits companies to make more extensive use of XBRL for internal decision making. By tagging data as information is processed, the data can be analyzed and used to create business intelligence for internal applications, in addition to external financial reporting. XBRL moves from being an additional cost to meet mandated requirements to adding value by creating business intelligence for decision making.

Organizations using integrated enterprise systems with a centralized database can use XBRL integrated tagging if they use an XBRL database. A conventional relational database can store data but not metadata. A special type of database, an XBRL database, can store both the data and the metadata. The data stored in an XBRL database is stored with its metadata, such as data about the time period, account, currency, and so on. If an XBRL database is used, then XBRL tags can be added before the data is stored in the database (Figure 9.7).

The Bank of Japan uses an XBRL database. Prior to switching to an XBRL database, the Bank of Japan stored XBRL data using simple CSV (comma separated values) that could be stored in a conventional relational database. However, using CSV resulted in loss of XBRL metadata. When the Bank of Japan switched to an XBRL database, both conventional and XBRL data could be stored and metadata preserved. Use of an XBRL database streamlined the XBRL tagging process and improved data quality and integrity. The Bank of Japan is also looking at XBRL data analyzing tools that would capitalize on the XBRL database (Wada, 2009).

United Technologies Corp. (UTC) first used XBRL bolt-on tagging to convert Word documents into XBRL for filing SEC Form 10-Q reports. After switching to integrated tagging, UTC saved 150 to 200 hours of labor during the quarterly reporting process, eliminating many nonvalue-added activities of proofing and rechecking. Furthermore, the company has applied XBRL internally to enhance cost accounting, performance measurement, analysis, and decision making (Stantial, 2007).

How XBRL Integrated Tagging Saved Wacoal Money...

Wacoal of Kyoto, Japan, uses XBRL to improve the quality, timeliness, and consistency of financial data to key decision makers. With 36 subsidiaries and operations in Japan, Asia, United States, and Europe, Wacoal's information technology consisted of 32 independent legacy systems. Its purchasing, sales, and payroll business systems were on various platforms, such as UNIX-based mainframes and Windows-based PC servers, with the financial system as a stand-alone system. The data flow from the business systems to the financial system was only partially automated, requiring employees to manually feed data into the financial system. This resulted in data errors, reduced timeliness, and excessive labor costs.

As you know from Chapter 6, some organizations with functional silos and legacy systems use spaghetti programming code to connect the various systems. Wacoal uses XBRL, instead of spaghetti code, to make data interchangeable among its systems. It turned to XBRL to solve the data interchangeability issue, tagging data during the information processing stage. XBRL is used to tag financial data that comes from the legacy systems for purchasing, sales, and payroll (Figure 9.8). Then the system uses an XBRL conversion engine to create XBRL data that can be transmitted to Wacoal's accounting system, thus automating data transfer using XBRL between the legacy systems. By tagging data during processing, the data becomes interchangeable between systems, programs, and platforms.

The new system was much quicker to implement than installing an integrated enterprise system, shortened month-end closing by two days, reduced errors, and increased timeliness of data (Sambuichi, 2004).

You're the Boss...

If you were the CFO of Wacoal, what would you do?
- Continue rekeying data?
- Use XBRL?
- Purchase a multimillion dollar integrated enterprise system?

FIGURE 9.6

XBRL Bolt-on Tagging

FIGURE 9.7

XBRL Integrated Tagging

Pair and Share: Compare Figures 9.6 and 9.7 with the previous two diagrams, Figures 9.4 and 9.5. What are the similarities between barcodes and XBRL tags?

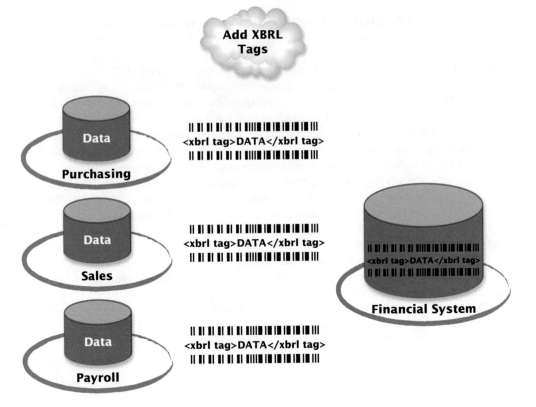

FIGURE 9.8

Wacoal's XBRL Integrated Tagging

Pair and Share: Explain the process of financial reporting if Wacoal used XBRL bolt-on tagging.

How Does XBRL Work?

What do you, as an accounting professional, need to know about how XBRL works? Do you need to write XBRL programming code?

The good news is that you do not need to become an XBRL programmer to understand the power of XBRL for intelligent financial reporting. To give you a competitive advantage, we share with you a few XBRL essentials so you are prepared to converse with IT professionals who write the XBRL programming code.

XBRL Essentials

Think of learning XBRL like learning a new language, such as Spanish, Italian, or German. After you learn a few essential words, you can become conversational in the language. The five XBRL terms you will need to know are:

- Taxonomy
- Instance document
- Elements
- Schema
- Linkbase

TAXONOMY A **taxonomy** is like a dictionary that defines the XBRL tags used for specific data items. You can see XBRL tags appearing between < > in Figure 9.1.

Tags are basically used to label or identify data and metadata. For example, an inventory balance might be expressed as follows:

<inventories balance> 100000 </inventories balance>

The opening tag is <inventories balance>. The closing tag is </inventories balance>. Note that the opening and closing tags are identical except that the closing tag contains a forward slash (/). This is the same syntax used by XML and HTML.

The data item is 100,000, which is defined by the tags as the amount of inventories balance. More tags could be added to the 100,000 to indicate the company, time period, and currency.

A taxonomy standardizes the tags used. With XBRL taxonomies, the account titles and structure have been standardized. For example, the XBRL Global Ledger taxonomy standardizes the accounts and structure of the general ledger for XBRL reports. This is the taxonomy used by Wacoal to standardize and transmit accounting data (Figure 9.8).

Prior to XBRL, companies used different account titles to refer to similar items for financial reporting. If you were an investor or financial analyst and wanted to compare similar items across different companies, it required extra time and effort to convert the data so it could be analyzed. Taxonomies, such as the XBRL Global Ledger taxonomy, standardize reporting of accounting information collected from various accounting systems with different charts of accounts. XBRL taxonomies permit users to compare and analyze financial results more quickly and accurately.

Several taxonomies have been officially recognized by XBRL International, a not-for-profit consortium of companies and agencies worldwide working to promote XBRL (xbrl.org). In addition to the XBRL Global Ledger taxonomy, other recognized taxonomies include U.S. generally accepted accounting principles (GAAP), International Financial Reporting Standards (IFRS), and the Global Reporting Initiative (GRI).

> **My Connection...**
> - Short Exercise 9.26
> - It's Your Call 9.29

INSTANCE DOCUMENT An **instance document** contains specific amounts for a taxonomy at one instance. For example, an instance document might contain income statement amounts for Wacoal for the year 2013. This would be one instance. Another instance would be income statement amounts for Wacoal for the year 2014. Wacoal uses one taxonomy for income statements but has an income statement instance for each year.

First, the taxonomy is selected, such as XBRL Global Ledger taxonomy. Then the taxonomy is used to create an instance document such as the one shown in Figures 9.1 and 9.2. XBRL software tools using a specified taxonomy transforms data into XBRL instance documents.

ELEMENTS Elements relate to data and metadata. Elements are shown in bold in the XBRL code (Figure 9.1). For example, notice the inventory XBRL statement balance shown from Figure 9.1.

<ifrs-gp:Inventories   contextRef="**Current_AsOf**"   unitRef="**U-Euros**"   decimals="**0**"> **100000**</ifrs-gp:Inventories>

From the tags we can tell the following:

1. The IFRS taxonomy is used.
2. The context in which inventory appears is current as of a specified date.
3. The unit of measure used is Euros.
4. No decimal places are used.
5. The amount of inventory is 100,000.

Different types of elements include the following:

- **Data elements** are numeric or nonnumeric facts. The 100,000 is a data element that is a numeric fact. It is defined by the tags as inventories.
- **Context elements** explain the context in which the data appears.
- **Unit elements** define the unit of measure, such as Euros or U.S. dollars. In Figure 9.1, the unit of measure is Euros.
- A **period element** defines the time period, such as 2013.
- An **entity element** defines the company or entity, such as Wacoal.
- An **identifier element** is a unique identifier for the element, such as an account number.

SCHEMA A taxonomy contains one or more schemas. The **schemas** define which elements are related to a particular taxonomy. There are a number of different elements possible. The schema identifies which elements are associated with the taxonomy that a company uses. United Technologies might use the U.S. GAAP taxonomy, and the schema would specify that the unit element was U.S. dollars.

LINKBASE An XBRL taxonomy also contains one or more linkbases. **XBRL linkbases** define relationships between data. How is the data linked?

For example, we know that assets must equal liabilities plus stockholders' equity. An XBRL linkbase would be required to define this relationship between assets, liabilities, and stockholders' equity.

XBRL uses the following types of linkbases to define relationships:

- **Definition links** define different kinds of relationships between elements. For example, ZIP code is the postal code used in the United States.
- **Calculation links** define basic validation rules. For example, assets equal liabilities plus stockholders' equity.
- **Presentation links** define how the elements are presented. For example, the balance sheet typically uses a tree-like, hierarchical structure where Total Assets are made up of Current Assets and Noncurrent Assets.
- **Label links** define the labels used in the document. Elements can be assigned to labels in different languages, such as English or Italian.
- **Reference links** define the relationships between the elements and the external regulations or standards, such as IFRS (iasb.org).

XBRL behind the Screen

The connection between the XBRL essentials (taxonomy, schema, element, linkbase, and instance document) is shown in Figure 9.9. The diagram is divided into three sections.

1. XBRL taxonomy. As you can see, the XBRL taxonomy consists of one or more schemas and linkbases.
2. Data. The data for a specific company is stored in a database. For example, account balances would be extracted from the company's database for use in preparing financial statements in XBRL.

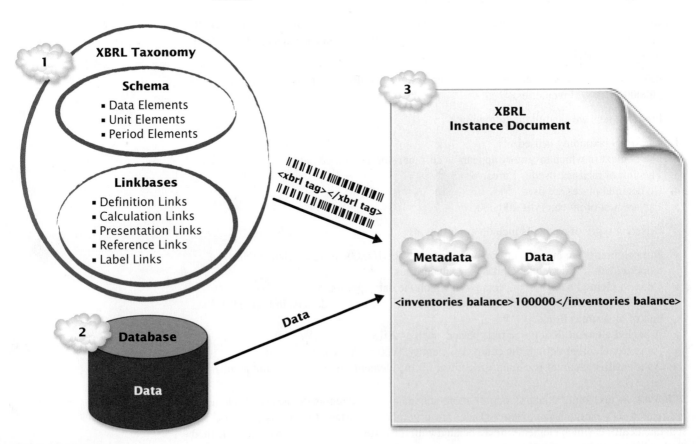

FIGURE 9.9

XBRL Essentials (Bolt-on Tagging)

Pair and Share: Can you explain how an XBRL taxonomy is used to build an instance document? Why is it called an instance document?

3. XBRL instance document. The XBRL taxonomy is used with a specific company's data to create an XBRL instance document. The instance document contains both data and meta-data. The metadata is contained in the XBRL tags that describe the data.

Samples of the XBRL essentials are shown in Figures 9.10 through 9.14. The samples shown are created using Altova® XMLSpy®, which is an XBRL development tool. These samples correspond to the three sections of Figure 9.9.

1. XBRL taxonomy. Portions of a sample taxonomy with schemas and linkbases are shown in Figure 9.10.
2. Data. The data for a sample company is shown in Figure 9.11. This data consists of account balances for a balance sheet. The data was extracted from an operational database and transferred to a spreadsheet.
3. XBRL instance document. The instance document with data and metadata is shown in Figure 9.12. The same instance document in human readable form is shown in Figure 9.13. Notice that in the Altova screen, the tabs across the bottom of the screen permit you to preview the instance document in HTML, rich text file, PDF, or Word. Altova also provides a design view to use in XBRL instance document development (Figure 9.14).

XBRL software tools, such as those provided by Altova, UBMatrix, SAP, and Rivet, convert data into XBRL instance documents using the selected taxonomy. Some firms choose to outsource the XBRL function, sending data to outside firms to convert the data into instance documents. Other firms choose to insource the XBRL function, tagging and storing the data in-house.

We hope this chapter has inspired you to explore XBRL further.

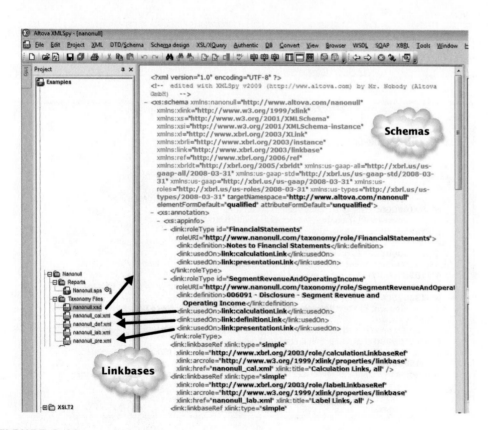

FIGURE 9.10

Sample XBRL Taxonomy Files

Pair and Share: What are the names of the linkbase files? (Hint: They end in .xml.)

This figure was created using Altova XMLSpy (Copyright 2003–2010 Altova GmbH) and is reprinted with permission of Altova. XMLSpy and Altova are trademarks of Altova GmbH and are registered in numerous countries.

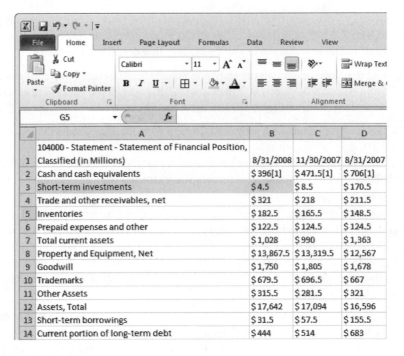

FIGURE 9.11

Sample XBRL Data

Pair and Share: Can you find short-term investments for 2008 in the XBRL instance document?

> **My Connection...**
> • Tech in Practice 9.34

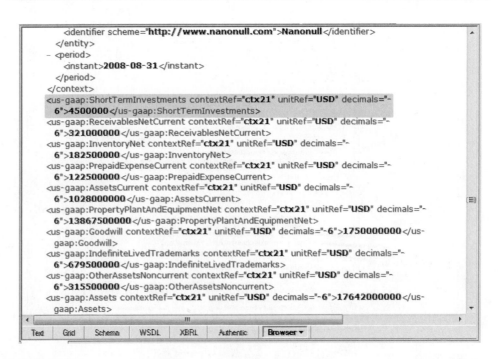

FIGURE 9.12

Sample XBRL Instance Document

Pair and Share: What is the currency used in this XBRL instance document?

This figure was created using Altova XMLSpy (Copyright 2003–2010 Altova GmbH) and is reprinted with permission of Altova.

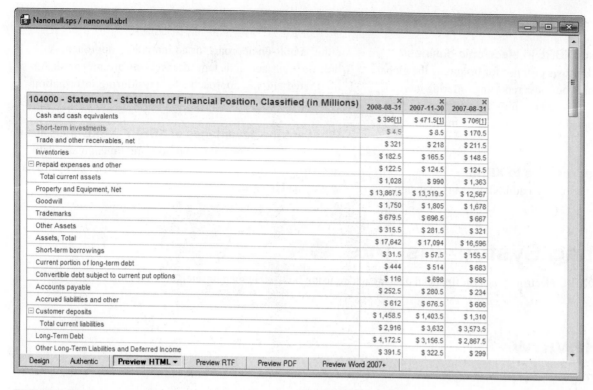

FIGURE 9.13

Sample XBRL Instance Document in HTML

This figure was created using Altova XMLSpy (Copyright 2003–2010 Altova GmbH) and is reprinted with permission of Altova.

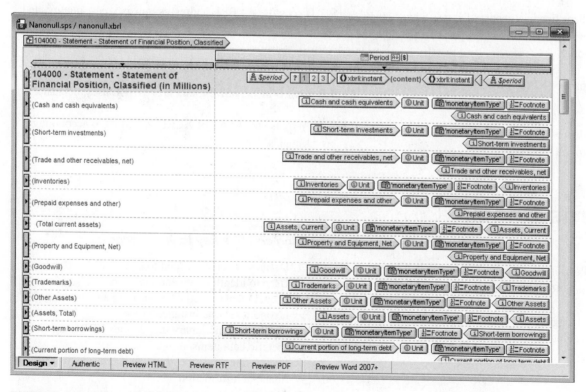

FIGURE 9.14

Sample XBRL Instance Document in Altova Design View

This figure was created using Altova XMLSpy (Copyright 2003–2010 Altova GmbH) and is reprinted with permission of Altova.

Chapter Highlights

What is the role of XBRL in electronic business reporting? XBRL shows promise for becoming the global standard for electronic business reporting, offering more intelligent reporting than ever before. From Europe to Asia, XBRL is being adopted for banking, capital markets, and internal applications.

What are two approaches to XBRL tagging? Organizations can add XBRL tags to data using either a bolt-on approach or an integrated approach. A bolt-on approach adds tags after reports are prepared. An integrated tagging approach adds tags during information processing.

What are the advantages of XBRL? XBRL offers many advantages including reduced processing time, greater data interchangeability, increased standardization, and higher data quality and integrity.

Accounting System Insights

Insight No. 18 XBRL electronic tags for financial data are added using bolt-on tagging or integrated tagging.

Active Review

Study less. Learn more. Make connections.

9.1 Refer to the chapter opener, *Meet Charlie Hoffman*. XBRL is being used around the globe for digital business and financial reporting purposes. In your opinion, why is XBRL becoming globally accepted for financial reporting?

9.2 XBRL standardizes financial reports. Discuss why standardization of business and financial reports is important in today's global economy.

9.3 Discuss the impact of XBRL on business intelligence applications.

9.4 Why are there different taxonomies? Why can't one taxonomy be used for all reporting?

9.5 Can companies reduce costs by using XBRL for reporting? How?

9.6 Discuss how organizations can benefit from XBRL.

9.7 Discuss how XBRL addresses transparency, quality, and timeliness issues.

9.8 Explain how XBRL reduces rekeying data.

9.9 What is metadata? Explain how XBRL uses metadata.

9.10 Why is knowledge of XBRL important to accounting professionals? Explain.

Key Terms Check

Understanding the language used at the crossroads of accounting and IT is key to your success.

9.11 Match the following terms and definitions.
a. eXtensible Business Reporting Language (XBRL)
b. metadata
c. XBRL integrated tagging
d. XBRL bolt-on tagging
e. taxonomy
f. elements
g. schema
h. XBRL linkbases
i. instance document

_____ 1. Defines elements related to a particular taxonomy
_____ 2. Used to identify data and metadata
_____ 3. A document that contains specific amounts for a taxonomy at one instance
_____ 4. Similar to a dictionary that defines XBRL tags for specific data items
_____ 5. Digital financial reporting that electronically tags financial information
_____ 6. Adds data tags after reports are created
_____ 7. Adds data tags during information processing
_____ 8. Data about data
_____ 9. Defines relationships between data

9.12 Match the following terms and definitions.

a. data element
b. context element
c. unit element
d. period element
e. entity element
f. identifier element

_____ 1. Defines the company
_____ 2. Numeric or nonnumeric facts
_____ 3. Defines the time period
_____ 4. Unique identifier, such as account number
_____ 5. Explains the context in which the data appears
_____ 6. Defines the unit of measure, such as U.S. dollars

9.13 Match the following terms and definitions.

a. definition links
b. calculation links
c. presentation links
d. label links
e. reference links

_____ 1. Defines the labels used in the document
_____ 2. Defines basic validation rules, such as assets equal liabilities plus equity
_____ 3. Defines the relationships between the elements and the external standards
_____ 4. Defines different kinds of relationships between elements
_____ 5. Defines how elements are presented

Practice Test

9.14 Which of the following is false?

a. XBRL is used for digital financial reporting around the globe.
b. XBRL is an extension of XML.
c. XBRL is a programming language that is used for writing accounting software.
d. XBRL provides the metadata capability.

9.15 What was XBRL developed to standardize and streamline?

a. Accounting software
b. Operational database
c. Decision making
d. Financial and business reporting

9.16 What is metadata?

a. Data about data
b. Secondary data
c. Data extracted from database
d. Virtual data

9.17 _____ tagging adds XBRL data tags after reports are created.

a. Built-in
b. Integrated
c. Quick-tag
d. Bolt-on

9.18 _____ tagging adds XBRL data tags as information is processed.

a. Integrated
b. Information
c. Process
d. Bolt-on

9.19 XBRL tags are similar to

a. A driver's license
b. A barcode
c. A house address
d. All of the above

9.20 Which of the following is NOT an XBRL essential?

a. Taxonomy
b. Integrated tagging
c. Schema
d. Instance document

9.21 Which of the following provides the most capability for sharing data between applications?

a. Spreadsheet
b. HTML
c. Text file
d. XBRL

9.22 Which of the XBRL essentials is like a dictionary?

a. Taxonomy
b. Instance document
c. Element
d. Schema

9.23 Which of the following is needed to create an XBRL instance document?

a. Data and XBRL tags
b. XBRL schema and data elements
c. XBRL taxonomy and data
d. XBRL programming language and data

Exercises

Each Exercise relates to one of the major questions addressed in the chapter and is labeled with the question number in green.

Short Exercises

Warm up with these short exercises.

9.24 Compare and contrast adding XBRL tags at the end of the financial reporting process (bolt-on tagging) versus during information processing (integrated tagging). Use the following organizer for your answer. **(Q9.5)**

Compare (Same)	and	Contrast (Different)

9.25 List the five different types of linkbases and describe the function of each. **(Q9.6)**

9.26 Review the XBRL programming code shown in Figure 9.1. Answer the following questions: **(Q9.6)**

1. What taxonomy is being used?
2. What currency is used?
3. How many decimal places will be displayed in the report?

9.27 Can a relational database be used to store XBRL metadata? Explain your answer. What other options are organizations using to store XBRL metadata in a database? **(Q9.5)**

It's Your Call

This is your training ground. These scenarios provide you with the opportunity to use your knowledge and professional skills.

9.28 You have been called in as an XBRL consultant. The president of the company has asked for your opinion regarding the costs and benefits of XBRL. What would you say? What benefits of XBRL do you see as the most important? What costs should an organization consider? **(Q9.4)**

9.29 At lunch one day, the topic of XBRL is mentioned. One of your colleagues says, "It has something to do with schemas, linkbases, and taxonomies—that is all I know." Then he turns to you and asks, "What do you know about XBRL?"

What would you say? How would you explain the relationship of schemas, linkbases, and taxonomies? **(Q9.6)**

9.30 You are serving as a liaison between accounting and IT. Your company is required to use XBRL for external financial reporting. IT would like to use XBRL integrated tagging and has asked for funding for an XBRL database. The accounting department doesn't see why IT needs funding for another new database.

What are the benefits of XBRL integrated tagging for internal use? Why would IT need a new XBRL database? What would you say at your meeting with accounting and IT? **(Q9.5, 9.6)**

9.31 Mark, chief financial officer (CFO) of iElectronics, and Brittany, chief information officer (CIO), would like to take advantage of XBRL technology for their company financial and accounting functions. They are both agreed that the company has several financial companies' reporting problems. They have prepared the following list of problems:

- The Security and Exchange Commission (SEC) reports have been late for the past 2 years.
- Their international subsidiaries in Canada and Mexico have been late sending their monthly closing information to the company's headquarters in St. Louis, Missouri.
- Their internal reports regarding key performance indicators (KPI) are also late and sometimes inaccurate.
- The company's reported financial data is not detailed enough for the company's analysts.

IT department programmers have been able to use XML to help the financial department, but the result is not satisfactory.

You have learned about XBRL in your accounting information course and have recently attended an XBRL workshop. Mark and Brittany are very excited to learn about the XBRL possibilities for helping iElectronics. In the last Friday meeting, Brittany asked, "So, what is XBRL and how could it help us?" After a brief explanation, you added that XBRL uses XML data tags plus some additional tags to describe financial statements. You assured them that XBRL could solve the company's reporting problems.

"How is that possible?" asked Mark. You responded that you would be more than happy to prepare a presentation for the next meeting, providing more information about XBRL and explaining how it could provide assistance to the iElectronics reporting and financial data exchange. "OK, this sounds great," responded Mark. Brittany asked you to include in your presentation the following topics:

a. What is XBRL?
b. How does it relate to XML?
c. What are integrated and bolt-on tagging?
d. How could XBRL solve the listed problems?
e. What are the advantages to iElectronics of adopting XBRL?

Prepare a summary that includes answers to Brittany's questions. **(Q9.1, 9.2, 9.3, 9.4, 9.5)**

Tech in Practice

These technology in practice exercises are perfect for both individuals and teams.

Tech Exercises

Sharpen your skills with these technology exercises. Download the data files for these Tech Exercises at www.pearsonhighered.com/kay.

9.32

Tech Tool: Spreadsheet Software

Valencia Orange Inc. has asked for your assistance in adding XBRL tags to its financial statements.

1. Download the data file for this exercise.
2. Use the information in Figure 9.12 to write the XBRL tags for the following selected items on Valencia Orange's statement of financial position at August 31, 2011.
   a. Short-term borrowings $31.5 million
   b. Accounts payable $252.5 million
   c. Accrued liabilities $612 million
   d. Customer deposits current $1,458.5 million

9.33

Tech Tool: Spreadsheet Software

Valencia Orange Inc. has asked for your assistance in adding some XBRL tags to its financial statements.

1. Download the data file for this exercise.
2. Use the information in Figure 9.12 to write the XBRL tags for the following selected items on Valencia Orange's statement of financial position at August 31, 2011.
   a. Long-term debt noncurrent $4,172.5 million
   b. Other liabilities noncurrent $391.5 million
   c. Commitments and contingencies $0
   d. Common stock $3 million

9.34

Tech Tool: Spreadsheet Software

Valencia Orange Inc. has asked for your assistance with XBRL tags for its financial statements.

1. Download the data file for this exercise.
2. Use the information in Figure 9.12 to answer the following questions about XBRL tags for the selected items on Valencia Orange's statement of financial position at August 31, 2011.
   a. What account and amount should appear on the financial statement for the XBRL tag labeled 2a in the spreadsheet data file for this exercise?
   b. What account and amount should appear on the financial statement for the XBRL tag labeled 2b in the spreadsheet data file for this exercise?
   c. What account and amount should appear on the financial statement for the XBRL tag labeled 2c in the spreadsheet data file for this exercise?
   d. What account and amount should appear on the financial statement for the XBRL tag labeled 2d in the spreadsheet data file for this exercise?

Go Online

In the fast-paced world of technology, your skill at finding answers fast can be vital. Go online and experience typical assignments you may encounter as a professional.

9.35 As an accounting intern, you have been asked by your supervisor to research software that can be used for XBRL bolt-on tagging. Go online and search for software that can be used for this purpose. Write a brief email to your supervisor with a summary of your findings.

9.36 You have been assigned to the XBRL project team for your company. Your assignment is to research available taxonomies. Go online and research the different taxonomies available. Write a brief email to your project team summarizing your findings.

9.37 XBRL stands for eXtensible Business Reporting Language. Your boss wants to know why. Go online and search for an explanation as to why it is called extensible. Write a brief email to your boss with your explanation.

Technology Projects

These technology projects are perfect for both individuals and teams.

Technology Project 9

Tech Tool: Internet

Software Video: Internet Research

iSportDesign is considering implementing XBRL for business reports. Nick, the owner, has asked for your assistance. He wants you to research the two options for XBRL: bolt-on tagging and integrated tagging.

Go online and research the XBRL software products available for each option. Prepare an executive summary for Nick with your recommendation and rationale.

Your deliverable for the project is as follows:

> Deliverable 1. An executive summary regarding which XBRL option and software is the best fit for iSportDesign.

Visit www.pearsonhighered.com/kay to do the following:

1. Download Technology Project 9 instructions.
2. Download files provided online for your convenience in completing the project deliverables.
3. Watch the video with software instructions to complete this project at www.pearsonhighered.com/kay.

Part Three *Security, Controls, and Risk* focuses on how to safeguard the information assets stored in the accounting and intelligence systems.

Part Three
Security, Controls, and Risk

Chapter 10
Fraud and Internal Control

Chapter 11
Cybersecurity

Chapter 12
The Risk Intelligent Enterprise:
Enterprise Risk Management

Safeguard Accounting Data

10

Fraud and Internal Control

How Does Someone Bilk His Clients for $50 Billion?
Meet a Ponzi Scheme.

Imagine on Monday that you borrow $1 from a friend to buy your favorite snack. On Tuesday to pay back friend no. 1, you borrow $2 from another friend, using the extra dollar to buy another snack for yourself. On Wednesday, you borrow $3 from a third friend to pay back friend no. 2 and buy yet another snack for yourself. By Friday, how much do you owe?

If you said $5, you are absolutely right. Meet a Ponzi scheme. Now imagine continuing this until you owe $50 billion!

Bernard Madoff in December 2008 admitted that he had basically been operating a Ponzi scheme. Client losses are estimated at $50 to $65 billion, amounting to Wall Street's largest investment fraud. Madoff confessed that instead of investing clients' funds, he used money deposited from new clients to finance the withdrawals of earlier clients. After the financial crisis in the fall of 2008, more and more of his investors were withdrawing funds and Madoff was unable to pay them. Madoff pleaded guilty to criminal charges including securities fraud and money laundering. He was sentenced to 150 years in federal prison. Madoff's auditor also faces criminal charges, allegedly failing to conduct due diligence (reuters.com, 2009).

> **Crossroads**
> At the crossroads of accounting and IT, the accounting professional must understand internal control, including IT controls.

My Questions

Q 10.1	Fraud: What will I tell my MOM?
Q 10.2	What is SOX?
Q 10.3	What is internal control?
Q 10.4	What are IT controls?
Q 10.5	What are service organization controls?

Fraud: What Will I Tell My MOM?

Can you imagine working as an auditor for a company and suddenly one day being jailed because you failed to uncover that the CEO was defrauding investors?

Dubbed *India's Madoff,* Ramalingam Raju, chairman of India's fourth largest IT outsourcing company, Satyam Computer Services, admitted that he had inflated cash by $1 billion and overstated profits by 97%. Despite claiming no knowledge of the fraud, Satyam's CFO and auditors were jailed.

Satyam's clients included large corporations such as Nestlé and General Electric. Earlier, the World Bank had banned Satyam from completing any further work after discovering that Satyam employees had hacked into its system to access sensitive information. One company, Unpaid Systems, filed suit charging Satyam with intellectual fraud and forgery (businessweek.com, 2009).

Fraud Triangle

Fraud is a deliberate, illegal, deceptive event which causes damage to others for the fraudster's benefit. The fraud triangle (Figure 10.1) depicts three conditions that typically must exist in order for a fraud to be perpetrated:

- Motive
- Opportunity
- Means

One way to remember the fraud triangle is *What will I tell my MOM?* When you are placed in a difficult position and are assessing whether to initiate or participate in fraud, ask yourself: *When the fraud is discovered and my photo is posted on the Internet as a fraudster, what will I tell my MOM?*

> **Crossroads**
>
> Both IT professionals and accounting professionals refer to a fraud triangle. They are just different fraud triangles.
>
> IT professionals refer to the fraud triangle as motive/opportunity/means (MOM).
>
> Accounting professionals often refer to the fraud triangle as incentive/opportunity/rationalization.

FIGURE 10.1

Fraud Triangle

In order for fraud to be committed, the perpetrator must have motive—reason for committing the fraud, such as financial difficulties. The perpetrator must have opportunity—access to the asset or financial statements in order to carry out the fraud. Finally, the perpetrator must have the means to carry out the fraud—knowledge or skills that permit the perpetrator to commit the crime. For fraud to occur, all three conditions must be present. Motive and opportunity without means will not result in fraud because the potential fraudster has no means of committing the fraud. Opportunity and means without motive will not result in fraud because the individual is not motivated to commit fraud. Motive and means without opportunity will not result in fraud, because even though the potential fraudster is motivated to commit fraud and has the means to do so, the individual does not have an opportunity. So one way to prevent fraud is to ensure that fraudsters do not have the opportunity to commit fraud.

Types of Fraud

The Association of Certified Fraud Examiners (ACFE) classifies occupational fraud into three general categories:

1. Corruption
2. Misappropriation of assets
3. Fraudulent financial reporting

CORRUPTION Corruption includes illegal acts such as bribery, kickbacks, money laundering and rigging bids.

MISAPPROPRIATION OF ASSETS Misappropriation of assets involves theft of assets for personal gain. Cash, inventory, and intellectual property are often top targets for theft.

FRAUDULENT FINANCIAL REPORTING Fraudulent financial reporting includes misstating financial statements to meet earnings targets. Examples of fraudulent financial reporting are overstating revenues, understating expenses, and failure to disclose pertinent information.

> ### Fraud Facts
>
> Most occupational frauds are committed by the accounting department (29% of cases) or upper management (19%).
>
> The typical fraud lasts two years before it is detected. Forty-six percent of frauds are detected by tips, which is the most likely means of detection. In 35% of the cases, inadequate internal controls were cited as a primary contributing factor (acfe.com, 2009).

> ### Why Does Fraud Occur?
> The two top reasons given for why executive fraud occurs are:
> • Pressure to meet goals (81%)
> • Personal gain (72%)

Fraud Risk Management

How do you manage the risk of fraud? To provide guidance in managing the risk of fraud, the Institute of Internal Auditors (IIA), the AICPA, and the Association of Certified Fraud Examiners (ACFE) issued a report entitled *Managing the Business Risk of Fraud: A Practical Guide.* The following five principles were identified to establish an environment to manage fraud risk effectively.

PRINCIPLE 1: FRAUD RISK GOVERNANCE As part of an organization's governance structure, a fraud risk management program should be in place, including a written policy (or policies) to convey the expectations of the board of directors and senior management regarding managing fraud risk.

PRINCIPLE 2: FRAUD RISK ASSESSMENT Fraud risk exposure should be assessed periodically by the organization to identify specific potential schemes and events that the organization needs to mitigate.

Fraud...

Typical organizations lose an estimated 5% of annual revenues to fraud, which is a potential projected global fraud loss exceeding $3.5 trillion according to an ACFE survey (acfe.com, 2012).

Effectively Fighting Fraud

Not even the strongest system of controls can eliminate all risk of organizations' being defrauded by employees who are sufficiently motivated to find loopholes, ways to override controls, or opportunities for collusion. While most accountants are familiar with methods for identifying manipulated accounting data, effectively fighting fraud involves going further and understanding the human elements involved.
—What's Your Fraud IQ?, JournalofAccountancy. com, August 2012

PRINCIPLE 3: FRAUD PREVENTION Prevention techniques to avoid potential key fraud risk events should be established, where feasible, to mitigate possible impacts on the organization.

PRINCIPLE 4: FRAUD DETECTION Detection techniques should be established to uncover fraud events when preventive measures fail or unmitigated risks are realized.

PRINCIPLE 5: FRAUD INVESTIGATION AND CORRECTIVE ACTION A reporting process should be in place to solicit input on potential fraud, and a coordinated approach to investigation and corrective action should be used to help ensure potential fraud is addressed appropriately and timely.

Key components of effective fraud risk management are controls to prevent, detect, and correct fraud. These controls attempt to prevent and detect both intentional errors (such as fraud) and unintentional errors (such as mistakes).

1. **Prevent:** controls designed to prevent or reduce the likelihood of a fraud risk occurring. This includes controls to prevent errors from occurring in the accounting system. An example of a preventive control would include restricting employee access to some parts of the accounting system and requiring an employee user ID and password to log into the system.
2. **Detect:** controls designed to discover fraud when it occurs and alert management. The purpose of detective controls is to detect if an error or issue occurs in your accounting system. An example of a detective control is conducting a physical inventory count on a regular basis to verify that the items on hand agree with the number of items recored in the accounting system. This detective control helps to detect inventory shrinkage (missing inventory) possibly due to theft.
3. **Correct:** investigate and take corrective action to remedy harm caused. Sometimes this step is referred to as respond instead of correct.

Where's the Line between Earnings Management and Fraud?

Often in accounting scandals, accounting numbers are misstated to make the company's financial performance appear better than it really is. Earnings management focuses on managing when revenues and expenses are recorded in order to favorably reflect a company's financial performance in a legal manner. Where is the line between earnings management and fraud? Fraud is earnings management gone amuck. Both Madoff and Raju admitted that their problems began with a marginal gap, but once they started down the path of misstating amounts, there was no turning back. The gap between the misstated amounts and the real amounts only grew wider. In many fraud cases, the perpetrator moves from a "gray area" into outright illegal activity.

The 2012 ACFE report on occupational fraud and abuse found that in 81% of cases, the fraudster displayed one or more behavioral warning signs. Top behavioral red flags of fraudsters were:

- Living beyond means (36% of cases)
- Financial difficulties (27% of cases)
- Unusually close association with vendors or customers (19% of cases)
- Excessive control issues, unwillingness to share duties (18% of cases) (acfe.com, 2012)

The challenge for you as an accounting professional is to safeguard the information assets in the accounting system, utilizing security and controls, as well as understanding behavioral aspects of fraud so you can identify and investigate red flags before it's too late.

Would You Like to Know More?
One type of fraud on the rise is cybercrime with new, more sophisticated cyberattacks.

See the next chapter, *Cybersecurity,* if you would like to know more.

My Connection...
- Active Review 10.2
- It's Your Call 10.36

What Is SOX?

The millennium began with the Enron accounting scandal in October 2001. Enron CEO Jeffrey Skilling was convicted and sentenced to 24 years in prison for conspiracy, securities fraud, insider trading, and lying to auditors (businessweek.com, 2009). Enron's many accounting problems led to its collapse.

After indictment for obstruction of justice, Enron's auditor, Arthur Andersen LLP, lost much of its client base. In June 2002, Andersen was found guilty of obstruction of justice for destroying documents related to Enron and surrendered its CPA license. Although the conviction was later overturned by the U.S. Supreme Court, Andersen virtually ceased operations (newsbbc. co.uk, 2002; time.com, 2002).

In June 2002, WorldCom revealed it had improperly booked $3.8 billion of operating expenses as capital expenditures to inflate profits. A month later, WorldCom declared bankruptcy (businessweek.com, 2002). The year 2002 also saw Tyco, Adelphia, and Global Crossing corporate scandals.

Losing billions of dollars as a result of these scandals, investors were losing confidence in the securities markets and the financial statements issued by publicly traded companies. In response to the frauds and accounting scandals of 2002, the U.S. Congress passed legislation—the Sarbanes-Oxley Act of 2002, which would become known as SOX. The legislation created the Public Company Accounting Oversight Board (PCAOB) to oversee and regulate public companies and their auditors. This was a turning point for the accounting profession, which prior to then had been self-regulated.

The Sarbanes-Oxley Act relates to corporate governance and financial disclosure requirements only for organizations registered with the Securities and Exchange Commission (SEC) and listed on the U.S. stock exchanges. SOX emphasized a strong system of internal control as a means of avoiding Enron-sized accounting frauds. In addition to establishing the PCAOB to regulate the auditors of publicly traded companies, SOX legislation contained the following sections that are still especially pertinent to the accounting profession.

SOX Requirements

SECTION 302. CORPORATE RESPONSIBILITY FOR FINANCIAL REPORTS Section 302 requires the chief executive officer and chief financial officer to certify in each annual or quarterly report that the signing officer reviewed the report and that the report does not contain any untrue or omission of material fact that made the statements misleading. Furthermore, the statements fairly present in all material aspects the financial condition and results of operations. The signing officers are responsible for establishing and maintaining internal controls, and evaluating and reporting the effectiveness of the internal controls. The officers are required to disclose to the auditors and the audit committee of the board of directors all significant deficiencies in internal controls, which could adversely affect the ability to record, process, summarize, and report financial data and any material weaknesses in internal controls. The officers are also required to disclose any fraud, whether material or immaterial, that involved management or employees who play a significant role in internal controls.

SECTION 404. MANAGEMENT ASSESSMENT OF INTERNAL CONTROLS This section of SOX requires each annual report of a publicly traded company to contain an internal control report stating management's responsibility to establish and maintain an adequate system of internal control for financial reporting as well as an assessment of the effectiveness of the internal control structure and procedures. The public accounting firm that audits the financial statements of the company must issue an attestation report regarding the effectiveness of the company's internal controls.

SECTION 806. PROTECTION FOR EMPLOYEES OF PUBLICLY TRADED COMPANIES WHO PROVIDE EVIDENCE OF FRAUD This section of SOX is known as *Whistleblower Protection for Employees of Publicly Traded Companies*. It provides protection against retaliation for employees, such as company accountants, who provide information in fraud cases of publicly traded companies.

SECTION 906. CORPORATE RESPONSIBILITY FOR FINANCIAL REPORTS Section 906 requires corporate management to certify reports filed with the SEC, such as the annual 10-K and quarterly 10-Q. This section also provides for criminal penalties of up to $5 million or 20 years imprisonment (Sarbanes-Oxley Act, 2002).

SOX legislation basically requires management of public companies to assess and report on the effectiveness of internal controls for financial reporting using a recognized framework. As SOX went into effect, third party review of internal controls, in essence, meant that the company would now need to have two audits: one to assess internal controls to comply with SOX and another to provide an audit of the financial statements. If the internal audit revealed any significant deficiencies, it is required to be disclosed by the signing officers of the company. Companies found it was in their best interests to address any internal control weaknesses before a third party review.

Audit and Internal Control

In 2007, the Public Company Accounting Oversight Board (PCAOB) issued Auditing Standard No. 5, an *Audit of Internal Control Over Financial Reporting That Is Integrated with An Audit of Financial Statements.* The standard establishes requirements and provides guidance for independent auditors attesting to management's assessment of internal control over financial reporting to comply with Section 404 of SOX. Using a more risk-based approach, the Accounting Standard No. 5 replaced Auditing Standard No. 2, which had proved unduly expensive and inefficient.

There are several different types of audits, all of which are addressed by Auditing Standard No. 5. An **audit of internal control** over financial reporting requires the auditor to conduct tests of controls to obtain evidence that internal control over financial reporting has operated effectively. The auditor tests the design and operating effectiveness of controls.

In an **audit of financial statements**, the auditor performs tests of controls and substantive procedures. Tests of controls assess control risk. Substantive procedures collect evidence regarding the accuracy, completeness, and validity of data produced by the accounting system. The auditor's assessment of control risk determines the extent of substantive procedures to perform.

The auditing standard requires the auditor to understand how IT affects the following:

1. The company's flow of transactions
2. Internal control over financial reporting

The standard specifies that the identification of risks and controls within IT is not a separate evaluation, but is an integral part of the top-down approach specified in the auditing standard. This is sometimes referred to as **IT audit**. In the past, it was not unusual for the auditor to bring in an IT audit specialist to conduct tests of IT controls. Increasingly, the PCAOB is expecting auditors to understand how IT affects the audit and integrate IT into the audit.

An **integrated audit**, as required by Auditing Standard No. 5, integrates an audit of internal control with an audit of financial statements. In an integrated audit of internal control over financial reporting and the financial statements, the auditor is required to design tests of controls so that the objective of both audits are accomplished simultaneously. Thus, the financial statement audit is combined with an attestation of the effectiveness of internal control over financial reporting. Note that Auditing Standard No. 5 also refers to integration of tests of IT controls into the audit. Thus, the integrated audit integrates tests of controls for an audit of internal control, tests of controls for the audit of financial statements, and tests of IT controls.

There are two types of deficiencies that may be found in internal control over financial reporting: a **material weakness**, which is the more serious of the two, and a **significant deficiency**. A material weakness in internal control over financial reporting is defined as a deficiency such that there is a reasonable possibility that a material misstatement of financial statements will not be prevented or detected on a timely basis. A significant deficiency is less severe, but nonetheless merits attention of those responsible for oversight of financial reporting. If even one material weakness is detected, the company's internal control over financial reporting cannot be considered effective. Note that it is possible for a material weakness in internal control over financial reporting to exist even though the financial statements are not materially misstated.

CIO...
One chief information officer of a hospital admits that IT audits can be disruptive as well as costly when taking systems offline. He reduces disruptions, however, by using software tools that clone the systems to be audited. The tools basically take a snapshot of the database, which is then run on a different server for the auditors to examine. This enables IT to provide uninterrupted service to the hospital (CIO Decisions Magazine, 2007).

XBRL + SOX...
XBRL, extensible Business Reporting Language, offers auditors benefits in complying with Sarbanes-Oxley Section 404. Because XBRL uses electronic tags on the financial data, auditors can search data faster and more accurately, with streamlined data analysis. When investigating fraud, XBRL enables auditors to extract, analyze, and interpret evidence to detect unusual patterns and irregularities. However, some of XBRL's benefits (for example, online, real-time) can present increased information security risks (Internal Auditor, 2004).

Generally accepted auditing standards (GAAS) require technical training and proficiency as an auditor, independence, and exercise of due professional care. Management is required by SEC rules to use a suitable, recognized framework established by a body or group that follows due-process procedures as a basis for its evaluation of the effectiveness of the company's internal control over financial reporting. The auditor is required to "use the same suitable, recognized control framework to perform his or her audit of internal control over financial reporting as management uses for its annual evaluation of the effectiveness of the company's internal control over financial reporting" (PCAOB Auditing Standard No. 5, 2007). Suitable frameworks for this purpose would include COSO's *Internal Control—Integrated Framework*.

My Connection...
- Active Review 10.3
- Active Review 10.4
- It's Your Call 10.37

What Is Internal Control?

Internal control is a key element of the Sarbanes-Oxley Act of 2002. A system of internal controls is required by SOX Section 404.

Internal control is a set of policies, procedures, and activities to achieve an organization's objectives related to the following:

1. Effective and efficient operations.
2. Reliable financial reporting, preventing and detecting both intentional errors (fraud) and unintentional errors (mistakes).
3. Safeguard assets including information assets associated with the accounting system.
4. Comply with applicable laws and regulations.

Note that objective 2 above relates to fraudulent financial reporting and objective 3 above relates to misappropriation of assets.

For internal control to be effective, an organization needs both:

1. Stated policies and procedures for internal controls, and
2. Compliance with internal controls (individuals comply with or follow the policies and procedures)

Internal Control...

... is a process, effected by an entity's board of directors, management, and other personnel. This process is designed to provide reasonable assurance regarding the achievement of objectives in effectiveness and efficiency of operations, reliability of financial reporting, and compliance with applicable laws and regulations (coso. org, 2009).

Five Categories of Internal Control

Statement on Auditing Standards No. 109 (SAS 109), a pronouncement related to privately held company audits, provides useful guidance regarding internal control policies, procedures, and activities.

There are five major categories for internal control.

1. Control environment
2. Risk assessment
3. Information and communications systems relevant to financial reporting
4. Control activities
5. Monitoring of controls

CONTROL ENVIRONMENT The control environment includes tone at the top and the ethical standards and values of an organization and its employees. In the movie about the Enron scandal, *Smartest Guys in the Room*, Enron employees bragged as they participated in unethical acts. This type of environment encourages rather than discourages unethical behavior.

RISK ASSESSMENT Risk assessment can be divided into:
- Financial statement risk assessment: Identify, analyze, and manage risks affecting ability to report financial data properly.
- Fraud risk assessment: Identify, analyze, and manage risks related to fraud.

INFORMATION AND COMMUNICATION SYSTEMS RELEVANT TO FINANCIAL REPORTING
Internal controls in this category include:

- Validity: Record all valid transactions.
- Classification: Properly classify transactions for financial reporting.

- Valuation: Record transactions at appropriate amount.
- Cutoff: Record transactions for the appropriate period.
- Presentation and disclosure: Properly present transactions and related disclosures in the financial statements.

CONTROL ACTIVITIES Controls activities include:
- Segregation of duties: Individuals with access to company assets, such as cash or inventory, do not also have access to the accounting records to cover up the theft. For example, roles to initiate transactions, authorization, custody of asset, record keeping and review are performed by different individuals.
- Reconciliation of assets and accounting records: Bank reconciliations and physical inventory counts are performed on a regular basis.
- Performance reviews: Actual performance results are compared to plans or goals, such as key performance indicators (KPI).
- Physical controls: Physical security to safeguard assets, such as locked cash drawers and security cameras.
- IT controls: IT security plays an important role in a sound system of internal controls, such as using login passwords for access control.

MONITORING OF CONTROLS Monitoring of controls might include the following activities:
- Internal auditor evaluation of compliance with internal control policies and procedures.
- Legal department's oversight of compliance with legal and ethical policies.
- Periodically assessing internal controls and taking corrective action.

COSO Internal Control Integrated Framework

The **Committee of Sponsoring Organizations of the Treadway Commission (COSO)** issued *Internal Control—Integrated Framework* in 1992 that became widely adopted to comply with the new SOX 404 legislation. COSO is a private organization comprised of the professional associations of the American Accounting Association (AAA), the American Institute of Certified Public Accountants (AICPA), the Financial Executives International (FEI), the Institute of Management Accountants (IMA), and the Institute of Internal Auditors (IIA). The framework was updated in 2012.

The COSO *Internal Control—Integrated Framework* provides a blueprint for implementing an internal control system to assist in ensuring the reliability of financial statements and compliance with Sarbanes-Oxley legislation. As stated in the COSO framework, the purpose of internal control is to provide reasonable assurance in achieving the following internal control objectives:

1. Effectiveness and efficiency of operations
2. Reliability of financial reporting
3. Compliance with laws and regulations

The COSO *Internal Control—Integrated Framework* specifies five essential components of an effective internal control system that basically correspond to the five categories of internal control discussed previously:

1. Control environment
2. Risk assessment
3. Control activities
4. Information and communication
5. Monitoring

These five internal control components are used to achieve the three objectives of effective operations, reliable financial reporting, and legal and regulatory compliance. The COSO Internal Control Framework Cube is shown in Figure 10.2.

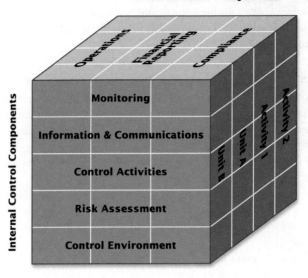

FIGURE 10.2

COSO Internal Control Framework Cube

Control Environment

The control environment is strongly influenced by the tone at the top of the organization set by top management and those charged with governance. The culture of the organization should foster an environment of control consciousness. Control environment factors include integrity and ethical values, importance of board of directors, management philosophy and operating style, organizational structure, commitment to financial reporting competencies, authority and responsibility, and human resources.

Effectively Fighting Fraud

What is considered legal versus ethical can shift over time with the passage of new legislation or regulations. The code of ethics can vary by profession and area of expertise. For example, within the accounting profession there is more than one code of ethics. Ethical codes of conduct for associations at the crossroads of accounting and IT include the following:

- Institute of Management Accountants (IMA)
- American Institute of Certified Public Accountants (AICPA)
- Institute of Internal Auditors (IIA)
- Information Systems Audit and Control Association (ISACA)
- International Federation of Accountants (IFA)
- International Information Systems Security Certification Consortium (ISC)[2]
- Institute of Electrical and Electronics Engineers (IEEE)
- The Hacker Ethic
- IT Code of Ethics

For your review, the code of ethics for the Institute of Internal Auditors (IIA) is contained in Chapter Extension 10.

Risk Assessment

Risk assessment involves identifying, analyzing, and managing risks that affect a company's ability to record, process, summarize, and report financial data properly. An entity can set entity-level and activity-level objectives that can identify critical success factors to be used for assessing risk and measuring performance. Three broad types of objectives are operations objectives pertaining to the effectiveness and efficiency of the entity's operations, financial reporting objectives pertaining to publishing reliable financial statements, and compliance objectives pertaining to an entity's adherence to applicable laws and regulations. After setting objectives, management can assess risks of not attaining these objectives.

Risk assessment control objectives include the following:

1. **Importance of financial reporting objectives**
2. **Identification and analysis of financial reporting risks**
3. **Assessment of fraud risk**

Control Activities

Control activities include policies and procedures to mitigate risks including:

- financial controls
- operational controls
- compliance controls

Examples of control activities include:

- Segregation of duties to divide authorization, recording, and asset custody among different individuals. For example, the person responsible for custody of an inventory of digital cameras should not also have access to the accounting records. If the inventory clerk stole 10 digital cameras to give to family and friends, the accounting records should show a discrepancy between the actual physical count of inventory that would be 10 cameras short versus the accounting records.
- Independent reconciliations of assets and accounting records, such as bank statement reconciliations and inventory reconciliations.
- Physical controls to provide for physical security of assets, such as security cameras and restricted access to corporate buildings.
- Information technology (IT) controls to ensure appropriate information processing, authorization, and data integrity. An example of an IT control would be data validation, techniques to ensure that only valid data is entered, such as five spaces for ZIP code.

Information and Communication

This component of internal control includes the accounting system for identifying, recording, processing, and reporting transactions and financial data. An organization's system produces reports containing operational, financial, and compliance information. Internal control principles related to this component include information technology, information needs, information control, management communication, upstream communication, board communication, and communication with external parties.

Monitoring

Monitoring involves assessing internal controls as well as the process for taking corrective action, if needed. Effective monitoring includes **ongoing monitoring**, such as controls over purchasing, and **separate evaluations**, such as an internal audit that assesses internal controls. Monitoring also includes upstream communication to report internal control deficiencies.

The control environment provides an atmosphere in which people conduct their activities and carry out their control responsibilities. It serves as the foundation for the other components. Within this environment, management assesses risks to the achievement of specified objectives. Control activities are implemented to help ensure that management directives to address the risks are carried out. Meanwhile, relevant information is captured and communicated throughout the organization. The entire process is monitored and modified as conditions warrant (Internal Control—Integrated Framework, 1994).

To comply with SOX, companies must use a framework for evaluating internal control, such as COSO's *Internal Control—Integrated Framework*. Information technology (IT) controls present unique challenges when implementing and assessing a system of internal controls. Information technology hardware, software, and systems require special consideration when implementing internal controls. PCAOB Auditing Standard No. 5 requires that assessment of the risks and controls within IT are integrated into the audit.

My Connection...
- Active Review 10.7
- Short Exercise 10.26
- It's Your Call 10.38

What Are IT Controls?

IT and Internal Control

...this situation creates a unique challenge: Many of the IT professionals being held accountable for the quality and integrity of information generated by their IT systems are not well-versed in the intricacies of internal control. This is not to suggest that risk is not being managed by IT, but rather that it may not be formalized or structured in a way required © by an organization's management or its auditors (IT Governance Institute, 2006).

While the auditor and the IT professional have specialized knowledge in their individual fields, increasingly the expectation is that each learns more about the other's field. To assist you in this quest, we share with you an accounting insight that is a blueprint for IT controls in the enterprise.

Accounting Insight No. 19: House of IT Controls

Accounting Insight No. 19 states that there are three zones in the house of IT controls (Figure 10.3):

- Top management: entity-level IT controls
- Business processes: application controls
- IT services: IT general controls

Each level of IT controls corresponds to a level within the enterprise. Like the foundation for a house, IT services provide support foundation for the business processes performed by the enterprise. Business processes consist of business activities that create value for the business, such as sales activities. Top management provides leadership for the enterprise, developing strategy and policy that guides the organization toward defined goals.

19

ACCOUNTING INSIGHT NO. 19
Three Zones in the House of IT Controls:
1. Top Management: Entity-Level IT Controls
2. Business Processes: Application Controls
3. IT Services: IT General Controls

ENTITY-LEVEL IT CONTROLS **Entity-level IT controls** include IT governance at top management levels where strategic business objectives are set and policies are established. Top management consists of the board of directors (BOD), chief security officer (CSO), chief executive officer (CEO), chief financial officer (CFO), chief information officer (CIO), and other executive-level positions in the enterprise. The audit committee (AC) under SOX legislation plays a greater role in corporate governance. Members of this committee are selected by the organization's board of directors. The audit committee's responsibilities include the following:

1. The integrity of the organization's financial statements and reports
2. The organization's internal controls
3. The organization's compliance with legal and regulatory requirements
4. The organization's policies regarding ethical conduct

Corporate and IT governance are influential in creating an organizational environment that is control conscious. ISACA defines IT governance as:

The responsibility of executives and the board of directors, and consists of the leadership, organizational structures and processes that ensure that the enterprise's IT sustains and extends the organization's strategies and objectives (http://isaca.org/glossary, 2009).

IT governance provides processes, organizational structure, and the leadership necessary for IT to support an organization's business strategy. Executives and boards play a crucial role in providing the leadership necessary to make IT governance effective.

Entity-level IT controls relate to the IT controls that influence the entire entity and include those listed in Figure 10.4. While entity-level IT controls are part of the entity's overall control environment, the next type of control is focused on business processes that create value for the organization.

Crossroads

IT controls are at the crossroads of accounting and IT. Internal controls for the accounting system are incomplete without IT controls.

Crossroads

Forty-two percent of organizations reported that their IT departments reported to the CFO. Thirty-three percent reported to the CEO (CFOs to CIOs: You Work For Me Now, cio.com, 2010).

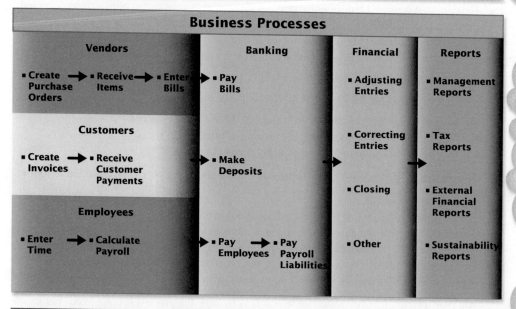

Entity-level Controls
These controls affect the enterprise's overall control environment including IT entity-level controls. Controls include risk assessment and internal audit.

Application Controls
Application controls are embedded within business process applications such as accounting applications. Integrated enterprise systems, such as SAP, contain application controls. Applications are designed with controls to prevent or detect unauthorized transactions. Application controls objectives for financial reporting include completeness, accuracy, authorization, and existence of transactions.

IT General Controls
Controls within IT processes support application controls and provide a reliable operating environment. Controls include program development, program changes, security access controls, and computer operations.

FIGURE 10.3

IT Controls

APPLICATION CONTROLS Application controls are controls embedded within business process applications (see Figure 10.3). Technology plays such an integral role in performing business processes today. Applications, such as accounting software, require application controls to ensure that financial reporting control objectives are achieved. Integrated enterprise systems, such as SAP and Oracle, include application controls within the financial applications of the integrated system.

FIGURE 10.4 Entity-Level IT Controls

Entity-Level IT Control
IT strategic plans
IT policies and procedures
IT risk management activities
IT professionals and end-user training and education
IT quality assurance
Monitor and evaluate IT performance
Monitor and evaluate internal control
Ensure legal and regulatory compliance
Provide IT governance

Application controls ensure completeness and accuracy of transaction processing, authorization, and validity. Such controls are intended to support control objectives of the following:

- Completeness: All transactions and accounts that should be presented in the financial statements are included.
- Accuracy: This refers to the accuracy of processing transactions as well as accuracy of accounts and information presented in the financial statements.
- Authorization: Transactions are recorded in accordance with authorization of management.
- Existence: Assets and liabilities exist at the given date and recorded transactions occurred during a given period.
- Disclosure: Processes are in place to ensure that all material information is disclosed in required reports and that disclosure is authorized, complete, accurate, and timely.

Application Control Classifications One way to classify application controls is by the control objectives specified in the COSO internal control framework:

1. Operations make effective and efficient use of the entity's resources.
2. Financial reporting produces reliable financial statements.
3. Compliance with applicable laws and regulations is achieved.

To correspond to the COSO control objectives, application controls can be classified as follows:

- **Operational controls**, such as controls to manage timing of cash disbursements to assure all discounts are taken and finance charges and late fees avoided
- **Financial controls**, such as controls to ensure that external financial reports are prepared on a timely basis in compliance with applicable laws, regulations, or contractual agreements
- **Compliance controls**, such as controls to maintain confidentiality of information in accordance with all applicable laws and regulations

Another way to classify application controls is by how the process is completed. For example, application controls can be completed manually, automatically, or some combination.

- **Manual controls:** Manual controls are performed without the assistance of technology. Manual controls include manually reconciling purchase orders to receiving reports to verify that goods received are the ones ordered.
- **Automated controls:** Automated controls are built into the system and performed automatically by computers. For example, automated controls can be used in IT systems so that exceptions are automatically reported. Automated application controls can be divided into input controls, processing controls, and output controls. An **input control** provides control over the data entered or input into the system. An example of an input control would be the database interface that contains input fields with data validation, such as nine spaces for the Social Security number field. Other input application controls might require a default value that is preassigned for all invoices. **Processing controls** ensure data integrity. For example, processed data might include control totals to verify that all amounts had been processed appropriately. Record count is another processing control to verify that all records had been processed properly. **Output controls** are used to ensure that reports and other output are distributed properly. For example, output (end-user) controls could prevent unauthorized users from accessing confidential salary reports.
- **Hybrid controls:** Hybrid controls are a combination of manual and automated processes. Reconciling inventory is an example of a hybrid control. The system automatically generates an inventory report on a scheduled basis (automated process). Then inventory is manually counted to verify inventory (manual process). The two results, automated and manual, are compared and any discrepancies resolved. Another example of a hybrid control is one used for accounts receivable. Application controls can be used to produce exception reports, such as accounts receivable that are 90 days or more past due (automated process). Then the responsible manager reviews the report and initiates follow-up activities to verify and resolve items on the exception report (manual process).

Application Control and Business Processes Sarbanes-Oxley legislation requires that public companies' internal control be evaluated, including documenting and testing of control activities and monitoring methods for business processes. Business processes for a baseline accounting system are shown in Figure 10.3. Each business process and accompanying accounting transaction cycle would need to have appropriate control activities identified and implemented. For business processes that involve IT systems, appropriate automated application controls should be identified.

When an audit of internal controls is conducted, the auditor would review the objectives and control activities, documenting compliance. A mechanism for reporting any internal control deficiencies would need to be established.

As Figure 10.3 shows, the purchasing cycle for a baseline accounting system might consist of creating a purchase order, receiving items ordered, receiving a bill for the items, and then paying the bill. Sometimes this is referred to as purchase-to-pay. A sample of application control objectives for the purchasing cycle is shown in Figure 10.5.

The sales cycle for a baseline accounting system consists of accepting a customer's order, recording the customer's payment, and then depositing the payment. Sometimes this is referred to as order-to-cash. See Figure 10.6 for a sample of application control objectives for the sales cycle.

Figure 10.7 lists examples of application control objectives for the payroll cycle. Sample objectives for banking or funds processing are listed in Figure 10.8. Figure 10.9 lists a sample of application control objectives for financial activities. A sample of reporting control objectives is shown in Figure 10.10.

IT GENERAL CONTROLS **IT general controls (ITGC),** sometimes referred to as simply general controls, apply to IT services in general and help to ensure continued proper IT operation and availability. IT general controls support application controls to provide a reliable operating environment.

IT general controls have a pervasive effect on all internal controls. For example, if a computer hacker gains access to the enterprise database management system, financial data stored in the database is at risk. Consequently, if the IT general control fails, it has a pervasive impact on all applications, including financial applications, that rely on those controls.

IT general controls are depicted in Figure 10.3 and typically include the following four categories:

- Program development controls
- Program change controls
- Computer operations controls
- Access security controls

FIGURE 10.5 Purchasing Cycle Application Control Objectives

Purchasing Cycle Application Control Objectives

Process Purchases
Order items meeting specifications
Receive items ordered on a timely basis
Record authorized purchase orders completely and accurately
Prevent unauthorized use of purchase orders*

Process Accounts Payable
Accurately record bills on a timely basis for all authorized and accepted purchases
Accurately record returns and allowances for all authorized credits
Ensure completeness and accuracy of accounts payable
Safeguard accounts payable records

Pay Bills
Manage timing of cash disbursements
Disburse cash only for authorized purchases**
Record cash disbursements completely and accurately

*An example of the related control activity for attaining this control objective would be consecutive prenumbering of purchase orders.

**Examples of related control activities include matching the purchase order, receiving report, and bill to verify that the items were authorized, received, and billed appropriately.

FIGURE 10.6 Sales Cycle Application Control Objectives

Sales Cycle Application Control Objectives

Process Customer Orders
Process orders only within approved customer credit limits
Process customer orders accurately
Process only valid customer orders
Transfer order data completely and accurately to shipping and accounts receivable

Process Shipments
All shipments are accurately documented and data transferred to accounts receivable
Ship customer orders in a timely manner

Process Accounts Receivable
All goods shipped are accurately billed in the proper period
Accurately record invoices for all authorized shipments
Ensure completeness and accuracy of accounts receivable
Safeguard accounts receivable records

Process Funds (Record Customer Payments)
Record cash receipts on accounts receivable completely and accurately*
Monitor timely collection of accounts receivable

*Examples of related control activities include using segregation of duties so that the person responsible for custody of cash received and bank deposits is not the same person who is responsible for recording customer cash received in the accounting records. Any possible deposits withheld would then be detected unless the accounting records were falsified.

FIGURE 10.7 Payroll Cycle Application Control Objectives

Payroll Cycle Application Control Objectives

Process Payroll
Enter and process time worked accurately
Calculate payroll and withholdings
Record payroll in the appropriate period
Record tax payments completely and accurately

Process Payroll Payments
Disburse payroll payments to appropriate employees
Make authorized tax payments

FIGURE 10.8 Banking/Cash Application Control Objectives

Banking/Cash Application Control Objectives

Process Funds (Cash)
Accurately forecast cash balances
Ensure financing is available in the event of a cash shortage
Accelerate cash collections
Record cash receipts on accounts receivable completely and accurately*
Manage timing of cash disbursements
Minimize cash disbursements using available discounts
Disburse cash only for authorized purchases**
Record cash disbursements completely and accurately
Safeguard cash and related accounting records, including reconciling bank accounts and segregation of duties

*Examples of related control activities include using segregation of duties so that the person responsible for custody of cash received and bank deposits is not the same person who is responsible for recording customer cash received in the accounting records. Any possible deposits withheld would then be detected unless the accounting records were falsified.

**Examples of related control activities include matching the purchase order, receiving report, and bill to verify that the items were authorized, received, and billed appropriately.

FIGURE 10.9 Financial Cycle Application Control Objectives

Financial Cycle Application Control Objectives

Analyze and Reconcile

Compare operating results with standards, such as budgets. Identify variances and trends.

Reconcile accounting records with physical assets to ensure internal consistency, such as bank reconciliations and physical inventory counts.

General Ledger

General ledger balances reconcile to subledger balances.

Access to general ledger records is appropriate and authorized.

System functionality supports the segregation of the posting and approval functions.

System controls are in place for appropriate approval of write-offs.

All transactions on exception reports are identified as either rejected or accepted.

Journal entries of exceptional amount posted to the general ledger are flagged by the system and reviewed for accuracy and approval.

Closing

Closing entries are complete and accurate.

Transactions cannot be recorded outside of financial close cutoff requirements.

FIGURE 10.10 Reporting Control Objectives

Reporting Control Objectives

Provide Financial and Management Reporting

Provide timely and accurate information needed by management and others to discharge their responsibility

Prepare external financial reports on a timely basis in compliance with applicable laws, regulations, or contractual agreements

Maintain confidentiality of financial information

Program Development Controls These are controls over developing an application. Controls include monitoring the phases of the SDLC for a new IT project. The phases of the SDLC are:

1. Plan the system development project including the budget and timeline.
2. Analyze user requirements to see how the new system could satisfy those requirements.
3. Design the system architecture of hardware and software.
4. Build or buy the system components.
5. Install and test the system.
6. Deploy the system by operating, maintaining, and supporting the new system.

Controls over the system development methodology require feasibility checkpoints and authorization of change requests with appropriate approvals and reviews. Controls for the SDLC also include appropriate documentation for each phase of the SDLC. IT auditors audit the SDLC process to verify that appropriate security and controls are used in each SDLC phase.

Program Change Controls The SDLC is also used for software upgrades and modifications. Program change controls include control over SDLC phases for software upgrades and modifications. These controls require appropriate authorization, documentation, and verification of changes made to IT systems and software.

Computer Operations Controls These controls cover acquisition, implementation, and maintenance of system software including the operating system, DBMS, network software, and security software.

Access Security Controls These controls prevent unauthorized access and use of the system, programs, and data. Another example would be data center operations controls, such as backup and recovery procedures.

What Is CAATT?
CAATT refers to computer assisted audit tools and techniques. These are software programs developed to assist auditors. ACL, Audit Command Language, is a specific type of CAATT.

IT Control Frameworks

There are a couple of IT control frameworks that organizations can use to address IT control needs and regulatory requirements. One IT control framework is ISO 27k (or ISO 27000). This framework for IT controls is shown in *Cybersecurity*, Chapter Extension 11. COBIT, another IT control framework, is also included in Chapter 11 Extension.

My Connection...
- Active Review 10.5
- Short Exercise 10.25
- Short Exercise 10.30

What Are Service Organization Controls?

Given the dramatic growth in outsourcing services and cloud computing services used by many organizations, the AICPA issued a reporting framework for Service Organization Control (SOC) reports. There are three SOC reports identified simply as:

- SOC 1
- SOC 2
- SOC 3

Service organizations are external organizations that perform services to the company being audited. For example, if your company outsources its IT services to a cloud computing provider, the cloud provider is considered a service organization to your company. When your company is being audited and your company's controls evaluated, your auditor also needs to consider the controls that the service company does (or doesn't) have. Also consider that the service organization that provides you with cloud computing services may outsource some of its services as well, such as database services or security services it purchases from other service organizations.

Your company may have superb internal controls and compliance. However, if your cloud service provider (or its outsourced service providers) do not have adequate controls, this deficiency might result in your customer credit card numbers being hacked, for example. Due to the increase in outsourcing and cloud computing services, concern about service organization controls, addressed in SOC 1, SOC 2, and SOC 3, have also increased.

SOC 1

Does the outsourcing organization that provides services to your company have controls relevant to your internal controls related to your financial reporting? If the answer is yes, then your auditor may need a SOC 1 report from the service organization to complete your audit.

SOC 1 reports are issued by the service organization to report on its controls relevant to your company's internal control over financial reporting. Statement on Standards for Attestation No. 16 (SSAE 16) provides guidance for preparing the SOC 1 report. SSAE 16 replaces Statement on Auditing Standards No. 70 (SAS 70).

There are two types of SOC 1 reports:

- **SOC 1 Type 1 Report:** The service auditor provides an opinion regarding fairness of the service organization's description of controls, but does not test the controls or express an opinion regarding the effectiveness of the controls.
- **SOC 1 Type 2 Report:** The Type 2 report includes Type 1 information plus the service auditor tests controls and expresses an opinion regarding the effectiveness of the controls.

Which report would you prefer to receive from your service organization providing you with cloud computing services? Type 1 or Type 2? Would you like to know that your service organization has controls (Type 1)? Or that the service organization has controls and the controls have been tested and operate effectively (Type 2)?

Examples of service organizations that might fall under the SOC 1 could include employee benefit plans or actuarial services.

SOC 2

Does the outsourcing organization that provides services to your company have controls outside those related to your financial reporting? If the answer is yes, then your auditor may a need a SOC 2 or 3 report from the service organization to complete your audit.

SOC 2 reports are issued by the service organization to report on controls other than those relevant to your internal control related to financial reporting. SOC 2 reports are prepared by the service organization's auditors using Attestation Standards (AT) Section 101. To attest is to express an opinion. So this attestation standard provides guidance to accounting professionals expressing an opinion on SOC 2 reports. In addition to AT Section 101, the AICPA audit guide, *Reports on Controls at a Service Organization over Security, Availability, Processing, Integrity, Confidentiality, or Privacy*, is also used when preparing a SOC 2 report.

Again, there are Type 1 and Type 2 for SOC 2 reports:

- **SOC 2 Type 1 Report:** The service auditor provides an opinion regarding fairness of the service organization's description of controls, but does not test the controls or express an opinion regarding the effectiveness of the controls.
- **SOC 2 Type 2 Report:** The Type 2 report includes Type 1 information plus the service auditor tests controls and expresses an opinion regarding the effectiveness of the controls.

Examples of service organizations that might fall under the SOC 2 could include cloud computing services.

SOC 3

As with SOC 2 reports, SOC 3 reports are prepared by the outsourcing organization that provides services to your company and report on controls outside those related to your financial reporting. The main difference between SOC 2 and SOC 3 reports is the guidance used when preparing the reports. SOC 3 reports are conducted by the service organization's auditors using Attestation Standards (AT) Section 101 and prepared using the AICPA Trust Services.

> **My Connection …**
> - Active Review 10.10
> - Short Exercise 10.35
> - It's Your Call 10.44

AICPA's Trust Services

Trust Services is a framework developed jointly by the American Institute of Certified Public Accountants (AICPA) and the Canadian Institute of Chartered Accountants (CICA). Originally issued in 2006, *Trust Services Principles, Criteria, and Illustrations* was updated in 2009. Trust Services principles provide guidance for practitioners providing attestation and/or advisory services for IT systems including e-commerce. The Trust Services include SysTrust and WebTrust. SysTrust is an assurance service for enterprise systems and databases while WebTrust includes WebTrust Confidentiality, WebTrust Online Privacy, and WebTrust Consumer Protection.

The Trust Services framework defines IT systems as consisting of the following five components:

- Infrastructure including computer and network hardware
- Software consisting of operating software, application software, and utilities
- People who are involved in operating and using the system including users and IT professionals
- Procedures consisting of the automated and manual procedures in operating the system
- Data such as transaction data, databases, tables, and files

Trust Services framework for evaluating information systems is based on five principles of security, availability, processing integrity, confidentiality, and online privacy.

Security. The system is protected against unauthorized access, both physical and logical.

Availability. The system is available for use as committed or agreed. This principle does not address system functionality (the functions performed by the system) or usability (how easy the system is to use). The principle, instead, addresses system availability (whether the system is available to use).

Processing Integrity. System processing is accurate, timely, complete, valid, and authorized. Processing integrity is different than data integrity. For example, an organization's system processing may be accurate; however, the data imported from external sites may contain errors, resulting in loss of data integrity.

Confidentiality. Confidential information is protected as committed or agreed. Whereas personal information is defined and subject to privacy regulations in a number of countries, confidential information is less well-defined. In business transactions, confidential information is often exchanged, intellectual property shared, and contractual information revealed. This principle refers to the organization's ability to protect designated confidential information as mutually agreed. The next chapter on Cybersecurity will cover in depth some of the specific IT measures used for ensuring confidentiality of data during transmission and storage.

Privacy. Personal information is collected, used, retained, disclosed, and destroyed in conformity with the commitments in the entity's privacy notice and with criteria set forth in GAPP issued by the AICPA and CICA. GAPP are essential to the proper protection and management of personal information. They are based on internationally known fair information practices included in many privacy laws and regulations of various jurisdictions around the world and recognized as good privacy practices.

Four aspects of the preceding principles of security, availability, processing integrity, confidentiality, and privacy are addressed in the Trust Services framework:

- Policies. The organization has defined and documented policies for the specific principle.
- Communications. The organization has communicated its policies to responsible parties and authorized users.
- Procedures. In accordance with its policies, the organization implemented procedures to achieve defined objectives.
- Monitoring. The organization monitors the system and takes corrective action to maintain compliance with its policies.

The purpose of this framework is to provide guiding principles for accounting practitioners who provide attestation and consulting services that involve IT-enabled systems, addressing both the risks and opportunities of IT (infotech.aicpa.org, 2009).

Ten Generally Accepted Privacy Principles

1. Management. The entity defines, documents, communicates, and assigns accountability for its privacy policies and procedures.
2. Notice. The entity provides notice about its privacy policies and procedures and identifies the purposes for which personal information is collected, used, retained, and disclosed.
3. Choice and consent. The entity describes the choices available to the individual and obtains implicit or explicit consent with respect to the collection, use, and disclosure of personal information.
4. Collection. The entity collects personal information only for the purposes identified in the notice.
5. Use and retention. The entity limits the use of personal information to the purposes identified in the notice and for which the individual has provided implicit or explicit consent. The entity retains personal information only for as long as necessary to fulfill the stated purposes.

6. **Access.** The entity provides individuals with access to their personal information for review and update.
7. **Disclosure to third parties.** The entity discloses personal information to third parties only for the purposes identified in the notice and with the implicit or explicit consent of the individual.
8. **Security for privacy.** The entity protects personal information against unauthorized access (both physical and logical).
9. **Quality.** The entity maintains accurate, complete, and relevant personal information for the purposes identified in the notice.
10. **Monitoring and enforcement.** The entity monitors compliance with its privacy policies and procedures and has procedures to address privacy-related complaints and disputes *(Trust Services Principles, Criteria, and Illustrations, 2009).*

Chapter Highlights

What is SOX and how does it affect the accounting system? Sarbanes-Oxley (SOX) legislation resulted from the accounting scandals of 2002. This legislation requires organizations to use recognized frameworks for internal control. As a result, many organizations adopted COSO's *Internal Control—Integrated Framework* and the COBIT framework for IT controls.

What is IT control architecture? IT control architecture is a blueprint for IT controls in the organization. This blueprint

(Figure 10.6) shows that internal control impacts IT at three levels within the organization resulting in three levels of IT controls:

1. Entity-level IT controls
2. Application controls
3. IT general controls

Chapter Extension 10

Code of Ethics Institute of Internal Auditors

The Institute of Internal Auditors (IIA) provides the following code of ethics that internal auditors are expected to follow in the conduct and performance of internal audits. The purpose of the code of ethics is to promote an ethical culture in the internal audit profession (Institute of Internal Auditors, 2009).

Code of Ethics

Principles
Internal auditors are expected to apply and uphold the following principles:

1. **Integrity**
   The integrity of internal auditors establishes trust and thus provides the basis for reliance on their judgment.
2. **Objectivity**
   Internal auditors exhibit the highest level of professional objectivity in gathering, evaluating, and communicating information about the activity or process being examined. Internal auditors make a balanced assessment of all the relevant circumstances and are not unduly influenced by their own interests or by others in forming judgments.
3. **Confidentiality**
   Internal auditors respect the value and ownership of information they receive and do not disclose information

without appropriate authority unless there is a legal or professional obligation to do so.
4. **Competency**
   Internal auditors apply the knowledge, skills, and experience needed in the performance of internal audit services.

Rules of Conduct

1. **Integrity**
   Internal auditors:
   1.1. Shall perform their work with honesty, diligence, and responsibility.
   1.2. Shall observe the law and make disclosures expected by the law and the profession.
   1.3. Shall not knowingly be a party to any illegal activity, or engage in acts that are discreditable to the profession of internal auditing or to the organization.
   1.4. Shall respect and contribute to the legitimate and ethical objectives of the organization.

2. **Objectivity**
Internal auditors:
2.1. Shall not participate in any activity or relationship that may impair or be presumed to impair their unbiased assessment. This participation includes those activities or relationships that may be in conflict with the interests of the organization.
2.2. Shall not accept anything that may impair or be presumed to impair their professional judgment.
2.3. Shall disclose all material facts known to them that, if not disclosed, may distort the reporting of activities under review.

3. **Confidentiality**
Internal auditors:
3.1. Shall be prudent in the use and protection of information acquired in the course of their duties.
3.2. Shall not use information for any personal gain or in any manner that would be contrary to the law or detrimental to the legitimate and ethical objectives of the organization.

4. **Competency**
Internal auditors:
4.1. Shall engage only in those services for which they have the necessary knowledge, skills, and experience.
4.2. Shall perform internal audit services in accordance with the International Standards for the Professional Practice of Internal Auditing.
4.3. Shall continually improve their proficiency and the effectiveness and quality of their services.

Accounting System Insights

Insight No. 19 In the house of IT controls, there are three zones: (1) top management: entity-level IT controls, (2) business processes: application controls, and (3) IT services: IT general controls.

Active Review

Study less. Learn more. Make connections.

10.1 Refer to the chapter opener, *Meet a Ponzi Scheme.* In your opinion, how much responsibility should Madoff's accountant bear for the billions lost?

10.2 Discuss earning management issues and its relationship with fraud.

10.3 Discuss how the Sarbanes-Oxley Act of 2002 affected organizations' internal control.

10.4 Compare the internal control element of the Sarbanes-Oxley Act of 2002 with COSO's *Internal Control—Integrated Framework.*

10.5 Discuss how the three levels of IT controls relate to three levels within an organization.

10.6 Discuss how an organization's network firewall fits into the three levels of IT controls.

10.7 Discuss how the Sarbanes-Oxley Act of 2002 affected internal control for publicly traded companies.

10.8 What positions within an organization are considered executive management? Discuss their roles in entity-level IT controls.

10.9 What are the five internal control components specified by COSO's *Internal Control—Integrated Framework*? How do COSO's internal control components relate to IT controls?

10.10 Discuss control issues with outsourcing IT services to a cloud computing services provider. How can organizations verify service organizations' controls?

Key Terms Check

Understanding the language used at the crossroads of accounting and IT is key to your success.

10.11 Match the following terms and definitions.

a. motive
b. opportunity
c. means
d. misappropriation of assets
e. fraudulent financial reporting
f. corruption
g. prevent
h. detect
i. correct

_____ 1. Access to the asset or financial statements in order to carry out the fraud

_____ 2. Controls designed to discover fraud when it occurs and alert management

_____ 3. Includes misstating financial statements to meet earnings targets

_____ 4. Includes illegal acts such as bribery, kickbacks, money laundering, and rigging bids

_____ 5. Knowledge or skills that permit the perpetrator to commit the crime

_____ 6. Investigate and take corrective action to remedy harm caused

_____ 7. Reason for committing the fraud, such as financial difficulties

_____ 8. Involves theft of assets for personal gain

_____ 9. Controls designed to prevent or reduce the likelihood of a fraud risk occurring

10.12 Match the following terms and definitions.

a. entity-level IT controls
b. application controls
c. IT general controls
d. operational controls
e. financial controls
f. compliance controls
g. manual controls
h. automated controls
i. input controls
j. processing controls
k. output controls
l. hybrid controls

_____ 1. Controls performed without the assistance of technology

_____ 2. Controls performed automatically by computers

_____ 3. Processes, organizational structure, and leadership for IT to support an organization's business strategy and objectives, such as internal audits

_____ 4. A combination of manual and automated controls

_____ 5. Controls embedded within business process applications, such as accounting software controls

_____ 6. Controls that apply to IT services in general and ensure continued IT operation and availability, such as change and access controls

_____ 7. Controls to ensure that external financial reports are prepared on a timely basis in compliance with laws, regulations, or contractual agreements

_____ 8. Controls to ensure that operations are completed appropriately, such as the timing of cash disbursements to ensure that late fees are avoided

_____ 9. Controls to maintain confidentiality of information in accordance with all applicable laws and regulations

_____ 10. Controls to ensure that amounts have been processed appropriately

_____ 11. Controls over data entered into the system

_____ 12. Controls to ensure that reports are distributed only to appropriate users

10.13 Match the following terms and definitions.

a. audit of internal control
b. audit of financial statements
c. IT audit
d. integrated audit
e. material weakness
f. significant deficiency
g. COSO

____ 1. Deficiency that results in a reasonable possibility that a material misstatement of financial statements will not be prevented or detected on a timely basis
____ 2. A deficiency in internal control over financial reporting that is less severe than a material weakness
____ 3. Tests of controls to obtain evidence that internal control over financial reporting has operated effectively
____ 4. Integrates an audit of internal control with an audit of financial statements
____ 5. Audit of IT controls
____ 6. Tests of controls to assess risk and substantive procedures to collect evidence regarding the accuracy, completeness, and validity of data produced by the accounting system
____ 7. Committee of Sponsoring Organizations of the Treadway Commission

10.14 Match the following terms and definitions.

a. segregation of duties
b. independent reconciliation of assets and accounting records
c. physical controls
d. information technology (IT) controls
e. ongoing monitoring
f. separate evaluations
g. Service Organization Control

____ 1. An example would be controls over purchasing activities
____ 2. Controls to ensure appropriate information processing, authorization, and data integrity
____ 3. Reports your auditor may need from the service organization to complete your audit
____ 4. Divides authorization, recording, and asset custody among different individuals
____ 5. An example would be assessing internal controls with an internal audit
____ 6. Control activities such as bank reconciliations and inventory counts
____ 7. Controls to provide for physical security of assets

Practice Test

10.15 Which of the following is not considered fraud?

a. Error in financial statements
b. Bribery
c. Stealing merchandise
d. Misstating financial statements

10.16 The three components of the fraud triangle are:

a. People, technology, database
b. Opportunity, database, accounting processes
c. Opportunity, motive, means
d. Motive, employees, means

10.17 Which of the following is NOT a key component of the effective fraud risk management?

a. Prevent
b. Evaluate
c. Detect
d. Correct

10.18 Which of the following is considered as a top behavioral red flag of a fraudster?

a. Buying a new house
b. Vacationing in Tuscany for a month
c. Having a large dollar amount of life insurance
d. Having all family members and relatives as customers

10.19 Which SOX section requires corporate management to certify reports filed with the SEC, such as the annual 10-K and quarterly 10-Q?

a. Section 302. Corporate Responsibility for Financial Reports
b. Section 404. Management Assessment of Internal Controls
c. Section 806. Protection for Employees of Publicly Traded Companies Who Provide Evidence of Fraud
d. Section 906. Corporate Responsibility for Financial Reports

10.20 Which of the following audits requires the auditors to conduct tests of controls and substantive procedures?

a. Audit of financial statement
b. Audit of internal control
c. Integral audit
d. All of the above

10.21 Internal control in the *information and communication systems relevant to financial reporting* category does NOT include:

a. Monitoring and control
b. Valuation
c. Classification
d. Record transactions for the appropriate period

10.22 Which organization did the Sarbanes-Oxley Act of 2002 create?

a. American Accounting Association (AAA)
b. Public Company Accounting Oversight Board (PCAOB)
c. Institute of Management Accountants (IMA)
d. Committee of Sponsoring Organizations of the Treadway Commission (COSO)

10.23 In the COSO *Internal Control—Integrated Framework*, control activities do not include:

a. Segregation of duties
b. Information technology
c. Project management
d. Physical controls

10.24 According to Accounting Insight No. 19, the three zones in the house of IT controls are:

a. Top Management, Business Process Applications, and IT Services
b. SOX, COSO, and COBIT
c. Top Management, IT Management, Operations
d. IT Control, Internal Control, External Controls

Exercises

Each Exercise relates to one of the major questions addressed in the chapter and is labeled with the question number in green.

Short Exercises

Warm up with these short exercises.

10.25 Match each of the following control items to the type of control. **(Q10.4)**

a. Entity-level IT controls
b. Application controls
c. IT general controls

____ 1. Computer operation controls
____ 2. Internal audit
____ 3. Program development controls
____ 4. Data validation for data entry
____ 5. Risk assessment
____ 6. Access security controls
____ 7. Record count
____ 8. Program change controls
____ 9. Auto-numbered invoices

10.26 Match each of the following control activities to the type of control activity. **(Q10.3)**

a. Segregation of duties
b. Reconcile assets to accounts
c. Physical controls

____ 1. Take a physical inventory count and compare it to the inventory balance in the accounting system.
____ 2. The cashier does not have access to the accounting records.
____ 3. Security cameras
____ 4. The sales clerks in a retail store do not have access to the accounting system.
____ 5. Bank reconciliations
____ 6. Key cards to access offices

10.27 Match each of the following application control objectives to the appropriate transaction cycle. **(Q10.4)**

a. Purchasing cycle
b. Sales cycle
c. Payroll cycle
d. Banking/Cash
e. Financial cycle

____ 1. All goods shipped are accurately billed in the proper period.
____ 2. Record cash receipts on accounts receivable completely and accurately.
____ 3. Enter and process time worked accurately.
____ 4. Ensure that items ordered are received on a timely basis.
____ 5. Disburse cash only for authorized purchases.
____ 6. System controls are in place for appropriate approval of write-offs.
____ 7. Record tax payments completely and accurately.
____ 8. Prevent unauthorized use of purchase orders.
____ 9. Process only valid customer orders.
____ 10. Reconcile accounting records with physical assets.

10.28 The following exercise relates to application control objectives for the purchasing cycle. (Q10.4)

1. List at least three application control objectives for the purchasing cycle.
2. Give an example of how the associated IT controls would be implemented for these control objectives.
3. How would this improve internal control?

10.29 The following exercise relates to application control objectives for the sales cycle. (Q10.4)

1. List at least three application controls used in the sales cycle.
2. Give an example of how the associated IT controls would be implemented for these control objectives.
3. How would this improve internal control?

10.30 The following exercise relates to application control objectives for the payroll cycle. (Q10.4)

1. List at least two application controls used in the payroll cycle.
2. Give an example of how the associated IT controls would be implemented for these control objectives.
3. How would this improve internal control?

10.31 The following exercise relates to application control objectives for the financial cycle. (Q10.4)

1. List at least two application controls used in the financial cycle.
2. Give an example of how the associated IT controls would be implemented for these control objectives.
3. How would this improve internal control?

10.32 Imagine that a CPA firm performing an audit of your company's financial statements sends Midwestern Bank a request for confirmation of your company's cash balance. However, Midwestern Bank uses a cloud service organization to provide confirmation responses to the CPA firm.

As part of the same audit, the CPA firm requests a confirmation from Aroma Coffee of the amount Aroma Coffee owes your company. Aroma Coffee uses the same cloud service organization used by Midwestern Bank to confirm the amount that Aroma Coffee owes your company. (Q10.4, 10.5)

Explain how the cloud service organization can provide assurance to your company, Midwestern Bank, and other customers regarding

a. the effectiveness of controls it implements on its customer's financial reporting.
b. the privacy, confidentiality, security, availability, and processing integrity of the cloud system that generates the confirmations.

(Source: http://www.aicpa.org)

10.33 EspressoCoffee uses EDA Bank to invest. When the EspressoCoffee financial statements are audited, the auditor needs information about the EspressoCoffee internal control over financial reporting, including controls at the EDA Bank that affect EspressoCoffee's financial statements. (Q10.5)

a. What type of information does the SOC 1 Type 1 report include?
b. What type of information does the SOC 1 Type 2 report include?

10.34 Think of an authentic enterprise of your choice. What internal control procedures does the enterprise use? Does the enterprise use any IT controls? (Q10.2, 10.3, 10.4)

10.35 CCS Inc. is a software as a service (SaaS) or cloud service organization that offers various computing services for your company. What types of information does the SOC 2 report include? (Q10.5)

It's Your Call

This is your training ground. These scenarios provide you with the opportunity to use your knowledge and professional skills.

10.36 You notice your coworker, another accountant, emailing confidential accounting documents to an outside supplier who is bidding on a contract. What action should you take? Explain your reasons. **(Q10.1)**

10.37 According to company policy, employees are not permitted to remove computers or external hard drives from the office because of the sensitivity of the data. It is now Friday afternoon at 5 PM. Because your high-priority project that is due Monday is not finished, you decide to take the external hard drive home so that you can meet the deadline.

On the way home Friday evening, you stop at a gas station for a snack and refuel. When you return to your car, the hard drive that was on the front passenger seat is gone. What would you do? **(Q10.2, 10.3, 10.4)**

10.38 You are the internal auditor for a company conducting internal audit tests. You discover that the company is misusing federal grant funds. Instead of the funds being used for the designated purpose, they are being used to fund vacation trips for management. What would you do? **(Q10.1, 10.2, 10.3)**

10.39 You are an external auditor conducting an internal audit for a client company. You discover that the company is misusing federal grant funds. Instead of the funds being used for the designated purpose, they are being used to fund vacation trips for management. What would you do? **(Q10.1, 10.2, 10.3)**

10.40 As an auditor, you are assigned to investigate a possible fraudulent situation characterized by the way the sales cycle application is conducted. During the course of investigation of the sales cycle processes, you determined the following when analyzing the generate invoice process map:

- Items unit prices are extracted from the item table.
- The number of items was multiplied by unit prices to calculate subtotals.
- A salesperson verifies possible discount and approves the discount amount.
- Tax was added.
- The shipment amount was extracted from the shipment table and added to the sales amount.
- The salesperson verifies invoice form on the computer screen. The salesperson has full access to the invoice form and can change any value on it.
- The invoice was printed after being verified by the salesperson, and account receivable tables were updated.

Prepare a report of your analysis of the generate invoice process, and include manual and automated controls situations as a possible indicator of fraud. **(Q10.1, 10.2, 10.3, 10.4)**

10.41 As an auditor, you are assigned to investigate the bonus system put in place by a retail store company. During the course of investigation of the bonus system process, you identified the following:

- $1,000 checks were issued and sent to privileged customers.
- The date on the checks was marked one month after the date being sent, so the check amounts were deposited a month after they were received by customers.
- Bonus policy requires customers to spend the $1,000 amount in one of the company's store within three days after receiving the checks.
- Customers should pay with cash or credit card for the purchased merchandise.

Prepare a report of your analysis of the bonus system process, and include manual and automated controls situations as a possible indicator of fraud. (Q10.1, 10.2, 10.3, 10.4)

10.42 In a store such as an electronics store, a cashier and a customer may conspire to steal items in the following manner:

- Customer brings many items to the cashier
- Cashier scans only a few items
- Customer pays for scanned items and leaves store with all items
- Later, cashier and customer sell stolen items for personal gain

As an auditor, you are assigned to investigate this situation. In your report to your supervisor, include what type of application controls are violated. How this fraudulent act detected, and how can it be prevented? (Q10.1, 10.2, 10.3, 10.4)

10.43 In your company, the payroll process is as follows:
- Employees return their time cards to the supervisor.
- At the end of the moth, supervisors send the time cards to the payroll department.
- The payroll department calculates employees' pay, prints paychecks, and sends checks to the supervisors.
- Supervisors distribute payroll checks to employees.
- According to the company regulations, supervisors must return unclaimed checks to the payroll department.

Your boss has asked you to evaluate the payroll process and find the possible fraudulent acts loopholes. In your report to your boss, include what type of application controls are violated. How this possible fraudulent act detected, and how can it be prevented? (Q10.4)

10.44 Your boss has asked you to prepare a report on control issues with outsourcing your company's financial reporting to a cloud service organization. Your company also needs to move its operational data to the same cloud service organization, he added. After a few calls to the IT department, you realize that the cloud service organization provides Software-as-a-Service (SaaS) and Infrastructure-as-a-Service. What are you going to include in your report? Prepare a summary and outline your findings. (Q10.5)

Tech in Practice

These technology in practice exercises are perfect for both individuals and teams.

Tech Exercises

Sharpen your skills with these technology exercises. Watch these software videos at www.pearsonhighered.com/kay.

10.45
Tech Tool: Spreadsheet Software
EspressoCoffee has asked for your assistance in assessing spreadsheet controls.

1. Select a specific spreadsheet software, such as Microsoft Excel, iWork Numbers, or Google Docs.
2. List the application controls embedded in the software.
3. Discuss any deficiencies in controls that you see.

10.46

Tech Tool: Accounting Software

EspressoCoffee has asked for your assistance in assessing controls in accounting software it is considering for adoption.

1. Select a specific accounting software, such as QuickBooks, Peachtree, or SAP Business One.
2. Identify the application controls embedded in the software.
3. Discuss any deficiencies in controls that you see.

10.47

Tech Tool: Database Software

EspressoCoffee's accounting professionals have asked for your assistance in assessing controls in the database software they use.

1. Using Microsoft Access database software, identify the application controls embedded in the software.
2. Discuss any deficiencies in controls that you see.

10.48

Tech Tool: Spreadsheet Software
Software Video: Spreadsheet Controls

EspressoCoffee has asked for your assistance in using formula auditing to improve spreadsheet controls.

1. Download the data file for this exercise.
2. Watch the software video for spreadsheet controls.
3. Use formula auditing with the spreadsheet data file to trace precedents for the cell labeled.
4. Identify any issues or errors. Print the spreadsheet. Clear precedents.
5. Use formula auditing with the spreadsheet data file to trace dependents for the cell labeled.
6. Identify any issues or errors. Print the spreadsheet. Clear dependents.
7. Use formula auditing to trace the error in the spreadsheet in the cell labeled.
8. Print the spreadsheet. How would you document the error? How would you fix this error?

Go Online

In the fast-paced world of technology, your skill at finding answers fast can be vital. Go online and experience typical assignments you may encounter as a professional.

10.49 You are the accounting representative on the IT project team for improving spreadsheet security and controls. You have been asked to investigate third-party add-in software for spreadsheets to improve controls. Go online and research spreadsheet add-ins, such as SpreadsheetProfessionals, used to improve spreadsheet controls. Write an email to your team, summarizing the software and features.

10.50 You are a staff accountant for a regional CPA firm. The partners of the firm are conducting a series of seminars for current and prospective clients. One of the partners has asked you to do research for the next seminar on the topic of COSO's internal control framework. Go online and search for information. Prepare a short presentation that the partner could use at the seminar.

10.51 You are a staff accountant for a regional CPA firm. The partners of the firm are conducting a series of seminars for current and prospective clients. One of the partners has asked you to do research for the next seminar on the topic of COBIT's framework for IT controls. Go online and search for information. Prepare a short presentation that the partner could use at the seminar.

10.52 You have been assigned to the project team to evaluate IT controls. The IT professionals specifically asked for you to be on the team because of your accounting and IT background. They have asked you to make a presentation at the next team meeting about the three levels of IT controls:

1. Entity-level controls
2. Application controls
3. IT general controls

Go online and search for information about these three types of IT controls. Draft a short email to send to the team leader, summarizing your findings and obtaining his feedback.

10.53 You have been assigned to gather information and prepare a presentation on service organization control reports. Your presentation must include information about SOC 1, SOC 2, and SOC 3 reports.
Go online and search for information about these three types of reports.

Technology Projects

These technology projects are perfect for both individuals and teams.

Tech Tool: Spreadsheet Software
iSportDesign would like to improve security and controls for its business processes.

Your deliverables for the project include the following:
Deliverable 1. Prepare a report on issues that should be considered by iSportDesign regarding using a service organization for all or part of its application, database, and reporting services.
Deliverable 2. Prepare a report regarding spreadsheet control.

Visit www.pearsonhighered.com/kay to download Technology Project 10 instructions.

11

Cybersecurity

How Secure Is Your Credit Card? Meet Heartland.

Heartland Payment Systems processed credit card transactions for Visa and MasterCard, approximately 100 million transactions per month for 175,000 merchants. When Heartland was contacted by Visa and MasterCard about suspicious fraudulent credit card transactions, Heartland initiated an investigation.

In January 2009, Heartland disclosed that a security breach had given hackers access to millions of debit and credit card numbers. Heartland was audited and certified by Payment Card Industry Data Security Standards (PCI-DSS), a global security standard for any company that has access to credit cards. The Heartland security breach demonstrated that even secure systems can be vulnerable.

Hackers and intruders are continuously searching for the most vulnerable point in an enterprise's cybersecurity. In the Heartland case, the sophisticated cyberattack included a sniffer, or data stealing program, planted by the hackers to intercept data in transit. The sniffer intercepted credit and debit card information as it traveled over Heartland's network (Davie, 2009).

Crossroads

At the crossroads of accounting and IT, accounting systems contain some of an enterprise's most confidential data. The IT used in the accounting system can actually create vulnerabilities to cyberattacks of this confidential data.

My Questions

Q 11.1	What are the 10 domains of cybersecurity?
Q 11.2	What are cyberlaw and cybercrime?
Q 11.3	What are information security and risk management?
Q 11.4	What are security architecture and design?
Q 11.5	What is telecommunications, network, and Internet security?
Q 11.6	What is access control?
Q 11.7	What is operations security?
Q 11.8	What is physical and environmental security?
Q 11.9	What is application security?
Q 11.10	What are business continuity and disaster recovery?
Q 11.11	What is cryptography?
Q 11.12	Why does cybersecurity for accounting require prudence?

What Are the 10 Domains of Cybersecurity?

When was the last time you used a debit or credit card? Did you think about the security to protect your debit or credit information?

In a world of fast-changing information and communication technology, the need for knowledge of information security has never been greater. The complexity and size of integrated enterprise systems makes safeguarding information assets a growing challenge.

Cybersecurity combines people, processes, and technology to continually monitor vulnerabilities and respond proactively to secure the system. Cybersecurity is a highly technical, specialized field, yet the confidential nature of data stored in accounting systems puts increasing pressure on accounting professionals to understand IT security.

A growing number of accounting professionals responsible for the security of confidential accounting data are obtaining the CISSP (Certified Information Systems Security Professionals) certification. This internationally recognized certification is administered by the (ISC)² (International Information Systems Security Certification Consortium). (ISC)² developed the 10-domain Common Body of Knowledge (CBK) for IT security and controls.

In this chapter, to make it easier for you to get up to speed quickly on this critical topic of cybersecurity, we share with you a summary of these 10 domains (isc2.org, 2009).

> ### Leave It in the Room...
> Are you familiar with hotel key cards? Did you know your personal data, such as home address and credit card number, are stored on those cards?
>
> As instructed, do you leave your key card in the hotel room when you check out? If so, you may want to reconsider.
>
> Security advisors recommend taking the cards with you and shredding them.

> ### Your Competitive Advantage...
> Familiarity with the 10 domains of the Common Body of Knowledge for information security and control provides you with a useful tool for understanding and communicating with IT security professionals responsible for the security of accounting systems.

Cybersecurity 10 Domains

	Domain	Domain Description
1	**L**egal, regulations, compliance, and investigations	Focuses on cybercrime and cyberlaw.
2	**I**nformation security and risk management	Focuses on preventive and proactive policies and procedures to secure information assets.
3	**S**ecurity architecture and design	Addresses security for IT architecture.
4	**T**elecommunications, network, and Internet security	Addresses security for data transmissions.
5	**A**ccess control	Addresses security for access to computers, networks, routers, and databases.
6	**O**perations security	Refers to activities and procedures to keep IT operations running securely.
7	**P**hysical and environmental security	Addresses physical security of facilities and IT components (hardware and software).
8	**A**pplication security	Addresses security and control for application software, such as accounting and spreadsheet software.
9	**B**usiness continuity and disaster recovery	Addresses backup and disaster recovery plans.
10	**C**ryptography	Focuses on encryption as a tool to secure data during transmission and storage.

Try this mnemonic to recall the 10 domins

Learn Info Security Tech, Avoid Oops Please, Accountants Beware Cybercrime!

FIGURE 11.1
Cybersecurity

Each of the 10 domains addresses different aspects of cybersecurity (Figure 11.1). Next, we explore how the following domains relate to the security and control of accounting systems.

1. Legal, regulations, compliance, and investigations
2. Information security and risk management
3. Security architecture and design
4. Telecommunications, network, and Internet security
5. Access control
6. Operations security
7. Physical and environmental security
8. Application security
9. Business continuity and disaster recovery
10. Cryptography

> **My Connection...**
> How do I study less and learn more? Make connections. Try Active Review 11.6.

What Are Cyberlaw and Cybercrime?

The legal, regulations, compliance, and investigations domain focuses on cybercrime and cyberlaw. **Cybercrimes** are crimes connected to information assets and IT. **Cyberlaw** relates to the laws and regulations to prevent, investigate, and prosecute cybercrimes.

Cybercrime

Cybercrime is on the rise. Who is behind the data breaches? Increasingly, cybercrime is traced to sophisticated organized crime that steals data for fraudulent use. Verizon's 2012 Data Breach Investigations Report found that 83% of the breaches were tied to organized criminal groups. The report concluded: "Bottom line: most data thieves are professional criminals deliberately trying to steal information they can turn to cash" (Verizon, 2012).

Verizon reported that 98% of the breaches came from external sources, and only 4% implicated internal employees. A significant development was the increased number of attacks from activist groups, accounting for 58% of all data theft.

How do cybersecurity breaches occur? Verizon's 2012 report found that 81% of data breaches were linked to hacking, often using stolen or guessed credentials to gain access. Malware (malicious software) was utilized in 69% of the breaches. Only 10% of the breaches occurred via physical attacks, such as theft of a company laptop. Successful data breaches may involve multiple means of attack and exploit mistakes made by the victim. For example, an employee of the victim organization might open an attachment in a phishing email that loads malware on the employee computer. The malware creates a backdoor for the hacker to gain and maintain access so the hacker can view email and other confidential data. The hacker may be able to gain access to the network and data stored on servers, providing an opportunity for him to access intellectual property and confidential customer information (Verizon, 2012).

Next, we will explore a few different types of cyberattacks. Some of the more well-known cyberattacks are salami, social engineering, and dumpster diving.

SALAMI Salami attacks, also known as skimming, usually target the accounting department. A common example of salami attacks is rounding additional digits in an interest calculation into the attacker's own account. For example, when interest is calculated on a customer's bank account with a balance of $103 at 5.27% interest, the interest amount equals $5.4281. Interest of $5.42 would be added to the customer's account. In a salami attack, the difference of $0.0081 ($5.4281 − $5.42) would be transferred to the attacker. Salami attacks are typically for very small amounts over numerous accounts that accumulate into significant sums.

SOCIAL ENGINEERING Social engineering attacks involve manipulating and tricking an individual into divulging confidential information to be used for fraudulent purposes. As an example, attackers might send out emails posing as the company IT department. The email will

---

Hack, Pump, and Dump...
What is hack, pump, and dump?

In April 2010, an Indian national was sentenced to 81 months in prison for conspiracy in an international hack, pump, and dump scheme.

1. Hack into unsuspecting online brokerage accounts.
2. Pump up the price of selected stocks using the funds in the unsuspecting person's brokerage account. These selected stocks were ones that the co-conspirators owned themselves.
3. Dump the stock from the unsuspecting brokerage account holders...after the co-conspirators had sold their stock at a greatly increased profit.

Coffee and Wireless?
Do you like to use the wireless network at your favorite coffee shop? Do you enter your passwords when you are using the wireless network? If an attacker is using a password sniffer, he or she can capture your password as it is transmitted over the unsecured wireless network.

Would You Like to Know More?
For more information about the latest cybercrimes, visit www.cybercrime.gov.

How Much Is Stolen Data Worth?

There is so much stolen magnetic-stripe data available on the underground markets that prices for it have dropped from between $10 and $16 per record in mid-2007 to less than 50 cents (Verizon Business 2009 Data Breach Investigations Report).

We Need to Talk....

What do you say when your stock broker calls and asks if you've been buying $500,000 of penny stocks...when you haven't been?

When this happened to one unsuspecting accountant, his response was "We need to talk."

The FBI was called in and discovered that while on a recent vacation, the accountant had checked his brokerage account from a hotel computer. When he had logged into the computer, his password and user ID had been stolen. This permitted cybercriminals to access his brokerage account (hack) and use funds in it to purchase penny stocks, driving up the price (pump). The cybercriminals sold their stocks after making their profits (dump).

Since the cybercriminals didn't actually steal any money from the accountant's brokerage account per se, just used his funds to purchase stocks that lost money, was a crime committed? What do you think?

request that you email back your password and ID in order to reset your account. The attacker then uses the information to hack into the company system.

Pretexting, a form of social engineering, is the act of creating a scenario and using deception for information gathering fraud. For example, because companies typically require only minimal or no client authentication, it is possible for an attacker to impersonate a client. If successful, the attacker can then ask questions to extract information from the company about the client.

Phishing is another type of social engineering to fraudulently obtain confidential information, such as financial data. The attacker fishes for sensitive, private data. An example of phishing is an attacker sending you an email stating that your account will be suspended unless you update your information. The link provided in the email takes you to the attacker's Web site, constructed to appear legitimate, where you are asked to update confidential information. If you enter your information into the Web site, the attacker then uses the information for fraudulent purposes.

DUMPSTER DIVING **Dumpster diving** refers to rummaging through garbage for discarded documents or digital media. The disposal area is often not as closely guarded as office and IT areas, offering easy access. While dumpster diving is unethical, it may not be illegal. An example of dumpster diving is collecting or buying discarded computer hardware and then extracting data left on the media. Even if data has been deleted and the drives reformatted, data can still be extracted. Special wiping software can be used to eliminate any trace of the data, or the hard drive can be permanently disabled by using a power drill to physically drill through it.

PASSWORD SNIFFING **Password sniffing** involves attempts to obtain passwords by sniffing messages sent between computers on the network. Do you use a hotel lobby computer when you travel? If you enter your password to access financial Web sites, such as your bank or brokerage accounts, your password is at risk for password sniffing.

Cyberlaw

Cyberlaw is complex and constantly evolving to meet more sophisticated cyberattacks. Laws related to cybersecurity originate from legislation, regulations, and case law.

LEGISLATION Legislation can be passed by federal or state legislatures specifying civil or criminal penalties. The civil code is enforced through litigation and monetary penalties. The criminal code is enforced by governmental agencies with monetary penalties and prison sentences.

Examples of legislation affecting cybersecurity include the following:

- Sarbanes-Oxley (SOX)
- Health Insurance Portability and Accountability Act (HIPPA)
- Gramm-Leach-Bliley Act of 1999 (GLBA)

- Computer Fraud and Abuse Act
- Federal Privacy Act of 1974
- Basel II
- Payment Card Industry Data Security Standards (PCI-DSS)
- Computer Security Act of 1987
- Economic Espionage Act of 1996
- Employee Privacy Issues
- Federal Information Security Management Act of 2002 (FISMA)
- Dodd-Frank Wall Street Reform and Consumer Protection Act

Many of these acts relate to protecting consumer and patient privacy, specifying penalties if an organization is negligent. Next, we will discuss briefly four pertinent pieces of legislation affecting cyberlaw.

SARBANES-OXLEY As discussed in the prior chapter, Sarbanes-Oxley legislation addresses requirements for proper internal control, including information security and controls. Thus, SOX impacts cybersecurity for financial data and its transmission.

GRAMM-LEACH-BLILEY ACT This legislation requires financial institutions to provide customers with privacy notices and prohibits the institutions from sharing customer information with nonaffiliated third parties. The institution must have adequate cybersecurity to prevent unauthorized sharing of customer data.

PAYMENT CARD INDUSTRY DATA SECURITY STANDARDS PCI-DSS legislation requires organizations that handle credit and debit card data to meet cybersecurity requirements to safeguard the data. These requirements cover not only the storage of payment card data, but also security during transmission of the data. Heartland Payment Systems was required to meet PCI-DSS requirements because it processed payment card transactions for Visa and MasterCard.

FEDERAL INFORMATION SECURITY MANAGEMENT ACT (FISMA) This legislation requires each federal agency to develop, document, and implement an agency-wide information security program. FISMA also pertains to agency contractors, companies, and consultants hired by federal agencies.

Cyber Forensics

Cyber forensics involves collecting, examining, and preserving evidence of cybercrimes. Typically, organizations do not have an in-house cyber forensics team. Most of the time, organizations turn to law enforcement, regulatory agencies, and outside consultants to conduct cyber forensics investigations. For example, when Heartland became aware of a cybersecurity issue, the company hired an outside consultant to investigate.

> **My Connection...**
> • Active Review 11.7

What Are Information Security and Risk Management?

Cybercrimes grab headlines about hackers, identity theft, and stolen credit card numbers. This domain, information security and risk management, consists of the preventive and proactive measures taken to prevent the hacker headlines from happening. Information security consists of the policies and procedures required to secure information assets, including IT hardware, software, and stored data. Information risk management is part of the larger enterprise risk management (ERM) framework covered in the next chapter.

Security Management Principles

Fundamental principles of information security include confidentiality, integrity, and availability (CIA).

Confidentiality. This security principle ensures that sensitive data at each point in information processing is secure and protected from unauthorized access. A confidentiality breach can result in disclosure of sensitive information, such as credit card numbers or Social Security numbers.

Integrity. Data integrity is a security principle that ensures data is accurate and reliable. Lack of data integrity is caused by data alteration, which can occur at any stage in information processing. Data can be altered when entered, transmitted, or extracted.

Availability. This security principle provides an acceptable level of performance so that required data is available as needed by the organization's users, such as its accountants. If data is destroyed by malicious malware, security measures should ensure the system recovers from disruption so data is available for users.

Information Classification

Information has different sensitivity levels for different users. To address this, information is often assigned a classification to designate its level of sensitivity.

INDUSTRY/PRIVATE SECTOR Information sensitivity classification for the private sector includes the following categories:

- Confidential: This classification is for extremely sensitive information. Disclosure would have serious adverse impact on the organization. Confidential information requires the highest level of security in all IT aspects.
- Private: Disclosure of private information could compromise employee or customer privacy. Disclosure would adversely impact the company. Private information requires tight security to protect employee and customer privacy.
- Sensitive: This type of information requires higher than normal security measures to ensure data integrity and security.
- Public: Disclosure of public information would not adversely affect the company. However, it might not be intended for public disclosure.

GOVERNMENT Information sensitivity classification for governmental use includes the following categories:

- Top Secret: This classification is reserved for information that if disclosed would cause grave damage to national security.
- Secret: Unauthorized disclosure could cause serious harm to national security.
- Confidential: Unauthorized disclosure might be harmful to national security.
- Sensitive But Unclassified (SBU): Disclosure could cause serious damage.
- Unclassified: Data is not sensitive nor classified.

The information sensitivity level determines the information security required.

Information Security Management

Information security management involves developing and enforcing security policies, standards, guidelines, and procedures for information. Three types of information security controls are as follows:

- Administrative controls consist of security policies, standards, guidelines, and procedures to screen employees and provide security training.
- Technical or logical controls consist of security policies, standards, guidelines, and procedures for access control and configuration of IT infrastructure.
- Physical controls include facility access control, environmental controls, and intrusion detection.

SDLC...
As you know, SDLC phases are used for developing accounting and other systems.
- Plan
- Analyze
- Design
- Build/Buy
- Install
- Deploy

Systems Development Life Cycle (SDLC) Security

During each phase of the SDLC, information security and control measures should be considered and implemented. A proactive approach is to design security measures into the accounting system as opposed to adding security and controls as an afterthought after the system is built. Examples include the following:

- During the planning phase, develop a threat profile to identify potential threats to the system.
- In the design phase, identify sensitive data storage and transmission.

- During the installation phase, configure the security measures to protect sensitive data in storage and transmission.
- In the deployment phase, conduct internal and external audits to ensure that security policies and procedures are followed.

Security Frameworks

A security framework provides a conceptual structure to address security and control. Security frameworks include the following:

- Control Objectives for Information and Related Technology (COBIT) was developed by Information Systems Audit and Control Association (ISACA) to manage IT security. This framework provides a model for IT governance (policies and procedures for IT security).
- Committee on Sponsoring Organizations of the Treadway Commission (COSO) provides a framework for corporate governance.
- ISO 27000 series, published by the International Organization for Standardization, consists of standards for information security management systems. See Chapter Extension 11 for more information about IT controls and the ISO 27000 series.

> **My Connection...**
> • Active Review 11.2

What Are Security Architecture and Design?

To understand cybersecurity and how to evaluate whether cybersecurity is adequate for an accounting system, a basic understanding of IT architecture proves essential. Businesses depend on computer and network technology for electronic communication, data transfer, funds transfer, and storage of confidential information. Information technology (IT) has become an integral part of business operations. Sales representatives in the field analyzing bid prices on their laptops, accountants closing accounts at year end, customers entering their orders online, and vendors updating shipping status online are all examples of how IT is integrated into business processes.

Next, we share with you what you need to know about IT architecture.

IT Architecture

IT architecture can be compared to architecture for your home. An architectural blueprint for your home shows electrical wiring, plumbing, walls, windows, doors, and closets. IT architecture is similar except that the components are different. Instead of electrical wiring, you have network wiring. Instead of closets, you have data storage. Instead of doors to a house, IT architecture has access points to the enterprise system.

IT architecture consists of architecture for computers, networks, and databases. Computer and network architecture are explored next. Databases are discussed in the application security domain.

Computer Architecture

Computer architecture consists of computer hardware components and computer software. The computer hardware and software interact to perform tasks, such as queries. Today, computers have the capability to multitask, executing more than one program at the same time. Types of computers include the following:

- Supercomputers are powerful, high-speed computers used for complex numerical calculations. For example, NASA uses supercomputers to calculate flight trajectories for space shuttles. Supercomputers can execute millions of instructions per second (MIPS).
- Mainframe computers are large, high-speed computers often used for high-volume transaction processing. IBM is a leading supplier of mainframe computers. Mainframes are often used by companies for maintaining legacy systems.
- Midrange computers (minicomputers) are used for moderate computing power. Midrange computers are used by companies for computer servers, including database servers.

- Microcomputers (personal computers and laptops) are relatively small computers. In contrast to the other types of computers, personal computers are used by one person at a time.
- Mobile devices can include smartphones, such as the iPhone, and other handheld devices, such as the iPad.

Regardless of the type, power, or size of the computer, all the preceding computers have the same basic hardware and software components.

COMPUTER HARDWARE Computer hardware consists of interconnected electronic devices. These devices execute software commands, store data, and transfer data. Computer hardware includes the following:

- Central processing unit (CPU) extracts instructions and data and decodes and executes the instructions. Computers must have at least one CPU. Some computers, however, have more than one CPU, which permits multiprocessing where more than one program is executed using two or more CPUs. The CPU consists of an arithmetic/logic unit (ALU) and a control unit (CU). The ALU performs arithmetic operations (for example, addition, subtraction, multiplication, and division) and logical comparisons (for example, compare two values to determine which is greater). The CU coordinates the CPU operations, such as when instructions are retrieved from primary memory.
- Primary or main memory stores data and programs for the CPU to execute. Random-access memory (RAM) and read-only memory (ROM) are two major components of main memory.
- Storage devices include hard disks, flash drives, compact disks (CD), and digital versatile disks (DVD). In contrast to RAM, which stores data as long as the computer is connected to electricity, these storage devices store data permanently.
- Input devices capture data from various sources and move the data into main memory. From there, the data may be moved to storage devices, such as a hard disk, or used by the CPU in executing instructions. Input devices include keyboards, mouses, barcode scanners, touch screens, magnetic ink character reader (MICR), point-of-sale (POS) recorders, and voice recognition.
- Output devices represent computer output in various forms. Examples of output devices include computer screens, printers, plotters, and speakers.

COMPUTER SOFTWARE Computer software are programs written by humans and executed by computer hardware. Software can be written in many programming languages including XML, XBRL, C#, and JAVA. Two major categories of computer software are systems software and applications software.

- **Systems software** are computer programs used for managing computer hardware. Systems software include operating systems, such as MS Windows, Linux, Unix, and Mountain Lion. Systems software also include utility programs that handle data manipulation, such as a database management systems (DBMS). Another example of a utility program is a compiler, a computer program that transforms a program into a language that the CPU understands (machine language).
- **Applications software** are computer programs for specific applications, such as spreadsheets and accounting software. As you know, accounting software can be divided into three tiers: low-end or small business accounting software, midrange, and high-end or integrated enterprise systems sometimes called ERPs. When application software is updated to fix an error or add a new feature, a section of coding called a **patch** is inserted into the program. Application software execution can be **real-time** (processing transactions at the current time) or **batch** processing (running a batch of transactions at a later time).

Network Architecture

Networks are interconnected computers and devices. **Network architecture** consists of network hardware and software. Network hardware and software interact to provide reliable communication channels between computers.

Networks can be categorized based on their size or their functionality (the way they function). Network categories based on size are as follows:

- **Local area networks (LANs)** consist of a few computers in a relatively small area, such as your college campus (Figure 11.2).
- **Metropolitan area networks (MANs)** shown in Figure 11.3 are networks that cover a metropolitan area, such as the city of San Antonio.
- **Wide area networks (WANs)** cover a large geographic region, such as a midwestern region of the United States (Figure 11.4).

The Internet is a collection of many networks of various types, connecting different LANs, MANs, and WANs together. An intranet consists of all of an organization's networks.

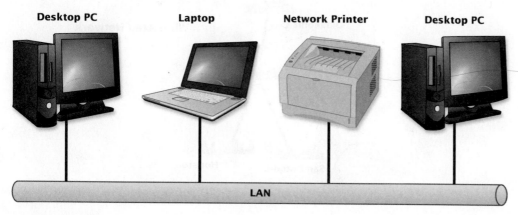

Desktop PC   **Laptop**   **Network Printer**   **Desktop PC**

LAN

FIGURE 11.2

Local Area Network (LAN)

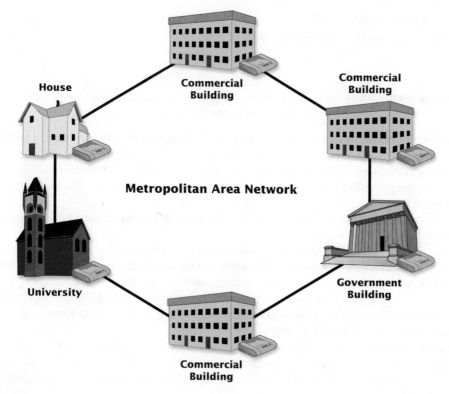

House   **Commercial Building**   **Commercial Building**

Metropolitan Area Network

University   **Government Building**

Commercial Building

FIGURE 11.3

Metropolitan Area Network (MAN)

Where would the LANs be in this MAN?

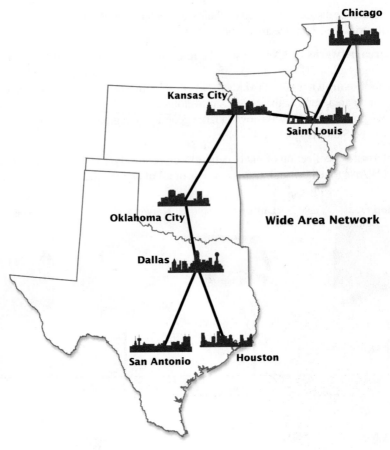

FIGURE 11.4

Wide Area Network (WAN)

Where would you find the MANs in this WAN?

NETWORK HARDWARE Network hardware consists of interconnected devices to form LANs, MANs, and WANs. Network hardware includes the following:

- **Workstation computers** are typically personal computers and laptops connected to the network.
- **Server computers** can be microcomputers, midrange computers, or a mainframe. These servers are generally used for a specific purpose, such as email servers, database servers, or Internet servers.
- **Peripherals** are utility devices connected to the network for shared use, such as a network printer or network storage device.
- **Routing devices** are special purpose computers without a keyboard or monitor that are used for routing messages over the network, similar to a traffic cop. Routing devices, or switches, include routers, gateways, and bridges. **Bridges**, as shown in Figure 11.5, connect one LAN to another LAN of the same type to create a **LAN cluster** (Figure 11.6). **Routers** can connect LANs of similar or different types to create an intranet (Figure 11.7). **Gateways** connect the enterprise's intranet to the Internet.
- **Network wiring (transmission media)** connects network devices to each other. Different types of network wiring (twisted-pair wire, coaxial cable, and fiber optics) offer different bandwidth or bit rates (number of bits per second). Fiber optics provide the highest bandwidth.

NETWORK SOFTWARE Network software connects network devices to each other in a specified way, such as client/server. Network software permits network devices to share peripherals, execute application programs on a remote computer, and access a database on a remote server.

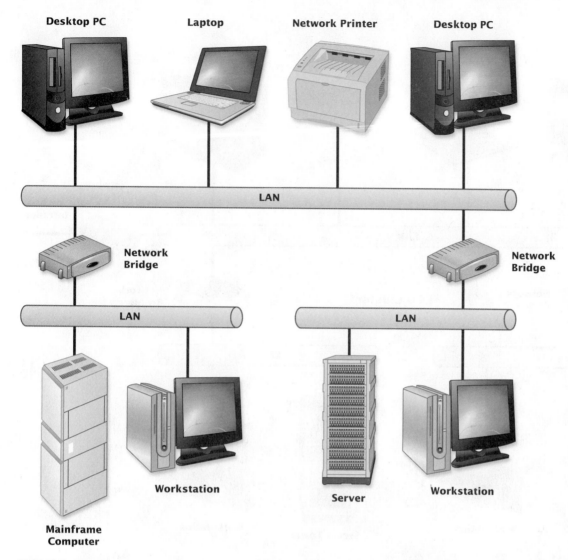

FIGURE 11.5

LANs with Similar LAN Protocol Connected Using a Network Bridge

Network software is called a protocol. The various types of protocols used by a network can include the following:

- **Ethernet protocol** is a software program commonly used to connect computers to create a LAN.
- **Internet protocol (IP)** is a software program that provides routing services to messages transmitted over the Internet. This protocol provides the IP addresses, which uniquely identify the sender and receiver's computers (for example, 193.168.0.103).
- **Transport control protocol (TCP)** provides message transportation services between sending and receiving computers. The Internet uses TCP and IP (TCP/IP suite) to address and transport messages from sender to receiver.
- **Electronic data interchange (EDI)** is a protocol that allows the enterprise network to connect to the network of vendors and suppliers through proprietary lines.

In addition to classifying networks by size, networks can be classified by functionality. Protocols determine the functionality of a network. Different categories of networks based on their functionality include the following:

- **Client/server network.** A client/server protocol allows client computers on the network to send a request to the server computer. The server computer responds to the request.

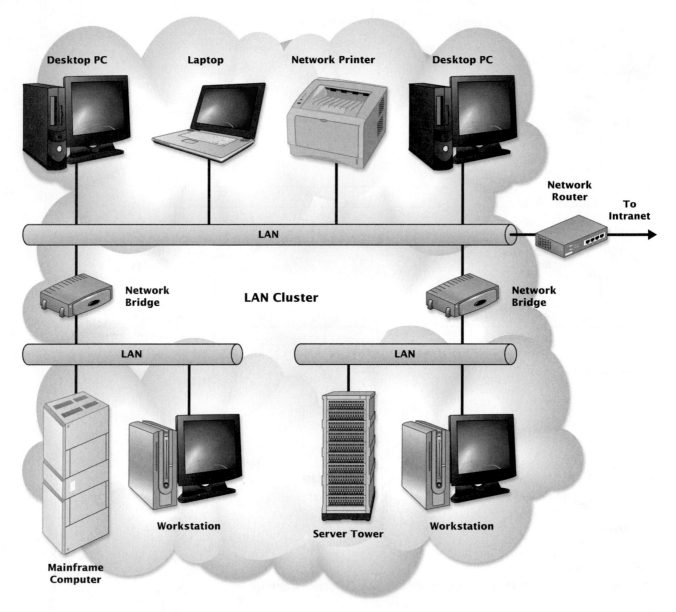

FIGURE 11.6

LAN Cluster

Compare the LAN cluster here with the LANs in the previous figure. What is the difference?

For example, if you need to update a customer record, your computer application sends a request for the record through a query to the database server. The database server extracts the record and sends it to your computer. Client/server networks can use centralized processing (processing occurs at one location with data distributed over many computers), decentralized processing (processing and data are stored on computers at multiple locations), or distributed processing (a single database is centralized with processing occurring at multiple sites in either a batch or real-time basis).

- **Value-added network (VAN)** allows an organization to share data with suppliers using EDI protocol. More and more organizations are moving from EDI systems to the Internet and the TCP/IP suite.

Now that you know about IT architecture, next you will discover how to secure it.

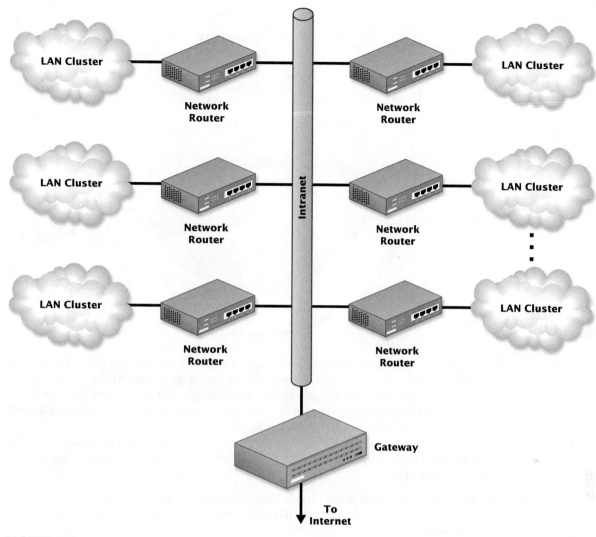

FIGURE 11.7

Enterprise Intranet

What is the difference between the network routers shown here and the network bridges shown in the prior figures?

Security Architecture

Security architecture addresses security for the IT architecture of the entire organization. One approach to security architecture is called **stovepipe**. This approach involves tossing in security patches, hoping that vulnerabilities are covered. However, this approach can result in constant fire drills as IT professionals continually work to put out fires from security breaches. This haphazard approach to cybersecurity can result in a high-stress, chaotic business environment.

Another approach, **enterprise security architecture**, studies the enterprise architecture and business environment to develop an overall strategy and plan that best fits enterprise-specific needs. This proactive approach develops policies and procedures to standardize solutions and address potential threats.

Security of the IT architecture should be considered in each phase of the system development life cycle (SDLC) to ensure that computer and network hardware and software are secure. As is often the case, it is much easier to design security into the system as opposed to adding security and controls after the system is operational. Granted, it may not be possible to foresee every event that could result in a security breach; however, anticipating and addressing security during system design offers many advantages.

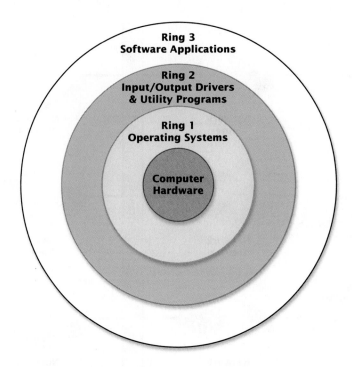

FIGURE 11.8
Rings of Protection

In general, securing computer architecture involves using layering and rings of protection. A computer hacker often targets application software first to obtain access. Then if the hacker's attempt is successful, he or she can gain access to input/output (I/O) drivers and utilities with the ultimate target being the operating system. If the hacker gains access to the operating system, data and applications can be disrupted, stolen, or destroyed.

To protect your computer architecture, access to these layers should be secured using the following rings of protection for software applications, I/O drivers and utilities, and operating systems (Figure 11.8).

- Ring 3: Software applications include Web browser, word processing, spreadsheet, and accounting software. Login passwords to open applications are an example of Ring 3 protection.
- Ring 2: Input/output drivers are programs that access input and output devices, such as printers or disks. Utilities include RDBMS for accessing a relational database. An example of Ring 2 protection would be to require a password to access a data file.
- Ring 1: Operating systems, such as Unix, are programs running computer hardware. Ring 1 protection might consist of limiting access to operating system commands based on the security level of the user.

Security for computer and network hardware will be addressed in the physical security domain. Computer and network software is addressed in the application security domain. Network security is discussed in the telecommunications, network, and Internet security domain next.

> **My Connection...**
> - Short Exercise 11.33
> - Short Exercise 11.34

What Is Telecommunications, Network, and Internet Security?

This domain covers security for telecommunications, networks, and the Internet. Telecommunications, networks, and the Internet all relate to data transmission.

Telecommunications Security

Telecommunications is the electrical transmission of data through analog or digital transmission media. Transmission media can include laser, fiber optics, coaxial cable, twisted-pair wire (phone wire), and airwaves (wireless). The data transmitted can be text, images, video, or audio. Telecommunications are used in many industries including financial institutions, stock exchanges, airlines, insurance, and health care. Telecommunications security includes controls to limit network access, ensure data integrity, and secure physical telecommunications facilities.

Network Security

As discussed in the security architecture and design domain, network architecture consists of network hardware and software. **Intranet** is an enterprise-wide network. An intranet may consist of several types of LANs including an ethernet LAN. Organizations use intranets to disseminate information to employees, such as human resources information, and share business intelligence digital dashboards. **Extranet** is a network used by external customers and/or suppliers. For example, extranets provide customers with online access to their account information and shipment tracking.

An important aspect of network security is the competence of the network administrator, who is responsible for operating the network. The network administrator must know how to identify potential vulnerabilities and troubleshoot effectively.

Network cyberattacks can occur from external or internal threats. Typically, there are **network access points (NAP)** that are targeted because these points offer access to the network. A computer, router, bridge, or gateway are access points that may be vulnerable to attack.

Since routers, bridges, and gateways are access points to the network, **firewalls** or software programs that control traffic between two networks can be installed on these routing devices to prevent unauthorized access (Figure 11.9).

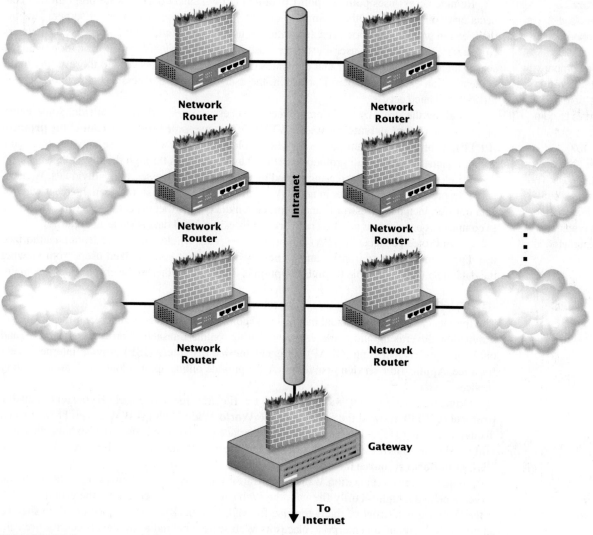

FIGURE 11.9

Enterprise Intranet with Firewalls

What is the purpose of the firewalls on these routers?

Every message that a router receives is checked by the firewall protocol to determine if the message is authorized to enter the network. If the firewall program suspects that the message is not authentic and authorized, the message is destroyed and information about the message is logged. Later, if network security is compromised, the log can be checked for the unauthorized message source (IP address). Firewalls can also be installed on servers and personal computers.

An enterprise may have many layers of firewalls with increasing levels of security to protect the network. For example, the firewall securing an enterprise's database should have the highest level of security. The enterprise might have a firewall on the gateway, another firewall on the network router, and another on the bridge leading to the database server, each with an increased security level.

Sophisticated techniques used to pass through firewalls undetected include SQL Injection. This technique involves adding unauthorized programming code to a valid SQL query. When the valid SQL query is run, the disguised code is also run, permitting it to pass through the firewall undetected. Increasingly sophisticated firewall programs are required to address newly emerging threats.

Another challenge for network security is permitting **remote access** to employees who need to access the enterprise network from offsite. Sales reps in the field, road warriors, and telecommuters require access to the enterprise network and database in order to conduct business. Network security must be configured to permit the employee to access the network without compromising network security.

Remote access uses **point-to-point protocol (PPP)**, a network software program that connects one computer to another computer or network server, such as an email server. This authentication protocol identifies and authenticates users who are attempting to access the network from a remote system. The user must enter a username and password for identification, which is sent to an authentication server that compares the username and password to those stored in the authentication database. If there is a match, the user is permitted access to the network. If not, the user is denied access.

To allow the organization's employees to access the network from outside, some enterprises use a **virtual private network (VPN)**. VPNs use **point-to-point tunneling protocol (PPTP)**, a software program permitting the employee to use the enterprise network through a secure channel. The firewall protocol lets PPTP messages pass through the firewall.

Wireless networks are increasingly used by universities, businesses, and individuals. Wireless networks present new challenges in network security. Hackers using sniffers can intercept wireless data transfer, including passwords and credit card numbers. Furthermore, hackers can gain access to computers on unsecured wireless networks and steal financial data, such as tax returns.

Wi-Fi Protected Access (WPA) can be used to secure wireless networks from unauthorized use. Furthermore, data in transit can be encrypted to prevent unauthorized users from viewing the data in an understandable form. Encryption is discussed further in the cryptography domain.

> **45.6 Million....**
>
> A Marshalls store's wireless network that connected credit-card processing hardware to the company server was not secured with WPA. This permitted cybercriminals to gain access to the computer network of the TJX Companies, Inc., the parent company of Marshalls. The attack resulted in an estimated theft of information on 45.6 million credit and debit cards (securityfocus.com, 2007).

Internet Security

The Internet can be used for social media, cloud computing, email, e-commerce, information dissemination, advertising and marketing, file sharing, online transaction processing (OLTP), and online analytical processing (OLAP). **Internet service providers (ISP)** provide Internet access for a fee. **Application service providers (ASP)** provide online applications, such as accounting services.

Originally, the Internet was only used for file transfer and email. **Hypertext transfer protocol (HTTP)** allowed the creation of the **World Wide Web (WWW)**. Web browsers can display files using HTTP in a graphical user interface (GUI). Web browsers also have the capability to display HTML, XML, and XBRL files. Every Web site has a Web address known as a **URL** or **uniform resource locator.**

Frequently, an organization wants high traffic on its Web site. However, if the Web site server is behind a high-security firewall, the Web site cannot be accessed by the general public. If the Web site is in front of the enterprise firewall, then hackers may deface the Web site. To address this dilemma, an enterprise places its Web servers behind a low-level security firewall, which is the first firewall to the outside world. Another high-level security firewall is located behind the Web servers. The area between the first firewall and the second firewall is called a **demilitarized zone** or **DMZ.**

Firewalls also play an important role in **e-commerce**, in which sales transactions are conducted online. Amazon.com is an example of an enterprise using e-commerce. To allow customers to pass the second firewall located behind the Web server yet protect the enterprise database, e-commerce servers are placed behind the second firewall. A third firewall is added behind the e-commerce server to protect the enterprise's database and applications (Figure 11.10). To further protect the enterprise database, some companies use two e-commerce servers. One e-commerce server accepts customer requests and queries, such as searching for a specific book on Amazon.com. Any customer requests requiring database access are forwarded to the second e-commerce server, which uses the DBMS to retrieve or update data in the database. An additional firewall is added between the two e-commerce servers (Figure 11.11).

Proxy firewall is a special type of firewall located on a proxy server used to intercept and inspect all incoming messages prior to delivering them to the intended recipients. The proxy firewall either will forward the message to the recipient or destroy suspicious messages.

A technique used to distract and sometimes catch hackers is use of a **honeypot**. A honeypot is a computer located in the DMZ with attractive, but irrelevant data (Figure 11.12). The honeypot is used to lure hackers, distracting them from bypassing other firewalls and hacking into the enterprise database. Some organizations use a honeypot to catch hackers by tracing them back to their source while the hackers are busy hacking the honeypot.

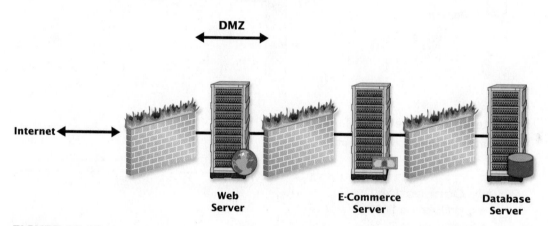

FIGURE 11.10

E-Commerce Architecture Using Firewalls and DMZ

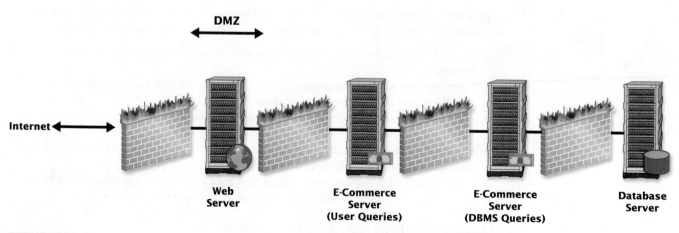

FIGURE 11.11

E-Commerce Architecture Using Four Layers of Firewall Protection

Can you find the difference between this e-commerce architecture and the e-commerce architecture in the previous figure?

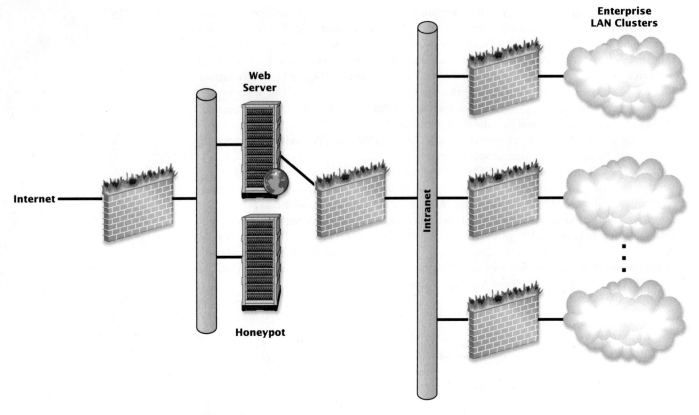

FIGURE 11.12

Enterprise Intranet with Honeypot

What is the role of the honeypot?

> **My Connection...**
> • Short Exercise 11.35
> • Short Exercise 11.38

What Is Access Control?

The access control domain addresses security for access to the enterprise system, including computers, networks, routers, and databases. Access control threats include the following:

- Network sniffers: These are programs or devices that examine traffic on the enterprise network.
- Phishing: This is social engineering used to obtain confidential information, such as a Social Security number or a credit card number.
- Identity theft: Sensitive personal data is stolen and used to impersonate individuals for fraudulent purposes.
- Password attack: Cyberattacks to obtain passwords may include hacking into the password table in a database or sniffing the network for passwords.
- Spoofing at log-on: A malicious program presents a fake login window that captures an individual's username and password information for fraudulent purposes.

Access Control Security Principles

Security principles for access control include identification, authentication, authorization, and accountability. For a user to be allowed access to a secured system (computers and network) the user should be identified, authenticated, and then authorized to access the system. Users are then held accountable for their actions and how they use the system.

Password Management

To identify users, usernames and passwords may be required to log into the system. Password management involves the number of passwords a user has, how frequently the password must be changed, the password format including length and type (for example, alphanumeric), and number of incorrect login attempts.

A **dynamic password** is used once and then changed. Virtual Private Networks (VPNs) may require dynamic passwords for identification and authentication. A **token device (TD)** is a hardware device containing a password generator protocol that creates a new password each time the token is used, thus eliminating the need for the user to memorize a password that is continually changing.

In many organizations, users often need to access several different systems, such as email systems, databases, and intranets. A **single sign-on (SSO)** permits the user to use one username and password to log into the various systems.

Biometric Access

Biometrics is an access method that identifies the user by analyzing his or her personal attributes, such as a fingerprint. Other forms of biometrics used include face recognition, retina scans, and palm scans.

Intrusion Prevention Systems

Intrusion Prevention Systems (IPS) are used by enterprises to address the various types of access control attacks with the intent to access and control corporate assets. New technologies are continually being developed to address these ongoing threats.

An Intrusion Detection System alone is inadequate because the attack has already occurred. An Intrusion Prevention System attempts to prevent the attack from occurring.

Just as cyberattackers can use sniffers, so can the enterprise. Some organizations use sniffers on their own networks to detect malicious messages, such as viruses. The malicious messages can be destroyed before harming the network or data.

> ### Online Banking?
> The vice president of finance for a retirement home confessed that he embezzled $693,000 from the California charity using online banking.
>
> The 66-year-old former VP admitted that he used the Internet to open unauthorized bank accounts for the retirement home. Then he transferred funds from the retirement home accounts into his own bank accounts.
>
> He was charged with money laundering and computer fraud.

> ### My Connection...
> • Active Review 11.8

What Is Operations Security?

Operations security refers to activities and procedures required to keep information technology running securely. IT security personnel are charged with responsibility for the security of the networks and computers, including hardware and software.

IT Security Management Responsibilities

IT security management includes responsibility for maintaining security devices and software, such as virus detection, firewalls, Intrusion Prevention Systems (IPS), and Intrusion Detection Systems (IDS). Security assessment is carried out on a scheduled basis to evaluate the security of the various components of the enterprise system.

Other responsibilities include password management and reviewing the security audit logs, such as the firewall logs to review blocked unauthorized network activity. User access is reviewed and controlled to ensure that users are not overprivileged.

IT Security Operational Responsibilities

Operational responsibilities for IT security relate to how the enterprise system operates. For example, operational responsibilities include input/output controls. **Input controls** ensure that data is valid and entered correctly. Input controls can include logs that document each time an online user views a Web site. **Output controls** ensure that reports and messages reach intended recipients, such as a publicly traded company's XBRL Form 10-K report reaching the SEC.

Operational responsibilities also include responsibility for a licensing system. Such a system ensures that all software used by the enterprise is legally purchased, licensed, installed, and configured. For example, if a software license permits 25 installations, IT personnel have responsibility for ensuring that the total number of installations does not exceed that number. Hefty fines can be imposed for use of pirated or unlicensed copies of software.

Data leakage is caused when employees unwittingly allow data leaks, such as leaving laptops unsecured or using public unsecured wireless networks. The IT security personnel are responsible for providing adequate training to all employees to inform and educate them regarding security policies and procedures.

Operational responsibilities also entail developing contingency plans for virus attacks, disk crashes, hardware failure, and software malfunction. Email security requires controlling email traffic from the outside to the email server located in the DMZ. Spam filters may be used to scan incoming email and quarantine or destroy suspicious messages. Periodically, highly trained IT security experts conduct vulnerability checks to detect and assess vulnerabilities, including attempts to hack into the system.

My Connection...
- Active Review 11.10
- It's Your Call 11.49

How Much Does a Laptop Cost? How Much Does a *Stolen* Laptop Cost? $20 Million.

In January 2009, the U.S. Department of Veterans Affairs agreed to pay $20 million to settle a class action lawsuit on behalf of current and former military personnel whose personal data was on a stolen laptop. The Veterans Affairs' laptop that disappeared in 2006 contained names, birth dates, and Social Security numbers of 26.5 million veterans and active duty military personnel (Frieden, 2009).

What Is Physical and Environmental Security?

The physical and environmental security domain addresses the physical security of information technology components, such as hardware and software. Physical threats include natural environmental disasters, such as fire and flood, supply system threats, man-made threats, and politically motivated threats.

Physical Security Framework

Physical security frameworks are useful to provide guidance on how to secure the physical facilities, grounds, and IT assets. Facilities and grounds should be constructed not only to protect assets, but also to deter intruders. Deterrents include security cameras, fencing, and locked doors. Organizations can use environmental design of their grounds and facilities for crime prevention. For example, a data center should be located at the center of the building in order to buffer physical damage through external walls. Procedures should be in place to detect a crime or disruption, assess the incidents that occur, and respond accordingly.

Information Asset Protection

Information assets include IT hardware and software, as well as the information assets stored in databases. Many security policies and procedures have been discussed already. One unique challenge to IT security is mobile IT assets that contain sensitive data, such as company laptops. First, all enterprise laptops should be inventoried with a serial number and responsible party. In addition to the typical user password login, a laptop might also require a hardware password. Laptop protection devices include laptop locks and GPS tracking. All data on the laptop should be encrypted. Road warriors traveling with laptops should not check laptops as luggage and should never leave the laptop unattended, especially when going through airport security.

Corporate espionage happens. Key employees may be targeted and followed by corporate spies who are waiting for an opportunity to swipe the company laptop. It can happen in the few seconds it takes to refill a cup of coffee at a cafe.

My Connection...
- Active Review 11.3

What Is Application Security?

The application security domain addresses security and controls for application software, including input, processing, and output. Application software includes accounting and spreadsheet software that accounting professionals use daily.

Application Security and Software Development

Software applications, such as accounting software, are developed with great care. In every phase of the system development life cycle (SDLC), the software engineer's goal is to reduce application vulnerabilities and the possibility of data corruption. At the same time, the hacker's goal is to use software vulnerabilities to steal or destroy data.

Although no software is guaranteed to be 100% secure, actions can be taken to reduce the probability of vulnerabilities. Software development projects may include IT security specialists in addition to software engineers on the project team. These specialists test to find vulnerable points in the software being developed. Some vulnerabilities may be discovered during the design and coding phases. Other vulnerabilities may not become apparent until the software interacts with another software, such as the accounting software interacting with DBMS. Furthermore, when the software is upgraded, additional vulnerabilities may surface.

Many software vulnerability issues are solved by firewalls. The firewall prevents intruders from reaching the application software to take advantage of the vulnerability. However, since most firewalls are software applications themselves, intruders may be able to use firewall vulnerabilities to access the system.

Intrusion Detection Systems (IDS), such as Symantec Enterprise Security Systems, are used to detect the damage caused by intruders and fix the applications.

Client/server architecture permits applications to be disbursed throughout the network. This offers the advantage of users being able to access the accounting system without having the entire application installed on the accountant's desktop computer. However, the disadvantage is that the interaction of the various applications may create additional vulnerabilities.

Database Applications Security

Database applications, such as database management systems (DBMS), are used to create a database, store data in the database, and retrieve data from the database. Hackers often target databases because of the information assets, such as credit card numbers, Social Security numbers, intellectual property, and financial information, stored in the database. To access the database, hackers must pass through the firewalls and capitalize on a DBMS application vulnerability. Open database connectivity (ODBC) is also a database application that is targeted by hackers.

A common practice in most organizations is to grant only partial database access to employees so that the employee is only able to access the needed data, such as accounts payable. However, partial database access itself is a vulnerability. A user with specialized knowledge can use partial database access to gain full access to the database.

Online transaction processing (OLTP) offers enterprises many benefits of permitting multiple users at various locations access to the enterprise database at the same time. To prevent two users from changing the same data at the same time, OLTP uses a record-locking and file-locking system.

Web Applications Security

Web applications include Web sites coded in HTML or XML. Because Web applications are stored on a Web server in the DMZ, which has limited security, these Web site applications are vulnerable to malicious attacks. For example, a hacker might deface a company's Web site by changing product prices from $200 to $2. Another type of malicious attack uses the e-commerce client application to access the enterprise's financial system for fraudulent purposes. Yet another type of attack is transaction information theft. Attackers track customer transactions and steal customers' payments or redirect goods to a different shipping address. In a denial-of-service attack, the hacker overloads the enterprise's bandwidth, effectively shutting down the Web site.

Malware

Malicious software, or malware, is written by hackers who are expert programmers. Malware is spread through the enterprise system by email, fraudulent customer requests, fake advertisements, sales messages, Internet downloads, and shared drives. Types of malware include the following:

- **Viruses**: A computer virus is a relatively small program that infects other application software by attaching to it and disrupting application function. The application, in this case, is called the host, just as a human cell is a host for a virus. Antivirus software removes the computer virus from the host application.

- **Bots**: Short for robots, bots are tiny pieces of programming code that install themselves on the infected computer called a Zombie. Bots monitor the Zombie computer's activity and transmit information back to the Master, typically a program on the hacker's computer (Figure 11.13). Bots can be used to transmit financial information to their Master without awareness of the Zombie computer user. Antivirus, or anti-malware, programs can scan for known bots and, if found, delete them.
- **Worms**: A worm is like a virus except it does not need a host application to function or reproduce. Antivirus programs can search for known worms and delete them from the system.
- **Logic Bombs**: This malicious software executes when a specified event happens within the computer, as for example, when the user logs into his or her bank account. The logic bomb is activated and steals bank account information. Logic bombs can be scanned for by antivirus software and removed.
- **Trojan horses**: A malware disguised as a legitimate program, a Trojan horse can be downloaded and installed by users without realizing it is a virus.
- **Spam**: Malware sent by email, spam can be a virus, bot, logic bomb, worm, or Trojan horse.

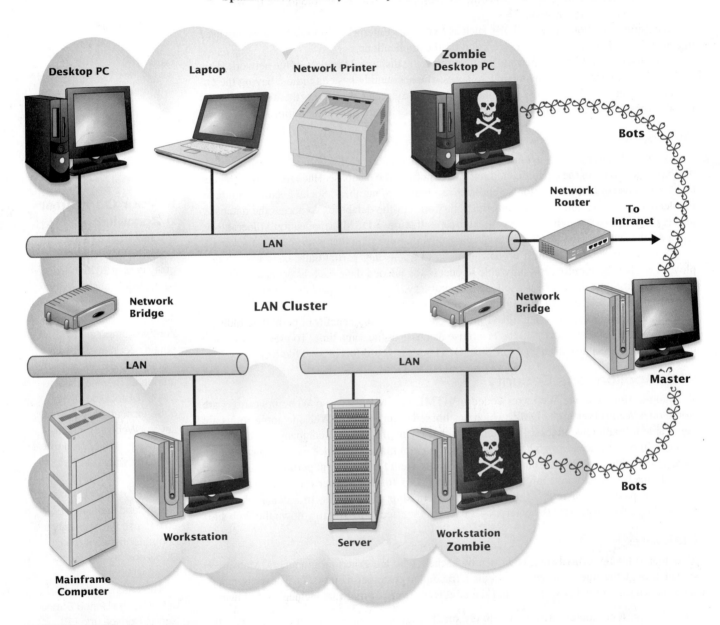

FIGURE 11.13

Bots and Zombie Computers

How does the Master control the Zombies?

My Connection...
- Short Exercise 11.39
- Short Exercise 11.43

What Are Business Continuity and Disaster Recovery?

This domain addresses an enterprise's business continuity and disaster recovery plan. Natural disasters, such as Hurricane Katrina in 2005, underscore the need for a comprehensive business continuity and disaster recovery plan. Lessons learned from Katrina are that companies with disaster recovery plans, such as SCP Pool Corp., are able to resume operations within 24 hours (CIO.com, 2005).

The goals of a disaster recovery plan include the following:

- Minimize disruption, damage, and loss from a disaster.
- Provide a temporary method for processing business and accounting transactions.
- Resume normal operations quickly.

Disaster Recovery Priorities

When developing a business continuity and disaster recovery plan, an impact analysis should be conducted and priorities identified for critical business processes, systems, and data. Downtime that can be tolerated by a business can be estimated and used to prioritize recovery. The maximum tolerable downtime (MTD) can be stated in days, hours, or minutes for each business function and asset. For example, processing customer orders might be classified as urgent with an MTD of 24 hours. The enterprise's Internet connection might be classified as critical with a one-hour MTD.

Backup Methods

There are different approaches used to back up an enterprise's critical hardware, software, and data. Accounting data backups are critical and should be scheduled on a regular basis. A recommended approach is to complete a full backup once a week with incremental backups of changes made daily. A common backup approach is the **Grandfather-Father-Son method**. For accounting, this method typically involves a daily backup of all accounting data. Imagine you made a backup at the end of the day on Monday, which becomes the grandfather. The backup on Tuesday is the father and the backup on Wednesday is the son. The purpose of having three or more backups is that if the Wednesday backup fails, you can rollback to Tuesday's backup. In any case, at least one off-site or remote backup is always recommended.

Backup Facilities

A disaster recovery plan should specify the backup facilities that will be used by the enterprise. Examples of backup facilities include the following:

- **Reciprocal agreements** between organizations can be used to provide backup services. In the event that one organization is down, the other organization would process the data.
- **Internal sites** can be used by large organizations with multiple locations. For example, a facility in the Midwest might provide backup services for the headquarters in California.
- **Hot site** is a commercial disaster recovery service that can be leased by an enterprise to provide IT services in the event of a disaster. A hot site can be fully operational in a few hours.
- **Warm site** is also a commercial disaster recovery service to provide IT services; however, it is only partially configured with some equipment and may take a few days to be operational.
- **Cold site** is a commercial disaster recovery service providing air conditioning, wiring, and plumbing, but it does not contain any IT equipment. It may take several days for the site to be operational.

A combination of the preceding backup facilities may be used in order to reduce risk of backup failure.

Would You Like to Know More?
For more information about backup methodology, visit the *Disaster Recovery Journal* (www.drj.com).

My Connection...
- It's Your Call 11.47

What Is Cryptography?

Accounting involves use of sensitive, confidential data that requires a high degree of accuracy. Therefore, encryption is a valuable tool that can be used to secure data during transmission and storage. Encryption is used to do the following:

- Ensure confidentiality of data by preventing hackers from reading the data
- Maintain data integrity by preventing hackers from altering data

Intruders may place malware on an organization's router to sniff for data as it passes through the network. Encryption makes the attacker's job more difficult because even if the attacker is able to access the encrypted data, to be readable the data must be decrypted.

Cryptography is encoding data in a form that only the sender and intended receiver can understand. Encryption is a method of converting plaintext data into an unreadable form called ciphertext. Ciphertext is converted back to plaintext using decryption (Figure 11.14).

The encryption process is accomplished using an algorithm and a key. An algorithm is a finite series of steps to accomplish an objective. The key is a value or method that converts the plaintext into ciphertext.

Encryption Keys

Various types of encryption keys can be used in conjunction with algorithms to create encrypted data. Types of encryption keys include the following.

1. **Substitution key**: The algorithm uses the key to substitute a letter or word for another letter or word.

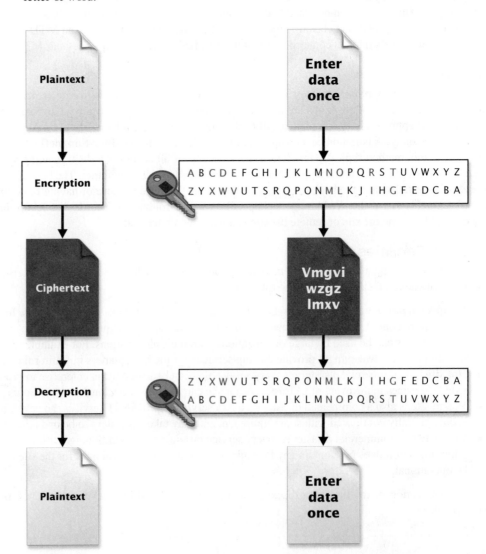

FIGURE 11.14

Cryptography

Pair and Share: Pick one of your favorite phrases or mottos. Encode it with the key shown in this figure. Exchange it with a classmate and decode each other's messages.

2. **Transposition key**: The algorithm uses the key to scramble the data.
3. **Product key**: A product key is a combination of substitution and transposition keys.

Substitution Cipher

A well-known encryption key uses a substitution cipher that employs a reverse cipher key. Each letter of the alphabet is substituted for another letter of the alphabet. For example, a reverse cipher key reverses the alphabet to determine the letter that will be substituted. The following simple example illustrates how the reverse cipher key works:

1. We take a plaintext message, **Enter data once**, as shown in Figure 11.14.
2. Then the reverse cipher key shown in the figure is used to encrypt the plaintext message. For simplicity, only capital letters are used in the key.
3. The ciphertext message results. The encrypted message is not understandable in this form.
4. To decrypt the message, the cipher key is applied to the ciphertext message.
5. The plaintext message is the final result.

Encryption Methods

Encryption methods determine the number of keys and how the keys are used to encode and decode data. Encryption methods include the following:

1. **Symmetric cryptography** or **1-key method**: This method uses one key to encode and the same key to decode. Thus, both the sender and the intended recipient must have the same key (Figure 11.15).
2. **Asymmetric cryptography** or **2-key method**: This method uses two keys with one key used to encode and a second related, but different, key to decode the message. The key used to encrypt the message is called a **public key**. The key used to decode is called a **private key** (Figure 11.16).
3. **Digital envelope** or **3-key method**: This method combines symmetric and asymmetric cryptography. First, the intended recipient's message is encoded using symmetric encryption, and then the key to decode the message is encrypted using recipient's public-key encryption.

Encryption is a useful tool for protecting data in transit and stored in databases. However, as encryption tools have improved, crackers (high-level hackers) are using even more sophisticated

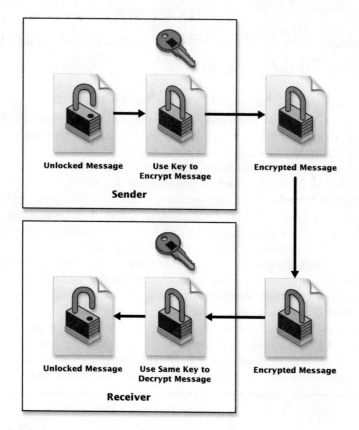

FIGURE 11.15

Symmetric Cryptography (1-Key Method)

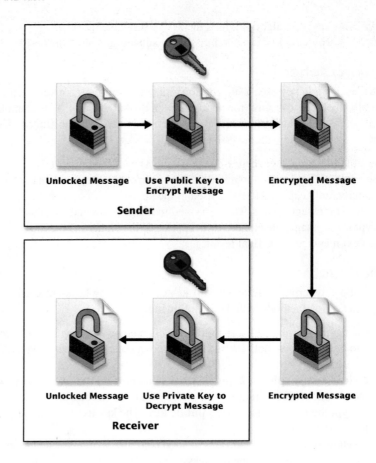

FIGURE 11.16

Asymmetric Cryptography (2-Key Method)

My Connection...
- Short Exercise 11.40
- It's Your Call 11.50

techniques to bypass data encryption. One example is using malware that captures the keystrokes for data as the end user is entering the data into the computer. Thus, the data is captured before there is a chance for it to be encrypted.

Why Does Cybersecurity for Accounting Require Prudence?

Accounting Insight No. 20: Prudence Principle

ACCOUNTING INSIGHT NO. 20
When It Comes to Cybersecurity at the Crossroads of Accounting and IT... Use the Prudence Principle

You may recall from your other accounting courses that there is a convention of conservatism (also called the prudence principle) used in accounting. Accountants are often characterized as conservative or cautious in their approach to matters. Accountants are often the voice of reason cautioning others to think of the downside of decisions and actions.

When it comes to cybersecurity at the crossroads of accounting and IT, use the prudence principle. While new technology may appear promising, it may also create vulnerabilities and risks to confidential data contained in the accounting system. Just because we can do something doesn't mean that we should. Just because there is the latest and greatest IT available, doesn't mean that it is secure enough to use for confidential accounting data.

Accounting professionals understand well the confidential nature of the accounting data with which they work. Accountants have access to confidential data that others inside an enterprise do not. For example, accountants may know how much each person in the enterprise makes while others in the enterprise have no clue.

Accounting systems contain some of an enterprise's most confidential data. The IT used can actually create vulnerabilities to cyberattacks on this confidential accounting data. For this reason, accountants need to be prudent when implementing new technology until it has been tested and proven reliable enough to adequately safeguard accounting data.

My Connection...
- It's Your Call 11.45

Chapter Highlights

What are the 10 domains of cybersecurity? This chapter provided you with an introduction to the 10 domains of cybersecurity:

- Legal, regulations, compliance, and investigations
- Information security and risk management
- Security architecture and design
- Telecommunications, network, and Internet security
- Control access
- Operations security
- Physical and environmental security
- Application security
- Business continuity and disaster recovery
- Cryptography

These domains provide an overall global framework for understanding the critical issues of enterprise information security management.

What is the scope of cybersecurity in the accounting system? Cybersecurity in an enterprise is not limited to just guarding against hackers and cyberattacks. It involves many aspects of enterprise operations, including how you train and educate your employees about security awareness to safeguarding information assets, how to implement new technologies in a security conscious manner, how to maintain backups in order to recover and continue business operations, and how to provide the highest level of security in a cost-effective way.

Why is encryption important in securing accounting data? For accounting purposes, encryption provides an especially valuable tool offering increased data integrity and confidentiality. Encryption can be used for accounting data in transit and for accounting data stored in the database. If an attacker is successful in penetrating the enterprise security and reaches the database, encryption of the stored data is an additional line of defense.

Chapter Extension 11

IT Control Frameworks

Two control frameworks are included in Chapter Extension 11. ISO 27k and COBIT. Organizations already using other ISO standards for quality control, enterprise risk management, and other areas may prefer the ISO 27k framework for IT controls. Furthermore, COBIT is in the process of being updated and revised and at the time of writing this text for you, it appears the new COBIT 5.0 will have less emphasis on control objectives, which actually may make it less useful for some accounting applications.

ISO 27k and IT Controls

The ISO 27000 series is also referred to as ISO 27k or the International Security Management Systems (ISMS) family of standards. ISO 27k consists of a series of standards related to information technology security techniques. Some of the standards include the following:

- ISO 27000 *Information security management systems—Overview and vocabulary*
- ISO 27001 *Information security management systems—Requirements*
- ISO 27002 *Code of practice for information security management*
- ISO 27003 *Information security management system implementation guidance*
- ISO 27004 *Information security management—Measurement*
- ISO 27005 *Information security risk management*
- ISO 27006 *Requirements for bodies providing audit and certification of information security management systems*
- ISO 27007 *Guidelines for information security management systems auditing*
- ISO 27011 *Information security management guidelines for telecommunications organizations based on ISO 27002*
- ISO 27799 *Information security management in health using ISO 27002*

Figure 11.17 diagrams the relationships of the ISO 27k standards. Notice in Figure 11.17 that ISO 27k can be grouped into four categories:

1. Terminology:
   - ISO 27000 *Information security management systems—Overview and vocabulary*

2. General requirements:
   - ISO 27001 *Information security management systems—Requirements*
   - ISO 27006 *Requirements for bodies providing audit and certification of information security management systems*

3. General guidelines:
   - ISO 27002 *Code of practice for information security management*
   - ISO 27003 *Information security management system implementation guidance*
   - ISO 27004 *Information security management—Measurement*
   - ISO 27005 *Information security risk management*
   - ISO 27007 *Guidelines for information security management systems auditing*

4. Sector-specific guidelines:
   - ISO 27011 *Information security management guidelines for telecommunications organizations based on ISO 27002*
   - ISO 27799 *Information security management in health using ISO 27002*

ISO 27002 provides a code of practice for information security management. IT control objectives are summarized in this standard and are organized into the following sections 4 through 15:

- Section 4: *Risk assessment and treatment*
  - 4.1 Assessing security risks
  - 4.2 Treating security risks

- Section 5: *Security policy*
  - 5.1 Information security policy

- Section 6: *Organization of information security*
  - 6.1 Internal organization
  - 6.2 External parties

- Section 7: *Asset management*
  - 7.1 Responsibility for [information] assets
  - 7.2 Information classification

- Section 8: *Human resources security*
  - 8.1 Prior to employment
  - 8.2 During employment
  - 8.3 Termination or change of employment

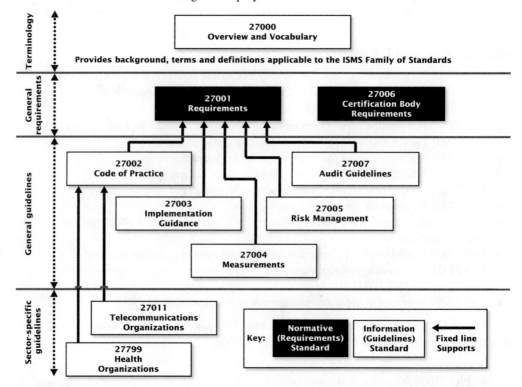

FIGURE 11.17

- Section 9: *Physical and environmental security*
  - 9.1 Secure areas
  - 9.2 Equipment security
- Section 10: *Communications and operations management*
  - 10.1 Operational procedures and responsibilities
  - 10.2 Third party service delivery management
  - 10.3 System planning and acceptance
  - 10.4 Protection against malicious and mobile code
  - 10.5 Back-up
  - 10.6 Network security management
  - 10.7 Media handling
  - 10.8 Exchange of information
  - 10.9 Electronic commerce services
  - 10.10 Monitoring
- Section 11: *Access control*
  - 11.1 Business requirement for access control
  - 11.2 User access management
  - 11.3 User responsibilities
  - 11.4 Network access control
  - 11.5 Operating system access control
  - 11.6 Application and information access control
  - 11.7 Mobile computing and teleworking
- Section 12: *Information systems acquisition, development, and maintenance*
  - 12.1 Security requirements of information systems
  - 12.2 Correct processing in application systems
  - 12.3 Cryptographic controls
  - 12.4 Security of system files
  - 12.5 Security in development and support processes
  - 12.6 Technical vulnerability management
- Section 13: Information security incident management
  - 13.1 Reporting in information security events and weaknesses
  - 13.2 Management of information security incidents and improvements
- Section 14: *Business continuity management*
  - 14.1 Information security aspects of business continuity management
- Section 15: *Compliance*
  - 15.1 Compliance with legal requirements
  - 15.2 Compliance with security policies and standards, and technical compliance
  - 15.3 Information systems audit considerations

The IT Controls Reference chart shown in Figure 11.18 maps ISO 27002 with:

- COBIT (Control OBjectives for Information and Related Technology)
- Sarbanes-Oxley
- COSO (Committee of Sponsoring Organizations of the Treadway Commission)
- HIPAA (Health Insurance Portability and Accountability Act)
- PCI-DSS (Payment Card Industry Data Security Standards)
- GLBA (Gramm-Leach-Bliley Act of 1999)

The chart on pages 370–372 illustrates the complexity of maintaining IT controls that comply with various legal and regulatory requirements. For more information about ISO 27k, see iso.org.

COBIT and IT Controls

In today's complex and global business organizations, information systems and technologies are integral components of business. The number and scope of government regulations for control and security of an organization's IT continue to grow. Hacker attacks on IT infrastructures are increasing at an alarming rate. Consequently, organizations are incurring increased costs to stay compliant with applicable laws and regulations while fighting hackers at the same time.

symantec™ IT Controls Reference

ISO 27002:2005	CobiT® 4.1	Sarbanes-Oxley COSO	HIPAA Requirements	Payment Card Industry PCI DSS 1.2	GLBA*	Symantec Products, Solutions & Capabilities
SECTION: 4 Risk Assessment and Treatment						
4.1 **Assessing Security Risks** Identify, quantify, and prioritize risks against criteria for risk acceptance relevant to the organization • Performed Periodically • Systematic Approach estimating risks • Clearly defined scope	**Plan and Organize:** • PO9 Assess and Manage IT Risks **Monitor and Evaluate:** • ME3 Ensure Compliance with External Requirements • ME4 Provide IT Governance	• Risk Assessment • Objective Setting • Event Identification	**Security Standard:** a) 1. Risk Analysis (R)	PCI is an audit standard and risks are quantified and prioritized within it Maintain an Information Security Policy: 12.1.2 - Includes an annual process that identifies threats, and vulnerabilities, and results in a formal risk assessment	III.B. Assess Risk	**Symantec™ Security Information Manager** Ability to associate risk scores to assets and discriminate threat response activities based on risk rating **Symantec™ Control Compliance Suite** Ability to group, trend and remediate asset vulnerabilities and configurations based on risk categorizations **Symantec Enterprise Vault™** Monitor, block and review email before it is sent **Symantec Consulting Services** Assess and prioritize risks against frameworks and standards Symantec Data Loss Prevention - Identify, classify, adn monitor critical information stores across hetergenous infrastructures
4.2 **Treating Security Risks** Before treating, organization must ascertain ability and level of risk acceptable to an organization • Knowing and objectively accepting risk in accordance with organizations risk tolerance • Avoiding risk by not engaging in activities that introduce risk • Transferring risks to other parties (insurance, partner, service provider)	**Plan and Organize:** • PO9 Assess and Manage IT Risks **Monitor and Evaluate:** • ME1 Monitor and Evaluate IT Performance • ME2 Monitor and Evaluate Internal Control	• Risk Response • Event Identification	**Security Standard:** a) 1. Risk Management (R)	**Protect Cardholder Data:** 3.4 - Render PAN, at a minimum, unreadable anywhere it is store (including on portable digital media, backup media, in logs) 6 - Develop and maintain secure systems and applications	III.C. Manage and Control Risk	**Symantec™ Security Information Manager** Discriminate threat response activities based on risk rating Symantec Altiris Inventory, treat, and manage information technology assets, ensuring the security posture throughout an assets lifecycle **Symantec Consulting Services** Assess and prioritize risks against frameworks and standards Symantec Data Loss Prevention - Gain visibility of data in motion and prevent sensitive data from being leaving an organi-zation
SECTION: 5 Security Policy						
5.1 **Information Security Policy** Information security policies should be sponsored/approved by management, published to all employees and relevant external parties Include within: • Definition of information security, objectives, scope, and importance • Statement of management intent, supporting goals and principles • Framework for setting control objectives and controls	**Plan and Organize:** • PO1 Define a Strategic IT Plan • PO4 Define the IT Processes, Organization and Relationships • PO6 Communicate Management Aims and Direction • PO7 Manage IT Human Resources	• Internal Environment • Objective Setting • Risk Assessment	**Security Standard:** a) 1. Sanction Policy (R) a) 2. Assigned Security Responsibility (R)	**Maintain an Information Security Policy:** 12.4 - Ensure that the security policy and procedures clearly define information security responsibilities for all employees and contractors. 12.5.1 - Establish, document, and distribute security policies and procedures	II.A. Information Security Program II.B. Objectives III.A. Invoice Board of Directors	**Symantec™ Control Compliance Suite** Ability to author, review, publish and gather approval on corporate policies **Symantec Consulting Services** Develop security strategy, security policy and security policy documentation
SECTION: 6 Organization of Information Security						
6.1 **Internal Organization** A management framework should be established to initiate and control the implementation of information security within the organization	**Deliver and Support:** • DS5 Ensure Systems Security	• Internal Environment • Control Activities • Information and Communication	**Security Standard:** a) 1. Information System Activity Review (R) a) 2. Assigned Security Responsibility (R)	**Maintain an Information Security Policy:** 12.4 - Ensure that the security policy and procedures clearly define information security responsibilities for all employees and contractors. 12.5.1 - Establish, document, and distribute security policies and procedures	II. A. Information Security Program II.B. Objectives III. A. Involve the Board of Directors III.C. Manage and Control Risk III.F. Report to the Board	**Symantec™ Security Information Manager** Provides a critical component of Information Security management process; implementing offers one way to establish the required control **Symantec™ Control Compliance Suite** Ability to ensure complete IT policy coverage and evidence of compliance across multiple management frameworks **Symantec Enterprise Vault™** Support Information security policy with audited roles based search and review of email, IM and files **Symantec Consulting Services** Help structure security organization and develop supporting policy
6.2 **External Parties** To maintain the security of information and information processing facilities that are accessed, processed, communicated to, or managed by external parties	**Plan and Organize:** • PO8 Manage Quality **Deliver and Support:** • DS1 Define and Manage Service Levels • DS2 Manage Third-Party Services • DS5 Ensure Systems Security	• Internal Environment • Risk Assessment • Control Activities • Information and Communication • Monitoring	**Security Standard:** b) 1. Written Contract or Other Arrangement (R)	**Maintain an Information Security Policy:** 12.8.2 - Maintain a written agreement that includes an acknowledgement that the service providers are responsible for the security of cardholder data the service providers posess.	III.C. Manage and Control Risk III.D. Oversee Service Provider Arrangements	**Symantec™ Security Information Manager** Ensure that information is secure and best practices are in place **Symantec Enterprise Protection** Ability to prevent introduction of non-compliant, insecure devices onto corporate network, reducing the likelihood of information being compromised Symantec Data Loss Prevention - Gain visibility of data in motion and ensure that sensiitive data is being shared with third parties in accordance with security policies and any relevant security controls Consulting Services Develop security policy for client external parties and conduct related security assessments
SECTION: 7 Asset Management						
7.1 **Responsibility for Assets** All assets should be accounted for and have a nominated owner	**Plan and Organize:** • PO4 Define the IT Processes, Organization and Relationships	• Control Activities	**Physical Standard:** d) 2. Device and Media Controls – Accountability (A)	Maintain an Information Security Policy: 12.3.4 Labeling of devices with owner, contact information, and purpose	N/A	**Symantec™ Security Information Manager** Ability to classify assets and reporting accordingly and allows for definition of asset owners **Symantec Consulting Services** Produce asset registers including asset valuation as part of risk assessments
7.2 **Information Classification** Information should be classified to indicate the need, priorities and expected degree of protection • Define an information classification scheme	**Plan and Organize:** • PO2 Define the Information Architecture • PO9 Assess and Manage IT Risks **Deliver and Support:** • DS5 Ensure Systems Security	• Risk Assessment • Event Identification	**Security Standard:** a) 1. Risk Analysis (R) a) 1. Risk Management (R)	**Implement Strong Access Control Measures:** 7.1 - Limit access to system components and cardholder data to only those individuals whose job requires such access. 7.2 - Establish an access control system for system components with multiple users that restricts access based on a user's need to know and is set to "deny all" unless specifically allowed.	N/A	**Symantec™ Security Information Manager** Ability to classify assets and reporting accordingly **Symantec™ Enterprise Vault** Automated classification and retention or expiry of email, IM, and files Symantec Data Loss Prevention - Identify, classify, adn monitor critical information stores across hetergenous infrastructures **Symantec Consulting Services** Produce Information Classification schemes, associated policies and detailed set of procedures as part of assessments
SECTION: 8 Human Resources Security						
8.1 **Prior to Employment** To ensure that employees, contractors and third party users understand responsibilities, and are suitable for their roles; reduce the risk of theft, fraud, and or misuse of facilities/resources	**Plan and Organize:** • PO7 Manage IT Human Resources **Deliver and Support:** • DS12 Manage the Physical Environment	• Internal Environment • Control Activities • Information and Communication	**Security Standard:** a) 1. Sanction Policy (R) a) 3. Authorization and/or Supervision (A) a) 3. Workforce Clearance Procedure (A) a) 5. Security Reminders (A)	**Maintain an Information Security Policy:** 12.7 - Screen potential employees prior to hire to minimize the risk of attacks from internal sources.	III.C. Manage and Control Risk	**Symantec Consulting Services** Develop policies and procedures covering Human Resources related information security
8.2 **During Employment** To ensure that employees, contractors and third party users are aware of information security threats and concerns, their responsibilities and liabilities, and are equipped to support security policy in the course of their normal work	**Plan and Organize:** • PO7 Manage IT Human Resources **Deliver and Support:** • DS7 Educate and Train Users	• Internal Environment • Control Activities • Information and Communication	**Security Standard:** a) 5. Security Reminders (A)	**Maintain an Information Security Policy:** 12.6 - Implement a formal security awareness program to make all employees aware of the importance of cardholder data security.	III.C. Manage and Control Risk	**Symantec™ Control Compliance Suite** Ability to disseminate policy to employees, contractors, and 3rd party and ensure sign-off; ensure, via controls self-assessment capability, that critical procedures are understood and implemented **Symantec Consulting Services** Develop policies and procedures covering Human Resources related information security
8.3 **Termination or Change of Employment** To ensure that employees, contractors and third party users exit an organization or change employment in an orderly manner	**Plan and Organize:** • PO4 Define the IT Processes, Organization and Relationships • PO7 Manage IT Human Resources	N/A	**Security Standard:** a) 3. Termination Procedures (A)	**Implement Strong Access Control Measures:** 8.5.4 - Immediately revoke access for any terminated users **Maintain an Information Security Policy:** 12. Maintain a policy that addresses information security for employees and contractors	N/A	**Symantec™ Security Information Manager** Ability to monitor, search and query on user activity **Symantec™ Control Compliance Suite** Ability to establish termination policies and track compliance to the requirements; help ensure, via controls self-assessment capability, that termination procedures are understood and implemented **Symantec Enterprise Vault™** Prevent the use of PST files and risk of PST files leaving the company **Symantec Consulting Services** Develop policies and procedures covering Human Resources related information security
SECTION: 9 Physical and Environmental Security						
9.1 **Secure Areas** To prevent unauthorized physical access, damage, and interference to the organization's premises and information • Critical or sensitive information processing facilities should be housed in secure areas • Protection provided should be commensurate with the identified risks	**Deliver and Support:** • DS5 Ensure Systems Security • DS11 Manage Data • DS12 Manage the Physical Environment	• Control Activities • Information and Communication • Monitoring	**Security Standard:** a) 3. Authorization and/or Supervision (A) a) 3. Workforce Clearance Procedure (A) **Physical Standard:** a) 1. Facility Access Control a) 2. Facility Security Plan a) 2. Access Control and Validation Procedures (A)	**Implement Strong Access Control Measures:** 9. Restrict physical access to cardholder data	III.C. Manage and Control Risk	**Symantec Consulting Services** Deliver physical security posture assessment; develop policies and procedures covering Physical and Environmental Security
9.2 **Equipment Security** To prevent loss, damage, theft or compromise of assets and interruption to the organization's activities	**Deliver and Support:** • DS12 Manage the Physical Environment	• Control Activities • Information and Communication	**Physical Standard:** a) 1. Facility Access Control b) Workstation Use (R) c) Workstation Security d) 1. Device and Media Controls – Disposal (R) d) 2. Media Re-use (R) d) 2. Device and Media Controls – Accountability (A)	**Implement Strong Access Control Measures:** 9.1.3 - Restrict physical access to wireless access points, gateways, and handheld devices	III.C. Manage and Control Risk	**Symantec Consulting Services** Develop policies and procedures covering Equipment Security

FIGURE 11.18

IT Controls Reference

SECTION: 10 Communications and Operations Management						
10.1 **OperationalProceduresandResponsibilities** Responsibilities and procedures for the management and operation of all information processing facilities should be established • Segregation of duties should be implemented	**Plan and Organize:** • PO4 Define the IT Processes, Organization and Relationships **Acquire and Implement:** • A16 Manage Changes **Deliver and Support:** • DS4 Ensure Continuous Service • DS13 Manage Operations	• Internal Environment • Risk Response • Control Activities • Monitoring	**Security Standard:** a) 1. Information System Activity Review (R) a) 1. Sanction Policy (R) a) 2. Assigned Security Responsibility (R) b) 1. Written Contract or Other Arrangement (R) a) 6. Response and Reporting (R) **Physical Standard:** a) 2. Contingency Operations (R)	**Maintain a Vulnerability Management Program** 6.3.3 - Separate development/test and production environments	III.C. Manage and Control Risk	**Symantec™ Security Information Manager** Ability to search and query on user activity and that best practices are in place **Symantec™ Control Compliance Suite** Gather permissions on control points data, provides a consolidated view of entitlements, and enable periodic approval workflow Symantec Altiris Inventory, treat, and manage information technology assets, ensuring the security posture throughout an assets lifecycle **Symantec Enterprise Vault™** Supports audited, roles based search and review of email, IM and files **Symantec Consulting Services** Develop policies, procedures, guidelines and standards covering Communications and Operations Management
10.2 **Third Party Service Delivery Management** Validate the implementation of agreements, monitor compliance, and manage changes to ensure that all services delivered meet requirements set out in agreements	**Plan and Organize:** • PO4 Define the IT Processes, Organization and Relationships • PO8 Manage Quality • PO10 Manage Projects **Deliver and Support:** • DS1 Define and Manage Service Levels • DS2 Manage Third-Party Services	• Internal Environment • Control Activities	**Security Standard:** b) 1. Written Contract or Other Arrangement	**Maintain an Information Security Policy:** 12.8.2 Maintain a written agreement that includes acknowledgement that the service providers are responsible for the security of cardholder data teh service providers posess.	III.D. Oversee Service Provider Arrangements	**Symantec™ Control Compliance Suite** Define and manage information security programs **Symantec Consulting Services** Develop policies, procedures, guidelines and standards covering Communications and Operations Management related to Third Party Service Delivery
10.3 **System Planning and Acceptance** To minimize the risk of systems failures • Advanced planning and preparation are required to ensure availability and adequate capacity of resources • Operational requirements of new systems should be established, documented, and tested	**Deliver and Support:** • DS3 Manage Performance and Capacity • DS4 Ensure Continuous Service	• Control Activities • Monitoring	N/A	**Maintain a Vulnerability Management Program:** 6. Develop and maintain secure systems and applications **Regularly Monitor and Test Networks:** 11. Regularly test security systems and processes	III.C. Manage and Control Risk	**Symantec™ Security Information Manager** **Symantec™ Control Compliance Suite** Ensure that systems are secure and best practices are in place Symantec Altiris Inventory, treat, and manage information technology assets, ensuring the security posture throughout an assets lifecycle **Symantec Consulting Services** Deliver Application Design Assessments, Application Architecture Assessments, Application Development Lifecycle Review, Code Review and Application Penetration Test
10.4 **Protection Against Malicious and Mobile Code** Precautions are required to prevent and detect the introduction of malicious code and unauthorized mobile code	**Deliver and Support:** • DS5 Ensure Systems Security • DS8 Manage Service Desk and Incidents • DS9 Manage the Configuration • DS10 Manage Problems	• Control Activities • Event Identification • Information and Communication	**Security Standard:** a) 4. Access Establishment and Modification (A) a) 5. Protection from Malicious Software	**Maintain a Vulnerability Management Program:** 5. Use and regularly update anti-virus software 6. Develop and maintain secure systems and applications	III.C. Manage and Control Risk	**Symantec™ Security Information Manager** Ability to manage response through incident notification and workflow **Symantec™ Endpoint Protection** Prevents, detects and remediates malicious and unauthorized code for managed endpoints (laptops, desktops and servers owned by the organization) **Symantec™ Mobile Security** Prevents, detects and remediates malicious and unauthorized code for managed endpoints (PDAs, handhelds, smartphones owned by the organization) Symantec Altiris Inventory, treat, and manage information technology assets, ensuring the security posture throughout an assets lifecycle **Symantec™ On-Demand Protection** Protects against malicious and unauthorized code for unmanaged endpoints (laptops, desktops and servers not owned by the organization) **Symantec™ Critical System Protection** Prevents, detects and remediates malicious and unauthorized code for heterogeneous servers that host sensitive and confidential information **Symantec Consulting Services** Deliver Application Design Assessments, Application Architecture Assessments, Application Development Lifecycle Review, Code Review and Application Penetration Test
10.5 **Back-up** To maintain the integrity and availability of information and information processing facilities	**Deliver and Support:** • DS4 Ensure Continuous Service • DS11 Manage Data	• Event Identification • Control Activities • Monitoring	**Security Standard:** a) 7. Data Backup Plan (R) a) 7. Disaster Recovery Plan (R) a) 7. Emergency Mode Operation Plan (R) a) 7. Testing And Revision Procedure (A) **Physical Standard:** a) 2. Contingency Operations (R) a) 2. Data Backup and Storage (A)	**Implement Strong Access Control Measures:** 9. Restrict physical access to cardholder data **Regularly Monitor and Test Networks:** 10. Track and monitor all access to network resources and cardholder data **Maintain an Information Security Policy:** 12. Maintain a policy that addresses information security for employees and contractors	III.C. Manage and Control Risk	**Symantec™ Security Information Manager** Ensure that systems are secure and best practices are in place **Symantec Enterprise Vault™** Facilitates faster backup and recovery of email applications and file systems **Veritas NetBackup™ Server** **Symantec Backup Exec™** Ability to conduct backup and recovery on all enterprise devices **Symantec Consulting Services** Policy Development Services, Residency Services to transfer best-practices for storage management to enterprise, Services to outsource storage management
10.6 **Network Security Management** To ensure the protection of information in networks and the protection of the supporting infrastructure	**Deliver and Support:** • DS5 Ensure Systems Security	• Risk Assessment • Control Activities • Monitoring	**Technical Standard:** a) 2. Encryption and Decryption (A) (e) 1. Transmission Security (e) 2. Integrity Controls (A)	**Build and Maintain a Secure Network:** 1. Install and maintain a firewall 2. Do not use vendor-supplied defaults for system passwords and other security parameters **Maintain a Vulnerability Management Program:** 5. Use and regularly update anti-virus software 6. Develop and maintain secure systems and applications	III.C. Manage and Control Risk	**Symantec™ Security Information Manager** Ensure that systems are secure and best practices are in place **Symantec Endpoint Protection** Ability to prevent introduction of non-compliant, insecure devices onto corporate network, reducing the likelihood of information being compromised Symantec Altiris Inventory, treat, and manage information technology assets, ensuring the security posture throughout an assets lifecycle Symantec Data Loss Prevention - Gain visibility of data in motion and ensure that sensitive data is being disseminated in accordance with security policies and any relevant security controls **Symantec Consulting Services** Deliver security reviews, penetration tests and vulnerability assessments of network security; provide monitoring of compliance of servers and devices through Symantec Operational Services
10.7 **Media Handling** To prevent unauthorized disclosure, modification, removal or destruction of assets, and interruption to business activities • Media should be controlled and physically protected • Appropriate operating procedures should be established to protect, documents, and computer media	**Deliver and Support:** • DS11 Manage Data	• Control Activities • Information and Communication	**Physical Standard:** d) 1. Device and Media Controls – Disposal (R) d) 2. Media Re-use (R) d) 2. Device and Media Controls - Accountability (A)	**Protect Cardholder Data:** 3. Protect stored data 4. Encrypt transmissions of cardholder data and sensitive information across public networks **Implement Strong Access Control Measures:** 7. Restrict access to data by business need-to-know 9. Restrict physical access to cardholder data **Regularly Monitor and Test Networks:** 11. Regularly test security systems and processes **Maintain an Information Security Policy:** 12. Maintain a policy that addresses information security for employees and contractors	III.C. Manage and Control Risk	**Symantec Enterprise Vault™** Prevent the use of PST files and risk of PST files leaving the company; enforce preservation of data with legal hold **Symantec Consulting Services** Provide policies, procedures, standards and guidelines covering Media Handling
10.8 **Exchange of Information** To maintain the security of information and software exchanged within an organization and with any external entity	**Deliver and Support:** • DS5 Ensure Systems Security	• Risk Assessment • Risk Response • Control Activities • Information and Communication • Monitoring	**Security Standard:** b) 1. Written Contract or Other Arrangement (R) **Technical Standard:** a) 2. Encryption and Decryption (A) (d) Person or Entity Authentication (R) (e) 1. Transmission Security (e) 2. Integrity Controls (A)	**Build and Maintain a Secure Network:** 1. Install and maintain a firewall **Protect Cardholder Data:** 4. Encrypt transmissions of cardholder data and sensitive information across public networks **Implement Strong Access Control Measures:** 7. Restrict access to data by business need-to-know **Implement Strong Access Control Measures:** 8. Assign a unique ID to each person with computer access **Maintain an Information Security Policy:** 12. Maintain a policy that addresses information security for employees and contractors	III.C. Manage and Control Risk	**Symantec Enterprise Vault™** Audited export of electronically stored information for E-discovery Symantec Data Loss Prevention - Gain visibility of data in motion and ensure that sensitive data is being shared with third parties in accordance with security policies and any relevant security controls **Symantec Consulting Services** Provide policies, procedures, standards and guidelines covering Exchange of Information
10.9 **Electronic Commerce Services** To ensure the security of electronic commerce services, and their secure use.	**Deliver and Support:** • DS5 Ensure Systems Security	• Event Identification • Control Activities	N/A	**Build and Maintain a Secure Network:** 1. Install and maintain a firewall configuration to protect data 2. Do not use vendor-supplied defaults for system passwords and other security parameters **Protect Cardholder Data:** 4. Encrypt transmissions of cardholder data and sensitive information across public networks **Maintain a Vulnerability Management Program:** 6. Develop and maintain secure systems and applications	III.C. Manage and Control Risk	Symantec Altiris Inventory, treat, and manage information technology assets, ensuring the security posture throughout an assets lifecycle **Symantec Consulting Services** Develop policies, procedures and standards covering Electronic Commerce Services; conduct vulnerability assessments; conduct security infrastructure review
10.10 **Monitoring** To detect unauthorized information processing activities including review of operator logs and fault logging • Systems should be monitored and information security events should be recorded • Organization should comply with all relevant legal requirements applicable to monitoring and logging • System monitoring should be used to check the effectiveness of controls adopted and to verify conformity to access policies	**Deliver and Support:** • DS5 Ensure Systems Security **Monitor and Evaluate:** • ME1 Monitor and Evaluate IT Performance • ME2 Monitor and Evaluate Internal Control	• Control Activities • Monitoring	**Security Standard:** a) 5. Log-In Monitoring (A) a) 1. Information System Activity Review (R) b) 8. Audit Controls (R)	**Implement Strong Access Control Measures:** 8. Assign a unique ID to each person with computer access **Regularly Monitor and Test Networks:** 10. Track and monitor all access to network resources and cardholder data	III.C. Manage and Control Risk	**Symantec™ Security Information Manager** Ability to consolidate logs and conduct period reviews of access Symantec Data Loss Prevention - Identify, classify, adn monitor critical information stores across hetergenous infrastructures **Symantec Consulting Services** Develop policies, procedures and standards covering Electronic Commerce Services; conduct vulnerability assessments; conduct security infrastructure review
SECTION: 11 Access Control						
11.1 **Business Requirement for Access Control** Access to information, information processing facilities, and business processes should be controlled based upon business and security requirements. • Access controls should take account policies for information dissemination and authorization	**Deliver and Support:** • DS5 Ensure Systems Security	• Internal Environment • Control Activities	**Security Standard:** a) 4. Access Authorization (A)	**Implement Strong Access Control Measures:** 8. Assign a unique ID to each person with computer access **Maintain an Information Security Policy:** 12. Maintain a policy that addresses information security for employees and contractors	III.C. Manage and Control Risk	**Symantec™ Security Information Manager** Ability to search, query and notify on user activity **Symantec™ Control Compliance Suite** Ability to author, review, publish, and ensure sign-off on access control policies **Symantec Consulting Services** Develop policies, procedures, standards and guidelines covering Access Control; conduct audits to ensure access control measures are in place and operational
11.2 **User Access Management** Formal procedures to control the allocation of access rights to information systems and services	**Deliver and Support:** • DS5 Ensure Systems Security	• Control Activities • Monitoring	**Security Standard:** a) 4. Access Authorization (A) a) 4. Access Establishment and Modification (A) a) 5. Password Management (A) **Technical Standard :** a) 2. Unique User Identification (R)	**Implement Strong Access Control Measures:** 7. Restrict access to data by business need-to-know 8. Assign a unique ID to each person with computer access	III.C. Manage and Control Risk	**Symantec™ Security Information Manager** Ability to search, query and notify on user activity **Symantec™ Control Compliance Suite** Gather permissions on control points data, provides a consolidated view of entitlements, and enable periodic approval workflow **Symantec Consulting Services** Develop policies, procedures, standards and guidelines covering User Access Management; conduct audits to ensure access control measures are in place and operational
11.3 **User Responsibilities** To prevent unauthorized user access, and compromise or theft of information and information processing capabilities	**Deliver and Support:** • DS5 Ensure Systems Security	• Internal Environment • Control Activities	**Security Standard:** a) 5. Password Management (A) **Physical Standard:** b) Workstation Use (R) c) Workstation Security	**Build and Maintain a Secure Network:** 2. Do not use vendor-supplied defaults for system passwords **Implement Strong Access Control Measures:** 8. Assign a unique ID to each person with computer access **Maintain an Information Security Policy:** 12. Maintain a policy that addresses information security for employees and contractors	III.C. Manage and Control Risk	**Symantec™ Control Compliance Suite** Ensure user awareness of control requirements via policy dissemination and acceptance tracking Symantec Altiris Inventory, treat, and manage information technology assets, ensuring the security posture throughout an assets lifecycle **Symantec Consulting Services** Develop policies, procedures, standards and guidelines covering User Responsibilities; conduct audits to ensure User Responsibilities policies are enforced
11.4 **Network Access Control** Ensure that appropriate interfaces and authentication mechanisms to networked services are in place	**Deliver and Support:** • DS5 Ensure Systems Security	• Internal Environment • Control Activities • Monitoring	**Security Standard:** a) 5. Password Management (A) **Technical Standard:** c) 2. Mechanism to Authenticate Electronic Protected Health Information (A) d) Person or Entity Authentication (R)	**Build and Maintain a Secure Network:** 2. Do not use vendor-supplied defaults for system passwords **Implement Strong Access Control Measures:** 8. Assign a unique ID to each person with computer access	III.C. Manage and Control Risk	**Symantec™ Security Information Manager** Ability to search, query and notify on user activity **Symantec™ Network Access Control** Enforces that managed endpoints (laptops, desktops and servers owned by the organization) meet minimum endpoint security requirements prior to allowing access to the corporate network; non-compliant endpoint can be automatically remediated **Symantec™ On-Demand Protection** Ensures that unmanaged endpoints (laptops, desktops and servers not owned by the organization) meet minimum endpoint security requirements prior to allowing access to the corporate network **Symantec Consulting Services** Develop policies, procedures, standards and guidelines covering Network Access Control; conduct audits to ensure Network Access Control measures are in place and operational
11.5 **Operating System Access Control** To prevent unauthorized access to operating systems. Some methods include: ensure quality passwords, user authentication, and the recording of successful and failed system accesses, providing appropriate authentication control means	**Deliver and Support:** • DS5 Ensure Systems Security	• Internal Environment • Control Activities • Monitoring	**Security Standard:** a) 4. Access Establishment and Modification (A) a) 5. Password Management (A) **Technical Standard:** a) 2. Unique User Identification (R) a) 2. Automatic Logoff (A) d) Person or Entity Authentication (R)	**Build and Maintain a Secure Network:** 2. Do not use vendor-supplied defaults for system passwords **Implement Strong Access Control Measures:** 8. Assign a unique ID to each person with computer access **Monitor and Test Networks:** 10. Track and monitor all access to network resources and cardholder data	III.C. Manage and Control Risk	**Symantec™ Security Information Manager** Ability to search, query and notify on user activity **Symantec™ Control Compliance Suite** Ensure system security by automating the management of deviations from technical standards/best practices and providing the ability to remediate misconfigurations Symantec Altiris Inventory, treat, and manage information technology assets, ensuring the security posture throughout an assets lifecycle **Symantec Consulting Services** Develop policies, procedures, standards and guidelines covering Operating System Access Control; conduct audits to ensure Operational System Access Control are in place and operational

FIGURE 11.18 Continued

IT Controls Reference

11.6 **ApplicationandInformationAccessControl** • To prevent unauthorized access to information held in application systems. • Security facilities should be used to restrict access to an within application systems • Logical access to application software and information system functions	**Deliver and Support:** • DS5 Ensure Systems Security	• Control Activities • Monitoring	**Security Standard:** a) 4. Access Establishment and Modification (A) a) 5. Password Management (A) **Technical Standard:** a) 2. Unique User Identification (R) d) Person or Entity Authentication (R)	**Build and Maintain a Secure Network:** 1. Do not use vendor-supplied defaults for system passwords **Maintain a Vulnerability Management System:** 6. Develop and maintain secure systems and applications **Implement Strong Access Control Measures:** 8. Assign a unique ID to each person with computer access	III.C. Manage and Control Risk	**Symantec™ Security Information Manager** Ability to search, query and notify on user activity Symantec Altiris Inventory, treat, and manage information technology assets, ensuring the security posture throughout an assets lifecycle **Symantec Consulting Services** Develop policies, procedures, standards and guidelines covering Application and Information Access Control; conduct audits to ensure Application and Information Access Control policies are enforced
11.7 **Mobile Computing and Teleworking** To ensure information security when using mobile computing and teleworking facilities	**Deliver and Support:** • DS5 Ensure Systems Security	• Internal Environment • Control Activities • Monitoring	**Security Standard:** a) 4. Access Establishment and Modification (A)	**Build and Maintain a Secure Network:** 1. Install and maintain a firewall configuration to protect data **Build and Maintain a Secure Network:** 2. Do not use vendor-supplied defaults for system passwords and other security parameters **Implement Strong Access Control Measures:** 8. Assign a unique ID to each person with computer access	III.C. Manage and Control Risk	**Symantec™ Endpoint Protection** Prevents, detects and remediates malicious and unauthorized code for mananged endpoints (laptops, desktops and servers owned by the organization) **Symantec™ Mobile Security** Prevents, detects and remediates malicious and unauthorized code for mananged endpoints (PDAs, handhelds, smartphones owned by the organization) **Symantec™ On-Demand Protection** Protects against malicious and unauthorized code for unmanged endpoints (laptops, desktops and servers not owned by the organization) Symantec Altiris Inventory, treat, and manage information technology assets, ensuring the security posture throughout an assets lifecycle **Symantec Consulting Services** Develop policies, procedures, standards and guidelines covering Mobile Computing and Teleworking; conduct audits to ensure Mobile Computing and Teleworking policies are enforced; conduct wireless assessments of client's network
SECTION: 12 Information Systems Acquisition, Development and Maintenance						
12.1 **Ensure that security is an integral part of information systems** Security should be built into operating systems, infrastructure, business applications, off the shelf products, and user-developed applications	**Acquire and Implement:** • A12 Acquire and Maintain Application Software • A13 Acquire and Maintain Technology Infrastructure	• Control Activities • Monitoring	N/A	**Maintain a Vulnerability Management Program:** 6. Develop and maintain secure systems and applications	N/A	**Symantec™ Security Information Manager** Ensure that systems are secure and best practices are in place **Symantec Consulting Services** Security Architecture and Design Assessments of infrastructure and applications to ensure security is a key design element; Application Development Lifecycle Reviews to ensure threat and security assessment is an integral part of the development process
12.2 **Correct Processing in Applications** To prevent errors, loss, unauthorized modification or misuse of information in applications	**Acquire and Implement:** • A12 Acquire and Maintain Application Software	• Control Activities	**Technical Standard:** e) 2. Transmission Security – Integrity Controls (A)	**Maintain a Vulnerability Management Program:** 6. Develop and maintain secure systems and applications	III.C. Manage and Control Risk	**Symantec Consulting Services** Security Architecture and Design Assessments of infrastructure and applications to ensure security is a key design element; Application Development Lifecycle Reviews to ensure threat and security assessment is an integral part of the development process
12.3 **Cryptographic Controls** • To protect the confidentiality, authenticity or integrity of information by cryptographic means. • Policy should be developed on the use of cryptographic controls • Key management should be in place to support cryptographic techniques	**Deliver and Support:** • DS5 Ensure Systems Security	• Control Activities • Monitoring	**Technical Standard:** a) 2. Encryption and Decryption (A) e) 2. Transmission Security – Encryption (A)	**Protect Cardholder Data:** 3. Protect stored data 4. Encrypt transmission of cardholder data and sensitive information across public networks	III.C. Manage and Control Risk	**Symantec™ Security Information Manager** Ensure that systems are secure and best practices are in place **Symantec Consulting Services** Design Assessments of applications to ensure encryption is correctly managed in applications; penetration assessments to ensure encryption is correctly implemented within applications
12.4 **Security of System Files** To ensure security of system files through the control of access to system files and program source code	**Acquire and Implement:** • A16 Manage Changes **Deliver and Support** • DS5 Ensure Systems Security	• Control Activities • Information and Communication Monitoring	N/A	**Build and Maintain a Secure Network:** 2. Do not use vendor-supplied defaults for system passwords and other security parameters	III.C. Manage and Control Risk	**Symantec™ Security Information Manager** Provide a watchlist for monitoring of critical system files **Symantec™ Control Compliance Suite** Gather permissions on control points data, provides a consolidated view of entitlements, and enable periodic approval workflow **Symantec Consulting Services** Host Security Assessments to validate system security posture; host Hardening and Secure Build Programs to manage system security
12.5 **Security in Development and Support Processes** Project and support environments should be strictly controlled	**Acquire and Implement:** • A16 Manage Changes **Deliver and Support** • DS5 Ensure Systems Security	• Control Activities • Monitoring	N/A	**Maintain a Vulnerability Management Program:** 6. Develop and maintain secure systems and applications	N/A	**Symantec™ Security Information Manager** Ensure that systems are secure and best practices are in place Symantec Altiris Inventory, treat, and manage information technology assets, ensuring the security posture throughout an assets lifecycle **Symantec Consulting Services** Host and Network Device Security Assessments to validate system security posture; Host Hardening, Network Device Hardening and Secure Build Programs to manage system security
12.6 **Technical Vulnerability Management** To reduce risks resulting from exploitation of published technical vulnerabilities • Technical vulnerability management should be effective, systematic, and repeatable	**Plan and Organize;** • PO9 Assess and Manage IT Risks **Deliver and Support:** • DS2 Manage Third-Party Services • DS4 Ensure Continuous Service • DS5 Ensure Systems Security • DS9 Manage the Configuration **Monitor and Evaluate:** • ME1 Monitor and Evaluate IT Performance	N/A	**Security Standard:** a) 6. Response and Reporting (R)	**Maintain a Vulnerability Management Program:** 5. Use and regularly update antivirus software 6. Develop and maintain secure systems and applications	III.C. Manage and Control Risk	**Symantec™ Security Information Manager** Manage response through workflow and distribute reporting automatically **Symantec™ Control Compliance Suite** Ensure system security by automates the management of deviations from technical standards/best practices and providing the ability to remediate misconfigurations Symantec Altiris Inventory, treat, and manage information technology assets, ensuring the security posture throughout an assets lifecycle **Symantec Consulting Services** Threat and Vulnerability Management Programs to provide an integrated approach to vulnerability management
SECTION: 13 Information Security Incident Management						
13.1 **InformationSecurityIncidentManagement** To ensure information security events and weaknesses associated with information systems are communicated in a manner allowing timely corrective action to be taken • Formal event reporting and and escalation procedures should be in place	**Deliver and Support:** • DS5 Ensure Systems Security • DS8 Manage Service Desk and Incidents • DS10 Manage Problems **Monitor and Evaluate:** • ME1 Monitor and Evaluate IT Performance • ME2 Monitor and Evaluate Internal Control	N/A	**Security Standard:** a) 6. Response and Reporting (R)	**Maintain a Vulnerability Management Program:** 6. Develop and maintain secure systems and applications **Regularly Monitor and Test Networks:** 11. Regularly test security systems and processes **Maintain an Information Security Policy:** 12. Maintain a policy that addresses information security for employees and contractors	III.C. Manage and Control Risk	**Symantec™ Security Information Manager** Ability to gather, alert, and trend on security events and weaknesses in real time **Symantec™ Control Compliance Suite** Ensure system security by automates the management of deviations from technical standards/best practices and providing the ability to remediate misconfigurations **Symantec Consulting Services** Develop policies, procedures, standards and guidelines covering Reporting Information Security Events and Weaknesses; Provide Incident Response Programs
13.2 **Management of Information Security** **Incidents and Improvements** • To ensure a consistent and effective approach is applied to the management of information security incidents	**Deliver and Support:** • DS5 Ensure Systems Security • DS8 Manage Service Desk and Incidents • DS10 Manage Problems **Monitor and Evaluate:** • ME1 Monitor and Evaluate IT Performance • ME2 Monitor and Evaluate Internal Control	N/A	N/A	**Maintain an Information Security Policy:** 12. Maintain a policy that addresses information security for employees and contractors	III.C. Manage and Control Risk	**Symantec™ Security Information Manager** Ability to manage security events through incident workflow and integration to change management systems **Symantec Consulting Services** Develop policies, procedures, standards and guidelines covering Management of Information Security Incidents; provide Incident Response Programs
SECTION: 14 Business Continuity Management						
14.1 **Information Security Aspects of Business Continuity Management** To counteract interruptions to business activities and to protect critical business processes from the effects of major failures or disasters and to ensure their timely resumption	**Deliver and Support:** • DS4 Ensure Continuous Service • DS10 Manage Problems • DS11 Manage Data	• Event Identification • Risk Response • Control Activities • Information and Communication • Monitoring	**Security Standard:** a) 7. Disaster Recovery Plan (R) a) 7. Testing and Revision Procedures (A) a) 7. Applications and Data Criticality Analysis (A)	**Maintain an Information Security Policy:** 12. Maintain a policy that addresses information security for employees and contractors	III.C. Manage and Control Risk	**Symantec™ Security Information Manager** Ensure that systems are secure and best practices are in place **Veritas™ product line** Ensure rapid data recovery from major failures **Symantec Consulting Services** Develop business continuity strategy, framework, plans, policies and procedures; conduct business impact analysis and operational risk assessments to develop business continuity plans
SECTION: 15 Compliance						
15.1 **Compliance with Legal Requirements** To avoid breaches of any law, statutory, regulatory or contractual obligations, and of any security requirements	**Monitor and Evaluate:** • ME3 Ensure Regulatory Compliance • ME4 Provide IT Governance	• Internal Environment • Event Identification • Risk Assessment • Control Activities • Information and Communication • Monitoring	**Security Standard:** a) 1. Sanction Policy (R) a) 6. Response and Reporting (R) b) 1. Written Contract or Other Arrangement (R)	**Maintain an Information Security Policy:** 12. Maintain a policy that addresses information security for employees and contractors	III.C. Manage and Control Risk III.F. Report to the Board	**Symantec™ Security Information Manager** Ensure that systems are secure and best practices are in place **Symantec™ Control Compliance Suite** Automate assessment of legal IT procedural and technical controls from across infrastructure management systems, and consolidate evidence into a single repository **Symantec Enterprise Vault™** Support email retention, monitoring and discovery requirements Symantec Data Loss Prevention - Identify, classify, and monitor movement of critical information stores across hetergenous infrastructures **Symantec Consulting Services** Conduct security audits to ensure Compliance with Legal Requirements; provide onsite compliance monitoring
15.2 **Compliance with Security Policies and Standards, and Technical Compliance** To ensure compliance of systems with organizational security policies and standards	**Acquire and Implement:** • AI7 Install and Accredit Solutions and Changes **Monitor and Evaluate:** • ME1 Monitor and Evaluate IT Performance • ME2 Monitor and Evaluate Internal Control • ME4 Provide IT Governance	• Internal Environment • Control Activities • Monitoring	**Security Standard:** a) 8. Technical evaluation that measures compliance with security requirements (R)	**Regularly Monitor and Test Networks:** 10. Track and monitor all access to network resources and cardholder data 11. Regularly test security systems and processes **Maintain an Information Security Policy:** 12. Maintain a policy that addresses information security for employees and contractors	III.C. Manage and Control Risk III.E. Adjust the Program III.F. Report to the Board	**Symantec™ Security Information Manager** Ensure that systems are secure and best practices are in place via integration with compliance tools like Symantec Control Compliance Suite **Symantec™ Network Access Control** Enforces that managed endpoints (laptops, desktops and servers owned by the organization) meet minimum endpoint security requirements/policies/standards prior to allowing access to the corporate network; non-compliant endpoint can be automatically remediated **Symantec™ On-Demand Protection** Enforces that unmanaged endpoints (laptops, desktops and servers not owned by the organization) meet minimum endpoint security requirements/policies/standards prior to allowing access to the corporate network **Symantec™ Control Compliance Suite** Ensure policy coverage via mapping to control objectives, and collect/trend evidence of compliance to key regulations and frameworks Symantec Data Loss Prevention - Identify, classify, and monitor critical information stores across hetergenous infrastructures ensuring compliance with regulatory requirements **Symantec Enterprise Vault™** Automatically enforce retention, preservation and expiry of unstructured content such as email, IM and files **Symantec Consulting Services** Conduct security audits to ensure Compliance with Legal Requirements; provide onsite compliance monitoring

www.symantec.com/compliance

FIGURE 11.18 Continued

IT Controls Reference

To manage costs and stay in compliance with laws and regulations, organizations are adopting recognized frameworks such as COBIT.

Control Objectives for Information and Related Technology (COBIT) was developed by the Information Systems Audit and Control Association (ISACA) and the Information Technology Governance Institute (ITGI). This framework defines goals and objectives for the controls that should be in place for management of information technology. Currently, ISACA is in the process of updating the COBIT framework.

The premise of the COBIT framework is that IT resources are used by IT processes to achieve IT goals related to business requirements. The COBIT cube (Figure 11.19) shows the three dimensions:

- IT resources
- IT processes
- Business requirements

IT Resources

IT resources can be divided into the following four categories:

- **Applications** consist of manual and programmed procedures to process information. An example of a manual procedure would be manually opening incoming mail containing customer checks. A programmed procedure would be processing the mail checks in the accounting system using accounting software.
- **Information** includes structured and unstructured data in any form, such as text, graphics, pictures, audio, and video. Data is input, processed, and output by the system.
- **Infrastructure** refers to IT technology including hardware and software. Infrastructure also includes physical structures, such as a data center facility.
- **People** include staff members as well as their knowledge and skills to plan, organize, acquire, implement, deliver, support, monitor, and evaluate IT processes and systems.

IT Processes

IT processes use the preceding IT resources. IT processes deliver information, run applications, and use infrastructure and people to accomplish IT goals in light of business requirements.

IT processes are grouped into the following four domains. Notice that these four domains and their order of execution roughly correspond to the system development life cycle (SDLC) phases.

- **Plan and Organize (PO) Domain.** This domain relates to IT strategy and tactics to contribute to attaining business goals. The plan and organize domain addresses organization and IT infrastructure. The COBIT framework has ten IT processes in the plan and organize domain.
- **Acquire and Implement (AI) Domain.** To attain the IT strategy, IT solutions must be identified, acquired (built or bought), and implemented. The acquire and implement domain also ensures that the proper SDLC phases and activities are used when upgrading and modifying current systems.
- **Deliver and Support (DS) Domain.** Concerned with the delivery of IT services, this domain encompasses IT operations, security, and training. It assures the continued support and maintenance of these services. The deliver and support domain is comprised of 13 processes.
- **Monitor and Evaluate (ME) Domain.** IT processes must be monitored for compliance with control requirements. The domain includes management oversight of control processes as well as independent assurance services provided by internal and external audits. The monitor and evaluate domain consists of four processes.

The COBIT framework breaks down each of the domains into a list of detailed processes and activities. For example, the plan and organize (PO) domain provides guidance to organizations when planning a strategic IT change or improvement.

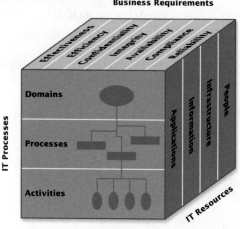

FIGURE 11.19

COBIT Cube

Information Criteria

Information criteria are criteria that information must meet in order to satisfy business goals and objectives.

Three of the information criteria relate to information security: confidentiality, integrity, and availability (CIA).

- **Confidentiality.** This criterion addresses the requirement to protect confidential data from unauthorized disclosure and use.
- **Integrity.** Data integrity refers to data accuracy, completeness, and validity.
- **Availability.** Data availability requires that data be available for use when needed for business processes. This criterion also addresses safeguarding information assets.

For the remaining four information criteria, COBIT relied upon definitions used by COSO's *Internal Control—Integrated Framework*.

- **Effectiveness.** The effectiveness of information criteria refers to the information being relevant and pertinent to business processes. In addition, the information should be timely, accurate, and usable.
- **Efficiency.** Efficiency of information refers to providing information using resources in the most productive and economic way.
- **Compliance.** This criterion refers to information conforming with laws and regulations, such as the Sarbanes-Oxley Act.
- **Reliability.** The reliability of information relates to providing information that management can rely upon to meet financial and compliance reporting responsibilities.

IT processes use IT resources to achieve IT goals related to the information criteria of confidentiality, integrity, availability, effectiveness, efficiency, compliance, and reliability.

Accounting System Insights

Insight No. 20 When it comes to cybersecurity at the crossroads of accounting and IT, use the prudence principle.

Active Review

Study less. Learn more. Make connections.

11.1 Refer to the chapter opener, *Meet Heartland.* In your opinion, how was it possible for Heartland to have been audited and certified by Payment Card Industry Data Security Standards and still have been hacked?

11.2 Discuss what motivates hackers use to break into computer systems.

11.3 Discuss the security of laptop computers versus desktop computers.

11.4 Why do organizations leave the DMZ less secure than the rest of the intranet?

11.5 What section of the enterprise-wide network is located in the DMZ? Why?

11.6 This text uses the ISC² 10 domain framework for cybersecurity. Discuss which of those domains are related to the IT controls in the previous chapter, *Fraud and Internal Control*.

11.7 In this text you learned about many types of malware (malicious software). In your opinion, which one is the most damaging to an organization's information assets and computer systems? Why?

11.8 Discuss why longer passwords are more secure than shorter ones. Why are passwords with a combination of characters and digits more secure than those with just alphabetic characters? Can you think of any 'cons' to longer, alphanumeric passwords that need to be changed frequently?

11.9 Discuss the Gramm-Leach-Bliley Act and its impact on cybersecurity.

11.10 Discuss how changes in information technology affect cybersecurity. Give an example to illustrate.

Key Terms Check

Understanding the language used at the crossroads of accounting and IT is key to your success.

11.11 Match the following terms and definitions.

a. cybercrime
b. cyberlaw
c. cyber forensics
d. pretexting
e. password sniffing
f. salami attacks
g. social engineering
h. phishing
i. dumpster diving

_____ 1. Usually targeting the accounting department, these attacks are electronic theft of very small amounts numerous times, such as rounding of fractions of a cent from interest calculations

_____ 2. A form of social engineering, the attacker fishes for sensitive, private data, such as using an authentic-looking fraudulent Web site

_____ 3. Attacks involving manipulating and tricking individuals into divulging confidential information, such as imposter emails

_____ 4. Social engineering attacks that involve creating a scenario and using deception for information gathering purposes

_____ 5. Rummaging through garbage for discarded documents or digital media

_____ 6. Attempts to obtain passwords by reading messages sent on a network

_____ 7. Involves collecting, examining, and preventing evidence of cybercrime

_____ 8. Crimes connected to information assets and IT

_____ 9. Laws and regulations to prevent, investigate, and prosecute cybercrimes

11.12 Match the following terms and definitions.

a. viruses
b. Trojan horse
c. worms
d. logic bombs
e. bots
f. spam

_____ 1. Malicious software that executes when a specified event occurs, such as logging into a bank account

_____ 2. Malware sent by email that can be a virus, a Trojan horse, worms, logic bombs, or bots

_____ 3. Malware disguised as a legitimate program

_____ 4. Tiny pieces of programming code that install themselves on an infected computer called a zombie and transmit data back to the hackers' computers without the awareness of the zombie computer user

_____ 5. Relatively small programs that infect other application software by attaching to it and disturbing application functioning

_____ 6. Similar to viruses except they do not need a host application to function or reproduce

11.13 Select the single best answer.

Identifying users by analyzing their personal attributes, such as face recognition, is called

a. honeypot.
b. firewall.
c. DMZ.
d. biometrics.

11.14 Select the single best answer.

Software generally located on routing devices (bridges, routers, and gateways) to monitor network traffic and prevent unauthorized access is

a. honeypot.
b. firewall.
c. DMZ.
d. biometrics.

11.15 Select the single best answer.

An area between the enterprise's first firewall to the outside world and the next firewall is called

a. honeypot.
b. firewall.
c. DMZ.
d. biometrics.

11.16 Select the single best answer.

A computer located in the DMZ with attractive but irrelevant data to distract and catch hackers would be

a. honeypot.
b. firewall.
c. DMZ.
d. biometrics.

11.17 Match the following terms and definitions.

a. IT architecture
b. computer architecture
c. network architecture
d. system software
e. application software
f. patch
g. real-time
h. batch

_____ 1. A small sequence of programming code inserted into a program to fix an error or add a new feature
_____ 2. Network hardware and software
_____ 3. Application software execution that runs a group of transactions at a later time
_____ 4. Application software execution that processes transactions at the current time
_____ 5. Computer hardware components and computer software
_____ 6. Computer programs for a specific application, such as accounting
_____ 7. A blueprint for computers, networks, and databases
_____ 8. Computer programs used for managing computer hardware

11.18 Match the following terms and definitions.

a. local area network (LAN)
b. metropolitan area network (MAN)
c. wide area network (WAN)
d. workstation computers
e. server computers
f. peripherals
g. routing devices
h. bridges
i. LAN cluster
j. routers
k. gateways
l. network wiring (transmission media)
m. ethernet protocol
n. Internet protocol (IP)
o. transport control protocol (TCP)
p. electronic data interchange (EDI)
q. client/server network
r. value-added network

_____ 1. A network that covers a large geographic region, such as several states
_____ 2. A device connecting an enterprise intranet to the Internet
_____ 3. Special-purpose computers that monitor network traffic and transfer messages from one network to another network
_____ 4. A software program that provides routing services to messages transmitted over the Internet
_____ 5. A network that allows computers to request data and other services from other specific computers on the network
_____ 6. A group of the same type of LANs connected to each other by bridges
_____ 7. A network covering a city
_____ 8. A software program commonly used to connect computers on a LAN
_____ 9. A computer that serves other computers with data and applications, such as an accounting database
_____ 10. A software program that allows the enterprise network to connect to the network of vendors through proprietary lines
_____ 11. Utility devices connected to a network for shared use, such as a printer
_____ 12. A personal computer or laptop connected to a network
_____ 13. Physical media connecting computers
_____ 14. A software program that provides transportation services to messages sent over the Internet
_____ 15. A Computer connected in a relatively small area, such as your college campus
_____ 16. A network that allows an organization to share data with suppliers
_____ 17. An electronic device that connects networks of different types
_____ 18. A device that connects two LANs of the same type

11.19 Match the following terms and definitions.

a. stovepipe
b. enterprise security architecture
c. telecommunication
d. intranet
e. extranet
f. network access point (NAP)
g. remote access
h. point-to-point protocol (PPP)
i. virtual private network (VPN)
j. point-to-point tunneling protocol (PPTP)
k. Internet service provider (ISP)
l. application service provider (ASP)
m. hypertext transfer protocol (HTTP)
n. uniform resource locator (URL)
o. e-commerce
p. proxy firewall

_____ 1. A provider of online applications, such as accounting applications, for a fee
_____ 2. A proactive approach to enterprise security that involves developing an overall plan
_____ 3. A network software program that connects one computer to another computer
_____ 4. An Internet protocol that allowed the creation of the World Wide Web
_____ 5. An enterprise-wide network
_____ 6. A software program permitting an employee to use the enterprise network through a secure channel
_____ 7. A point on the network that offers access to the network, such as an accountant's computer
_____ 8. A provider of access to the Internet for a fee
_____ 9. Online sales transactions
_____ 10. A network that provides a secure channel to access the enterprise network
_____ 11. Electrical transmission of data through analog or digital networks
_____ 12. A wide network used by external customers and suppliers
_____ 13. Accessing a computer from a remote location
_____ 14. Tossing in security patches, hoping to cover vulnerabilities
_____ 15. Located on a proxy server and used to intercept and inspect all incoming messages prior to delivering them to the intended recipient
_____ 16. A Web site address

11.20 Match the following terms and definitions.

a. dynamic password
b. token device (TD)
c. single sign-on (SSO)
d. Intrusion Prevention System (IPS)
e. input controls
f. output controls
g. Grandfather-Father-Son method
h. reciprocal agreement
i. internal sites
j. hot sites
k. warm sites
l. cold sites
m. substitution key
n. transposition key
o. product key
p. symmetric cryptography (1-key method)
q. asymmetric cryptography (2-key method)
r. digital envelope (3-key method)
s. public key
t. private key

_____ 1. A commercial disaster recovery service that provides a fully operational site within a few hours
_____ 2. A hardware device that contains a password generator protocol
_____ 3. A commercial disaster recovery service that provides a partially configured site that is operational within a few days
_____ 4. A commercial disaster recovery service that provides a site with air conditioning, wiring, and plumbing but no IT equipment
_____ 5. A backup technique that keeps multiple backups
_____ 6. Backup services shared between two organizations
_____ 7. Controls that ensure reports and messages reach intended recipients
_____ 8. In asymmetric cryptography, the key used to decode the message
_____ 9. Backup services distributed among an organization's multiple locations
_____ 10. Systems used to prevent access control attacks
_____ 11. A software that permits the user to use one username and password to log in to various systems
_____ 12. A cryptography key that substitutes one letter for another letter
_____ 13. A cryptography key that scrambles the data
_____ 14. A cryptography key that uses a combination of substitution and transposition keys
_____ 15. Controls that ensure that data is valid and entered correctly
_____ 16. Cryptography that uses one key to encode and a second key to decode
_____ 17. A password used once and then changed
_____ 18. Cryptography that uses both symmetric and asymmetric cryptography
_____ 19. Cryptography that uses the same key to encode and deco᠍
_____ 20. In asymmetric cryptography, the key used to encode tʰ

Practice Test

11.21 Which of the following is NOT part of the 10 domains of cybersecurity?

a. Network security
b. Business continuity and disaster recovery
c. Operational security
d. Information security and risk management

11.22 Which of the following is NOT part of the fundamental principles of information security?

a. Confidentiality
b. Timeliness
c. Integrity
d. Availability

11.23 Cybercrimes are crimes connected to what? (Select the best answer.)

a. Information assets and IT
b. Electronic data interchange (EDI)
c. The Internet and intranet
d. Electronic payments

11.24 Which of the following is considered a social engineering cyberattack?

a. Salami attack
b. Dumpster diving
c. Password sniffing
d. Phishing

11.25 Which of the following legislations is related to agency contractors, companies, and consultants hired by federal agencies?

a. Sarbanes-Oxley
b. Gramm-Leach-Bliley Act
c. Federal Information Security Management ACT (FISMA)
d. Payment Card Industry Data Security Standards (PCI-DSS)

11.26 In the industry/private sector, unauthorized disclosure of data with this classification would have a serious adverse impact on the organization.

a. Sensitive
b. Private
c. Top Secret
d. Confidential

11.27 _____ is considered computer hardware.

a. Network protocol
b. RAM
c. Operating system
d. Application software

11.28 What types of networks are connected by a network bridge?

a. Same type of intranets
b. Same type of local area networks
c. Same type of networks
d. Same type of metropolitan area networks

11.29 What is the purpose of installing firewalls on bridges, routers, and gateways?

a. Ensuring unauthorized access to the network
b. Preventing unauthorized access to the network
c. Detecting unauthorized access to the network
d. Preventing data from moving too quickly over the network

11.30 Which of the encryption techniques is used by digital signature?

a. Symmetric

b. Substitution

c. Asymmetric

d. a and c

Exercises

Each Exercise relates to one of the major questions addressed in the chapter and is labeled with the question number in green.

Short Exercises

Warm up with these short exercises.

11.31 Compare and contrast LANs, MANs, and WANs. Use the following organizer for your answer. **(Q11.4)**

Compare (Same)	and	Contrast (Different)

11.32 Compare and contrast Internet, intranet, and extranet. Use the following organizer for your answer. **(Q11.4)**

Compare (Same)	and	Contrast (Different)

11.33 Compare and contrast routers, bridges, and gateways. Use the following organizer for your answer. **(Q11.4)**

Compare (Same)	and	Contrast (Different)

11.34 Which of the rings of protection for IT architecture contain accounting software applications? What security measures are used in that ring to protect accounting software applications? **(Q11.4)**

11.35 If an organization's first firewall to the outside world fails, what are the risks to the organization? What are the possible consequences? **(Q11.5)**

11.36 What is a network access point? List at least two examples and what can be done to secure those access points. **(Q11.5)**

11.37 Explain why an organization puts its Web server in the DMZ instead of in the more-secure areas of the network. **(Q11.5)**

11.38 Explain how a honeypot can be used as part of an organization's cybersecurity. **(Q11.5)**

11.39 Explain the differences between Intrusion Prevention Systems (IPS) and Intrusion Detection Systems (IDS). **(Q11.6)**

11.40 Using the encryption key shown in Figure 11.14, encrypt the following plaintext message: *Cybersecurity Rules*. **(Q11.11)**

11.41 Explain the differences between symmetric and asymmetric cryptography. Which is more secure? **(Q11.11)**

11.42 Computer viruses could damage data and applications on an infected computer. Detective techniques can minimize the damage by detecting the virus program and type and removing it from the infected computers. The preventive techniques can confine the damage to infected computers. **(Q11.9)**

- What is a computer virus?
- Explain why a computer cannot be 100% secure from viruses.
- A virus could damage data or applications. In your opinion, which virus damage is more severe? Why?
- How can a computer that is not connected to the network be infected?

11.43 John, an accountant, noticed the QuickBooks application was running very slowly on his computer. He was suspicious since, except for QuickBooks, no other application was running at that time. His computer is a PC running Windows 7 and is connected to the company's intranet and the Internet. He opened the Windows task manager and realized that a suspicious process was running. He also checked network activities on the task manager and saw unexplained data transmission. To the best of your knowledge, what is wrong with his computer? Do you think John must report his computer problem to the IT department and his coworkers? Why? **(Q11.9)**

It's Your Call

This is your training ground. These scenarios provide you with the opportunity to use your knowledge and professional skills.

11.44 As the new accounting intern, the controller asked you to explain the importance of firewalls in securing the accounting system. Prepare a short presentation for the accounting staff on this topic. Discuss why some organizations are now using up to four firewall levels to protect the enterprise database. **(Q11.5)**

11.45 You just landed a job as an accounting intern for the Veterans Administration. Clearly there is a cost associated with securing information assets as well as a cost associated with lack of security. In the case of the stolen Veterans Administration laptop, the court case was settled for $20 million; however, there were also other costs involved in defending against the suit, the cost of investigating the theft of the laptop, and measures taken to try to address the potential identify theft of the military personnel. Prepare a cost-benefit analysis to the best of your ability by researching various costs to obtain estimates for securing the stolen laptop versus the cost of its theft. Write an email summarizing your findings and recommendations to the Veterans Administration. **(Q11.12)**

11.46 Refer to *It's Your Call* 11.45. Prepare a plan for the Veterans Administration to better secure its laptops in the future. **(Q11.10)**

11.47 You are on the team charged with business continuity and disaster recovery. Your role in the team is to focus on disaster recovery for the accounting system and financial data. At the first meeting, you learn that the remote backup site is located in Boca Raton, Florida. Prepare your notes for the next meeting to address the advisability of that location for a remote backup. **(Q11.10)**

11.48 One of your responsibilities as a staff accountant is to prepare and transmit your company's XBRL financial statements to the Securities and Exchange Commission (SEC). What cybersecurity measures would you implement to ensure data integrity and security? Provide your supporting rationale. **(Q11.11, 11.5, 11.6)**

11.49 Your company is planning to move certain systems, such as accounting, into the cloud. You are a member of a team responsible for evaluation of the advantages and disadvantages of the cloud accounting systems. Your team leader has asked you to prepare a presentation on the cloud accounting system security.

Prepare a paper summarizing your presentation. In your summary, include cloud access, data transmission, data storage security, and financial reporting issues. **(Q11.6 11.7, 11.9)**

11.50 You are on the team charged with data transmission and storage security. Your team leader has asked you to prepare a PowerPoint presentation on data transmission encryption techniques. He specifically is interested to know about various types of Advanced Encryption Standard (AES) methods.

Prepare a paper summarizing your presentation. In your paper include AES 64 and AES 128 encryption techniques. **(Q11.11)**

11.51 Since your supervisor knows that you took an accounting information system course in college, she has asked you to make a presentation to the accounting department on various types of computer malware and the ways in which malware affect computer systems.

Prepare a summary of your presentation. Extend your summary beyond the information that is provided in this chapter. **(Q11.11)**

Tech in Practice

These technology in practice exercises are perfect for both individuals and teams.

Tech Exercises

Sharpen your skills with these technology exercises. Watch these software videos at www.pearsonhighered.com/kay.

11.52
Tech Tool: Spreadsheet Software or Visio Software
Software Video: Cybersecurity Design

EspressoCoffee is concerned about securing accounting data transmitted over its network. The company has asked for your assistance in designing cybersecurity for its network.

1. Download the data file for this exercise.
2. Using the intranet diagram for EspressoCoffee's network, add firewalls to the network access points to control network traffic.

11.53

Tech Tool: Spreadsheet Software or Visio Software
Software Video: Cybersecurity Design

EspressoCoffee has asked for your assistance in designing cybersecurity for its e-commerce architecture.

1. Download the data file for this exercise.
2. Using the enterprise intranet diagram for EspressoCoffee's network, add firewalls to the network access points to control network traffic.
3. Label the DMZ in the intranet diagram.
4. EspressoCoffee would like to use a honeypot to distract and trace intruders. Insert the honeypot in the intranet diagram.

11.54

Tech Tool: Spreadsheet Software or Visio Software
Software Video: Cybersecurity Design

EspressoCoffee asked for your assistance in designing cybersecurity for its accounting LAN cluster. EspressoCoffee started with one LAN for accounting, and as accounting demands for IT grew, two more LANS were added to create a LAN cluster.

1. Download the data file for this exercise.
2. Using the appropriate network symbols, build a LAN cluster for accounting similar to the LAN cluster shown in Figure 11.6. The LAN cluster should contain the following:
    a. Three LANs.
    b. One LAN with the accounting application server and one workstation.
    c. One LAN with a mainframe used for the enterprise database and one workstation. The enterprise database is located in the accounting LAN cluster because accounting has the highest level of security.
    d. One LAN including three desktop PCs with the accounting interface software, one shared printer, and two laptops.
3. Add firewalls to the network access point(s) to control network traffic.
4. Because the accounting department requires tight security for its LANs, IT would like to monitor traffic between the LANs. Add firewalls to the routing devices connecting the LANs.
5. What other security and controls measures could be used for the accounting LAN cluster?

11.55

Tech Tool: Spreadsheet Software or Visio Software
Software Video: Cybersecurity Design

EspressoCoffee has asked for your assistance in designing cybersecurity for its enterprise network.

1. Download the data file for this exercise.
2. Using the appropriate network symbols, build EspressoCoffee's enterprise network using the following information:
    a. EspressoCoffee has five LAN clusters, one each for accounting, human resources, production, e-commerce, and management.
    b. The LAN clusters are connected to the intranet using routers with firewalls.
    c. The intranet is connected to the DMZ using a firewall router.
    d. Within the DMZ, there is a Web server and honeypot.
    e. The enterprise network is connected to the Internet using a gateway with a firewall.

Go Online

In the fast-paced world of technology, your skill at finding answers fast can be vital. Go online and experience typical assignments you may encounter as a professional.

11.56 You have been appointed the lead for the task force researching the use of biometrics to improve security at your company. Go online and research biometrics. Prepare a summary of your findings for the team. Include answers to the following questions that your teammates have asked:

- What is biometrics?
- What are examples of how biometrics can be used to prevent unauthorized access?
- What are the latest advances in biometrics?
- What are the advantages and disadvantages it offers?

11.57 You are a consultant to Shufang Company, responsible for providing recommendations about how encryption can improve security for confidential accounting data. Go online and search for information about encryption. What are the latest developments in encryption technology? How do you see encryption being used in accounting?

Prepare an email to the CFO with your recommendations regarding encryption for the accounting system. Provide a brief explanation of the rationale and support for your recommendations.

11.58 Your organization has a remote backup in another state. The backup facility is classified as a warm site. Go online and research hot and warm sites. Discuss the readiness of the current backup site. Prepare a plan with specific action steps that would need to be taken to upgrade to a hot site.

11.59 You are a member of the accounting information system development team. Your team leader has asked you to prepare a presentation on encryption techniques used for safeguarding accounting data in the cloud accounting system provided by service organizations. Go online and research encryption techniques that are used in cloud computing.

Technology Projects

These technology projects are perfect for both individuals and teams.

Technology Project 11

Tech Tool: Spreadsheet Software or Visio Software

Software Videos: Cybersecurity Design

iSportDesign asked for your assistance in designing cybersecurity for the enterprise network with a focus on securing accounting data.

Your deliverables for the project include the following:

Deliverable 1. A diagram of iSportDesign's accounting LAN cluster with firewalls

Deliverable 2. A diagram of iSportDesign's enterprise network with firewalls

Deliverable 3. A diagram of iSportDesign's e-commerce architecture with DMZ and honeypot

Deliverable 4. An executive summary with a recommendation for backup and disaster recovery based on your Internet research for cold, warm, and hot sites

Visit www.pearsonhighered.com/kay to do the following:

1. Download Technology Project 11 instructions.
2. Download files provided online for your convenience in completing the project deliverables.
3. Watch the videos with software instructions to complete this project at www.pearsonhighered.com/kay.

12

The Risk Intelligent Enterprise: Enterprise Risk Management

When You Need Advice about Enterprise Risk Management, Whom Do You Call?

Meet the CFO.

A recent IBM Global CFO study found that 83% of chief financial officers advise on risk mitigation.

The Securities and Exchange Commission (SEC) proposed rule changes that became effective in 2010 to require enterprise risk management (ERM) accountability. The SEC acknowledged that the root cause of the recent economic downturn was lack of risk management competency in corporate America.

The SEC now requires company boards to report in-depth on how their enterprises identify risk, set risk tolerances, and manage risk/reward trade-offs.

Crossroads

At the crossroads of accounting and IT, the chief financial officer (CFO) plays a growing role in managing IT and ERM.

My Questions

Q 12.1	Beyond security and control, what is risk intelligence?
Q 12.2	What's the COSO ERM Cube?
Q 12.3	What do I need to know about COSO's ERM Cube components?
Q 12.4	What is the ISO 31000 Risk Management Standard?
Q 12.5	How can sustainability improve risk intelligence?
Q 12.6	What are the top 10 tips for spreadsheet risk management?

Beyond Security and Control, What Is Risk Intelligence?

Have you ever done something that you knew you probably shouldn't (for example, drive too fast)? Did you think about the downside risk of events not turning out well (for example, getting a speeding ticket)? Did that risk weigh in your decision?

This chapter is all about risk. Every day, you are weighing risks, even if you don't think about it explicitly. Just as you do, enterprises face risks, manage risks, and mitigate risks.

One way to view enterprise risk management is to compare it to security for your home. There are various risks to your home, such as robbery, storms, lightning strikes, flooding, and so on. You may have a security system for your home, but does that protect you from all risks to your home? If you leave a door unlocked, does the security system work? Does the security system protect your home from an unexpected storm that blows shingles off your roof? How do you mitigate that risk? Do you purchase homeowner's insurance?

As you can see, a security system cannot address all risks. Enterprises can approach risk management in the same way. Enterprise risk management (ERM) goes beyond just security and controls.

It is simply not possible to develop security and controls to address every threat that an enterprise might face. Identifying, assessing, and mitigating risks has been shown to produce better business performance.

Risk Intelligence

Risk is defined as "the effect of uncertainty on objectives." Risk has both an upside and a downside. The downside of risk could be threats to success at attaining objectives. The upside to risk could be opportunities for benefits.

Risk intelligence moves beyond just managing risk to using risk intelligently to improve business performance and create value for the enterprise. Some risk has only a downside or loss associated with it, such as computer viruses that destroy corporate emails. Risk intelligence includes managing not only downside risks, but also capitalizing on upside risk that presents the enterprise with opportunities to create value, such as evaluating risk associated with a new business acquisition. Although the new acquisition may have risk associated with it, the venture also presents the possibility of generating additional income. A venture with upside risk presents the possibility of a benefit accompanying the associated risk.

> **After All...**
> *After all, controls are risk-driven, so understanding risk is a prerequisite to the appreciation and application of control (ITAudit, 2004).*

> **Risk Intelligence...**
> *Risk intelligence, simply stated, is improved intelligence about your organization's internal and external environments and how prepared your organization is to prevent or quickly detect and correct potentially high-impact risk events.*
>
> *Risk intelligence enables risk informed decision making (Deloitte, 2004).*

Downside risks have no benefits, only threats to success. There is only a downside or negative result associated with the risk, for example, the risk of denial of service attacks that overwhelm and shut down the enterprise's technology or unauthorized access and theft of confidential customer credit card information. There is only the downside risk of preventing the negative from occurring.

Upside risk, on the other hand, is a risk that has the possibility of a benefit associated with it, such as a business acquisition or merger. Risk intelligence involves using risk in a proactive, constructive way to create additional value for the enterprise. Risk management shifts an enterprise from a reactive, putting-out-fires approach to a proactive approach of anticipating and mitigating future risks before incidents occur.

The risk intelligent enterprise strives for an integrated comprehensive approach to risk and security. Instead of handling physical security and cybersecurity as separate silos, some enterprises, such as the company SAP AG, have integrated physical and cybersecurity to provide a more cohesive enterprise plan.

A comprehensive enterprise risk management program uses a top-down approach. Initiation, support, and direction come from executives at the top levels of the organization. A silo approach with separate departments, such as IT, developing separate security programs without consideration of comprehensive risk management can prove to be ineffective. For example, if the IT department begins installing firewalls to secure databases but fails to understand the value of the data, such as accounting data, the appropriate level of security may not be achieved.

IT Controls, Internal Controls, and ERM

How are risk management and controls related? Figure 12.1 depicts the relationship using three rings:

1. IT controls
2. Internal controls
3. Enterprise risk management

As you can see in Figure 12.1, IT controls can be viewed as three zones:

- Entity-level controls for top management
- Application controls for business processes
- IT general controls for IT services

At the top management level, entity-level IT controls provide IT governance that sets the tone from the top of the enterprise. Application controls are controls embedded in business processes where a majority of security breaches occur. IT general controls are controls over IT services, such as networks and database systems. As the figure illustrates, internal control encompasses IT controls. Internal control is a system of controls used to safeguard assets and prevent and detect errors. Enterprise risk management encompasses internal control and IT controls. ERM assesses the cause of risks that threaten to materialize. Then the enterprise evaluates what can be done to prevent those threats.

SEC Rule Change...

The SEC, in 2010, made rule changes requiring companies to report on ERM accountability. Specifically, the SEC wants companies to provide information to investors about the following:

- What is the board's role in ERM?
- What is the relationship between the board and top management in managing risks?

Where's the C-Suite?

The C-Suite refers to the people who's titles begin with C:
- CEO: Chief Executive Officer
- CFO: Chief Financial Officer
- CIO: Chief Information Officer
- CSO: Chief Sustainability Officer
- and so on....

The CFO is the chief financial officer responsible for the accounting and financial functions in the organization.

What does a CFO need to know?

Eighty-three percent of CFOs advise on ERM. Seventy-two percent advise on IT (IBM Global CFO Study, 2010).

Both of these topics are covered in your book to give you a competitive advantage on your way to the C-Suite.

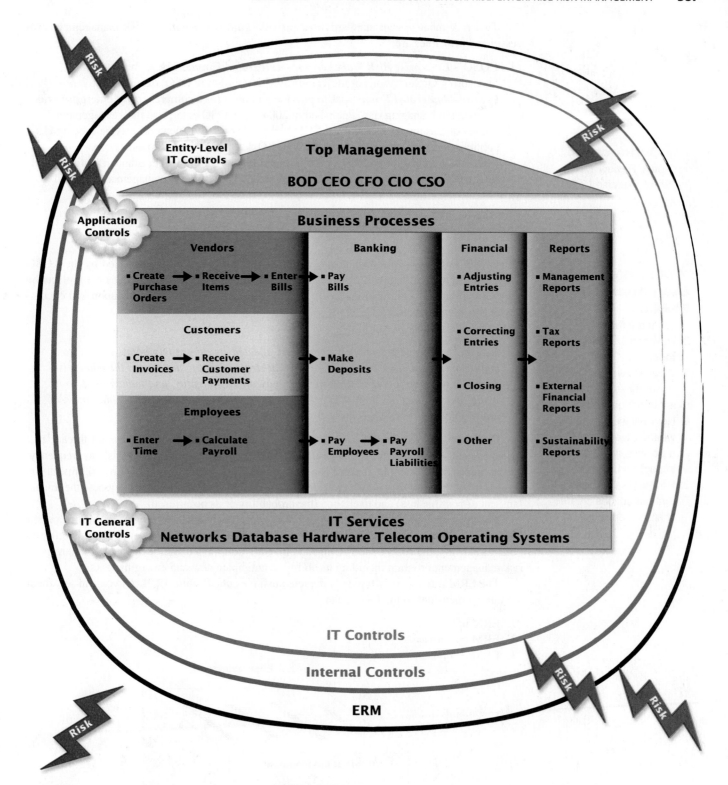

FIGURE 12.1

Enterprise Risk Management

What level of penetration do these risks present?

Two risk management standards that provide guidance regarding risk management processes and principles are:

1. **COSO's *Enterprise Risk Management—Integrated Framework*.** Committee of Sponsoring Organizations of the Treadway Commission (COSO) expanded the *Internal Control—Integrated Framework* to provide guidance for a comprehensive enterprise-wide approach to managing risk. Published in 2004, the COSO enterprise risk management framework, as an extension of the COSO internal control framework, may be used by U.S. publicly traded companies to meet Sarbanes-Oxley (SOX) requirements.
2. **ISO 31000.** Published in 2009 by the International Organization for Standardization (ISO), ISO 31000 is the only internationally recognized enterprise risk management standard.

My Connection...
- Active Review 12.1
- Short Exercise 12.27

What's the COSO ERM Cube?

> **Walmart's Five-Step Approach to ERM...**
> 1. What are the risks?
> 2. How can we mitigate those risks?
> 3. What are we going to do about these risks? What is our action plan?
> 4. How will we measure whether we are having a positive or negative impact on those risks?
> 5. How will we demonstrate that our actions created shareholder value?

The COSO *Enterprise Risk Management—Integrated Framework* is represented by the COSO ERM Cube shown in Figure 12.2. This ERM framework for managing risk does not replace the prior COSO internal control framework. Instead, the ERM framework builds upon and encompasses the internal control framework.

COSO defines ERM as follows:

Enterprise risk management is a process, effected by an entity's board of directors, management and other personnel, applied in strategy setting and across the enterprise, designed to identify potential events that may affect the entity, and manage risk to be within its risk appetite, to provide reasonable assurance regarding the achievement of entity objectives (COSO, 2004).

Given the impossibility of foreseeing every conceivable control to address all threats, risk management uses the approach of assessing risk to determine the probability of risk, its frequency, and its impact. For example, if there is a risk of a $2 loss, how much is it worth to prevent the loss? Is it worth $10,000 to prevent a $2 loss? Obviously, an enterprise wants to assess the impact (amount of possible loss) and likelihood (the probability of its occurrence).

The growing importance of enterprise risk management is the adoption of ERM in Standard & Poor's evaluation of company credit ratings. Credit ratings affect an enterprise's ability to obtain financing, the costs of borrowing, and investor confidence. S&P evaluates an enterprise's risk management program including its ability to anticipate new and emerging risks.

The ERM framework is typically depicted using a cube (Figure 12.2). As you can see, there are three dimensions to the ERM cube:

1. ERM units
2. ERM objectives
3. ERM components

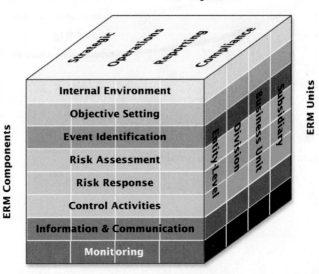

FIGURE 12.2
ERM Cube

ERM Units

Enterprise units may consist of entity-level units, divisions, business units, and/or subsidiaries. ERM units are basically how we view the enterprise in terms of implementing ERM.

ERM Objectives

The ERM framework specifies four categories of an enterprise's objectives:

- Strategic objectives relate to goals that support the entity's mission.
- Operational objectives relate to the effective and efficient use of the entity's resources.
- Reporting objectives relate to the reliability of the enterprise's reporting, both internal and external.
- Compliance objectives relate to the entity's compliance with all applicable laws and regulations.

Note that three of the preceding objectives were used in the COSO internal control framework. Strategic objectives are new to the ERM framework. The other difference is that the reporting objective in the internal control framework focused on financial statement reporting, primarily for external users. ERM, on the other hand, uses a reporting objective that includes both internal reports for management and external reports.

ERM Components

The COSO enterprise risk management framework consists of eight interrelated components. Risk management is an iterative process whereby the ERM components influence each other.

- **Internal Environment.** The internal environment of an enterprise involves the risk management philosophy of the enterprise, including the tone set by top management. Risk resilience, risk appetite, risk tolerance, integrity, and ethical values also affect the internal environment.
- **Objective Setting.** ERM ensures that the enterprise has a process for setting objectives that are consistent with the entity's mission and risk appetite.
- **Event Identification.** Events, both internal and external, that affect an enterprise's ability to attain its objectives, are identified. In addition to distinguishing between internal and external events, events can be further classified as risks and opportunities. Identified opportunities can subsequently influence the ERM objective setting component.
- **Risk Assessment.** Risks are assessed by analyzing the risk with consideration for the probability of occurrence and impact. The risk analysis provides a basis for determining how the risk should be managed.
- **Risk Response.** The enterprise's response to the risk is selected. The enterprise may choose to avoid, accept, reduce, or share the risk. The actions to respond to the risk are specified, consistent with the entity's risk tolerance and appetite.
- **Control Activities.** Control activities are comprised of policies and procedures established and implemented to ensure risk responses are effective.
- **Information and Communication.** Relevant information is captured and communicated effectively throughout the organization to appropriate individuals in a timely manner. Timely communication of relevant information is essential in implementing risk responses.
- **Monitoring.** An enterprise's risk management is monitored with evaluation and feedback that permits modifications as needed.

Note that some of the ERM components are named the same as the COSO internal control framework components. Risk assessment, control activities, information and communication, and monitoring are the same. The control environment component of the internal control framework is changed to internal environment. The other difference is that the components related to risk are expanded to include objective setting, event identification, and risk response.

ERM Limitations

The ERM framework provides guidance to organizations in addressing risk. In assessing risks, human judgment plays an important role. Human judgment, however, is subjective. When assessing risk, human judgment may under- or overestimate the impact and likelihood of risk. This is a significant limitation of the ERM framework. Although controls may be in place to

My Connection...
• Short Exercise 12.28

reduce risks, controls can be circumvented through collusion, and more advanced technology permits hackers to bypass the IT controls that were once effective. So it is never possible to have complete assurance or be 100% risk free.

What Do I Need to Know about COSO's ERM Cube Components?

Eight ERM Components...
• Internal environment
• Objective setting
• Event identification
• Risk assessment
• Risk response
• Control activities
• Information and communication
• Monitoring

The eight ERM components are combined with the four ERM objectives to create an ERM framework. This framework provides guidance to organizations implementing enterprise-wide risk management programs. Next, we explore each of the eight ERM components in more detail.

Internal Environment

The internal environment relates to the culture of the organization and its risk consciousness. The internal environment affects the remaining ERM components of objective setting, event identification, risk assessment, risk response, control activities, information and communication, and monitoring.

Influenced by the tone set by top management, the internal environment is also reflected in policies and procedures as well as the organizational structure. The entity's risk management philosophy reflects the organization's values, which in turn affects its risk assessment and risk responses. The philosophy may be affected by adverse external events, such as an economic downturn or a highly regulated industry. A risk management philosophy influences the entity's culture and operating style. If well-developed and articulated, a risk management philosophy can provide consistency in risk attitudes throughout the entire entity.

An entity's risk management philosophy affects its **risk appetite**, the amount of risk it is willing to accept in pursuit of value. Enterprise risk management involves developing strategy and objectives that are consistent with an entity's risk appetite.

The leadership provided by top management is a critical factor in influencing the corporate culture. The corporate culture, such as at Enron, can encourage fraud. Other cultures discourage fraud. Management incentives, such as bonuses based on profit, may promote a culture focused on "meeting the numbers, no matter what." The internal environment is also impacted by human resource policies, including hiring practices. Hiring competent employees who are provided ongoing training can reduce risk from accidents and errors.

Objective Setting

Strategic objectives, sometimes called mission or vision, establish the entity's purpose. Critical success factors can be identified both at the entity and activity levels to facilitate measurement of the attainment of strategic objectives.

The strategic objectives, in turn, form the basis for operations, reporting, and compliance objectives. Operations objectives relate to the effective and efficient use of the entity's resources. For example, operational objectives might include safeguarding assets, profitability goals, and quality standards. Reporting objectives relates to the reliability of both internal and external reports, including both financial and nonfinancial information. Compliance objectives relate to an entity's compliance with applicable laws and regulations. For example, compliance with the Sarbanes-Oxley Act and HIPAA would fall under compliance objectives.

An entity's objective setting process considers the entity's risk appetite, which affects risk tolerance. The risk appetite, the level of risk the entity considers acceptable in creating value, is often viewed as a balance between risk and return. The higher the return, typically, the higher the risk. When setting strategy objectives, different strategies may have different risk levels and the entity's risk appetite may be a determining factor in the final objectives selected.

Risk tolerance is the acceptable level of variation in attaining objectives. For an IT support desk, the objective might be to resolve 100% of client issues during the client's first call. An acceptable variation might be to resolve 85% of client issues on the first call. The amount of acceptable variation can differ by objective with high priority objectives having smaller variation and lower risk tolerance.

Event Identification

This component, **event identification**, involves identifying potential events that might affect the entity (Figure 12.1). Events can be either internal events or external events that might affect the entity's ability to achieve objectives. Events can be opportunities that provide positive effects or incidents that could negatively impact the entity.

External factors are incidents or occurrences that originate outside the entity. Examples include the following:

- Economic events include liquidity and competition factors. Examples might be higher interest rates or limited financing.
- Natural environment can include waste, energy, natural disasters, or sustainability. Examples are natural disasters such as fire or hurricane.
- Political events include new legislation, regulations, or public policy.
- Social events would include changes in consumer behavior, privacy, or demographics.
- Technological events include interruptions, electronic commerce, and emerging technology, such as cloud computing.

In addition to external events, an entity also identifies internal events that result from management choices. Examples of internal events include the following:

- Infrastructures include events related to availability and capability of assets, access to capital, and complexity.
- People relates to events that involve people such as fraud enacted by employees, health and safety of employees, and employee competence.
- Process refers to events related to capacity, design, execution, and suppliers. An example would be changing firewalls without adequate documentation and testing.
- Technology events might include data integrity, data and system availability, development, and maintenance. An example might be a new backup and recovery system.

Events can be classified as producing negative impacts (risk) or positive impacts (opportunities).

Risk Assessment

A **risk** is the possibility that an event will occur and negatively impact the entity's ability to achieve its stated objectives (Figure 12.1). **Risk assessment** is the process of assessing the extent to which events would impact an entity's ability to achieve its objectives.

There are two aspects to risk assessment:

- **Impact:** the effect that an event will have on the entity's ability to achieve its objectives if the event occurs
- **Likelihood:** the possibility or probability that a potential event will occur

In assessing risk impact, pertinent questions are as follows:

1. What is the asset's value? What is the value of customer payment card data stored in the enterprise database? What is the cost to the enterprise if a hacker steals the payment card information?
2. How much is the asset, such as information, worth to the competition? These assets might include intellectual property, such as the engineering designs for the latest computer chip. What is the value of that intellectual property to the competition? What is the risk of the competition accessing the enterprise server that stores the intellectual property?
3. What is the estimated potential loss per threat?

In assessing risk likelihood, pertinent questions are as follows:

1. What is the possibility or probability of the event (threat) occurring?
2. What is the estimated frequency of the threat occurring?

In assessing risk, the annual loss potential can be estimated by combining the impact and the frequency of the threat. There might be a low impact but high frequency associated with a threat. For example, salami attacks involve rounding fractions of cents into a hacker's account. This would be low impact (for example, $0.002). Combined with high frequency, however, the total annual loss potential can be significant. An example of high impact but low frequency would be a hacker's destruction of accounting data, which could be crippling to the business.

In the context of ERM risk assessment, the terms *possibility* and *probability* can have different definitions. **Possibility** may refer to assessing likelihood using qualitative measures, such as high, medium, or low. **Probability** may refer to assessing likelihood using a quantitative measure, such as percentages.

The assessment techniques that can be used to assess risk can be grouped into two general types:

> **Would You Like to Know More?**
> See Chapter 8, *Accounting and Sustainability Intelligence*, for more about how qualitative data can be quantified.

1. Quantitative techniques, such as mathematical models, may be used to assess the probability of occurrence. Benchmarking can provide common metrics with which to compare an entity's performance with others or assess the impact and likelihood of potential events for a particular industry, such as the alternative energy industry. Quantitative measures include percentages, means, standard deviations, and regression.

2. Qualitative techniques may be used when it is impossible for the entity to quantify the risk. Qualitative techniques may include conducting focus groups or individual interviews to obtain different views on the impact and likelihood of potential events. Qualitative measures can include ranking risk likelihood as high, medium, or low.

Risk Response

After risks have been assessed, the next component addresses how the entity will respond to the risk. In general, there are four categories of risk response.

- Avoidance. This risk response involves avoiding or exiting the activities that give rise to the risk. For example, given the risk of changing consumer behavior adversely affecting product sales, the entity may choose to exit the product line by selling it.
- Reduction. This risk response refers to actions taken to reduce risk likelihood, risk impact, or both. For example, an organization that could not afford a comprehensive security system might instead install firewalls to reduce the risk likelihood that a hacker will be able to access the enterprise database.
- Sharing. An entity reduces risk likelihood or risk impact by sharing the risk with another entity. For example, if you purchase car insurance, you are sharing risk with the auto insurance company.
- Acceptance. When an entity responds to risk with acceptance, the entity takes no action to affect risk likelihood or risk impact.

When risk responses are being considered, the costs and benefits of options may play a major role in the final decision. Another consideration is which risk response best aligns with the entity's risk tolerance. Some entities might be comfortable accepting risk while others might share, reduce, or avoid the risk entirely.

When evaluating risk responses, entity risk management takes an entity-wide or portfolio view. While consideration of risks for individual units, such as divisions within the entity, are important, when implementing enterprise risk management, entities also take a comprehensive view of how the risk affects the entire enterprise.

Control Activities

In the context of enterprise risk management, control activities are policies and procedures to ensure management's risk responses are implemented in a timely manner. Control activities can be classified by related objectives: strategic objectives, operations objectives, reporting objectives, and compliance objectives.

After an entity has identified risk responses, the next step is to identify the appropriate control activities to ensure that risk responses are implemented as planned, so that objectives, risk responses, and control activities are linked.

Examples of control activities include performance reviews, physical controls, and segregation of duties.

As discussed in Chapters 10 and 11, information technology, because of its integral nature in organizations today, requires special consideration to see that control activities are adequately addressed. As shown in Figure 12.1, three levels of IT control activities correspond to three levels within the enterprise:

- Entity-level IT controls, such as IT governance
- Application controls over business processes
- IT general controls (ITGC) over IT processes and services

These three levels of controls work together to ensure risk responses are addressed for the IT systems within the enterprise.

Would You Like to Know More?
For more information about the three types of IT controls, see Chapters 10 and 11.

Information and Communication

This component refers to the process of identifying, capturing, and communicating information accurately, completely, and in a timely manner to enable employees to carry out responsibilities including risk management responsibilities.

The entity's IT architecture and services are critical to achieving the entity's objectives. Technology itself can create new opportunities to provide services. Changing technology can also impact the enterprise's business processes. For example, at one time accounting clerks entered accounting transactions manually without the assistance of computers. Now it is rare to find an accounting system that does not use a computer.

As you know, integrated enterprise systems have resulted in technology being integrated throughout the enterprise, impacting almost all business processes in some way. The integrated enterprise system can provide management with additional data and information for use in making enterprise risk management assessments and decisions. Furthermore, business intelligence capabilities offer management the ability to gain further insights into enterprise risk management.

Monitoring

In the context of enterprise risk management, monitoring refers to the process of monitoring an entity's enterprise risk management. As with internal control, approaches to monitoring include the following:

- Monitoring activities that occur on an ongoing basis, such as weekly reviews, training seminars, and ongoing feedback regarding regulatory compliance
- Separate evaluations, such as an internal audit
- A combination of both ongoing monitoring and separate evaluations

Documentation of monitoring activities may be formal, such as a written report, or informal, such as an informational meeting. Enterprise risk management deficiencies are communicated upstream. Serious deficiencies, such as material deficiencies in internal control, are reported to top management and the board of directors.

My Connection...
- Active Review 12.5
- Short Exercise 12.29

What Is the ISO 31000 Risk Management Standard?

Introduced in 2009 after the 2008 global economic crisis, ISO 31000 is the only internationally accepted enterprise risk management standard. Based in Switzerland, the International Organization for Standardization (ISO) has also issued standards for quality control, social responsibility, environmental management, security management, and more. For enterprises with international operations and using other ISO standards, ISO 31000 for risk management is a logical choice.

ISO 31000 provides principles and guidelines for the design, implementation, maintenance, and improvement of enterprise risk management processes.

Efficient Operations, Effective Tactics, and Efficacious Strategy

Risk can impact an organization during different time frames, from the short term to the long term. A useful way to classify risk relates to the time frame that the risk impacts, as well as whether the risk is related to efficient operations, effective tactics, or efficacious strategy.

In general, the short term relates to operations and routine activities. The medium term relates to tactics, such as new projects that initiate change. The long term typically relates to the organization's strategy, affecting three to five years or longer.

For example, if you are considering a new accounting system, there could be significant risks associated with switching to a new system. There could also be significant risks associated with continuing to use an outdated accounting system that might not have adequate security and controls. For the new system, the long-term risks would relate to the strategic choice of accounting software and accompanying hardware. This strategic decision and accompanying risk will impact the organization for a lengthy period of time, typically at least three years and often much longer. Both upside and downside risk might be associated with this strategic choice of accounting system. A downside risk might be that the new accounting system is not compatible with other systems that must interact. An upside risk might be that the new system drastically reduces person hours required and eliminates redundancy in the system as well as providing better security and control.

Medium term risk might relate to the new accounting system project implementation. What are the risks associated with the project being on time? Going over budget? Not meeting user requirements and specifications?

For a new accounting system, short term risks relate to routine operations, such as maintaining daily backups of the system in case the system crashes.

7Rs and 4Ts of Risk Management

The risk management process consists of coordinated activities that span various levels within an organization. Risk management activities can be described by the following 7Rs and 4Ts of risk management:

1. Recognize (identify) risks
2. Rank (evaluate) risks
3. Respond to significant risks using the 4Ts of risk treatment:
   a. Tolerate risk
   b. Treat risk
   c. Transfer risk
   d. Terminate risk
4. Resource controls
5. Reaction planning (such as business continuity and disaster recovery)
6. Report and monitor risk performance
7. Review the risk management framework

The first two Rs of risk management, recognize risk and rank risk, pertain to risk assessment. The third R relates to how to treat the risk. Should you tolerate the risk (take no action)? Should you treat the risk (for example, develop plans to reduce the risk of a possible hazard)? Should you transfer the risk (for example, buy insurance)? Should you terminate the risk (for example, terminate a project to eliminate the associated risk)?

Note that many of these risk management activities are similar to those of the COSO ERM Cube.

My Connection...
- Active Review 12.6
- Short Exercise 12.36

How Can Sustainability Improve Risk Intelligence?

Increasingly enterprises are faced with more regulation and growing challenges to obtain scarce resources. Sustainability practices offer a solution to reduce risk. Focusing on sustainable operations reduces the risk of dependence on dwindling natural resources that may become cost prohibitive in the future. Furthermore, with the growing concerns about the natural environment, sustainable practices may offer an enterprise advantages with regard to reduced risk in an increasingly regulated environment with greater demand for transparency. As discussed in Chapter 8, *Accounting and Sustainability Intelligence*, innovation can play an important role in transforming risks into opportunities.

For an example of how sustainability can play a role in reducing risk, let's consider an IT compliance roadmap for IT professionals to address Sarbanes-Oxley requirements. The roadmap consists of the following six steps, the last of which is to build sustainability.

1. Plan and scope IT controls. Scoping involves evaluating and determining which IT applications and related systems should be included in the IT compliance review. This determination is influenced by the financial risk assessment for the organization. For example, applications and systems affecting the financial reporting process are included in the scope if the objective is in compliance with Sarbanes-Oxley. If the objective goes beyond just compliance with Sarbanes-Oxley and encompasses additional objectives such as those considered in enterprise risk management, then the scope would be expanded. In-scope applications are inventoried, application controls identified, in-scope IT infrastructure and databases identified, and relevant third-party dependencies (outsourcing) evaluated. Planning involves developing a timeline with scheduled activities and deliverables needed to complete the project, assigning responsibility for activities and tasks to specific individuals, and establishing a means of monitoring progress on the compliance project.

2. Assess IT risks. Assess the risk of IT systems and services causing financial statement errors or fraud. As mentioned earlier, when assessing risk, the impact and the likelihood of the event occurring is analyzed.

3. Document controls. Identify and document the three levels of IT controls within the organization: entity-level IT controls, application controls, and IT general controls.

4. Evaluate control design and operating effectiveness. Assess the design of controls, and then test the controls to confirm they operate effectively.

5. Prioritize and remediate deficiencies. Deficiencies can result from control design deficiencies, such as inadequate controls, or operating effectiveness deficiencies, such as a control being overridden by management. When control deficiencies are discovered, assess the deficiency's impact and likelihood of causing financial statement error or fraud.

6. Build sustainability. Redesign or reconfigure controls to build sustainability into IT controls. One way to make controls more sustainable is to configure an application so the controls are automated, improving reliability. For example, automating electronic workflows with enforced controls for authorizations might improve sustainability of the controls going forward (IT Governance Institute, 2006).

Whether enterprise risk management is effective and sustainable may depend upon the weakest link in the system. An expensive security system and extensive enterprise risk management are only as strong as the weakest link. This was demonstrated by the Marshalls store with one unsecured wireless network that permitted hackers access to information on 45.6 million payment cards. Next, we look at one of the weak links for many organizations: spreadsheets.

> **My Connection...**
> • Active Review 12.8

What Are the Top 10 Tips for Spreadsheet Risk Management?

Accounting Insight No. 21: **Spreadsheet Risk Management**

Spreadsheets introduce significant risks into the financial reporting process for some organizations. These organizations might have thousands of spreadsheets in shadow data. Although spreadsheet use is typically widespread, controls over spreadsheets tend to be limited. For example, access security controls and change management controls, discussed in Chapter 10 as required for SOX compliance, may not be used with an enterprise's spreadsheets.

Because of widespread spreadsheet use with limited controls, enterprises may integrate controls into spreadsheet management to reduce risk. Accounting Insight No. 21 states that shadow data ERM uses the top 10 tips for improved spreadsheet risk management.

ACCOUNTING INSIGHT NO. 21
Shadow Data ERM:
Uses the
Top 10 Tips
for Improved
Spreadsheet
Risk Management

A $24 Million Spreadsheet Error...
A spreadsheet error cost TransAlta $24 million. The spreadsheet error resulted in TransAlta buying more U.S. power transmission hedging contracts at higher prices. The CEO of the large Canadian power generator said the error was due to "literally a cut-and-paste error in an Excel spreadsheet that we did not detect when we did our final sorting and ranking bids prior to submission" (theregister.co.uk, 2003).

A 2011 study found that 87% of the CFOs surveyed relied heavily on Excel for financial tasks.

Top 10 Tips

The top 10 tips for improved spreadsheet risk management are as follows:

1. Inventory all spreadsheets using a global spreadsheet identification system. Each spreadsheet is assigned a unique spreadsheet ID number (SSID). Then the spreadsheets are inventoried in a global SSID log for tracking. A minimum of the filename, location, and purpose of the spreadsheet should be logged (Figure 12.3). Additional useful information includes:
   - The latest version date included in the filename
   - The related business process, if any
   - Any accounts affected by the spreadsheet
   - The financial statement item(s) affected
   - Dollar value of amounts in order to assess materiality
2. Assign risk for each inventoried spreadsheet by assessing the following:
   - The impact of a financial statement error resulting from the spreadsheet's use
   - The likelihood of a financial statement error

   The impact of a spreadsheet error is affected by the dollar value and the spreadsheet's use. The likelihood of error can be affected by the number of users and their training, frequency of use, and complexity of the spreadsheet. As shown in Figure 12.4, risk impact and risk likelihood can be ranked as high, medium, and low. The higher the risk associated with a given spreadsheet, the higher the level of controls that should be implemented.
3. Store all spreadsheets on a network server. This accomplishes a number of control objectives:
   - Access security codes. Access security controls can be implemented by assigning access logins and password protection.
   - Identification. A global spreadsheet ID can be assigned when the spreadsheet is stored on the server, facilitating use of a spreadsheet inventory and tracking log.
   - Firewall protection. Network firewalls can provide extra layers of protection that a spreadsheet on a mobile laptop does not afford.
   - Virtual private network. Mobile IT assets, such as laptops, are often at greater risk. Storing spreadsheets on a network server ensures that the user accessing the spreadsheet from offsite uses a VPN (virtual private network) that provides a higher security level.
   - Spreadsheet changes. Storing the spreadsheet on the server facilitates changes made by multiple users. Controls, such as spreadsheet lock, can be implemented to prevent more than one user making changes to the same spreadsheet at the same time.
4. Implement spreadsheet change controls using two logs:
   - User log
   - Change log

   A **user log** tracks users accessing the specific spreadsheet. The user log includes the date, user identification, and purpose, such as enter data, analysis, or reporting.

	A	B	C	D	E	F
1	SSID	SSNAME	FILENAME	AUTHORIZED USERS	LOCATION STORED	PURPOSE
2	SSID0127	Consolidation	Consolidate.xls	Accounting: Consolidation Specialist	Network Server	Prepare Consolidated Financial Statements
3	SSID0450	Securities Valuation	SecuritiesVal.xls	Finance: Market Analyst	Network Server	Value Securities for FS Preparation
4						
5						

Global SSID Log | SS Risk Assessment

FIGURE 12.3
Global Spreadsheet Identification (SSID) Log

	A	G	H	I	J	K	L	M
1	SSID	RELATED BUSINESS PROCESS	RELATED ACCOUNTS	FINANACIAL STATEMENT LINE ITEM	DOLLAR VALUE	COMPLEXITY H/M/L	RISK IMPACT H/M/L	RISK LIKELIHOOD H/M/L
2	SSID0127	Financial Cycle	All	All	$10.5 M	H	H	L
3	SSID0450	Financial Cycle	Securities	Securities	$1.2 M	M	H	L
4								
5								

Global SSID Log | SS Risk Assessment

FIGURE 12.4

Spreadsheet Risk Assessment

Which spreadsheet (SSID0127 or SSID0450) should have higher security?

A **change log** documents changes made to spreadsheet design, such as changes to formulas. Use the change log to document the date of change, user making the change, the type of change (for example, formulas), change specifications, and what initiated the change. Each change should be documented so that if new errors begin occurring in a previously correct spreadsheet, there is an audit trail for tracking the changes made. The user log and change log can be added to the workbook as two additional worksheets, labeling the worksheet tabs accordingly (Figures 12.5 and 12.6).

5. Add a contents tab to the spreadsheet to create a spreadsheet table of contents. Typically the first tab, the contents sheet, lists all authorized sheets in the workbook. The contents sheet can include sheet names, purpose of each sheet, and a hyperlink to each sheet. Accidental sheet deletions or unauthorized sheet additions can be tracked by comparing to the contents sheet (Figure 12.7).

6. Add a documentation tab to record proper documentation for the spreadsheet. This documentation sheet can include information about the purpose of the spreadsheet and its authorized uses. User instructions can also be included to reduce the likelihood of user error. Other documentation might include developer notes such as formula specifications, formula links, and any macros and algorithms used.

7. Use data validation controls in spreadsheets as much as possible to reduce data entry errors. Data validation can be used for input controls, such as drop-down lists. Using menus instead of hard keying data entry reduces the likelihood of typing and formatting errors in entering data.

	A	B	C	D	E
1	DATE	TIME	USER ID	DATA: ENTRY/ANALYSIS/REPORT	NOTES
2	10.04.2014	9:00 AM	ajaan	DATA ENTRY	Updated September sales
3	10.20.2014	2:30 PM	ajaan	DATA ANALYSIS	Forecast Q1 2014 sales
4					
5					

User Log / Change Log

FIGURE 12.5

Spreadsheet User Log

	A	B	C	D	E	F	G
1	DATE	TIME	USER ID	DESIGN CHANGE: FORMULA/SHEET/DATA	FROM:	TO:	NOTES: REASON FOR CHANGE
2	11.30.2014	10:58 AM	djaan	SHEET		+SHEEET10	Added sheet fro new subsidiary
3	11.30.2014	11:30 AM	djaan	FORMULA	SHEET9.AJ13 (SHEET5!AJ14+ SHEET8!AJ13)	SHEET9.AJ13 (SHEET5!AJ14+ SHEET8!AJ13+SHEET10!AJ13)	Updated formulas
4							
5							

User Log | Change Log

FIGURE 12.6

Spreadsheet Change Log

EspressoCoffee
Company

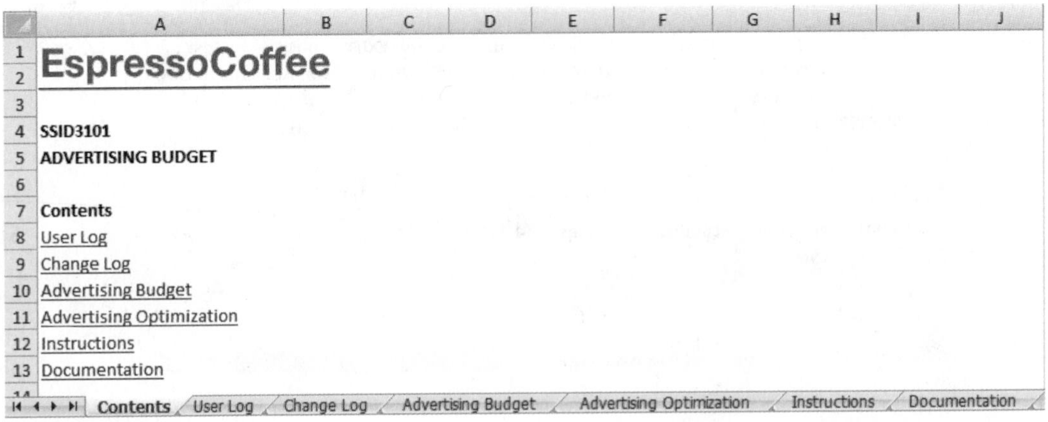

FIGURE 12.7

Spreadsheet Contents

How are the spreadsheets in this figure and the prior two figures related?

8. Use the spreadsheet protection feature for an access security control. Password protect the spreadsheet and specific cells to prevent unauthorized use or accidental data deletion.

9. Test the spreadsheet to assure that it is functioning properly. One technique is to enter "1" into each spreadsheet cell used for data entry. This makes it easier to see where an error is occurring during testing. Use the spreadsheet auditing tool to track errors and verify formula links. Enlist other users to test the spreadsheet to verify that it is functioning as planned. Testers should evaluate whether the correct numbers are calculated and whether the spreadsheet's logic is sound. Document the testing.

10. Remember the 80/20 rule for accounting design. Accounting Insight No. 10 also applies to spreadsheet design. Invest 80% of your time in the design of the spreadsheet and only 20% of your time maintaining it. One good example of the 80/20 rule for spreadsheet design is using a proper system development life cycle (SDLC) methodology to design and build your spreadsheets. Design spreadsheets so that you are never hard-keying data into formulas. If necessary, redesign your spreadsheet so you can use a formula and then use a data entry section, referring to the cell address for data to enter. One company hard-keyed data into complex spreadsheet formulas. This worked fine until the spreadsheet needed to be updated. Remember to include a rigorous backup schedule in the maintenance phase of your spreadsheet SDLC.

> Understanding how spreadsheets are used and the adequacy of related controls is a critical part of management's assessment of the effectiveness of its internal control over financial reporting under SOX Section 404 (PWC 2004).

My Connection...
- It's Your Call 12.43
- Tech Exercise 12.48

Chapter Highlights

What is a risk intelligent enterprise? The risk intelligent enterprise moves beyond security and controls to managing risk and then to using risk to create value.

What is the COSO ERM Cube? The COSO ERM framework offers guidance to enterprises implementing enterprise risk management. The framework consists of four ERM objectives: strategic, operational, reporting, and compliance. The eight ERM components consist of internal environment, objective setting, event identification, risk assessment, risk response, control activities, information and communication, and monitoring.

What is the ISO 31000 Risk Management Standard?
ISO 31000 is an internationally recognized risk management standard that was published by the International Standards for Organizations in 2009.

What is spreadsheet risk management? A significant risk for many enterprises is the widespread use of spreadsheets

with limited controls. A spreadsheet risk management program includes using access and change controls with spreadsheets in order to be SOX compliant.

Accounting System Insights

Insight No. 21 Shadow data ERM uses the top 10 tips for improved spreadsheet risk management.

Active Review

Study less. Learn more. Make connections.

12.1 Refer to the chapter opener, *Meet the CFO*. In your opinion, how could enterprise risk management affect a company's financial performance during an economic downturn? Why is the CFO well suited to advise about enterprise risk management?

12.2 Discuss how enterprise risk management, internal control, and IT controls are related.

12.3 Discuss how opportunity and risk are related.

12.4 Discuss the difference between possibility and probability as related to risk.

12.5 Discuss how governance, including the tone at the top of the organization and policies and procedures, affects an organization's risk management.

12.6 Discuss what caused the development of the ISO 31000 risk management standard.

12.7 Discuss the differences between risk management and risk intelligence.

12.8 Discuss how incorporating sustainability practices supports an organization's enterprise risk management efforts.

12.9 Discuss why the simple spreadsheet can represent a significant risk to organizations.

12.10 Discuss the benefits of a global spreadsheet identification system.

Key Terms Check

Understanding the language used at the crossroads of accounting and IT is key to your success.

12.11 Select the single best answer.
The level of variation an enterprise is willing to accept in attaining objectives is
a. risk appetite.
b. risk tolerance.
c. risk assessment.
d. none of the above.

12.12 Select the single best answer.
The amount of risk an enterprise is willing to accept pursuing value is
a. risk appetite.
b. risk tolerance.
c. risk assessment.
d. none of the above.

12.13 Select the single best answer.
When an enterprise evaluates the extent to which events would impact its ability to achieve objectives, it is conducting
a. risk appetite.
b. risk tolerance.
c. risk assessment.
d. none of the above.

12.14 Select the single best answer.

Adding impact and likelihood columns to a spreadsheet to evaluate risk associated with its use is an example of

a. risk appetite.

b. risk tolerance.

c. risk assessment.

d. none of the above.

12.15 Select the single best answer.

A policy of reconciling a bank statement to within $5 of balancing is an example of

a. risk appetite.

b. risk tolerance.

c. risk assessment.

d. none of the above.

12.16 Match the following terms and definitions.

a. risk

b. event identification

c. likelihood

d. impact

e. possibility

f. probability

g. user log

h. change log

_____ 1. The likelihood of an event occurring using qualitative measures, such as high, medium, or low

_____ 2. The possibility that an event will occur and negatively impact the entity's ability to achieve its stated objectives

_____ 3. The likelihood of an event occurring using quantitative measures, such as percentages

_____ 4. A document that records changes

_____ 5. The possibility or probability that a potential event will occur

_____ 6. A document that records user access

_____ 7. The process of determining events that effect an enterprise's ability to attain its objectives

_____ 8. The effect that an event will have on the enterprise's ability to achieve its objectives if the event occurs

Practice Test

12.17 The relationship between risk management and control is identified in three rings. These rings are:

a. Processes, database, and employees

b. IT control, internal control, and enterprise risk management

c. IT control, internal processes, and enterprise resource planning

d. Enterprise information system, enterprise resource planning, and accounting system

12.18 In the context of ERM, the C-Suite refers to:

a. CEO, CFO, CIO

b. People who are involved with IT control

c. People in an organization, whose titles begin with *C*

d. People who are involved with computers and networks

12.19 ERM framework is typically depicted using a cube. The three dimensions of this cube are:

a. ERM components, ERM objectives, ERM units

b. ERM monitoring, ERM strategic, and ERM business units

c. ERM risk assessments, ERM operations, and ERM entity level

d. ERM control activities, ERM reporting, and ERM division

12.20 Which of the following is NOT part of ERM components?

a. Reporting
b. Risk response
c. Internal environment
d. Control activities

12.21 In the context of ERM, event identification involves identifying

a. potential threats to the organization.
b. potential events that might affect the IT control.
c. potential events that might affect the entity.
d. potential events that might affect the application control.

12.22 In the context of ERM, risk is defined as:

a. Possibility that an event will occur and impact the entity's ability to achieve its stated objectives
b. Possibility that an event will occur and negatively impact the entity's ability to achieve its stated objectives
c. Possibility that an event will occur and impact the entity's ability to conduct its daily activities
d. Possibility that an event will occur and negatively impact the entity's ability to conduct its daily activities

12.23 Focusing on sustainable operations reduces the risk of:

a. Economic downturns
b. Dependence on dwindling natural resources
c. Inflation
d. Dependence on vendors

12.24 How can a risk management philosophy provide consistency in risk attitudes throughout an organization?

a. By setting employee expectations
b. By anticipating all possible risks
c. By providing event-specific examples
d. By being well developed and articulated

12.25 Which of the following is not one of the 10 tips for improving spreadsheet risk management?

a. Store all spreadsheets on a network server
b. Implement spreadsheet changes controls using daily log
c. Use data violation controls in spreadsheets
d. Remember the 80/20 rule accounting design

12.26 In the context of the ISO 31000 risk management standard, the response to significant risk consists of:

a. Tolerate risk, treat risk, transfer risk, and terminate risk
b. Avoid risk, reduce risk, share risk, and accept risk
c. Monitor risk, isolate risk, transfer risk, and terminate risk
d. Quantify risk, evaluate risk, resolve risk, and report risk

Exercises

Each Exercise relates to one of the major questions addressed in the chapter and is labeled with the question number in green.

Short Exercises

Warm up with these short exercises.

12.27 Compare and contrast COSO's *Enterprise Risk Management—Integrated Framework* and COSO's *Internal Control—Integrated Framework.* **(Q12.1)**

Compare (Same)	and	Contrast (Different)

12.28 List and explain the four enterprise risk management objectives specified in the ERM framework. **(Q12.2)**

12.29 List and explain the eight enterprise risk management components specified in the ERM framework. **(Q12.3)**

12.30 Discuss the different types of external events that correspond to the event identification component of the ERM framework. Provide examples. **(Q12.3)**

12.31 Discuss the different types of internal events that correspond to the event identification component of the ERM framework. Provide examples. **(Q12.3)**

12.32 Explain the two aspects of risk assessment. What are pertinent questions in assessing each? **(Q12.3)**

12.33 Risk assessment techniques can be classified as either quantitative or qualitative. Discuss how each type of technique can be used to assess risk. **(Q12.3)**

12.34 Refer to Figure 12.1. Identify the different risks that each of the three levels of IT control addresses. **(Q12.1)**

12.35 Explain the two monitoring approaches suggested in the ERM framework: ongoing monitoring and separate evaluation. Provide examples of each. **(Q12.3)**

12.36 Compare ERM components of the COSO's Enterprise Risk Management Cube and risk management activities described in the ISO 31000. **(Q12.4)**

COSO's ERM Cube Components	and	ISO 31000

12.37 Give an example for each of the 7Rs and 4Ts of the ISO 31000 risk management standard. **(Q12.4)**

12.38 Explain the impact of the organization culture on the organization risk management. What are the two areas of business that are most affected by the organization culture and consequently impact the organization's approach to risk management? **(Q12.3, 12.4)**

12.39 Identify control objectives, risks, and control activities for the account payable process. **(Q12.3, 12.4)**

12.40 Use the following template to assess the level of risk by identifying the level of impact and probability of a call center risk. In this exercise, a risk level is assessed based on a combination of the impact and probability level of an event. The impact and probability level range is low or high. A risk level range is low, medium, or high. For example, if impact and probability are both low, then the risk level is low; if the impact is high and probability is low or vice versa, then the risk level is medium; and if impact and probability are both high, then the risk level is also high. **(Q12.3, 12.4)**

Call Center Risks	Impact	Probability	Risk Level
Loss of call center phone (damaged or stolen)			
Loss of call center computer (damaged or stolen)			
Caller bad credit			
Fraud			
Lost transactions			
Data entry error			
Customer experiences long wait time			
Customer can't get through to the call center			
Call center employee bad behavior			
Call center employee cannot answer customer questions			
Obsolete computers, phones, and internal communications			

It's Your Call

This is your training ground. These scenarios provide you with the opportunity to use your knowledge and professional skills.

12.41 You have been hired as a consultant to an organization that owns a social networking Web site. The president is considering implementing enterprise risk management. He has asked you to summarize for him the benefits and limitations of an enterprise risk management system. Prepare a brief email to the president summarizing the benefits and limitations of enterprise risk management. **(Q12.1, 12.2, 12.3)**

12.42 You are the new accounting intern. You have been charged with improving risk intelligence related to the organization's 1,000 spreadsheets. You have been asked to make a presentation to the CFO and controller with your findings. For your presentation, summarize the risks associated with an enterprise using spreadsheets without implementing spreadsheet risk management. Include a summary of your recommendations in your presentation. Do you anticipate any resistance from the accountants? How would you address this? **(Q12.5)**

12.43 You recently accepted a new accounting position. The accountant who preceded you prepared numerous spreadsheets but did not follow the top 10 tips for spreadsheet risk management. Explain specifically the issues that you, as a successor, may encounter as a result of this oversight. What risks does this present to the organization? Prepare a short email to your supervisor addressing this issue. **(Q12.5)**

12.44 You are a member of a project team responsible for evaluating whether your company should switch from its current silo IT architecture to an integrated enterprise architecture. Recently, the CFO asked you how work was progressing on the team. She wanted to know if the project team was considering enterprise risk management. She's in charge of the new ERM initiative and suggested that you consider ERM in your evaluation of the IT architecture. She asked you to send her a brief email summarizing the advantages and disadvantages of the two types of IT architecture with respect to ERM. **(Q12.2, 12.3)**

12.45 You have been hired as a member of a consultant team by an organization that needs to implement enterprise risk management. Your job is to come up with the key questions when it comes to determining the risk appetite. You have already prepared three sample areas:

1. Environment or quality compromises
2. New product lines
3. Gross profit vs. market share

State your questions in a brief document. **(Q12.2, 12.3)**

12.46 This morning while checking your emails, you noticed an urgent message from your supervisor. He wants you to prepare a short summary before 2:00 PM about ISO 31000, explaining whether your organization needs to comply with this standard or not. Prepare a brief email to your supervisor summarizing the ISO 31000 Risk Management Standard and specifying which type of organizations would mostly benefit from adopting this standard. **(Q12.4)**

12.47 You have just been hired as an accountant in a local bank. You are called to a meeting with the ERM director. He tells you that the bank is considering a new accounting system and mentions the risks associated with switching to a new system as well as the risks associated with the current accounting system. Then he asks you to come up with a short list of risks associated with both systems. Provide the requested list and include opportunities related to each decision. **(Q12.3, 12.4)**

Tech in Practice

These technology in practice exercises are perfect for both individuals and teams.

Tech Exercises

Sharpen your skills with these technology exercises. Watch these software videos at www.pearsonhighered.com/kay.

12.48

Tech Tool: Spreadsheet Software
Software Video: Spreadsheet ERM

EspressoCoffee has asked for your assistance in organizing the many spreadsheets scattered throughout the enterprise.

1. Download the data file for this exercise.
2. Using the data file, create a global spreadsheet identification log that EspressoCoffee can use to track its spreadsheets.

3. Using the data file, create a spreadsheet risk assessment sheet for EspressoCoffee.
4. Print the sheets.

12.49

Tech Tool: Spreadsheet Software
Software Video: Spreadsheet ERM

To assist EspressoCoffee in its spreadsheet risk management efforts, you have decided to create a template that users can request when they are building new spreadsheets. The template will accomplish two objectives. First, the spreadsheets will be more standardized. Second, when the template is requested, the spreadsheet will be assigned a global spreadsheet identifier (SSID) that is logged.

1. Download the data file for this exercise.
2. Create a Contents sheet for the template. See Figure 12.7 for the format.
3. Create a User Log sheet for the template. See Figure 12.5 for the format. Enter the data shown on row 2 as an example in the User Log sheet.
4. Create a Change Log sheet for the template. See Figure 12.6 for the format. Enter the data shown on row 2 as an example in the Change Log sheet.
5. Enter hyperlinks in the Contents sheet.
6. Print the sheets.

Go Online

In the fast-paced world of technology, your skill at finding answers fast can be vital. Go online and experience typical assignments you may encounter as a professional.

12.50 You have been assigned to the project team responsible for implementing enterprise risk management. Your task is to research best practices of other organizations. Go online and search for ERM best practices. Summarize your findings in an email to your project teammates.

12.51 You are an accounting intern at Joseph Enterprises. Recently, an error in an accountant's spreadsheet caused a loss of over $100,000 on a company bid. The controller has come under increasing pressure from the CFO to impress upon all the accounting professionals the importance of error-free spreadsheets. The controller has asked you to go online and search for cases of spreadsheet errors that had a significant adverse impact.

Write an email to the controller summarizing your findings that he can use for training purposes. Apply the top 10 tips for spreadsheet risk management to develop an action plan for Joseph Enterprises to prevent such errors in the future.

12.52 You are an accountant in a rental car company. Your employer rents luxury cars in both the United States and Europe. You have just been assigned to the company's risk management project. Your first assignment is to prepare a presentation on the COSO ERM framework and the ISO 31000 standard. Go online and search for both standards. Summarize your findings.

Technology Projects

These technology projects are perfect for both individuals and teams.

Technology Project 12

Tech Tool: Spreadsheet Software
Software Videos: Spreadsheet ERM

iSportDesign has asked for your assistance in organizing and documenting the organization's spreadsheets, consistent with ERM.

Your deliverables for the project include the following:

Deliverable 1. A global spreadsheet identification log for iSportDesign

Deliverable 2. An ERM spreadsheet template

Visit www.pearsonhighered.com/kay to do the following:

1. Download Technology Project 12 instructions.
2. Download files provided online for your convenience in completing the project deliverables.
3. Watch the video with software instructions to complete this project at www.pearsonhighered.com/kay.

LIVE Project 3

LIVE projects give you an opportunity to apply your accounting and technology skills to LIVE applications. LIVE Project 3 lets you apply enterprise risk management to an organization's spreadsheets.

To view the LIVE projects, visit www.pearsonhighered.com/kay and click on online Chapter 16, *Accounting Systems in Action: LIVE Projects.* You will find the following:

1. LIVE Project 3 with milestones and deliverables
2. Project management training
3. Team coaching

Part Four *Designing and Developing Accounting Systems*
explores the process for developing accounting systems and
tools for accounting database design.

Part Four
Designing and Developing
Accounting Systems

**System
Design**

Chapter 13
Accounting System Development

Chapter 14
Database Design: ERD, REA, and SQL

13

Accounting System Development

How Are Accounting Systems Developed in Practice Today? Meet ABC Methodology.

Can you imagine shopping for a new car and the car dealer asks you if you want four wheels on your car? Do you want a steering wheel? An engine in the car? Car seats?

Does it feel like you are "reinventing the wheel"? Wouldn't it be more effective to start with a base model car and select options, such as a sunroof, to customize your car?

Would you like to learn accounting information systems using the approach the car dealer used, "reinventing the wheel" for each and every accounting system? Is there a more effective way?

Meet ABC methodology. The ABC methodology reflects how accounting systems are developed in practice today. The accounting system consists of a baseline system that is typically purchased and then customized or configured to meet the enterprise's specific needs.

Crossroads

At the crossroads of accounting and IT, when designing and developing a new accounting system, what IT professionals call *user requirements*, accounting professionals refer to as: *This is what I need*.

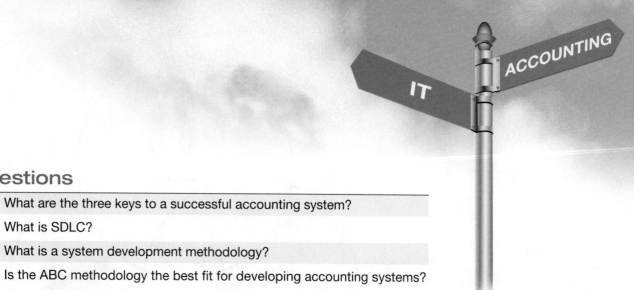

My Questions

Q 13.1	What are the three keys to a successful accounting system?
Q 13.2	What is SDLC?
Q 13.3	What is a system development methodology?
Q 13.4	Is the ABC methodology the best fit for developing accounting systems?

What Are the Three Keys to a Successful Accounting System?

What is required to create an accounting system? Databases, business process maps, database forms, database queries, database reports, database fields, records, tables, RDBMS, accounting software, cybersecurity, internal control... and the list goes on and on.

When there are so many components that must work in an interrelated fashion, it is imperative to stay organized!

In this chapter, we share with you some of the tools that IT professionals use to stay organized when working with interrelated, complex systems. And accounting tends to be one of the most complex and interconnected systems on which IT professionals work.

First, let's review three main functions of the accounting system, and then look at three keys to success in fulfilling those functions. As you know, three main functions of the accounting system are:

1. Store data. This is usually accomplished using a relational database.
2. Analyze and use data. This may be accomplished using shadow data in spreadsheets or business intelligence technologies.
3. Safeguard the accounting data. Internal control and cybersecurity are used to safeguard the data stored and used by the accounting system.

Three keys (Figure 13.1) to success in fulfilling these accounting system functions are:

1. People
2. Processes
3. Technology

People

Who are the people involved in designing and developing an accounting system? What are their roles?

Accounting professionals are often the end users of the accounting system. Because of the complexity of the accounting system, however, the accounting professional typically needs to be involved in the design and development of the system. The IT professionals responsible for designing and developing the accounting system cannot be expected to know everything that the accountants know about accounting. For this reason, it is important that the development team for the accounting system includes accounting professionals who have knowledge of accounting and IT.

3 + 3
3 main functions of the accounting system:
1. Store data.
2. Analyze data.
3. Safeguard data.

3 keys to success in fulfilling those functions:
1. People
2. Processes
3. Technology

Project Management...
...is an important aspect of successful accounting system projects. Project management uses techniques to organize and streamline the project. Project management questions are now included on the CPA Examination.

Would you like to know more about project management? See our online Chapter 16, *Accounting Systems in Action: LIVE Projects.*

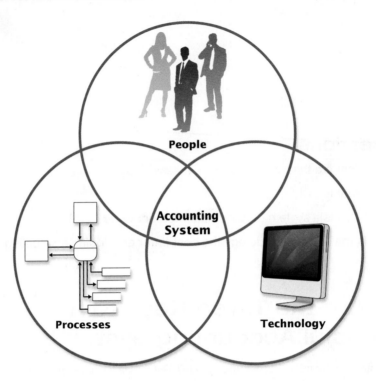

FIGURE 13.1

Three Keys to a Successful Accounting System: People, Processes, and Technology

The IT professionals involved in the design and development of the accounting system include:

- System analysts who design the system, specifying the components needed for the accounting system
- Database designers who create the design for the accounting database
- Database developers who build the database using the database design and DBMS software
- Application developers or programmers who design and write the software for applications, such as accounting software
- Network specialists who design the network for a new system

Processes

What are the processes involved in developing an accounting system? What are the steps in the processes?

IT professionals use the following two tools to define and structure the process for developing systems, including accounting systems.

- **System development life cycle (SDLC)** is a series of phases used to create a system: plan, analyze, design, build/buy, install, and deploy.
- **System development methodology (SDM)** is the order and timing of when the SDLC phases are completed.

Why should you, as an accounting professional, care about the SDLC? Why do accountants need to know about the processes IT professionals use for system development?

One reason is that accountants are often asked to participate in the accounting system development process. Knowledge of the SDLC and SDM is vital if the accountant is to be an informed participant in the process. Often as an accounting professional, you are asked by IT professionals to approve various aspects of the design before proceeding. Later, if there are problems, you must be prepared to take responsibility because you approved the design.

Another reason you should care is that accountants must audit the SDLC as the system is being developed. In order to audit the SDLC, the accountant must understand the phases of system development and the methodology used.

Technology

What technology is used by the accounting system? You have been introduced to various technologies used by an accounting system throughout this book. To briefly summarize for you, accounting system technology might include:

- Accounting software
- Database and DBMS
- Network and protocols
- Desktop and laptop computers
- Cybersecurity and technology to safeguard information assets

The three keys of people, processes, and technology are combined to design and build an accounting system. Next, we explore in greater depth the SDLC process for organizing these three keys.

> **My Connection...**
> How do I study less and learn more? Make connections. Try Active Review 13.1.

What Is SDLC?

The system development life cycle (SDLC) is a process for analyzing, designing, organizing, and integrating the three keys (people, processes, technology) to a successful accounting system. The SDLC is an effective tool for learning how to design accounting systems.

Just as accounting provides a common language for business, the SDLC provides a common language for communicating with programmers, system analysts, database administrators, and other IT professionals engaged in accounting system development.

The SDLC is a series of phases to create a system (Figures 13.2 and 13.3). We will use the following six phases representative of the typical phases of an SDLC for an accounting system:

- Plan
- Analyze
- Design
- Build/Buy
- Install
- Deploy

> **SDLC...**
> The system development life cycle is a series of phases to create a system:
> 1. Plan
> 2. Analyze
> 3. Design
> 4. Build/Buy
> 5. Install
> 6. Deploy
> You can remember the phases by thinking of PAD-BID....
> Did the system developer PAD the BID?

SDLC Phases

Each SDLC phase consists of specific activities. Next, we explore the activities comprising each of the SDLC phases. To start the process, a new opportunity or issue with the current system typically triggers the first phase, planning.

SDLC

Plan

Analyze

Design

Build/Buy

Install

Deploy

FIGURE 13.2

System Development Life Cycle (SDLC)

FIGURE 13.3 System Development Life Cycle (SDLC) Phases

Plan	Identify the problem, need, or opportunity that a new system would address. Plan the system development project.
Analyze	Analyze user requirements. Models for the current system, such as database models and business process models, are analyzed to determine modifications required.
Design	Design new system models based on your system analysis.
Build/Buy	Build/buy and test the new system. In this phase, the models are transformed into software programming code, which is then tested.
Install	Install the new system, including hardware and software. Train users. Convert data from the current system to the new system and begin using the new system.
Deploy	Deploy the new system. Operate the new system as users enter data, execute processing, and generate reports. Maintain the system as new updates or requirements emerge. Support the system providing ongoing user care and training.

Plan. The planning phase is triggered by problems with the current system, by opportunities that the current system does not take advantage of, or by governmental regulations not satisfied by the current system. This phase involves first identifying the problem, need, or opportunity that a new system would address. Then plans, schedules, and budgets are prepared to successfully complete the system development project.

Analyze. In the second phase of the SDLC, user requirements for the new system are collected and analyzed. What do the accounting and business professionals using the system need? How can user requirements be satisfied with the new system? Models for the current system, such as database models and business process models, are analyzed to determine required modifications.

Design. The system design phase involves designing new system models to satisfy user requirements, either by creating a new model or by modifying existing models.

Build/Buy. During the system build/buy phase, system builders and software engineers transform the system models into applications (computer software) and databases. The newly developed system software applications and databases are tested using test data. Final fine tuning is completed.

Install. The system install phase involves installing the final product on enterprise servers and user computers (client workstations). The database is populated with the enterprise's real data (accounting data). Users of the system, such as accountants, are trained.

Deploy. Typically, this is the longest phase of the SDLC. It involves operating and maintaining the new system until it no longer satisfies the organization's needs. Activities in this phase include operating the system as users enter data, execute processing, and generate reports. System maintenance involves installing new updates, patches, and new version upgrades. System support includes ongoing user care and training to resolve issues. When a system can no longer be maintained or new opportunities arise, the development of a new system begins.

SDLC...

Each SDLC phase (plan, analyze, design, build, install, and deploy) consists of specific activities. Some activities are performed only once while cross-life-cycle activities are conducted in more than one SDLC phase. Cross-life-cycle activities include documentation and presentations. Documentation is the process of recording notes, models, specifications, requirements, and solutions in both a hardcopy printout and electronic form. Activities conducted in each phase of the SDLC should be well documented because system designers and developers will use this documentation in the subsequent phase of the SDLC. Periodically, the project team presents project progress to interested parties. The presentations can be live or virtual.

My Connection...
- Active Review 13.3
- Short Exercise 13.16

What Is a System Development Methodology?

A system development methodology determines the specific order and progression of how and when the phases of the SDLC are performed.

The system development life cycle lists *what* steps to complete. The system development methodology determines *when* the steps are performed.

For example, let's say EspressoCoffee is sending you on a European business trip to Florence, Geneva, Monte Carlo, Nice, Paris, and Zurich. The SDLC is similar to the list of cities that you would visit. The system development methodology can be compared to your itinerary of the particular route, order, and frequency in which you visit these European cities.

There are many system development methodologies, and which one is the best fit for a particular project depends upon the nature of the project and its specific requirements. Traditional system development methodologies used by IT professionals include waterfall, prototyping, spiral, and agile methodologies. Among the traditional methodologies, the waterfall methodology is often used for learning system development methodologies.

EspressoCoffee
Company

Waterfall Methodology

The waterfall methodology completes the SDLC phases in a waterfall order starting with the planning phase and completing each phase, one after the other in PAD-BID order. The waterfall methodology collects *all* user requirements at the beginning of the analysis phase. These requirements are analyzed and current system models are modified or new system models are designed.

Enterprise technology (hardware and software) together with the new system models are used to build (or buy) and test the new system. Then the system is installed. Figure 13.4 summarizes the steps in the SDLC phases using the waterfall methodology.

Prototyping Methodology

The prototyping methodology collects *some* user requirements to analyze, design, and build a prototype. The prototype or sample is shown to the user to obtain feedback. The revised user requirements are utilized to analyze, design, and revise the prototype. This is repeated as necessary until the prototype is complete and meets user requirements. When the prototype is approved, it is built, tested, installed, and operated. Figure 13.5 summarizes the prototyping methodology phases.

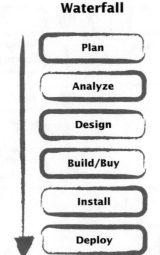

FIGURE 13.4
Waterfall Methodology

Prototyping

> Plan
>
> Analyze
>
> Design Prototype
>
> Build Prototype
>
> Install
>
> Deploy

FIGURE 13.5

Prototyping Methodology

Pair and Share: Compare the prototyping methodology illustrated here with the waterfall methodology. What are the differences?

ABC Methodology

The ABC methodology (Figure 13.6) more closely reflects the methodology used in practice today for most systems development. The ABC methodology starts with a baseline system. Then the baseline system is customized to meet the enterprise's specific needs. The baseline stage resembles the waterfall methodology. The customization stage resembles the prototyping methodology where customization may involve several iterations of prototypes.

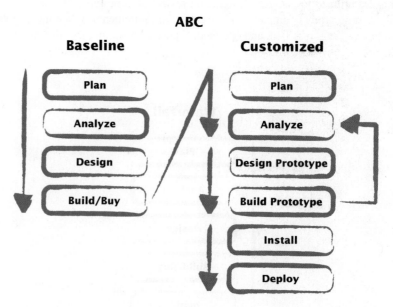

ABC

| Baseline | Customized |

FIGURE 13.6

ABC Methodology

Pair and Share: Compare the ABC methodology with the waterfall and prototyping methodologies. What are the similarities? What are the differences?

My Connection...
- Active Review 13.8
- Short Exercise 13.17

Illustration: Waterfall and Prototyping Methodologies

Let's assume that before you worked at EspressoCoffee you were a designer for a company that makes Italian handmade sports cars, Ferrari. One of your customers wants you to build him a car.

WATERFALL METHODOLOGY Using the waterfall approach to design and build the car, you would do the following:

Step 1: You meet customer and ask him all the things he needs for the new car.

Step 2: With your customer requirements, you design the new car.

Step 3: When the design is complete, your company builds the car. Your company's designated driver tests the car.

Step 4: If the car passes the test, then it is delivered to the customer.

Step 5: The customer operates and maintains the car.

PROTOTYPING METHODOLOGY Using the prototyping approach to design and build the car, you would do the following:

Step 1: You meet with your customer and ask him for some requirements for the car. For example, you would obtain user requirements for the car engine, such as horsepower and so on.

Step 2: With your customer's requirements, you design the car engine.

Step 3: You build a prototype of the engine.

Step 4: You show the customer the prototype. The customer adds more requirements, such as a turbocharger.

Step 5: You design a new prototype with the new requirements.

Step 6: You build the new prototype based on the new requirements.

Step 7: This process continues, repeating steps 4 through 6 until the customer has no more requirements. Then you test the car.

Step 8: If the car passes the test, it is delivered to the customer.

Step 9: The customer operates and maintains the car.

Illustration: ABC Methodology

To return to the handmade Italian sports car example, if you used the ABC methodology you would complete the following steps.

BASELINE STAGE In the baseline stage of designing and building the car, you would do the following:

Step 1: You already know the requirements to build a base model car, such as four wheels, an engine, and a steering wheel.

Step 2: With these basic requirements you build a baseline working model or prototype.

Step 3: Test the baseline model to see if it satisfies those requirements.

CUSTOMIZATION STAGE In the customization stage, you would do the following:

Step 1: Show the customer the baseline model. The customer may add a set of requirements to customize a component of the baseline model for his specific needs, such as the car engine. If the customer has no additional requirements, the prototype is used to create the final product.

Step 2: With the new requirements for the component, design the customized features of the engine.

Step 3: You build the new component prototype based on the new requirements.

Step 4: This process continues, repeating steps 1 through 3 until the customer has no more requirements and is satisfied with the component. Test the component.

Step 5: Repeat the customization process for each component until the car is complete.

Step 6: Test and deliver the car.

Is the ABC Methodology the Best Fit for Developing Accounting Systems?

With the advent of computers, the first software to perform accounting functions often was custom written by programmers. Each company would hire its own in-house or outsourced programmers to write custom programs to process accounting transactions. When each enterprise had its own computer programmers write custom programming code for its accounting applications, a system development methodology, such as the waterfall methodology, might have been a good option. However, today, for most enterprises it is not cost-effective to hire programmers to write custom software programs for all of their accounting functions.

Today, there is widespread use of commercial accounting software (off-the-shelf software) that is then customized to meet an enterprise's specific needs. QuickBooks accounting software is an example of this for small businesses. Most entrepreneurs do not need to hire custom programmers to write accounting programs. Instead, the entrepreneur can purchase QuickBooks accounting software for approximately $200 to $500 and then hire an in-house accountant or a CPA firm to customize the QuickBooks software.

SAP enterprise software is an example of this approach for large-scale enterprises. SAP AG, headquartered in Germany, released R/3 in 1992. This was the dawn of a new era for enterprise systems. Since then, large-scale enterprises can purchase baseline enterprise software off the shelf from commercial vendors, such as SAP. Enterprises then hire in-house programmers or consultants to customize the baseline enterprise software to meet enterprise-specific needs.

ACCOUNTING INSIGHT NO. 22
Accounting Systems Today
Are Built Using an
ABC Methodology:
Accounting System =
Baseline System + Customization

Accounting Insight No. 22: **ABC Methodology**

Accounting Insight No. 22 states that accounting systems today are built using an ABC methodology:

$$\text{ACCOUNTING SYSTEM} = \text{BASELINE SYSTEM} + \text{CUSTOMIZATION}$$

Today, most enterprises, from small to large-scale, use a two-stage process for developing accounting systems. First, a baseline software is selected and purchased. Second, the baseline software is configured or customized to meet the enterprise's specific needs. The system development methodology that most closely resembles actual practice in developing accounting systems is the ABC methodology.

The baseline stage focuses on the baseline accounting system that contains features common to most accounting systems. This is represented by the model shown in Figure 13.7. The customization stage involves customizing the baseline system to meet the specific needs of the particular enterprise. The two-stage approach accelerates the customization of the accounting system, saving time and money.

ABC Methodology Phases

The ABC methodology involves customizing the baseline system to meet enterprise-specific needs. Thus, there are two distinct system development stages: baseline and customization.

The baseline accounting system is a generic or basic accounting system that includes the workflow and business processes frequently used by most enterprises. Modules in a baseline system include the vendors, customers, employees, banking, financial, and reporting modules (Figure 13.7). The baseline accounting system is typically selected from among available commercial accounting or enterprise software.

Next, the baseline accounting system is configured or customized to meet the unique requirements and needs of the specific enterprise. The baseline modules for vendors, customers, employees, banking, financial, and reports are customized to meet enterprise requirements.

Each module of the baseline model is expanded and customized to show the detail of the business processes of the specific enterprise. Models, such as business process maps, are used to illustrate the business processes of the enterprise and document the data flow. When a new accounting system is developed, organizations often use business process management (BPM) to streamline operations and business processes to improve effectiveness.

There may be many iterations for each module as user requirements are collected, prototypes built and tested, and user feedback obtained. The requirements for customization may be

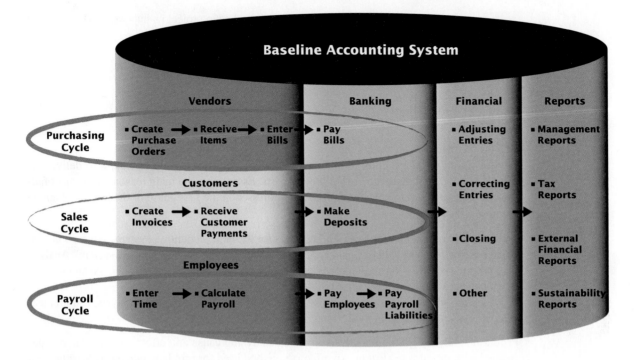

FIGURE 13.7

Baseline Accounting System with Transaction Cycles

provided by accounting professionals. IT professionals, such as consultants or in-house programmers, may build the customization requirements for the system.

BASELINE SYSTEM STAGE In the baseline stage, the following steps would be followed to develop a baseline system:

- Plan
- Analyze
- Design
- Build/Buy

Plan Identify the problem, need, or opportunity that a new system would address. Plan the system development project. Form a team charged with overseeing new project planning, conduct an initial feasibility analysis to assess the viability of a new system, and plan project management activities. The project team consists of senior management, system users, IT professionals, accounting and accounting system professionals, and consultants. Since the project affects many business activities and functions, the team should have representatives from various departments and areas. The system project users, referred to as clients, should be included on the project team. Clients, such as the accountants using the new system, are included on an accounting system development project team to provide adequate and proper input and feedback. In order for accountants to be able to communicate effectively and contribute to the success of the project, it is vital for accountants to have knowledge of IT and accounting systems.

The project team is charged with overseeing the initial feasibility analysis and project management activities. Initial feasibility analysis for the project is performed to determine if a new system is viable and effective for the enterprise. The current system is evaluated to determine the main reasons for modifying or replacing it. Typically, initial feasibility analysis views the new system from the enterprise point of view and provides an overall assessment of the new project. It focuses on economic feasibility by analyzing the costs and benefits of the new system. In addition, customer satisfaction as well as security and control issues are evaluated.

Initial project feasibility analysis is usually summarized in a one-page document consisting of two sections. The first section, the *Issue/Opportunity* section, addresses the issues with the current system or the opportunities that a new system presents. The second section, entitled *Rationale* or *Risks,* specifies the consequences of not addressing such issues or opportunities.

Other activities conducted in the planning phase relate to project management. These project management activities include:

- Establish a vision and broad strategic framework for a new system.
- Develop a timeline and schedule for the SDLC phases.
- Identify and specify due dates for deliverables for each phase.
- Develop budgets.
- Prepare an executive summary proposal to obtain project approval.

Project management is crucial to the success of any systems project. Common reasons for project failure include failure to deliver a system that satisfies the client, failure to deliver the system on time, and underestimating project costs. Essentially, the main reasons for project failure relate to activities that were not properly addressed in the first phase of the SDLC, planning the new system project.

Analyze Collect and analyze user requirements for the new accounting system. What do the users need from the system? How can we satisfy user requirements with the new system? Analyze the current system and business processes for information about user requirements, and streamline business processes whenever possible.

We can break the system analysis phase into three parts: problem analysis, requirement analysis, and current system model analysis.

Problem Analysis. Problem analysis involves analyzing cause and effects of a problem experienced with the current system. An effective method used for problem analysis is Weatherbe's PIECES framework, which classifies the problem into one or more of the following categories:

- **Performance problem.** If the problem affects business performance, such as the current system requiring 10 hours to run a simple customer query, it is classified as a performance problem.
- **Information problem.** If the problem relates to confidentiality, integrity (accuracy and completeness), or availability of information, then it is an information problem. This is referred to as information CIA (confidentiality, integrity, and availability). For example, if information is not tracked about the trucks in a trucking company's fleet, the accountants cannot accurately track assets or develop depreciation schedules.
- **Economic problem.** An economic problem affects revenues (benefits) or costs. For example, if the current system is not cost effective because it requires expensive manual data entry, that would be classified as an economic problem.
- **Control problem.** A control problem relates to security and control of the system. For example, if the current system has no means of tracking which user is making adjustments to the accounting records, this is classified as a control problem.
- **Efficiency problem.** Efficiency problems pertain to the efficiency of the current system. If the same data must be reentered into three different systems in order to update accounts, this is an efficiency problem.
- **Service problem.** A service problem relates to system problems with service either to enterprise users or customers. An example would be an online sales system that does not provide technical support for the online customer who experiences technical difficulties with the Web site storefront.

By categorizing the problem, system analysts are able to identify system requirements to solve the problem.

Requirement Analysis. Requirement analysis involves analyzing user requirements for the new system. System analysts conduct fact-finding about user requirements through surveys, observations, document review, and interviews. Based on these fact-finding results, user requirements are analyzed. Requirement analysis involves asking questions, such as *What specific reports will management need? What information does management require to make business decisions? What information does your accounting system need to collect in order to produce the required reports?* Answers to these questions become user requirements in the analysis phase of system development.

Current System Model Analysis. After conducting problem analysis and user requirement analysis, the next activity is to collect current system models consisting of database models, business process models, and people models (organization charts) (Figure 13.8). The problem and

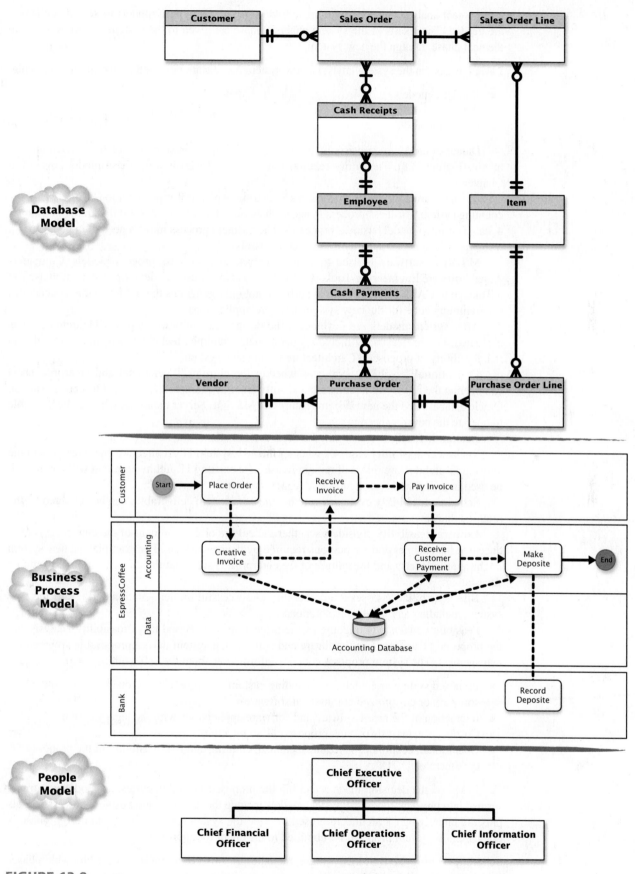

FIGURE 13.8

System Models

Pair and Share: Match the database tables in the database model to the business process model.

requirement analysis results are compared with the current system models to see what changes are needed. The results of the system analysis phase are given to the system designers to use in the next phase: Design the new system.

Design Based on the system analysis, new system models are designed including the following:

- Database models
- Business process models
- People models

Database modeling consists of preparing a pictorial representation of the accounting database (Figure 13.8). The entity relationship diagram (ERD) is a database model covered in Chapter 14.

Business process modeling involves preparing a pictorial representation of the entire accounting system. Business process maps, such as flowcharts or BPMN 2.0 illustrated in Chapter 4, can be used to model business processes. The business process models need to include control techniques designed to safeguard information assets.

MS Visio software is used to create database and business process models. Computer-Aided Software Engineering Tools (CASE Tools) also are used to develop system models. The advantage to CASE Tools is that the software not only generates the models but also generates programming code for the new system software applications.

After system models are developed, the design feasibility of proposed IT architecture is evaluated. Design feasibility includes operational, economic, technical, schedule, cultural, and risk feasibility of proposed IT architecture for the new system.

Operational feasibility evaluates whether the current IT personnel and enterprise users can operate the new system hardware and software. For example, if the client has been using an Oracle database and the new system requires an MS SQL Server database, will the client be able to operate the new database?

Economic feasibility analyzes the costs and benefits of the new system.

Technical feasibility assesses whether the new system IT architecture can interact with the existing IT architecture that will remain in use. The existing IT architecture that will continue to be used in the future is referred to as a **legacy system**.

Schedule feasibility evaluates whether the new system deliverables can be delivered by the required due dates.

Cultural feasibility considers whether the culture or environment of the enterprise is conducive to the changes and adaptations required by the new system. For example, the new system might require layoffs and the culture of the enterprise is such that the effect on morale would be devastating.

Risk feasibility assesses the probability of successful implementation and use of the new system, including any legal considerations.

Feasibility analysis is ongoing as the project unfolds. Based upon feasibility analysis and the proposed IT architecture (hardware and software), a system design proposal is prepared for management. The system proposal contains information about the following:

- Proposed system architectures, including custom software, commercial or off-the-shelf software, or customized commercial software
- Interaction of the new hardware and software applications with the legacy system
- Cost/benefit analysis of each proposed IT architecture
- Operational, economic, schedule, technical, cultural, and risk feasibility of the proposed IT architectures

Based on the decision made regarding the proposed IT architectures, all models are transformed into physical models. Physical models include the database and business process models plus the underlying IT architecture used to build the system. After the system design phase is complete, the system proposal is submitted to the client for approval.

Build/Buy During the Build/Buy phase, the enterprise makes a decision regarding which baseline system it will build or buy. If the enterprise builds the system, it will use programmers to write code. If the system is bought, a commercial accounting software selection is made based upon the best fit with user requirements. For example, a small enterprise might purchase QuickBooks accounting software. A large-scale enterprise might select SAP enterprise software for the baseline system.

CUSTOMIZED SYSTEM STAGE The customization stage involves customizing the baseline system. The following steps would be used to complete this customization process:

- Plan
- Analyze
- Design
- Build/Buy
- Install
- Deploy

Plan Based on the baseline accounting system selected, update the plan for the system development project adding customization of the accounting system. Identify and address any new issues, problems, or opportunities that have arisen.

Analyze Review and update user requirements for each module of the system, considering the baseline accounting system selected. Conduct a gap analysis, identifying any gaps between the specifications of the baseline accounting system and the enterprise-specific user requirements.

Design Based on your system analysis, design new system models that include customization.

Build/Buy Build a prototype that includes customization features by developing the programming code for customizing the baseline modules or buy the customization features from consultants or business solution providers. The prototype is shown to the user to obtain feedback. Any revised user requirements are used to analyze, design, and revise the prototype. This is repeated as necessary until the prototype is complete and meets user requirements. When the prototype is approved, it is built, tested, installed, and operated. This process is repeated for each module of the system until all the modules have user approval and are complete.

Install Deliver and install the customized system, including hardware and software. Train users on using the new system. Convert data from the current (legacy) system to the new system and begin using the new system.

The old system (legacy system) may be run in parallel with the new system for two reasons:

1. The legacy system backs up the new system until there is full confidence in the new system.
2. The legacy system serves as a crosscheck on the results generated by the new system.

Deploy Operate the new system as users enter data, execute processing, and generate reports. Maintain the system by upgrading software as needed. Update with new features. Provide routine, ongoing support and maintenance including backup and recovery. Provide ongoing user care and training as needed to resolve issues that arise.

Eventually, when a system can no longer be maintained, no longer satisfies enterprise requirements, or fails to address new opportunities, it will be replaced with a new system, and a new system development life cycle begins.

The ABC methodology phases are summarized in Figure 13.6 with supporting details provided in Figure 13.9.

Illustration: EspressoCoffee ABC Methodology

EspressoCoffee
Company

Now, let's turn our attention to applying the ABC methodology to designing an accounting system for EspressoCoffee Company. Due to a significant number of accounting errors in its current system, EspressoCoffee management would like to update its accounting system. So a system development project is initiated. The phases EspressoCoffee would use in applying the ABC methodology are summarized as follows.

BASELINE STAGE In the baseline stage, EspressoCoffee would verify consistency of the baseline model with its accounting system needs.

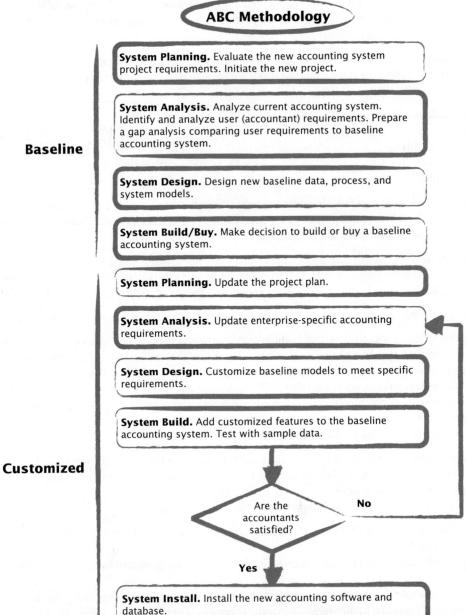

FIGURE 13.9

ABC Methodology Phases

Which of the ABC methodology phases relate to prototyping?

Plan

1. In conjunction with EspressoCoffee management, establish a vision and broad strategic framework for a new system.
2. Conduct an initial feasibility analysis.
3. Evaluate the legacy system—in this case the manual accounting system currently used by EspressoCoffee—and assess how much of the manual system will be computerized.
4. Conduct appropriate project management activities including the following:

   - Identify the project team and team members.
   - Develop a timeline and schedule for the SDLC phases.

- Identify and specify due dates for deliverables for each phase.
- Develop budgets.
- Prepare a proposal to obtain project approval.

Analyze

1. **Analyze Problem.** Using the PIECES framework, classify EspressoCoffee's problems with its current manual system.

   - **Performance Problem.** The manual system slows the operations of the business due to lags in processing orders.
   - **Information Problem.** EspressoCoffee's current system results in data entry errors and information processing errors.
   - **Economic Problem.** EspressoCoffee's manual system causes cash flow problems because of slow customer billing.
   - **Control Problem.** The accounting errors in the current system adversely affect EspressoCoffee's ability to manage and control inventory.
   - **Efficiency Problem.** Both data entry errors and slow processing cause inefficiencies.
   - **Service Problem.** Customer service is adversely affected due to customer complaints resulting from billing errors and incorrect shipments.

2. **Analyze Requirements.** Baseline requirements and components to build a baseline accounting system are shown in the baseline model (Figure 13.7). The requirements for EspressoCoffee's baseline accounting system are detailed in conjunction with fact finding, such as surveys, observations, document review, and interviews. EspressoCoffee compares and verifies its baseline requirements with the baseline model.

Design Using its requirements, EspressoCoffee would build models for databases, business processes, and security and controls.

1. Identify system architecture options including the following:
   - Custom software
   - Commercial or off-the-shelf software, such as QuickBooks or Peachtree
2. Evaluate feasibility and cost-effectiveness of each of these system options.
3. Prepare a system proposal for EspressoCoffee's IT architecture options.
4. EspressoCoffee's management makes a decision to select QuickBooks software for the following reasons:

   - **User Requirements.** QuickBooks software meets EspressoCoffee's user requirements, including its user requirement for multiple currencies. QuickBooks provides this required functionality.
   - **Operational Feasibility.** EspressoCoffee is a relatively small enterprise and QuickBooks software is designed for ease of use by small businesses.
   - **Economic Feasibility.** QuickBooks is affordable and cost-effective.
   - **Technical Feasibility.** QuickBooks will run on EspressoCoffee's existing computers.
   - **Schedule Feasibility.** QuickBooks is readily available and would meet EspressoCoffee's due dates.
   - **Cultural Feasibility.** Because QuickBooks uses onscreen forms that resemble source documents used in EspressoCoffee's existing manual system, QuickBooks would require only minimal retraining and change for employees.
   - **Risk Feasibility.** Because QuickBooks accounts for approximately 90% of small business accounting software sales, it is a proven, reliable software.

5. Design a physical model for EspressoCoffee's new system that integrates database models, accounting system models, controls, and IT architecture (hardware and software).

Build/Buy EspressoCoffee decides to select QuickBooks Premier accounting software as its baseline accounting system.

CUSTOMIZATION STAGE In this stage, the baseline accounting system model is customized based on specific user requirements to meet EspressoCoffee's needs.

Plan Review the planning activities performed in the baseline stage and make any necessary modifications or updates.

Analyze

1. **Analyze Problem.** Review problem analysis from the baseline stage and update as needed.
2. **Analyze Requirements.** Using baseline system requirements, collect and analyze an updated set of EspressoCoffee's enterprise-specific accounting requirements including a gap analysis for particular modules.

Design

1. Using the enterprise-specific requirements from the customization analysis phase, modify EspressoCoffee's baseline system models to develop customized system models. Repeat for each module of the baseline system (vendors, customers, employees, banking, financial, and reports) that requires customization. Repeat for any additional customization required in terms of additional modules needed, such as manufacturing.
2. Design physical models for EspressoCoffee's new system that integrate database models, accounting system models, controls, and IT architecture (hardware and software).

Build/Buy

1. Based on EspressoCoffee's decision to select QuickBooks as the system solution, the enterprise purchases QuickBooks Premier software.
2. EspressoCoffee runs its legacy system (old accounting system) in parallel with QuickBooks.
3. Preferences are selected in QuickBooks to customize it to meet user requirements.
4. Test the customization.
5. Demonstrate to the client and obtain feedback.
6. Revise as needed, repeating the customization process until EspressoCoffee has no additional requirements and is fully satisfied with the QuickBooks software solution.

Install Install the customized accounting system and make it available for EspressoCoffee to use as its primary system. Employee training occurs in this phase.

Deploy Operate the new system as users enter data, execute processing, and generate reports. Maintain the system as new updates or requirements emerge. QuickBooks auto-update feature is turned on to automatically download updates. QuickBooks is upgraded each year as new versions become available. Support the system, providing ongoing user care and training as needed.

Why Is Baseline Plus Customization Widely Used in Practice Today?

The baseline plus customization approach is well suited to the unique needs of accounting system design. Most accounting systems have certain business processes and activities in common, yet need to have certain features customized for the particular enterprise.

Benefits of the ABC approach to accounting system development include:

- Portable: The ABC methodology is portable to any organization.
- Flexible: The ABC approach is flexible to meet the varying needs of the enterprise through customization. Extra modules for customization can be modified and added to the baseline model.
- Effective: This design approach is effective because time and resources are saved since the baseline model does not have to be developed, just the customization features.

What Are the Advantages of Using a Baseline Model?

- Saves time since you do not need to "reinvent the wheel" for basic requirements common to most enterprises.
- Improves efficiency since it provides a model that can be shared with clients to create quickly a common framework for understanding.
- Reduces the opportunity for design errors.

My Connection...
- Short Exercise 13.14
- Short Exercise 13.15

Chapter Highlights

What are the three keys to a successful accounting system? The three keys to a successful accounting system include people, processes, and technology.

What is the SDLC? System development life cycle (SDLC) is a framework that identifies phases of developing a system. Phases of the SDLC are PAD-BID:

1. Plan
2. Analyze
3. Design
4. Build/Buy
5. Install
6. Deploy

What are system development methodologies? A system development methodology is an organized, systematic approach for developing an accounting system. The system development methodology determines the order in which the SDLC phases are completed. System development methodologies include waterfall, prototyping, and ABC methodologies.

What is waterfall methodology? The waterfall methodology completes the SDLC phases in a waterfall order starting with the planning phase and completing each phase, one after the other in PAD-BID order.

What is prototyping methodology? The prototyping methodology completes the SDLC phases by designing prototypes until the user's approval is obtained. Then the final prototype is built, installed, and deployed.

How are most accounting systems developed in practice today? Most accounting systems today are developed in two stages. First, a baseline accounting system is identified. Then the baseline accounting system is customized to meet enterprise-specific needs. The ABC methodology is a system development methodology that resembles what is found in practice.

What are the modules in the baseline accounting system? Typically, a baseline system consists of the following modules:

- Vendors
- Customers
- Employees
- Banking
- Financial
- Reports

Each module contains related events.

The vendors module, also called the purchasing cycle, consists of the following events:

- Create purchase orders
- Receive items
- Enter bills

The customers module, also called the sales cycle, consists of the following events:

- Create invoices
- Receive customer payments

The employees module, also called the payroll cycle, consists of the following events:

- Enter time
- Calculate payroll

The banking module is interrelated to the other modules. Typically, it consists of the following:

- Pay bills
- Make deposits
- Pay employees
- Pay payroll liabilities

The financial module contains all events not in the prior modules. Typically, it would include the following:

- Adjusting entries
- Correcting entries
- Closing entries
- General ledger

The reports module typically consists of four major types of reports:

- Financial reports
- Tax reports
- Management reports
- Sustainability reports

Accounting System Insights

Insight No. 22 Accounting systems today are built using an ABC methodology: Accounting system = Baseline system + Customization.

Active Review

Study less. Learn more. Make connections.

13.1 Refer to the chapter opener, *Meet ABC Methodology*. In your opinion, why is this approach to developing accounting systems commonly found in practice today?

13.2 Discuss how user requirements influence the design and development of a new accounting system.

13.3 As an accounting professional, why is it important for you to know about SDLC and system development methodologies?

13.4 Discuss the differences between a conventional system development project with custom programming from scratch versus a system development project with an off-the-shelf system that is purchased.

13.5 Discuss the reasons why EspressoCoffee management decided to use QuickBooks. Do you agree? Why or why not?

13.6 Discuss the possible roles of accounting professionals in an accounting system development project.

13.7 Discuss what might trigger a systems development project.

13.8 Discuss how development of an accounting system differs from the development of other systems, such as customer relationship management.

13.9 Discuss important benefits of purchasing an off-the-shelf accounting system.

13.10 Discuss some potential drawbacks associated with off-the-shelf accounting solutions.

Key Terms Check

Understanding the language used at the crossroads of accounting and IT is key to your success.

13.11 Match the following terms and definitions.
a. system development life cycle
b. system development methodology
c. legacy system
d. plan
e. analyze
f. design
g. build/buy
h. install
i. deploy

_____ 1. This SDLC phase includes creating new system models
_____ 2. The order and timing of when SDLC phases are completed
_____ 3. The SDLC phase that involves delivering the final product
_____ 4. This SDLC phase includes purchasing software or transforming system models into programming code
_____ 5. An SDLC phase that includes collecting requirements
_____ 6. A series of phases to create a system
_____ 7. The SDLC phase that involves operating, maintaining, and supporting the new system
_____ 8. A prior system that may be run in parallel with a new system
_____ 9. This SDLC phase includes preparing a schedule and a budget

13.12 Match the following terms and definitions.
a. performance problem
b. information problem
c. economic problem
d. control problem
e. efficiency problem
f. service problem

_____ 1. A problem that relates to data confidentiality, integrity, or availability
_____ 2. This problem pertains to efficacy of the current system
_____ 3. A problem that relates to security of the system
_____ 4. A problem that affects business results
_____ 5. This problem affects the enterprise users or customers
_____ 6. This problem affects an organization's costs and benefits

13.13 Match the following terms and definitions.

a. operational feasibility

b. economic feasibility

c. technical feasibility

d. schedule feasibility

e. cultural feasibility

f. risk feasibility

_____ 1. Relates to costs and benefits of the new system

_____ 2. Considers whether the culture or environment of the enterprise is ready to adapt to the new system

_____ 3. Relates to whether the new IT architecture can interact with the existing one

_____ 4. Relates to whether current IT personnel and users can operate the new system

_____ 5. Evaluates whether the new system deliverables can be provided on time

_____ 6. Assesses the probability of the successful implementation and use of the new system

Practice Test

13.14 The three main functions of the accounting systems are:

a. Store data, analyze and use, and safeguard data

b. Store data, report data, and safeguard data

c. Capture data, store data, report data

d. Perform accounting activities

13.15 Which IT professionals typically create the design for the accounting database?

a. Database designers

b. Systems analyst

c. Network specialist

d. Database developer

13.16 What does the system development life cycle define?

a. The life cycle of a computer program from its installation until crash

b. A series of phases used to create a system

c. The order and timing of steps needed for the system development

d. None of the above

13.17 What does the system development methodology define?

a. A series of phases used to create a system

b. The order and timing of steps needed for the system development

c. A series of steps to create a software

d. None of the above

13.18 What phase of SDLC deals with user requirement and current system models?

a. Design

b. Plan

c. Build

d. Analyze

13.19 In what phase of the SDLC are current system problems, needs, or opportunities identified?

a. Design

b. Plan

c. Buy/Build

d. Analyze

13.20 Which phase in the SDLC typically takes the longest?

a. Buy/Build

b. Plan

c. Design

d. Deploy

13.21 Which methodology more closely reflects the methodology used today by businesses to develop an accounting system?

a. Waterfall
b. ABC
c. Rapid prototyping
d. Spiral

13.22 PIECES framework is used to

a. Classify the current system problems
b. Identify current system problems
c. Identify new system requirements
d. Classify new accounting system technology

13.23 In ABC methodology, what steps are not included in the baseline stage?

a. Plan and analyze
b. Design and build/buy
c. Install and deploy
d. Analyze and design

Exercises

Each Exercise relates to one of the major questions addressed in the chapter and is labeled with the question number in green.

Short Exercises

Warm up with these short exercises.

13.24 Match each of the following items to the type of problem. **(Q13.4)**

a. Performance problem
b. Information problem
c. Economic problem
d. Control problem
e. Efficiency problem
f. Service problem

_____ 1. The system is not able to detect duplicate purchase orders.
_____ 2. The system takes 24 hours to process a query request.
_____ 3. In stock status of inventory cannot be determined when customers want to place orders.
_____ 4. The cost of maintaining the current system exceeds the estimated cost of a new system.
_____ 5. Customers are confused by the new Web site.
_____ 6. The current system requires eight screens and an average of 20 minutes to enter an order.

13.25 Match each of the following items to the type of feasibility. **(Q13.4)**

a. operational feasibility
b. economic feasibility
c. technical feasibility
d. schedule feasibility
e. cultural feasibility
f. risk feasibility

_____ 1. The estimated cost of the new system exceeds the budget.
_____ 2. The accounting department staff do not like the format of the reports generated by the new system.
_____ 3. The new system software program does not match the current system hardware.
_____ 4. IT staff are not familiar with the new system hardware.
_____ 5. The new system cannot be delivered as scheduled.
_____ 6. There is a possibility that the hardware for the new system will no longer be in production after one year.

13.26 Match each of the following items to the correct phase of the SDLC in which it would occur. **(Q13.2, 13.3)**

a. plan

b. analyze

c. design

d. build/buy

e. install

f. deploy

_____ 1. The project team creates new system models.

_____ 2. Patches are downloaded and installed.

_____ 3. Based on the recommendation of the project team, the company purchases the new accounting system software.

_____ 4. The project team is formed.

_____ 5. IT staff configure the new system.

_____ 6. The project team collects user requirements.

13.27 List the order of the SDLC phases as used in the waterfall methodology. Why is it called waterfall? **(Q13.3)**

13.28 List the order of the SDLC phases as used in the ABC methodology. Why are some of the SDLC phases repeated in this methodology? **(Q13.3, 13.4)**

13.29 Using the following organizer, compare and contrast the waterfall methodology and the ABC methodology for developing accounting systems. **(Q13.3, 13.4)**

Compare (Same)	and	Contrast (Different)

13.30 Complete the following:

1. Select an authentic enterprise or system development project of your choice.
2. Apply the waterfall methodology, listing the steps and order of the steps you would complete.
3. Apply the ABC methodology, listing the steps and order of the steps you would complete.
4. Compare and contrast the advantages and disadvantages that each methodology offers for the selected situation. **(Q13.3, 13.4)**

It's Your Call

This is your training ground. These scenarios provide you with the opportunity to use your knowledge and professional skills.

13.31 JB Brothers is a home appliance retailer. JB owns one retail store in St. Louis and one in Kansas City. The company also owns three warehouses in St. Louis and one warehouse in Kansas City. JB is losing sales due to order fulfillment problems.

You have been hired as a consultant to investigate and report back to the CFO on the problem. You discover that sales are entered into cash registers manually in the retail stores. All inventory updates are manually entered into the system. You notice that to reduce customer wait time when the stores are busy, the cashiers sometimes set aside the inventory updates to enter them later.

Jeff Bume, director of inventory and purchasing management, complains to you that he is coming under increasing pressure from the chief operations officer about problems with stock outs and inability to fill customer orders quickly. An increasing number of customers are canceling orders and then placing the order with a competitor who can deliver faster.

Use the PIECES framework to analyze JB Brothers' problem. What is the effect of this problem on JB Brothers' accounting. Write a brief summary of your analysis to send to the CFO. Make assumptions as required, and include your assumptions in your response. **(Q13.4)**

13.32 You are an accounting intern for Pacioli Accountants. You notice that the staff accountants must enter client tax information into three different systems: one to track customer information, another for tax information, and a third for billing information.

After taking your accounting information systems course, you share Accounting Insight No. 9, *Enter Data Once*, with your supervisor. The supervisor asks you to prepare a short email with your recommendations for implementing this accounting insight. **(Q13.2, 13.3, 13.4)**

13.33 You are a consultant for Austin Consulting. The organization would like to reduce the time required for system design and development, to increase its consultants' productivity. You have been asked by the president of Austin Consulting to prepare an executive summary with recommendations on how this could be accomplished with respect to accounting system design and development. **(Q13.4)**

13.34 Your company is planning to develop a new accounting system. The ABC methodology is used for this project. The current system is custom made, and Microsoft Excel is used for data entry and output reports. As an accountant and a member of the project team, you have already been through the planning, analysis, and design phases.

a. List all the common user requirements that have been documented for the new system.
b. What is the next phase, and how many times do you think that the next phase will be performed?
c. What are the current system models?
d. What are you suggesting for the new system—build or buy? Explain your answer.

Tech in Practice

These technology in practice exercises are perfect for both individuals and teams.

Tech Exercises

Sharpen your skills with these technology exercises. Watch these software videos at www.pearsonhighered.com/kay.

13.35

Tech Tool: Spreadsheet Software
EspressoCoffee has asked for your assistance developing a schedule for a new accounting system development project.

1. Download the data file for this exercise.
2. The data file contains a list of all activities for the project, with estimated completion times. Using this list and the schedule template, prepare a timeline for the project.
3. Print the timeline.

13.36

Tech Tool: Spreadsheet Software
Kolbe & Co. has asked for your assistance in developing a schedule for a new accounting system development project.

1. Download the data file for this exercise.
2. The data file contains a list of all activities for the project, with estimated completion times. Using this list and the schedule template, prepare a timeline for the project.
3. Print the timeline.

13.37

Tech Tool: Spreadsheet Software

Software Video: Spreadsheet ERM

Kolbe & Co. has asked for your assistance in training its project development team in the PIECES framework. To prepare for the training session, you decide to develop a PIECES framework template to share with the team. The template will standardize the PIECES analysis performed by various team members. It also serves as a visual for your presentation.

1. Download the data file for this exercise.
2. Follow the instructions in the data file to build a PIECES framework template.
3. Print the template.

13.38

Tech Tool: Spreadsheet Software

Management at Lakeview Restaurant has many suppliers. These suppliers supply frozen food packages, fresh meat, chicken, and fish, as well as fresh produce. Lakeview would like to notify its supplier when the quantity of an inventory item reaches the critical level. The project management team at Lakeview Restaurant has prepared the following list of requirements.

a. To be able to extract and view specific supplier information
b. Automatic transmission of notification messages with a list of needed items to a specific supplier
c. To be able to extract and view a list of all suppliers

Management intends to use this information to manage its inventory and suppliers. Lakeview already has a computerized system, but this system does not satisfy the above requirements. The current system BPMN 2.0 diagrams are shown below. The current system database consists of only two tables: Inventory and Sales.

a. In what phase or phases of SDLC is this project right now?
b. Prepare a document to list all changes that should be implemented on the current system's process and data models.
c. Redesign the BPMN 2.0 diagrams to satisfy the new requirements.

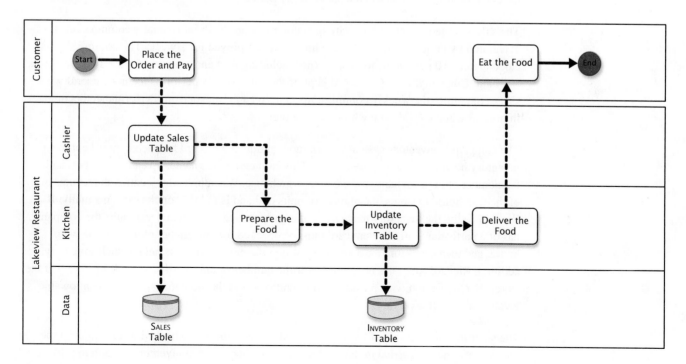

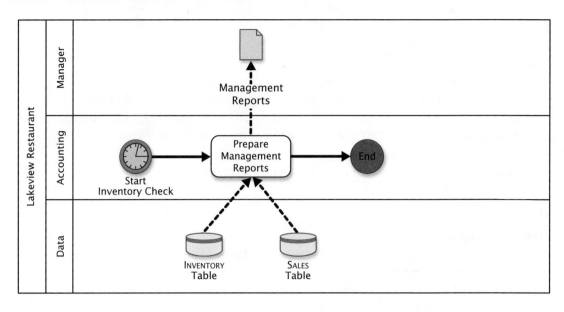

13.39

Tech Tool: Spreadsheet Software

Despite the fact that the iElectronics company has had a computer for the past 10 years, all data collections still rely on written documents. Only data processing activities are carried out on the computer. For example, the company payroll system has all the processing on the computer, and all payroll records are kept in a database. Time cards are still used to collect the hours worked by employees, but the total hours that each employee works for the week are typed into the database from terminals at the end of a pay period.

The salespeople are paid a base rate plus commission. Each individual's commission is calculated by collecting all the sales slips for an employee for a week. The commission is calculated as 10 percent of total sales (not including tax) and entered into the system from a terminal. Currently, the only record kept of the sales staff's performance is a general work sheet containing the weekly commissions paid to each salesperson. Performance becomes important when considering whom to promote.

The company's inventory system is even more antiquated. A card for each item is kept in an inventory book at the central warehouse. This card carries the name, inventory number, and the number of units on hand in the central warehouse. When inventory control ships items out of the warehouse to stores, the number of units on hand is reduced on the card, manually. If Richard Kelly, the inventory manager, wants to know the actual number of units the company has of a particular item, the item card must be checked for the number of units in the ware-house, and then each store must be called to find the number of units held in shelf inventory. In addition, Richard Kelly has no control over the number of units carried as shelf inventory at the stores. Rachel Burton, vice president for operations, and the store managers set the allowable levels of the shelf inventory.

The shelf inventory levels of the items carried by each store are checked weekly against the reorder information carried in the master inventory book. When inventory for a item falls below the reorder point, the item's inventory card is tagged, and the buyer for that item is notified. If the item is to be reordered, the buyer sends a purchase order to the supplier and a copy to the Finance Department. At the end of each quarter, the buyers receive a list from the Inventory Department of the items below the reorder point and tell the Inventory Department which items to drop from inventory.

When a shipment of items arrives at the central warehouse in Bridgton, the inventory clerks check each order against the enclosed invoice and send copies of the invoice to both the item buyer and the Finance Department. If the item received already has a card that has been tagged, a new card is created with the new inventory count. If the item is new, a card is created for it, and the store managers are notified that the item is in the warehouse.

The system runs fairly smoothly, but several problems have cost the company money. Most of them have occurred because the company never knows exactly what its inventory is for a given item. Items have had high actual inventory counts long after the buyer has said the item should be dropped, thus increasing cash tied up in inventory and causing losses when inventory is sold in the end-of-season sales. Sales have been lost because items were unavailable or were available at one store but not another. Regularly, items in the warehouse are found to be out of stock. This results in lots of small backorders before completing the sale. Finally, items have come into the central warehouse unexpectedly, with no room available to store them. The unexpected inventory required Richard Kelly to either send other items to the stores to make room or rent additional warehouse space on a short-term basis.

1. Download the data file for this exercise
2. Follow the instructions in the data file to build a PIECES framework template
3. Use the PIECES framework to analyze problems with the iElectronics inventory and sales system. Make assumptions if necessary. In your opinion, which problem must be fixed first? Why?

Go Online

In the fast-paced world of technology, your skill at finding answers fast can be vital. Go online and experience typical assignments you may encounter as a professional.

13.40 You have been assigned to a project team to develop a new accounting system for Shepperd Inc. You are part of the task force to evaluate small business software available in the market. Go online and research accounting software packages, such as QuickBooks, Peachtree, and SAP Business One. Become an expert on the software. What are the advantages and disadvantages of the selected software?

Write a brief summary of your findings to share with the project team.

13.41 You have been assigned to a project team to develop a new accounting system for Roxanne Inc. You are part of the task force to evaluate midrange accounting software available in the market. Go online and research accounting software packages, such as QuickBooks Enterprise, MS Dynamics GP, SAP Business All-in-One, and Oracle's JD Edwards. Become an expert on the software. What are the advantages and disadvantages of the selected software?

Write a brief summary of your findings to share with the project team.

13.42 You have been assigned to a project team to develop a new accounting system for SLM Inc. You are part of the task force to evaluate large-scale enterprise software with an accounting/financial module available in the market. Go online and research such applications, including SAP Business Suite and Oracle's E-Business Applications. Become an expert on the software. What are the advantages and disadvantages of the selected software?

Write a brief summary of your findings to share with the project team.

13.43 You have been asked to serve as the lead for a project team to develop a new accounting system for your company. At the first team meeting, the IT and accounting professionals had different opinions regarding the phases that should be used in the system development life cycle. You are familiar with the PAD-BID (plan, analyze, design, build/buy, install, and deploy) approach that is representative of the phases commonly used in the SDLC. You are also aware that different solution providers use variations of these phases. Go online and research the SDLC and compile a summary of the different phases that can be used in the SDLC. Prepare your notes to present to your team at the next meeting. How will you facilitate communication and consensus for your team?

Technology Projects

These technology projects are perfect for both individuals and teams.

Technology Project 13

Tech Tool: Spreadsheet Software
iSportDesign is implementing a new accounting system, and you have been asked to join the project team.

Your deliverables for this project include the following:

Deliverable 1. A project schedule
Deliverable 2. A list of user requirements
Deliverable 3. A PIECES analysis

Visit www.pearsonhighered.com/kay to do the following:

1. Download Technology Project 13 instructions.
2. Download files provided online for your convenience in completing the project deliverables.

LIVE Project 4

LIVE projects give you an opportunity to apply your accounting and technology skills to LIVE applications. LIVE Project 4 explores the system development life cycle for an accounting system.

To view the LIVE projects, visit www.pearsonhighered.com/kay and click on online Chapter 16, *Accounting Systems in Action: LIVE Projects.* You will find the following:

1. LIVE Project 4 with milestones and deliverables
2. Project management training
3. Team coaching

14

Database Design: ERD, REA, and SQL

What Is the World's Most Valuable Relational Database?

Meet Oracle.

In 2010, the global database market was over $22 billion. Who had the largest share of that market?

Meet Oracle. Oracle had approximately 45% of the database market in that year, with over $10 billion in database sales.

In 2009, Oracle acquired Sun Microsystems Inc. for $7.4 billion. With Oracle's acquisition of Sun, it now owns the most popular open-source database, MySQL, used by Google Inc., YouTube, and Craigslist.

Salesforce, which sells software as a service through the cloud, runs much of its operations on Oracle relational databases. Interestingly, in 2011 Oracle began buying companies providing cloud-based computing services.

Crossroads

At the crossroads of accounting and IT, well-designed databases and queries determine whether accounting professionals are able to retrieve accurate accounting data.

My Questions

Q 14.1	What do I need to know about databases?
Q 14.2	What is ERD (entity relationship diagram)?
Q 14.3	What is REA (resources, events, and agents)?
Q 14.4	How is SQL used in database queries?

What Do I Need to Know about Databases?

How many databases do you think you used today? How many queries did you use?

Did you use Google? Did you log in to your student account? Your online course? Did you use your phone today? Text someone today?

Yes, all of these applications use databases and queries. What determines whether the database and query are successful is the design of the database and query. In this chapter we share with you the basics of database design and database queries.

Information assets are the new currency of business. Databases are the storehouses for that information. They are a crucial component of the enterprise system, containing some of the most sensitive and confidential data and intellectual property. The database design can affect how well the database serves the needs of the enterprise.

Database Types

As you know from previous chapters, one enterprise may have many types of databases. Databases serve many purposes in the enterprise. For example, relational databases store data about accounting transactions. Data warehouses store data that is analyzed for business intelligence to enhance tactical and strategic decision making.

In general, there are external databases and internal databases. External databases contain data collected by other organizations and agencies, such as the Securities and Exchange Commission (SEC). Internal databases can be classified as (1) operational databases, (2) data warehouses, or (3) XBRL databases. These internal databases differ not only in use, but also in their structure.

1. **Operational database.** These databases are used in operating the business. Data stored in operational databases include data collected from enterprise transactions, such as vendor transactions, customer transactions, and employee payroll. The operational database also includes data about people or agents, including vendors, customers, and employees. Today, most operational databases are relational databases. The largest provider of relational database development tools is Oracle.
2. **Data warehouse.** The data warehouse contains data collected by an organization from a variety of sources, including the operational database. The difference between the operational database and the data warehouse is that the data warehouse is not used for routine business activities. Instead, the data warehouse is often used for business intelligence purposes to improve management decision making, such as targeting specific customers. Data collected and stored in the data warehouse may be current data, historical data, or future estimates. The data may not be as well structured as the operational database. As you know from Chapter 7, ETL tools are used to extract data from the operational database and other sources, transform it into the data warehouse required structure, and load it into the data warehouse.
3. **XBRL database.** A relatively new type of database, the XBRL database was introduced to you in Chapter 9. XBRL databases contain XBRL data and metadata used for creating XBRL reports. In the future, expect to see more XBRL databases as more financial reporting requires XBRL and as management becomes more aware of XBRL benefits for internal analysis and business intelligence.

> **Crossroads**
> What IT professionals call *objects*, accounting professionals usually call *people* or *things*.

Database Structure

Databases can be built using different structures. The structures include relational, hierarchical, network, and object-oriented. Today, operational databases almost exclusively use the relational structure. The first reason for this is because the relational structure uses less processing time to store and extract data. Secondly, the relational database requires less storage space than other database structures. Furthermore, the structured query language (SQL) for a relational database is relatively easy to code and interpret.

The dimensional database structure is used by data warehouses. One type of dimensional database is the star structure discussed in Chapter 7. The dimensional structure speeds up query processing time. The other database structures mentioned are beyond the scope of this text.

RDBMS

Accounting software relies on relational database management system (RDBMS) software to process accounting data stored in the accounting database. As you know from prior chapters, RDBMS is software used to create, manage, maintain, and manipulate a relational database. Database manipulation includes inserting, updating, and deleting data.

All database programs, from MS Access to large Oracle databases, use RDBMS software. Accounting software, from QuickBooks to SAP, interacts with the RDBMS software to enter accounting transactions and generate accounting reports.

Accounting data is entered into the computer using onscreen forms. The accounting software interacts with the RDBMS software to transfer the accounting data and store it in the appropriate tables in the accounting database.

When the accounting user wants to generate an accounting report, the user requests the report, and the accounting software interacts with the RDBMS software to retrieve the requested data from the specific table in the accounting database and to generate the report.

Data, such as accounting data, can be facts or properties related to:

- **Objects**, such as people including vendors, customers, and employees
- **Events**, such as transactions including vendor transactions, customer transactions, or employee transactions

For example, properties about an object, such as an employee, that would be considered data include employee name, employee address, and employee salary amount. Properties about an event, such as a sales transaction, that would be considered data include sales date, invoice number, and items sold.

Database Essentials Revisited

As discussed earlier, the database essentials that an accountant needs to know include certain database terms and definitions. The relational database hierarchy that shows how the following four database elements are interrelated is shown in Figure 14.1.

- **Field** is a piece of information about events and objects.
- **Record** is a collection of related fields.
- **Table** is a collection of related records with a unique table name.
- **Database** is a collection of related tables with a unique database name.

Additional database essentials include database forms, queries, and reports that form the accounting interface.

A relational database used for business operations should be accurate and complete. Accuracy and completeness is achieved by maintaining database integrity and removing anomalies.

Database Integrity

Data integrity refers to data being accurate and complete. **Database integrity** refers to the database containing accurate and complete data. The following four rules help to ensure database integrity.

RULE 1. ENTITY INTEGRITY Each record in the database must have a unique identifier called a primary key. No two records in the database table can have the same primary key value.

RULE 2. PRIMARY KEY INTEGRITY The primary key value cannot be null (empty). Each record must have a value for the primary key field.

RULE 3. DOMAIN INTEGRITY The field values must be from a predefined domain. For example, the Date field must have a date and no other values. In some database development software, such as Oracle, this is referred to as a Validation Rule.

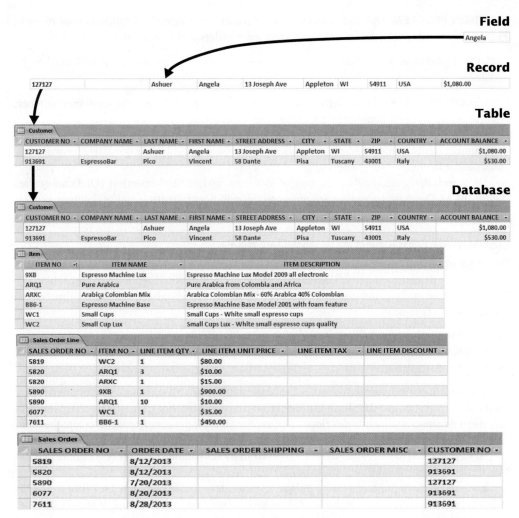

FIGURE 14.1

Relational Database Hierarchy

RULE 4. REFERENTIAL INTEGRITY Data referenced and stored in related tables must be consistent across the database. For example, a customer address should be the same in any table in which it is referenced. Referential integrity is improved when the customer address, for example, is stored in one location only, eliminating the possibility of the address differing from table to table.

Database Anomalies

Database anomalies are problems within a database table that result in inaccurate or incomplete data. Three types of anomalies are shown in the database table in Figure 14.2 and discussed next.

CUSTOMER NO	NAME	ADDRESS	TOTAL BALANCE	ORDER NO	ORDER DATE	ORDER LINE BAL	ITEM NO	QTY	UNIT PRICE
913691	Vincent	58 Dante	$530.00	5820	8/12/2013	$30.00	ARQ1	3	$10.00
913691	Vincent	58 Dante	$530.00	5820	8/12/2013	$15.00	ARXC	1	$15.00
913691	Vincent	58 Dante	$530.00	6077	8/20/2013	$35.00	WC1	1	$35.00
913691	Vincent	58 Dante	$530.00	7611	8/28/2013	$450.00	BB6-1	1	$450.00
127127	Angela	13 Joseph Ave	$1,080.00	5890	7/20/2013	$900.00	9XB	1	$900.00
127127	Angela	13 Joseph Ave	$1,080.00	5890	7/20/2013	$100.00	ARQ1	10	$10.00
127127	Angela	13 Joseph Ave	$1,080.00	5819	8/12/2013	$80.00	WC2	1	$80.00

FIGURE 14.2

Database Table with Anomalies

To update Vincent's address, how many records do you need to change?

DELETION PROBLEM Deleting Vincent as a customer will cause the deletion of four records. These four records hold vital information about three orders and four items.

UPDATE PROBLEM To update Vincent's customer address, four records would need to be updated.

INSERTION PROBLEM To identify a unique record, we have to use the customer number, order number, and item number. That means these three fields together form the primary key. If we want to insert a new customer who hasn't placed an order yet, then the order number and item number fields would be empty. This violates database integrity rule no. 2: The primary key value cannot be null.

So a well-designed database is free of deletion, update, and insertion (DUI) anomalies (Figure 14.3). Database anomalies are removed through **normalization** and/or database modeling. Both methods can be used to design an accurate and complete relational database.

Database Modeling

Database modeling, also called data modeling, is a technique used to develop an anomaly-free database with database integrity. Database modeling uses a pictorial representation of the database elements to analyze and design a database. The following **database realms** are timeframes in database development:

- Database designer realm
- Database builder realm
- Database user realm

The **database designer** designs the database model. Using the database model prepared by the database designer, the **database builder** builds the database. For example, database builders may use a database application developer tool and/or SQL programming code to create the database. The **database user** uses the database to enter, update, delete, search (query), and sort data.

Note that a single individual can be involved in more than one realm. For example, a database designer might also be a database builder and user.

Each database realm has its own unique database terminology. Figure 14.4 lists examples of how terms can differ from realm to realm. As an accounting professional, you may be most accustomed to the terminology of the user realm. Today more accounting professionals need to communicate with IT professionals, database designers, and database builders. As a result,

FIGURE 14.3 Database Anomalies

Database Anomalies	
Deletion	Deleting one record may cause deletion of unintended relevant information.
Update	Updating data requires updating multiple records.
Insertion	Inserting a record is prevented if the primary key value is unknown.

FIGURE 14.4 Database Realms and Terminologies

Example	Database Designer Realm	Database Builder Realm	Database User Realm
Customer	Entity	Table	List
Vincent	Entity occurrence	Record	Information
Customer ZIP	Entity attribute	Field	Form entries
Customer No. and SS No.	Entity identifier	Candidate Key	N/A
Customer No.	Entity identifier to select an entity occurrence	Primary Key	ID
Customer No. in SALES ORDER table	Entity identifier to link related entities	Foreign Key	N/A

accountants need to be familiar with the corresponding terms in the other realms. In the remainder of this chapter, although we are discussing activities in the database design timeframe, to facilitate learning about databases, we will use terminology from both the database design and builder realms (Figure 14.4).

To create well-designed, relational databases free of anomalies, database designers use a modeling approach. Next, you will see how to design a database using a database modeling technique called entity relationship diagram (ERD).

Accounting Insight No. 10: 80/20 Rule

Accounting Insight No. 10 that you saw in earlier chapters also applies to this chapter: Invest 80% of you time designing the database and 20% of your time maintaining it.

This underscores the importance of good database design. If a database is designed well, it provides accurate data that can be retrieved easily. If a database is not well designed, then 80% of your time can be spent maintaining a poorly designed database. In addition, the result may be poor quality data that is inaccurate or irretrievable.

Database modeling may require additional investment of time as the database is being developed. This time is recovered later when time required for errors and maintenance is reduced.

ACCOUNTING INSIGHT NO. 10
Use the 80/20 Rule When Designing Accounting Databases...
80% Design
20% Maintenance

My Connection...
Try the following:
- Active Review 14.2
- Go Online 14.51

> **A Model...**
> A model is a representation of real objects, events, or systems. Most models are built using specific symbols. Models are used for understanding, analyzing, and documenting real systems.

What Is ERD (Entity Relationship Diagram)?

Entity relationship diagram (ERD) depicts the relationship among entities in the database. Although there are many different data modeling approaches, we will use the relational ERD with crow's feet symbols.

The ERD in Figure 14.5 shows the following:

- Entities: customer and sales order
- Relationship between entities: customer places an order
- Relationship cardinality: one-to-many relationship because one customer can place many orders

> **Entity Relationships...**
> Sometimes the entity relationship is written on the relationship line. For example, if the relationship between entities is "customer places an order," then the word "places" can be written on the relationship line connecting the customer and order entities.

An order is placed by only one customer

Customer Entity		Sales Order Entity

A customer may place zero or more orders

FIGURE 14.5

Entity Relationship Diagram (ERD)

In database modeling performed in the database designer realm, the term **entity** can refer to the following:

- object, such as people (customer or vendor)
- event, such as transactions (sales or purchases)

See Figure 14.6 for an example of database entities.

Using database design terminology, customer is an entity. A specific customer, such as Vincent, is an **entity occurrence**. A field in the CUSTOMER table is an **entity attribute**. As shown in Figure 14.7, the entity (customer) will become a database table and the specific entity occurrence (Vincent) becomes a record in the CUSTOMER table. Thus, the ability to distinguish between an entity and an entity occurrence is very important in designing the database tables and records.

An entity attribute describes a property of the entity (an object or event). For example, for the customer entity, entity attributes (properties) would include customer company name and Customer No.

Entity identifiers are attributes that uniquely identify an entity occurrence. For example, Customer No. is an entity identifier for the customer entity (see Figure 14.7). Furthermore, Customer No. identifies the entity occurrence (Vincent Pico) uniquely. An entity may have more than one entity identifier that uniquely identifies the entity. For example, a customer may have a unique Customer No. and a unique Social Security No.

All the entity identifiers that uniquely identify the entity are called **candidate keys** in the database builder realm. In the previous example, Customer No. and Social Security No. would be candidate keys. The candidate key you select for identifying the entity occurrence will be the primary key. For example, the IRS uses Social Security No. as the primary key, while a company, such as EspressoCoffee, uses Customer No. as the primary key to identify customers.

Entity Relationships

An entity relationship diagram shows relationships among entities. The database designer creates an ERD to assist in understanding, analyzing, and building an error-free database. To identify entity relationships in a specific organization, a database designer needs to understand how a business conducts its operations. Business rules describe how a business operates. Business rules define the following:

- **Attribute limitations:** For example, date of birth must be month, day, and year.
- **Referential integrity:** For example, a customer address should be the same in any table in which it is referenced and stored.
- **Cardinality of relationships:** For example, one customer can place many orders.

Three different types of relationships among entities are:

- One-to-one relationships
- One-to-many relationships
- Many-to-many relationships

For a single occurrence of one entity (one customer), cardinality defines the maximum and minimum number of occurrences that might relate to the other entity (sales orders). One customer can place a maximum of many orders and a minimum of zero orders.

FIGURE 14.6 Database Entities

Database Entities			Database Tables
Objects	➤ People	➤ Customers	➤ CUSTOMER Table
Events	➤ Transactions	➤ Sales Orders	➤ SALES ORDER Table

FIGURE 14.7 Example: Entity Occurrence

Entity (Object Type)	Entity Occurrence (Object)	Entity Identifier
Customer	Vincent Pico	Customer No.
Vendor	Roberto Dino	Vendor No.

The name given to the relationship (one-to-one, one-to-many, and many-to-many) refers to the maximum cardinalities (steps 1 and 3 in Figure 14.8). In MS Access, for example, only maximum cardinalities are used. However, as shown in steps 2 and 4 in Figure 14.8, there are also minimum cardinalities for each relationship.

Entity Relationship Diagram (ERD) with Crow's Feet Symbols

Step 1:
What is the *maximum* number of *orders* a customer can place? ***Many***.
To represent this, draw crow's feet on the line next to the sales order entity.

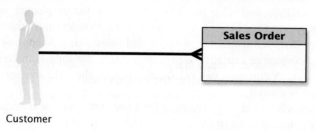

Customer

Step 2:
What is the *minimum* number of *orders* a customer can place? ***Zero***.
To represent this, draw 0 on the line next to the crow's feet.

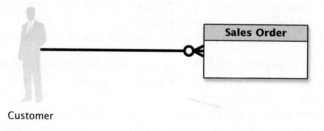

Customer

Step 3:
What is the *maximum* number of *customers* who can place a specific order? ***One***.
Draw a 1 on the line next to the customer entity.

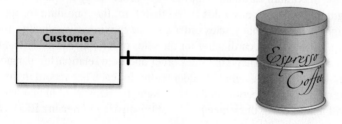

Step 4:
What is the *minimum* number of *customers* who can place a specific order? ***One***.
Draw a 1 on the line next to the first 1 by the customer entity.

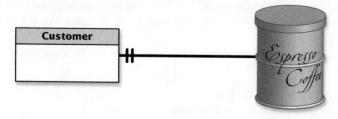

FIGURE 14.8

ERD with Crow's Feet Symbols

How many different entities are shown in this figure?

EspressoCoffee
Company

ONE-TO-ONE RELATIONSHIPS In designer terminology, for a one-to-one relationship, the maximum occurrence possible for each entity is one.

To restate this using terminology of the database builder realm, for each one record in one database table there is one record in the related table. For example, there is one record for each employee in the EMPLOYEE table, and there is one corresponding record in the 401K RETIREMENT ACCOUNT INFORMATION table for that specific employee.

ONE-TO-MANY RELATIONSHIPS In designer terminology, for a one-to-many relationship, the maximum possible for one entity is one occurrence and the maximum possible for the other entity is many occurrences. Most entity relationships in an ERD are one-to-many.

For example, EspressoCoffee's business rules specify that you can be listed as a customer when you contact EspressoCoffee for information, even before placing your first order. So at EspressoCoffee, one customer can place a minimum of zero orders and a maximum of many orders.

The entities involved would be customer and sales order. According to EspressoCoffee's business rules, a customer can have zero orders. Thus, the minimum cardinality for the sales order entity is zero. A customer can place many orders; thus, the maximum cardinality for the sales order entity is many.

Since a sales order must be placed by at least one customer, the minimum cardinality for the customer entity is one. A sales order can be placed by a maximum of one customer, so the maximum cardinality for the customer entity is one.

Since the maximum cardinality for the customer entity is one and the maximum cardinality for the sales order entity is many, the customer and sales order relationship is one-to-many.

Using terminology from the database builder realm, for each one record in the CUSTOMER table there can be many related records in the SALES ORDER table for the many orders placed by that one customer. In a one-to-many relationship, the entity on the one side (customer) is called a **parent entity** and the entity on the many side (sales order) is called a **child entity** or **dependent entity**.

MANY-TO-MANY RELATIONSHIPS In a many-to-many relationship, the maximum occurrence possible for each entity is many. As you will learn later, a many-to-many relationship is problematic when building a database.

For EspressoCoffee, a specific sales order has a minimum of one item (for example, an espresso machine) and a maximum of many items. An item can be in a minimum of zero sales orders and a maximum of many sales orders.

Sales order and item are the two entities. A sales order must have at least one item; therefore, the minimum cardinality for the sales order entity is one. A sales order can have many items; therefore, the maximum cardinality for the sales order entity is many.

An item might not appear in any sales order; therefore, the minimum for the item entity is zero. An item might appear on many sales orders, so the maximum cardinality for the item entity is many. Since the maximum cardinality for the sales order entity is many and the maximum cardinality for the item entity is many, the sales order and item relationship is many-to-many.

Using terminology from the database builder realm, for each one record in the SALES ORDER table there can be many related records in the ITEM table for items sold in that one sales order.

Next, you will learn how to draw an entity relationship diagram using ERD symbols.

How to Build an ERD

There are many different symbols used for ERD and cardinalities. In this text, we use Martin/Information Engineering (IE)/Crow's Foot notation. This notation is provided by ERD software tools, such as MS Visio (PC) and Omnigraffle (Mac). The other popular database modeling tool is Unified Modeling Language (UML). The UML tools are complex and are used by software engineers and programmers.

The ERD symbols used to represent entity relationships for database modeling include the following:

1. Entity: a square (or rectangular) box
2. Entity relationship: a connector line between two entities
3. Relationship cardinality: crow's feet symbols
4. Entity attributes: listed in the entity box
5. Entity identifier or primary key: PK symbol listed by attribute; attribute is bolded

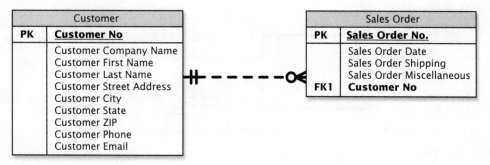

FIGURE 14.9

Entity Relationship Diagram Symbols

In this figure, to what does PK refer?

Figure 14.9 shows ERD symbols for customer and sales order entities and the customer and sales order relationship. Notice that Customer No. and Sales Order No. are the primary keys (entity identifiers) that uniquely identify a specific record (entity occurrence).

Next, let's focus on the crow's feet symbols for diagramming relationship cardinalities for an ERD. For example, EspressoCoffee's business rule specifies that each customer can place zero or more orders, and each order can be placed by one customer. Thus, each customer places a minimum of zero orders and a maximum of many orders. An order can be placed by a minimum of one customer and a maximum of one customer. Thus, there is no sales order without a customer (Figure 14.10).

In Figure 14.8, steps 1 and 2 show sales order entity cardinality. Steps 3 and 4 show customer entity cardinality.

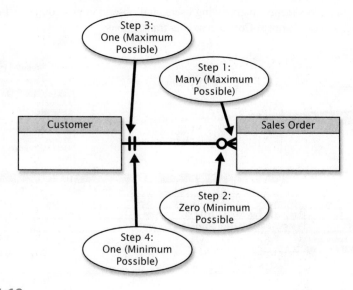

FIGURE 14.10

ERD Relationship Cardinality Symbols

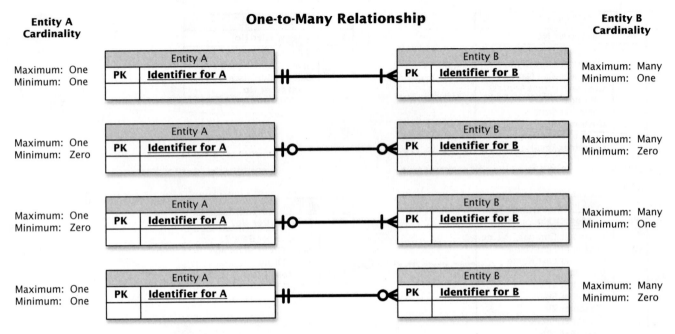

FIGURE 14.11

ERD One-to-Many Relationship Possibilities

Figure 14.11 shows different possible cardinalities for a one-to-many relationship. Entity A's maximum cardinality is one. Entity B's maximum cardinality is many. Notice that the minimums differ for the four possibilities. Similar possible cardinalities exist for one-to-one and many-to-many relationships.

In the following steps, we will cover the required activities for designing an ERD for sales order transactions for EspressoCoffee Company. Using EspressoCoffee's business rules and information from the sales order (invoice) shown in Figure 14.12, you will learn how to identify business entities and the relationship among those entities.

STEP 1: DETERMINE THE RELEVANT BUSINESS TRANSACTIONS THAT THE ORGANIZATION MUST SUPPORT For an accounting database in a baseline accounting system, for example, the organization must support vendor transactions, customer transactions, and employee transactions. By determining and using business transactions to design ERD, we ensure that our database will support data needed by the enterprise. You can collect information about business transactions by reviewing source documents, interviewing users, and observing procedures and operations. In this example, we will use EspressoCoffee customer transactions.

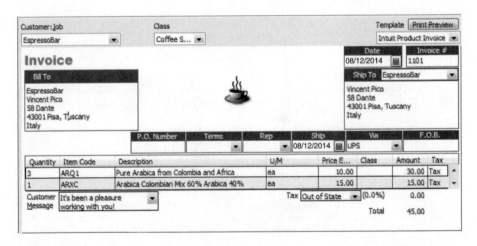

FIGURE 14.12

EspressoCoffee Sales Order (Invoice)

STEP 2: DETERMINE THE BUSINESS RULES FOR A SPECIFIC BUSINESS TRANSACTION
Business rules define attribute limitations, referential integrity, and cardinality of relationships among entities. In our example, EspressoCoffee's business rule is that customers can place a maximum of many orders and a minimum of zero orders. A specific sales order is placed by a maximum of one customer and a minimum of one customer.

Another business rule for EspressoCoffee is that a sales order can have a maximum of many items and a minimum of one item. An item can be listed on a maximum of many sales orders and a minimum of zero orders. Thus, you may have an item that does not appear on any sales orders.

STEP 3: DETERMINE BUSINESS ENTITIES AND THE RELATIONSHIP AMONG THEM To identify the database entities, you analyze business transactions. To identify the relationships, you analyze business rules.

By analyzing the EspressoCoffee sales invoice (Figure 14.12), we identify the following entities:

1. Customer
2. Sales order
3. Item

EspressoCoffee Company's business rules for sales order transactions state the following:

- A customer may place one or many sales orders. However, there are some customers who haven't placed a sales order yet, such as new customers.
- A sales invoice could have one or many items. Obviously a sales order cannot exist without any item in it.
- An item can be in one or many sales orders.
- EspressoCoffee will not accept a sales order for an item that is not already registered in the ITEM table. There are some items in the ITEM table that customers have not ordered yet.

These business rules clearly specify a one-to-many relationship between a customer entity and sales order entity. In addition, these rules specify a many-to-many relationship between item entity and sales order entity. The ITEM table contains a listing of all inventory items that EspressoCoffee currently lists in a spreadsheet.

STEP 4: DETERMINE THE ENTITY IDENTIFIER(S) FOR EACH ENTITY In database design, entity properties are called entity attributes. Properties that identify a specific entity occurrence are called candidate keys. Furthermore, the candidate key we choose to identify entity occurrences in our database is called a primary key.

In our example, we have identified three entities: customer, sales order, and item. Next, we need to identify primary keys for each of these entities. For the customer entity, some of the customer entity properties are customer name, address, email, and account balance. How does EspressoCoffee identify specific customers?

Clearly, customer name, address, email, and account balance attributes cannot be considered candidate keys. For example, EspressoCoffee might have two customers with the same name. Customer No. and Social Security No. are candidate keys and either of them can be selected as the primary key. EspressoCoffee selects Customer No. as the primary key because EspressoCoffee prefers to safeguard confidential customer information such as Social Security No. The Sales Order No. and Item No. are candidate keys selected as primary keys for sales order and item entities, respectively.

STEP 5: DRAW ENTITY RELATIONSHIP DIAGRAM Using ERD symbols and the information collected in steps 2 and 3 about business entities and entity relationships, we can draw the ERD. Figure 14.13 shows the entity relationship diagram for the sales order transaction database.

This model shows the following:

- The three entities: customer, sales order, and item.
- The relationship between customer and sales order is one-to-many.
- The relationship between sales order and item is many-to-many.

> **Entities and Relationships...**
> Experience as well as business transaction analysis helps database designers define business entities and relationships among those entities.

FIGURE 14.13

Sales Order ERD

Pair and Share:
What is the relationship
between customer and sales
order? What is the
relationship between item and
sales order? What is the
cardinality of these
relationships?

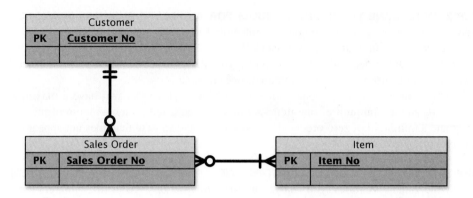

STEP 6: OPTIMIZE THE ENTITY RELATIONSHIP DIAGRAM BY REMOVING MANY-TO-MANY RELATIONSHIPS While an ERD with one-to-one and one-to-many relationships can immediately be mapped into database tables, an ERD with many-to-many relationships cannot. Therefore, we have to convert any many-to-many relationships into one-to-many relationships using intersection tables.

The following steps show how we convert a many-to-many relationship into a one-to-many relationship.

1. For each many-to-many relationship, create an intersection (junction) entity. The relationship between sales order and item is a many-to-many relationship. We create an intersection entity and put it between the sales order and item entities. We call this entity sales order line (Figure 14.14).
2. Create two new one-to-many relationships, each of which connects one of the entities involved in the many-to-many relationship to the intersection entity. Notice the intersection entity is the many side of the relationship. The relationship between sales order and sales order line as well as between item and sales order line is now one-to-many (Figure 14.15).
3. The intersection entity will inherit the primary keys of the two entities involved in the many-to-many relationship as its own primary key. However, sometimes other attributes of the intersection entity can also participate in the primary key. The intersection entity's primary key is a composite primary key, which means that more than one attribute is required to uniquely identify a record (entity occurrence) in the entity. In this case, the primary key for the sales order line entity is a combination of Sales Order No. and Item No. (Figure 14.16).

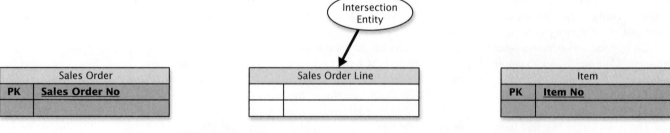

FIGURE 14.14
ERD Intersection Entity

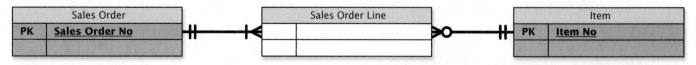

FIGURE 14.15
ERD Intersection Entity Relationships

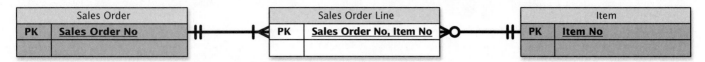

FIGURE 14.16
ERD Intersection Entity Primary Keys

Let's go back to EspressoCoffee's sales order transaction. We see in the sales order (invoice) form (Figure 14.12), for each item ordered, the item number (item code), description, quantity, unit price (price each), and total price (amount) are written in one line of the sales order (line item).

When we add the intersection entity, the relationship between the original entities and the new intersection table (entity) automatically becomes one-to-many. Why do the relationships between the original entities and the intersection entity become one-to-many?

First, let's look at the relationship between the sales order entity and the sales order line entity (Figure 14.17):

- Each record (entity occurrence) in the SALES ORDER LINE intersection table represents a line in the sales order form.
- Every sales order has a maximum of many sales order lines.
- A sales order has a minimum of one sales order line.
- A sales order line belongs to one sales order, so the sales order line has a maximum and minimum of one sales order.

Since relationships are named based on the maximums, the relationship between the sales order entity and the sales order line entity is one-to-many. Next, let's look at the relationship between the item entity and the sales order line entity:

- An item type can appear a maximum of many times in the SALES ORDER LINE intersection table.
- An item type may appear a minimum of zero times in the SALES ORDER LINE intersection table because an item may not be ordered.
- A sales order line has a maximum and a minimum of one item type.

Since relationships are named based on the maximums, the relationship between the item entity and the sales order line entity is one-to-many. From the preceding information, we conclude that there is a one-to-many relationship between SALES ORDER and SALES ORDER LINE tables (entities) and a one-to-many relationship between ITEM and SALES ORDER LINE tables (entities). The ERD shown in Figure 14.17 is the optimized version of the sales order transaction ERD. Figure 14.18 summarizes the steps in an ERD using an intersection table to remove many-to-many relationships.

> **Microsoft Visio...**
> is a software used to design ERD models. It automatically copies the primary key of the parent entity into the child entity when you connect two entities with a one-to-many relationship.

> **Microsoft Visio and Identifying Relationships...**
> In some instances, an entity occurrence in the child entity cannot exist if there is not a corresponding entity occurrence in the parent entity. For example, a sales order cannot exist without a customer placing it. This is called an identifying relationship between parent and child. In identifying relationships, Visio automatically makes the foreign key part of the primary key in the child entity. Visio represents identifying relationships as a straight line instead of a dotted line (Figure 14.21).

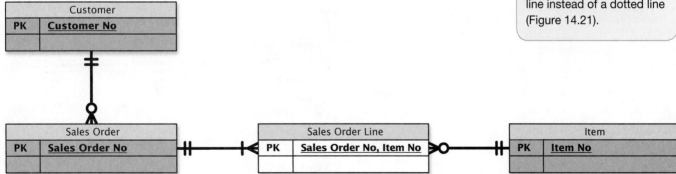

FIGURE 14.17
ERD with Intersection Table

Pair and Share:
What is the relationship between sales order and sales order line? What is the relationship between item and sales order line? What is the cardinality of these relationships?

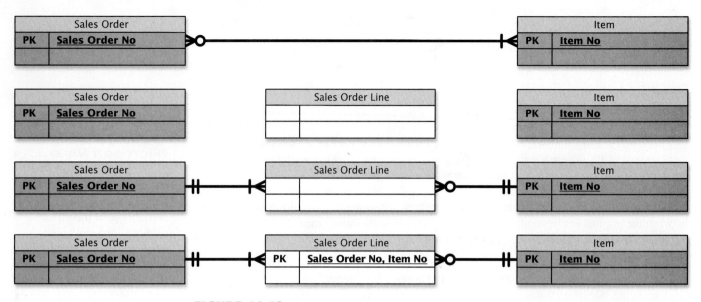

FIGURE 14.18

ERD Using Intersection Table to Remove Many-to-Many Relationships

STEP 7: ADD BUSINESS-RELATED ATTRIBUTES TO THE ENTITY RELATIONSHIP DIAGRAM

Now it is time to complete the database model. To do so, first we have to identify entity attributes that serve business requirements. For example, a customer entity attribute is marital status, but EspressoCoffee doesn't have a business need to know marital status. Therefore, we would not identify marital status as an entity attribute for the customer entity. Database designers prepare a list of entities and entity attributes called an entity definition matrix. Figure 14.19 shows an entity definition matrix related to the sales order transaction.

You may notice that some attributes from the sales order form are not listed in Figure 14.19, such as item quantity, discount value, tax, unit price, and line total. These attributes do not belong to any entities listed in Figure 14.19. Later, these attributes will be included in the intersection

FIGURE 14.19 Entity Definition Matrix: EspressoCoffee Sales Transaction Entities and Attributes

Entity	Attributes
Customer	Customer No.
	Customer Company Name
	Customer First Name
	Customer Last Name
	Customer Street Address
	Customer City
	Customer State
	Customer ZIP
	Customer Phone
	Customer Email
Sales Order	Sales Order No.
	Sales Order Date
	Sales Order Shipping
	Sales Order Miscellaneous
Item	Item No.
	Item Name
	Item Description

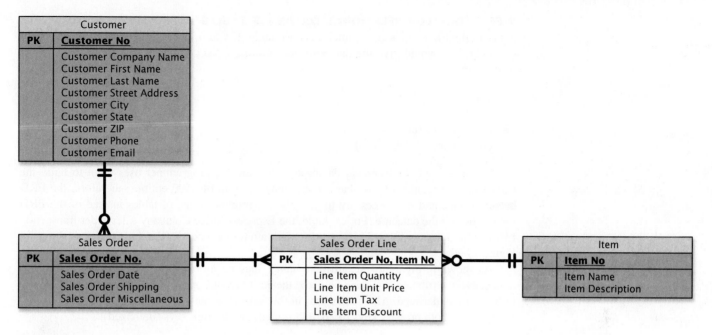

FIGURE 14.20

EspressoCoffee Sales Transaction ERD with Attributes

table created to remove many-to-many relationships. Figure 14.20 shows the EspressoCoffee sales order transaction ERD including attributes.

STEP 8: IMPLEMENT RELATIONSHIPS Next, we need to implement the relationship lines into the database tables to connect the tables. We do this by copying the primary key of a parent entity into the child entity. For the child entity, this field is called the foreign key. Thus, the foreign key is a primary key of a parent entity copied into the child entity in a one-to-many relationship.

In Figure 14.21, we redo the EspressoCoffee sales transaction ERD to include foreign keys. You will notice that foreign keys are marked with FK. Because the table may have many foreign keys, the foreign keys are numbered.

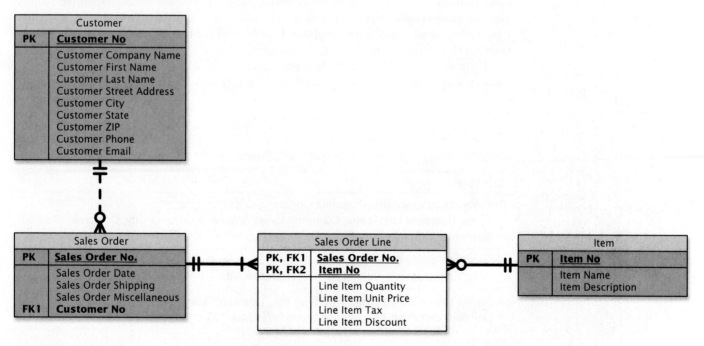

FIGURE 14.21

EspressoCoffee Sales Transaction ERD with Foreign Keys

STEP 9: DEVELOP RELATIONAL DATABASE TABLES In this step we transform each entity in the ERD into a conceptual database table. If you were working with a database programmer, you would give the database programmer a list containing information about the following:

- Tables
- Attributes
- Primary keys (bold, underline)
- Foreign keys (bold, italics)

These are called conceptual database tables and the programmer uses them to build the database. An organization database model may have 400 to 500 entities; therefore, the ERD becomes huge and it is necessary to give the programmer a list of tables instead of the ERD used to design the database. For example, the EspressoCoffee Company sales order transaction ERD includes four entities. These entities map into four conceptual database tables as shown in Figure 14.22.

As shown in Figure 14.22, attribute names may be shortened to save space. As you may notice, every attribute becomes a field and the entity identifier becomes the primary key shown in bold and underlined. Also notice that in the SALES ORDER LINE table, Sales Order No. and Item No. are both primary keys (bold, underlined) and foreign keys (italicized).

STEP 10: BUILD RELATIONAL DATABASE TABLES At this step we have to select the database application software we will use to build our database. Among our many choices are Oracle, MS SQL Server, MySQL, and MS Access. Detail of the ERD and information about the tables' fields, such as their size and type, are stored in a document called the data dictionary. Database programmers use the data dictionary to build the database tables. Figure 14.23 shows the EspressoCoffee sales order transaction database implemented in MS Access and MS SQL Server. You can see that the MS SQL Server screen provides more information about the database tables.

After table relationships (one-to-one, one-to-many) are added, database users can extract related data from multiple tables of the database. Database designers cannot build a many-to-many relationship in a database program, such as MS Access, SQL Server, or Oracle. In a database program, we can build only one-to-many and one-to-one relationships. Thus, all many-to-many relationships must be removed, using intersection tables. When we remove many-to-many relationships by adding a new intersection table (for example, SALES ORDER LINE table), we also remove the duplicate records from the two tables (ITEM table and SALES ORDER table) that have a many-to-many relationship.

Up to step 10, the database design is not related to a particular type of database development application. In step 10, to build the database, it is necessary to select a database development

---

FIGURE 14.22 Conceptual Database Tables

Attributes
CUSTOMER (**<u>Customer No.,</u>** Customer Company, Customer First Name, Customer Last Name, Customer Street Address, Customer City, Customer State, Customer ZIP, Customer Phone, Customer Email)
SALES ORDER (**<u>Sales Order No.,</u>** Sales Order Date, Sales Order Shipping, Sales Order Miscellaneous, *Customer No.*)
SALES ORDER LINE (**<u>Sales Order No., Item No.,</u>** Line Item Quantity, Line Item Unit Price, Line Item Tax, Line Item Discount)
ITEM (**<u>Item No.,</u>** Item Name, Item Description)

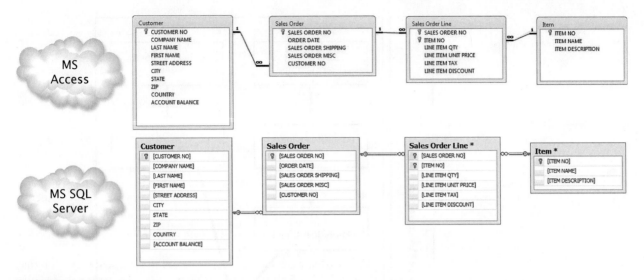

FIGURE 14.23

MS Access and MS SQL Server EspressoCoffee Sales Transaction ERD

Pair and Share: Compare the MS Access screen and the MS SQL Server screen. What is similar? What is different?

software, such as Oracle. The steps in relational database design and development are summarized in Figure 14.24.

Database Normalization

Besides database modeling, normalization can be used to design a database. When using normalization for database development, all the attributes are placed in one huge table. Then the table is normalized using five normalization rules that are discussed in more detail later. The outcome will be normalized database tables.

Database designers also use the normalization technique to remove anomalies. The database table shown in Figure 14.2 contains data about specific objects (specific customers) and events (specific sales orders). The problem with the table is that it contains data about multiple objects and events: two objects (item and customer) and an event (sales order). When using the divide-and-conquer principle, we divide the two objects (item and customer) into two different, but related tables: CUSTOMER table and ITEM table.

We record the event in yet another table: SALES ORDER table. The SALES ORDER table has information about only the order event. Separating the database into related tables instead of using just one large table helps to eliminate deletion, update, and insertion problems.

During the normalization process, different causes of anomalies are removed. Next you will learn how the normalization technique removes database table anomalies. The normalization technique consists of five rules, three of which are listed next.

RULE 1: FIRST NORMAL FORM (1NF) No field can have multiple values. For example, if one customer had multiple orders, then you cannot place all orders in one field in the CUSTOMER table. Instead, you would need another table to hold the customer orders.

RULE 2: SECOND NORMAL FORM (2NF) If a table identifier (primary key) is not a composite identifier, then the table is in 2NF. Otherwise, the composite identifier should identify all other attributes. For example, in the database table shown in Figure 14.2 the quantity of a specific item ordered by a specific customer on a specific order requires you to use Customer No., Order No., and Item No. to identify the quantity. The identifier in the table consists of a Customer No., Order No., and Item No. together, which is a composite key. At the same time,

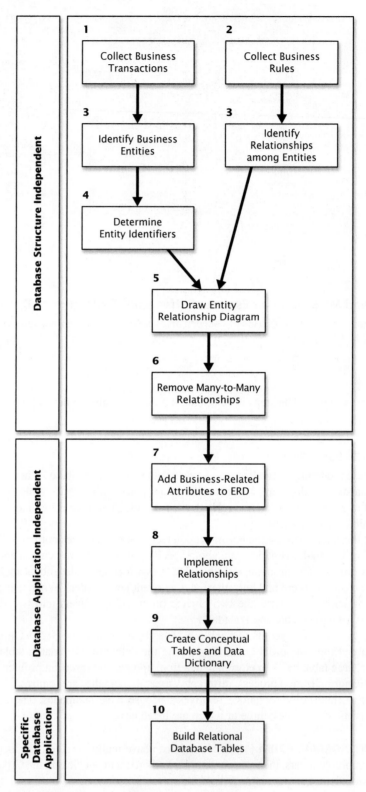

FIGURE 14.24

Relational Database Design and Development

if you wanted to retrieve a customer address, you would use only the Customer No. instead of the composite identifier. That indicates that the customer address is only identified by Customer No., and this violates the second normal form. Database designers divide the table that is not in 2NF into two or more tables to satisfy the 2NF rule. It is beyond the scope of this text to further show how that work is done.

RULE 3. BOYCE-CODD NORMAL FORM (BCNF) To remove more anomalies from the database, database designers were using the third normal form (3NF). However, 3NF was not effective in certain situations as proved by Raymond Boyce and Edgar Codd, two IBM computer scientists who went on to develop the Boyce-Codd Normal Form (BCNF). In BCNF every identifier should be a candidate key. In the database table shown in Figure 14.2, Customer No. is enough to identify customer name and customer address. Therefore, Customer No. is an identifier. However, Customer No. cannot identify items ordered by a customer on a specific order. This indicates that the table shown in Figure 14.2 is not in BCNF. To normalize to the BCNF, database designers split the table into two or more tables, each table complying with BCNF rules.

The normalization process goes beyond BCNF. There is a fourth and fifth normal form. However, after BCNF, rarely does a database table need further normalization.

After normalization, the single table shown in Figure 14.2 would be split into four tables: CUSTOMER table, SALES ORDER table, SALES ORDER LINE table, and ITEM table.

> **My Connection...**
> • Short Exercise 14.29
> • Short Exercise 14.30
> • Short Exercise 14.32

What Is REA (Resources, Events, and Agents)?

Accounting Database Semantic Modeling

Up to this point, we discussed the traditional modeling procedure used by IT professionals for designing a relational database. The outcome of that procedure was an entity relationship diagram (ERD).

REA (resources, events, and agents) is a database modeling tool that is sometimes used to teach accounting databases. However, it is not used by IT professional database designers. Instead, database designers use ERD or UML to design and develop relational databases.

The primary difference between ERD and REA is how entities are defined. In an ERD, entities are business objects or events. In REA, entities can be resources, events, or agents. Basically, the business object in the ERD is subcategorized in the REA model as either a resource or agent.

In REA modeling, a resource has economic value to the enterprise, such as inventory, cash, or other assets. An agent is a person or organization involved in events and can include a vendor, employee, or customer. An event is the same as under the ERD modeling and includes business activities and transactions, such as sales, orders, and purchases. Both REA and ERD should result in the same number of entities and relationships.

REA Modeling

To design an REA diagram for a specific business transaction, first identify agents, resources, and events. Let's consider the sales order transaction. In this transaction the agent is the customer. The resource is the item the customer is ordering. The event is the sales order event.

An agent is related to a resource through an event. In this case, the customer (agent) is related to the items (resource) ordered through the sales order (event). The customer places many orders, and in every order there is one or more items. The relationship between the sales order event and the item is many-to-many since the customer's order can contain many items and an item can appear on many different customer orders. The resulting REA diagram (Figure 14.25) corresponds to what you saw in Figure 14.20 for an ERD.

The REA model shows what is given and what is taken in a business exchange. The giving and taking concept provides a guideline to identify entities involved and draw the REA model.

Figure 14.26 shows the basic REA template. The *giving* event consumes business resources and the *taking* event compensates the consumed resource with a different or same type of resource. The relationship between the two events is called economic duality and represents resource exchange. The economic duality relationship is the essence of a business in the market economy. As you recall, we need business rules to be able to identify relationships among entities. For every instance of the *giving* of a business resource there must be one or more instances of the *taking* of a resource.

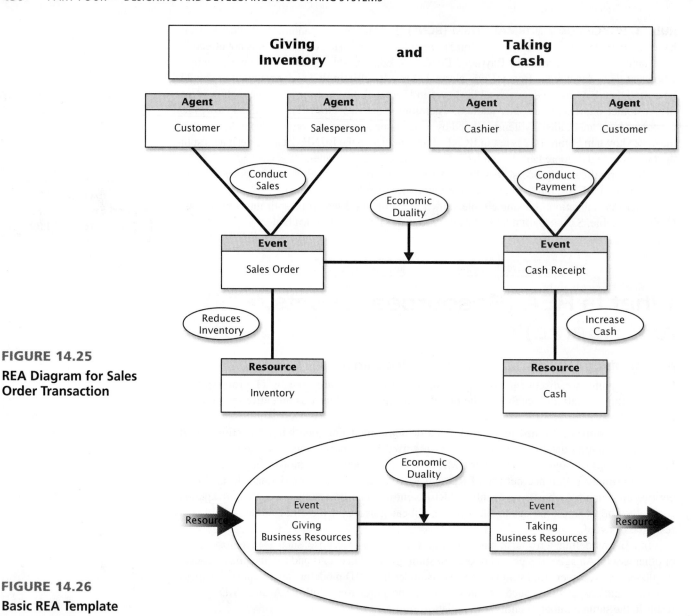

FIGURE 14.25

REA Diagram for Sales Order Transaction

FIGURE 14.26

Basic REA Template

Applying the basic REA template in Figure 14.26 to the revenue, expenditure, payroll, and financial modules results in the REA diagrams shown in Figure 14.27. The four rules for drawing REA diagrams are as follows.

RULE 1. RESOURCE-EVENT RELATIONSHIP Every event entity must relate to a resource entity. In an event, resources are given or taken. Thus, there is at least one resource for every event. For example, a sales event is related to the inventory entity. The relationship between an event and a resource is called stockflow since the relationship represents moving business stock (resources).

RULE 2. EVENT-EVENT RELATIONSHIP An event entity is related to at least one other event entity. This is an obvious postulate since a *giving* event requires a *taking* event. The relationship between two events is called economic duality.

RULE 3. AGENT-EVENT RELATIONSHIP At least two agent entities are required for an event entity. An agent entity can be a person, department, or another system. In our example, the customer entity initiates the sales event. However, for accountability, the employee agent is included to monitor the sales order event. Every business transaction requires two participants: the giver and the taker. The relationship between agent and event is called participation. The agent can be an internal agent (such as an employee) or an external agent (such as a customer).

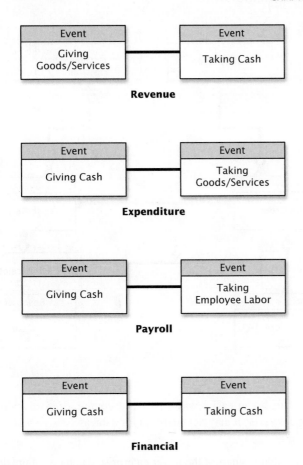

FIGURE 14.27

Basic REA Templates for Modules

RULE 4. AGENT-AGENT RELATIONSHIP There is no relationship between two agents. This is a rule for REA modeling that may create an issue for IT professionals developing databases. Consider the human resources database that includes data about employees and employee dependents. There is a one-to-many relationship between employee and employee dependents. An REA diagram would not depict employee dependents, which the database developer would need in order to develop an accurate enterprise database. An ERD depicts the relationship between two agents, such as employee and employee dependents, in order to build an anomaly-free enterprise database.

Figure 14.28 shows an REA diagram for customer transactions including internal agents and relationships among involved entities.

To analyze the expenditure cycle for REA modeling, resources, agents, and events are identified for the vendor module activities including creating a purchase order, receiving items, and receiving the bill.

- Create Purchase Orders. This event requires two agent entities: an employee (internal agent) and a vendor (external agent). The resource entity required for this event is the item (inventory). A vendor handles zero or many purchase orders. The purchase department or an employee monitors zero or many purchase orders. There are one or more items in a purchase order. An item may appear in zero, one, or many purchase orders.
- Receive Items. The *receive item* event requires two agent entities, an employee (for example, the receiving department) and the vendor. The resource entity is the same as the previous event. A vendor supplies zero or many items. The receiving department or an employee verifies zero or many items. There are zero or many of a received item. There are one or many of a received item in the item list.
- Receive Bills. This event needs an employee (for example, a cashier) and the vendor. The resource entity is cash. A vendor receives zero or many payments and a specific payment belongs to only one vendor. The cashier issues zero or many payments and a specific payment is issued by only one cashier. There are zero or many payments from cash and every payment is recorded once in cash.

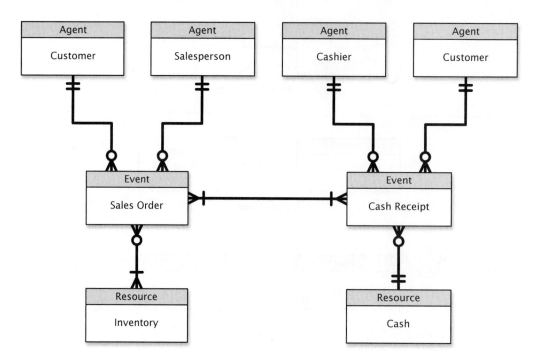

FIGURE 14.28

REA Diagram for Complete Customer Module

Pair and Share: Compare this REA diagram to the ERD diagram for the EspressoCoffee sales transaction. What is similar? What are the differences?

REA may appear to be an easier way to learn accounting information systems. From a practical perspective, however, it may not be useful for database design and development for the following reasons:

1. The accounting database is part of the larger enterprise database. Many database tables are shared among enterprise functions such as employee information is shared among accounting and human resources. Using the REA rules to develop an accounting database could obscure or omit vital information for sound database design related to shared data, such as employee and employee dependents.

2. REA modeling rules can result in entity duplication in the REA diagram. For example, an REA diagram may show many Employee entities. However, for a redundant-free database, there should be only one EMPLOYEE database table. For the database designer, every entity in the database model should represent a database table. Because the REA model shows multiple entities for Employee, for example, this creates confusion for the IT professional database developer.

3. Although widely used in academic AIS texts, REA is not widely used among IT professionals. As an accountant, it is imperative to have a common language so that meaningful, constructive conversations with IT professionals occur without technical miscommunication. Furthermore, as you know, increasingly accountants are expected to perform integrated audits including auditing the system development life cycle (SDLC). To perform such integrated audits, an understanding of the ERD models used by database designers and developers is essential. REA may be beneficial as a teaching tool; however, it has limitations for the accountant's toolkit on the job.

My Connection...
- Active Review 14.10
- Short Exercise 14.34
- Go Online 14.51

How Is SQL Used in Database Queries?

Structured query language (SQL) is a fourth generation, nonprocedural language designed to define and manipulate relational database objects. The relational database objects are databases, tables, records, and fields. A record-oriented language, SQL can query many records from one or more tables with a single statement. Other programming languages, such as C++, require many statements to accomplish the same query that SQL can accomplish with one statement.

Another advantage of SQL over other languages is that it is a nonprocedural language. Procedural languages, such as C#, C++, and Java, require programmers to specifically state how a task is accomplished.

In a nonprocedural language, such as SQL, programmers just state what they want accomplished (for example, find a customer record with Customer No. 2727 from the database). The how part of the task is done behind the scene by the RDBMS.

SQL statements, also called commands, are divided into two distinct categories:

1. Data definition language (DDL)
2. Data manipulation language (DML)

DDL statements create, alter, and drop database objects. Examples of each command follow:

- CREATE statement is used to create relational database objects such as creating a database or a table.
- ALTER statement is used to change the relational database object such as adding a new field to a specific table.
- DROP statement is used to delete a database object such as deleting a table or removing an existing field from a specific table.

DML statements are used to manipulate data within a relational database. These statements select, insert, update, and delete database records. Of these four statements, the SELECT statement is the primary one used to create database queries. The SELECT statement retrieves one or more records from one or more tables from a relational database. SELECT statements also allow programmers to specify particular fields of the retrieved records.

The output of a SELECT statement is a table with the selected records and fields. This table is called a **database view**. A database view can be stored as a table or moved into a spreadsheet program for further data analysis.

SQL Statements: Data Definition Language (DDL)

SQL data definition statements are for creating a new database, adding tables to the database, altering the structure of one or more tables, deleting a field from a table, deleting a table, or deleting the entire database. Because of the complexity and variety of formats used for these statements, we provide two simple examples for creating a database and a table.

DDL EXAMPLE 1 The CREATE statement creates a relational database as specified in the CREATE statement. The SQL statement shown in Figure 14.29 creates the Accounting_db database and

---

Do You Need a Book from the Library?

As an illustration of how nonprocedural languages function, imagine you ask a friend to get a book from the library for you.

If you used a procedural approach, you would need to specify each step in detail. Go to the door, turn left, cross the street, open the library door, go to the first floor, go to row 15, go to shelf 2, pick the third book from the left.

In a nonprocedural approach, you would just tell your friend to get the book from the library. You would just need to specify the library name and book name.

SQL is a nonprocedural language.

FIGURE 14.29 SQL Statements to Create a Database and Table

SQL DDL CREATE Statements

DDL Example 1
```
CREATE DATABASE Accounting_db
ON (NAME=Accounting_db,
    FILENAME='C:\accountingdata\accountingdb.mdf,
SIZE=10,
MAXSIZE=100,
FILEGROWTH=5);
```

DDL Example 2
```
CREATE TABLE Customer
(Customer No. INTEGER NOT NULL CONSTRAINT prim_customer
    PRIMARY KEY,
Customer First Name (CHAR(20) NOT NULL,
Customer Last Name (CHAR(20) NOT NULL,
Customer Phone (CHAR(14) );
```

FIGURE 14.30 **SQL Statements to Select Records from Database Tables**

How many tables are accessed by the SQL query in DML Example 2? How many fields are accessed?

SQL DML SELECT Statements
DML Example 1
SELECT Employee First Name, Employee Last Name FROM Employee WHERE Employee No. = '9444';
DML Example 2
SELECT Employee First Name, Employee Last Name FROM Employee, Department WHERE Employee. Department No. = Department. Department No. AND Department No. = Department Name='Accounting';

stores it in the accountingdb.mdf file. The initial size of the file is 10MB and can increase by 5MB if needed. The maximum size the database can reach is 100MB.

There are many varieties of CREATE statements to allow the database developer to add specific features to the database created.

DDL EXAMPLE 2 Figure 14.29 also shows how a CREATE statement is used to create a table. In this example, a CUSTOMER table with three fields is created and Customer No. is specified as the primary key of the table.

SQL Statements: Data Manipulation Language (DML)

The SQL data manipulation statements are used to select specific records from one or more tables, insert a record into a table, delete one or more records, or update one or more record contents. DML statements are only applied to database records.

In this section we explain two examples of SELECT statements (Figure 14.30). The first example uses only one table (EMPLOYEE) and the second example uses two tables (EMPLOYEE AND DEPARTMENT). Notice the role of the foreign key in connecting the related tables in the second example.

DML EXAMPLE 1 This SELECT statement would select the record from the EMPLOYEE table where the Employee No. is equal to 9444. The output view will be the first name and last name of that employee.

DML EXAMPLE 2 This SELECT statement joins the EMPLOYEE table and the DEPARTMENT table on the Department No. field, the foreign key. The output view will be the first names and last names of all employees working in the accounting department.

Figure 14.31 shows the EMPLOYEE and DEPARTMENT tables and their relationship. As you can see, Department No. is a foreign key (FK) in the EMPLOYEE table and is used in the SELECT statement to join the DEPARTMENT and EMPLOYEE tables.

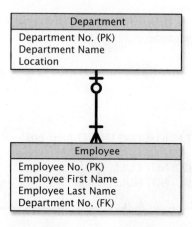

FIGURE 14.31

Database Tables Used in SQL SELECT Statements

SQL DML statements are used to build queries required for accounting and financial applications. SQL statements are embedded into accounting software. When accounting software commands are executed, the SQL statements are passed to RDBMS. RDBMS interprets and executes the SQL statements, retrieving the designated records from the database.

SQL is the language for relational databases. SQL is supported by relational database development software including MS Access, MS SQL Server, and Oracle databases. Because it is a nonprocedural language, SQL's ease of use is one reason for the popularity of relational databases. Today, most database development software even includes a graphical user interface (GUI) that permits developers to create queries and database objects without writing SQL programming code. Behind the screen, the database development software generates the accompanying SQL programming code needed to execute the task.

> **My Connection...**
> • Short Exercise 14.36

Chapter Highlights

What is the role of database modeling in developing a well-designed database? Relational databases are used to store data about accounting transactions and other operational data. A well-designed database is easy to maintain and provides accurate and complete data. Through database modeling, database designers and developers can analyze business requirements and see how the database can satisfy those requirements.

What is an ERD? Entity relationship diagram (ERD) is a database modeling technique used by database designers to visualize user requirements from the database and be able to create an accurate database without data duplication and redundancy.

What is REA? REA is another database modeling technique that is similar to ERD except entities are classified as resources, agents, and events. REA is primarily used for teaching purposes and not widely used by IT professionals.

What is SQL? SQL, or structured query language, is a nonprocedural programming language used with relational databases. SQL statements are divided into two categories: (1) data definition language (DDL) that is used to create relational databases, alter the database structure, delete database objects, and manipulate the database contents, and (2) data manipulation language (DML) that is used for selecting specific records from the database as specified in queries. A high percentage of operational databases are relational databases using SQL as the query language. Oracle and Microsoft provide relational database development software.

Accounting System Insights

Insight No. 10 Invest 80% of your time designing the database and 20% of your time maintaining it.

Active Review

Study less. Learn more. Make connections.

14.1 Refer to the chapter opener, *Meet Oracle*. In your opinion, why do companies spend millions of dollars on databases?

14.2 Discuss the advantages of relational databases for recording accounting transactions.

14.3 Discuss considerations for selecting a primary key.

14.4 Discuss the advantages that the structure query language (SQL) offers.

14.5 Discuss the differences between procedural and nonprocedural programming languages.

14.6 Discuss database anomalies and the three categories used to classify anomalies. Which anomaly is caused by data duplication?

14.7 Discuss the different types of relationships among entities. Which are problematic? Why?

14.8 Discuss the reasons why a well-designed database is important.

14.9 Why is it important to identify relationships among entities before building a database?

14.10 Discuss the concept of economic duality as used in REA. How does this relate to double entry accounting?

Key Terms Check

Understanding the language used at the crossroads of accounting and IT is key to your success.

14.11 Match the following terms and definitions.

a. fields
b. records
c. tables
d. database
e. objects
f. events

_____ 1. Collection of related tables
_____ 2. Collection of related fields
_____ 3. Collection of related records
_____ 4. Pieces of information about events and objects
_____ 5. People and things
_____ 6. Transactions

14.12 Match the following terms and definitions.

a. database modeling
b. entity relationship diagram (ERD)
c. resources, events, and agents (REA)
d. data integrity
e. database integrity
f. normalization
g. database view

_____ 1. The output of a SELECT statement in a table with the selected records and fields
_____ 2. A database modeling tool that depicts the relationship among entities in the database
_____ 3. A set of steps to remove anomalies from a database
_____ 4. A technique used to develop an anomaly-free database with database integrity
_____ 5. Data is accurate and complete
_____ 6. A database modeling tool that uses economic duality sometimes used to teach accounting databases
_____ 7. The database contains accurate and complete data

14.13 Match the following terms and definitions.

a. entity
b. entity occurrence
c. entity attribute
d. entity identifier
e. candidate key
f. parent entity
g. child entity
h. dependent entity

_____ 1. In a one-to-many relationship, the entity on the many side
_____ 2. An attribute that uniquely identifies an entity occurrence
_____ 3. Can refer to an object or event
_____ 4. This entity is also known as a child entity
_____ 5. A specific object or event
_____ 6. A property of an entity
_____ 7. In a one-to-many relationship, the entity on the one side
_____ 8. One of the entity identifiers that uniquely identifies an entity occurrence

14.14 Select the single best answer.
Professionals modeling the database are called

a. database realms.
b. database designers.
c. database builders.
d. database users.

14.15 Select the single best answer.

Professionals constructing the database tables, records, and fields are called

a. database realms.   **c.** database builders.
b. database designers.   **d.** database users.

14.16 Select the single best answer.

Professionals who enter, update, delete, or search the database are called

a. database realms.   **c.** database builders.
b. database designers.   **d.** database users.

14.17 Select the single best answer.

Timeframes in the development of a database in which different terminology may be used are

a. database realms.   **c.** database builders.
b. database designers.   **d.** database users.

Practice Test

14.18 In which database structure is SQL used?

a. Hierarchical
b. Network
c. Relational X
d. Object-oriented

14.19 Which of the database integrity rules addresses data consistency across the database?

a. Referential integrity X
b. Entity integrity
c. Domain integrity
d. Primary key integrity

14.20 Which of the database anomalies is related to the primary key value?

a. Update
b. Insertion X
c. Deletion
d. None of the above

14.21 Which of the following does NOT represent an entity?

a. Customer
b. Supplier
c. Address
d. Item

14.22 Which of the following does NOT represent an entity attribute?

a. Street name
b. Account number
c. Customer order X
d. Item code

14.23 What is described by the business rules?

a. Entity relationship cardinality
b. Database anomalies
c. Entity integrity
d. Attribute name

14.24 Entity identifiers that uniquely identify the entity are called

a. composite key.

b. foreign key.

c. primary key.

d. candidate key.

14.25 What type of relationship cannot be mapped into database tables?

a. One-to-one

b. Many-to-many

c. One-to-many

d. None of the above

14.26 In building an ERD, in which step is the database application chosen?

a. Step 2: Determine the business rules for a specific business transaction.

b. Step 5: Draw entity relationship diagram.

c. Step 9: Develop relational database tables.

d. Step 10: Build relational database tables.

14.27 Database normalization are performed to

a. remove redundant tables from the database.

b. remove redundant relationships from the database.

c. remove the database anomalies.

d. remove non-normal data from the database.

Exercises

Each Exercise relates to one of the major questions addressed in the chapter and is labeled with the question number in green.

Short Exercises

Warm up with these short exercises.

14.28 A credit card company allows a customer to have many credit cards. A credit card belongs to only one customer. What is the relationship between customer and credit card? What is the cardinality of the relationships? **(Q14.2)**

14.29 A company allows sales representatives to serve many customers. A customer can be served by only one sales representative. What is the relationship between customer and sales representative? What is the cardinality of the relationships? **(Q14.2)**

14.30 A sales order has many items. An item can be in many sales orders. What is the relationship between sales order and item? What is the cardinality of the relationships? **(Q14.2)**

14.31 A car in a car rental agency can have many types of repairs. A type of repair may be performed on many different cars. What is the relationship between car and type of repair? What is the cardinality of the relationships? **(Q14.2)**

14.32 Use the following ERD to answer the accompanying questions. **(Q14.2)**

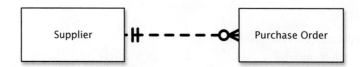

1. What is the relationship between the two tables in the ERD?
2. What is the cardinality of the relationships?

14.33 How do you remove the many-to-many relationship in the following ERD? **(Q14.2)**

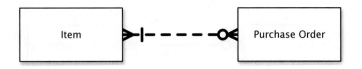

14.34 Use the following REA diagram to answer the accompanying questions. **(Q14.3)**

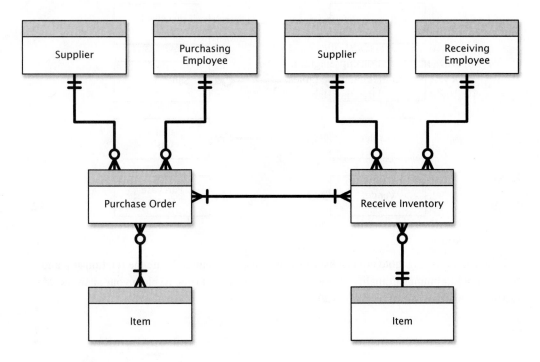

1. Who are the agents?
2. What are the events?
3. What are the resources?

14.35 Using the ERD shown in Figure 14.13, identify the following: **(Q14.2)**

1. SALES ORDER table minimum
2. SALES ORDER table maximum
3. ITEM table minimum
4. ITEM table maximum

14.36 Using the SQL statement provided, answer the following questions. **(Q14.4)**

1. Identify the database tables used by the SQL query.
2. Identify the fields retrieved by the SQL query.
3. Identify the specific record that is retrieved by the query.
4. What is the name of the output of this query?

SELECT.Developer First Name, Developer Last Name, Date Created

FROM Accountant, Spreadsheet

WHERE SSID = "SSID041201";

14.37 Explain why the following relationship cardinalities are incorrect. Why? Provide the correct relationship cardinalities. **(Q14.2)**

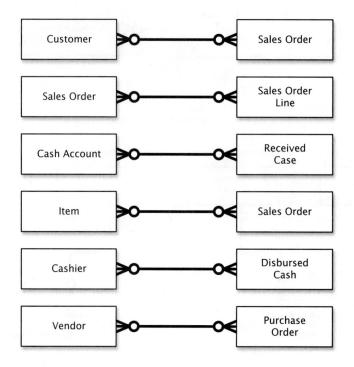

14.38 The following table holds a list of entities in each column. Write the relationship and maximum/minimum cardinality between two entities in each row. Explain your answers. Make assumptions where necessary. **(Q14.2)**

Sales Order	Item
Cash Received	Sales Order
Item Received	Disbursed Cash
Employee	Sales Order
Customer	Sales Order
Supplier	Disbursed Cash

It's Your Call

This is your training ground. These scenarios provide you with the opportunity to use your knowledge and professional skills.

14.39 Your friend is designing a database as part of her internship assignment. She calls you with the following question: "Should I use Social Security No., Customer No., or Customer Credit Card No. for the primary key of the CUSTOMER database table?" What is your response? What are your reasons for your answer? **(Q14.1)**

14.40 You are a member of a project team created to develop a database for online sales transactions. The IT professionals on the team asked you to provide them with the accounting data that needs to be captured in the online sales transactions. Write an email to your team members summarizing the attributes and their definitions. **(Q14.2)**

Tech in Practice

These technology in practice exercises are perfect for both individuals and teams.

Tech Exercises

Sharpen your skills with these technology exercises. Watch these software videos at www.pearsonhighered.com/kay.

14.41

Tech Tool: Spreadsheet Software or Visio Software

Software Video: ERD and REA Drawing

Refer to the EspressoCoffee invoice shown in Figure 14.12 and the 10 steps to relational database design and development in Figure 14.24. Then complete the following steps.

1. Identify entities involved.
2. Identify the relationships among entities.
3. Identify entity identifiers.
4. Draw an entity relationship diagram.
5. Remove many-to-many relationships, if necessary.
6. Add entity attributes.
7. Print your ERD.

14.42

Tech Tool: Spreadsheet Software or Visio Software

Software Video: ERD and REA Drawing

Your organization would like to implement better security and control over the numerous spreadsheets that the accountants are using. You have been asked to design ERD for a proposed database to document spreadsheets using the following business rules:

a. An accountant creates many spreadsheets.
b. A spreadsheet is created by only one accountant.
c. A project uses many spreadsheets.
d. A spreadsheet can be used in many projects.

1. Draw an ERD.
2. Remove many-to-many relationships, if necessary.
3. Print the ERD.

14.43

Tech Tool: Spreadsheet Software or Visio Software

Software Video: ERD and REA Drawing

You have been asked to design an ERD for a database to better track employees and their skills. You identified three entities: department, employee, and employee skills.

1. Making assumptions regarding business rules as appropriate, define the relationship among department, employee, and employee skills.
2. Draw an entity relationship diagram.
3. Identify an identifier for each entity.
4. Remove many-to-many relationships, if necessary.
5. Print your ERD.

14.44

Tech Tool: Spreadsheet Software or Visio Software

Software Video: ERD and REA Drawing

Kolbe & Co. has asked for your assistance in designing an ERD for a new database.

1. Download the data file for this exercise.
2. Follow the instructions in the data file to build an ERD for Kolbe & Co.
3. Print the ERD diagram.

14.45

Tech Tool: Database Software

Software Video: Database Tables, Database Relationships

Kolbe & Co. has asked for your assistance in building a MS Access database from an ERD.

1. Download the data file for this exercise.
2. Follow the instructions in the data file to build Access database tables from an ERD for Kolbe & Co. Identify the primary key for each table.
3. Build the table relationships.
4. Print the relationships.

14.46

Tech Tool: Database Software

Software Video: Advanced Database Forms and Queries

Kolbe & Co. has asked for your assistance to create a SQL query.

1. Download the data file for this exercise.
2. Build a query to retrieve customers who live in Canada with a balance greater than $1,000.
3. Run the query and print the result.

14.47

Tech Tool: Spreadsheet Software or Visio Software

Software Video: ERD and REA Drawing

Jordan & Co. has asked for your assistance in building an REA diagram for a new database.

1. Download the data file for this exercise.
2. Follow the instructions in the data file to build an REA diagram for Jordan & Co.
3. Print the REA diagram.

14.48

Tech Tool: Database Spreadsheet Software or Visio Software

Software Video: ERD and REA Drawing

Use information provided on the following Project Purchasing Summary Report and construct an ERD. Remove many-to-many relationships if necessary. Make assumptions where necessary.

Project Purchasing Summary Report

Project Name: High-speed line

Project No: PR1

Report Date: 3/19/2014

Project Manager: John Smith

Part No.	Supplier No.	Quantity	Unit Price
M128	S100	4	$120
M129	S101	3	$150
R234	S100	4	$230

1. Draw and print the ERD diagram.
2. Draw and print the REA diagram.

14.49
Tech Tool: Database Spreadsheet Software or Visio Software
Software Video: ERD and REA Drawing

Sam's repair shop has many employees who use an electronic time clock to record their working time. Working-time process records the starting and ending time and date. Some of the employees are floor supervisors. One of the supervisors' responsibilities is to check the employees' working times. Employee paychecks are verified and signed by an accountant and handed out to employees. Paycheck disbursement occurs twice a month.

1. Identify resources, events, and agents.
2. Draw the REA diagram.
3. Print the REA diagram.

Go Online

In the fast-paced world of technology, your skill at finding answers fast can be vital. Go online and experience typical assignments you may encounter as a professional.

14.50 Due to recent budget cuts, your department is looking for ways to reduce costs. The CFO tells you he has heard about open-source databases that are free. He asks you to investigate open-source databases and report back to him about the feasibility of switching to a free open-source database for accounting.

Go online and search for open-source databases. Summarize your findings in an email to the CFO. Include advantages and disadvantages of the open-source database as compared to purchased database engines.

14.51 You have been assigned to the project team developing a new accounting database. In your accounting information systems class, you studied REA. The IT professionals on the project team have never heard of REA. They ask you to send them a summary of what REA is and some examples of companies that have used it for database development.

Go online and search for information about REA diagrams. Did you find any examples of corporate systems using the REA modeling for database development? Write an email to the IT professionals on your team summarizing your findings.

14.52 You are a member of the project team for developing a new accounting database. At the last project meeting, some team members suggested using database structures other than a relational database. You have been assigned the task of researching other database structures and reporting back to the team at the next meeting.

Go online and search for information about network, hierarchical, and object-oriented database structures. Compare the advantages and disadvantages of each with the relational database structure used for most operational databases such as accounting. Who are the solution providers for the other types of database structures? Write a summary of your findings that you can distribute to the team members at the next meeting.

Technology Projects

These technology projects are perfect for both individuals and teams.

Technology Project 14

Tech Tool: Spreadsheet Software or Visio Software

Software Videos: ERD and REA Drawing

iSportDesign needs a new database for its purchasing cycle. You have been asked to assist with the database modeling.

Your deliverables for the project include the following:

Deliverable 1. An ERD

Deliverable 2. Access database tables

Visit www.pearsonhighered.com/kay to do the following:

1. Download Technology Project 14 instructions.
2. Download files provided online for your convenience in completing the project deliverables.
3. Watch the videos with software instructions to complete this project at www.pearsonhighered.com/kay.

Chapters 15 and 16 are available online at your text Web site.

Part Five *Enterprise Accounting Systems: Capstone* explores emerging trends and technologies impacting accounting systems in Chapter 15. Chapter 16 offers you practice with project management and live consulting projects to apply your accounting system knowledge and skills.

Part Five
Enterprise Accounting
Systems: Capstone

Chapter 15
Emerging Trends and Technologies

Chapter 16
Accounting Systems in Action: LIVE Projects

Appendix A:
Accounting Insights

INSIGHT No. 1	Use satellite mapping to view accounting systems. Zoom out to see the entire system...zoom in to focus on detail.
INSIGHT No. 2	Most accounting information is not entered using debits and credits.
INSIGHT No. 3	Accounting information is often entered using onscreen forms, such as checks and invoices.
INSIGHT No. 4	Nearly all accounting systems use databases to store accounting information.
INSIGHT No. 5	To understand accounting systems, the accountant must understand databases.
INSIGHT No. 6	When designing databases, begin with the outcome in mind.
INSIGHT No. 7	Business intelligence provides organizations with competitive advantage.
INSIGHT No. 8	Because information assets have value, the accounting system must safeguard the information stored.
INSIGHT No. 9	Enter data once.
INSIGHT No. 10	Design accounting databases using the 80/20 rule. Invest 80% of the time designing the database and 20% of the time maintaining the database.
INSIGHT No. 11	To save time entering data, mirror database forms and paper forms.
INSIGHT No. 12	Use database queries to extract data from multiple related database tables.
INSIGHT No. 13	The ABCs of accounting systems are the accounting system equals the baseline system plus customization.
INSIGHT No. 14	Gap analysis is the difference between the baseline system and the customization desired.
INSIGHT No. 15	Integrated systems share data...let others enter data for you.
INSIGHT No. 16	While relational databases are well suited for storing data, intelligence tools are better suited for analysis.
INSIGHT No. 17	Use satellite mapping for sustainability accounting. Zoom out to see business in a global worldview considering economic, social, and environmental sustainability.
INSIGHT No. 18	XBRL electronic tags for financial data are added using bolt-on tagging or integrated tagging.
INSIGHT No. 19	In the house of IT controls, there are three zones: (1) top management: entity-level IT controls; (2) business processes: application controls; and (3) IT services: IT general controls.
INSIGHT No. 20	When it comes to cybersecurity at the crossroads of accounting and IT, use the prudence principle.
INSIGHT No. 21	Shadow data ERM uses the top 10 tips for improved spreadsheet risk management.
INSIGHT No. 22	Accounting systems today are built using an ABC methodology: Accounting system = Baseline system + Customization.

Appendix B:
Acronyms and Abbreviations

3BL	Triple Bottom Line
AAA	American Accounting Association
ACFE	Association of Certified Fraud Examiners
AICPA	American Institute of Certified Public Accountants
AIS	Accounting Information Systems
ALU	Arithmetic/Logic Unit
AS	Accounting System
ASP	Application Service Provider
BI	Business Intelligence
BPMN	Business Process Modeling and Notation
BPMS	Business Process Management System
CBK	Common Body of Knowledge
CEO	Chief Executive Officer
CFO	Chief Financial Officer
CIA	Confidentiality, Integrity, Availability
CICA	Canadian Institute of Chartered Accountants
CIO	Chief Information/Intelligence Officer
CISO	Chief Information Security Officer
CISSP	Certified Information Systems Security Professional
COBIT	Control Objectives for Information and related Technology
COO	Chief Operations Officer
COSO	Committee of Sponsoring Organizations
CPO	Chief Privacy Officer
CPU	Central Processing Unit
CRM	Customer Relationship Management
CRO	Chief Risk Officer
CU	Control Unit
DBA	Database Administrator
DBMS	Database Management System
DDL	Data Definition Language
DFD	Data Flow Diagram

DML	Data Manipulation Language
DMZ	Demilitarized Zone
EAS	Enterprise Accounting System
ECA	Enterprise Carbon Accounting
EDI	Electronic Data Interchange
EIS	Enterprise Information System
EMAS	European Union Eco-Management and Audit Scheme
EMS	Environmental Management System
ERD	Entity Relationship Diagram
ERM	Enterprise Risk Management
ERP	Enterprise Resource Planning
ESA	Enterprise Sustainability Accounting
ETL	Extract, Transfer, Load
EU	European Union
FDIC	Federal Deposit Insurance Corporation
FEI	Financial Executives International
FISMA	Federal Information Security Management Act of 2002
GAAP	Generally Accepted Accounting Principles
GAAS	Generally Accepted Auditing Standards
GAPP	Generally Accepted Privacy Principles
GLBA	Gramm-Leach-Bliley Act of 1999
GRI	Global Reporting Initiative
GUI	Graphical User Interface
HIPAA	Health Insurance Portability and Accountability Act
HRM	Human Resource Management
HTML	HyperText Markup Language
HTTP	HyperText Transfer Protocol
IDS	Intrusion Detection System
IES	Integrated Enterprise System
IFAC	International Federation of Accountants
IFRS	International Financial Reporting Standards
IIA	Institute of Internal Auditors
IMA	Institute of Management Accountants
IP	Internet Protocol
IPS	Intrusion Prevention Systems
IR	Integrated Report
IRS	Internal Revenue Service

ISACA	Information Systems Audit and Control Association
ISC2	International Information Systems Security Certification Consortium
ISO	International Organization for Standardization
ISP	Internet Service Provider
IT	Information Technology
ITGI	Information Technology Governance Institute
LAN	Local Area Network
MAN	Metropolitan Area Network
MICR	Magnetic Ink Character Reader
MIPS	Million Instructions Per Second
NAP	Network Access Points
NGO	Nongovernmental Organization
ODBC	Open Database Connectivity
OLAP	Online Analytical Processing
OLTP	Online Transaction Processing
OPS	Operation/Production System
PAD-BIO	Plan, Analyze, Design, Build/Buy, Install, Operate
PCAOB	Public Company Accounting Oversight Board
PCI-DSS	Payment Card Industry Data Security Standards
POS	Point-of-Sale
PPP	Point-to-Point Protocol
PPTP	Point-to-Point Tunneling Protocol
RAM	Random Access Memory
RDB	Relational Database
RDBMS	Relational Database Management System
REA	Resources, Events, Agents
ROM	Read Only Memory
SCM	Supply Chain Management
SDLC	System Development Life Cycle
SEC	Securities and Exchange Commission
SIGMA	Sustainability Integrated Guidelines for Management
SOX	Sarbanes-Oxley Act of 2002
SQL	Structured Query Language
SSID	Spreadsheet Identification
SSO	Single Sign-On
STR	Straight Through Reporting
TCP	Transport Control Protocol

TD	Token Device
UML	Unified Modeling Language
VAN	Value-Added Network
VPN	Virtual Private Network
WAN	Wide Area Network
WPA	Wi-Fi Protected Access
WWW	World Wide Web
XBRL	eXtensible Business Reporting Language
XML	eXtensible Markup Language

Glossary

A

adjusting entry A journal entry made at year end to bring accounts up to date.

agent A person, system, or part of an organization.

algorithm A step-by-step solution to a problem.

analyze The second phase of the SDLC, in which user requirements for the new system are collected and analyzed.

application A manual or programmed procedure to process information.

application control A control embedded within a business process application.

application service provider (ASP) A provider of online applications.

applications software Computer programs for specific applications.

application tier Part of the three-tier architecture that consists of application servers, specialized computers that store and run the applications.

asymmetric cryptography or 2-key method An encryption method that uses two keys, with one key used to encode and a second related, but different, key to decode the message.

audit of financial statements Tests of controls to assess risk and substantive procedures to collect evidence regarding the accuracy, completeness, and validity of data produced by the accounting system.

audit of internal control An audit that requires the auditor to conduct tests of controls to obtain evidence that internal control over financial reporting has operated effectively.

automated control A control that is built into the system and performed automatically by a computer.

availability An information criterion that requires that data be available for use when needed for business processes.

B

banking module A module that involves cash received (deposits) or cash paid (checks/withdrawals) by the enterprise.

baseline accounting system A model that provides an enterprise-wide view of the firm's accounting system similar to the aerial, global view for satellite mapping.

batch A type of application software execution in which a batch of transactions is run at a later time.

big bang An approach to customization that involves customizing and installing customer, vendor, employee, and remaining modules for the entire enterprise at the same time.

biometrics An access method that identifies a user by analyzing his or her personal attributes.

black hole A BPMN error that occurs when the data is shown going into an activity, but no data exits.

bot A tiny piece of programming code that installs itself on the infected computer called a zombie.

bridge A routing device that connects one LAN to another LAN of the same type to create a LAN cluster.

build/buy The fourth phase of the SDLC, during which system builders and software engineers transform the system models into applications (computer software) and databases.

business intelligence (BI) Analysis of data to make more intelligent decisions to improve business performance.

business process management (BPM) The practice of streamlining operations and business processes to improve effectiveness.

business processes Related activities performed by an enterprise to create value by transforming input into output (a product or service sold to customers).

C

calculation link An XBRL linkbase that defines basic validation rules.

candidate keys All the entity identifiers that uniquely identify an entity occurrence.

change log A document that records changes.

child entity In a database one-to-many relationship, the entity on the many side. Also called a dependent entity.

client/server network A network that allows client computers on the network to send a request to the server computer. The server computer then responds to the request.

closing entries Journal entries made to close out Income and Expense accounts at year end so the enterprise can begin the new year with $-0- balances in all Income and Expense accounts.

cold site A commercial disaster recovery service that provides a site with air conditioning, wiring, and plumbing but no IT equipment.

Committee of Sponsoring Organizations of the Treadway Commission (COSO) A private organization comprised of the professional associations of the American Accounting Association (AAA), the American Institute of Certified Public Accountants (AICPA), the Financial Executives International (FEI), the Institute of Management Accountants (IMA), and the Institute of Internal Auditors (IIA).

compliance An information criterion that refers to information conforming with laws and regulations.

compliance control A control to maintain confidentiality of information in accordance with all applicable laws and regulations.

composite primary key A type of primary key in which more than one field is required to uniquely identify a database record.

computer architecture Computer hardware components and computer software.

confidentiality An information criterion that addresses the requirement to protect confidential data from unauthorized disclosure and use.

context element An XBRL element that explains the context in which data appears.

control problem A problem that relates to security and control of the system.

correcting entry A journal entry made to correct an error.

cultural feasibility A type of design feasibility that considers whether the culture or environment of the enterprise is conducive to the changes and adaptations required by the new system.

customers module A module that is composed of transactions with customers, such as selling the customer a product or service.

cyber forensics The collection, examination, and preservation of evidence of cybercrimes.

cybercrimes Crimes connected to information assets and IT.

cyberlaw The laws and regulations to prevent, investigate, and prosecute cybercrimes.

data element An XBRL element that specifies numeric or nonnumeric facts, such as dollar amount.

data flow A DFD component represented by lines and arrows that show how data enters, moves through, and exits a system.

data flow diagrams (DFDs) One of the techniques commonly used to document the detail of business processes for an enterprise.

data integrity The accuracy and completeness of data.

data list A spreadsheet that uses columns for fields and rows for records. Also called a data table.

data mining A business intelligence technology that uses mathematical algorithms to find patterns, trends, and relationships among data, such as customer purchasing patterns.

data store A DFD component, represented by an open rectangle, that shows the database table where data is stored.

data validation A type of tool used to help ensure that only valid data is entered.

data warehouse Contains data collected by an organization from a variety of sources and is often used for business intelligence purposes.

database A collection of related database tables.

database administrator (DBA) A person responsible for managing the enterprise's databases.

database builders Professionals constructing the database tables, records, and fields.

database designers Professionals modeling the database.

database fields Pieces of information about events, people, and objects.

database form An onscreen form or screen interface used for entering and updating data in a database.

database integrity The accuracy, validity, and completeness of data in a database.

database modeling The process of developing a pictorial representation of a database. Also called data modeling.

database queries Search and retrieval of specific data from one or more database tables.

database realms Timeframes in the development of the database in which different terminology may be used.

database records A collection of related database fields, populated with data.

database reports The screen interface used to display the database output.

database table A collection of related database records with a unique table name.

database tier One tier in three-tier architecture comprised of a large centralized relational database.

database user Professionals who enter, update, delete, or search the database.

database view The output of a SQL SELECT statement in a table with the selected records and fields.

definition link An XBRL linkbase that defines different kinds of relationships between elements.

demilitarized zone (DMZ) An area between an enterprise's first firewall to the outside world and the next firewall where Web site servers are located.

dependent entity In a database one-to-many relationship, the entity on the many side. Also called a child entity.

deploy The sixth and longest phase of the SDLC, which involves operating and maintaining the new system until it no longer satisfies the organization's needs.

design The third phase of the SDLC, which involves designing new system models to satisfy user requirements, either by creating a new model or by modifying existing models.

DFD fragment A DFD of a single event.

digital dashboard A combination of visualization tools that is often interactive, permitting the viewer to see the effect of changes in various scenarios, parameters, and variables.

digital envelope or 3-key method An encryption method that combines symmetric and asymmetric cryptography.

dimensional database A database that has one fact table and two or more dimension (Dim) tables.

dumpster diving The act of rummaging through garbage for discarded documents or digital media.

dynamic password A password that is used once and then changed.

e-commerce A type of commerce in which sales transactions are conducted online.

economic feasibility A type of design feasibility that analyzes the costs and benefits of the new system.

economic problem A problem that affects revenues (benefits) or costs.

e-cycling Recycling of electronic equipment such as computers and monitors.

effectiveness An information criterion that refers to the information being relevant and pertinent to business processes. In addition, the information should be timely, accurate, and usable.

efficiency An information criterion that refers to providing information using resources in the most productive and economic way.

efficiency problem A problem that pertains to the efficiency of the current system.

electronic data interchange (EDI) A protocol that allows the enterprise network to connect to the network of vendors and suppliers through proprietary lines.

employees module A module that consists of transactions related to employees and payroll.

enterprise security architecture An approach to security architecture that studies the enterprise architecture and business environment to develop an overall strategy and plan that best fits enterprise-specific needs.

enterprise system A system that supports people conducting business activities throughout the enterprise. The three basic functions of an enterprise system involve input, processing, and output.

entity An object or event.

entity attribute An entity identifier that describes a property of an entity.

entity element An XBRL element that defines the company or the entity.

entity identifier An attribute that uniquely identifies an entity occurrence.

entity-level IT controls Controls that include IT governance at top management levels where strategic business objectives are set and policies are established.

entity occurrence A specific object or event.

entity relationship diagram (ERD) A diagram that depicts the relationship among entities in the database.

ethernet protocol A software program commonly used to connect computers to create a LAN.

event A DFD component, represented by a rounded rectangle, that describes a process.

event-agent-database (EAD) table A table used for DFDs summarizing events, agents, and database tables.

event identification The identification of potential events that might affect an entity.

external agent An agent who is outside the business for which the accounting system is designed.

extranet A network used by external customers and/or suppliers.

F

field A piece of information about events and objects stored in a database.

financial controls Controls to ensure that external financial reports are prepared on a timely basis in compliance with applicable laws, regulations, or contractual agreements.

financial module A module that consists of other events and transactions that do not fall into the other modules.

financial reports Reports often given to external investors and creditors to report on an organization's financial performance. Includes financial statements included in a company's annual report given to investors.

firewall A software program on the router that controls traffic between two networks, preventing unauthorized access to servers.

G

gap analysis Analysis of the gap between the baseline modules and the customization required to meet enterprise-specific needs.

gateway A routing device that connects the enterprise's intranet to the Internet.

Global Reporting Initiative (GRI) A sustainability reporting framework that includes performance indicators for measuring social and environmental issues.

Grandfather-Father-Son method A backup technique that keeps multiple backups.

graphical user interfaces (GUI) User interfaces containing images and icons.

gray hole A BPMN error that occurs when the input data does not generate the output information.

green IT Environmentally friendly information technology equipment.

H

honeypot A computer located in the DMZ with attractive, but irrelevant data, used to lure hackers, distracting them from bypassing other firewalls and hacking into the enterprise database.

hot site A commercial disaster recovery service that provides a fully operational site within a few hours.

hybrid controls A combination of manual and automated processes.

hypertext transfer protocol (HTTP) A programming language that allowed the creation of the World Wide Web.

I

identifier element A XBRL element that is a unique identifier, such as account number.

impact The effect that an event will have on an entity's ability to achieve its objectives if the event occurs.

information Structured and unstructured data in any form, such as text, graphics, pictures, audio, and video.

information criteria Criteria that information must meet in order to satisfy business goals and objectives.

information problem A problem that relates to confidentiality, integrity (accuracy and completeness), or availability of information.

information technology (IT) The software, hardware, and network technology used by an organization.

information technology (IT) controls Control activities that ensure appropriate information processing, authorization, and data integrity.

input control An automated control that provides control over the data input into the system to ensure that the data is valid and entered correctly.

install The fifth phase of the SDLC, which involves installing the final product on the enterprise's servers and users' computers (client workstations).

instance document An XBRL document that is created by using a specific company's data and an XBRL taxonomy. It contains both data and metadata with specific amounts for the taxonomy at one instance.

integrated audit An audit that integrates an audit of internal control with an audit of financial statements.

integrated enterprise system A system that shares data across functional areas within the enterprise.

integrated decision model (IDM) A model that provides a framework to structure and organize the decision-making process and integrates consideration of qualitative and quantitative factors in the decision.

integrity An information criterion that refers to data accuracy, completeness, and validity.

internal agent An employee who holds a position within the organization.

internal site Backup services distributed among an organization's multiple locations.

Internet protocol (IP) A software program that provides routing services to messages transmitted over the Internet.

Internet service provider (ISP) A provider of Internet access for a fee.

intersection tables Database tables that are placed at the intersection or junction of the two tables with a many-to-many relationship. Also called junction tables.

intranet An enterprise-wide network.

Intrusion Prevention System (IPS) A system used by an enterprise to prevent the various types of access control attacks with the intent to access and control corporate assets.

IT architecture The design architecture or blueprint for an enterprise's information technology (computers, networks, and databases).

IT audit Audit of IT controls.

IT general controls (ITGC) Controls that apply to IT services in general and help to ensure continued proper IT operation and availability. Also referred to as general controls.

IT infrastructure Information technology (specific software, hardware, and networks) used to build IT architecture for an enterprise.

IT processes Processes that use IT resources to deliver information, run applications, and use infrastructure and people to accomplish IT goals in light of business requirements.

IT resources The resources used by IT processes to achieve IT goals related to business requirements.

L

label link An XBRL linkbase that defines the labels used in an XBRL document.

LAN cluster LANs of the same type connected by bridges.

legacy system A prior system that will continue to be used in the future alongside a new system.

likelihood The possibility or probability that a potential event will occur.

live reports Reports that continuously provide live, up-to-the-minute data.

local area network (LAN) A network that consists of a few computers in a relatively small area.

logic bomb Malicious software that executes when a specified event happens within the computer.

M

macro An instruction that can be used with Excel to automatically perform a sequence of tasks, step by step.

management reports Reports provided to management of the enterprise. These reports are prepared as needed to assist management in decision making.

manual controls Controls performed without the assistance of technology.

material weakness A deficiency such that there is a reasonable possibility that a material misstatement of financial statements will not be prevented or detected on a timely basis.

metadata Electronic tags that are data about data.

metropolitan area network (MAN) A network that covers a metropolitan area.

miracle A BPMN error that occurs when miraculously something comes out of a process, but there was no input into the process.

N

network access points (NAP) Points in a network that are targeted by cyberattacks because these points offer access to the network.

network architecture Network hardware and software.

network wiring (transmission media) Hardware that connects network devices to each other.

normalization A process in which database anomalies such as redundancy and inconsistencies are removed.

O

objects People—including vendors, customers, and employees—that data can be related to.

OLAP cubes (online analytical processing cubes) An online application that permits a user to view data in a multidimensional way.

Open Database Connectivity (ODBC) Software that translates data analysis query commands into commands that are compatible with RDBMS commands.

operational controls Controls to ensure that operations are completed appropriately, such as the timing of cash disbursements to ensure that late fees are avoided.

operational database A relational database that stores data related to operating a business, such as accounting transactions.

operational feasibility A type of design feasibility that evaluates whether the current IT personnel and enterprise users can operate the new system hardware and software.

order-to-cash The sales cycle, which starts with the customer's orders and ends with the collection of cash.

output control A control that ensures that reports and messages are distributed properly to reach intended recipients.

P

parent entity In a database one-to-many relationship, the entity on the one side.

password sniffing The act of attempting to obtain passwords by sniffing messages sent between computers on the network.

patch A section of coding that is inserted into a program when the application software is updated to fix an error or add a new feature.

payroll cycle A transaction cycle consisting of employee and payroll transactions.

people One of the three keys of opportunity that focuses on how employees, customers, and vendors are impacted.

performance problem A problem that affects business performance.

period element An XBRL element that defines the time period, such as the year 2013.

peripheral A utility device connected to the network for shared use.

phishing A form of social engineering to fraudulently obtain confidential information, such as financial data.

physical controls Control activities that provide for physical security of assets.

plan The first phase of the SDLC, which involves first identifying the problem, need, or opportunity that a new system would address and then preparing plans to successfully complete the system development project.

point-to-point protocol (PPP) A network software program that connects one computer to another computer or network server.

point-to-point tunneling protocol (PPTP) A software program permitting an employee to use an enterprise network through a secure channel.

possibility The assessment of likelihood using qualitative measures.

predictive modeling A business intelligence technology that uses mathematical algorithms to predict future trends, such as future customer purchases.

presentation link An XBRL linkbase that defines how the XBRL elements are presented.

pretexting A form of social engineering that is the act of creating a scenario and using deception for information gathering fraud.

primary key A unique identifier for each database record.

private key The key used to decode the message in asymmetric cryptography.

probability The assessment of likelihood using a quantitative measure.

processes One of the three keys of opportunity that focuses on how business activities are impacted.

processing control An automated control that ensures data integrity.

procure-to-pay The purchasing cycle, typically starting with a purchase order and ending with payment to the vendor.

product key A combination of substitution and transposition keys for cryptography.

proxy firewall A special type of firewall located on a proxy server used to intercept and inspect all incoming messages prior to delivering them to the intended recipients.

public key The key used to encrypt the message in asymmetric cryptography.

purchasing cycle A transaction cycle consisting of vendor and purchasing transactions.

Q

query builder tools User-friendly tools used to streamline database query development.

R

REA (resources, events, and agents) A database modeling tool that uses economic duality and is sometimes used to teach accounting databases.

real-time A type of application software execution in which transactions are processed at the current time.

real-time reports Reports that provide up-to-the-minute data without a time lag.

reciprocal agreement An agreement between organizations that can be used to provide backup services. In the event that one organization is down, the other organization would process the data.

record A collection of related database fields.

reference link An XBRL linkbase that defines the relationships between XBRL elements and external regulations or standards.

relational database A database in which the tables are related or connected through fields that are common to two or more tables.

reliability An information criterion that relates to providing information that management can rely upon to meet financial and compliance reporting responsibilities.

remote access The ability of employees to access an enterprise network from offsite.

reports module A module that relates to output from the accounting system.

risk The possibility that an event will occur and negatively impact an entity's ability to achieve its stated objectives.

risk appetite The amount of risk an entity is willing to accept in pursuit of value.

risk assessment The process of assessing the extent to which events would impact an entity's ability to achieve its objectives.

risk feasibility A type of design feasibility that assesses the probability of successful implementation and use of the new system, including any legal considerations.

risk tolerance The acceptable level of variation in attaining objectives.

router A routing device used to connect LANs of similar or different types to create an intranet.

routine operational decisions Decisions that are recurring and typically relate to ongoing business operations.

routing device A special purpose computer without a keyboard or monitor that is used for routing messages over the network.

S

salami attack Usually targeting the accounting department, these attacks are electronic theft of very small amounts numerous times, such as rounding of fractions of a cent from interest calculations.

sales cycle A transaction cycle that involves exchanges or transactions between an enterprise and its customers.

SAP *Systeme, Anwendungen, und Produkte in Datenverarbeitung Aktiengesellschaft* (English translation: Systems, Applications, and Products in Data Processing AG or SAP AG).

schedule feasibility A type of design feasibility that evaluates whether the new system deliverables can be delivered by the required due dates.

schema An XBRL taxonomy component that defines which elements are related to the particular taxonomy, such as the schema for the U.S. GAAP taxonomy specifies a unit element of U.S. dollars.

segregation of duties A control activity that divides authorization, recording, and asset custody among different individuals.

server computers Computers (microcomputers, midrange computers, or mainframes) that serve other computers with data and applications, such as an accounting database.

service problem A problem that relates to system problems with service either to enterprise users or customers.

significant deficiency A deficiency that is less severe than a material weakness but that still merits attention of those responsible for oversight of financial reporting.

single sign-on (SSO) A type of password management that permits a user to use one username and password to log into various systems.

social engineering A cyberattack that involves manipulating and tricking an individual into divulging confidential information to be used for fraudulent purposes.

spaghetti code Programming code used to connect stand-alone systems.

spam Malware sent by email.

stages An approach to customization that customizes one module or geographic location at a time, stage by stage, until the entire enterprise has been converted to the new system.

stovepipe An approach to security architecture that involves tossing in security patches, hoping that vulnerabilities are covered.

strategic decisions Decisions that are usually long term in nature and unstructured with a high degree of ambiguity.

structured query language (SQL) Programming code used to search and retrieve data from a database.

substitution key A type of encryption key in which the algorithm uses the key to substitute a letter or word for another letter or word.

sustainability A measure of an organization's ability to sustain an action in the future on an ongoing basis.

sustainability accounting A type of accounting that involves collecting, storing, organizing, and reporting economic, social, and environmental information for two general purposes: making decisions and evaluating performance.

sustainability IDa (Integrated Decision analysis) model An expanded decision model that provides an organizing framework for considering both qualitative and quantitative aspects of economic, social, and environmental factors in making decisions.

sustainability reports Reports used for decision making and performance evaluation related to an enterprise's sustainability practices.

symmetric cryptography or 1-key method An encryption method that uses one key to encode and the same key to decode. Thus, both the sender and the intended recipient must have the same key.

system development life cycle (SDLC) A structured approach consisting of a series of phases used to create a system: plan, analyze, design, build/buy, install, and deploy.

system development methodology (SDM) The order and timing of when the SDLC phases are completed.

systems software Computer programs used for managing computer hardware.

T

table A collection of related database records with a unique table name.

tactical decisions Decisions that are typically short term, impacting one year or less.

tax reports Reports used when filing federal, state, and local taxes.

taxonomy A dictionary that defines the XBRL tags used for specific data items.

technical feasibility A type of design feasibility that assesses whether the new system IT architecture can interact with the existing IT architecture that will remain in use.

technology One of the three keys of opportunity that focuses on software, hardware, and networks.

telecommunications The electrical transmission of data through analog or digital transmission media.

text mining BI analysis tool that can be used to mine text stored in various enterprise documents, including emails, word processing documents, and reports.

three-tier architecture A system format in which the system relies upon three tiers of information technology components: database tier, application tier, and user tier.

token device (TD) A hardware device containing a password generator protocol that creates a new password each time the token is used, thus eliminating the need for the user to memorize a password that is continually changing.

transaction cycles Accounting transactions related to specific business processes.

transport control protocol (TCP) Protocol that provides message transportation services between sending and receiving computers.

transposition key A type of encryption key in which the algorithm uses the key to scramble data.

triple bottom line Measurement of an organization's performance in terms of economic, social, and environmental results.

Trojan horse Malware disguised as a legitimate program that can be downloaded and installed by users without realizing it is a virus.

U

uniform resource locator (URL) A Web address unique to a particular Web site.

unit element An XBRL element that defines the unit of measure, such as euros.

user log A document that records user access.

user tier A tier in three-tier architecture that consists of front-end client computers.

V

value-added network (VAN) A network that allows an organization to share data with suppliers using EDI protocol.

value chain An organizing framework for business processes that is useful in coordinating activities with suppliers and customers.

vendors module A module related to transactions with vendors, such as purchasing goods or services.

virtual private network (VPN) A network that uses point-to-point tunneling protocol (PPTP) to allow an organization's employees to access the network from outside.

virus A relatively small program that infects other application software by attaching to it and disrupting the application's function.

W

warm site A commercial disaster recovery service that provides a partially configured site that is operational within a few days.

web mining BI analysis tool that searches the Internet for specific patterns on Web sites.

wide area network (WAN) A network that covers a large geographic region.

workstation computers Personal computers and laptops connected to the network.

worm A type of malware that is like a virus except it does not need a host application to function or reproduce.

X

XBRL (eXtensible Business Reporting Language) A web-based programming language used for digital financial reporting around the globe.

XBRL bolt-on tagging The approach to adding XBRL tags in which the XBRL tags are added after reports are created.

XBRL element A specific XBRL term or code which identifies specific data or metadata.

XBRL integrated tagging The approach to adding XBRL tags in which XBRL tags are added to data during information processing.

XBRL linkbases The component of an XBRL taxonomy that defines relationships between data.

References

Preface

American Institute of Certified Public Accountants. (2002). "The CPA Vision Project: 2011 and Beyond." New York, NY: American Institute of Certified Public Accountants.

Chapter One

Dove Consulting. "Retail Bank and Deposit Summary Statistics." fdic.gov/unbankedsurveys/unbankedstudy/FDICBankSurvey_AppendixB.pdf (accessed May 2010).

Duff, M. (2009, January). "Dunnhumby Complicates Outlook for Tesco, Kroger, Wal-Mart." industry.bnet.com/retail (accessed May 2010).

Hitachi Consulting. "Case Study: Southwest Airlines, Business Intelligence Challenge Leadership." hitachi-consulting.com/files/pdfRepository/CS_SWA_BIChangeLeadership.pdf (accessed May 2010).

Jelter, J. (2005, November). "Kodak Restates, Adds $9 Million to Loss." MarketWatch. marketwatch.com/story/kodak-restates-earnings-adds-9-million-to-latest-loss?dist=rss&siteid=mktw (accessed June 2009).

Manu, A. (2006). *The Imagination Challenge: Strategic Foresight and Innovation in the Global Economy.* Berkeley, CA: Pearson Education, Peachpit Press.

Tempero, S. (2006, May). "Focus on: Technology Tax Dodgers Beware." *Dayton Business Journal*, Vol. 17, No. 19. teradataservicesnetwork.com/t/article-reprints/Tax-dodgers-beware-Dayton-Business-Journal-ar4886/ (accessed May 2010).

Teradata. (2010). "Coca-Cola Enterprise Data Warehouse (EDW)." teradata.com/t/customers/manufacturing-Coca-Cola/ (accessed May 2010).

Teradata. (2010). "Travel-Travelocity: Being the Customer's Champion with Teradata CRM." teradata.com/t/customers/Travel-Travelocity/ (accessed May 2010).

Teradata. (2010). "Wells Fargo Beyond Internet Banking." teradata.com/customers/Financial-Services-Wells-Fargo/ (accessed May 2010).

Wailgum, T. (2010, March). "What Does ERP really cost?" cio.com/article/40323/ERP_Definition_and_Solutions?page=3 (accessed May 2010).

Wells Fargo & Company, Annual Report 2009. (2010). "The Vision That Works." wellsfargo.com/downloads/pdf/invest_relations/wf2009annualreport.pdf (accessed May 2010).

Chapter Two

Amazon.com. (2010). "2009 Annual Report." phx.corporate-ir.net/phoenix.zhtml?c=97664&p=irol-reportsannual (accessed May 2009).

Associate Press. (2009, June). "Database Takes Patients for Billion, Study Finds." *New York Times Business.* nytimes.com/2009/06/25/business/25insure.html (accessed May 2010).

Clusterstock. (2010, May). "ZOMG: Accenture Stock Briefly Had a Bid at $0.01 (ACN)." politifi.com/news/ZOMG-Accenture-Stock-Briefly-Had-A-Bid-At-001-ACN-598561.html (accessed May 2010).

Daley, J.B. (2004), "Do You Really Know Who Your Customers Are? An Interview with Shep Parke of Accenture." The Siebel Observer. slideshare.net/ShepParke/Parke-Siebel-Observer-Interview (accessed May 2010).

Kirk, J. (2006, June). "Oracle's Security Chief Lambasted Faulty Code." *itworld Canada.* itworldcanada.com/news/oracles-security-chief-lambastes-faulty-code/99110-pg2 (accessed May 2010).

Mearian, L. (2010, May). "Sharp Stock Market Drop Likely Human, Computer Error." computerworld.com/s/article (accessed May 2010).

Chapter Three

Forbes. (2010, March). "The World Billionaires #937 Scott Cook." *Forbes.com.* forbes.com/lists/2010/10/billionaires-2010_Scott-Cook_J8AI.html (accessed May 2010).

Intuit. (2010, May). "INTU: Stock & Summary Data." nasdaq.com/asp/SummaryQuote.asp symbol=INTU&selected=INTU (accessed May 2010).

Chapter Four

Altova. (2012). "Business Process Modeling." altova.com/umodel/business-process-modeling.html (accessed January 2012).

Earls, A. (2011, February). "Ebiz. BPMN 2.0: The emerging star of business process modeling." ebiz. ebiz.net (accessed January 2012).

Jacka, M. (2002). "The Four Steps of Business Process Mapping." Smartpros.com/x33396.xml (accessed March 2012).

Object Management Group, Inc. (2010, January). "BPMN 2.0 by Example." omg.org/spec/BPMN/2.0/examples/PDF/ (accessed January 2012).

Object Management Group, Inc. (2011, January). "Business Process Model and Notation (BPMN) Version 2.0." omg.org/spec/BPMN/2.0/examples/PDF/ (accessed January 2012).

Owen, M., and Raj, J. (2003). "BPMN and Business Process Management, Introduction to the New Business Process Modeling Standard." Popkin Software, Popkin.com (accessed January 2012).

Sandy, K. (2011). "Business Process Modeling." TIBCO Software Inc., TIBCO.com (accessed January 2012).

Sayer, P. (2010, March). "Software AG Opens BPM Social Networking Beta Test." cio.com, cio.com/article (accessed May 2010).

Software AG. Press Release. (2010, March). "Software AG at CEBIT 2010: Announces Open Beta for Its First Social BPM Platform-ArisAlign." softwareag.com/corporate/Press/pressreleases/20100302_ARISAlign_Announcement_page.asp (accessed May 2010).

SPARX Systems. (2012, January). "The Business Process Model." SPARX Systems, sparxsystems.com/business_process_model.html (accessed February 2012).

Wikipedia. (2012). "Business Process Model and Notation." en.wikipedia.org/wiki/Business_Process_Modeling_Notation (accessed February 2012).

Chapter Five

Osterland, A. (2001, January). "Blaming ERP" CFO Magazine, January 2001 issue, cfo.com/article.cfm/2987370 (accessed September 2009).

Wikipedia. (2010). "SAP History." en.wikipedia.org/wiki/SAP_AG#History (accessed June 2010).

Chapter Six

Benchpress.com. (1997, March). "Installing R/3 Is the Corporate Equivalent of a Root Canal." *The Wall Street Journal.* benchpress.com/Sapsd.htm (accessed June May 2010).

Hardy, Q. (2012, February). "Oracle to Buy Taleo, Speeding the Shift to the Cloud." *The New York Times.* bits.blogs.nytimes.com/2012/02/09/oracle-1-9-billion-more-to-change-everything/?ref=oraclecorporation (accessed February 2012).

Harman, P. (2002). "Nestle USA Installed SAP." BP Trend Newsletter.

Kalakota, R., and Robinson, M. (1999). *E-business: Roadmap for Success.* 2nd Edition. MA Reading: Addison Wesley.

News.bbc.co.uk. (2012, January). "Quantum computing could head to 'the cloud,' study says." news.bbc.co.uk/news/science-environment-16636580 (accessed March 2012).

Rusli, E. (2012, February). "Oracle Embraces the Cloud with $1.9 Billion Taleo Deal." *The New York Times.* dealbook.nytimes.com/2012/02/09/oracle-to-buy-taleo-for-1-9-billion/?ref=oraclecorporation (accessed February 2012).

Smith, H., and Fingar, P. (2003). *Business Process Management: The Third Wave.* Tampa, FL: Meghan-Kiffer Press.

Teuke, M. R. (2006, May). "The Big Squeeze, Built-in Best Practices Help Welch's Get the Most from ERP." Profit Online, oracle.com/profit/apps_strategy/p26consumer.html (accessed September 2009).

Waldman, L. (2011, December). "Cloud-Safe: 10 Considerations around Cloud Computing Security." Frank, The Nextpoint Blog. nextpoint.wordpress.com/2011/12/06/top-10-security-provisions-in-the-cloud/ (accessed March 2012).

Wallgum, T. (2010, May). "Oracle vs. SAP: Battle of the Spring 2010 Balance Sheets." *CIO.com.* cio.com/article/593571/Oracle_vs._SAP_Battle_of_the_Spring_2010_Balance_Sheets_ (accessed June 2010).

White, B., Clark, D., and Ascarelli, S. (1997, March 14). "Program of Pain: This German Software Is Complex, Expensive, and Wildly Popular." *The Wall Street Journal* Central Edition.

Worthen, B. (2007, July). "Nestlé's ERP Odyssey." http://www.web.eng.fiu.edu/~ronald/ERP/Nestle.pdf (accessed May 2010).

Chapter Seven

bbc.co.uk. (2012, January). "Newspaper Review: Papers Mull Tesco Share Price Drop." bbc.co.uk/news/uk-16541307 (accessed March 2012)

bbc.co.uk. (2012, March). "Business Turns to Ants and Algorithms in Search for Profit." bbc.co.uk/news/business-17034801 (accessed March 2012)

Boyle, M. (2007, November). "Kroger's Secret Weapon." CNNMoney. money.cnn.com/2007/11/21/magazines/fortune/boyle_datamining.fortune/index.htm (accessed February 2012).

Brandon, A. (2010, December). "Acting on Data Analytics—More Than Food for Thought." spotfireblog.tibco.com/?p=4236 (accessed February 2012)

Dubler, C., and Wilcox, C. (2002, April). "Just What Are Cubes Anyway? (A Painless Introduction to OLAP Technology)." Microsoft Excel 2002 Technical Articles. msdn.microsoft.com/en-us/library/aa140038 (office.10,printer).aspx (accessed July 2009).

Gartner Business Intelligence Summit in The Hague, Netherlands. (2009, January 20–22). gartner.com/it/page.jsp?id=856714 (accessed May 2009).

Gartner. (2012). "Magic Quadrant for Business Intelligence Platforms Report." Microstrategy. microstrategy.com/company/gartnerquadrant.asp (accessed February 2012).

IBM Press Release. (2011, November). "IBM Social Media Analysis Points to Lower Heels, Bucking Economic Trend." IBM Corporation. -03.ibm.com/press/us/en/pressrelease/35985.wss (accessed February 2012).

IBM White Paper. (2011, March). "Business Analytics and Optimization: The New Competitive Edge Using the Power of Insight to Shape Business Outcomes." IBM Corporation. www-03.ibm.com/press/us/en/pressrelease/35985.wss (accessed March 2012.).

Inmon, W. H., and Nesavich, A. (2008). *Tapping into Unstructured Data: Integrating Unstructured Data and Textual Analytics into Business Intelligence*. Upper Saddle River, NJ: Pearson Education.

Kanaracus, C. (2010, May). "IBM Points Predicitve Analysis at Social Web." *Computerworld*. computerworld.com/s/article/9176581/IBM_points_predictive_analytics_at_social_Web?taxonomyId=9 (accessed June 2010).

Kypost.com. (2010). "Data Mining Is Big Business for Kroger & Getting Bigger All the Time." kypost.com/dpp/news/region_central_cincinnati/downtown/data-mining-is-big-business-for-kroger-&-getting-bigger-all-the-time (accessed February 2012).

Luhn, H. P. (1958, October). "A Business Intelligence System." *IBM Journal,* Vol. 2, Issue 4. portal.acm.org/citation.cfm?id=1662381&CFID=103341642&CFTOKEN=98995673 (accessed June 2010).

PriceWaterhouseCooper. (2004, July). "The Use of Spreadsheets: Considerations for Section 404 of the Sarbanes-Oxley Act." whitepapers.techrepublic.com.com/abstract.aspx?docid=129345 (accessed June 2009).

Turban E., et al. (2008). *Business Intelligence: A Managerial Approach*. Upper Saddle River, NJ: Pearson Education.

Vox Marketing. (2009, January)."Kroger Targets Coupons with Customer-Loyalty Data." marketingvox.com/kroger-targets-coupons-with-customer-loyalty-data-042711/ (accessed February 2012).

Wallgum, T. (2010, March). "Inside the CIO's 'Big Four' Application Priorities." *Computerworld*. computerworld.com/s/article/9174225/Inside_the_CIO_s_Big_Four_Application_Priorities?taxonomyId=9 (accessed June 2010).

Chapter Eight

bbc.co.uk. (2012, January). "Electronic Waste: EU Adopts New WEEE Law." bbc.co.uk/news/world-europe-16633940 (accessed March 2012).

BITC Newsletter. (2012, February). "Trends in Sustainability Reporting." businessinthecommunity.newsweaver.co.uk/bitcnewsletter/vzas9fduievnkdv89usw6o (accessed April 2012).

Buytendijk, F., and O'Rourke, J. (2008, March). "Sustainability Matters: Why and How Business Is Widening Its Focus to Consider the Needs of All Stakeholders." *Oracle White Paper*. oracle.com/dm/09q1field/sustainability_matters_wp.pdf (accessed May 2009).

Chi, M. (1997, July). "Quantifying Qualitative Analysis of Verbal Data: A Practical Guide." *Journal of the Learning Sciences*. Vol. 6, Issue 3.

D'Aquila, J. (2012, April). "Sustainability into the Reporting Process and Elsewhere." *The CPA Journal*. cpaj.com (accessed April 2012).

Eccles, R., Cheng, B., and Saltzman, D. (2010). "The Landscape of Integrated Reporting: Reflections and Next Steps." Harvard Business School. Smartwords Edition eBook. (accessed April 2012).

Eccles, R., and Saltzman, D. (2012). "Achieving Sustainability through Integrated Reporting." *Stanford Social Innovation Review*. ssireview.org (accessed April 2012).

Epstein, M. (2008). *Making Sustainability Work: Best Practices in Managing and Measuring Corporate Social, Environmental, and Economic Impacts*. San Francisco, CA: Berrett-Koehler.

Epstein, M., and Roy, M. (1998, June). "Managing Corporate Environmental Performance: A Multinational Perspective." *European Management Journal.* Vol. 16, Issue 3.

Fisse, B., and Braithwaite, J. (1983). *The Impact of Publicity on Corporate Offenders.* Albany, NY: SUNY Press.

ISO – News. (2012, March). "Turning Waste into Gold with New ISO Standard for Environmental Management Accounting." iso.org/iso/pressrelease.htm?;refid=Ref1527 (accessed April 2012).

ISO Focus+. (2012, January). "Sustainability." ISO Focus+, Vol. 3, No 1. (accessed April 2012).

King, R. (2009, June). "U.S. Corporations Size Up Their Carbon Footprints." *Bloomberg Businessweek.* businessweek.com/technology/content/jun2009/tc2009061_692661.htm (accessed June 2010).

Kiron, D., and Kruschwitz, N. (2012). "Sustainability Nears a Tipping Point." *MIT Sloan Management Review.* sloanreview.MIT.EDU (accessed April 2012).

Knickie, K, (2011, February). "Sustainability Intelligence from Integrated Reporting." Sustainable Business Forum. sustainablebusinessforum.com/kim-knickle/49864/sustainability-intelligence-integrated-reporting (accessed April 2012).

Lamoreaux, M. (2010, August). "Accounting Groups Back Integrating Sustainability, Financial Reports." *Journal of Accountancy.* journalofaccountancy.com (accessed February 2011).

Mahler, D., et al. (2009). "Green Winners: The Performance of Sustainability-Focused Companies during the Financial Crisis." *A.T. Kearney.* atkearney.com (accessed June 2009).

Messina, L. (2010, May). "West Virginia Coal Mine Explosion: 25 Dead after Massey Blast." *The Huffington Post.* huffingtonpost.com/2010/04/05/west-virginia-coal-mine-e_n_526151.html (accessed June 2010).

Newsweek Green Rankings. (2012). "Global Companies." thedailybeast.com/newsweek/features/green-rankings/2011/international.html (accessed April 2012).

Newsweek Green Rankings. (2012). "The World's Greenest Companies, the 2012 Rankings." thedailybeast.com/newsweek/features/2012/newsweek-green-rankings.html (accessed April 2012).

PepsiCo. (2010). "Performance with Purpose: The Promise of PepsiCo, Sustainability Summary 2010." PepsiCo.com. pepsico.com/Download/PepsiCo_2010_Sustainability_Summary.pdf (accessed May 2012).

Plungis, J. (2010, May). "Toyota Sudden Acceleration May Be Tied to 89 Deaths, U.S. Says." *BusinessWeek.* businessweek.com/news/2010-05-25/toyota-sudden-acceleration-may-be-tied-to-89-deaths-u-s-says.html (accessed June 2010).

Rapid Library.com. (2011, September). "IR Discussion Paper Presentation." rapidlibrary.com/files/ir-discussion-paper-presentation-sep2011-ppt_ulcfcqcenzi89on.html (accessed April 2012).

Roben, F. (2009, May). "Israel's New Pioneers Cash in on CleanTech." *BusinessWeek.* businessweek.com/magazine/content/09_20/b4131034558887.htm (accessed May 2009).

Savitz, A. W., and Weber, K. (2006). *The Triple Bottom Line.* Hoboken, NJ: Wiley.

Southwest One Report. (2010). "Planet." southwestonereport.com/planet.php (accessed April 2012).

Stevens, H. (2011, October). "Justmeans Insights Brings Corporate Social Responsibility Reporting to Life." Justmeans. justmeans.com/blogs/Justmeans-Insights-Brings-Corporate-Social-Responsibility-Reporting-to-Life/1227.html (accessed April 2012).

Chapter Nine

AICPA.org. (2006, November). "Charles Hoffman Receives AICPA Special Recognition Award for Contributions to the Development of XBRL." aicpa.org/download/news/2006 (accessed June 2009).

Edgar-online.com. (2009, June). "That's the Wow." edgar-online.com/flash/imetrix (accessed June 2009).

Fujitsu.com (2009). "Customer Success Story." fujitsu.com/downloads/INTSTG/conference (accessed June 2009).

Hoffam, C., et al. (2005, July). "Business Case for XBRL." xml.coverpages.org/UBmatrix-BusinessCaseForXBRL.pdf (accessed June 2009).

Kernan K. (2008). "XBRL around the World." Journal of Accountancy. journalofaccountancy.com/Issues/2008/Oct (accessed June 2009).

Sambuichi, N. (2004, March). "Breathing New Life into Old Systems with XBRL-GL." *Strategic Finance.* allbusiness.com/technology/172158-1.html (accessed June 2009).

SEC.gov. (2009, April). "Final Rule: Interactive Data to Improve Financial Reporting." sec.gov/rules/final/2009/33-9002.pdf (accessed June 2009).

SEC.gov (2009, June). "Test Drive Interactive Data." viewerprototype1.com/viewer (accessed June 2009).

Software AG. (2002, December). "XBRL: Understanding the XML Standard for Business Reporting and Finance." softwareag.com (accessed April 2009).

Stantial, J. (2007, June). "ROI on XBRL." *Journal of Accountancy.* journalofaccountancy.com/Issues/2007/June (accessed June 2009).

Wada, Y. (2009, May). "Background Information and Future Plans of the Bank of Japan's XBRL Project." hitachidatainteractive.com/2009/05/11 (accessed June 2009).

XBRL.org. (2009, June). "Introduction to XBRL." xbrl.org/WhatISXBRL (accessed June 2009).

XBRL.US (2009). "SEC Activities and Resources." xbrl.us/Learn/Pages/SECAcivtiesandHelp.aspx (accessed June 2009).

Chapter Ten

ACFE.com. (2008). "Report to the Nation on the Occupational Fraud & Abuse." ACFE.com (accessed June 2009).

AICPA Case Study, (2012). "Putting Soc Reports to Work at confirmation.com." AICPA.org. aicpa.org/interestareas/frc/assuranceadvisoryservices/downloadabledocuments/soc_reports_case_study_serviceorg_final.pdf (accessed June 2012)

AICPA. (2006). "Trust Services Principles, Criteria, and Illustrations." American Institute of Certified Public Accountants, Inc., and Canadian Institute of Chartered Accountants. aicpa.org (accessed June 2009).

Black, C. (1979). *Black's Law Dictionary*. 5th Edition. St. Paul, MN: West Publishing Co.

Bostick, L., and Luehlfing, M. (2009). "Auditors' Responsibilities Formalized under SAS 109. Understanding Risks Associated with the Legal and Regulatory Environment." *The CPA Journal*. nysscpa.org/cpajournal/2007/207/essentials/p23.htm (accessed May 2012).

Business.com. (2009, January). "India's Madoff? Satyam Scandal Rocks Outsourcing." businessweek.com/globalbiz/content/jan2009/gb2009017_807784_page_2.htm *(accessed June 2009).*

Businessweek.com. (2009, June). "Employee Fraud and Misconduct." businessweek.com/managing/content/jun2009/ca20090612_156983.htm (accessed June 2009).

Coderre, D. (2004, August). "Are you ready for XBRL? The de-facto standard for electronic business reporting provides auditors with an opportunity to increase efficiency and add value." Internal Auditor, thefreelibrary.com/ (accessed June 2009).

Coso.org. (1994). "Internal Control-Integrated Framework, Committee of Sponsoring Organizations of the Treadway Commission." coso.org (accessed June 2009).

Gibney, A. (2005, January). "Enron: The Smartest Guys in the Room, Movie." imdb.com/title/tt0413845/ (accessed June 2009).

Govindaraj, S., and Sampath, V. (2009, May). "Learning from Satyam: How to Detect Fraud." businessweek.com/globalbiz/content/may2009/gb20090521_309883.htm (accessed June 2009).

Graybow, M. (2009, March). "Hunt for Madoff Money to Drag On for Years." reuters.com/article/reutersEdge/ (accessed June 2009).

Institute of Internal Auditors. (2009, January). "Code of Ethics." theiia.org/guidance/standards-and-guidance/ippf/code-of-ethics (accessed June 2009).

IT Governance Institute. (2006, September). *IT Control Objectives for Sarbanes-Oxley: The Role of IT in the Design and Implementation of Internal Control over Financial Reporting*. 2nd Edition. Rolling Meadows, IL: IT Governance Institute.

IT Governance Institute. (2007). "COBIT. 4.1.itgi.org (accessed June 2009).

Journal of Accountancy. (2012, August). "Fraud: Behavioral Red Flags of Perpetrators." journalofaccountancy.com (accessed April 2012).

Katcher, A., Parthum, J., and Stewart, C. (2010). "Service Organization Controls, Managing Risks by Obtaining a Service Auditor's Report." AICPA. aicpa.org/interestareas/informationtechnology/resources/trustservices/downloadabledocuments/10957-378%20soc%20whitepaper.pdf (accessed June 2012).

Lakshman, N. (2009, April). "Nine Charged in Hyderabad in Satyam Fraud." businessweek.com/globalbiz/content/apr2009/gb2009047_927710.htm (accessed June 2009).

Lawrence, M., and Wells, J. (2004, October). "Basic Legal Concepts, Beware Insufficient Knowledge of the Law." journalofaccountancy.com/Issues/2004/Oct/BasicLegalConcepts.htm (accessed June 2009).

News.bbc.co.uk. (2002, June). "Andersen Guilty in Enron Case." news.bbc.co.uk/2/hi/business/2047122.stm (accessed June 2009).

Oray, M. (2009, January). "Enron's Skilling Loses Appeal." businessweek.com/bwdaily/dnflash/content/jan2009/db2009016_313568.htm (accessed June 2009).

Oversightsystems.com. (2007). "The 2007 Oversight Systems Report on Corporate Fraud." oversightsystems.com (accessed June 2009).

PCAOB. (2007). "Auditing Standard No. 5." pcaobus.org/Standards/Auditing/Pages/Auditing_Standard_5.aspx (accessed May 2012).

PCAOB. File No. PCAOB-2007-02. (2007, June). "Auditing Standards 5." pcaobus.org/standards/index.aspx (accessed June 2009).

Public Law 107–204 107th Congress [H.R. 3763]. (2002, July). Sarbanes-Oxley Act of 2002. Corporate responsibility 15 USC 7201 note.

Ratcliffe, T. (2005, December). "To Consolidate or Not—For Some Companies, That IS the Question." journalofaccountancy.com/Issues/2005/Dec/ToConsolidateOrNot (accessed June 2009).

Reuters.com. (2009, May). "2-Settlements Could Soon Boost Madoff Client Recovery." reuters.com/article/rbssInvestmentServices/idUSN1448649320090514 (accessed June 2009).

Richards, D., Melancon, B., and Ratley, J. "Managing the Business Risk of Fraud: A Practical Guide." The Institute of Internal Auditors, AICAPA, ACFE. acfe.com/uploadedFiles/ACFE_Website/Content/documents/managing-business-risk.pdf (accessed May 2012).

RubinBrown. (2007). "Focus on Internal Audit: Integrating Process Improvements and Internal Controls." RubinBrowm.com. rubinbrown.com/contents/view/1262/101 (accessed January 2009).

RubinBrown. (2012, January). "Focus on Business Advisory Services: COSO Integrated Framework." rubinbrown.com/professional-news/1914-focus-on-business-advisory-services-coso-integrated-framework (accessed May 2012).

Sec.gov. (2002, July). "Public Law 107–204 107th Congress [H.R. 3763]: Sarbanes-Oxley Act of 2002. Corporate responsibility 15 USC 7201 note." sec.gov/about/laws/soa2002.pdf (accessed June 2009).

Sec.gov. (2007, July). "SEC Approves PCAOB Auditing Standard No. 5 Regarding Audits of Internal Control over Financial Reporting; Adopts Definition of "Significant Deficiency." sec.gov/news/press/2007/2007-144.htm (accessed June 2009).

Stone, A. "How Everyone Missed WorldCom." businessweek.com/bwdaily/dnflash/jul2002/nf2002073_5726.htm (accessed June 2009).

THEIIA.org. (2009). "Managing the Business Risk of Fraud: A Practical Guide." The Institute of Internal Auditors. fvs.aicpa.org/NR/rdonlyres/98BD10EC-CC12-4D14-848D-E5BDB181F4EE/0/managing_business_risk_fraud.pdf (accessed June 2009).

Thomas, B. (2002, June). "Called to Account." time.com/time/business/article/0,8599,263006,00.html (accessed June 2009).

Wells, J., and Gill, J. (2007, October). "Assessing Fraud Risk." journalofaccounancy.com (accessed April 2012).

Xiong, Y., and Martin, M. (2006). "Mapping Internal Controls Using System Documentation Tools." *The Review of Business Information Systems*, Vol. 10, No. 1.

Younglai, R. (2009, May). "SEC Proposes Tougher Investment Adviser Rules." reuters.com/article/businessNews/idUSTRE54D3MT20090514 (accessed June 2009).

Chapter Eleven

Accenture. (2011). "The Dodd-Frank Wall Street Reform Act. Implications for Energy Companies, Utilities and Other Over-the-Counter Market Participants." accenture.com/SiteCollectionDocuments/PDF/Accenture_The_Dodd_Frank_Wall_Street_Reform_Act.pdf (accessed May 2012).

Acohido, B. (2009, January). "Hackers Breach Heartland Payment Credit Card System." *USA Today*. usatoday.com/money/perfi/credit/2009-01-20-heartland-credit-card-security-breach_N.htm (accessed July 2009).

bbc.co.uk. (2011, November). "US dismantles 'massive' cyber crime syndicate." bbc.co.uk/news/business-15668377 (accessed May 2012).

Davie, P. (2009, May). "PCI in the Age of the Heartland." *E-Commerce Times*. newsworld.com/perl/section/computing (accessed May 2009).

Department of Justice. (2010, April). "Indian National Sentenced to 81 Months in Prison for Role in International Online Brokerage 'Hack, Pump and Dump' Scheme." cybercrime.gov/marimuthuSent.pdf (accessed June 2010).

Department of Justice. (2010, May). "Chico Man Pleads Guilty to Embezzling $693,000 from Charity." justice.gov/criminal/cybercrime/randlePlea.pdf (accessed June 2010).

Department of Justice. (2010, May). "Student Charged with Using University Computer Network for Denial of Service Attacks and to Control Other Computers (via 'BotNet' Zombies)." cybercrime.gov/frostChar.pdf (accessed June 2010).

Federal Trade Commission. (2012, May). "How Not to Get Hooked by a 'Phishing' Scam." ftc.gov/bcp/edu/pubs/consumer/alerts/alt127.shtm (accessed May 2012).

Frieden, T. (2009, January). "VA Will Pay $20 Million to Settle Lawsuit over Stolen Laptop's Data." cnn.com/2009/POLITICS/01/27/va.data.theft/ (accessed June 2009).

International Standard. (2005). "ISO/IEC 27002: 2005 Information Technology—Security Techniques—Code of Practice for Information Security Management." iso27001security.com/html/27002.html#StructureAndFormatOfISO17799 (accessed April 2012).

International Standard. (2009, May). "ISO/IEC 27000 Information Security Management Systems (ISMS) Family." ISO.org (accessed May 2012).

International Standard. (2011, December). "ISO IEC 27002 (17799) Information Security Control Objectives." praxiom.com/iso-17799-objectives.htm (accessed April 2012)

Isc2.org (2009, June). "Certified Information Systems Security Professional." isc2.org/cissp/default.aspx (accessed June 2009).

Journalofaccountancy.com. (2008, October). "High-Tech Fraud Prevention." *Journal of Accountancy.* journalofaccountancy.com/Issues/2008/Oct/High_Tech_Fraud_Prevention.htm (accessed July 2009).

Marcella, A., and Menendez, D. (2007). *Cyber Forensics.* 2nd Edition. Boca Raton, FL: CRC Press.

Russo, C., and Tucci, L. (2005, September). "Katrina: IT Lesson in Disaster Recovery." *SearchCIO.com.* searchcio.techtarget.com/news/article/0,289142,sid182_gci1122305,00.html (accessed June 2009).

Securityfocus.com. (2007, May). "TJX Thieves Exploited Wireless Insecurities." securityfocus.com/brief/496 (accessed June 2009).

Symantec White Paper: IT Compliance. (2012, January). "Compliance Field Guide—Symantec Control Compliance Suite." www4.symantec.com/mktginfo/RSA_2011/ComplianceFieldGuide_Jan11.pdf (accessed April 2012).

Verizon White Paper. (2012). "2012 Data Breach Investigations Report." verizon.com/enterprise (accessed April 2012).

Wikipedia. (2012). "ISO/IEC 27000-series." en.wikipedia.org/wiki/ISO/IEC_27000-series (accessed April 2012).

Wikipedia. (2012, January). "ISO/IEC 27007." en.wikipedia.org/wiki/ISO/IEC_27007 (accessed April 2012).

Chapter Twelve

AESRM. (2007). "The Convergence of Physical and Information Security in the Context of Enterprise Risk Management." aesrm.org (accessed June 2009).

AIRMIC, Alarm, IRM. (2010). "A structured approach to Enterprise Risk Management (ERM) and the Requirements of ISO 31000." The Institute of Risk Management. theirm.org/ISO31000guide.htm (accessed May 2012).

Atkinson, W. (2003, December). "Enterprise Risk Management at Wal-Mart." *AllBusiness.com.* allbusiness.com/finance/insurance-risk-management/1025647-1.html (accessed May 2010).

Chan, S. (2004, October). "Mapping COSO and COBIT for Sarbanes-Oxley Compliance." *ITAudit.* theiia.org/itaudit/index.cfm?fuseaction=print&fid=5553 (accessed June 2009).

Coso.org. (2004, September). "Enterprise Risk Management – Integrated Framework, Committee of Sponsoring Organizations of the Treadway Commission." coso.org (accessed June 2009).

Cullen, D. (2003, June). "Excel Snafu Costs Firm $24m." *The Register.* theregister.co.uk/2003/06/19/excel_snafu_costs_firm_24m/ (accessed June 2009).

Deloitte. (2004). "Beyond 404: Responding to COSO's New Enterprise Risk Management Framework." deloitte.com/dtt/cda/doc/content/us_ers_COSOerm.pdf (accessed July 2009).

Higher Education Information Security Council. (2012). "Risk Management (ISO 4)." Internet2 Wiki. wiki.internet2.edu/confluence/display/itsg2/Risk+Management+(ISO+4) (accessed June 2012)

IT Governance Institute. (2006, September). *IT Control Objectives for Sarbanes-Oxley: The Role of IT in the Design and Implementation of Internal Control over Financial Reporting.* 2nd Edition. Rolling Meadows, IL: IT Governance Institute.

Jelter, J. (2005, November). "Kodak Restates, Adds $9 Million to Loss." *MarketWatch.* marketwatch.com/story/kodak-restates-earnings-adds-9-million-to-latest-loss?dist=rss&siteid=mktw (accessed June 2009).

Loughridge, M. (2010, March). "The New Value Integrator, Insight from the Global, Chief Financial Officer Study." IBM Global Business Services. http://www-935.ibm.com/services/us/cfo/cfostudy2010/ (accessed June 2010).

PricewaterhouseCoopers. (2004, July). "The Use of Spreadsheets: Considerations for Section 404 of the Sarbanes-Oxley Act." us.pwc.com (accessed May 2009).

PricewaterhouseCoopers. (2008, October). "Safeguarding the New Currency of Business." us.pwc.com (accessed June 2009).

PricewaterhouseCoopers. (2009). "Internal Audit Perspective on Sustainability." us.pwc.com (accessed June 2009).

Rosenbaum, D. (2012, January). "Imagine There's No Excel." CFO Magazine. cfo.com/Print/PrintArticle?;pageId=d5ab5025-dac1-4e04-a118-49337ce22932 (accessed May 2012)

Sec.gov. (2009, July). "Securities and Exchange Commission Release Nos. 33-9052; 34-60280; IC-28817: File No. S7-13-09." sec.gov/rules/proposed/2009/33-9052.pdf (accessed June 2010).

Chapter Thirteen

Weatherbe, J., and Vitalari, N. (1994). *System Analysis and Design: Traditional, Best Practices*. 4th Edition. St. Paul, MN: West Publishing.

Chapter Fourteen

Lai, E. (2009, April). "Experts: Oracle and MySQL Don't Create Database Monopoly." *CIO.com*. cio.com/article/490134/Experts_Oracle_and_MySQL_Don_t_Create_Database_Monopoly (accessed June 2010).

Index

S